COLLINS

BUTTERFLY GUIDE

COLLINS BUTTERFLY GUIDE

TOM TOLMAN

ILLUSTRATED BY
RICHARD LEWINGTON

HarperCollins Publishers
1 London Bridge Street
London SE1 9GF

WilliamCollinsBooks.com

First published in 1997 as *Collins Field Guide to the Butterflies of Britain and Europe*
This edition first published in 2008
Paperback edition first published in 2009

18 17 16 15 14
10 9 8 7 6 5 4

ISBN: 978 0 00 727977 7

Edited and designed by Fluke Art, UK
Colour reproduction by Colourscan, Singapore
Printed and bound by Printing Express in Hong Kong

Contents

This volume is dedicated to the memory of Dr Lionel G Higgins and Mr Norman D Riley, and to all entomologists, amateur and professional, past and present, who, collectively, are responsible for the vast, accumulated knowledge of the western Palearctic butterfly fauna.

A Personal Tribute to the Memory of Lionel G. Higgins and Norman D. Riley

In the course of almost three decades, *A Field Guide to the Butterflies of Britain and Europe* by L. G. Higgins and N. D. Riley has become an almost indispensable travelling companion for many general naturalists and butterfly specialists alike. As a familiar prelude to many a reference to the European butterflies, the words '....according to Higgins and Riley.....' testify to the heavy reliance placed upon this standard work, as well as the high esteem in which these authors are universally held.

Norman Riley died in 1979, at about the time I began to take an active interest in the butterflies of continental Europe, and, although I never met with this gentleman, I was privileged to develop a close association with Lionel Higgins in the latter years of his life. This man, characterized by his mild, unassuming manner, incisive mind, great enthusiasm, gentle humour and generous nature, seemed never too busy to give attention to problems of butterfly identification for which I invariably sought his help. I was also impressed by his uncommon, although tacit regard for the need for circumspection in the pursuit of science: indeed, I do not believe we ever provided a complete solution to any problem. Our best efforts invariably raised more questions than answers, conclusions were, accordingly, always tentative, always calling for more data, more material and, of course, more work. The commendable caution of Lionel Higgins is well epitomized by the last example of our many co-operative efforts to resolve ambiguities in the characters of 'difficult' butterflies. Two days were spent preparing and comparing dissected components of insects. We each had our allotted tasks, and, as work progressed, silence prevailed except for essential exchanges, mostly to predetermine the availability of the one and only binocular microscope – the preferred instrument for insect dissection. During this period, the cramped conditions of Lionel's insect-storage room/laboratory/library were transformed into a state of near chaos, with every available work-surface strewn with books, journals, insect drawers, microscope slides, test-tube racks and a host of other paraphernalia. Only at the end of the second day, when all available avenues of investigation had been exhausted, did I ask the inevitable question 'Well, what do you think?' Lionel's furrowed brow provided the answer before he spoke 'Hmmm.... any chance of getting more material?'. Lionel Higgins will always stand out in my mind as one who needed no reminding that only fools rush in where wise men fear to tread.

After a brief illness, Lionel George Higgins died on October 9th 1985, at the age of 94. We spoke for the last time, by telephone, shortly before his death. The brief conversation – about butterflies, as usual – ended with Lionel making a joke, and the very last thing I recall were not words, but hearty laughter. A fitting, final farewell from a very fine, old gentleman and one whom I shall always feel honoured to have been able to call my friend.

Preface

Since the first edition of *A Field Guide to the Butterflies of Britain and Europe* by L. G. Higgins and N. D. Riley in 1970, Europeans have witnessed many changes. Overall economic growth, reflected in greatly enhanced personal disposable income, increased leisure time, a vastly improved road network and, in most recent times, the very welcome removal of previously inhibiting travel restrictions in eastern Europe, have concerted in presenting the butterfly enthusiast with greater opportunities for travel within the subcontinent than perhaps might have been imagined or hoped for three decades ago. In direct consequence of one change, namely, the ever-growing interest in the butterflies of the Greek islands, those of the eastern Aegean region are covered by the Field Guide for the first time. These islands hold several species which are to be found nowhere else in the geo-political region of Europe. In the last decade or so, other additions to the list of Europe's butterfly fauna have brought the total, recognized and described in this work, to 440.

The previous field guide was intended largely for use in the field for the purpose of butterfly identification. The present volume, whilst, hopefully, fulfilling this same basic need, endeavours to encourage wider and deeper interest in the butterflies themselves. As most people, including most children know, a butterfly arises from a chrysalis, which, in turn, comes from a caterpillar. That these three states of development equate to one and the same entity, argues convincingly that no knowledge of the adult butterfly, however extensive, can be complete without that of its life-history. Moreover, the benefits bestowed by a wider understanding of the biology, ecology and behaviour of butterflies extends significantly beyond any theoretical consideration. In illustration of the practical benefit of wider knowledge, familiarity with habitat character, coupled with awareness of larval host-plants, is a general and often considerable advantage in locating adult butterflies, especially those of very restricted or uncertain distribution. Again, for purely practical purposes, knowledge of the early-stages of butterflies commends itself as a tool of potentially considerable convenience for searching out these insects even when they are not flying. As an activity far less susceptible to the vagaries of the weather, and one offering greater option in the use of time, searching for eggs or caterpillars can, through choice, be conducted in much more leisurely fashion. Of course, the concomitant advantage of almost inevitable, incidental discoveries of value to science is the greater source of gratification.

Within the constraints imposed by the size of this volume, every effort has been made to facilitate and encourage these potentially highly rewarding pursuits. A strong, personal commitment to the notion that no facet of butterfly science should suffer needless neglect, has provided more than sufficient stimulus for the task of extending the previous field guide. If this stimulates the reader to peer amongst leaves and flowers for butterfly eggs or caterpillars, or to pay closer attention to the activities of the adult insects, as well as the character of the habitat in which they reside, then the effort expended in preparing this work will have been justified.

Acknowledgements

No work of the present kind is possible without the collective efforts of a great many people. As the content of scientific journals provide the indispensable basis of this volume, the author is deeply indebted to all who have taken the trouble to publish their observations. For their direct assistance, in providing information, helpful discussion and access to private butterfly collections, the writer also wishes to express his gratitude to the following – Dr Stanislav Abadjiev (Institute of Zoology, Bulgarian Academy of Sciences, Sofia - BU), Professor Zolta Balint (Magyar Természettudományi Múzeum Állattára, Budapest - H), Mr Dubi Benyamini (Santiago - Chile [Israel]), Mr Lubos Bieber (Lipuvka - Czech Republic), Dr Jean-Pierre Borie, (Compiègne - F), Mr Nils Brostrom (Hässelby - S), Dr John Brown (Department of Physiology, University of Cambridge - U.K.), Dr Clair Brunton (Department of Genetics, University of Cambridge - U.K.), Professor Jaroslaw Buszko (Institute of Biology, Copernicus University, Torun - PL), Mr Paola Casini (Firenze - I), Sir Cyril Clarke (West Kirby - U.K.), Mr John Coutsis (Athens - GR), Professor Sir John Dacie (Wimbledon - U.K.), Mr Charles Derry (Ironbridge - U.K.), Mr Jos Dils (Hoevenen - B), Mr Roland Essayan (Dijon - F), Mr David Hall (Litchfield - UK), Mr Hans Forslind (Kalmar - S), Mr Jürgen Fuchs (Feucht - D), Mr Nicos Ghavalas (Athens - GR), Mr Yves Gonseth (Neuchâtel - CH), Dr Jacques Hutsebaut (Brussels - B), Mr and Mrs David Howell (Broadstairs - U.K.), Mr Hans Henrickson (Stenstrup - DK), Mr David Jutzeler (Effretikon - CH), Mr Ib Kreutzer (Arden - DK), Dr Torben Larsen (London - U.K.), Mr Ronnie Leestmans (Vilvoorde - B), Mr and Mrs Staf de Louker (Bouwel - B), Dr Marchi (Universitá degli studi di Cagliari, Sardinia - I), Mr Francisco Martinex (Valencia - E), Professor Steffen Oemig (Leverkusen - D), Mr Alain Olivier (Antwerp - B), Professor Denis Owen (Oxford Brookes University - U.K.), Mr Jim Phelpstead (Southampton - U.K.), Mr Tony Pittaway (Moulsford - U.K.), Mr Dirk van der Poorten (Antwerp - B), Mr Willy de Prins (Antwerp - B), Mr Alex Riemis (Turnhout - B), Dr Patrick Roche (Sant Julià de Lòria - Andorra), Dr Klaus Schurian (Kelkeim-Fischbach - D), Professor C. B. Stace (Department of Botany, Leicester University - U.K.), Mr Per Tangen (Askim - N), Monsieur Michel Tarrier (Malaga - E[F]), Dr George Thomson (Lochmaben - U.K.), Mr Gerry Tremewan (Truro - U.K.), Mr Rainer Ulrich (Wiesbach - D), Mr Ken Wilmott (Leatherhead - UK), Mr and Mrs Joachim Wolf (Neu-Isenburg - D).

Staff of the Departments of Entomology of – Institut voor Taxonomische Zoologie, Amsterdam (Holland); Natural History Museum, London (U.K.); Oxford University Museum [Hope Department] (U.K.) for arranging access to butterfly collections and entomological libraries. Also, to Dr Stephen Simpson and Dr George McGavin of the Hope Department, and members of Vlaamse Vereniging Voor Entomologie, Antwerp for the loan of specimens used for illustration.

Dr Roberto Crnjar (Universitá degli studi di Cagliari, Sardinia - I) for checking and amending the text relating to the butterflies of Sardinia and Corsica: Mr Martin Gascoigne-Pees (Stonesfield - U.K.) and Dr Peter Russell (East Wittering - U.K.) for checking the main text, furnishing much useful comment and the loan of many specimens used for illustration: Dr N. Savenkov (Latvijas Dabas Muzejs - Latvia) for detailed distributional and historical data on the butterflies of Latvia: Mr John Tennent (Fylingthorpe - U.K.) for very extensive and much needed information on the butterflies of Morocco, Algeria and Tunisia.

For their willing assistance in the identification of larval host-plants – Dr Brian Adams and Professor Frank Bisby (Department of Botanical Taxonomy, University of Southampton - U.K.); Professor K. Browicz (Pozan - PL); Mr Thomas Cope and Mr David Gardner (Royal Botanic Gardens, Kew - U.K.), Dr D. Champluria and Professor D. Fergusson (Rijksuniversitair Centrum Antwerpen (Antwerp - B); Mr Wolfram Hannig (Schladming - A); Dr Alfred Hansen (Botanical Museum, Copenhagen - DK); Dr Stephen Blackmore and Mr Nick Turland (Botany Department, Natural History Museum, London).

Dr P. H. Boting (Antwerp - B) for identifying many ant species, and to Dr Konrad Fiedler

(Theodor-Boveri-Institut für Biowissenschaften [Biozentrum] der Universität Würzberg - D) for rendering a similar and extensive service, and for many helpful discussions on the Lycaenid butterflies: for assisting Dr Fiedler in the identification of some ant species from Greece, thanks are also due to Dr Donat Agosti (Zürich - CH).

Finally, it is with particular pleasure that I express my deep and heartfelt gratitude to my wife, Sally, for her dedicated and indispensable assistance in field work, especially in connection with the tedious and time-consuming tasks of locating and rearing the early-stages of butterflies: invaluable help in literature research is no less appreciated, as is her uncommon capacity to respond with patience and tolerance to the often immoderate restrictions imposed upon her life by her husband's entomological pursuits.

Abbreviations

Bco.	Barranco
CN	chromosome number
Dj.	Djebel (Mount/Mountain)
E	east
f.	form
fw	fore-wing
fwl	fore-wing length (from apex to point of attachment to thorax)
gc	ground-colour
hw	hind-wing
LHP(s)	larval host-plant(s)
m	metre
mm	millimetre
Mt./Mts.	Mountain/Mountains
Mte.	Mount/Mountain
N	north
NE	northeast
NW	northwest
pd	postdiscal
Pl.	Planina (mountains)
Pso.	Passo
Pto.	Puerto
s	space (referring to the area of wing-membrane between the veins)
S	south
SE	southeast
SW	southwest
S.	Sierra
sp./spp.	species (singular)/species (plural)
ssp./sspp.	subspecies (singular)/subspecies (plural)
syn:	synonym
TL:	type locality
unf	fore-wing underside
unh	hind-wing underside
uns	fore-wing and hind-wing undersides
upf	fore-wing upperside
uph	hind-wing upperside
ups	fore-wing and hind-wing uppersides
v	vein
var.	variety
W	west
♂	male
♀	female

Introduction

Butterflies (Rhopalocera) and moths (Heterocera) together comprise the vast order of insects known as the Lepidoptera – a word of Greek origin meaning wings with scales (*lepis* = scale, *pteron* = wing). In most of Europe, butterflies may be distinguished from moths by one or more of the following characteristics:

1) Butterflies have clubbed antennae: those of moths are usually fine and filamentous and often markedly different between the sexes.
2) Unlike butterflies, moths possess a coupling device, linking fore-wing to the hind-wing during flight.
3) Butterflies roost with their wings tightly closed in the vertical plane above the body: moths usually roost and rest with the wings in roughly the horizontal plane with the fore-wing obscuring the hind-wing.
4) The flight of butterflies is confined mostly to sunny or at least bright conditions: most moths fly at night; those that fly in the day-time are easily recognized by their antennae and resting pose.

The basic external anatomy of a butterfly

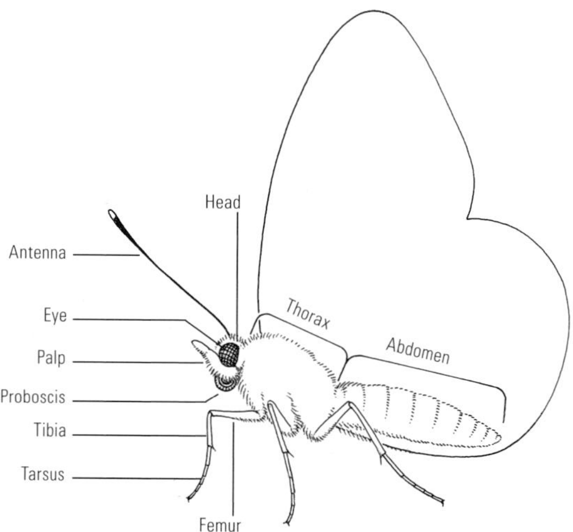

Figure 1. Main external features

The head, which is capable of very limited movement, carries two large, compound eyes giving virtually all-round vision, but of low resolutional quality: the eyes are, however, very sensitive to movement in the field of vision. The frons – 'face' – is located between the eyes often bearing a hair-tuft. In place of jaws, the coiled and extendable proboscis, formed from two, co-acting tubes, finely tapered at their extremities, is an organ through which fluid nutrients are obtained by sucking. Located symmetrically about the proboscis, is a pair of jointed sensory organs known as the palpi. The clubbed antennae, important sensory organs, arise from the upper part of the head from between the eyes. Behind the head is the thorax, which carry the two pairs of wings and three pairs of legs: in

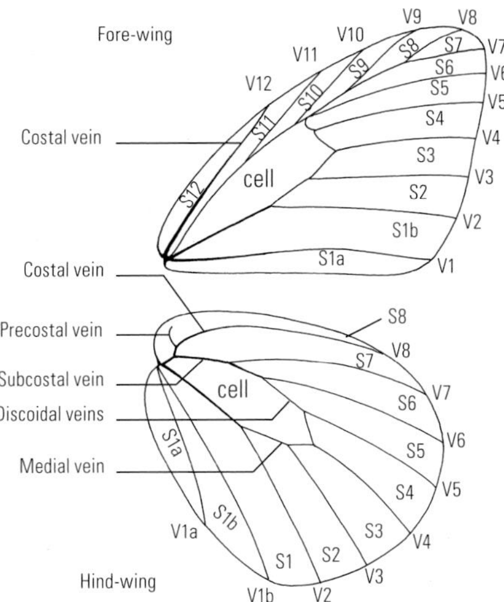

Figure 2. Wing venation

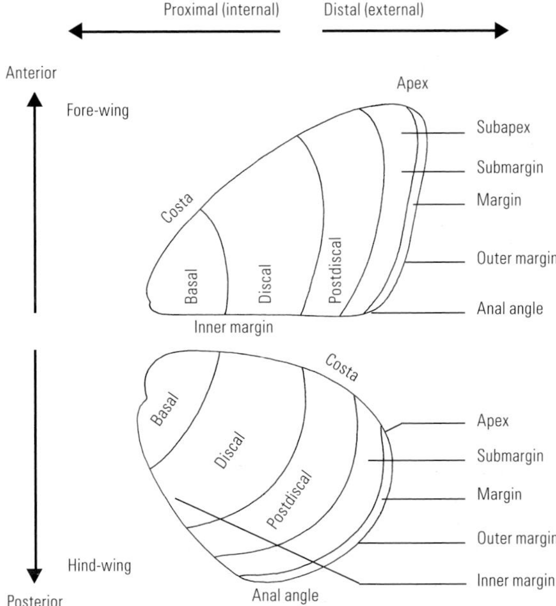

Figure 3. Wing-area notation

some groups, the first pair of legs are degenerate and useless for walking, and may not be apparent without close inspection. All functional legs are jointed and comprise a femur, tibia and tarsus: the structure of the tarsus varies but usually terminates in a pair of claws. Olfactory sensors are present on the antennae, palpi, head, proboscis and legs. Compared to the head and thorax, the abdomen is soft and relatively much more flexible. It contains the organs of digestion and reproduction. The abdomen of a female, as it contains the eggs, is usually noticeably 'fatter' than that of the male. Male genitalia are often of critical value in the identification/separation of species. However, as the structural complexity of these essentially internal anatomical organs are not adequately describable without pictorial representation, reference to genitalia is limited to those instances where alternative, superficial diagnostic features are absent.

Androconia (singular, androconium) are specialized wing-scales (often referred to as scent-scales or androconial scales) possessing gland cells containing chemicals known as pheromones which are released by male butterflies in courtship. Androconia usually differ markedly in shape from ordinary scales and often have a terminal fibrous tuft. Androconia may be distributed and effectively hidden amongst ordinary wing-scales, or grouped in conspicuous patches: these sex-brands, as they are often called, are usually located on the upper surface of the fore-wing. In a few species, androconia are held in a kind of envelope formed by a fold in the fore-wing costal membrane.

An ordinary wing-scale is a very small, thin, chitinous platelet with a tiny peg at its base by which means it is attached to the wing-membrane. Wing-scales are usually pigmented, but bright 'metallic' colours of butterflies, such as the 'blues' and 'coppers', are due entirely to the diffraction of incidence light by the microscopic structure of the scale. The same phenomenon is responsible for the 'rainbow' colours created by a thin film of oil on water. The colours of these interference patterns, as they are called, are very sensitive to viewing angle, and explains why the purple flush of the Purple Emperor, for example, is not visible on both sets of wings at the same time. The subtle variations in the tone of the greenish or brassy iridescent sheen of many satyrid butterflies is similarly explained.

The wings are of prime importance in the identification of butterflies. To facilitate the description of wing-markings, the wing-surface is divided into specific areas as shown in figures 2 and 3.

The terminology and vein-notation is standard. Although demarcation of adjacent wing-areas is somewhat arbitrary, confusion over the described location of markings need never arise: for example, whether a row of spots is designated as 'postdiscal' or 'submarginal' is immaterial if no other markings are present in this general region. All terms are explained in the glossary (page 363): abbreviations are given on page 13. The notation used for the veins and intervening spaces is self-explanatory, and designed to accommodate slight differences in venation between families without the need for altering the numbering system. Where, for example, one or more of the veins branching from the fore-wing subcostal vein (v7, v8 or v9) are absent, the space above vein 6 is still called space 6. In the case of the Papilionidae, where v1a is absent on the hind-wing, v1b becomes v1 and the spaces below and above v1 becomes s1a and s1 respectively. One or more of the three discocellular veins on the hind-wing may be absent, in which case the cell is said to be open. The finer detail of venation in a dead butterfly can be seen more easily if the wings are moistened with a drop of petroleum spirit: this renders the wings briefly translucent without damage to the scales. (Organic solvents should only be used in well-ventilated areas, well away from naked flames: inhalation and contact with the skin should be avoided).

The life-cycle of a butterfly

The egg (ovum), caterpillar (larva), chrysalis (pupa) and adult butterfly (imago) are the four distinct stages in the life-cycle. This remarkable process of transformations is known as metamorphosis.

Ova are usually laid on the plants upon which the larvae subsequently feed. Ova vary considerably in external appearance, and may be bottle-shaped, disc-shaped, spherical or dome-shaped according to the family to which they belong. The ovum stage lasts a few days, a few weeks or several months if hibernation (over-wintering) occurs in this stage.

Larval development proceeds in stages (instars) corresponding to the need for skin-changes to accommodate growth. Most European species hibernate in the larval stage. Between families, a considerable variance in larval shape, colouring and markings, together with a wide range of adaptive behaviour, reflect a correspondingly wide range of survival strategies: similar adaptive variation is shown by pupae, the hibernation stage for many species.

Butterfly identification

With the exception of the Danaidae (which comprises two very distinctive species) a representative sample of each European butterfly family is illustrated on pages 24–27. A comparison of one or more of the characters of size, wing-shape and wing-markings of an unidentified specimen with those of the sample will show the group to which the specimen most probably belongs. By referring to the page indicated by the number adjacent to the species bearing the closest resemblance to the unknown specimen, an immediate identification is sometimes possible; if not, reference to neighbouring plates, illustrating other species within the same family or genus, will usually prove more productive. All possible checks should be made, including a comparison with similar species and of the site of observation of the newly identified butterfly with its known geographical/altitudinal range. It is prudent, of course, to assume that not all is known about the distribution of European butterflies; it is, accordingly, always best to expect the unexpected. In particularly difficult cases, it may be helpful to list all possible candidates, and, after systematic elimination of the least likely, focus attention on the diagnostic features of those remaining.

Arrangement of the Main Text

The following annotated description of subtitled elements of the main text, is intended to illustrate the essentially interactive nature of insect behaviour, ecology and biology, including that pertaining to early-stages, as well as demonstrating its relevance to the identification of butterflies and the investigation of their taxonomic relationships.

Range

Unless otherwise qualified, range denotes the known, global limits of distribution.

Species name, author and date: type-locality: synonymy

This brief, unsubtitled section, gives the Latin (scientific) name of the species, along with the author and date of its original description: the origin of the specimen (the type specimen) pertaining to this description is the type locality. The Latin name may be written as binomen or trinomen, e.g., *Pieris napi* (in abbreviation, *P. napi*) or *Pieris napi napi* (in abbreviation, *P. n. napi*): these names refer to exactly the same entity: the trinomen is required only to distinguish the nominate subspecies from other subspecies; e.g., *Pieris napi napi* and *Pieris napi segonzaci*. Only the more recent or commonly encountered synonyms are given, and are restricted to species name.

Taxonomic classification is often the subject of much contention. However, such matters need not be a source of confusion or consternation if it is recognized that, in reality, a great deal of taxonomic classification equates to hypotheses yet to be tested by the rigorous application of investigative biological methods.

As no universally accepted arrangement of butterfly taxa appears to exist, the systematic order adopted by Higgins and Riley (1983), with a few minor adjustments, has been followed: this may prove convenient for readers familiar with the previous field guide. For the general purpose of this book, departures from the more recent and possibly more rigorous taxonomic evaluations is of little consequence. All butterfly taxa are indexed, and their location within the text should present no difficulty.

Distribution

The geographical area covered is indicated on the map in figure 4 and includes the Canary Islands, Madeira, the Azores, and the Aegean Islands of Greece, but excludes Cyprus and eastern Mediterranean islands not under European political administration. The map provided with each species is intended as a rough, graphical summary of distribution. It will be appreciated that information is often incomplete, especially in some eastern regions. It should also be noted that, in general, a species will not be found at all sites within the designated area of distribution. The regions of temporary occupancy of migrants is indicated by a tint. The predictability of migration near the limits of migratory range, varies appreciably for each migrant species as does uncertainty regarding residency near the often ill-defined boundaries of permanent occupancy.

Altitudinal range is included with distribution. Apart from the advantage in locating butterfly habitats, knowledge of altitudinal range usually serves to account for otherwise anomalous disjunctions in the two-dimensional distributional representation of many species: a cursory inspection of the maps will reveal recurring distributional patterns closely associated with higher mountain massifs, suggesting a restriction to colder conditions at higher altitude, a situation usually confirmed by the altitudinal range given in the text. Cold conditions also occur in higher latitudes, and some species found in central Europe only at high altitude, 'reappear' at or near sea-level in the arctic region. Whilst these examples furnish useful ecological information, other disjunctive patterns, equally evident in the maps, reveal, or at least suggest, a continuity of distribution in the distant past, subsequently disrupted by climatic change in more recent geological time: the study of these and related events in respect of other animals as well as plants – palaeobiogeography – often provides significant clues to the processes of evolution.

The quoted lower limit of altitudinal range, approximating to sea-level, has been refined, as far as available data allow, in an attempt to accommodate the significant and often rapid transition

Figure 4. Region covered by this book

in habitat character, reflected in vegetation zones, which can occur between low-lying, inland coastal districts and the shoreline itself.

Description

For several reasons, quantified estimates of butterfly size have been omitted; the best indication of approximate size is provided by the illustrations. No valid representation of size-variance is easily interpretable, nor indeed, easily obtainable: an estimate of the range of fore-wing length is apt to be misleading, as geographical variation is often appreciable and it is almost always possible to find individuals whose size falls beyond either limit of the range commonly quoted for most species.

With few exceptions, descriptions are restricted to important diagnostic features and characters not apparent in the illustrations. In cases where confusion between closely similar species may arise, comparative data are included with each description.

Variation

The great many types and sources of variation, including that of larvae and pupae, are given in the text.

Flight-time

For many geographically wide-ranging species, voltinism, the number of annual broods (generations), may vary appreciably according to general geographical location, altitude and regional climatic conditions. A species, single-brooded in colder, more northerly locations or at higher altitudes, may produce two or more broods in warmer regions at low altitudes. Some multiple-brooded (polyvoltine) species may be on the wing from early Spring until late Summer or Autumn in North Africa or coastal Mediterranean regions, or throughout the year in the Canary Islands. As a rule, a species occurring at low altitude in more southerly regions will emerge earlier. Emergence dates may also be influenced significantly by seasonal conditions and may even affect voltinism. A late Spring, combined with a cool Summer, can delay the emergence of some arctic species by more than a month: prolonged periods of drought may delay entirely the emergence of some desert-dwelling (eremic) butterflies for one or more seasons.

Habitat

Whilst many widespread species are frequently found in commonly occurring habitats, others live in relative isolation in habitats of special character. The general character of habitat is described, along with any readily discernible features. Geology/soil-type is a factor of considerable, and sometimes definitive importance in respect to the character of vegetation, including, of course, larval host-plants. In company with other information, a knowledge of habitats is often very useful in locating butterflies, especially those having very specific requirements.

Life-history

The limitation of space precludes detailed description of life-history. Larval host-plant (LHP) data have either been personally verified, or taken from sources deemed to be reliable. Uncertainties, in plant identity and use as LHPs, are indicated as appropriate: thus; (?)*Centaurea scabiosa* signifies confirmation of plant identity at species level, but only its suspected use as a LHP: *Centaurea* (?)*scabiosa* signifies a confirmed LHP whose identity has been determined with certainty at generic level, but only tentatively at species level: *Centaurea* sp. indicates confirmation of a LHP whose identity has been confirmed at generic, but not species level. Suspected, but unconfirmed errors in LHP records are indicated by the expressed need for confirmation. Where the reliability of a data source cannot be established with confidence, many, often very old records have been omitted without comment. Wherever possible, plant taxonomy/nomenclature follows that of *Flora Europaea*: beyond the geographical range covered by this work, other standard floras, e.g., *Flora of Turkey*, and original publications have been consulted.

The distinction between the plants that butterfly larvae will accept as food in captivity and those selected in nature is very important. The behaviour of any animal can be expected to change according to circumstance, most especially where survival is threatened. It should not be assumed that a species that accepts a particular plant as a food-source in captivity would thrive or survive, or, indeed, make any attempt to exploit the same plant in the wild. As the captive behaviour of larvae, as well as that of butterflies themselves, provides no dependable guide to natural behaviour, the sole, reliable criterion of a LHP is the plant upon which larvae are known to feed in nature. That not all butterflies lay their eggs on the plants upon which their larvae subsequently feed, indicates the need for caution in the interpretation of field observations.

For many reasons, a knowledge of LHPs is of great importance. Their distribution may reveal much of interest concerning that of the butterfly itself: in some cases, for example, the rarity and/or distributional pattern of a butterfly may correspond very closely with that of its LHP. Such information may be quite sufficient to locate a butterfly in its early stages, including that of hibernation: on this account, and as already indicated in the Preface, the field study of butterflies need not necessarily be confined to the period in which they normally fly.

For many reasons, it makes good sense to ensure that all necessary care is exercised in effecting the identification of LHPs. Given that mainland Europe hosts something of the order of 20,000 flowering plants, the scope for misidentification is considerable, and the responsibility for identifying LHPs is, in general, best delegated to the professional botanist.

Behaviour

For our own species, success in life very much depends upon our behaviour. This is no less true of a butterfly. Of course, butterflies do not make choices, in the sense that we understand, but respond instinctively to specific stimuli as well as gradual seasonal or other changes in its environment. For this reason it is probably more useful, and certainly instructive, to regard a butterfly, not as a living creature, but as a small miniaturized, biological machine equipped with an array of sensors linked to a central processing unit (equivalent more to a computer than a brain) preprogrammed with all necessary inherited information required to ensure its survival. On this premise, we would at once dispose of any notion that a butterfly is capable of being 'frightened': instead, we would consider that it was programmed to react swiftly to any sudden movement in its immediate vicinity, simply to avoid being eaten by a bird: in reality, the butterfly is probably incapable of distinguishing a bird from a butterfly net or a windblown leaf. Through the process of natural selection, the genes carried by those insects failing to react appropriately to threat, would be quickly eliminated. By this means, the need for choice of action, which would imply intelligent behaviour, is also eliminated. In more complicated examples of behaviour, it would appear that programmes are often interactive. For example, in considering the factors controlling the emergence date of a spring butterfly which has hibernated as a pupa, it is clear that temperature is not the sole determinant: if it were, the insect might well emerge, prematurely, in winter and well out of synchronization with, say, the development of its LHP. In fact, it is virtually certain that butterflies have built-in clocks (just like modern computers) and are able to respond to the seasonal changes in day-length (photoperiod).

In view of the importance of camouflage as a survival strategy, it is not surprising that the behaviour of a butterfly is often highly correlated with its physical appearance and the character of its habitat. The presumed need for good underside camouflage of the Purple Hair-streak (*Quercusia quercus*) for example, required to evade the predatory attentions of birds whilst sitting on the leaves of oak trees – a common occupation – explains, so it would appear, the otherwise anomalous underside markings, namely, the silvery-greyish ground-colour which mimics, not the green pigment of the leaf itself, but the reflections of the shiny leaf-surface, and the white discal line which corresponds to the highlighted reflection from a leaf-vein. As may be confirmed by reference to the illustrations and main text, the underside ground-colours of the Brimstone (*Gonepteryx rhamni*), the Peacock (*Inachis io*) and the Comma (*Polygonia c-album*), three species which hibernate as adults, corresponds closely with the character of their respective hibernation quarters.

Refinement in the adaptive colouring of a species to suit the particular character of a particular habitat is also to be expected and in company with butterfly behaviour, often appears to explain local variation in wing-markings. In the genus *Pseudochazara*, for example, local variation in wing colouring and pattern, especially on the underside of the hind-wing, is observed frequently and is often presented as justification for subspecific separation. However, considering the unvarying preference of the genus for resting on or amongst rocks, superficial differences between populations, corresponding to refined adjustment to local geological conditions, are as readily attributable to the need for good camouflage. Roosting occurs in concealment amongst stones or in rock crevices. That such retreats are invariably cool, relative to ambient, surface conditions, precludes the predatory attention of lizards – always a serious threat to adult *Pseudochazara* species – but a roosted insect loses this security once it has crawled up towards the light, seeking the warmth of the morning sun, for then it becomes visible and, in its still torpid state, especially vulnerable: here, the importance of underside hind-wing camouflage is most obvious. The warming-up process always seems to be conducted in the same way, with the same meticulous care: thus, situated very close to or even in contact with a stone, the insect adjusts the plane of its tightly closed wings perpendicularly to the sun, thereby maximising exposure to its rays. Some vertical tilting is often necessary to gain precise adjustment, and it is noteworthy that subtle corrections corresponding to the movement of the sun are often observed during this normally lengthy procedure. It is apparent from these observations, that by exploiting the potential for heating both hind-wing surfaces simultaneously – the stone against which the butterfly stations itself will already have warmed – the period of greatest threat from predation is minimized. Here, it is interesting to reflect upon the interaction of elements within an ecosystem, for it appears that the behaviour and adaptation of a *Pseudochazara* species is intimately and competitively associated with the behaviour and adaptation of lizards.

A parallel example of adaptive colouring is apparent for the genus *Hipparchia*. However, it is often found that the range of variation in the underside hind-wing is greater than at first sight might be expected; possibly, because of equivalent variation in the character of the surfaces upon which the butterflies rest or roost: for example, the bark of a pine tree, a favoured resting site, usually displays a most complex array of colours, pattern and hard shadows created by texture.

An interesting survival strategy adopted by some species is that of migration. With seasonal regularity, such species – the 'nomads' of the butterfly world – disperse, sometimes in prodigious numbers, from areas of permanent residence, taking up accommodation in more or less any suitable site encountered along migratory routes. Colonies thus established, provide for further migration and colonization. In this way, the Painted Lady (*Vanessa cardui*), one of the better known migrants, extends its range progressively from early Spring onwards through Summer, from north Africa, throughout Europe, to well within the Arctic Circle: it is one of very few migrants to reach Iceland. The process of breeding and dispersion continues until the onset of cold weather, when all or nearly all colonists and offspring are presumed to perish in the winter months: however, the loss of such huge numbers of butterflies is of little or no consequence, as it is not the survival of individuals, but that of the species which determines its overall success. As a broad, unrefined hypotheses, the basis of migratory behaviour as a survival strategy is easily understood, for in the event of general climatic change, inevitable in geological time, some colonies, somewhere, are likely to be favourably placed for the purpose of establishing a new, permanent base from which future generations can migrate. Characteristically, migrants have, through necessity, adapted either to a wide variety of larval host-plants or at least one of common and widespread occurrence.

A few species, such as the Swallowtail (*Papilio machaon*) and the Nettle-tree Butterfly (*Libythea celtis*), appear to disperse with seasonal regularity, as indicated by their frequent occurrence in locations well-removed from potential breeding sites, that is, those containing larval host-plants. However, unlike typical migrants, dispersion is confined largely within the boundaries of permanent residence.

Conservation

Nature conservation is the collective responsibility of all individuals, not just the relatively very few, active conservationists. Securing the very necessary wider commitment to the protection of the environment presents a problem of truly global dimensions for which no proportionately adequate solutions are currently available.

Enhancing the security of the natural world means damaging or destroying as little of it as possible. Given our present circumstances, responding to the challenge of meeting our responsibility to future generations will doubtless call for very profound and, quite possibly, very rapid changes to social, economic and, by implication, personal philosophies. It is all but a certainty that our survival depends upon divesting ourselves of the mythical belief in our own adaptability. Contrary to popular conviction, man is not the most adaptable of species: indeed, in direct consequence of his much celebrated superior intelligence, man distinguishes himself by being the only species not to have adjusted to his environment. In contradistinction, the butterfly – a 'humble' creature of no intelligence – 'learned' to look after itself, with great proficiency, many millions of years before man first walked the Earth. It continues to live in harmony with the rest of nature. To ensure our own survival, we must learn to do the same.

Exploiting the popular appeal of creatures of great natural beauty, such as, but not exclusively butterflies, which arouse spontaneously our protective instincts, would appear to afford the best chance of securing the all-important protection of natural habitats. The late L. G. Higgins once remarked to the writer, that 'all butterflies must have a happy home', and, as a truism no less applicable to other animals and plants, the protection of a butterfly habitat serves, automatically, to protect all wildlife residing within the same domain. Assuming the efficacy of this aim and method, how is it best exploited? Widespread enlightenment – education – provides the general answer, but since children are the future custodians of our planet, it is perhaps their instruction which matters most. There are nothing but good reasons for encouraging children to take an interest in their planet. The wider and deeper the interest, the greater the desire to protect. The mind of a child is active, alert and inquisitive, but above all, it is impressionable, and, like a clean sheet of white paper, it may be the best place – it may be the only place – to write the messages required to reverse the fortunes of our species.

PAPILIONIDAE Pages 28–41

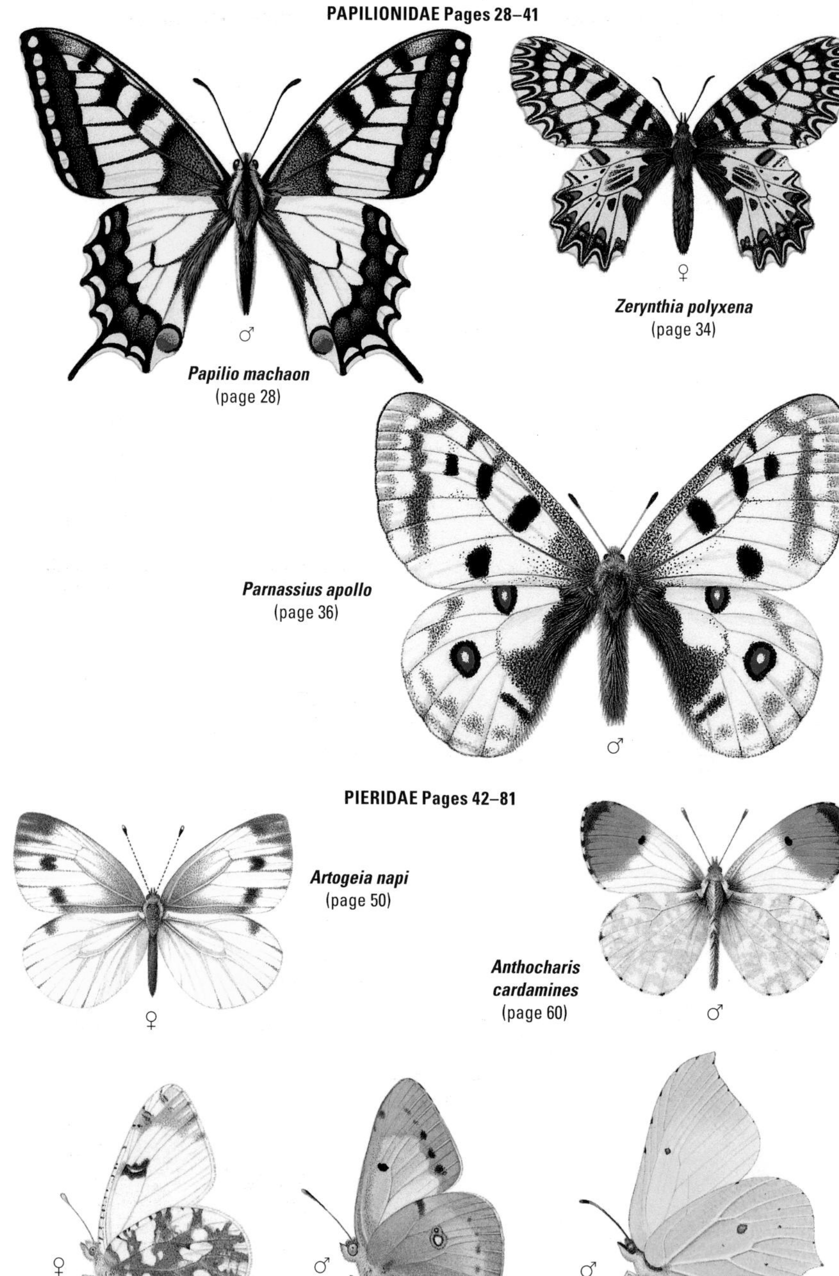

Papilio machaon (page 28)

Zerynthia polyxena (page 34)

Parnassius apollo (page 36)

PIERIDAE Pages 42–81

Artogeia napi (page 50)

Anthocharis cardamines (page 60)

Euchloe ausonia (page 56)

Colias crocea (page 72)

Gonepteryx rhamni (page 74)

LIBYTHEIDAE Page 158

Libythea celtis
(page 158)

RIODINIDAE Page 158

Hamearis lucina
(page 158)

LYCAENIDAE Pages 82–158

Satyrium ilicis
(page 86)

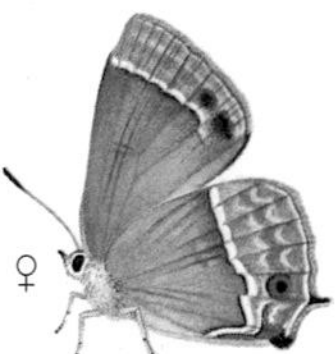

Quercusia quercus
(page 84)

Thecla betulae
(page 84)

Callophrys rubi
(page 90)

Lycaena phlaeas
(page 92)

Aricia agestis
(page 128)

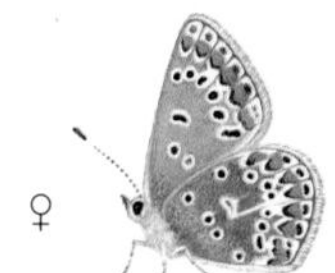

Polyommatus icarus
(page 156)

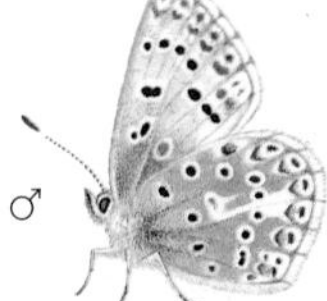

Lysandra coridon
(page 150)

HESPERIIDAE Pages 326–350

Pyrgus malvae
(page 326)

Thymelicus sylvestris
(page 346)

NYMPHALIDAE Pages 162–217

Apatura iris
(page 164)

Limenitis camilla
(page 170)

Polygonia c-album
(page 180)

Vanessa atalanta
(page 176)

Mellicta athalia
(page 208)

Euphydryas aurinia
(page 216)

SATYRIDAE Pages 218–325

Melanargia galathea
(page 218)

Hipparchia semele
(page 230)

Satyrus ferula
(page 256)

Erebia aethiops
(page 272)

♂

Erebia epiphron
(page 268)

Erebia tyndarus
(page 284)

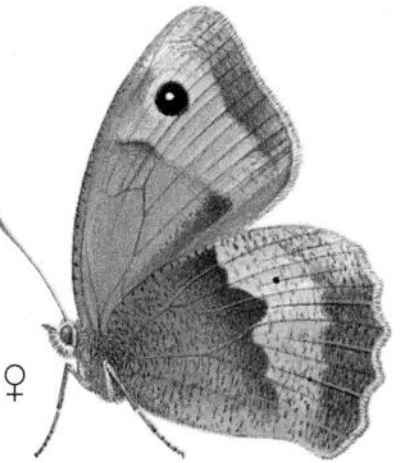

Maniola jurtina
(page 300)

Lasiommata megera
(page 320)

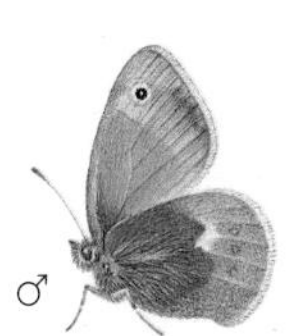

Coenonympha pamphilus
(page 310)

Coenonympha hero
(page 316)

Pararge aegeria
(page 318)

PAPILIONIDAE Latreille 1802

The twelve European representatives of this family include some very large and colourful butterflies, of which the swallowtails are perhaps the best known. Sexual dimorphism is generally not well marked in wing-characters, but appreciable differences in abdominal size, shape, colour or colour-pattern enables sexual determination to be made with no difficulty. With the exception of the Scarce Swallowtail, larvae have bright 'warning' colours and are often conspicuous when feeding or resting. As an additional deterrent to predators, the larvae of some species possess an osmeterium, a soft, fleshy, orange-coloured, eversible, forked organ concealed within the first thoracic segment: when erected, this organ emits a powerful and offensive odour, which, coupled with the startling appearance of the osmeterium itself, is said to be an effective defence against predatory birds. Swallowtail (*Papilio*) pupae, as well as those of the festoons (*Zerynthia*), are cryptically coloured: pupae of other species are secreted amongst moss/leaf-litter, under stones or in loose soil.

Swallowtail *Papilio machaon*

RANGE NW Africa and Europe, through Middle East, Near East, Asia (30-70°N) to Japan. Represented in N America by several subspecies/forms.

P. machaon Linnaeus 1758 TL: Sweden (Verity 1947).
syn: *sphyrus* Hübner 1823.

DISTRIBUTION Mediterranean coastal districts of NW Africa. Europe to N Fennoscandia and most Mediterranean islands. Absent from Atlantic Islands and British Isles, except for a very restricted area of SE England (Norfolk). Wide-ranging but usually encountered only in small numbers in any given site. 0-3000m: common occurrence at 1000-2000m above limit of available LHPs due to strong dispersive/migratory tendency.

DESCRIPTION Second brood: ups black markings lightly dusted with pale yellow scales; black markings slightly reduced; blue markings better defined. Superficially indistinguishable from *P. saharae* (see *P. saharae*).

FLIGHT-PERIOD Univoltine, bivoltine or trivoltine according to latitude, altitude and seasonal conditions: February/October. Impression of flight-period in any given site may be confounded by occurrence of vagrant specimens.

HABITAT Diverse. In N Europe, mostly wet places: marshes; fens; river banks. In C Europe, dry or damp, grassy places. In Mediterranean region, general habitat character appears to be relatively unimportant, relating more to the fortuitous occurrence of LHPs and opportunism of vagrant, ovipositing females. At low/moderate altitudes, most egg-laying sites, which may contain very few LHP specimens, comprise hot, dry, sunny places, often areas of cultivation, roadsides, disturbed ground etc., and are often abundant in robust, nectar-rich plants such as thistles, which offer an efficient means of acquiring the energy needed to sustain a large insect (cf. *A. crataegi*; *P. brassicae*; *P. apollo*).

LIFE-HISTORY LHPs: Apiaceae. In S Europe, *F. vulgare* is perhaps the most commonly used LHP: in England, exclusively *P. palustre*. Ova laid on leaves. Larvae feed on leaves and/or flowers, depending on LHP. Larvae which lack the normal green colouring may be either substantially black or white with the usual orange segmental dots; such forms have been recorded from very hot localities in the Mediterranean region. Hibernates as a pupa. Pupates on robust stems or dead, woody plants. Pupa variable, light green or greyish-buff.

BEHAVIOUR Males frequently 'hilltop'; several may remain flying together for some hours at mountain summit.

Desert Swallowtail *Papilio saharae*

RANGE E Morocco, N and SE Algeria, C Tunisia, N Libya, N Egypt, W Saudi Arabia, W Yemen. Replaces *P. machaon* in N Africa south and east of Atlas Mts.

P. saharae Oberthür 1879 TL: Laghouat (Algeria).

DISTRIBUTION Morocco: Erfoud; Zagora; Tizi-n-Tinififft; Tizi-n-Bachkoum. Algeria: El Kantara; Laghouat; Biskra; Bou Saâda; Oued Mya; Oued Nsa; El Oulaya. Tunisia: Gafsa; Gabès; Djerba. 100-2000m. Overlaps with *P. machaon* in some areas, e.g. Tizi-n-Bachkoum.

DESCRIPTION Indistinguishable from *P. machaon* on basis of wing-markings; genitalia differ but are too variable for reliable separation; antennal segments 30-31 (33-36 for *P. machaon*) – low-power magnification provides ready means of determination in the field; larvae morphologically distinct; divergent ecological needs and hybridization experiments provide evidence of separation at species level.

FLIGHT-PERIOD Univoltine. Generally mid April/late May; records span February/October. Records for most summer months in Middle East suggest partial bivoltinism/polyvoltinism or delayed emergence due to exceptionally dry conditions. Pupal diapause may extend over two or more years, with seasonal population density varying accordingly: in consecutive seasons of exceptional dryness, the butterfly may fail to appear (cf. *E. falloui*).

HABITAT Rocky slopes or gullies with an abundance of LHP; arid, stony, flattish ground with sparse, low-growing vegetation; desert oases.

LIFE-HISTORY LHPs principally *Deverra chloranthus*: also, *D. scopularia*; *Seseli varium*: elsewhere in range, *D. tortuosus*; *Ferula communis sinaica*; *Pycnocyla glauca*. Ovipositing and larval feeding behaviour similar to that of *P. machaon*. Larval markings (colour/pattern) differ considerably from those of *P. machaon*: also, in *P. saharae*, osmeterium is brown and twice the length of that of *P. machaon* which is orange. Hibernates as a pupa.

SWALLOWTAIL

P. m. gorganus
(Continental Europe)

P. m. britannicus
(East Anglia, England)

Swallowtail

Desert Swallowtail

BEHAVIOUR Males frequently 'hilltop': general behaviour very similar to that of *P. hospiton*.

NOTE Apparently closely related to *P. hospiton*. Relationship between *P. saharae* and P. *machaon* appears to parallel that of *P. glaucus* Linnaeus and *P. canadensis* Rothschild and Jordan in N America.

Corsican Swallowtail *Papilio hospiton*

RANGE Corsica, Sardinia.

P. hospiton Géné 1839 TL: Tortoli, Sardinia.

DISTRIBUTION Corsica and Sardinia. Generally 500-1200m, but records range from sea-level to summits of highest mountains.

FLIGHT-PERIOD Univoltine. Generally mid May/late July in prolonged emergence: records span mid March/mid August.

HABITAT Open, grassy hillsides and valleys, often amongst bushes and rocks.

LIFE-HISTORY LHPs: Corsica, *Ferula communis*; *Ruta corsica*; *Peucedanum paniculatum*: Sardinia, *F. communis*. Ova laid mostly near leaf-tips on plants in partial shade, or on lower, shaded leaves of plants growing in full sun. Larvae feed on leaves. Captive larvae readily accept *R. graveolans*. Captive larvae accept *Skimmia* (?)*japonia* cultivars (Rutaceae) – plant genus not indigenous in Europe. Hibernates as a pupa. Larvae often parasitized by a large, inky-blue hymenopteran (*Trogus violaceus*), which hibernates as a pupa within the pupal case of *P. hospiton*, or that of *P. machaon* subsequent to autumn emergence and parasitization of larvae of the latter species.

BEHAVIOUR Males regularly 'hilltop' late morning and early afternoon. Females show no tendency to 'hilltop', but territorial range is extensive. Natural hybrids with *P. machaon* have been reported from Corsica and Sardinia.

CONSERVATION Protective European legislation for this species appears to be unwarranted: widely held to be under no threat from any cause.

Southern Swallowtail *Papilio alexanor*

RANGE SE France, NW and SE Italy, W Croatia, S Balkans, Greece, Turkey, Israel, Lebanon, N Iraq, Iran, Transcaucasus, Turkmenistan, Uzbekistan, S Kazakhstan, Afghanistan, Tajikistan, Kyrgyzstan, W Pakistan.

P. alexanor Esper 1799 TL: Nice and Provence.

DISTRIBUTION SE France: Var; Alpes-Maritimes; Alpes-de-Haute-Provençe; Drôme; Hautes-Alpes; Isère; S Savoie. Extinct in Ardèche. Italy: Maritime Alps; Aspromonte; NE Sicily (Monti Peloritani). W Croatia: Istria; Dalmatia. Albania. Republic of Macedonia: Treska Valley; Titov Veles (Vardar River system). Greece: Mitzekeli Mts.; Parnassos massif (including Delphi; Arahova); Ghiona massif (including Amfissia); Mt. Hymettus; Mt. Parnis; northern coast of Peloponnesos; Panahaikion Mts.; Mt. Chelmos and environs (including Kalavrita; Zachlorou); Foli Mts.; Taygetos Mts.; Gythion; Corfu; Kefalonia; Lesbos; Samos. 0-1700m: generally below 1100m.

DESCRIPTION Female larger; ups gc distinctly paler yellow.

VARIATION On Lesbos and Samos, *eitschbergeri* Bollino and Sala: larger; ups gc paler; pd band narrower. (Typical form in W and C Turkey.)

FLIGHT-PERIOD Univoltine. Mid April/mid July in prolonged emergence.

HABITAT AND BEHAVIOUR Hot, dry, usually steep slopes on limestone or other consolidated calcareous substrates. In gliding or hovering fashion, both sexes exploit air currents associated with the topography of the terrain for their respective purposes – males in pursuit of females, females in search of egg-laying sites and both sexes open to any opportunity to take nectar. Frequently, habitats provide ideal conditions for *Centranthus ruber* (Red Valerian) – a much favoured nectar source.

LIFE-HISTORY LHPs: France and Italy, *Opopanax chironium*; *Seseli montanum*; *Ptychotis saxifraga* [=*P. heterophylla*]; *Trinia glauca* [=*T. vulgaris*]: Greece, *Opopanax hispidus*; *Pimpinella saxifraga*; *Scaligeria cretica* [=*S. napiformis*]; *Ferula communis*; *Pastinaca sativa*. Captive larvae readily accept *Carum carvi*. Ova laid on floret-stem or calyx, or close to tips of filamentous leaves of plants so structured. Larvae feed on flowers or developing seeds. Hibernates as a pupa on robust stems of dead plants, sometimes at base of large rocks. In captivity, pupal diapause may extend over two seasonal cycles.

Corsican Swallowtail

Southern Swallowtail

CORSICAN SWALLOWTAIL

♂

Inner and outer edge of submarginal band scalloped

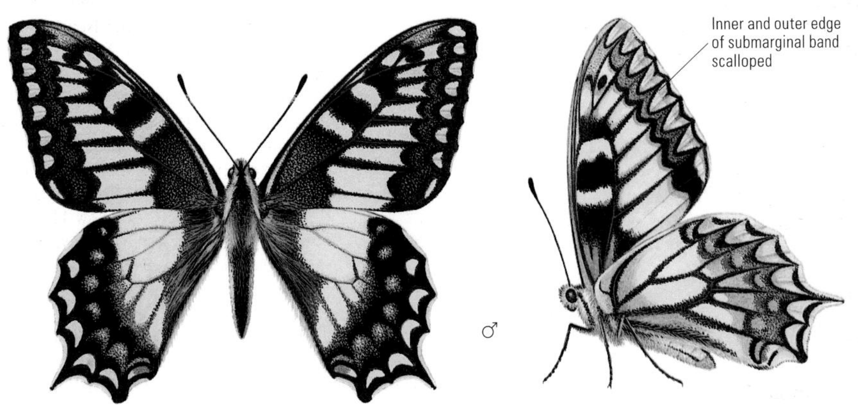

Restricted to Corsica and Sardinia

SOUTHERN SWALLOWTAIL

Appears more striped than other *Papilio* species, more closely resembling markings of Scarce Swallowtail but bars blunter and less elongated

Antennae straight, tipped with white

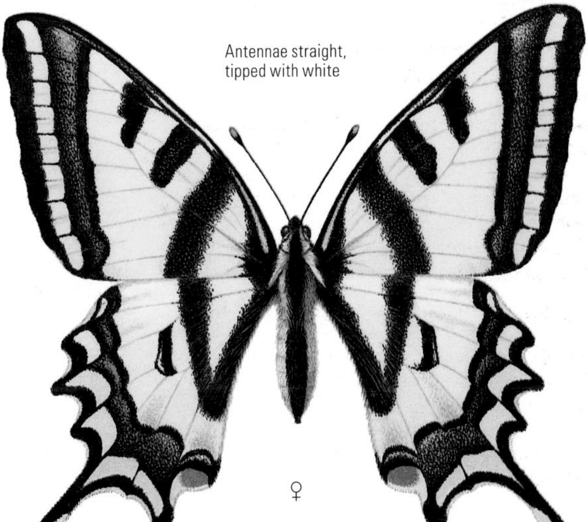

♀

♂

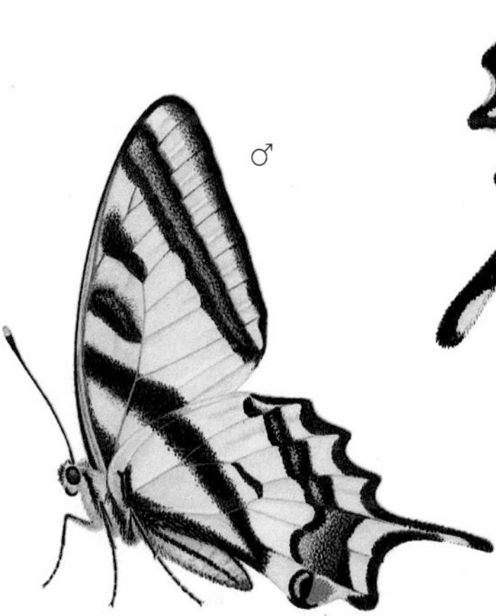

Scarce Swallowtail *Iphiclides podalirius*

RANGE N Africa, S and C Europe, Turkey, Middle East, Near East, through temperate Asia to W China.

I. podalirius Linnaeus 1758 TL: Livorno, Tuscany (Verity 1947).

DISTRIBUTION Widespread, locally common. N Africa. 0-2700m: generally below 2400m. N France and Baltic coast to S Europe and most Mediterranean islands including Corsica but reportedly absent from Sardinia. 0-1500m.

DESCRIPTION First brood: ups gc pale yellow; abdomen black. Second brood: ups gc whiter; black markings reduced; uph inner submarginal and pd bands narrow, greyish, often diffuse; unh twin black discal lines not filled with yellow-orange: female larger; abdomen greyish-white with dark grey dorsal line.

VARIATION In NW Africa, Iberian Peninsula and S France (E Pyrenees), *feisthameli* Duponchel: first brood; ups gc greyish-white in male; with faint yellow flush in female; black markings heavier; uph inner black marginal border broad, solid. Second brood; ups gc white in male, female often with pale yellow flush; dark inner marginal and submarginal bands reduced, divided by pale line or narrow band.

FLIGHT-PERIOD Univoltine, bivoltine or trivoltine according to locality and altitude: March/early October.

HABITAT Diverse. Bushy places; woodland margins; open grassy places, rocky slopes or gullies, sometimes containing few and isolated LHP specimens; orchards of *Prunus* cultivars: often in very hot and dry situations.

LIFE-HISTORY LHPs principally *Prunus*, including most cultivated species. Ova laid on leaves. Larvae feed on leaves. In later instars, the green larva is shorter in proportion to its maximum diameter than any other European species and smoothly tapered towards its 'tail': in colour, texture and markings, well-camouflaged amongst leaves of principal LHP, *Prunus spinosa*. When crawling, the larva sways gently backwards and forwards: the reason for this curious behaviour is not clear – possibly it confuses predators: other well-camouflaged but very different animals, such as the chameleon and some mantid species, move in a similar fashion. Pupates on thicker stems of LHP. Hibernates as a pupa. Pupa is green or buff, according to pupation site and season: pupae which hibernate – on plant stems devoid of leaves – are buff.

BEHAVIOUR Adults are greatly attracted to nectar-rich shrubs and trees such as apple, cherry, lilac and buddleia. Air currents are often exploited in aiding flight. Males sometimes 'hilltop'.

NOTE ONE *I. p. feisthameli* considered specifically distinct by some authors: confirmatory experimental evidence (biochemical comparisons, hybridization experiments, etc.) appears to be lacking.

NOTE TWO Apparent absence from Sardinia is curious in view of widespread occurrence in coastal districts of S Corsica and the scope for fortuitous introduction in consequence of strong, prevailing north-westerly winds.

CONSERVATION Becoming increasingly scarce in C Europe, reputedly in consequence of changes in agricultural practices.

Scarce Swallowtail

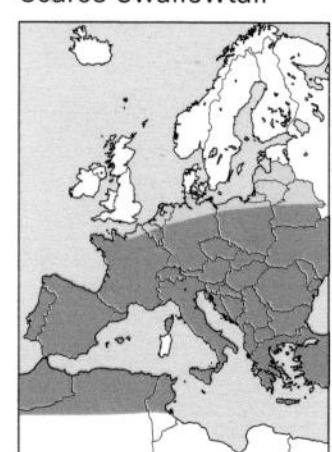

Eastern Festoon

Eastern Festoon *Zerynthia cerisy*

RANGE SE Europe, Turkey, Cyprus, Israel, Lebanon, Iraq, Iran.

Z. cerisy Godart 1824 TL: Ourlac [Province of Izmir].

DISTRIBUTION SE Serbia. S Romania. Albania. Republic of Macedonia. Bulgaria. European Turkey. N Greece: provinces of Kastoria, Drama and Evros: very sporadic and generally local: 75-1000m: Aegean Islands of Lesbos, Chios, Samos, Kos, Simi, Rhodes, Kastellorizo and Crete (0-1100m).

VARIATION Uph submarginal red spots variable in size. Female gc sometimes replaced by ochreous-yellow. On Samos: smaller; female ups gc appreciably darker yellow, red spots prominent. On Rhodes: both sexes: red spots replaced with orange in about 70% of specimens. On Crete, *cretica* Rebel: smaller; markings reduced; hw outer margin rounded: accorded specific status by some authors.

FLIGHT-PERIOD Univoltine. Mid March/late July in prolonged emergence: at highest altitude, emergence generally delayed by 3-4 weeks.

HABITAT Open, hot, sunny, dry, grassy places amongst thickets of mature bushes with dense undergrowth, or bordered by hedgerows with sparse deciduous trees: often in river valleys and cultivated areas.

LIFE-HISTORY LHPs: N Greece and Bulgaria, *Aristolochia clematitis*: Samos, *A. bodamae*: Rhodes *A. (?) guichardii*; *A. (?) parvifolia*: Crete, *A. cretica*; *A. (?) sempervirens*. Ova laid singly or in small numbers on upperside of leaf: plants in close proximity to bushes or well-shaded by trees are favoured for oviposition. Captive larvae accept *A. rotunda*. Pupates at base of woody plants or rocks. Hibernates as a pupa.

SCARCE SWALLOWTAIL

Fw and hw black bands prominent

♂

♂

I. p. feisthamelii

EASTERN FESTOON

Fw lacking red markings

Z. c. cerisy (Samos)

Smaller, heavily marked

♀

♂

♂

Z. c. cretica (Crete)

Smaller, paler, all markings reduced, hw 'tail' absent

♀

Southern Festoon *Zerynthia polyxena*

RANGE Central S and SE Europe, NW Turkey, S Urals, NW Kazakhstan.

Z. polyxena Denis and Schiffermüller 1775 TL: Vienna.

syn: *hypsipyle* Schulze 1776: *hypermnestra* Scopoli 1763 (invalid homonym).

DISTRIBUTION Widespread but local. SE France: Hérault to Ardèche, Hautes-Alpes and Alpes-Maritimes. Italy. Sicily. S Switzerland: S Tessin: very local. SE Austria. SE Poland. Slovakia. Hungary. Balkans. Greece. European Turkey. Absent from Greek islands. 0-1700m – generally below 900m.

DESCRIPTION Upf without red spots in s1b, s4-6, s9 or cell (cf. *Z. rumina*).

VARIATION In S Europe, females with ochreous ups gc are common (f. *ochracea* Staudinger). In S France and Italy, f. *cassandra* Geyer: ups black markings more extensive; upf red spot usually absent in s9.

FLIGHT-PERIOD Univoltine. Late March/early July in prolonged emergence.

HABITAT Hot, dry grassy and bushy places; rocky slopes and gullies; cultivated areas, especially neglected terraces.

LIFE-HISTORY LHPs *Aristolochia clematitis*; *A. rotunda*; *A. pallida*; *A. pistolochia*. Ova laid singly or in small batches on leaves, usually underside. Once established on a particular *Aristolochia* species, captive larvae may be reluctant to accept other, natural LHPs. Larvae often rest in full sun, usually on LHP leaves. Pupates on plant-stems, tree-bark or underside of stones. Hibernates as a pupa.

Spanish Festoon *Zerynthia rumina*

RANGE NW Africa, SW Europe.

Z. rumina Linnaeus 1758 TL: S Europe.

DISTRIBUTION Widespread, locally common. Morocco. Algeria. Tunisia. 0-2100m, generally below 1600m. Portugal. Spain. S France: Pyrénées-Orientales to Lozère and Provence: sporadic and local. 0-1500m, generally below 1000m.

DESCRIPTION Upf with red spots in s1b, s4-6, s7 and cell (cf. *Z. polyxena*).

VARIATION F. *medesicaste* Hoffmannsegg: uph red spot sometimes present at cell-base – common in some localities in S France. F. *honnoratii* Boisduval (often spelt *honoratii* in error): ups and unh red markings greatly extended. In female, f. *canteneri* Staudinger: ups gc yellow-ochreous (a rare variant in male). In N Africa, f. *africana* Stichel: larger; all markings bolder, well developed; upf without red spot in s1b – replaced by black; uph with solid black pd band enclosing red spots: closely similar forms are common in S Spain.

FLIGHT-PERIOD Generally univoltine (late March/May) in prolonged emergence: records span February/July: a second brood (August/October) has been reported from N Africa and S Spain.

HABITAT Hot, dry rocky places amongst scrub, including coastal gullies; margins of dry riverbeds; cultivated areas; flowery meadows.

LIFE-HISTORY LHPs: N Africa, *Aristolochia longa paucinervis*; *A. fontanesi*; *A. rotunda*; (?)*A. pallida*: Europe, *A. pistolochia*; *A. rotunda*; *A. longa*; *A. baetica*. Ova laid singly or in small batches on leaves: subsequent development similar to that for *Z. polyxena*.

Southern Festoon

Spanish Festoon

SOUTHERN FESTOON

Upf red spot in S9 small, often obsure

♂

♂

f. ***cassandra***

♀

♀

Uph and unh cell-spot often broken

f. ***ochracea***

SPANISH FESTOON

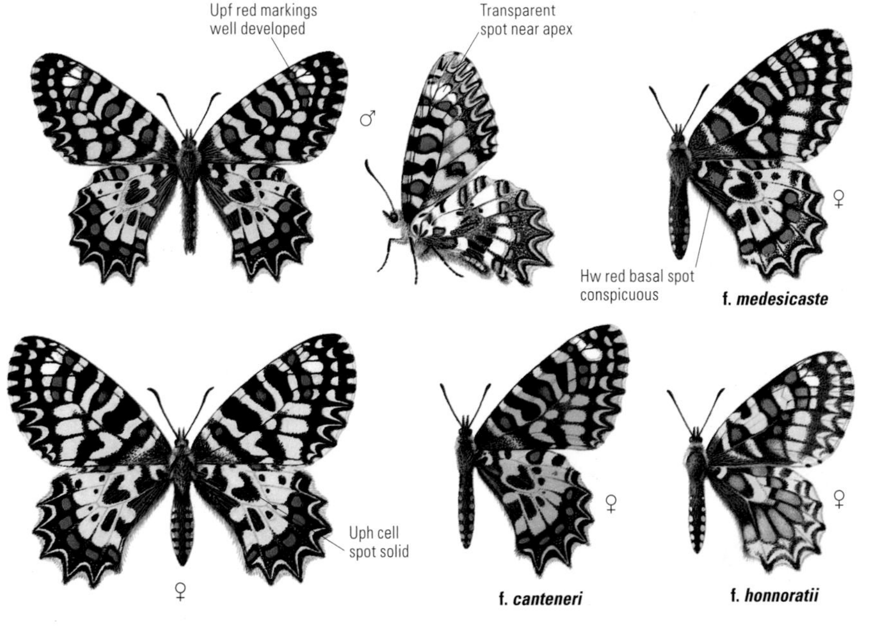

Upf red markings well developed

Transparent spot near apex

♂

♀

Hw red basal spot conspicuous

f. ***medesicaste***

Uph cell spot solid

♀

♀

f. ***canteneri***

♀

f. ***honnoratii***

Apollo *Parnassius apollo*

RANGE Most larger mountainous regions of Europe to Tian Shan and W Siberia.

P. apollo Linnaeus 1758 TL: Sweden.

DISTRIBUTION Most larger mountain ranges from Spain to S Fennoscandia, Balkans and Greece, including NW Peloponnesos. Absent from British Isles and Mediterranean islands except Sicily. Extinct in C Germany, Denmark and Czech Republic. 500-2400m: generally above 1000m in S Europe.

DESCRIPTION Male upf without red pd spot in s8; black pd spot in s5 rarely with obscure red centre: equivalent markings in female variable but averagely slightly better developed – sometimes conspicuous. Antennal shaft pale grey, narrowly ringed darker grey (cf. *P. phoebus*).

VARIATION A large accumulation of formal descriptions has resulted from attempts to account for local/regional variation in size, gc and development of markings. Many named forms differ only slightly, falling within an overall range of variation which might be considered normal for other species attracting less attention. An extensive, and therefore disproportionate account of racial differences may serve only to mislead. Amongst the more superficially distinctive forms are colour variants occurring at SW and SE extremes of European range: in S Spain, *nevadensis* Oberthür (Sierra Nevada), *filabricus* de Sagarra (S. de los Filabres) and *gadorensis* Rougeot and Capdeville (S. de Gádor); all red markings replaced by yellow-orange: in S Greece (Mt. Erimanthos, NW Peloponnesos), *atrides* van der Poorten and Dils: similarly coloured. Other races of Spain (*hispanicus* Oberthür), Greece and S Balkans (*rhodopensis* Markovic) have the more usual red markings.

FLIGHT-PERIOD Univoltine. Early May/September according to locality, altitude and season.

HABITAT Breeding-grounds comprise rocky places with areas favouring the establishment of LHP (Sedum) and the general exclusion of plant species requiring a more substantial soil-base – a condition met partly by the relatively high tolerance of LHP to desiccating conditions. Well-drained, often precipitous rocky slopes; limestone pavements with narrow crevices or hollows, or other flat, stony surfaces provide typical habitats where these occur in proximity to deeper soils supporting robust nectar-rich plants such as knapweeds and thistles.

LIFE-HISTORY LHPs principally *Sedum album*: less often, *S. telephium*. Other *Sedum* spp. and allied genera are often quoted in the literature – *S. roseum*; *S. annuum*; *S. villosum*; *Sempervivum tectorum*; *Rhodiola rosea*. Ova laid on dead or living woody plant stems, and the leaves of evergreen shrubs such as juniper or lichens. Usually hibernates as a fully formed larva within ovum-case, less often externally: may remain in diapause for two seasonal cycles: feeds in full sun on leaves. Larva, velvety black, lateral spots yellow or brilliant orange-red according to locality. Pupates in a flimsy cocoon under stones or moss.

NOTE Declined rapidly in Germany, Norway, Sweden and parts of France during the present century: climatic change appears primarily responsible.

Apollo

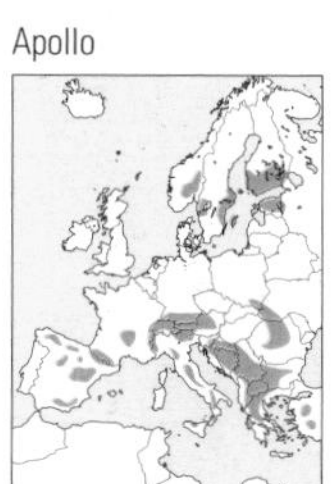

P. a. nevadensis
(Sierra Nevada)

APOLLO

P. a. atrides
(S Greece)

P. a. rhodopensis
(S Balklans)

Small Apollo *Parnassius phoebus*

RANGE Central European Alps, C and Polar Urals, Altai, Tian Shan, S and C Siberia, Yakutia, Magadan, Kamchatka, N America (Rocky Mts.).

P. phoebus sacerdos Stichel 1906 TL: Pontresina, Engadin. syn: *delius* Esper 1800 (invalid homonym).

DISTRIBUTION Central European Alps of France (Alpes-Maritimes to Haute-Savoie), Italy (Maritime Alps to E Alps), S Switzerland (Valais to Engadine) and S Austria (S Tirol to Styria and Carinthia). 1600-2800m: generally 1800-2200m.

DESCRIPTION Male upf often with black-edged red pd spots in s5 and s8: equivalent markings better developed in female and usually contiguous with additional red spot in s6. Antennal shaft alternately ringed greyish-white and dark grey. (cf. *P. apollo*).

VARIATION In Maritime Alps, f. *gazeli* Praviel: ups gc white; upf grey marginal border wider; black pd spot in s8 without red centre; uph black-ringed red ocelli smaller, without white pupils: variable and transitional to f. *sacerdos* in Hautes-Alpes. In E Switzerland, f. *cardinalis* Oberthür occurs frequently as a variant: ups dark markings more extensive; uph red ocelli joined by black bar. In Austrian Alps (Styria and Carinthia), f. *styriacus* Frühstorfer: resembles f. *gazeli*.

FLIGHT-PERIOD Univoltine. Late June/late August, according to altitude.

HABITAT Damp, sheltered gullies or hollows, often near the boggy margins of streams or similar sites suiting the needs of LHP.

LIFE-HISTORY LHP *Saxifraga aizoides*. Ova laid on various substrates in vicinity of LHP, including moss, dead vegetation, stones and soil; less often on host-plant leaves. Hibernates as a fully formed larva within ovum-case or externally. Pupates in a flimsy cocoon, in leaf-mould beneath LHP or amongst moss. (In N America, *P. phoebus* larvae feed on *Sedum* and other Crassulaceae, whilst captive larvae reportedly reject *S. aizoides*: the acceptability, or otherwise, of *Sedum* to European larvae does not appear to have been investigated).

Small Apollo

SMALL APOLLO

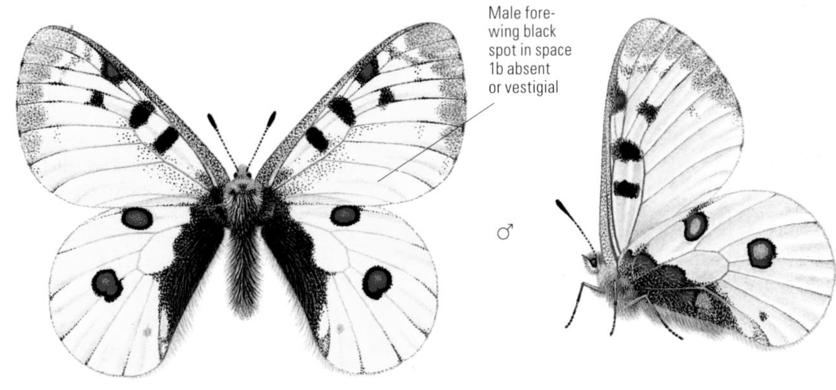

f. *cardinalis*
(E Switzerland)

False Apollo *Archon apollinus*

RANGE Bulgaria, Greece, Turkey, Jordan, Israel, Lebanon, Syria, N Iraq, N Iran.

A. apollinus Herbst 1798 TL: Ourlac (Bay of Izmir).

DISTRIBUTION SW Bulgaria: reported in 1991 from Sandanski (Struma Valley). Greece: district of Thessalonika; Aegean Islands of Lesbos, Chios, Samos, Kos and Rhodes. European Turkey: Keban; Kuru Dag; Gelibolu Peninsula. 0-1100m. Records from Thrace (NE Greece and E Bulgaria) are somewhat confused by alterations in political boundaries and place names around the time of the Great War, but appear to relate solely to attempted introductions. In 1918 and 1919, larvae from European Turkey (Kuru Dag) were introduced by Iltschev to Badoma (presently known as Avas or Avandas), an area north of Alexandroupolis. Searches for the species in this area in 1914 and 1915 had proved negative: several, recent searches (1987-1993) have also been unsuccessful.

FLIGHT-PERIOD Univoltine. Mid March/mid April.

HABITAT Olive-groves; vineyards; rocky places amongst scrub or open woodland.

LIFE-HISTORY LHPs: Lesbos and Samos, *Aristolochia bodamae*: Bulgaria, *A. clematitis*: Rhodes, *A. (?) guichardii*; *A. (?) parvifolia*. Ova bright green, laid on leaves. Larva black with red spots, feeding in small companies when young in loosely spun-up leaves. In later instars, larva feeds in a 'tent' fashioned from a leaf bound elaborately with silk – a curious practice, unique amongst European Papilionidae, for a larva with warning colours and an osmeterium to deter predators: however, the physical barrier would seem to offer some protection from dipterous and hymenopterous parasites. Captive larvae readily accept *A. clematitis* and *A. rotunda*. Pupates 1-2cm below ground-level in loose soil. Hibernates as a pupa.

CONSERVATION Use of herbicides in olive-groves and vineyards, the principal residual habitats, appears to have been responsible for extensive local extinction.

Clouded Apollo *Parnassius mnemosyne*

RANGE Pyrenees, C and NE Europe, Turkey, Transcaucasus, Lebanon, Syria, Iraq, Iran, Afghanistan, C Urals, Siberia, Tian Shan.

P. mnemosyne Linnaeus 1758 TL: Finland.

DISTRIBUTION Sporadic and often local. Pyrenees and Massif Central through C Alps, Italy and N Sicily to S Poland, Balkans, Greece and European Turkey: rare and local in S Fennoscandia (except Denmark) and Baltic states. 75-2300m: generally 1000-1700m.

VARIATION Many local variants have been described to account for development of ups dark suffusion. On Mt. Parnassos and mountains of Peloponnesos, *athene* Stichel: upf with 4-6 white pd spots in apical area: occurs as a variant in most S European populations, including Pyrenees, SE France, Apennines, Sicily and Republic of Macedonia: similar forms occur in Turkey, Middle East, Near East and C Asia.

FLIGHT-PERIOD Univoltine. Mid April/late August according to locality and altitude.

HABITAT Diverse. Light deciduous/coniferous/mixed woodland clearings, bushy places, open rocky and grassy slopes/gullies: in dry, damp or wet conditions in coastal and inland areas: less often, in hot, dry places near sea-level.

LIFE-HISTORY LHPs *Corydalis solida*; *C. bulbosa* [=*C. cava*]; *C. intermedia* [=*C. fabacea*]. In some sites where two host-plant species are present, e.g., *C. solida* and *C. bulbosa*, it appears that only one or other is used. Ova laid mostly on wilted leaves/stems of LHP; also, other dead plant stems, small stones or large rocks providing these are in close proximity to LHP. Hibernates as a fully formed larva within ovum-case or externally.

False Apollo

Clouded Apollo

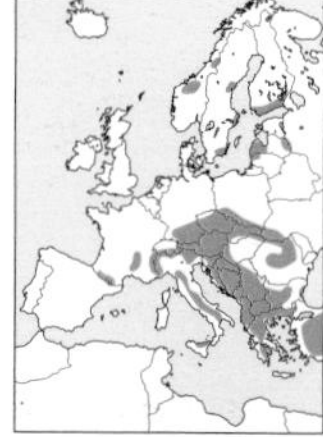

FALSE APOLLO

CLOUDED APOLLO

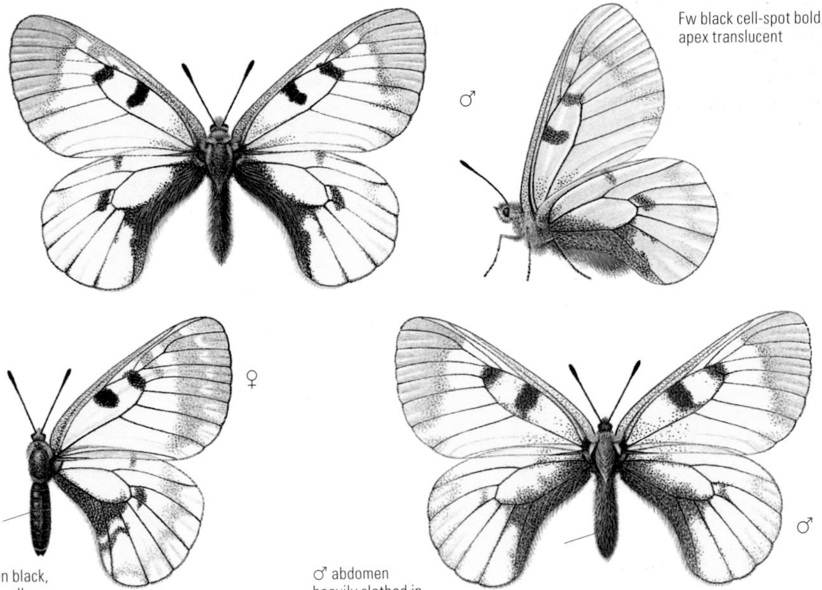

Fw black cell-spot bold,
apex translucent

♂

♀

♂

bdomen black,
ny with yellow
eral markings

P. m. athene
(Peloponnesos)

♂ abdomen
heavily clothed in
dark, greyish hairs

P. m. mnemosyne

PIERIDAE Duponchel 1835

Included in this large family, well-represented in Europe, are several of the more common and easily recognized butterflies, as well as some of the best known migrants, e.g., the Large White, Small White, Bath White and Clouded Yellow. Sexual dimorphism is generally well marked. The larvae of some species are cryptically coloured, whilst others are brightly marked with 'warning colours': larvae of the Large White and Small White, two very common pests on cabbages, exemplify the two extremes of these larval survival strategies.

Black-veined White *Aporia crataegi*

RANGE NW Africa, Europe, Turkey, Cyprus, Israel, Jordan, Lebanon, Syria, NE Iraq, N Iran, Transcaucasus, Asia (40-70°N), Japan.

A. crataegi Linnaeus 1758 TL: Sweden (Verity 1947).

DISTRIBUTION Widespread and common. Morocco. Algeria. Tunisia. Generally 500-2000m: occasional vagrants/(?)-migrants to 2600m. South of 64°N in Fennoscandia, throughout most of Europe including Sicily, Limnos, Lesbos, Chios, Samos, Ikaria and Rhodes. 0-2000m. Absent from C Norway, central W Sweden, Atlantic Islands, Balearic Islands, Corsica, Sardinia, Ionian Islands, Crete, Kykladian Archpeligo. Extinct in British Isles.

VARIATION Rhodes (common and widespread), f. *fert* Turati and Fiori: uns veins with heavy black suffusion, expanding into triangular markings towards outer margins.

FLIGHT-PERIOD Univoltine. In N Europe, late May/early July: in S Europe, mid April/July according to altitude, locality and season.

HABITAT AND BEHAVIOUR Diverse. Warm, sunny, bushy places; cultivated areas, especially orchards comprising species of LHP. Shows a marked preference for open ground containing an abundance of robust thistles upon which, during peak emergence, several butterflies may be found taking nectar on the same flower-head. Often found in areas devoid of LHPs, including high mountains. A dispersive/(?)migratory tendency would seem advantageous to a large species capable of very rapid population expansion: even at low population density, larvae may defoliate much of the available LHP: dispersion may be of further benefit in disrupting parallel population growth of larval parasites (commonly *Apanteles* spp.) which may infest over 90% of larvae.

LIFE-HISTORY LHPs *Prunus spinosa* and most *Prunus* cultivars including *P. domestica* (plum); *P. avium* (wild cherry); *P. persica* (peach); *P. armeniaca* (apricot); *P. amygdalus* [=*P. dulcis*; *Amygdalus communis*; *A. dulcis*; *Pyrus communis*] (almond): also, *P. mahaleb*; *P. padus* (Bird Cherry); *Crataegus monogyna*; *C. pycnoloba*; *C. laciniata*; *Pyrus communis* (pear); *Malus domestica* [=*Pyrus malus*] (apple); *Sorbus aucuparia*; also, in Atlas Mts., *Euproctis chrysorrhoea*. Bright yellow ova laid in batches on underside of leaves. Small larvae feed in a silken web which also serves as a hibernaculum. In later instars, after hibernation, larvae feed singly or in small groups. Often pupates on grass stems.

African Migrant *Catopsilia florella*

RANGE All Africa south of the Sahara, Canary Islands, through Egypt to India and China.

C. florella Fabricus 1775 TL: Sierra Leone.

DISTRIBUTION First reported in Canary Islands from Tenerife in 1965: recorded subsequently from Gran Canaria (1966), Gomera, Fuerteventura and Lanzarote (1976), La Palma (1986) and Hierro (1995): residency now well established in coastal districts, rarely recorded above 500m. Occasional in S Morocco (possibly resident in Drâa Valley), S Algeria (Tamanrasset). Recorded from Malta in 1963.

DESCRIPTION AND VARIATION Male ups and uns gc white: female dimorphic: yellow gc sometimes replaced by greenish-white (f. *pyrene* Swainson): both forms common in Canary Islands.

FLIGHT-PERIOD Polyvoltine. Recorded in all months in a succession of perhaps 8 or 9 broods: no diapause stage.

HABITAT Flowery places: gardens, parks etc.

LIFE-HISTORY LHPs: Canary Islands, *Cassia didymobotrya* (an ornamental plant introduced from Africa); possibly other introduced *Cassia* spp.: elsewhere in range, *C. odorata*; *C. occidentalis*; *C. petersiana*; *C. corymbosa*; *C. aschrek*. Ova laid singly on leaves, sometimes in large numbers, resulting in subsequent defoliation of LHP. Larval colouring depends on plant parts ingested: larvae feeding on leaves are green, those feeding on the yellow flowers are usually yellow – larval coloration unrelated to female dimorphism. Larvae are heavily parasitized by dipterans (Braconidae; Tachididae).

BEHAVIOUR Strongly migratory.

Black-veined White

BLACK-VEINED WHITE

Black veins conspicuous

♂

Fw translucent

♀

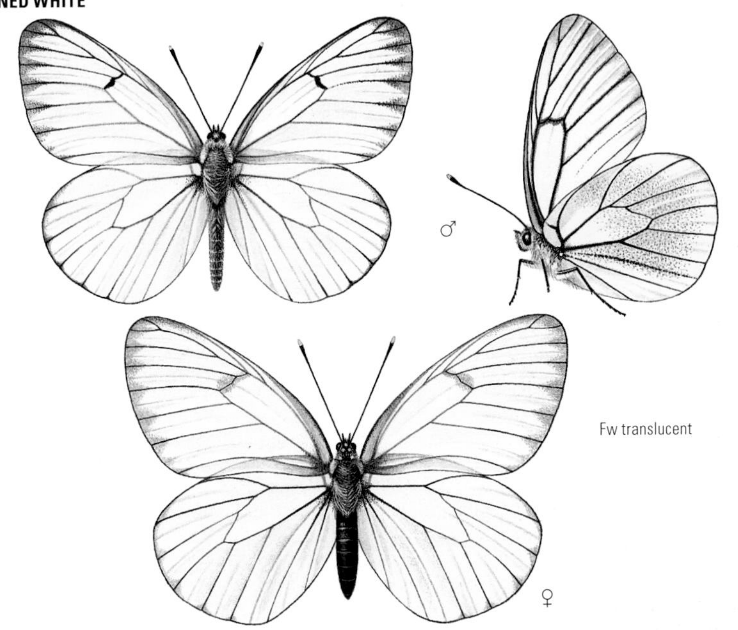

AFRICAN MIGRANT

♂

♀

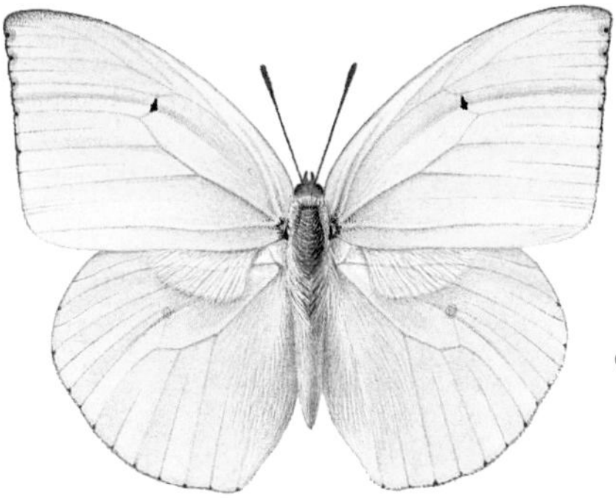

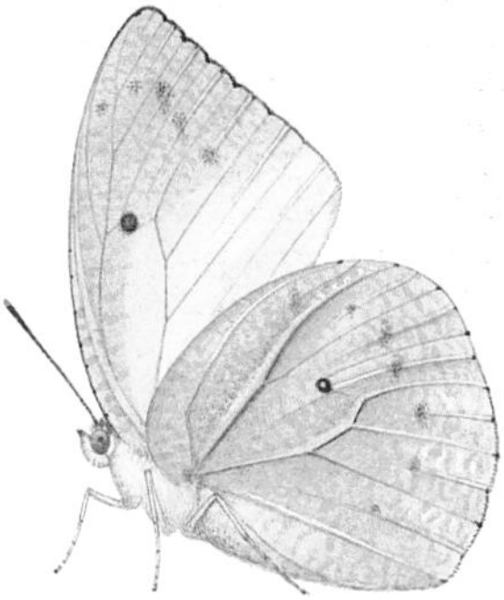

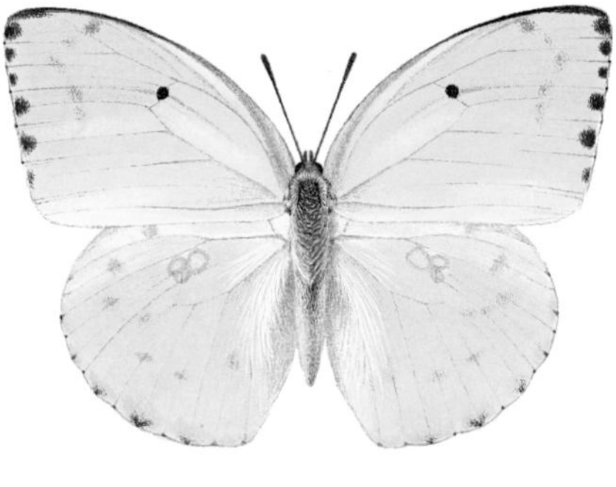

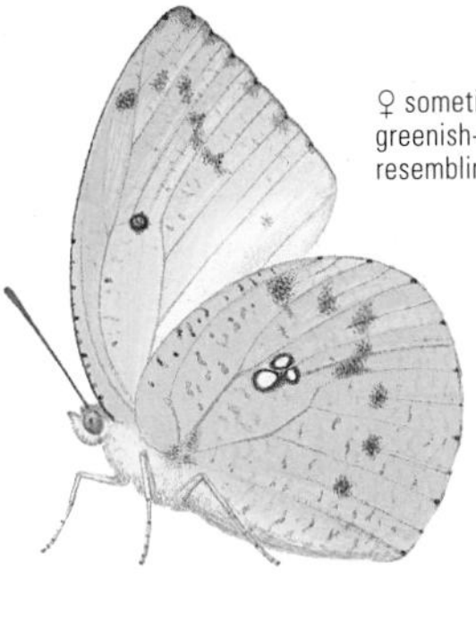

♀ sometimes greenish-white, resembling ♂

Large White *Pieris brassicae*

RANGE N Africa, Europe, Middle East and Asia to Himalayas. Naturalized in Chile.

P. brassicae Linnaeus 1758 TL: Sweden (Verity 1947).

DISTRIBUTION Widespread and common. Throughout N Africa and Europe to 66°N in Fennoscandia: at higher latitudes, appearance depends largely on migration. Recorded from most Mediterranean islands. Infrequent reports from Canary Islands most probably relate to accidental introduction or confusion with *P. cheiranthi* (below). 0-2600m: records at highest altitudes more probably relate to migrants.

DESCRIPTION AND VARIATION First brood: unh dusted with dark scales; male upf dark apical patch extending along outer margin to v3 or v2 (cf. *A rapae*). Second brood: unh dark colouring reduced or absent; male upf apical patch intensely black. On Madeira, f. *wollastoni* Butler (possibly extinct): ups markings with some of the character of *P. cheiranthi* (below). Wing-characters of captively produced hybrids of *P. brassicae* and *P. cheiranthi* resemble f. *wollastoni*.

FLIGHT-PERIOD Polyvoltine. March/late October.

HABITAT Diverse. Most habitat-types containing LHPs and an adequate supply of robust, nectar-rich plants, commonly thistles and knapweeds.

LIFE-HISTORY LHPs: diverse genera and species of Brassicaceae: also *Capparis spinosa* (Capparaceae); *Tropaeolum majus* (Tropaeolaceae). A frequent pest on *T. majus* and *Brassica* cultivars. Ova laid in batches. Young larvae feed synchronously in close companies, dispersing in late instars. Larvae have conspicuous 'warning' colours and a chemical defence derived from sulphur-bearing compounds (mustard oils) assimilated from LHP. Larvae often parasitized by *Apanteles* spp. (Hymenoptera). Hibernates as a pupa.

BEHAVIOUR A powerful migrant: vagrant specimens not uncommon on barren ground at high altitudes.

Large White

Canary Islands' Large White *Pieris cheiranthi*

RANGE Canary Islands.

P. cheiranthi Hubner 1808 TL: Canary Islands.

DISTRIBUTION La Palma: widespread, locally common. N Tenerife: apparently restricted to northern coastal districts. 200-1400m. Presumed extinct on Gomera – last recorded 1975. Records for Gran Canaria require confirmation: a record for Lanzarote appears to have arisen from mis-identification.

VARIATION On La Palma and (?)Gomera, f. *benchoavensis* Pinker: upf proximal border of black apical patch more sharply defined, extending to v2: upf and unf black discal markings averagely slightly reduced, showing tendency towards disconnection: characters are said to associate with smaller specimens and are suspected of being ecological in origin: closely similar forms occur sporadically on Tenerife.

FLIGHT-PERIOD Polyvoltine. Recorded in all months in a succession of 7 or 8 slightly overlapping broods. No diapause stage reported.

HABITAT Wet, shaded gullies in laurel forests appear to comprise the primary (natural) habitat. Areas with equivalent microclimate outside of laurel zone, such as wet cliffs, provide alternative, secondary habitats.

LIFE-HISTORY LHPs *Tropaeolum majus* (Tropaeolaceae); *Crambe strigosa* (Brassicaceae). *C. strigosa*, an endemic species confined to wet, rocky places in laurel forests, appears to be the only known, strictly natural LHP: *T. majus* (Nasturtium), an introduction from S America, is ecologically much more versatile. Ova laid on underside of leaves in batches of 5-50, batch-size roughly proportional to plant-size. Feeding behaviour and development similar to that of *P. brassicae*. Captive larvae accept many Brassicaceae species including *Brassica oleracea* (cabbage) which, if growing in appropriate microclimatic conditions (relatively cool/shady/damp) also appears to be acceptable in nature. Cabbage cultivars grown in more usual conditions, warm and dry, seem unattractive to the butterfly. In captive rearing, attempts to induce diapause by reduction of photo-period have been unsuccessful.

NOTE Specific separation from *P. brassicae* supported by differences in:- biochemistry; early-stages (especially ovum: 13-14 longitudinal ribs in *P. cheiranthi*, 17-18 in *P. brassicae*); voltinism (*P. cheiranthi* has no diapause stage); ecological requirements; migratory behaviour (*P. cheiranthi* is essentially sedentary).

CONSERVATION Destruction of primary, natural habitat appears largely responsible for decline in many areas and possibly extinction on some islands.

Higgins and Riley (1983) cite adult morphology as a basis for generic separation of *Pieris* from the following, seven allied species. This proposal has been largely disregarded by subsequent authors. However, as other taxonomically relevant differences are no less apparent (chromosome number, ovipositing behaviour and larval survival strategy – the latter reflected in morphology, behaviour and biochemistry), the proposal of Higgins and Riley is followed in the present treatment.

LARGE WHITE

Unf black spots faintly visible on upf

♂

1st brood

♀

1st brood

Black apex and marginal border dusted white in 1st brood, intense black in 2nd brood

♀

2nd brood

CANARY ISLAND'S LARGE WHITE

Pd black spots fused into solid band: upf basal area heavily suffused grey

Restricted to certain Canary Islands

♀

Small White *Artogeia rapae*

RANGE N Africa, Europe, Asia, Japan. Introduced to N America, Australia.
A. rapae Linnaeus 1758 TL: Sweden (Verity 1947).

DISTRIBUTION Azores. Madeira. Canary Islands (rare on Fuerteventura; a single record for Lanzarote). NW Africa. Throughout Europe, from Lapland to Mediterranean islands. Generally very common: less frequent in N Fennoscandia where occurrence may depend more on migration. 0-3000m: records at highest altitudes more probably relate to migrants.

DESCRIPTION Upf apical patch extends along outer margin to v7 or v6 (cf. *A. mannii*).

FLIGHT-PERIOD Polyvoltine. Generally early March/November: recorded in all months in Canary Islands.

HABITAT AND LIFE-HISTORY Diverse. Almost anywhere containing LHPs, principally Brassicaceae: also Capparaceae (*Capparis spinosa*); Tropaeolaceae; Resedaceae; Chenopodiaceae (*Atriplex* sp.). A common pest on cultivated Brassicaceae. Ova laid singly on leaves. Larva green, densely clothed with very short, whitish hairs – cryptically coloured and similar to other European *Artogeia* (cf. *P. brassicae* and *P. cheiranthi*). Larvae often parasitized by *Apanteles* spp. (Hymenoptera). Hibernates as a pupa, often at 1-3m above ground-level on walls, fences, etc.

Southern Small White *Artogeia mannii*

RANGE Morocco across S Europe to Turkey and Syria.
A. mannii Mayer 1851 TL: Split, Dalmatia.

DISTRIBUTION Morocco: Middle Atlas 2000m. Spain: very local: Provinces of Madrid and Málaga to Gerona and Huesca. SW and S France. S Switzerland: Valais; Tessin. Italy, eastwards to 51°N. Absent from Mediterranean islands except Sicily and Samos – possibly more widespread in E Aegean Islands. 0-2000m. Records for S Greece (Peloponnesos) require confirmation.

DESCRIPTION Upf apex black, extending along outer margin to v4 or v3; distal margin of spot in s3 concave or linear (not round), often linked to outer margin by black scaling along v3 and v4 (usually only apparent in second brood); uph, distal margin of costal mark concave. (cf. *P. rapae*).

FLIGHT-PERIOD Generally polyvoltine, March/September: in Morocco, only one brood has been reported (July/August).

HABITAT Dry, usually hot, rocky places, often amongst sparse bushes or trees.

LIFE-HISTORY LHPs *Iberis sempervirens*; *I. saxatilis*. Hibernates as a pupa.

Small White

Southern Small White

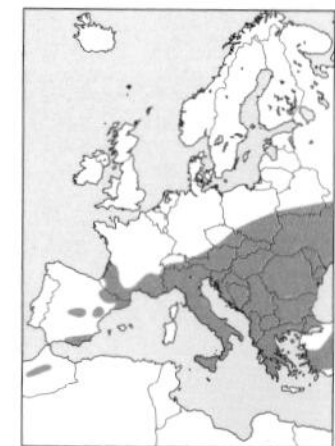

SMALL WHITE

Upf greyish apical patch extends further along costa than outer margin

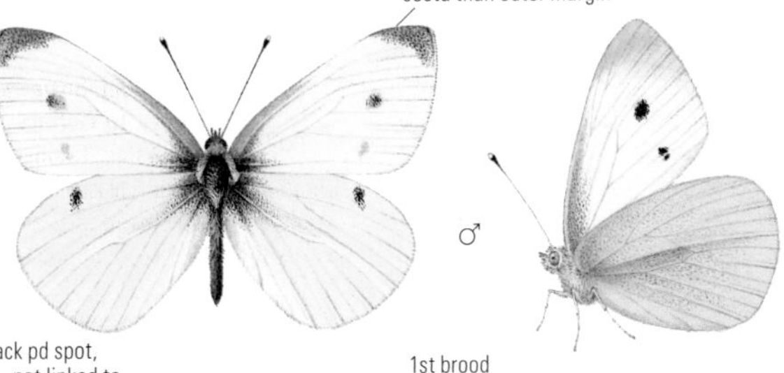

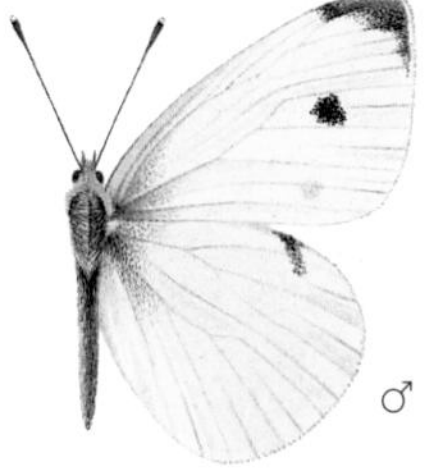

Upf black pd spot, round – not linked to outer margin by dark scaling along veins

♂

1st brood

♂

summer brood

♀

1st brood

♀

summer brood

SOUTHERN SMALL WHITE

Black apical patch extending to v3 or v4

♂

1st brood

♂

summer brood

Upf black pd spot concave on outer margin or linear: often linked to outer margin by black scaling along veins

♀

1st brood

♀

summer brood

Mountain Small White *Artogeia ergane*

RANGE Spain, S France, N and C Italy, Balkans, Greece, Turkey, Middle East, Iran.

A. ergane Geyer 1828 TL: Ragusa (Hemming 1937).

DISTRIBUTION Spain: very local: Provinces of Palencia; Cuenca; Huesca; Lérida; Gerona. S France: Pyrenees to Provence. Italy: extremely local in northern districts, commoner in C Apennines. Austria. Hungary. Balkans and Greece: widespread, often local. Absent from Mediterranean islands: records for Thassos and Crete require confirmation. 75-1850m: generally above 500m.

DESCRIPTION Upf without black spot (cf. *P. rapae*). Second brood: ups markings greyish, somewhat diffuse.

FLIGHT-PERIOD Bivoltine/trivoltine according to locality: early April/late August.

HABITAT Hot, dry bushy and rocky places, on limestone or base rich-soils; also dry, grassy slopes and gullies at higher altitudes.

LIFE-HISTORY LHP principally *Aethionema saxatile*: also, *A. orbiculatum*; *Isatis tinctoria*. Hibernates as a pupa.

BEHAVIOUR Males often gather in large companies on damp soil.

Balkan Green-veined White *Artogeia balcana*

RANGE Bosnia-Herzegovina, Republic of Macedonia, Bulgaria, N Greece.

A. balcana Lorkovic 1970 TL: Treska Valley [Republic of Macedonia].

syn: *canidiaformis* Drenowsky 1910 (nom. nud.)

DISTRIBUTION Bosnia-Herzegovina: Hrcavka; Zelenogora Pl. Republic of Macedonia: Treska Valley; Titov Veles; Katlanovo; Nikolic. Bulgaria: Osogovo Mts. (Kyustendil); Iskar Valley (Pancharevo Gorge); Struma Valley (Kresna Gorge). Greece: Phalakron massif: very local. 300-900m. Distributional relationship with *A. napi* unknown.

DESCRIPTION Resembles *A. napi* closely: unh veins more poorly defined in summer broods. Sexual and reproductive isolation (pre-mating barrier and low fertility) from *A. napi* has been demonstrated in cross-pairing experiments (male *napi* x female *balcana* and female *napi* x male *balcana*).

FLIGHT-PERIOD Bivoltine or trivoltine according to locality and altitude: early April/October.

HABITAT Superficially indistinguishable from that of nominate form.

Mountain Green-veined White *Artogeia bryoniae*

RANGE C European Alps, Tatra Mts., Carpathian Mts., Turkey, Caucasus, Tian Shan, Altai.

A. bryoniae Hübner 1806 TL: Geneva.

DISTRIBUTION Jura Mts.; Central European High Alps; Julian Alps; Tatra Mts.; Carpathian Mts. 800-2700m.

DESCRIPTION Male resembles first brood *A. napi*: female ups variable; pale cream-yellow, suffused greyish/greyish-brown; upf with narrow, greyish streak in s1b connecting outer margin to pd mark; uns veins well defined.

FLIGHT-PERIOD Generally univoltine. Mid June/early August: a partial second brood (August/September) has been recorded in warmer localities in S Switzerland.

HABITAT Damp alpine/subalpine meadows; flowery margins of streams.

LIFE-HISTORY LHPs (Brassicaceae) include *Cardamine bellidifolia alpina*; *C. resedifolia*; *Biscutella laevigata*; *Thlaspi alpinum*; *T. montanum*. Ova laid singly on flowers or leaves.

NOTE Hybrids with *A. napi* in areas of distributional overlap are reportedly infrequent: in captivity, cross-pairings result in progeny of poor viability. No significant biochemical difference between the two species has been discovered: greater differences have been found between different populations of *A. napi*.

Mountain Small White

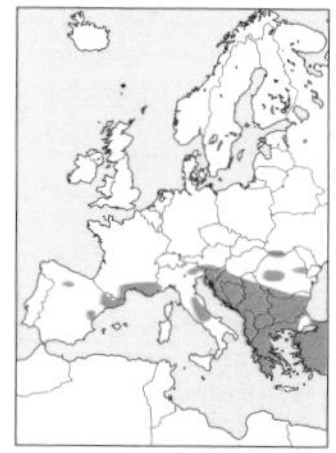

Balkan Green-veined White

Mountain Green-veined White

MOUNTAIN SMALL WHITE

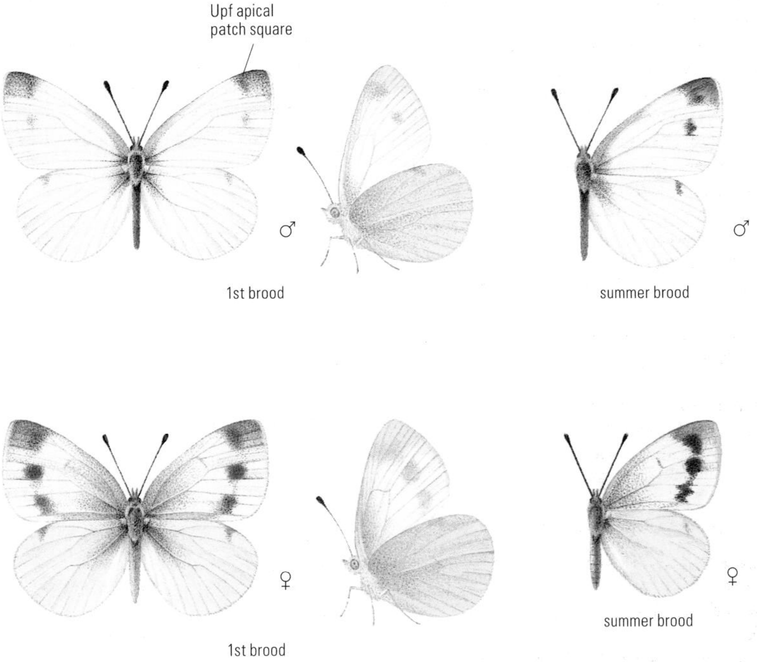

Upf apical patch square
♂
1st brood
♂
summer brood
♀
summer brood
♀
1st brood

MOUNTAIN GREEN-VEINED WHITE

♂
♀ ups dark suffusion distinctive
♀

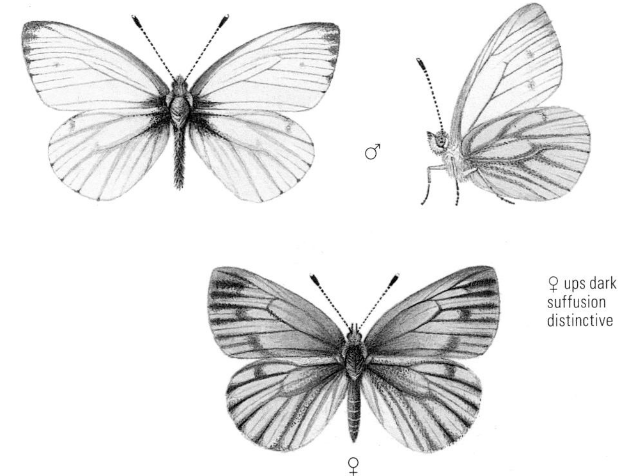

Green-veined White *Artogeia napi*

RANGE NW Africa, Europe, Middle East, Near East, Asia (40-70°N), N America.

A. napi napi Linnaeus 1758 TL: Sweden.

DISTRIBUTION Much of Europe, including Mediterranean islands of Corsica, Elba, Sicily, Corfu, Thassos and Lesbos. Generally widespread and common: more local in S Spain and S Greece. Absent from Atlantic islands, Shetland Islands, Sardinia and Crete. 0-2000m.

DESCRIPTION First brood: ups veins lined greyish; unh yellow, veins suffused greenish: male upf apical black scaling on veins variable, sometimes vestigial; spot in s3 variable, sometimes absent: female ups and uns black markings better developed, with additional spot in s1b and s5 upf. Summer broods: ups grey scaling along veins reduced or absent, but usually with black scaling near outer margin; unh paler yellow, variable – sometimes almost white: female black markings well developed. Female upf with greyish line in s1b connecting outer margin to pd mark – the so-called *bryoniae*-streak – occurs occasionally in England, commonly in Scotland and is typical in N Scandinavia (cf. *A. bryoniae*). In S Italy and sporadically elsewhere in S Europe, f. *meridionalis* Heyne: first brood indistinguishable from nominate form: summer broods: generally larger; unh gc very pale yellow, geyish markings greatly reduced. A rare but recurrent aberration in most populations has white gc on all wing-surfaces replaced by bright yellow (f. *sulphurea* Schoyen): intermediate forms with yellowish-buff gc (f. *flavescens* Tutt) are more common, especially in northern range.

VARIATION Considerable variation within European range is the subject of extensive research and debate. The species appears to be in an active state of evolution. The results of many experimental investigations are largely inconclusive and in some cases contradictory. The formal description of a great many local/regional ssp./forms presents a complicated and confused picture of biological relationships in which the contribution of ecological factors is very probably significant but difficult to isolate. The taxonomic status of the regional forms/sspp. described below is presently unclear.

FLIGHT-PERIOD Voltinism and emergence date dependent on locality, altitude and season: bivoltine (April/May and mid June/July) or trivoltine (April/early September) in N Europe, with a partial fourth brood in warmer areas (late September) in favourable seasons: in S Europe, three or more partially overlapping broods (March/October).

HABITAT AND BEHAVIOUR Damp, grassy and flowery places with some shade; woodland margins; hedgerows; fertile meadows; wooded river valleys. In later broods, females may extend their local range to drier terrain in search of alternative LHPs: such habitats include dry, often rocky, flowery gullies; open bushy places; areas of neglected cultivation. In Mediterranean region, bushy margins of mountain streams/springs, or flood-plains of rivers comprise a common habitat-type in which *Nasturtium officinale* (watercress) is a common LHP.

LIFE-HISTORY LHPs: Brassicaceae, including:- *Cardamine pratensis*; *C. amara*; *C. palustris*; *Nasturtium officinale*; *Lepidium heterophyllum*; *Lunaria rediviva*; *Hesperia matronalis*; *Arabis turrita*; *A. glabra*; *A. hirsuta*; *Sisymbrium officinale*; *Alliaria petiolata*; *Sinapis arvensis*; *Alyssum spinosum*; *A. saxatile*; *Cheiranthus cheiri*. Ova laid singly on underside of leaves, usually on smaller plants in partial shade. Larva usually feeds on developing leaves: in the case of *L. rediviva* (Honesty), oviposition/larval feeding appears to be restricted to young seed-capsules. *Barbarea vulgaris*, a frequently quoted LHP, appears to be unacceptable to captive larvae. Hibernates as a pupa.

A. napi segonzaci le Cerf 1923 TL: High Atlas.

DISTRIBUTION Morocco: High Atlas (Toubkal Massif; Tizi-n-Test; Dj. Ayachi). 1900-3800m.

DESCRIPTION Large; unh pale yellow; veins broadly lined greyish: male upf black spots in s3, s5 and s6 prominent: female ups veins lined grey.

FLIGHT-PERIOD Voltinism uncertain: records span May/early July.

A. napi maura Verity 1911 TL: Glacières de Blida, Algeria.

DISTRIBUTION Algeria: Glacières de Blida; Kabylie Mts. W Tunisia: Kroumerie. 900-1500m. Reported from Portugal.

DESCRIPTION Resembles summer broods of nominate form closely.

FLIGHT-PERIOD Trivoltine. April/September.

LIFE-HISTORY LHP *Ptilotrichum spinosum*.

A. napi atlantis Oberthür 1923 TL: Azrou, Morocco. Middle Atlas

DISTRIBUTION Morocco: Middle Atlas (Taghzeft Pass; Azrou; Dayet Achlef; Timhadit; Col de Tambrata): very local and uncommon. 1500m.

DESCRIPTION Large: unh veins almost without greyish suffusion: male upf black spot in s3 prominent.

FLIGHT-PERIOD Voltinism uncertain: possibly bivoltine: recorded in May and mid July.

A. napi adalwinda Frühstorfer 1909 TL: Finnmark.

DISTRIBUTION Fennoscandia north of 65°N. 0-500m.

DESCRIPTION Male indistinguishable from *A. bryoniae* or spring brood of nominate form from N Britain: female ups resembles *A. bryoniae*; variable, gc white to creamy-yellow, veins suffused greyish or greyish-brown, often extending to whole wing surface; upf usually with narrow, greyish streak in s1b connecting outer margin to pd mark (cf. *A. napi* and *A. bryoniae*). Local variation is marked but a systematic difference between mountain and lowland populations south of the Arctic Circle is apparent in the gc of females which are more yellow (*bicolorata* Petersen): although some ecological differences are associated with these two forms, their taxonomic relationship is unclear.

FLIGHT-PERIOD Generally univoltine, mid June/mid July, partially bivoltine in favourable seasons.

HABITAT Flowery mountain slopes/meadows; lowland grassland often near birch woods: often associated with human habitation.

A. napi flavescens Wagner 1903 TL: Mödling [E Austria].

DISTRIBUTION Central E Europe: E Austria; E Slovakia; Carpathian Mts. 300-1200m.

GREEN-VEINED WHITE

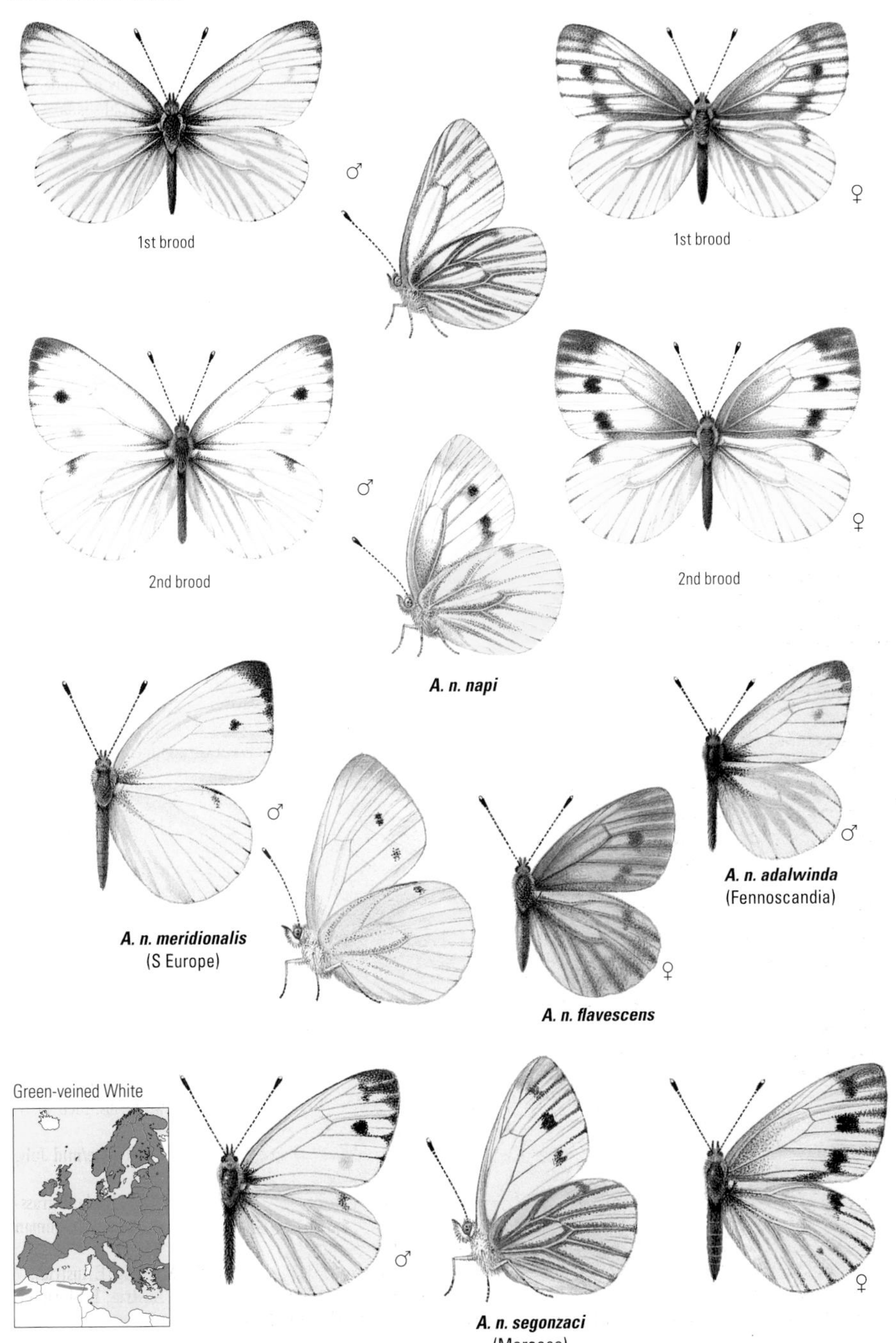

DESCRIPTION AND VARIATION Male resembles nominate form but variable; ups and uns dark markings and greyish suffusion along veins sometimes greatly reduced, unh gc sometimes white (f. *subtalba* Schima) – common or predominant in some localities: female extremely variable, ranging in overall character from *A. napi* to *A. bryoniae* (below): such variability may be expressed in the progeny of a single female. No ecological separation of *flavescens* and nominate form is apparent, and cross-pairing experiments indicate a high degree of genetic compatibility.

Krueper's Small White *Artogeia krueperi*

RANGE S Balkans, Greece, Turkey, Syria, Oman, N Iraq, Iran, Baluchistan, Afghanistan, Turkmenistan, N Pakistan, NW India.

A. krueperi Staudinger 1860 TL: Arcana, Greece.

DISTRIBUTION Widespread but very local. Albania. Republic of Macedonia. Bulgaria. Greece, including Corfu, Samos, Chios and Kos. 75-1250m – generally above 600m.

VARIATION In second and subsequent broods, unh markings progressively reduced, becoming paler and yellowish. Sporadic occurrence of typical first brood specimens in second generation suggests delayed emergence of hibernated pupae.

FLIGHT-PERIOD Polyvoltine. Late March/late August.

HABITAT AND BEHAVIOUR Hot, dry, precipitous slopes of limestone or other calcareous rocks hosting a wide range of flowering plants, including LHP, in rock crevices or on small ledges. Patrolling males appear to exploit air currents, generated over areas of naked rock, in search of females: similar behaviour is shown by females in search of ovipositing sites and nectar.

LIFE-HISTORY LHPs *Alyssum saxatile*; *A. montanum*. Ova laid singly on calyx. Larvae feed on flowers and developing seeds. Hibernates as a pupa.

Eastern Bath White *Pontia edusa*

RANGE C, E and SE Europe, Turkey, N Iraq, N and NW Iran, C and E Asia (40-65°N).

P. edusa Fabricius 1777 TL: Kiel.

DISTRIBUTION NW France (Finistère and Ille-et-Vilaine): E France (E of Saône Valley and Basses Alps), through S Switzerland (Valais), Italy (including Elba and Sicily), Germany (E of Rhine Valley and Bremen) to Gotland, Latvia, Balkans, Greece, European Turkey and most E Mediterranean islands. Recorded rarely as a migrant in S Ireland and S England. Occurrence in NE Europe largely dependent upon migration: with the exception of Gotland, no longer resident in Scandinavia. Distribution in N and E France and W Germany uncertain owing to possible confusion with *P. daplidice* and migratory behaviour of both species. 0-1500m, with migrants to at least 2300m.

DESCRIPTION Morphologically inseparable from *P. daplidice* but biochemically distinct. Differences in male genitalia, although statistically significant, are too small to allow reliable separation. Specific distinction is supported by poor viability of progeny arising from hybridization: no pre-copulative barriers appear to separate the two species.

VARIATION Second and subsequent broods, uns green markings less intense, tending to yellow. Size variable, sometimes very large; extremely small specimens appear to result from adverse effect of excessively hot/dry conditions on nutritional quality of LHP; similar observations apply to *P. daplidice* (below).

FLIGHT-PERIOD Polyvoltine. March/late October.

HABITAT Diverse – determined largely by presence of LHP. Open, hot, dry, sometimes barren, usually flattish, stony places: common on disturbed ground – roadsides, areas of cultivation, disused quarries and similar sites favouring colonization by LHPs.

LIFE-HISTORY. LHPs principally *Reseda alba*; *R. lutea*; *R. luteola*: in Scandinavia, *Descurainia sophia* [=*Sisymbrium sophia*]; *Teesdalia nudicaulis*; *Lepidium* sp. Ova laid mostly on underside of leaves. Larvae usually feed on flowers and developing seeds. Parasitization of larvae normally extensive and may exceed 99% (parasites often *Apanteles* spp., commonly *A. glomeratus* (Hymenoptera)). Hibernates as a pupa.

NOTE Identification of British migrants are based on superficial characters only and must, therefore, be considered tentative.

Bath White *Pontia daplidice*

RANGE Canary Islands, N Africa, SW Europe, SE Turkey, Middle East, W and S Iran to Afghanistan, Kazakhstan and Tahkistan.

P. daplidice Linnaeus 1758 TL: NW Africa (Wagener 1988).

DISTRIBUTION Canary Islands (La Palma; Gomera; Hierro; Gran Canaria; Fuerteventura; Tenerife: widespread and common (0-2400m); absent from Lanzarote except as a rare migrant – last recorded 1967. Madeira: as a very rare migrant. NW Africa 0-2700m. Portugal. Spain. Mallorca. France: west of Saône Valley; Provence. Corsica. Sardinia. Germany: west of Rhine Valley and Bremen. 0-2000m: migrants recorded at 2900m. Exact distribution and residential status uncertain in some regions (see *P. edusa*).

DESCRIPTION AND VARIATION See *P. edusa*.

FLIGHT-PERIOD Polyvoltine. Recorded in all months in Canary Islands. In Europe, March/October according to locality: generally more abundant in late summer/autumn brood.

Krueper's Small White

Eastern Bath White

KRUEPER'S SMALL WHITE

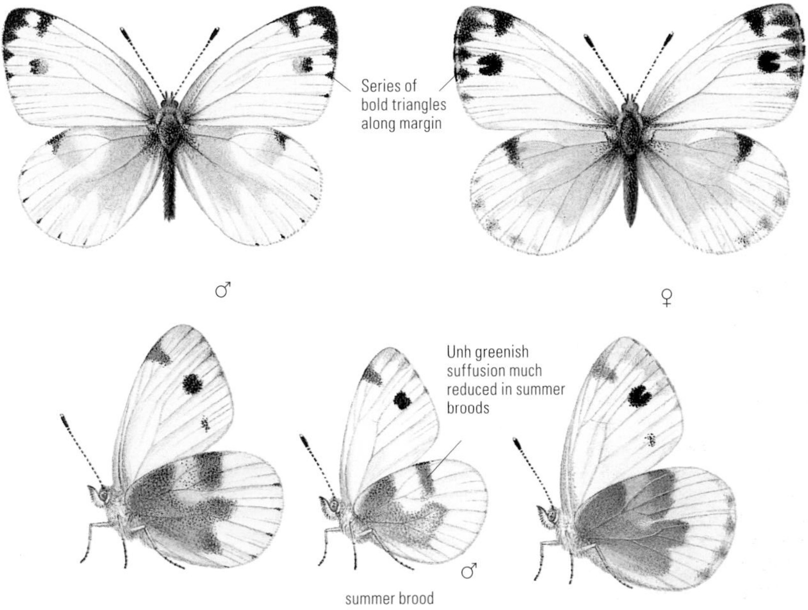

Series of
bold triangles
along margin
♂
♀
Unh greenish
suffusion much
reduced in summer
broods
♂
summer brood

BATH WHITE

♂
♀

Bath White

Unh white marginal
markings 'waisted'
2nd brood
2nd brood

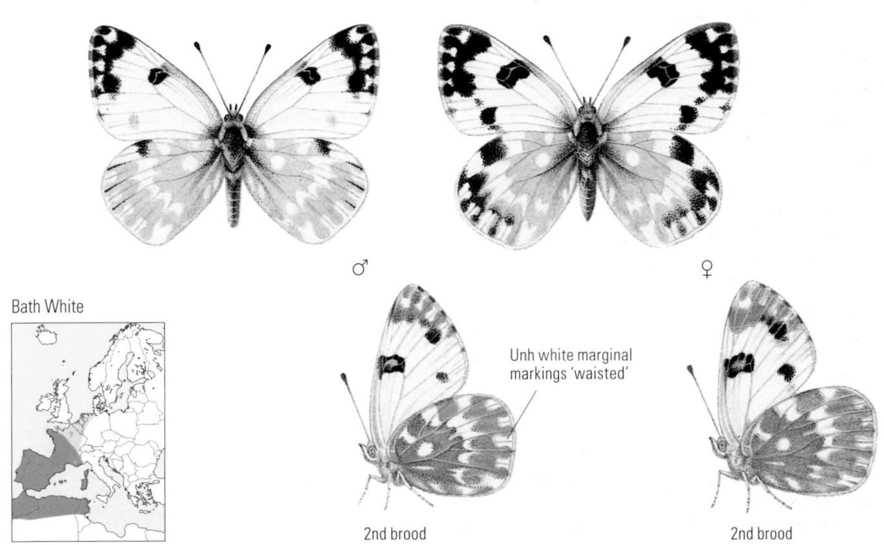

HABITAT As for *P. edusa*.
LIFE-HISTORY LHPs principally *Reseda luteola*; *R. alba*; *R. lutea*: several genera of Brassicaceae have been reported, including:- *Sisymbrium*; *Erysimum*; *Ptilotrichum*; *Arabis* [=*Turritis*]; *Moricandia*; *Alyssum*; *Sinapis*; *Iberis*; *Diplotaxis*; *Descurainia*; *Lepidium*; *Raphanus*; *Thlaspi*; *Fibigia* [=*Farsetia*]. Early-stage development as for *P. edusa*.
NOTE Occurrence of migrants in Britain cannot be excluded (see *P. edusa*).

Small Bath White *Pontia chloridice*

RANGE Republic of Macedonia, Bulgaria, NE Greece, Turkey, Iran, W and C Asia, N Pakistan, Siberia, Mongolia.
P. chloridice Hübner 1808 TL: not stated.
DISTRIBUTION Very local in widely scattered colonies. Republic of Macedonia: Vardar Valley (Titov Veles; Gradsko; Gevegelija). Bulgaria: Sliven; Belassisa Mts.; Arda Valley. NE Greece: Evros. European Turkey. 25-500m. Reported rarely from S Finland: a single record (1932) exists for Latvia. A record from Thessalonika (N Greece) requires confirmation (possibly a vagrant).
VARIATION Second brood, ups black markings slightly reduced; uns green markings slightly paler, tending to yellow.
FLIGHT-PERIOD Bivoltine. Mid April/late May and June/July in prolonged emergence.
HABITAT Stony places; gravelly river-banks; dry river beds and associated sites containing rounded stones, often amongst low scrub.
LIFE-HISTORY LHP *Cleome ornithopodioides*. Ova laid mostly on leaves. Larvae feed on leaves, flowers, and developing seeds. Pupates and hibernates on smooth, rounded stones. Pupa is remarkable in its striking resemblance to a bird-dropping. In captivity, pupa obtained from second brood enter diapause. (In Asia, *Cymatocarpus popovi*, *Sisymbrium polymorphum* [= *S. junceum*] and *Descurainia sophia* have been recorded as LHPs: the latter two species occur in SE Europe and may offer alternatives to the very rare and local *C. ornithopodioides*).
BEHAVIOUR Population density subject to marked fluctuation. Dispersion accompanies rapid population growth, resulting in the sporadic occurrence of both sexes in seemingly unsuitable terrain – devoid of known LHPs.
CONSERVATION Grazing, water extraction for agriculture and, most particularly, gravel extraction threaten most habitats associated with river systems.

NOTE Differences in larva and pupa indicates specific distinction from *P. beckerii* Edwards, a closely allied taxon in N America.

Peak White *Pontia callidice*

RANGE Pyrenees, C European Alps, Turkey, Middle East to Mongolia, China, N America.
P. callidice Hübner 1800 TL: Swiss Alps.
DISTRIBUTION Pyrenees. C European Alps: Alpes-Maritimes to Haute-Savoie; S Switzerland; N Italy, including Dolomites; Bavaria; Austria. 1500-3400m.
FLIGHT-PERIOD Univoltine. Early June/early August.
HABITAT Open, grassy and rocky alpine slopes.
LIFE-HISTORY LHPs *Erysimum helveticum* [=*E. pumilum*]; *Reseda glauca*; *Cardamine bellidifolia*; *Hutchinsia alpina*. Hibernates as a pupa.

Western Dappled White *Euchloe crameri*

RANGE NW Africa, Iberian Peninsula, S and SE France, NW Italy, E Libya, Egypt.
E. crameri Butler 1869 TL: S Spain.
DISTRIBUTION Widespread and common. NW Africa. 0-2700m. Iberian Peninsula. S and SE France. N Italy: Ligurian Alps to Bologna. 0-2000m. Limited distributional overlap with *E. simplonia* occurs in E Pyrenees and SE France.
DESCRIPTION First brood, ups discoidal spot usually not projecting along costal vein (cf. *E. simplonia*); hw apex (v8) conspicuously angled (cf. *E. tagis*). Second brood: larger; upf costa usually clear white – lacking dark striae; upf and unf discoidal spot often large, but variable; unf apex and unh markings yellowish-green, often interspersed with small patches of yellow, especially on veins. Resembles *E. ausonia* closely: variation in wing-characters largely precludes reliable separation without reference to distributional data – itself inadequate in areas of possible overlap.
FLIGHT-PERIOD Bivoltine. March/July, with prolonged and overlapping broods. Very large specimens with paler yellow-green uns, which usually accompany the first brood, are possibly the progeny of the first brood of the previous season – partial univoltinism: an extended period for larval/pupal development under different conditions (temperature/humidity) may account for differences in size and markings.

Small Bath White

Peak White

Western Dappled White

SMALL BATH WHITE

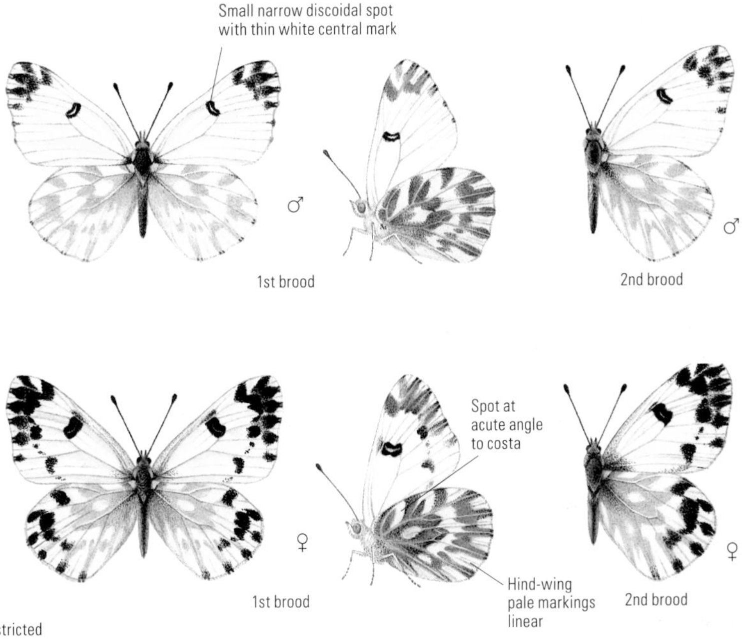

Small narrow discoidal spot
with thin white central mark
♂
1st brood
♂
2nd brood
Spot at
acute angle
to costa
♀
1st brood
Hind-wing
pale markings
linear
2nd brood
♀

Restricted
to SE Europe

PEAK WHITE

Restricted to
mountains

♂
Unh markings
distinctive
♀

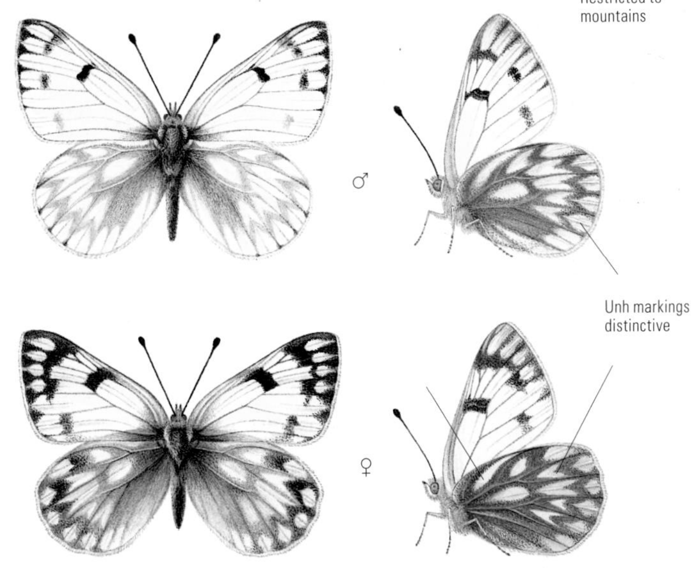

HABITAT Open, hot, dry, flowery places: common on disturbed ground, especially in cultivated areas.

LIFE-HISTORY LHPs include *Sinapis arvensis*; *Biscutella laevigata*; *Raphanus raphanistrum*; *Moricandia arvensis*; *Iberis sempervirens*; *I. pinnata*; *Isatis tinctoria*. Ova laid on flower-buds. Larvae feed on flowers and developing seeds. Hibernates as a pupa. May remain in diapause for two or more seasonal cycles.

Mountain Dappled White *Euchloe simplonia*

RANGE N Spain (Cantabrian Mts.), Pyrenees, Alps of France, SW Switzerland and NW Italy. (Closely allied taxa occur in NE Asia and N America).

E. simplonia Freyer 1829 TL: Croatia [?].

DISTRIBUTION N Spain: Cantabrian Mts.; Pyrenees. SE France: Basses Alpes; Hautes Alpes. SW Switzerland: Valais (Pennine, Bernese and W Lepontine Alps; Rhône Valley). NW Italy: higher slopes of S Alps. 400-2400m, usually above 1500m.

DESCRIPTION Upf black discoidal spot variable, usually narrow, curved, with short distal and proximal projections near costal vein (cf. *E. ausonia*; *E. crameri*). Hw apex (v8) conspicuously angled (cf. *E. tagis*).

FLIGHT-PERIOD Univoltine. April/August in prolonged emergence.

HABITAT Alpine/subalpine flowery meadows; grassy, rocky slopes.

LIFE-HISTORY LHPs include *Biscutella laevigata*; *Iberis spathulata*; *Erucastrum nasturtiifolium*. Ova laid on flower-buds. Larvae feed on flowers and developing seed capsules. Hibernates as a pupa. May remain in diapause for two or more seasonal cycles.

Eastern Dappled White *Euchloe ausonia*

RANGE C and S Italy, Balkans, Greece, Turkey, Israel, Jordan, N Iraq, N Iran, Transcaucasus, Afghanistan, S Kazakhstan, Tibet. (Closely allied taxa occur in N America).

E. ausonia Hübner 1803 TL: Italy.

DISTRIBUTION Widespread and common. C and S Italy. Elba. Sicily. Balkans. Greece, including Crete, Limnos, Lesbos, Inousses, Chios, Fourni, Samos, Ikaria, Kos, Rhodes and Kastellorizo. 0-1600m.

DESCRIPTION Resembles *E. crameri* very closely (See *E. crameri* and *E. simplonia*).

FLIGHT-PERIOD Bivoltine. Early March/early July in prolonged, overlapping broods. Variation between broods as for *E. crameri*.

HABITAT As for *E. crameri*.

LIFE-HISTORY LHPs *Sinapis arvensis*; *Isatis tinctoria*; *I. glauca*; *Aethionema saxatile*; *Iberis sempervirens*; *Biscutella mollis*; *B. laevigata*; *Bunias erucago*; *Alyssum saxatile*. Ova laid on flower-buds. Larvae feed on flowers and developing seed-capsules. Hibernates as a pupa. May remain in diapause for two or more seasonal cycles.

Corsican Dappled White *Euchloe insularis*

RANGE Corsica, Sardinia.

E. insularis Staudinger 1861 TL: Corsica.

DISTRIBUTION Corsica and Sardinia. 0-1300m. Common and widespread.

DESCRIPTION Upf black discoidal spot narrow with fine proximal taper projecting along v12; unf black discoidal spot small; hw apex (v8) conspicuously angled (cf. *E. tagis*); unh white spots small (cf. *E. ausonia*; *E. simplonia*).

FLIGHT-PERIOD Bivoltine. Mid March/April and mid May/late June: second brood partial, generally of very low abundance.

HABITAT Flowery scrub, rocky slopes and gullies.

LIFE-HISTORY LHPs include: *Iberis pinnata* (Corsica); *Sinapis* sp.; *Hirschfeldia incana*.

Mountain Dappled White

Eastern Dappled White

Corsican Dappled White

Portuguese Dappled White

Scarce Green-striped White

Green-striped White

MOUNTAIN DAPPLED WHITE

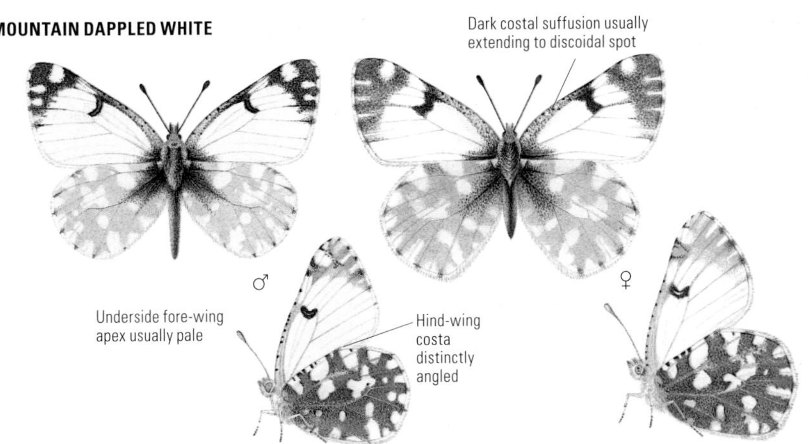

EASTERN DAPPLED WHITE

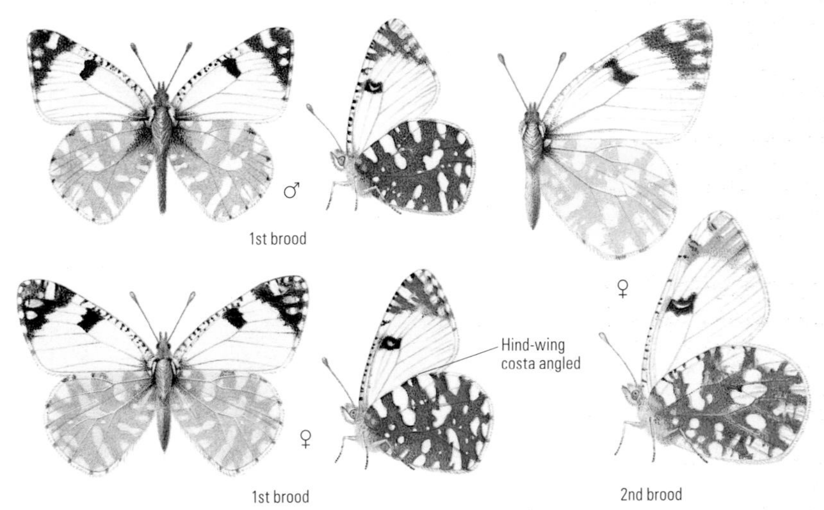

CORSICAN DAPPLED WHITE

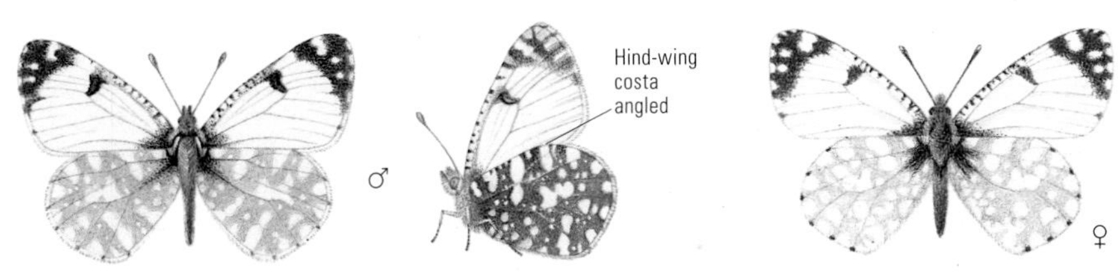

Portuguese Dappled White *Euchloe tagis*

RANGE Morocco, Algeria, Portugal, Spain, S France, NW Italy.

E. tagis Hübner 1804 TL: Peidade, Portugal.
syn: *lusitanica* Oberthür 1909.

DISTRIBUTION Colonies very local, widely dispersed. Morocco: Middle Atlas (Ifrane; Immouzer-du-Kandar; Annoceur; 1600m); Rif Mts. (Chefchaoune; Dj. Tizuka; Dj. Lakraa; 1400-1600m). Algeria: Dj. Aurès; Batna; Dj. Kaïder; El Kantara; Guelt-Es-Stel; Dj. Senalba; Lambessa; 600-1200m. Portugal: Tagus Valley; Algarve. Gibraltar. Spain: Provinces of Cádiz; Málaga; Granada; Alicanti; Toledo; Madrid; Lérida; Burgos; Vitoria. S France: Hérault; Gard; Vaucluse; Bouches-du-Rhône; Var; Alpes-de-Haute-Provençe; Alpes-Maritimes; Lot; Lozère; Ardèche; Drôme; Ain. NW Italy: Maritime Alps; Apuane Alps (coastal foothills); Monti Calvi. 300-2400m: generally below 1000m in Europe.

DESCRIPTION Hw apex smoothly curved (cf. *E. ausonia*; *E. simplonia*; *E. insularis*; *E. crameri*).

VARIATION Marked regional variation, especially development of unh white markings, has given rise to many named forms/ssp. However, these taxa appear to conform to a well-defined, although slightly erratic cline. In Europe, unh white markings show progressive development from Portugal and SW Spain (*davidi* Torrez Mendez and Verdugo Paez, *granadensis* Ribbe and nominate form) through C and E Spain (*castellana* Verity) and S France and NW Italy (Maritime Alps)(*bellezina* Boisduval) to west-central Italy (Monti Calvi, Livorno) (*calvensis* Casini). From SW Iberian Peninsula through Morocco (*reisseri* Back and Reissinger; *atlasica* Rungs), a general clinal reduction in unh white markings is apparent, culminating in NE Algeria (Aures Mts.) with *pechi* Staudinger in which the uns is uniform green except for small pale discoidal spot. Local and individual variation is significant, sometimes overlapping that of other regionally well-separated races; e.g., forms resembling *pechi* occur in Morocco and S Spain as occasional variants, whilst examples typical of French colonies occur in C Spain and *vice versa*.

FLIGHT-PERIOD Univoltine. N Africa, February/June: Europe, late March/May: according to locality, altitude and season.

HABITAT Hot, dry, rocky, slopes or gullies; rocky, flowery places, often amongst sparse scrub: usually on limestone.

LIFE-HISTORY LHPs: N Africa, *Iberis grosmiqueli*; *I. linifolia*; *I. odorata*; *I.* (?)*ciliata* and *I.* (?)*taurica*: Europe, *I. pinnata*; *I. linifolia* (?)*welwitschii*; *I. saxatilis saxatilis*; *I. s. cinerea*; *I. sempervirens*; *I. ciliata*; *I. amara*; *I. umbellata*; (?)*Biscutella laevigata*. Larvae feed on flowers and young seed capsules. Hibernates as a pupa.

Scarce Green-striped White *Euchloe falloui*

RANGE Mauritania, eastwards to Sinai and Saudi Arabia.

E. falloui Allard 1867 TL: Biskra, Algeria.

DISTRIBUTION Morocco: Anti Atlas (Tafilalet; Tizi-n-Tinififft; Tafraoute); High Atlas; Middle Atlas. Algeria: (Biskra; Bou Saâda). Tunisia. 200-1800m.

DESCRIPTION AND VARIATION Upf black discal spot without white centre (cf. *E. belemia*). Unf apical and unh markings vary from yellowish, through greyish-yellow to greyish-green.

FLIGHT-PERIOD Generally bivoltine, February/June, emergence prolonged in both broods: whilst records for September/October have been attributed to a third brood, the possibility of delayed emergence of second brood, due to weather conditions, does not appear to have been excluded.

HABITAT Dry, stony ground; dry gullies; desert oases.

LIFE-HISTORY LHP *Moricandia arvensis*: elsewhere in range, *M. sinaica*; *Diplotaxis acris*; *Schouwia thebaica*; *Zilla spinosa*; *Reseda muricata*. Ova laid on flowers/flower-buds. In Saudi Arabia, ovum/larval stage may occupy as little as 7 days: a possible survival strategy to offset the risk of rapid dessication of LHP. Prolonged pupal diapause may occur in years of persistent drought.

BEHAVIOUR Rarely strays far from LHP.

Green-striped White *Euchloe belemia*

RANGE Canary Islands, SW Europe, N Africa, N Chad, Middle East, Turkey, Iran, SW Pakistan.

E. belemia belemia Esper 1800 TL: Belem, Portugal.

DISTRIBUTION Generally widespread and common. Morocco Algeria. Tunisia. 0-1500m. Portugal: S. da Estrêla to Algarve. Spain: common in Andalusia; less frequent in Cuenca; Teruel; Madrid; Guadalajara; Valladolid; Burgos. 0-1350m.

DESCRIPTION Upf black discal spot with white centre (cf. *E. falloui*). First brood, upf apical patch and unh green stripes dark, well defined: second brood larger; uns stripes paler green tending to yellowish, somewhat diffuse.

FLIGHT-PERIOD Bivoltine. February/mid April and late April/early June, in overlapping broods. Occasionally, single specimens have been observed in late summer/early autumn.

HABITAT Dry, flowery, often rocky places, amongst scrub or open woodland; neglected areas of cultivation; olive-groves; orchards.

LIFE-HISTORY LHPs: Iberian Peninsula, *Diplotaxis siifolia*; *Biscutella laevigata*; *Sisymbrium*: NW Africa, *Diplotaxis tennuisiliqua*; *Biscutella didyma*. Larvae feed on developing seeds. Diapause stage: pupa.

E. belemia hesperidum Rothschild 1913 TL: Canary Islands.

DISTRIBUTION Fuerteventura 200-400m; Tenerife 1800-2300m; Gran Canaria 200-1000m. Reports from Gomera require confirmation.

DESCRIPTION AND VARIATION Similar to nominate form: smaller; upf black discal spot narrower; unh, margins of green stripes somewhat diffuse in both broods. On Tenerife, f. *eversi* Stamm: unf apical patch whitish.

FLIGHT-PERIOD Bivoltine. Gran Canaria and Fuerteventura, late December/early May: Tenerife, late March/early June. (Occasionally, single specimens have been observed well outside normal flight-times).

Maps on p. 56

PORTUGUESE DAPPLED WHITE

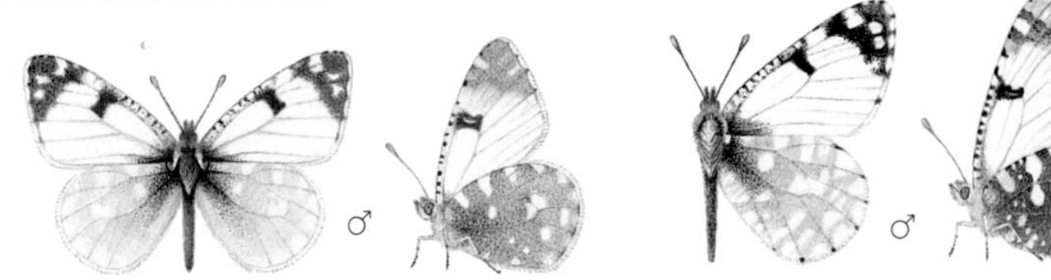

E. t. tagis

Hind-wing costa smoothly curved – distinctive

E. t. bellezina

E. t. castellana

E. t. pechi
(Restricted to Algeria)

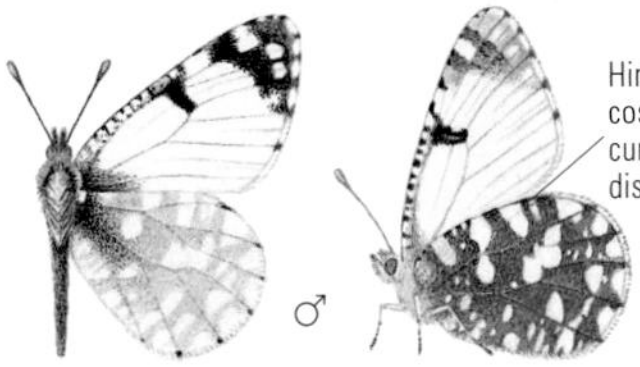

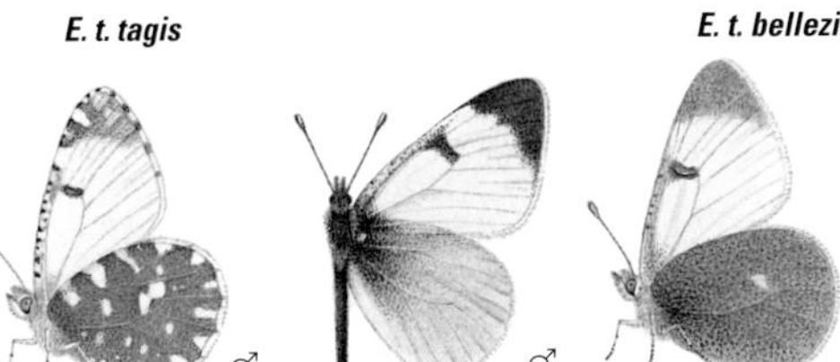

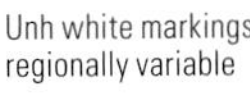

Unh white markings regionally variable

SCARCE GREEN-STRIPED WHITE

Discoidal spot solid and isolated from costa, bolder in female

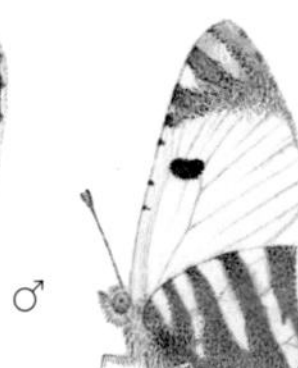

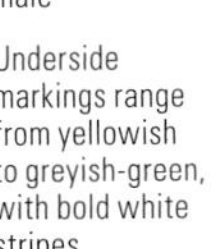

Underside markings range from yellowish to greyish-green, with bold white stripes

Distribution restricted to N Africa

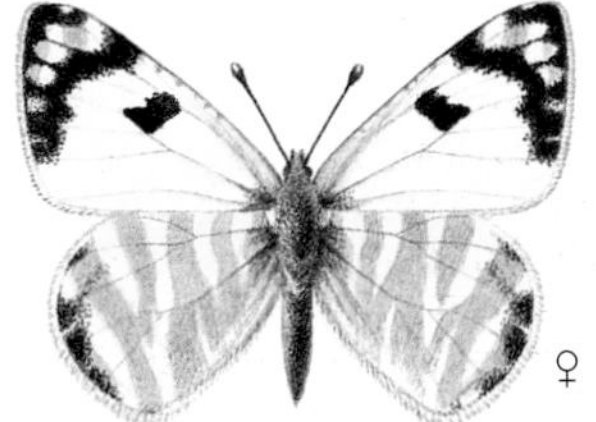

GREEN-STRIPED WHITE

Unh markings distinctive

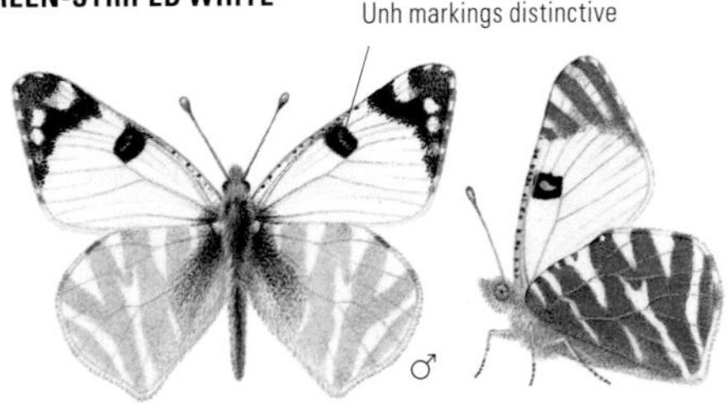

1st brood

E. b. belemia

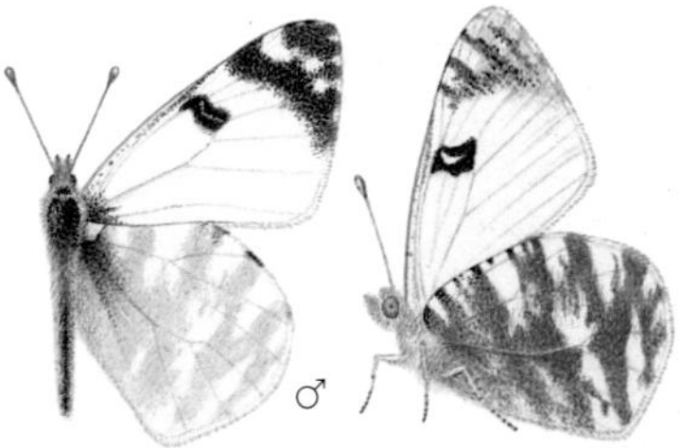

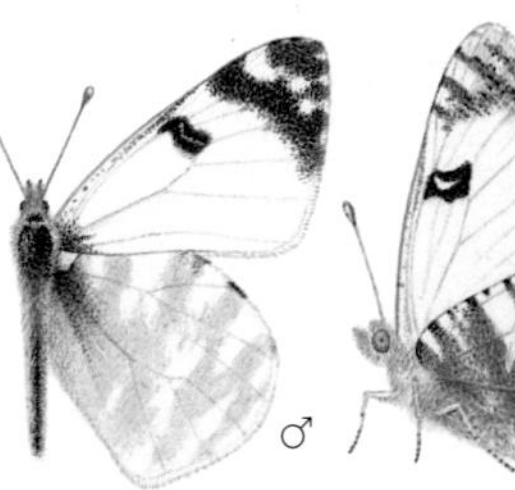

2nd brood

Second brood larger, underside markings yellowish-green

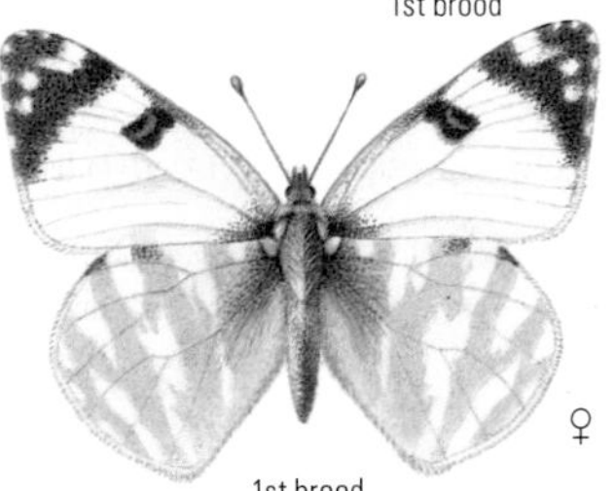

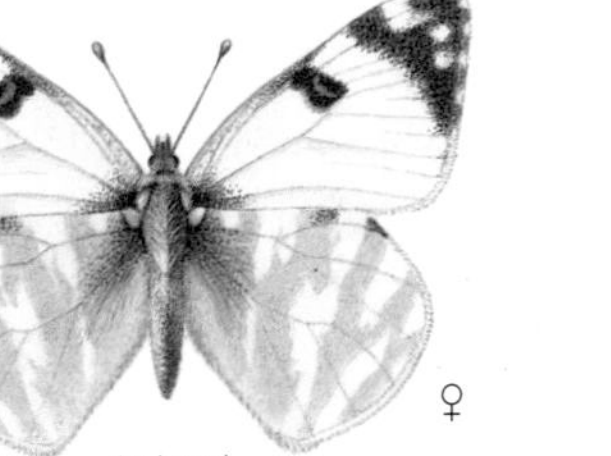

1st brood

E. b. belemia

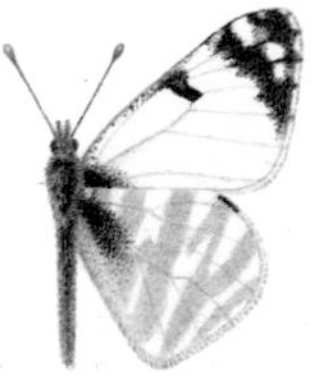

E. b. hesperidum
(Restricted to Canary Islands)

HABITAT Gran Canaria; dry, uncultivated places with *Sisymbrium*. Tenerife; sparse pinewood; semi-desert. Fuerteventura; damp meadows; neglected areas of cultivation containing *Sisymbrium*.

LIFE-HISTORY. LHPs: Tenerife, *Descurainia bourgeana*: Fuerteventura, *Carrichtera annua*; *Sisymbrium erysimoides*. Development as for nominate form.

Greenish Black-tip *Elphinstonia charlonia*

RANGE Canary Islands, Morocco, Algeria, Tunisia, Spain, N Chad, Egypt, Sudan, Saudi Arabia, Oman, Jordan, Israel, Lebanon, Syria, Iraq, Iran, Turkmenistan, Pakistan, NW India.

E. charlonia Donzal 1842 TL: Emsilah, Algeria.

DISTRIBUTION Canary Islands: Fuerteventura; Lanzarote; Graciosa. 0-400m. Morocco: S coastal region (Sidi R'bat); Middle Atlas; High Atlas (N'fiss Valley 1100m); Rif Mts. Algeria. Tunisia. 200-2000m. Spain: Granada (Baza 800m); Huesca (Fraga).

DESCRIPTION AND VARIATION Ups gc sulphur-yellow; apical patch dark brown with pale distal markings, proximal margin almost black, unmarked; unf costa and outer margin thinly lined red; discal spot solid black (cf. *E. penia*), appreciably variable in size; unh with a few obscure pale markings: hair-collar between head and thorax rose-pink (cf. *E. penia*). In Granada, S Spain, f. *bazae* Fabiano: all characters appear to be within range of variation of nominate form.

FLIGHT-PERIOD Bivoltine or polyvoltine according to locality: emergence in very arid regions appears to be governed by rainfall. Canary Islands, December/May: NW Africa, records span all months, more generally February/October: Spain, late February/late May (information limited).

HABITAT Hot, dry, rocky slopes; arid valleys; desert oases.

LIFE-HISTORY LHPs: Canary Islands, *Reseda lancerotae* [= *R. crystallina*]; *Carrichtera annua*; reported use of *Kickxia sagittata* [=*K. heterophylla*] (Scrophulariaceae), which captive larvae reject, has been discredited: Morocco, *Reseda villosa*; *Succowia balaerica*; *Moricandia arvensis*; *Eryngium tenue*; *Eruca vesicaria*; *Diplotaxis pendula*: Algeria, *Cleome arabica*; *Lonchophora capiomontana*: Tunisia, *Diplotaxis acris*: Spain, *E. vesicaria*. Ova laid on underside of leaves. Larvae feed on leaves and developing seeds. Hibernates as a pupa, which, on Fuerteventura, reportedly has a more pointed head than non-hibernating pupae.

BEHAVIOUR Recorded 'hilltopping' at 3000m in Atlas Mts.

NOTE Range overlaps that of *E. penia* in S Syria and Jordan: limited sympatry reported for S Syria.

Eastern Greenish Black-tip *Elphinstonia penia*

RANGE Republic of Macedonia, Bulgaria, Greece, Turkey, Lebanon, Syria, N Iraq.

E. penia Freyer 1851 TL: not stated.

DISTRIBUTION Republic of Macedonia: Treska Gorge (Skopje); Placenska Pl.; Pletvar Pass (Prilep); Vardar Valley (Tetovo). SW Bulgaria: Pirin Mts. (850m). Greece: Mt. Orvilos Mt.; W Phalakron massif; Mt. Pangeon; Lake Vegoritis; Vermion Mts.; Askion Mts.; Vourinos Mts.; Mt. Olympus; Mt. Chelmos. European Turkey. 700-1750m.

DESCRIPTION AND VARIATION All black markings subject to appreciable individual, inter-seasonal and intra-seasonal variation, with no clearly defined systematic differences between broods. Upf black apical patch variable, sometimes solid black, more often broken with yellow marks; discal spot very variable in size and shape; unf outer margin and costa sometimes lined rose-red; unf with black discal spot showing through from ups – shadowy, not solid black (cf. *E. charlonia*); unh gc greyish-green with variable pale obscure spots, more evident along costa: hair-collar between head and thorax pale yellow, sometimes with interspersed rose-pink dorsal hair (cf. *E. charlonia*). In addition to unf discal spot, distinctive characters in male genitalia and larval/pupal morphology serve to distinguish this species from *E. charlonia*. In Askion Mts. and Vourinos Mts., upf black discal mark generally larger, roughly rectilinear, atypically extending across costal vein to wing-edge – a relatively constant and distinctive feature.

FLIGHT-PERIOD Voltinism uncertain: at least bivoltine in a prolonged emergence, early May/late July (in captivity, pupae obtained from second brood usually enter diapause, emerging the following spring).

HABITAT Hot, dry, often precipitous limestone formations, where, evidently, topography affords some protection of LHP from grazing animals.

LIFE-HISTORY LHP *Matthiola tessela*. Ova laid on uns of leaves, less often on seed-pods. Pupates at base of woody plant stems or rocks. Pupa may remain in diapause for two seasonal cycles.

BEHAVIOUR In hot, overcast conditions, both sexes often sit on warm rocks with half-open wings. Seeks shelter under rock-ledges in hottest part of day. Males show some tendency to 'hilltop'.

Orange Tip *Anthocharis cardamines*

RANGE Europe, Middle East, eastwards through temperate Asia to Japan.

A. cardamines Linnaeus 1758 TL: Sweden (Verity 1947).

DISTRIBUTION Common and widespread in most of Europe to 69°N in Fennoscandia, including Ireland, Britain, Baltic Islands, Corsica, Sardinia (above 500m), Sicily, Corfu, Thassos, Lesbos, Chios, Samos, Tinos and Kastellorizo. Absent

Greenish Black-tip

Eastern Greenish Black-tip

GREENISH BLACK-TIP

Very local in Spain, Canary Islands and N Africa

EASTERN GREENISH BLACK-TIP

Very local in southern Balkans

ORANGE TIP

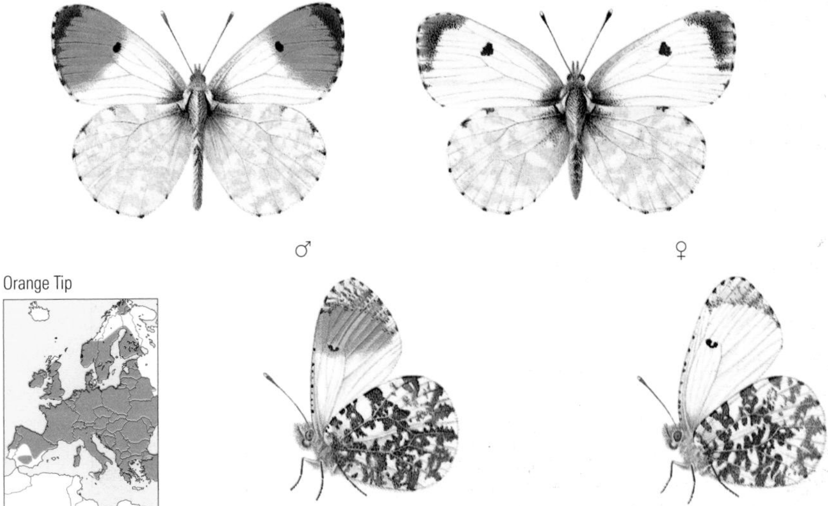

from NW Africa, parts of SW Iberian Peninsula, Balearic Islands, Malta, Crete and Rhodes. 0-2100m.

FLIGHT-PERIOD Univoltine. Late March/June according to locality and altitude.

HABITAT Diverse. Damp meadows; marshes; dry, lowland scrub; forest clearings; alpine grassland. On acidic or base-rich soils.

LIFE-HISTORY LHPs include *Cardamines pratensis*; *Alliaria petiolata*; *Arabis turrita*; *Lunaria annua*; *Biscutella mollis*; *Hesperis lacinata*. Hibernates as a pupa on plant-stems.

Moroccan Orange Tip *Anthocharis belia*

RANGE NW Africa, SW Europe.

A. belia belia Linnaeus 1767 TL:'Barbaria'Algeria.
syn: eupheno Linnaeus 1767.

DISTRIBUTION Widespread, generally common. Morocco. Algeria. Tunisia. 0-2000m.

DESCRIPTION AND VARIATION Both sexes: unh greyish markings indistinct: female uph often flushed ochreous-yellow. In S Morocco, *androgyne* Leech: both sexes, unh markings reduced, sometimes restricted to indistinct wedge-shaped marks on costa; female ups lightly flushed lemon yellow: distributional relationship with nominate form imperfectly known.

FLIGHT-PERIOD Univoltine. N Morocco, Algeria and Tunisia, April/May with sporadic occurrence of fresh specimens in June/early July: S Morocco, late February/April.

HABITAT Flowery places; woodland clearings.

LIFE-HISTORY. LHPs *Biscutella lyrata*; *B. didyma*; *B. raphanifolia*.

A. belia euphenoides Staudinger 1869 TL: Gibraltar.

DISTRIBUTION Widespread and common in Iberian Peninsula except NW Portugal. France: Haute-Garonne, through S Massif Central to Provence. S Switzerland: very local, restricted to Tessin. Italy: very local: Cottian Alps; Ticino; Abruzzi; Lazio. 0-1800m.

DESCRIPTION AND VARIATION Resembles nominate form: unh greyish markings more extensive, better developed. No significant variation noted in male unh gc. Female upf orange apical patch with variable black suffusion.

FLIGHT-PERIOD Univoltine. Generally April/June according to locality: reported from Gibraltar in early March.

HABITAT Dry, often hot, flowery places; margins of cultivated ground.

LIFE-HISTORY LHPs *Biscutella laevigata*; *B. auriculata*; *B. ambigua*. Larva feeds on developing seeds. Pupates and hibernates on dead plant-stems.

Eastern Orange Tip *Anthocharis damone*

RANGE Sicily, S Italy, Greece, Republic of Macedonia, Turkey, Israel, Lebanon, Syria, N Iraq, Iran.

A. damone Boisduval 1836 TL: Sicily.

DISTRIBUTION Italy: Sicily (Mt. Etna); Calabria; Aspromonte. Republic of Macedonia: Radika Valley; Treska Valley; Galicica Pl. Greece: Corfu (Mt. Pantokrator); Mitsikeli Mts.; Parnassus and Ghiona massifs; Taygetos Mts. 350-1300m. European Turkey. Not reported from Albania. A record for Mt. Chelmos requires confirmation.

FLIGHT-PERIOD Univoltine. Early April/late May, according to season.

HABITAT Hot, rocky, south-facing, usually precipitous slopes on limestone.

LIFE-HISTORY LHP *Isatis tinctoria*. Ova laid on flower buds. Larvae feed on flowers and developing seeds. Pupates on dried plant-stems.

Gruner's Orange Tip *Anthocharis gruneri*

RANGE Albania, Republic of Macedonia, Bulgaria, Greece, Turkey, Israel, Syria, N Iraq, Iran.

A. gruneri Herrich-Schäffer 1851 TL:'Crete'[(?)Greece].

DISTRIBUTION Albania. Republic of Macedonia: Galicica Pl; Radika Valley; Vardar Valley and associated river systems. SW Bulgaria: Slavayanka Mts.; Belassisa Mts. Greece: widespread but local: not reported from extreme NW Greece, E Thrace or Greek islands. 100-1800m.

FLIGHT-PERIOD Univoltine. Generally late March/May according to altitude: fresh males have been recorded in early July.

HABITAT Hot, dry, rocky calcareous slopes, often amongst scrub or small trees.

LIFE-HISTORY LHPs *Aethionema saxatile*; *A. orbiculatum*. Larva feeds on leaves and developing seeds. Pupates on dried plant-stems. Pupa, light green or buff.

Moroccan Orange Tip

Eastern Orange Tip

Gruner's Orange Tip

MOROCCAN ORANGE TIP

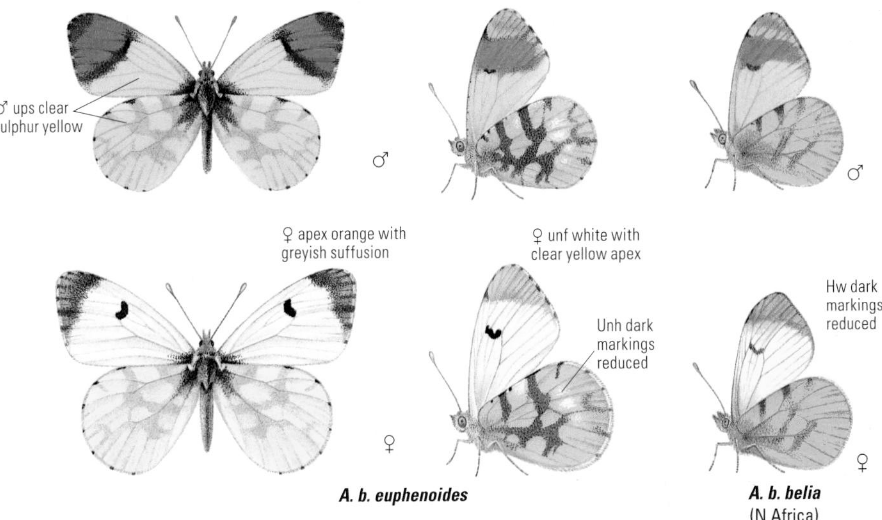

A. b. euphenoides

A. b. belia (N Africa)

EASTERN ORANGE TIP

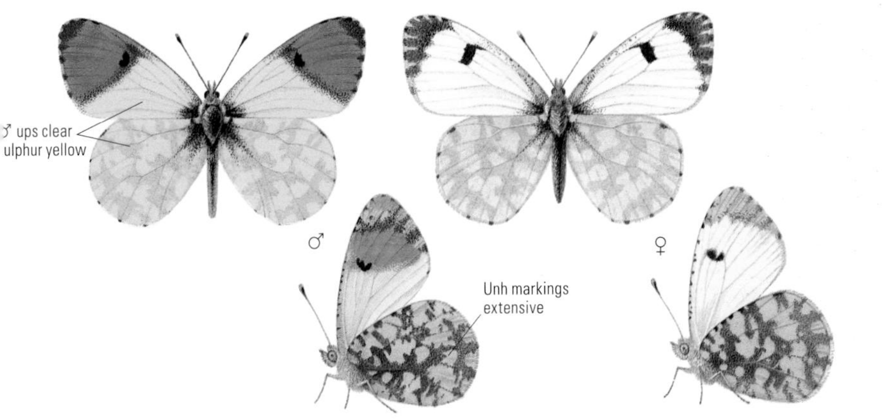

GRUNER'S ORANGE TIP

Sooty Orange Tip *Zegris eupheme*

RANGE Morocco, S Spain, Turkey, Saudi Arabia, Iran, Caucasus, Ukraine, Volga, S Urals, Kazakhstan, Altai.

Z. eupheme meridionalis Lederer 1852 TL: Andalusia.

DISTRIBUTION Local, in widely separated colonies. Morocco: Middle Atlas (Anosseur, Ifrane, Forum-Kaharig, Azrou 1200-1800m); High Atlas (Oukaïmeden; Tizi-n'Ouguerd-Zegzaoune; Lake Tislit, 1200-2750m. Spain: Andalusia to Provinces of Salamanca; Burgos; Soria; Zaragosa; Huesca; Lérida; Alicante. 500-1400m.

VARIATION Female ups orange apical patch sometimes reduced, rarely absent. In Morocco, f. *maroccana* Bernardi: superficially indistinguishable from f. *meridionalis*.

FLIGHT-PERIOD Univoltine. Late March/mid June according to locality.

HABITAT Dry, flowery often rocky places; most frequent in margins of cultivated land, neglected orchards and olive-groves.

LIFE-HISTORY LHPs *Hirschfeldia incana* [=*Sinapis incana*]; *Isatis tinctoria*. Hibernates as a pupa.

Desert Orange Tip *Colotis evagore*

RANGE NW Africa, S Spain, SW Saudi Arabia, Ethiopia, Somalia.

C. evagore nouna Lucas 1849 TL: Oran, Algeria.

DISTRIBUTION Morocco: Middle Atlas; High Atlas. Algeria. Tunisia. Generally 800-2200m: recorded at 2500m in High Atlas. S Spain: mainly coastal areas below 100m: Provinces of Cádiz; Málaga; Granada; Almeria; Murcia. 0-400m.

VARIATION Both sexes, ups black and grey markings follow a very complex, but systematic pattern of development through the broods: first brood, lightly marked, late summer broods heavily suffused black, with complementary greyish markings in nearly all wing-areas.

FLIGHT-PERIOD Polyvoltine. Spain, April/October: Morocco, generally February/November, but records span all months.

HABITAT Hot, dry gullies; steep, rocky slopes; stony margins of cultivated ground.

LIFE-HISTORY LHPs: NW Africa, *Capparis spinosa*; *C. droserifolia*: Spain, *Capparis spinosa*. Ova laid on leaves, upon which larvae feed. Hibernates as a pupa.

BEHAVIOUR In S Spain, population density increases progressively with each brood, apparently inducing territorial expansion and establishment of temporary colonies away from coastal regions in late summer/early autumn. In autumn, recorded from Middle Atlas and Rif Mts. in areas apparently devoid of LHPs.

Mountain Clouded Yellow *Colias phicomone*

RANGE Europe (Cantabrian Mts., Pyrenees, Central Alps, Carpathians).

C. phicomone Esper 1780 TL: Styria.

DISTRIBUTION Spain: Cantabrian Mts. above 1800m; Pyrenees. France: Pyrenees. Alps of France; Italy; S, C and E Switzerland; Germany; Austria. Romania: N Carpathian Mts. 900-2500m.

VARIATION At lower altitudes, ups greyish suffusion reduced; male gc brighter yellow.

FLIGHT-PERIOD Univoltine. Generally mid June/mid August, emerging late May at lowest altitudes: a partial second brood has been reported in warm localities in favourable seasons.

HABITAT Grassy slopes; alpine pasture.

LIFE-HISTORY. LHPs *Hippocrepis comosa*; *Trifolium repens*; *Lotus corniculatus*. Ova laid singly on upperside of leaves. Hibernates as a small larva.

Sooty Orange Tip

Desert Orange Tip

Mountain Clouded Yellow

SOOTY ORANGE TIP

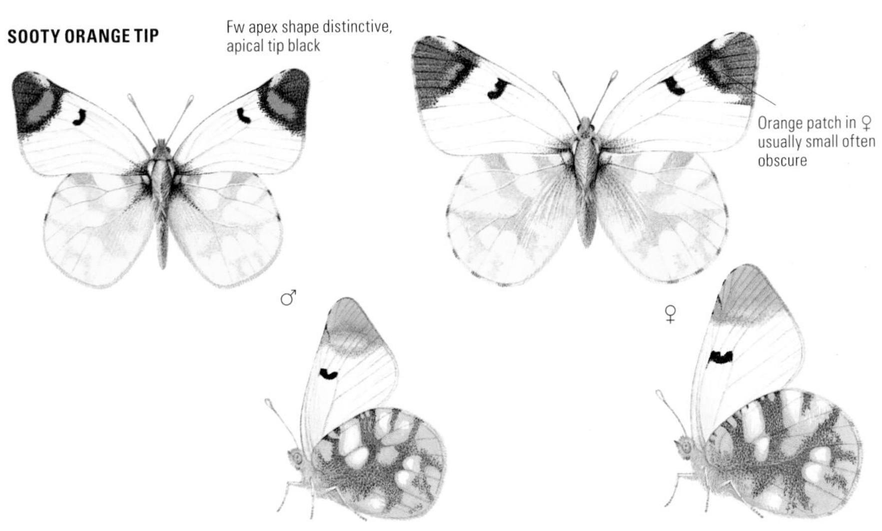

DESERT ORANGE TIP

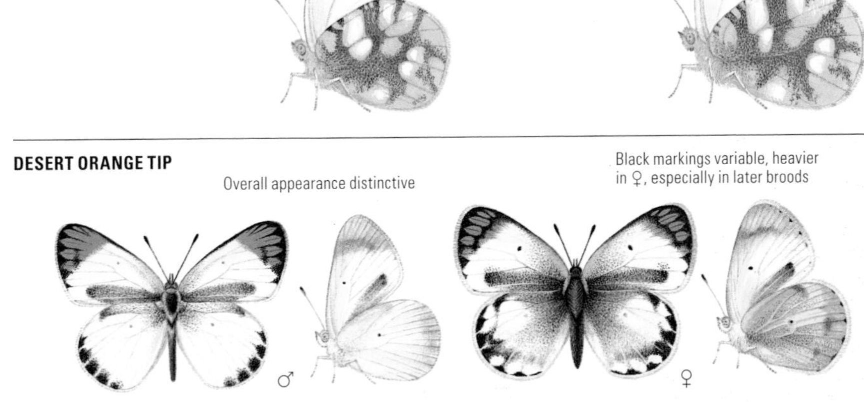

MOUNTAIN CLOUDED YELLOW

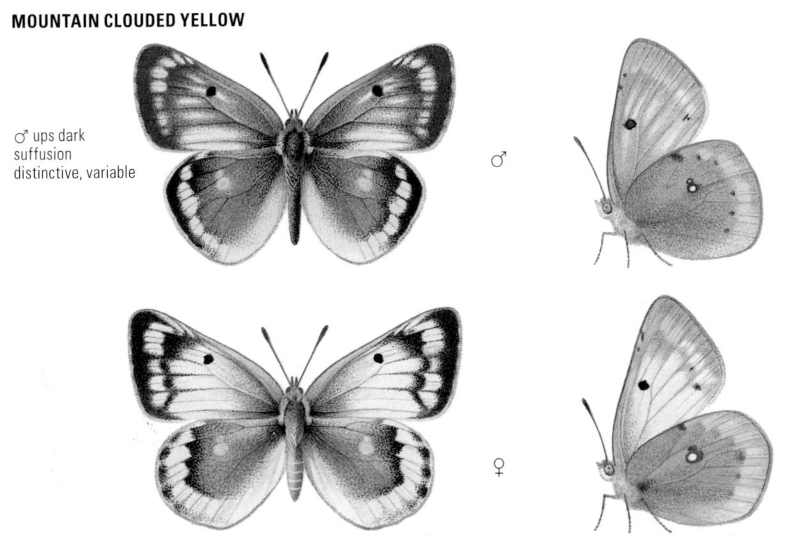

Pale Arctic Clouded Yellow *Colias nastes*

RANGE Arctic Fennoscandia, Taimyr, Yamal Peninsula, Novaya Zemlya, Polar Urals, N America (including Rocky Mts.), Greenland.

C. nastes werdandi Zetterstedt 1840 TL: Torne-Lapland.

DISTRIBUTION Norway: just S of Arctic Circle to Arctic Sea. N Sweden. NW Finland. 100-1100m.

VARIATION Male ups gc various delicate shades of whitish-yellow or green; marginal borders variable, light grey to black; upf proximal dark border of submarginal pale spots often reduced, sometimes absent. Males reflect UV light. Female uph dark markings sometimes limited to greyish dusting on veins at outer margin. Yellowish-orange variants (f. *christiernssoni* Lampa) are believed to result from hybridization with *C. hecla*.

FLIGHT-PERIOD Univoltine. Mid May/early July according to locality and season.

HABITAT Open grassy areas amongst scrub; gentle heathland slopes near marshes; dry grassy and rocky slopes in mountains.

LIFE-HISTORY LHP *Vaccinium* spp. at lowest altitudes, *Astragalus alpinus* in mountains. Ova laid on leaves. Hibernates as a larva or pupa. Full larval development may require two seasonal cycles.

Moorland Clouded Yellow *Colias palaeno*

RANGE C, E and NE Europe, W and C Asia (50-70°N), Siberia, Sakhalin, Mongolia, NE China, Korea, Japan, N America.

C. palaeno Linnaeus 1761 TL: Uppsala.

DISTRIBUTION France: Jura; Vosges. Italy: very restricted in S Alps. Switzerland: Jura Mts.; C and S Alps. Germany to N Fennoscandia, Baltic states and N Balkans (Carpathian Mts.). 100-2500m. Extinct in Belgium.

VARIATION Male ups gc ranges from white, faintly tinged with yellow, to pale sulphur-yellow: palest forms predominate in Lapland, yellowish forms in southern range (f. *europome* Esper); upf black discoidal spot variable; sometimes very small or absent, or replaced by thin oval ring, usually very faint in specimens from highest altitudes. In Central Alps, female ups sometimes pale lemon yellow (f. *illgneri* Rühl). At high altitudes, unh in both sexes more heavily dusted with dark scales (f. *europomene* Ochsenheimer).

FLIGHT-PERIOD Univoltine. Late June/early August in Lapland: mid June/July in S Scandinavia and C Alps: mid June/late August: emergence depending on altitude, locality and season.

HABITAT Acidic marshes and bogs with *Vaccinium* and other shrubs, usually near deciduous or coniferous woodland. At highest level in C Alps, habitats somewhat drier, more open and frequently associated with *Juniperous communis*.

LIFE-HISTORY LHPs *Vaccinium uliginosum*; *V. myrtillus*. Ova laid on upperside of leaves. Larvae are said to feed at night, concealing themselves during the day. Hibernates as a larva.

CONSERVATION Habitat loss arising from land drainage has been responsible for widespread local extinction in many low-lying areas of C Europe.

Lesser Clouded Yellow *Colias chrysotheme*

RANGE E Europe, C and E Asia (50-57°N), NE China.

C. chrysotheme Esper 1781 TL: Cremnitz, Hungary.

DISTRIBUTION Small, widely dispersed colonies. E Austria. Slovakia. Hungary. Romania. 300-1000m. Apparently extinct in Czech Republic. Records for Bulgaria appear to have arisen from misidentification.

DESCRIPTION AND VARIATION Male ups dark marginal borders crossed proximally by yellow veins; uph costa without androconial patch (cf. *C. crocea* and *C. myrmidone*): female fw pointed; upf costa dusky-green; uph lemon yellow submarginal spots well developed, extending to costa (cf. *C. crocea*): white female form is said to be very rare. First brood appreciably smaller than late summer brood.

FLIGHT-PERIOD Polyvoltine. Late April/late October in three or four broods according to season.

HABITAT Grassy, flowery bushy places.

LIFE-HISTORY LHPs *Vicia hirsuta*; *Astragalus austriacus*. Captive larvae accept *A. glycyphyllos* readily.

Pale Arctic Clouded Yellow

Moorland Clouded Yellow

Lesser Clouded Yellow

PALE ARCTIC CLOUDED YELLOW

♂ and ♀ markings distictive
Restricted to Arctic Fennoscandia
♂
♀

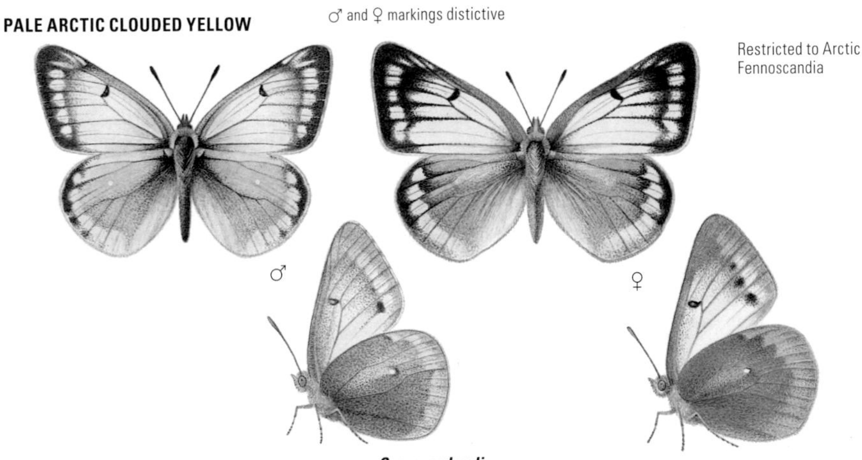

C. a. werdandi

MOORLAND CLOUDED YELLOW

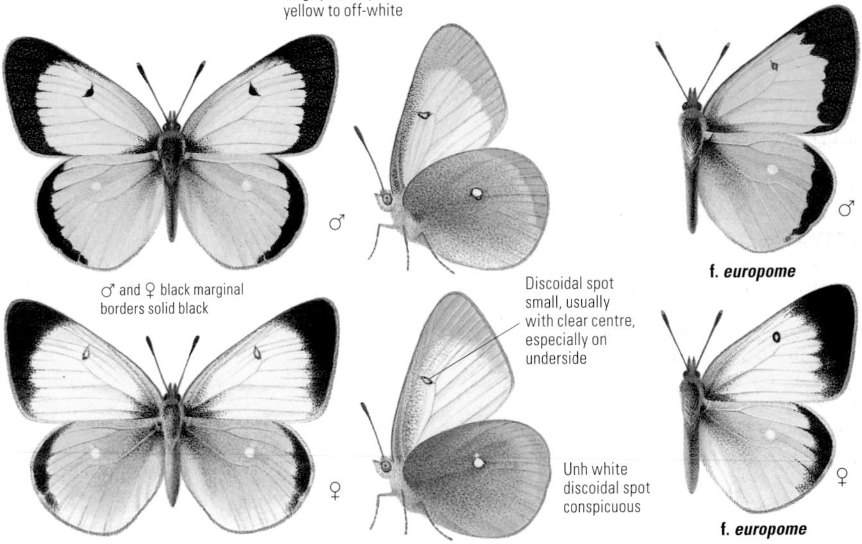

♂ gc pale sulphur yellow to off-white
♂
♂
f. *europome*
♂ and ♀ black marginal borders solid black
Discoidal spot small, usually with clear centre, especially on underside
Unh white discoidal spot conspicuous
♀
♀
f. *europome*

LESSER CLOUDED YELLOW

Uns dark pd spots usually well developed
Costa greyish-green
♀
♂
Discoidal spot deep orange, lemon submarginal spots

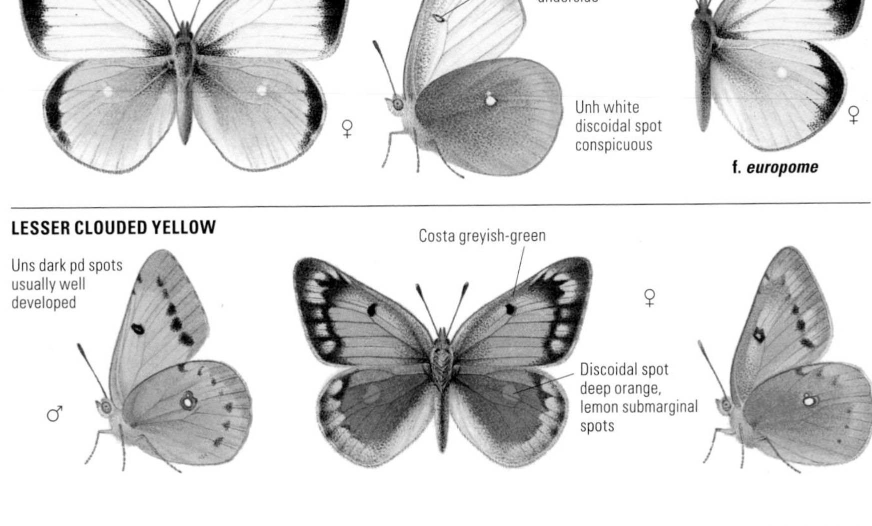

Greek Clouded Yellow *Colias aurorina*

RANGE Greece, Turkey, Lebanon, Syria, N Iraq, NW Iran, Caucasus, Transcaucasus.
C. aurorina heldreichii Staudinger 1862 TL: Mt. Veluchi [=Mt. Timphristos].
syn: *libanotica* Lederer 1858

DISTRIBUTION Restricted to Greece: Pindos Mts. (Grammos massif; N Smolikas massif; Timfi Mts.; Mt. Vardhousia; Mt. Tymphristos; Mt. Iti; Mt. Ghiona; Mt. Kaliakouda; Mt. Parnassos). 550-2000m. Peloponnesos: Aroanian Mts. (Mt. Chelmos; mountains W of Vouraitis Gorge; Panahaikon Mts.). 1100-1800m.

VARIATION Female f. *fountainei* Aigner [=*alba* Rühl]: orange gc replaced by white: progressively commoner towards end of flight-period.

FLIGHT-PERIOD Univoltine. Mid May/mid July, emergence dependent upon altitude and locality: rarely, worn examples may occur in late August.

HABITAT Dry, usually open terrain, dominated by LHP: on limestone or base-rich soils.

LIFE-HISTORY LHPs: Timfi Mts. and Smolikas massif, *Astracantha rumelica* [= *Astragalus creticus rumelicus*]: S Pindos Mts. and Aroanian Mts., *Astragalus parnassi cyllenus*. Ova laid on upperside of leaves. Hibernates as a small larva. Hibernated larvae feed quickly, completing their development within 14 days. In later instars, larva very distinctive: very dark olive-green with yellowish markings.

Danube Clouded Yellow *Colias myrmidone*

RANGE E Europe, Ukraine, Volga, C and S Urals, NW Kazakhstan.
C. myrmidone Esper 1781 TL: Turnau, Hungary.

DISTRIBUTION SE Germany. Austria. Czech Republic. Slovakia. Poland. S Lithuania. (?)Hungary. Romania. In SE Range, closely associated with Danube River system. Very local and sporadic. Recorded only once from Latvia (1949). Not confirmed for Bulgaria. 100-500m.

DESCRIPTION AND VARIATION Male ups gc deep yellow; upf outer margin straight; black marginal borders unmarked by yellow veins but with tendency to faint yellow superscaling; uph costa, oval androconial patch conspicuous: female uph submarginal lemon yellow spots conspicuous; f. *alba* Staudinger, orange gc and yellow spots replaced by white, faintly tinged green. (cf. *C. crocea* and *C. chrysotheme*).

FLIGHT-PERIOD Bivoltine. Late May/mid June and mid July/mid September.

HABITAT Open bushy areas, dominated by LHP.

LIFE-HISTORY LHPs *Cytisus ratisbonensis*; *C. capitatus*. Ova laid on upperside of leaves.

NOTE Adverse climatic factors, coupled with poor viabilty of small, fragmented habitats appears to be responsible for recent, accelerated decline in Germany, Czech Republic and Hungary: possibly now extinct in the latter country.

Greek Clouded Yellow

Danube Clouded Yellow

GREEK CLOUDED YELLOW

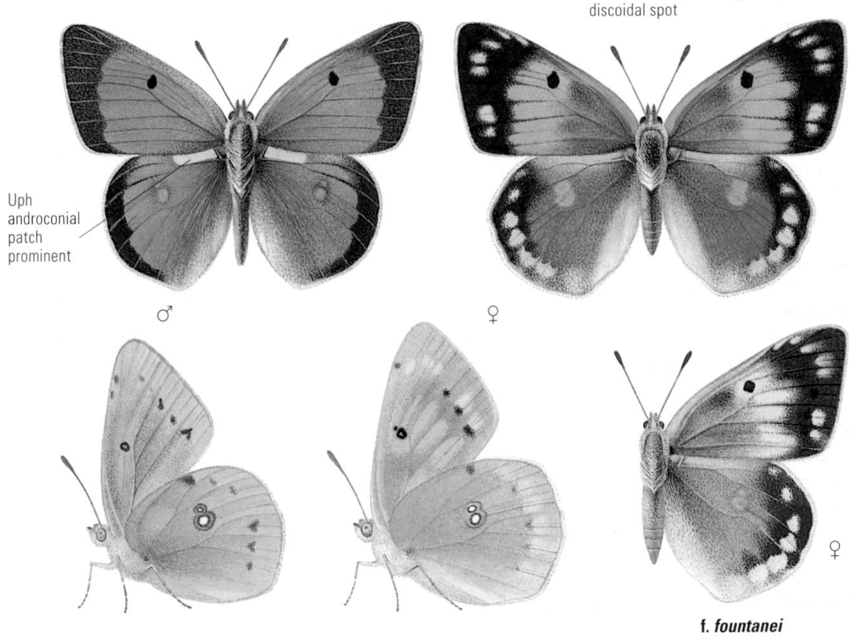
♂ ups deep orange with purple reflection
♀ upf basal suffusion clearly defined, almost reaching discoidal spot
Uph androconial patch prominent
♂
♀
♀
f. *fountanei*

DANUBE CLOUDED YELLOW

♂ ups gc deep yellow
Hw yellow submarginal spots prominent
♀
♂
Uns submarginal dark spots often reduced or absent
♀
f. *alba*

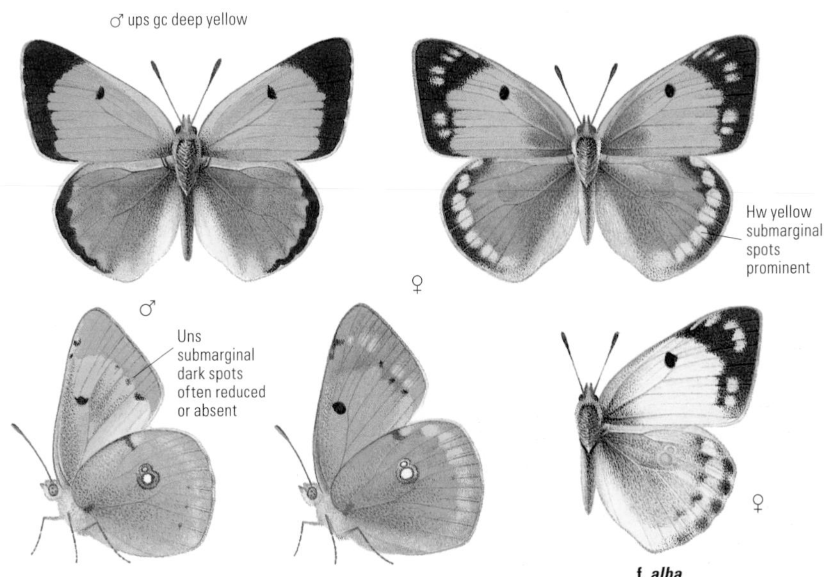

Northern Clouded Yellow *Colias hecla*

RANGE Arctic Fennoscandia, Kola and Yamal Peninsulas, Polar Urals, Polar Siberia, Arctic N America, Greenland.
C. hecla sulitelma Aurivillius 1890 TL: Mt. Sulitelma, Sweden.
DISTRIBUTION Norway: just south of Arctic Circle to Arctic Sea. Extreme north of Sweden and Finland. 50-900m – occurs near sea-level on Porsanger Peninsula.
DESCRIPTION Male uph costa without androconial patch.
VARIATION Male ups borders sometimes brownish with uniform whitish suffusion; ups gc occasionally with distinct pinkish-violet reflections – males reflect UV light. Female ups gc sometimes very pale yellowish-white. Believed to hybridize with *C. nastes* (see *C. nastes*).
FLIGHT-PERIOD Univoltine. Mid June/early August, emergence dependent on seasonal conditions.
HABITAT Open grassy slopes with low-growing shrubs.
LIFE-HISTORY LHP *Astragalus alpinus*. Ova laid on LHP as well as other low-growing plants. Larvae feed on leaves, flowers and stems. Captive larvae readily accept *Medicago sativa*. Hibernates as a larva or pupa. Larvae require two seasonal cycles for full development.

Pale Clouded Yellow *Colias hyale*

RANGE C Europe, NE Turkey, NW Asia, C Asia 43-63°N, NE China.
C. hyale Linnaeus 1758 TL: S England (Verity 1947).
DISTRIBUTION Spain: Granada (S. de Alfacar); Palencia; Guipuzeoa; Navarra; Catalonia (many records uncertain due to possible confusion with *C. alfacariensis*). Pyrenees to Denmark, Gotland (resident), Baltic states, S Finland and N Bulgaria. Migrants occur very rarely in Britain and S Norway, more frequently N Germany and S Sweden. 0-1800m. Absent from Italy, W and SW Balkans, Greece and Mediterranean islands.
DESCRIPTION See *C. alfacariensis* (below).
VARIATION Female white gc rarely replaced by yellow.
FLIGHT-PERIOD Bivoltine or trivoltine according to locality: early May/early October.
HABITAT Flowery, grassy places on base-rich soils; commonly associated with *Medicago sativa* (lucerne, alfalfa) under cultivation.
LIFE-HISTORY LHPs, principally *Medicago sativa* (widely cultivated and naturalized): also, *M. lupulina*; *Lotus corniculatus*; *Trifolium pratense*; *Hippocrepis comosa*; *Securigera varia*; *Vicia cracca*. Hibernates as a small larva. Mature larva green with pale yellow subspiracular line (cf. *C. alfacariensis*).

Berger's Clouded Yellow *Colias alfacariensis*

RANGE S and C Europe, Turkey. Eastern range uncertain due to possible confusion with *C. hyale*.
C. alfacariensis Ribbe 1905 TL: Sierra de Alfacar, Spain.
syn: *australis* Verity 1911
DISTRIBUTION Most of C and S Europe, including Balearic Islands, Corsica and Sicily, to 54°N in Poland. Absent from Britain, N Holland and N Germany except as a rare migrant: also absent from N Africa, S Greece, E Thrace, European Turkey and Sardinia. 0-2100m.
DESCRIPTION Resembles *C. hyale* closely: distinction often difficult, especially in female. Genitalia very similar: chromosome numbers identical (CN=31). Readily separable in larval stage. For the male, the following wing-characters of *C. alfacariensis*, considered collectively, usually allow separation from *C. hyale*:-

1. Fw outer margin and apex relatively more rounded.
2. Ups gc slightly deeper tone – 'warmer' yellow.
3. Upf dark basal shading wedge-shaped, extending along inner margin. (In *C. hyale*, radially more uniform – fan-shaped).
4. Uph marginal black border often narrower and less extensive; submarginal markings absent or restricted to s6 and s7.
5. Uph discoidal spot usually larger and deeper orange.

VARIATION Female white ups and uns gc rarely replaced by yellow.
FLIGHT-PERIOD Bivoltine or trivoltine. April/October according to locality.
HABITAT Rocky slopes, gullies, dry grassy places, often with open scrub: almost invariably on calcareous soils.
LIFE-HISTORY LHPs *Hippocrepis comosa*; *Coronilla varia*; oviposition on upperside of leaves appears to be restricted to one or other of these plant species when both are present. In Slovakia, where *H. comosa* is not native, restricted to *C. varia*. Larva very distinctive: green with yellow dorsal/subspiracular lines and black segmental spots (cf. *C. hyale*). Hibernates as a small larva.

Northern Clouded Yellow

Pale Clouded Yellow

Berger's Clouded yellow

NORTHERN CLOUDED YELLOW

PALE CLOUDED YELLOW

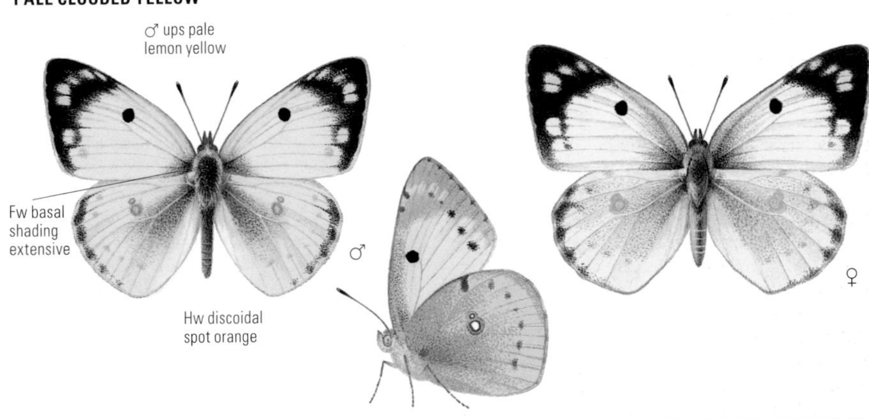

BERGER'S CLOUDED YELLOW

Clouded Yellow *Colias crocea*

RANGE N Africa, S and C Europe, Middle East, Turkey, Iran, Central W Asia C and S Urals.
C. crocea Geoffroy in Fourcroy 1785 TL: Paris.
syn: *edusa* Fabricus 1787.

DISTRIBUTION N Africa, Canary Islands, Azores, Madeira and Europe (including Mediterranean islands) to S Scandinavia and Baltic states. Appearance in Ireland, Britain, including Scotland, S Scandinavia and Baltic states depends exclusively on migration. Common and widespread in C and S Europe but probably not resident except in warmer regions of Mediterranean: resident in Rhône Valley and SW Iberian Peninsula (see Life-history). 0-3200m: more generally below 1600m: at highest altitudes observations more probably relate to migrants.

VARIATION Male uph with oval androconial patch (cf. C. erate): ups orange gc sometimes replaced by pure yellow; rare in Greece, more frequent in Azores (5-10% of population). Female f. *helice* Hübner: gc replaced by pale creamy-white; outer marginal borders dark brown: comprises 5-10% of all populations.

FLIGHT-PERIOD Polyvoltine. March/November in warmer Mediterranean region: in Canary Islands, continuously brooded.

HABITAT Diverse. Found in most habitat-types; more common in warm/hot places with an abundance of flowers.

LIFE-HISTORY LHPs: a wide range of genera and species of Fabaceae, including *Medicago sativa*; *M. lupulina*; *M. polymorpha*; *M. lappacea*; *M. hispida*; *M. sulcata*; *Trifolium pratense*; *Onobrychis viciifolia*; *Lotus*; *Coronilla*; *Melilotus*; *Hippocrepis*; *Astragalus*; *Astracanthus*; *Vicia*; *Chamaecytisus*; *Colutea*; *Erophaca*; *Acanthyllis*; *Anthyllis*. Ova laid on upperside of leaves, appears to be restricted to a single plant species at any given site. No diapause stage: most N and C European populations probably succumb to winter cold: in frost-free regions of S Europe, larvae continue to feed and develop slowly during winter.

NOTE Hybridizes freely with *C. erate* in E and SE Europe.

Eastern Pale Clouded Yellow *Colias erate*

RANGE SE Europe, NW Turkey, Central W Asia to E Kazakhstan, NW Siberia, Afghanistan, N Pakistan, N India, S Mongolia, China, Korea, Japan. Also Ethiopia and Somalia.
C. erate Esper 1804 TL: Sarepta, S Russia.

DISTRIBUTION SE Europe: distributional detail poorly known owing to migration and establishment of colonies of indefinite persistance. Resident in Slovakia, SE Poland, E Hungary, Romania, Bulgaria, NE Greece and European Turkey. Since about 1986, a progressive expansion in S Balkans has resulted in persistent colonies throughout Bulgaria (previously known only from Black Sea coast, Danube Plain and Mt. Sakar). Present situation in Republic of Macedonia unclear. Colonies established in N Greece (Lake Doirani, Phalakron massif, Rhodopi Mts. and Evros) in 1986/87 from extensive cross-border migration from generally low-lying areas of Republic of Macedonia and Bulgaria had largely expired during 1988/89. Very small, isolated colonies persist in Evros (NE Greece), but their existence before the 1987 influx cannot be precluded. 0-1700m.

DESCRIPTION AND VARIATION Male fw pointed, outer margin linear; ups gc pure lemon yellow; upf marginal borders uniformly black, but often with yellow spots (f. *poliographus* Motschulsky) – the dominant form in some colonies (see Note 1). Female ups gc and upf spots in marginal borders yellow or white.

FLIGHT-PERIOD Polyvoltine. Mid March/October, voltinism and emergence dependent on locality – in Slovakia and Bulgaria, 3 to 5 broods.

HABITAT Found in a wide variety of situations, mostly in regions containing an abundance of LHP in cultivation.

LIFE-HISTORY LHP: Europe, *Medicago sativa*: other genera/species of Fabaceae have been reported from eastern range. Hibernates as a pupa.

NOTE ONE *C. erate* (?)f. *poliographus* accorded specific rank by some authors: distribution reportedly overlaps that of *C. erate* in Romania, NW Siberia and Afghanistan, extending eastwards through N Pakistan, Kashmir, S Mongolia, China and Korea to Japan.

NOTE TWO Hybridization with *C. crocea* well documented: in E Thrace (NE Greece), specimens sharing characters of the two species – presumed to be hybrids – are common.

Clouded Yellow

Eastern Pale Clouded Yellow

CLOUDED YELLOW

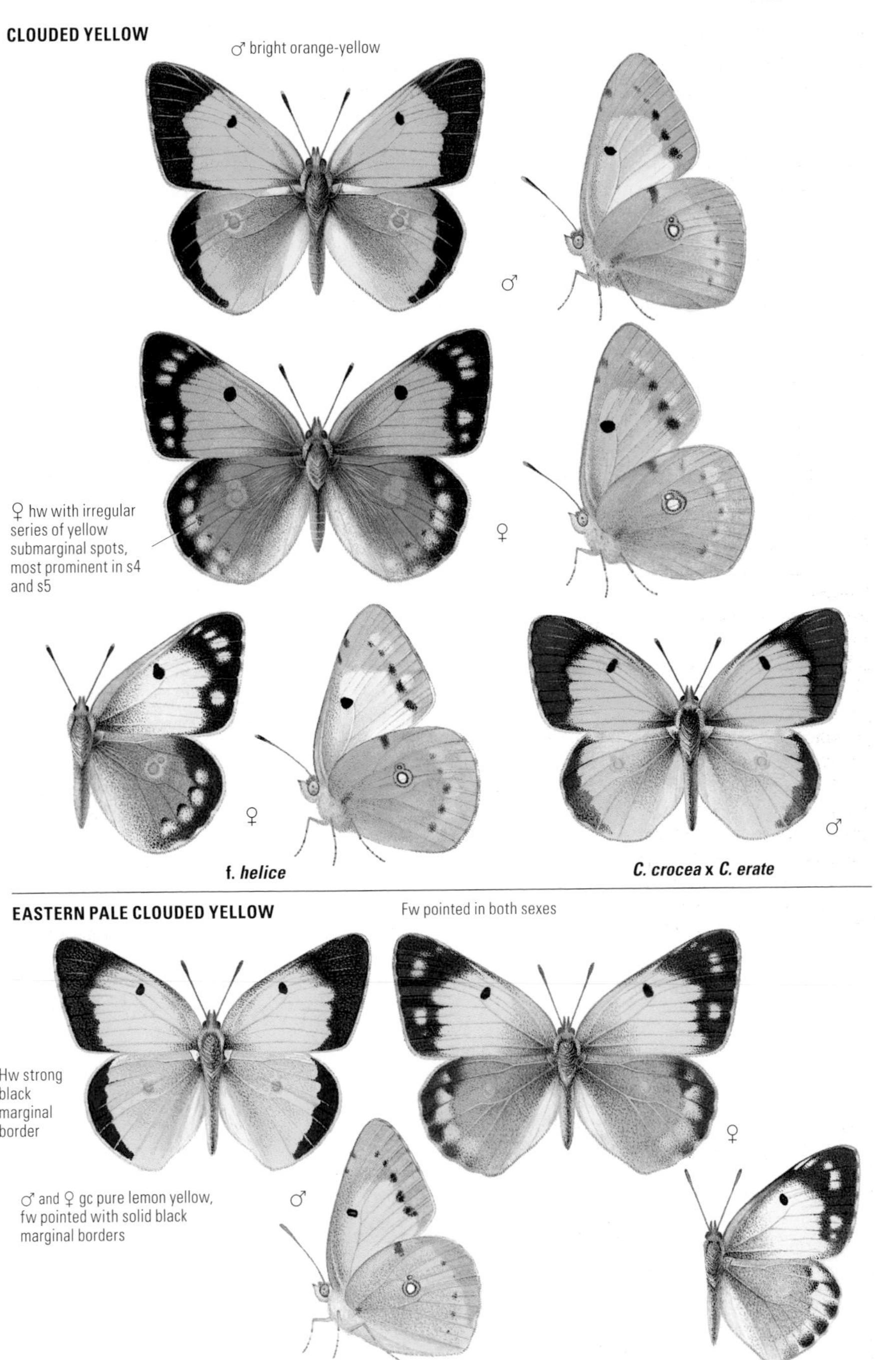

Balkan Clouded Yellow *Colias caucasica*

RANGE S Balkans, Greece.

C. caucasica balcanica Rebel 1903 TL: Bulgaria.

DISTRIBUTION Bosnia-Herzegovina: Jahorina Pl. (Trebevic); Ljubisnja Pl. SW Serbia (Montenegro): Mt. Durmitor; Sinjavina Pl. Republic of Macedonia: Sar Pl.; Bistra Pl.; Galicica Pl.; Mt. Pelister; Osogovska Pl. Bulgaria: Osogovo Mts.; Rila Mts.; Rhodopi Mts. Greece: Varnous Mts.; Voras Mts. 1200-2150m.

DESCRIPTION AND VARIATION Resembles *C. myrmidone*: larger; male ups gc deeper orange: female upf yellow spots in black marginal border variable in size and number, sometimes absent. Female f. *rebeli* Schawerda: orange gc replaced by white.

FLIGHT-PERIOD Univoltine. Mid June/mid August according to altitude.

HABITAT Open alpine grassland, rocky slopes or gullies dominated by LHP (1700-2100m); bushy clearings in beech or pine forests at lower altitudes. In Greece, on acidic soil-base (granite).

LIFE-HISTORY LHPs: Greece and Bosnia-Herzegovina, *Chamaecytisus hirsutus*; Bulgaria (Rila Mts.), *C. eriocarpus* [=*Cytisus absinthoides*]. Ova laid on upperside of leaves. Larvae feed on leaves. A second brood is easily produced in captive rearing: in Greece, in near natural conditions (normal photo-period) larval development is rapid, with 100% of pupae consistently producing imagines in August (cf. *C. myrmidone*). *Chamaecytisus hirsutus* is apparently repellent to grazing animals.

Brimstone *Gonepteryx rhamni*

RANGE NW Africa, Europe, Turkey to W Siberia, Kyrgyzstan and Mongolia.

G. rhamni Linnaeus 1758 TL: Sweden (Verity 1947).

DISTRIBUTION Widespread and common. Mountainous regions of NW Africa. 0-2800m. Europe, south of Scotland and 64°N in Fennoscandia. Mediterranean islands of Corsica, Sardinia, Sicily, Corfu, Kefalonia, Zakynthos and Kastellorizo. Absent from Atlantic Islands. 0-2500m.

DESCRIPTION Male ups yellow gc uniform (cf. male *G. farinosa*): female hw shape variable but dentation of inner margin better developed than that of *G. cleopatra*. Distinction from female *G. farinosa* often difficult: ups and uns white, faintly tinged greenish.

VARIATION Throughout range, hw shape variable. In NW Africa and S Europe, often very large (f. *meridionalis* Röber) but size locally and regionally variable. Gynandromorphism commonly reported.

FLIGHT-PERIOD Univoltine. In N and C Europe, June/July: in S Europe and NW Africa, May/October: hibernated specimens re-appear March/early May. Confirmation of partial bivoltinism reported for N Africa and S Europe requires detection of early stages in mid/late summer to eliminate possible confusion caused by disruption of diapause in summer/autumn: males, especially, are readily inclined to leave hibernation on warm days in late winter.

HABITAT Damp or dry bushy places especially associated with woodland; open grassy and rocky slopes with sparse bushes. Sympatric with *G. cleopatra* and *G. farinosa* in some areas of Greece.

LIFE-HISTORY LHPs *Frangula alnus*; *Rhamnus catharticus*; *R. alaternus*; *R. alpinus* (?)*alpinus*; *R. a. fallax*; *R. myrtifolia*; *R. oleoides*. Ova laid singly on developing leaves or stems. Larva feeds on leaves. Pupates on LHP stems. Hibernates as an adult, often amongst the leaves of evergreen shrubs and trees.

Balkan Clouded Yellow

Brimstone

BALKAN CLOUDED YELLOW

Gc deeper orange

♀ hw yellow submarginal spots conspicuous within dark border

♂

♀

♀

f. ***rebeli***

BRIMSTONE

Ups uniform lemon yellow

♂

'Tail' well developed

Apical 'hook' well developed

♀

Cleopatra *Gonepteryx cleopatra*

RANGE Canary Islands, Madeira, NW Africa, S Europe, Turkey, Middle East.

G. cleopatra cleopatra Linnaeus 1767 TL: Barbaria, Algeria.

DISTRIBUTION Widespread, generally common. Morocco. Algeria. Tunisia. 0-3000m. Portugal. Spain. Balearic Islands. S and C France: Pyrenees and Provence to Vendée and Ain. Corsica. Peninsular Italy except C Apennines; sporadic in northern districts. Sardinia. Sicily. Dalmatian coast: sporadic. C and S Greece, Corfu, Kefalonia, Zakynthos, Lesbos, Chios, Samos, Ikaria, Rhodes, Karpathos, Crete, Skiathos, Skyros, Sifnos, Paros and Milos. European Turkey. Not reported from Albania and Republic of Macedonia. Records for S Switzerland, Bulgaria and N Greece appear to relate to vagrant specimens only. 0-1600m: generally below 1200m. **DESCRIPTION** Male ups gc yellow; upf with deep orange discal patch; unf discal area yellow, unh and unf costa pale yellowish-green or whitish: in f. *italica* Gerhard [=f. *massiliensis* Foulquier], uns dull yellow, except for slightly brighter upf discal area. Whilst these colour forms occur together in varying ratio in most regions, including NW Africa, f. *italica* becomes increasingly common in E Mediterranean, comprising 100% of specimens on some E Aegean islands. Female unf with delicate, pale orange streak above median vein; uph often with faint orange flush; hw angular projection at v3 very shallow (cf. female *G. rhamni* and *G. farinosa*). **VARIATION** Male upf orange flush variable in size and intensity. On Mallorca, male upf orange flush averagely smaller and paler. In SE Europe, female white gc (normal) sometimes replaced by pale yellow or bright sulphur-yellow (resembling male *G. rhamni*); these forms sometimes occur together, in locally or regionally widely varying ratios: in N and C Greece, white form preponderates: on Mt. Chelmos, mostly bright yellow: in Taygetos Mts., normal and intermediate forms common, the brightest yellow forms infrequent: on Rhodes (f. *fiorii* Turati and Fiori), universally bright yellow (a similar form has been reported from Tunisia): yellow variants appear to be rare on Karpathos and absent from Crete and some other E Aegean islands: an intermediate yellow form has been reported from Milos. **FLIGHT-PERIOD** Univoltine. Mid May/August with hibernated specimens re-appearing in early spring (late February/late April). Reportedly bivoltine in S Spain and N Africa, but possible, temporary suspension of diapause in late summer is a potential source of confusion. **HABITAT** Open bushy, often rocky places: often associated with light woodland. **LIFE-HISTORY** LHPs *Rhamnus catharticus*; *R. alaternus*; *R. myrtifolia*; *R. oleoides*; *R. alpinus*; *R. sibthorpianus*; *R.* (?)*persicifolius* (Sardinia). Ova laid singly on developing leaves or stems. Larva feeds on leaves. Pupates on LHP stems. Hibernates as an adult.

G. cleopatra maderensis Felder 1862 TL: Madeira.

DISTRIBUTION Madeira: Terreirro da Luta; Ribeiro Frio; Encumeada Pass. 500-1500m. **DESCRIPTION** Male upf deep orange with very narrow, yellow marginal borders; fw and hw well marked with a reddish-brown marginal line, slightly expanded at veins: female ups pale greenish with faint yellow flush; unh and unf costal areas dull greenish; unf disc whitish. **FLIGHT-PERIOD** Voltinism uncertain due to longevity of adults and perhaps sporadic, temporary suspension of diapause – if any. Recorded in all months but commoner April/September. **HABITAT** Dense laurel forest containing other trees and shrubs including LHP. Butterfly appears to be confined to such areas – not as wide-ranging as Canary Island *Gonepteryx*. **LIFE-HISTORY** LHP *Rhamnus glandulosa*. **NOTE** Visible areas of female underside at rest (hw and fw costa) are non-reflective in UV-light, as are the leaves of laurel (*Laurus laurocerasus*) amongst which females normally roost, often rest and possibly hibernate: as insectivorous birds have good UV-colour vision, cryptic UV-coloration is an obvious functional advantage in habitat dominated by laurel. Canary Island *Gonepteryx* butterflies (below) have followed a different evolutionary path, resulting in strongly UV-reflective female undersides – an adaptive consequence, apparently, of less parochial behaviour in a more botanically diverse environment containing plants, e.g., bramble (*Rubus fruticosus*), whose leaves are also UV-reflective. Recent DNA studies have demonstrated a much closer affinity of *maderensis* to the nominate form than the *Gonepteryx* of the Canary Islands.

G. cleopatra cleobule Hübner 1825 TL: Tenerife.

DISTRIBUTION N Tenerife: Las Mercedes; Icod Alto; Anaga; Chinobre. 500-2000m. **DESCRIPTION** Fw outer margin almost linear; hw dentation very shallow; fw and hw with conspicuous, often striking, reddish-brown marginal line, slightly expanded at veins: male upf gc deep orange, extending almost to margins; uph yellow; unf greenish-yellow; unh greenish: female ups gc yellow, flushed orange; strongly UV-reflective. **FLIGHT-PERIOD** Voltinism uncertain (see *maderensis*). Recorded in all months. **HABITAT AND BEHAVIOUR** Sunny clearings in laurel forests, but habitat of more diverse character than that of maderensis. Both sexes tend to fly at lower altitudes in winter and often feed on *Cedronella canariensis* blossom. **LIFE-HISTORY** LHPs *Rhamnus glandulosa*; *R. crenulata*. Larvae have been recorded in April, August and December. Early stages do not appear to differ from *palmae* or *eversi* (below). Captive larvae accept *R. catharticus*. **NOTE** Considered specifically distinct by many authors: recent, comparative DNA studies of this and related taxa have proved inconclusive.

G. cleopatra palmae Stamm 1963 TL: La Palma.

DISTRIBUTION La Palma: Santa Cruz; Quintero; Rio de las Nieves; Barranco del Agua; Bco. de la Galga; Bco. de Jieque; Los Sauces; Los Tilos. 300-1600m. **DESCRIPTION** Fw outer margin almost linear; hw dentation very shallow: male upf yellow with diffuse orange discal flush, variable; uph yellow; unh and unf costal area greenish-yellow: female ups very pale yellow – fw discal area almost white, hw and fw costal areas flushed pale yellow-orange; uns similar. Female ups non-reflective in UV-light. **FLIGHT-PERIOD** Voltinism uncertain (see *maderensis*). Recorded in March/April, June/September and December. **HABITAT, BEHAVIOUR AND LIFE-HISTORY** As for *G. c. cleobule*.

G. cleopatra eversi **continued on p. 350**

CLEOPATRA

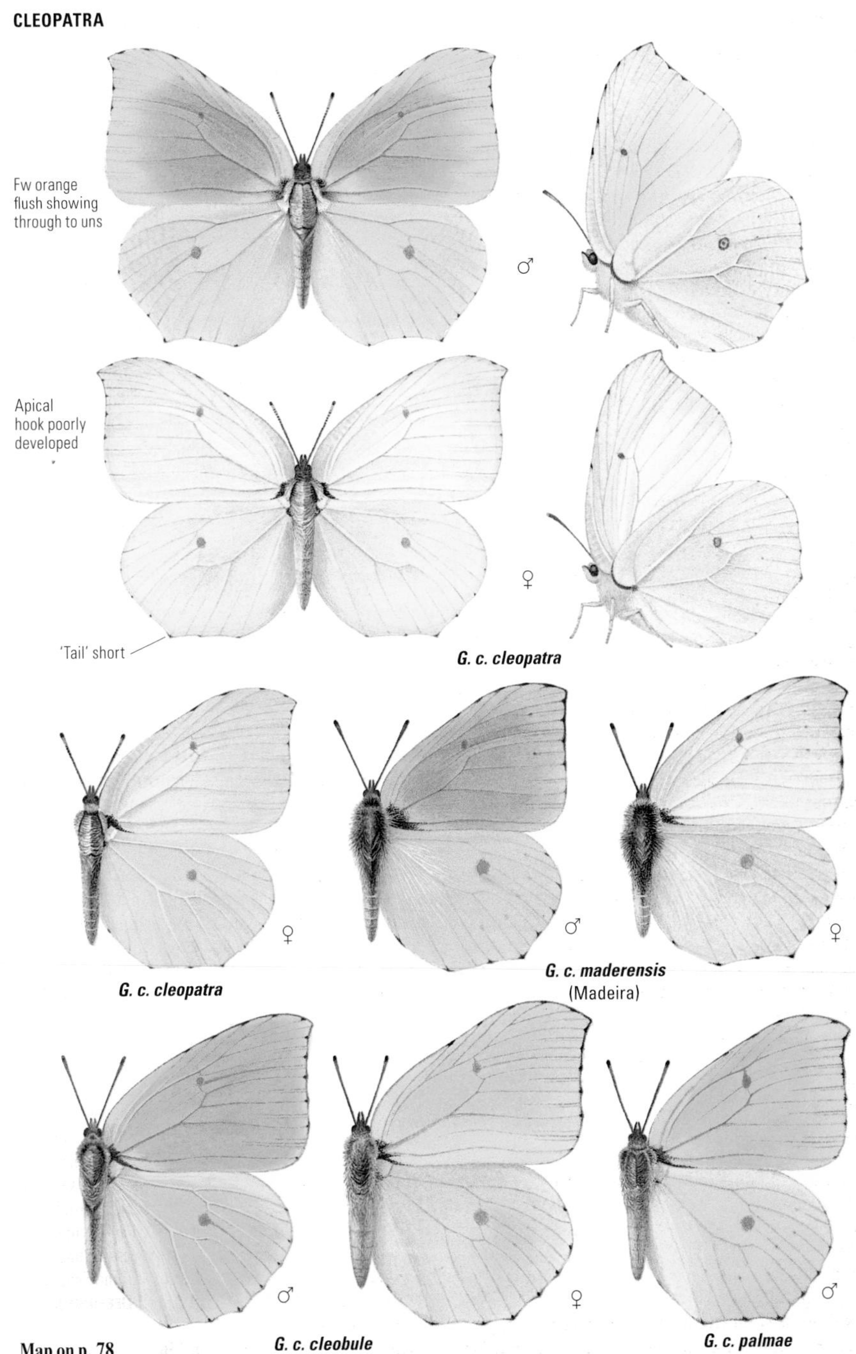

Map on p. 78

Powdered Brimstone *Gonepteryx farinosa*

RANGE Albania, Republic of Macedonia, Bulgaria, Greece, Turkey, Israel, Lebanon, Syria, N Iraq, N and W Iran, Caucasus to Tajikistan.

G. farinosa Zeller 1847 TL: Macri (Fethiye), SW Turkey.

DISTRIBUTION Albania. Republic of Macedonia. Bulgaria: a single site in Struma Valley. Greece: E Thessaly; Sterea Ellas; Attika; Peloponnesos: very restricted in N districts (Kastoria; Kozani; Drama; Evros): recorded from Levkas, Kefalonia, Rhodes, Kastellorizo. European Turkey. 25-1450m.

DESCRIPTION Male upf lemon yellow, with slightly roughened appearance; uph distinctly paler – constrast with fw apparent in flight: female ups white, sometimes faintly tinged bluish (cf. *G. rhamni*).

FLIGHT-PERIOD Univoltine. Mid June/July: hibernated specimens re-appear March/April.

HABITAT AND BEHAVIOUR Hot, dry, bushy places, often on rocky slopes at higher altitudes; very hot, dry low coastal hills amongst sparse bushes of *Paliurus spina-christi*. In some localities, often roosts in bushes of *Phlomis fruticosa*.

LIFE-HISTORY LHPs *Rhamnus alpinus fallax*; *R. sibthorpianus*; *R. lycioides graecus*; *Paliurus spina-christi*. Ova laid at leaf-nodes on stems.

Wood White *Leptidea sinapis*

RANGE Europe, Turkey, Lebanon, Syria, Caucasus to W Siberia and Tian Shan.

L. sinapis Linnaeus 1758 TL: Sweden (Verity 1947).

DISTRIBUTION Widespread and common in most of Europe south of 66°N in Fennoscandia (very local north of Arctic Circle), including Mediterranean islands of Mallorca, Corsica, Sardinia, Elba, Sicily, Corfu, Levkas, Kefalonia, Zakynthos, Skyros, Thassos, Lesbos, Chios, Samos and Crete. Absent from Scotland, N England, Holland, N Germany and Denmark except Bornholm. 0-2300m: generally below 1900m.

DESCRIPTION Antennal club black with extreme tip brown and small white ventral patch (cf. *L. duponcheli*). Second/third broods, dark markings reduced. Resembles *L. reali* closely.

FLIGHT-PERIOD Generally univoltine in N and C Fennoscandia, June/early August: bivoltine in most of C Europe May/June and July/August: trivoltine in parts of S Europe, late March/September according to locality and altitude.

HABITAT Diverse. Mature deciduous/coniferous/mixed forest clearings/margins; sparse woodland; bushy places; flowery meadows; coastal scrub; less often, grassy, rocky slopes/gullies above treeline: most habitat-types associate with a wide range of temperature, geology and ground-water conditions.

LIFE-HISTORY. LHPs *Lathyrus pratensis*; *L. grandiflorus*; *L. tuberosus*; *L. montanus*; *L. linifolius*; *L. vernus*; *L. niger*; *L. aphaca*; *Lotus uliginosus*; *L. corniculatus*. Ova laid on underside of leaves of partially shaded LHPs. Larvae feed on leaves. Pupates on robust plant-stems, usually in concealment amongst grasses. Hibernates as a pupa.

Cleopatra

Powdered Brimstone

Wood White

POWDERED BRIMSTONE

♂ fw with rough texture, distinctly darker than hw

♂

'Tail' short

Margin clearly scalloped

Discoidal spots usually very small

Costal margin contrasting with rest of fw

♀

WOOD WHITE

♂

1st brood

Antennal club black with orange tip, white on uns

♀

1st brood

In 2nd brood unh markings reduced in both sexes

♂

2nd brood

♀

2nd brood

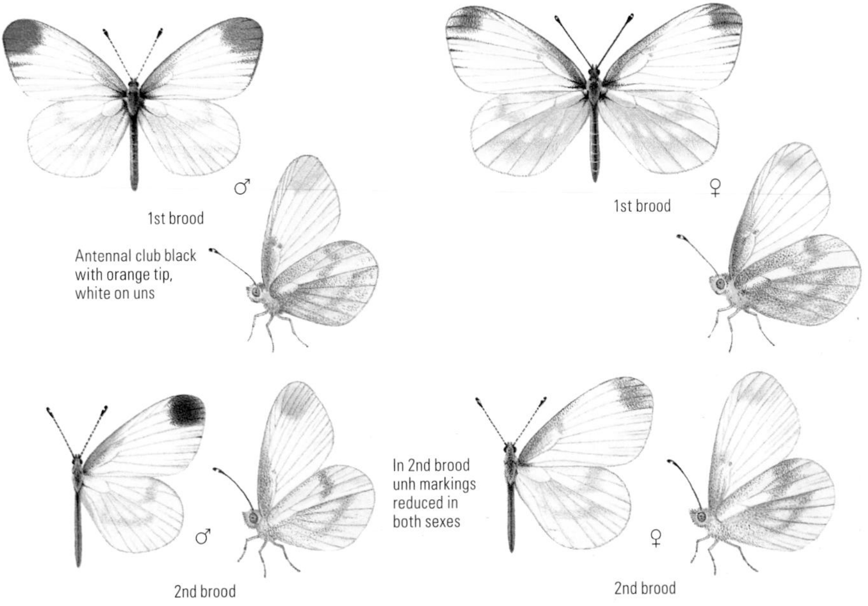

Eastern Wood White *Leptidea duponcheli*

RANGE SE France, S Balkans, Turkey, Lebanon, N Iraq, N and W Iran, Transcaucasus.

L. duponcheli Staudinger 1871 TL: S France.

syn: *lathyri* Duponchel (invalid homonym)

DISTRIBUTION SE France: Var and Alpes-Maritimes to Drôme and Hautes-Savoie. NW Italy: Maritime Alps: very local. SW Serbia (Montenegro). Albania. Republic of Macedonia. Bulgaria: very local and sporadic. N and C Greece, including Zakynthos: local but widespread. 50-1150m.

DESCRIPTION Fw pointed; uns of antennal club brown (white in *L. sinapis*); upf v1 with pronounced 'hump' below cell – curvature relatively slight in *L. sinapis*. First brood: colour and pattern of heavy uns markings distinctive, showing through to ups. Second brood: markings less intense. Separable from *L. sinapis* and *L. reali* in all broods and both sexes by wing-markings, antennal club and fw venation.

FLIGHT-PERIOD Bivoltine. Mid April/mid May and late June/July.

HABITAT Hot, sunny, bushy places; open woodland; rocky gullies. Habitats more restricted and averagely hotter/drier than those of the more ecologically diverse *L. sinapis* with which it usually occurs.

LIFE-HISTORY LHPs *Lathyrus aphaca*; *L. pratense*; *Lotus uliginosus*. Ova laid on underside of leaves of LHP specimens usually well-shaded by undergrowth or large rocks. Larvae feed on leaves. Hibernates as a pupa.

Réal's Wood White *Leptidea reali*

RANGE Spain, France, S Belgium, N Switzerland, Austria, Slovenia, Croatia, SW Serbia, S Poland, SE Sweden, Ukraine.

L. reali Reissinger 1989 TL: La Montailla, E Pyrenees.

syn: lorkovicii Réal 1988 (invalid homonym)

DISTRIBUTION Spain: provinces of Cuenca (Uña); Teruel (Albarracin); Alava (Cantabrian Mts.); Lérida (Caldos de Bohit); Gerona. France: Ariège; Pyrénées-Orientales; Aude; Alpes-Maritimes; Alpes-de-Haute-Provençe; Hautes-Alpes; Ardèche; Isère; Jura; Moselle; Meuse. S Belgium: province of Luxembourg. N Switzerland: canton of Luzern (Herigswald; Sörenburg). Slovenia. Croatia. SW Serbia: Mt. Maglic. SE Poland. SE Sweden: Söndermanland (including Island of Ingarö); Uppland. Tentative records for province of Alicante and Corsica require confirmation. 100-2000m. Geographical/altitudinal distribution uncertain due to probable confusion with *L. sinapis*: distribution possibly much less disjunctive than present records indicate.

DESCRIPTION Resembles *L. sinapis* but density of black pigmentation in wing-markings averagely greater; in summer broods, female upf black, roundish apical patch usually well represented. Wing-characters variable, inadequate for reliable determination, but, in either sex, readily separable from *L. sinapis* by substantial morphological and reproductively significant differences in genitalia: field observations and laboratory experiments indicate a significant pre-mating barrier between the two species: natural hybrids unknown.

FLIGHT-PERIOD Limited data indicate voltinism/flight-times similar to that of *L. sinapis*.

HABITAT Similar to that of *L. sinapis* with which it is usually to be found.

LIFE-HISTORY LHP *Lathyrus pratensis*. Life-cycle/early-stages similar to that of *L. sinapis*: pupa slightly more yellowish, reddish lateral lines and wing-case markings less distinct.

Fenton's Wood White *Leptidea morsei*

RANGE Central E Europe to C and S Urals, SE Turkey, Altai, W Siberia to Japan.

L. morsei major Grund 1905 TL: Zagreb, Yugoslavia.

DISTRIBUTION S Poland. Slovakia. SE Austria. Hungary. Slovenia, N Croatia. Romania. Bulgaria. 150-1400m.

DESCRIPTION Fw apex falcate – rounded in *L. sinapis* and L. reali. First brood, unh pattern and tone of greyish markings distinctive. Second brood, larger; markings greatly reduced. Antennal club resembles *L. sinapis*.

FLIGHT-PERIOD Bivoltine. Mid April/mid May and mid June/late July.

HABITAT Margins/clearings associated with mature, damp deciduous woodland. Habitat and LHP often shared with *Neptis sappho*.

LIFE-HISTORY LHPs *Lathyrus vernus*; *L. niger*: the latter appears to be the sole LHP in some habitats of N Croatia, despite presence of both plant species.

Eastern Wood White

Réal's Wood White

Fenton's Wood White

EASTERN WOOD WHITE

♂
1st brood
Antennal club black with orange tip, no white on uns
♀
1st brood
1st brood hw markings bold and distinctive
♂
2nd brood
2nd brood flushed yellow, faint markings
♀
2nd brood

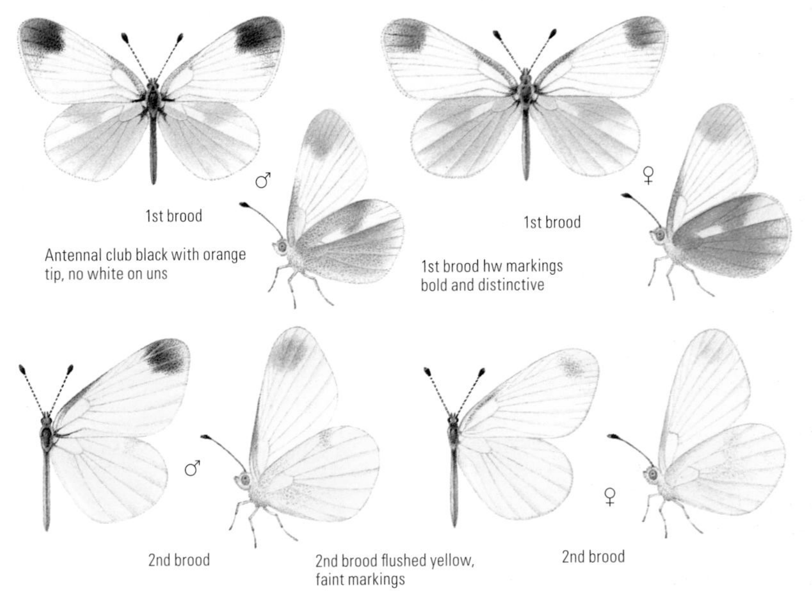

FENTON'S WOOD WHITE

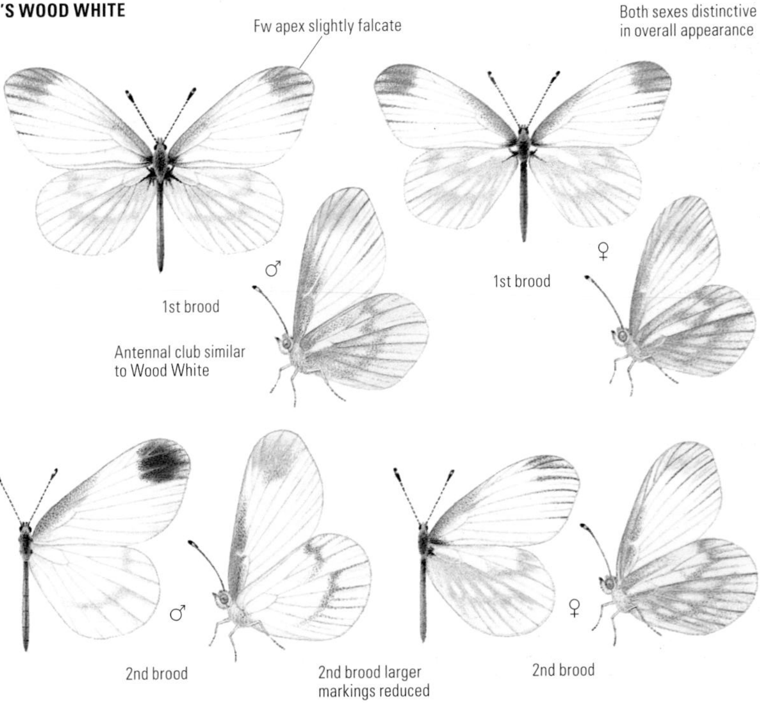

Fw apex slightly falcate
Both sexes distinctive in overall appearance
♂
1st brood
Antennal club similar to Wood White
♀
1st brood
♂
2nd brood
2nd brood larger markings reduced
♀
2nd brood

LYCAENIDAE Linnaeus 1758

This very large family of generally small butterflies, represented in Europe by over one hundred species, include the blues, hairstreaks and coppers. For most species, sexual dimorphism is especially well marked, and the females of many'blue'butterflies are brown. Close similarity between species sometimes renders identification difficult, but differences – often more easily seen than described – in ground colour and the pattern of markings, particularly on the hind-wing underside, are generally clear. The greatest difficulties in determination are presented by the distinctive group known as the 'anomalous blues', so-called because the uppersides of both sexes are brown: sexual distinction is, however, clearly indicated by a sex-brand on the upper fore-wing of the male. The males of many species will often gather, sometimes in huge numbers and for prolonged periods, on damp ground for the purpose of extracting sodium salts from the water. The larvae of the Lycaenidae are shaped much like a woodlouse, are usually well-camouflaged, and often show a high order of adaptation to larval host-plants. For most species, a 'honey' gland (dorsal nectary organ) on the 10th larval segment exudes a sugary fluid – a high-energy food – which is very attractive to ants. In exchange for this secretion, attending ants actively afford some protection against parasitic flies (Diptera) and wasps (Hymenoptera). Whilst some associations (facultative), although mutually advantageous, are not essential, others (obligate) are quite necessary for the survival of some lycaenid species such as the Large Blue, whose symbiotic relationship has evolved to the point of total dependence on (particular) ants species within whose nests the latter stages of larval, as well as pupal development occurs: the butterfly larvae feed exclusively on ant larvae, whilst receiving the full co-operation and protection of the adult ants. The association of many lycaenid larvae with ants (myrmecophily) is well-documented, but, as the rapid progress of research suggests, much detail remains to be discovered about these interesting relationships. Pupae are characteristically'dumpy' – short in proportion to diameter. According to species, pupae may be secured by a girdle of fine silk to a leaf or stem, often of the larval host-plant, or, with no attachment, secreted in rolled-up leaves, secured by a few strands of silk, under basal leaves of the larval host-plant, or on the ground under stones, amongst leaf-litter, moss, etc.

Donzel's Silver-line *Cigaritis zohra*

RANGE Morocco, Algeria.

C. zohra zohra Donzel 1847 TL: Djebel Amour, Algeria.

DISTRIBUTION W and C Algeria: widespread but local: Sebdou; El Bayadh; Aflou; Djelfa; Saïda; Kralfalih. Records from Tunisia (Tozeur; Gafsa; Moulares) require confirmation.

DESCRIPTION Male ups gc orange-brown; submarginal and marginal dark spots usually confluent; upf markings variable but usually well developed; unh gc brown. All markings subject to marked local variation.

FLIGHT-PERIOD Univoltine. Records span May/June.

C. zohra monticola Riley 1925 TL: Aghbalu Larbi, Taghzeff Pass, Morocco.

DISTRIBUTION Morocco: widespread but local: Middle and High Atlas (Annoceur; Ifrane; Tizi-n-Tretten; Boulmane; Col du Zad; Tizi-n-Taghzeft). 1600-2200m.

DESCRIPTION Resembles nominate form: smaller; ups gc deeper orange: all markings subject to appreciable variation.

FLIGHT-PERIOD Univoltine. March/June according to season, generally late April/May.

HABITAT Grassy slopes.

LIFE-HISTORY First and second instar larvae feed on *Coronilla minima*, thereafter, living in nests of *Crematogaster laestrygon* until adulthood.

BEHAVIOUR Flies close to the ground: fond of resting on bare ground with wings closed.

Common Silver-line *Cigaritis siphax*

RANGE Algeria, Tunisia.

C. siphax Lucas 1849 TL: Constantine, Algeria.

DISTRIBUTION Algeria: Collo; Bône; Aflou; Khenchala; Timgad; Djurdjura massif. Tunisia: Aïn Draham; Cap Bon; Hammamet. 100-1000m.

VARIATION Ups markings variable; black marginal spots sometimes absent; unh gc brown to purplish.

FLIGHT-PERIOD Voltinism uncertain, possibly trivoltine. Records span March/October.

HABITAT Dry hillsides with *Cistus*.

Allard's Silver-line *Cigaritis allardi*

RANGE Morocco, Algeria.

C. allardi Oberthür 1909 TL: Sebdou, Algeria.

DISTRIBUTION Morocco: W Middle Atlas (Abu Safra; Azrou; Immouzer; El Harcha; El Ksiba; 1200-1600m; W Anti-Atlas (Agadir; Tafraoute; Col du Kerdous; 800-1100m); High Atlas (Dj. Aourach; Tizi-n'Ouguerd-Zegzaoune 2000-2400m). Algeria: Sebdou; Masser Mines; Dj. Maktar; 1500-1800m.

VARIATION Subject to variation in ups black markings and gc variable: the following taxa relate to small but systematic, regional differences: Middle Atlas Mts., *occidentalis* Le Cerf: High Atlas Mts. (Morocco and W Algeria), *meridionalis* Riley: Anti-Atlas Mts. *estherae* Brevignon.

FLIGHT-PERIOD Univoltine. March/June according to location and season.

HABITAT Hot, dry, rocky slopes, sometimes scrub-covered.

LIFE-HISTORY LHPs *Genista quadriflora*; *Cistus salvifolius*; *Fumana thymifolia*; *Helianthemum hirtum ruficomum*. Larvae strongly myrmecophilous, attended by *Crematogaster auberti*; *C. antaris*; *C. scutellaris*.

BEHAVIOUR Flight very rapid in hot conditions. Both sexes rest on low-growing shrubs and are easily disturbed.

DONZEL'S SILVER LINE

Ups black markings variable, submarginal spots usually well developed

♂

♀

'Tails' short

Unh white gc white obscured by brown markings

COMMON SILVER-LINE

Ups variable, markings usually poorly developed

♂

♀

'Tails' short

Unh gc orange-brown, markings obscure

ALLARD'S SILVER-LINE

Ups variable, markings well developed

♂

♀

'Tails' well developed

Unh gc white, basal, discal and pd spots in linear rows

Donzel's Silver-line

Common Silver-line

Allard's Silver-line

Desert Leopard *Apharitis myrmecophila*

RANGE Tunisia, S and E Algeria, Libya, Egypt, Jordan, Cyprus, Saudi Arabia, Oman.

A. myrmecophila Dumont 1922 TL: Tozeur, Tunisia.

DISTRIBUTION E Algeria: Biskra. 100m. Extremely local, usually occurring in very small numbers. More widespread in S Algeria (Hoggar Mts.; Tassili n'Ajjer) and S Tunisia (Tozeur; Nefta).

DESCRIPTION Ups gc bright orange; marginal borders thinly black; upf dark markings variable, prominent or absent; uph without submarginal and discal markings: both sexes, upf apex with distinctive creamy-white patch (*Cigaritis* spp. and *A. acamas*, a closely similar species from S Algeria, are without a white apical patch).

FLIGHT-PERIOD Voltinism uncertain: possibly bivoltine or polyvoltine: records span April/July.

HABITAT Very hot sandy places.

LIFE-HISTORY LHP *Calligonum comosum* (Polygonaceae). Larvae strongly myrmecophilous, attended by *Crematogaster auberti*; (?)*Cataglyphis bicolor*. Larvae feed at night, residing in ants nest during the day. Pupates in ants nest.

BEHAVIOUR Adults often rest on small stones in full sun in the hottest parts of habitat, or bushes to which they quickly return when disturbed.

Brown Hairstreak *Thecla betulae*

RANGE Europe through Asia to Korea.

T. betulae Linnaeus 1758 TL: Sweden (Verity 1943)

DISTRIBUTION Spain: S. de Gata; Cantabrian Mts.; Catalonia. E Pyrenees through most of Europe, including W Ireland and S England to S Fennoscandia, Balkans, N Greece (Voras Mts., Phalakron massif and N Pindos Mts.) and European Turkey. Absent from Portugal, S Italy and Mediterranean islands. 50-1500m.

FLIGHT-PERIOD Univoltine. Late July/early September.

HABITAT Deciduous woodland or mature scrub with open, sunny clearings containing an abundance of blackthorn (*Prunus spinosa*).

LIFE-HISTORY LHP *Prunus spinosa*. Ova laid, often in pairs, mainly in forks at stem-junctions, usually on young plants. Hibernates as an ovum. Pupae attended by *Lasius niger*.

Purple Hairstreak *Quercusia quercus*

RANGE N Africa, Europe, Middle East, Turkey, Caucasus, Russia, S Urals, Kazakhstan.

Q. quercus quercus Linnaeus 1758 TL: England (Verity 1943).

DISTRIBUTION Common and widespread from Pyrenees, eastwards through most of Europe, including Britain, to S Fennoscandia, Greece, European Turkey and Mediterranean islands of Sicily, Corsica, Sardinia, Crete, Lesbos, Samos and Rhodes. 0-2000m. (Vagrant specimens have been found at 2300m).

FLIGHT-PERIOD Univoltine. Late June/early September.

HABITAT Diverse. Hot, dry oak scrub; damp or dry deciduous or mixed forests containing oak.

LIFE-HISTORY LHPs *Quercus* spp., including *Q. robur*; *Q. coccifera*; *Q. petraea*; *Q. ilex*; *Q. cerris*; *Q. pubescens*. Ova laid at base of leaf buds. Hibernates as an ovum.

BEHAVIOUR Adults show little interest in the nectar of plants, carrion or excrement, and only rarely visit damp soil: nutrients seem to be obtained largely from aphid secretion ('honeydew') on leaves of trees, especially LHP, to which adult activity is largely confined.

Q. quercus ibericus Staudinger 1901 TL: S Spain and Morocco.

DISTRIBUTION Morocco: Middle Atlas; Rif Mts. Algeria: Middle Atlas. 1200-2200m. Portugal. Spain. 900-2100m.

DESCRIPTION Resembles nominate form except uns very pale silvery-grey, markings reduced, including anal orange spot and ring.

FLIGHT-PERIOD Univoltine. June/mid September.

HABITAT Oak (*Quercus*) scrub; dry, oak woodland: often in very hot places.

LIFE-HISTORY LHP *Quercus* spp., including *Q. coccifera*; *Q. ilex*.

NOTE Intermediate forms, some closely approaching *ibericus*, occur north of Pyrenees in Haute Garonne. Captive rearing in cool conditions produce specimens indistinguishable from nominate form, indicating at least some ecological control over distinctive characters.

Spanish Purple Hairstreak *Laeosopis roboris*

RANGE Portugal, Spain, S France.

L. roboris Esper 1793 TL: Stated in error as 'Frankfurt am Main'

DISTRIBUTION Portugal except extreme south (Algarve). Throughout Spain in scattered colonies. France: E Pyrenees to Provence. 100-1600m.

FLIGHT-PERIOD Univoltine. Late May/late July according to locality and altitude.

HABITAT Open flowery bushy places with ash trees.

LIFE-HISTORY LHP *Fraxinus excelsior*. Ova laid near dormant leaf-buds or main trunk of host-tree, sometimes near ground-level. Larvae feed on flowers and developing leaves. Hibernates as an ovum.

BEHAVIOUR In early morning, both sexes often assemble in large numbers to feed on tall umbellifers (Apiaceae), including fennel (*Foeniculum vulgare*). Flight is confined mostly to higher branches of LHP in cooler conditions late afternoon/early evening: adults rest on leaves of trees/shrubs during hottest periods.

BROWN HAIRSTREAK

PURPLE HAIRSTREAK

SPANISH PURPLE HAIRSTREAK

Desert Leopard

Brown Hairstreak

Purple Hairstreak

Spanish Purple Hairstreak

Sloe Hairstreak *Satyrium acaciae*

RANGE Spain, S Europe, Turkey, S Russia.
S. acaciae Fabricus 1787 TL: S Russia.
DISTRIBUTION N Spain and Montes Universales, eastwards through France (to 49°N), Germany and Poland (to 51°N), N Italy to Greece and European Turkey. Absent from Portugal, S Italy and Mediterranean islands. 0-2000m.
DESCRIPTION Male ups without sex-brand. Female abdomen with black anal hair-tuft.
FLIGHT-PERIOD Univoltine. June/July.
HABITAT Diverse. Dry scrub; open woodland; occasionally, damp forest clearings and open terrain above tree-line.
LIFE-HISTORY LHP *Prunus spinosa*. Ova laid mostly at stem junctions. Immediately after ovipositing, the female uses the dark abdominal tuft to brush hair-like scales onto the whitish egg, rendering it less visible: as these scales are easily removed (hibernated ova are devoid of scales), the purpose of this practice is obscure. Hibernates as an ovum.
BEHAVIOUR Both sexes attracted to flowers of *Achillea* and *Thymus*.

Ilex Hairstreak *Satyrium ilicis*

RANGE Europe, S Fennoscandia, Israel, Lebanon, Turkey, W and S Urals, NW Asia.
S. Ilicis Esper 1779 TL: Erlangen, Germany.
DISTRIBUTION Portugal. N and E Spain: scattered colonies; Balearic Islands, eastwards to S Fennoscandia, Baltic states, Balkans, European Turkey and Greece, including Corfu, Thassos, Limnos, Lesbos, Samos, Ikaria, Chios, Kos, Simi, Poros and Tinos. 0-1600m. Absent from Britain, Corsica, Sardinia, Sicily and Crete.
DESCRIPTION AND VARIATION Male upf without sex-brand. Unh submarginal orange spots in s1b-s5 clearly defined, conspicuously edged black; white marginal line usually prominent (cf. *S. esculi*). In Portugal, Spain and S France, *cerri* Hübner: upf with variable orange discal patch, usually better developed in female.
FLIGHT-PERIOD Univoltine. Late May/early August according to altitude.
HABITAT Diverse. Hot, dry *Quercus coccifera* scrub; damp/dry heaths; forest clearings.
LIFE-HISTORY LHP *Quercus* spp., including *Q. coccifera*; *Q. ilex*; *Q. robur*. Ova laid near dormant leaf-buds. Hibernates as an ovum. Larvae attended by *Camponotus aethiops*; *Crematogastor schmidti* or (?)*ionia*.
BEHAVIOUR Attracted to flowers of *Thymus* and *Sambucus ebulus*.

False Ilex Hairstreak *Satyrium esculi*

RANGE N Africa, SW Europe.
S. esculi Hübner 1804 TL: Portugal.
DISTRIBUTION Morocco. Algeria. Tunisia. 900-2400m. Iberian peninsula except extreme N and NW; Balearic Islands (Ibiza and Mallorca). France: E Pyrenees to Alpes-Maritimes. 500-1300m.
DESCRIPTION AND VARIATION Male upf without sex-brand; ups gc light greyish-brown to dark brown; dull yellow-orange suffusion on fw disc and hw submargin extremely variable, often absent; unh reddish-orange submarginal spots in s1b-s5 clearly defined, internally finely edged black; marginal white line vestigial (cf. *S. ilicis*): female ups and uns gc generally paler; ups pattern of orange suffusion similar, averagely better developed. In N Africa (*mauretanica* Staudinger), range of variation in wing-markings similar: in some localities, ups orange suffusion extensive and constant (f. *powelli* Oberthür): similar forms occur in Spain (*illicioides* Gerhard).
FLIGHT-PERIOD Univoltine. Late May/August according to locality.
HABITAT Hot, dry flowery scrub or sparse deciduous or mixed woodland.
LIFE-HISTORY LHPs *Quercus coccifera*; *Q. ilex*. Larvae attended by *Camponotus cruetatus*.

Blue-spot Hairstreak *Satyrium spini*

RANGE S and C Europe to Turkey, Lebanon, Iraq and Iran.
S. spini Denis and Schiffermüller 1775 TL: Vienna.
DISTRIBUTION Most of Europe to about 54°N in Baltic states. Absent from N France, Belgium, Holland, Fennoscandia, Estonia, Latvia, S Italy and Mediterranean islands, except Mallorca, Corfu, Zakynthos, Kithira and Lesbos. 0-2000m.
DESCRIPTION Male upf with sex-brand. Both sexes, unh with blue spot in anal angle.
VARIATION In Iberian peninsula, female ups with variable orange suffusion, ranging from small, diffuse patch on fw disc and hw anal angle (f. *vandalusica* Lederer [=f. *lynceus* Hübner]) to most of ups except marginal, costal and basal areas (f. *leonensis* Manley): female ups orange suffusion rare elsewhere in Europe.
FLIGHT-PERIOD Univoltine. Late May/late July according to locality.
HABITAT Hot, dry scrub; grassy, bushy places; woodland clearings; exposed mountain meadows with light scrub.
LIFE-HISTORY LHPs Rhamnaceae, including *Rhamnus alaternus*, *R. lycioides*, *R. alpinus*: also, *Paliurus spina-christi* (Rhamnaceae) in Greece. Hibernates as an ovum.

Sloe Hairstreak

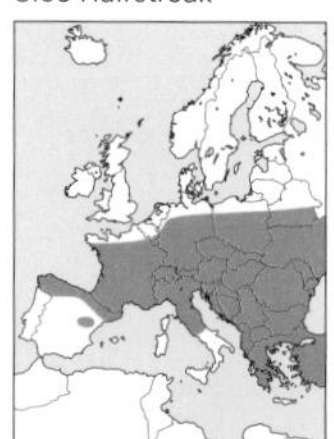

Ilex Hairstreak

SLOE HAIRSTREAK

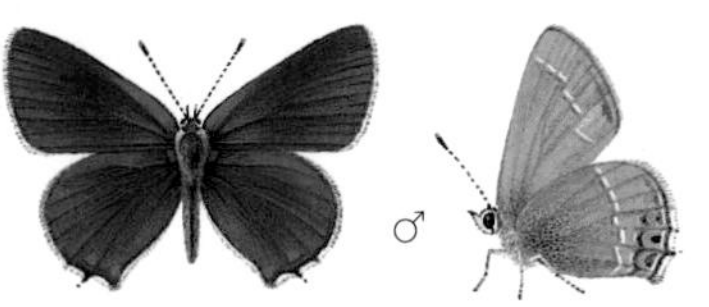

Unh gc and orange spots pale

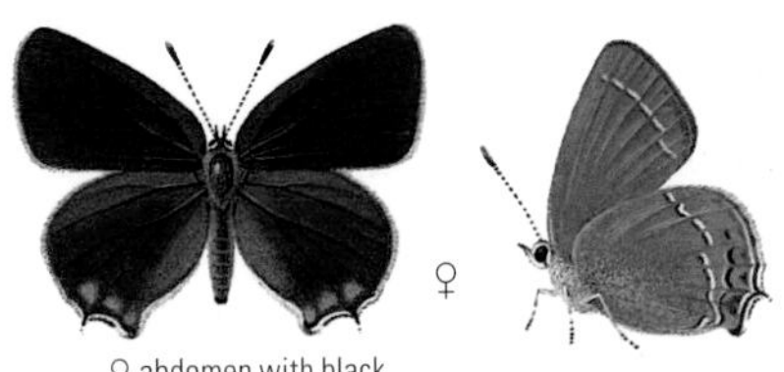

♀ abdomen with black hair-tuft at tip

ILEX HAIRSTREAK

Unh orange spots edged with black internally and externally

f. *cerri* (Portugal, Spain and S France)

FALSE ILEX HAIRSTREAK

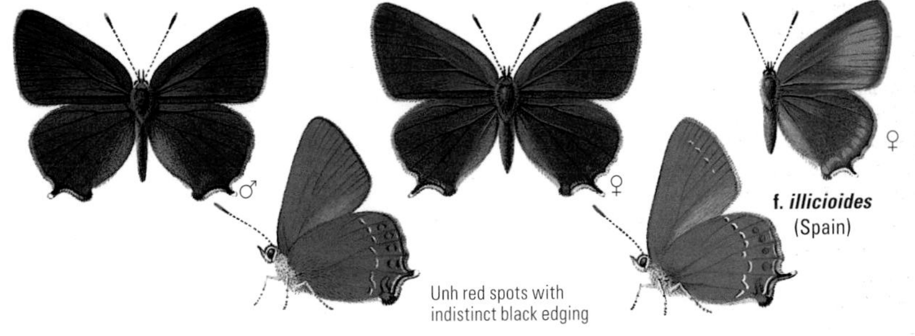

f. *illicioides* (Spain)

Unh red spots with indistinct black edging

BLUE-SPOT HAIRSTREAK

False Ilex Hairstreak

Blue-spot Hairstreak

Unh blue spot in anal angle distinctive

White-letter Hairstreak *Satyrium w-album*

RANGE C and E Europe, Turkey, Urals, Kazakhstan, Japan. *S. w-album* Knoch 1782 TL: Leipzig.

DISTRIBUTION From N Spain (Cantabrian Mts.), Italy (including Sicily) and Greece (in Peloponnesos, reported only from Mt. Chelmos) to S England and S Fennoscandia. Absent from European Turkey and Mediterranean islands except Sicily. 100-1300m.

DESCRIPTION Male upf with small sex-brand above cell.

FLIGHT-PERIOD Univoltine. Generally mid June/late July: emergence may be delayed until August in S Scandinavia in unfavourable seasons.

HABITAT Mature woodland with open, sunny clearings.

LIFE-HISTORY LHP *Ulmus*, principally *U. glabra*. Ova laid at base of terminal leaf buds. Hibernates as an ovum. Newly-hatched larvae feed on developing flower-buds in early spring.

BEHAVIOUR Both sexes attracted to bramble blossom.

Black Hairstreak *Satyrium pruni*

RANGE C and E Europe, S Siberia, Mongolia, Korea, Japan.

S. pruni Linnaeus 1758 TL Germany (Verity 1943).

DISTRIBUTION From E Pyrenees, N Italy (sporadic and very local) and N Greece (district of Drama: extremely local) to central S England, Denmark (restricted to Sjælland and Falster: very local), S Sweden (Skåne, Blekinge, Småland and Öland: very local), Lativa (widespread but scarce), (?) Estonia and S Finland. Absent from coastal Mediterranean districts and islands. 200-750m.

DESCRIPTION AND VARIATION Male upf with small sex-brand above cell. Ups submarginal orange markings variable, better developed in female.

FLIGHT-PERIOD Univoltine. Generally mid June/late July: mid May/early July in central E Europe.

HABITAT Mature blackthorn (*Prunus spinosa*) thickets in sheltered, sunny clearings or at margins of mature, deciduous woodland.

LIFE-HISTORY LHP *Prunus spinosa*. Ova laid mostly at stem junctions on taller plants. Hibernates as a fully-formed larva within ovum-case. Newly-hatched larvae feed on flower-buds in early spring and developing leaf-buds towards maturity.

BEHAVIOUR Adults take nectar from the blossom of shrubs, especially privet (*Lingustrum vulgare*) and bramble (*Rubus fruticosus*) rather than low herbage: often rest for prolonged periods in higher parts of LHP.

Orange-banded Hairstreak *Satyrium ledereri*

RANGE Greece (Samos), Turkey, Lebanon, Iran, Transcaucasus. *S. ledereri* Boisduval 1848 TL: Caucasus.

DISTRIBUTION Greece: known only from Mt. Karvouni (1050-1145m) and Mt. Kerketefs (1000-1400m) on E Aegean island of Samos.

VARIATION On Samos, *christianae* Olivier: wing-characters and male genitalia within range of variation of nominate form.

FLIGHT-PERIOD Univoltine. June.

HABITAT Above tree-line on exposed, dry, craggy limestone supporting sparse, low-growing vegetation.

LIFE-HISTORY LHP *Atraphaxis billardieri* var. *billardieri* (Polygonaceae). Ova laid on woody stems of LHP. Hibernation stage uncertain: in early spring, torpid, second instar larvae have been found under bark and in crevices on stems of dormant LHP: in captivity, hibernates as a fully-formed larva within ovum-case (cf. *S. pruni*). Larvae feed on leaves. In captivity, larvae reject *Rumex acetosella*, *R. acetosa* and *Polygonum aviculare*.

NOTE In North America, Polygonaceae shrubs are widely used by 'hairstreaks' of the genera *Callophrys* and *Strymon*.

Nogel's Hairstreak *Tomares nogelii*

RANGE Romania, Turkey, Ukraine, Crimea, Syria, Lebanon, N Iran.

T. nogelii dobrogensis Caradja 1895 TL: Tulcea, Romania.

DISTRIBUTION Information limited. SE Romania: known only from the district of Dobrogea (Galati; Tulcea).

FLIGHT-PERIOD Univoltine. May/early July.

HABITAT Grassy scrub.

LIFE-HISTORY LHP *Astragalus ponticus*.

White-letter Hairstreak

Black Hairstreak

Nogel's Hairstreak

WHITE-LETTER HAIRSTREAK

Unh white line forms a distinct 'W'

BLACK HAIRSTREAK

Unh orange submarginal spots confluent and distinctive

ORANGE-BANDED HAIRSTREAK

NOGEL'S HAIRSTREAK

Provence Hairstreak *Tomares ballus*

RANGE Morocco, Algeria, Tunisia, Lybia, Egypt, Portugal, Spain, S France.
T. ballus Fabricus 1787 TL: Spain.

DISTRIBUTION Morocco: Anti-Atlas (Aït-Abdallah; Tafraoute). Algeria: El Kantara. Tunisia: Hammamet. 0-1700m. Portugal and Spain: scattered colonies: absent from northern provinces and W Pyrenees. France: E Pyrenees to Alpes-Maritimes. 300-1300m.

VARIATION Male uns green or bluish-green disc sometimes greatly reduced; uph marginal orange spots in anal angle variable in number and size, sometimes absent: female ups orange areas sometimes replaced with dull yellow.

FLIGHT-PERIOD Univoltine. January/mid May according to locality and altitude.

HABITAT Open, dry, meadows and slopes with short grass-turf.

LIFE-HISTORY LHPs principally *Medicago*: S Portugal, *Dorycnium hirsutum*; S Spain, *Medicago littoralis*; *M. truncatula*; *M. minima*; S France, *M. lupulina*: N Africa, *M. turbinata*; *Lotus hispidus*; *Anthyllis tetraphylla*. Ova laid singly in folds of developing leaves. Captive full-grown larvae, are extremely restless and many die without pupating, suggesting that, in nature, pupation occurs within an ants'nest. Larvae are cannibalistic. Larvae attended by *Plagiolepis pygmaea*. Hibernates as a pupa.

BEHAVIOUR At higher altitudes, after severe overnight ground frost, very torpid adults have been observed laying with closed wings on rocks warmed by the early morning sun: after regaining the use of the legs, the insect raises itself from the prone position, adjusting the ventral surface of its wings perpendicular to the angle of the sun's rays: as warming progresses, further advantageous changes in wing-angle are made.

Moroccan Hairstreak *Tomares mauretanicus*

RANGE NW Africa.
T. mauretanicus Lucas 1849 TL: Algeria.

DISTRIBUTION Widespread, often common. Morocco. Algeria. Tunisia. 0-2400m.

VARIATION Subject to considerable local and individual variation: male uph orange markings in anal angle virtually absent or well represented (f. *undulatus* Gerhard), sometimes projecting to pd area: female uns black markings well developed or greatly reduced.

FLIGHT-PERIOD Univoltine. January/April at sea-level, early March/June at higher altitudes.

HABITAT Grassy places; hot, dry stony slopes.

LIFE-HISTORY LHPs *Astragalus epiglottis*; *A. pentaglottis*; *Hedysarum pallidum*; *Hippocrepis multisiliquosa*; *H. minor*. Ova laid on leaves in small batches – an unusual practice for Lycaenidae.

Green Hairstreak *Callophrys rubi*

RANGE N Africa, Europe, Turkey, Russia, Siberia, Amur.
C. rubi Linnaeus 1758 TL: Sweden (Verity 1943).

DISTRIBUTION Widespread and common. Morocco. Algeria. Tunisia. 0-2500m. Throughout Europe, including arctic Fennoscandia, Baltic Islands and most Mediterranean islands: reported from all Greek island-groups but apparently absent from Crete. Absent from Atlantic Islands (a record for Tenerife (1963) remains unconfirmed), Outer Hebrides, Orkney and Shetland Islands. 0-2300m: generally below 2000m.

DESCRIPTION AND VARIATION Frons green, eyes with very narrow white borders (cf. *C. avis*). Both sexes: ups smoky, greyish-brown; unh usually with white mark on costa, sometimes developed into a dotted white mediodiscal line, more rarely extending across unf: latter form relatively common in habitats shared with the similarly marked *C. avis*. In S Europe and NW Africa, f. *fervida* Staudinger: ups gc often more reddish-brown.

FLIGHT-PERIOD Univoltine. Generally March/June: single, fresh specimens are often recorded in July.

HABITAT Diverse. Woodland clearings; bushy places; scrubland; flowery meadows; heaths; marshes; sheltered rocky places or alpine grassland well above tree-line. Adapted to a remarkable range of climatic and other ecological conditions.

LIFE-HISTORY LHPs include *Cytisus scoparius*; *C. nigricans*; *C. villosus*; *Genista tinctoria*; *G. angelica*; *G. pilosa*; *G. germanica*; *G.* (?)*corsica* (Corsica and Sardinia); *Chamaespartium sagittale*; *Chamaecytisus hirsutus*; *C. ciliatus*; *C. eriocarpus*; *Ulex europaeus*; *U. minor*; *Anthyllis vulneraria*; *Dorycnium hirsutum*; *D. suffruticosum* (Algeria); *Onobrychis viciifolia*; *Heliathemun nummularium*; flower-buds/fruits of *Arbutus*; *Vaccinium*; *Rhamnus*; *Frangula*; *Cornus*; *Rubus*. Larvae polymorphic, displaying a wide colour-range – pale greenish-blue, grass green or reddish. Pupa has an ability to make faint sounds by moving its abdominal segments – stridulation. Hibernates as a pupa under stones, leaves or moss at base of trees/shrubs or amongst leaves on LHP.

Chapman's Green Hairstreak *Callophrys avis*

RANGE NW Africa, SW Europe.
C. avis Chapman 1909 TL: S France and Morocco.

DISTRIBUTION Morocco: Tangiers. Algeria: Algiers; Khenchela; Zehroun. Tunisia: Aïn Draham. 200-1700m. Portugal. Spain: provinces of Cádiz, Málaga, Barcelona, Gerona and Teruel. S France: Pyrénées-Orientalis to Alpes-Maritimes. 100-1000m: usually below 700m.

DESCRIPTION AND VARIATION Resembles *C. rubi*. Frons and eye borders rusty-red; ups reddish-brown; uns thin white mediodiscal line on both wings (cf. *C. rubi*).

FLIGHT-PERIOD Univoltine. Late March/mid June according to locality and altitude.

HABITAT Dry scrub containing *Arbutus unedo* – usually in abundance.

PROVENCE HAIRSTREAK

MOROCCAN HAIRSTREAK

GREEN HAIRSTREAK

Unh white discal line, often reduced to a white spot on costa

CHAPMAN'S GREEN HAIRSTREAK

Unh white discal line complete, usually extending into fw

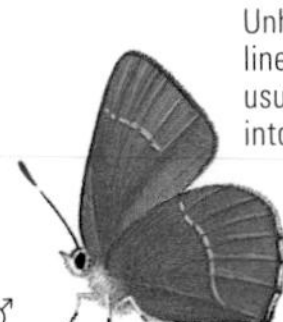

Provence Hairstreak

Moroccan Hairstreak

Green Hairstreak

Chapman's Green Hairstreak

LIFE-HISTORY LHP principally *Arbutus unedo*: also, *Salvia verbenaca*; *Vibernum tinus* (NW Africa) and *Coriara myrtifolia* (NW Africa and Spain). Reported use of *Cytisus malacitanus catalaunicus* [=*Sarothamnus catalaunicus*] and *C. grandiflorus* [=*Sarothamnus grandiflorus*] requires confirmation. On *A. unedo*, ova laid on developing leaves adjacent to withered flowers or fruits on mature plants – young or newly coppiced plants are avoided. Hibernates as a pupa.

Violet Copper *Lycaena helle*

RANGE C and N Europe, W Russia, C and S Siberia, Mongolia, Transbaikal, Amur.

L. helle Denis and Schiffermüller 1775 TL: Vienna.

DISTRIBUTION Locally very common in small, widely dispersed colonies. France: E Pyrenees (Ariège) to Jura Mts.; Doubs. NW Switzerland: Vaud; Valais; Fribourg; Berne; Luzern; Obwald. S Belgium: Ardennes. S Germany. Poland (very rare). Czech Republic. Slovakia. Fennoscandia, except S Norway and Denmark. Extinct in Latvia. 100-1800m.

VARIATION In Fennoscandia, ups markings generally much reduced.

FLIGHT-PERIOD Univoltine. May/July, according latitude and altitude.

HABITAT Flowery, marshy meadows, usually associated with rivers or lakes; sphagnum bogs, often associated with Vaccinium and open woodland.

LIFE-HISTORY LHPs: C Europe, principally *Polygonum bistorta*: N and C Fennoscandia, *P. viviparum*: reputed use of *Rumex acetosella* and *R. acetosa* in S Scandinavia requires confirmation. Ova laid on underside of leaves. Small larvae feed on lower cuticle creating a characteristic pattern of translucent 'windows'. Hibernates as a pupa.

CONSERVATION Drainage and afforestation of habitats poses a serious threat in C and E Europe.

Small Copper *Lycaena phlaeas*

RANGE Canary Islands, N and E Central Africa, Europe, temperate Asia, Japan, NE North America.

L. phlaeas phlaeas Linnaeus 1761 TL: Westermannia, Sweden.

DISTRIBUTION Widespread and common. Canary Islands (rare on Lanzarote: a record for Fuerteventura requires confirmation). NW Africa (0-2700m). South of Arctic Circle to all larger Mediterranean islands and island-groups. Absent from Outer Hebrides, Shetland and Orkney Islands. 0-2400m.

VARIATION First brood: male ups brightly marked: subsequent broods: ups often suffused smoky greyish-brown, sometimes almost obscuring orange gc; hw 'tail' at v2 usually prominent, less marked in female (f. *elea* Fabricius). Uph sometimes with blue pd spots (f. *caeruleopunctata* Rühl). Extremely small specimens, common in late broods in very hot localities, appear to result from premature pupation induced by LHP desiccation.

FLIGHT-PERIOD Bivoltine in N Europe, May/early October: at least trivoltine in S Europe and N Africa, February/late October: polyvoltine in Canary Islands, throughout the year in a succession of overlapping broods.

HABITAT Diverse. Adapted to most habitat-types.

LIFE-HISTORY LHPs *Rumex* spp., including *R. acetosella*; *R. acetosa*; *R. hydrolapathum*; *R. scutatus*: also, in N Africa, *R. thyrsoideus*; *R. papilio*; *R. vesicarius*; *R. tingitanus*: Gran Canaria, LHP determined as R. maderensis or R. vesicarius. Less commonly, *Polygonum* spp., including *P. aviculare*, especially in very arid places where *Rumex* spp. are scarce or absent. Hibernates as a small larva.

L. phlaeas polaris Courvoisier 1911 TL: Norwegian Lapland.

DISTRIBUTION Arctic Fennoscandia (66-70°N): generally local. 0-400m.

DESCRIPTION Ups resembles nominate form: unh gc dove-grey or greyish-buff, black spots prominent in contrast, pd series externally edged with whitish striae; submarginal red spots conspicuous.

FLIGHT-PERIOD Univoltine. Mid June/late July according to season and locality.

HABITAT Warm, sheltered, grassy, flowery places. 0-350m.

L. phlaeas phlaeoides Staudinger 1901 TL: Madeira.

DISTRIBUTION Madeira. 50-1800m.

DESCRIPTION AND VARIATION Ups resembles nominate form: unh colour and pattern distinctive: in late summer broods, ups darker; hw with 'tail' at v2.

FLIGHT-PERIOD Polyvoltine. March/October.

HABITAT As for nominate form.

LIFE-HISTORY LHP unknown. Captive larvae accept *Rumex acetosella* and *R. acetosa*.

Large Copper *Lycaena dispar*

RANGE Europe, N Turkey.

L. dispar dispar Haworth 1803 TL: Cambridgeshire, England.

DISTRIBUTION Restricted to Friesland, Holland. Became extinct in about 1848 in the fens of E England. Since 1927, a colony originating from Dutch race has been maintained at Woodwalton Fen, Huntingdonshire, England.

VARIATION In Holland, *batava* Oberthür: resembles nominate form closely.

FLIGHT-PERIOD Univoltine. June/July.

HABITAT Fenland.

LIFE-HISTORY LHP *Rumex hydrolapathum*. Ova laid mostly on upperside of leaves; small larvae feed by excavating lower cuticle. Hibernates as a small larvae. A second or third brood may be induced in captive rearing.

L. dispar rutila Werneburg 1864 TL: Berlin.

DISTRIBUTION Extremely local in widely dispersed colonies. France: Gironde; Doubs; Haute-Rhin; Bas-Rhin; Meuse; Ardennes; Nièvre; Côte d'Or; Haute-Marne; Aube. Doubtful in NW Switzerland. N Italy: W coastal Italy to Golfo di Gaeta. Germany. Latvia. S Finland. Poland to Balkans, N and C Greece. European Turkey. 0-1000m.

DESCRIPTION AND VARIATION Resembles nominate form: smaller; unh variable, but generally duller, tending to yellowish-grey; orange submarginal band paler. In Greece and Hungary, individuals of second brood sometimes approach or exceed size of *batava*.

VIOLET COPPER

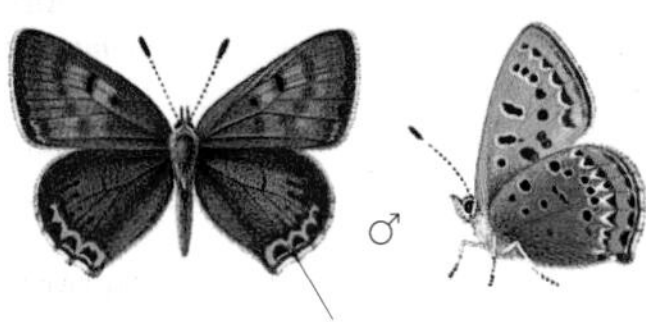

♂ small, ups with distinctive deep-violet sheen over orange and black, bright orange submarginal band on hw

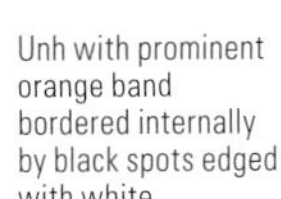

Unh with prominent orange band bordered internally by black spots edged with white

♀ larger, more boldly marked, violet suffusion reduced or more often absent

SMALL COPPER

3rd brood

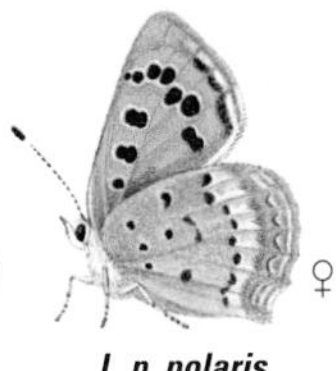

L. p. polaris
(Arctic Fennoscandia)

L. p. phlaeoides
(Madeira)

LARGE COPPER

Violet Copper

Small Copper

Large Copper

L. d. rutila

FLIGHT-PERIOD Bivoltine in most localities: late May/June and August: univoltine in colder, northern districts: a third brood has been reported from some localities in S Europe.
HABITAT Boggy margins of lakes, rivers, ditches and canals.
LIFE-HISTORY LHPs *Rumex hydrolapathum*; *R. crispus*; *R. aquaticus*. In second brood, oviposition and development as for nominate form. In Greece, larvae of the first brood have been known to enter diapause in June, remaining inactive until following spring.
CONSERVATION Changes in land use, particularly drainage of wetlands, pose a serious threat: in Greece, all known colonies appear to be at imminent risk on this account.
NOTE Variation in voltinism and size tends to diffuse the taxonomic boundary separating *rutila* and *batava*. In general, variation in these two parameters provides an inadequate basis for subspecific differentiation, especially as voltinism and size are significantly correlated, effectively halving the number of allowable taxonomic discriminators: in the present case, averagely greater size of *batava* may be attributed to the longer period available for larval growth and therefore causally related to voltinism. Such minor differences in wing-markings as are evident for the above forms, appear to fall within the variance of that which may be regarded as normal for most species.

Scarce Copper *Lycaena virgaureae*

RANGE Europe, Turkey, C Asia, Mongolia.
L. virgaureae virgaureae Linnaeus 1758 TL: Sweden (Verity 1943).
DISTRIBUTION N Spain: N Cantabrian Mts.; Pyrenees. S France: Massif Central. From E Alps eastwards to Arctic Circle in Fennoscandia and NW and N central Greece. Absent from Britain, Belgium and Holland. 1000-2000m.
VARIATION In N Europe, smaller. In Lapland, f. *oranulus* Freyer, male ups yellower; black marginal borders sometimes slightly wider: female ups suffused grey.
FLIGHT-PERIOD Univoltine. Mid July/mid September, according to altitude and locality.
HABITAT Flowery places, often dampish clearings or hillside bogs in woodland.
LIFE-HISTORY LHPs *Rumex* spp., commonly *R. acetosa*. Hibernates as an ovum or small larva below crown of LHP. In habitats prone to flooding, hibernating larvae are often inundated for prolonged periods.
L. virgaureae montanus Meyer-Dür 1851 TL: Rhône Glacier.
DISTRIBUTION Alps of France, Switzerland, Italy, Germany, Austria. 1700-2000m.
DESCRIPTION AND VARIATION Male ups black marginal borders wider, sometimes with very small black discoidal spot: female ups dull golden-yellow with variable greyish suffusion, sometimes obscuring gc.
FLIGHT-PERIOD Univoltine. Late June/early September.
HABITAT Sheltered hollows and gullies on open flowery grassland.
LIFE-HISTORY As for nominate form.
L. virgaureae miegii Vogel 1857 TL: Guardarrama, C Spain.
DISTRIBUTION N and C Spain: S. de Guardarrama; S. de Gredos; S. del Moncayo; Picos de Europa (Pto. de Pajares; Pto. de los Fierros). 600-1600m. No recent records from N Portugal.
DESCRIPTION AND VARIATION Upf with black cell-bar; black borders wider; 3-5 black pd spots in s2-6; uph with black cell-bar and sometimes 3 or 4 small, black pd spots.
FLIGHT-PERIOD Univoltine. July/August.
HABITAT AND LIFE-HISTORY As for nominate form.

Grecian Copper *Lycaena ottomana*

RANGE S Balkans, Greece, Turkey.
L. ottomana Lefèbvre 1830 TL: Greece.
DISTRIBUTION SW Serbia (Montenegro): Vipazar. Republic of Macedonia. Albania. Bulgaria. Greece, including Corfu and Evia. Absent from S Peloponnesos. A record for Thassos requires confirmation. Widespread but often very local. 50-1500m – generally below 1000m. Often occurs with *L. thersamon*.
VARIATION Second brood: unh gc colour somewhat yellowish; hw 'tail' at v2 generally better developed but variable.
FLIGHT-PERIOD Bivoltine. Mid April/late May and July/early August.
HABITAT Dry, generally hot, grassy, flowery places, often amongst bushes or in light woodland.
LIFE-HISTORY LHP *Rumex acetosella*. Ova laid on all plants parts. Larvae feed on leaves, less often on flowers. Captive larvae accept *Rumex hydrolapathum*, *R. acetosa* and *Polygonum aviculare*.
BEHAVIOUR Males of summer brood are especially attracted to flowers of *Sambucus ebulus*. Females appear to retire to a different part of their habitat after pairing. This behaviour, coupled with relatively subdued female activity, may account for the commonly reported 'rarity' of females, even in colonies where males are abundant.

Sooty Copper *Lycaena tityrus*

RANGE Europe, Turkey, Siberia, Urals, Kazakhstan, Altai Mts.
L. tityrus tityrus Poda 1761 TL: Graz, S Austria.
syn: *dorilis* Hufnagel 1766
DISTRIBUTION From N Spain (Cantabrian Mts. and Pyrenees) throughout Europe to about 58°N in Lithuania. Absent from Britain, Fennoscandia (except Fyen, Denmark) and Mediterranean islands except Sicily and Samos. 50-2500m.
VARIATION First brood: male ups gc dark grey-brown; female ups orange submarginal bands and orange basal suffusion extensive: in later broods, male ups often with orange submarginal spots on hw, sometimes extending to fw; female ups brown, sometimes with orange discal suffusion; orange submarginal spots reduced.
FLIGHT-PERIOD Polyvoltine in hot, low-lying regions, mid April/October: bivoltine in cooler localities, late April/June and July/September.

Maps on p. 97

SCARCE COPPER

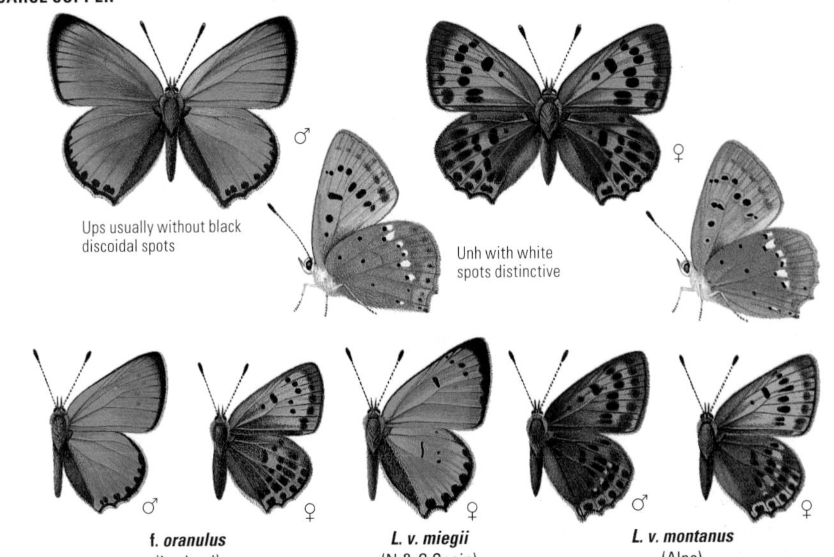

GRECIAN COPPER

SOOTY COPPER

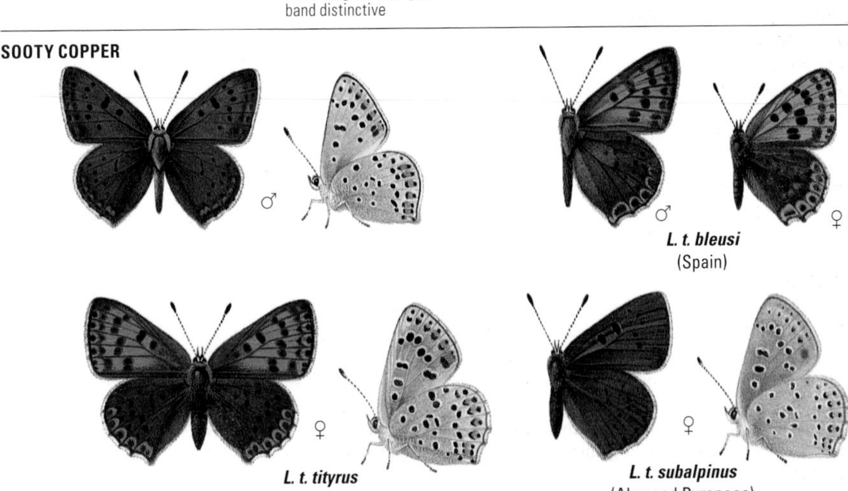

HABITAT Diverse. Flowery grassy meadows; dry scrub; damp woodland clearings; sheltered alpine gullies.
LIFE-HISTORY LHP *Rumex* spp., especially *R. acetosa*. Hibernates as a small larva at base of LHP.
L. tityrus subalpinus Speyer 1851 TL: Innsbruck, N Tyrol.
DISTRIBUTION Pyrenees (2100m). Alps of France, Switzerland, Italy, Germany, Austria. 1200-2500m.
DESCRIPTION Ups dark brown in both sexes, unmarked except dark cell-bar and occasional submarginal orange markings, especially in female; uns gc yellowish-grey.
FLIGHT-PERIOD Bivoltine at lower altitudes, April/June and July/early September: univoltine above (?)1500m, late June/September.
HABITAT Sheltered grassy and flowery places.
LIFE-HISTORY LHP *Rumex scutatus*.
L. tityrus bleusei Oberthür 1884 TL: Escorial and Madrid, Spain.
DISTRIBUTION Spain: S. de Guardarrama; S. de Guadalupe; S. de Gredos. 900-1100m.
DESCRIPTION Male upf gc orange, spots large; female ups orange markings extensive.
FLIGHT-PERIOD Voltinism uncertain: probably as for nominate form.
HABITAT Grassy, flowery, bushy places.

Purple-shot Copper *Lycaena alciphron*

RANGE Morocco, Europe, Turkey, Iran, S Siberia, S Urals, Mongolia, Altai.
L. alciphron alciphron Rottemburg 1775 TL: Berlin.
DISTRIBUTION S France. Germany. Czech Republic. Slovakia. Hungary. Lithuania. Latvia. (?)Estonia. 50-900m. Very sporadic and local.
FLIGHT-PERIOD Univoltine. Generally June/July: recorded in April from coastal districts of S France.
HABITAT Grassy, flowery places.
LIFE-HISTORY LHP *Rumex acetosa*.
L. alciphron melibaeus Staudinger 1879 TL: Greece.
DISTRIBUTION Widespread and common. Balkans. N and C Greece, including Lesbos. European Turkey. 50-1750m.
DESCRIPTION Male ups gc orange, suffused greyish with violet or pinkish tones: female ups gc medium brown with variable, sometimes extensive orange suffusion.
FLIGHT-PERIOD Univoltine. Mid June/July.
HABITAT Grassy flowery banks and meadows, sometimes in damp places; sheltered gullies above tree-line.
LIFE-HISTORY LHP *Rumex* spp. near polymorphic *R. acetosa*. Ova laid mostly at stem-leaf junctions, less often on flowers. Hibernates as a small larva at base of LHP.
BEHAVIOUR Both sexes attracted to flowers of *Thymus*.
L. alciphron gordius Sulzer 1776 TL: Graubünden, Switzerland.
DISTRIBUTION N Portugal. Spain: widespread in mountains. Andorra. S and C France: E Pyrenees; Massif Central; SW Alps. S Switzerland: Valais to Graubünden. Italy: Maritime Alps to Dolomites and Calabria (Aspromonte); generally absent from eastern coast. NE Sicily (Monti Nebrodi; Mt. Etna). Generally 800-2000m: Sierra Nevada, 1100-2500m.
DESCRIPTION Male ups violet suffusion reduced; uns brighter: female ups clear, bright orange; black markings bold.
FLIGHT-PERIOD Univoltine. Late June/early August.
HABITAT Sheltered, flowery hollows and gullies.
LIFE-HISTORY LHP *Rumex scutatus*.
L. alciphron heracleana Blachier 1908 TL: High Atlas, Morocco.
DISTRIBUTION Morocco: High Atlas; known only from Toubkal massif and Dj. Siroua. 1700-2650m.
DESCRIPTION Resembles *gordius*: large; male ups yellowish-orange without violet or greyish suffusion. Female ups deeper yellow-orange, black markings more prominent.
FLIGHT-PERIOD Univoltine. Mid June/July.
HABITAT Damp grassy places.
BEHAVIOUR Males often 'hilltop', congregating on barren, stony ground – recorded at 3000m.
LIFE-HISTORY LHP *Rumex scutatus*; possibly also *R. acetosa*.

Fiery Copper *Lycaena thetis*

RANGE Greece, Turkey, Lebanon, Syria, Iraq, Iran.
L. thetis Klug 1834 TL: Syria.
DISTRIBUTION C and S Greece: Mt. Tymphristos; Mt. Ghiona; Mt. Kaliakouda; Mt. Iti; Mt. Chelmos; Taygetos Mts. 1500-2300m. A record for former S Yugoslavia appears to have arisen from confusion with *L. ottomana* or *L. thersamon*.
VARIATION Hw 'tail' at v2 sometimes well developed (f. *caudata* Staudinger): although reputedly associated with a second brood, the species appears to be univoltine through-out its range. In Greece, *hephetstos* Dils and van der Poorten: wing-characters and male genitalia indistinguishable from nominate form.
FLIGHT-PERIOD Univoltine. Mid July/August.
HABITAT Open, dry, rocky sites on limestone supporting low-growing shrubs, including the spiny, cushion-forming LHP which shows a marked preference for consolidated rock formations in upper half of altitudinal range. Habitats may be as small as 2500m^2. All known habitats in Peloponnesos shared with *Turanana endymion*.
LIFE-HISTORY LHP *Acantholimon androsaceum* (Plumbaginaceae). Oviposition not observed in Europe: in Turkey, females have been seen to eject ova into the centre of LHP. Hibernates as a small larva concealed amongst the densely packed stems and dead stem-leaves of LHP. Post-hibernated larvae feed on leaves and are evidently very closely adapted to LHP. Appears to be unique amongst the European Lycaeninae – 'coppers' – for its independence from the Polygonaceae – the 'dock' family. Although LHP is shared with *Turanana endymion* in the same habitats, competition between the two species appears to be negligible.
BEHAVIOUR Both sexes strongly attracted to nectar of *Thymus*.
CONSERVATION Exploitation of many of the higher mountains of Greece for recreational and other purposes poses a direct threat to habitats.

PURPLE-SHOT COPPER

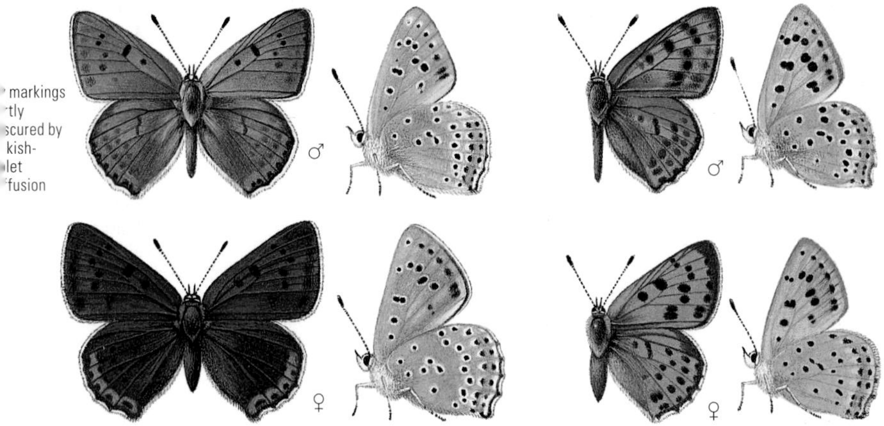

markings
tly
scured by
kish-
let
fusion
♂
♂
♀
♀

♀ ups with variable, sometimes extensive orange suffusion

L. a. alciphron

♀ ups lacking violet suffusion

L. a. gordius
(SW Europe)

♂
♀
♂
♀

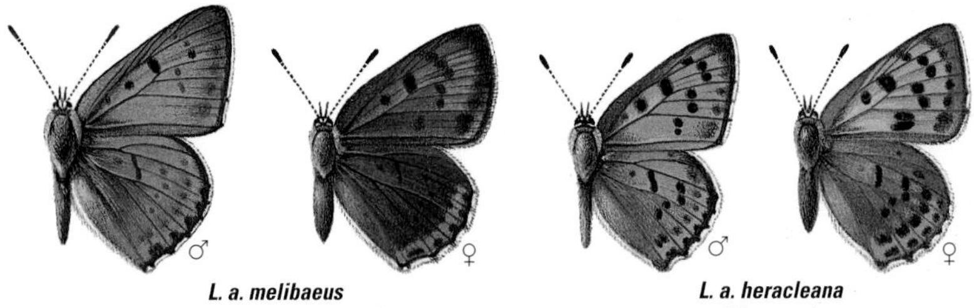

L. a. melibaeus
(Balkans, N & C Greece)

L. a. heracleana
(Morocco)

FIERY COPPER

Fw black apical patch distinctive
♂
♀
Small 'tail' at vein 2 sometimes well developed

Scarce Copper

Grecian Copper

Sooty Copper

Purple-shot Copper

Fiery Copper

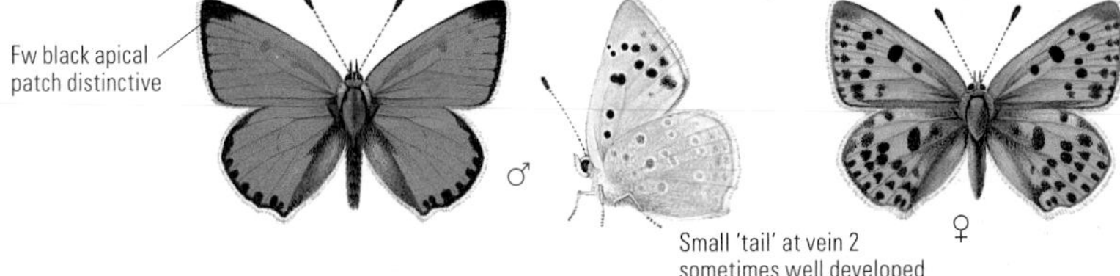

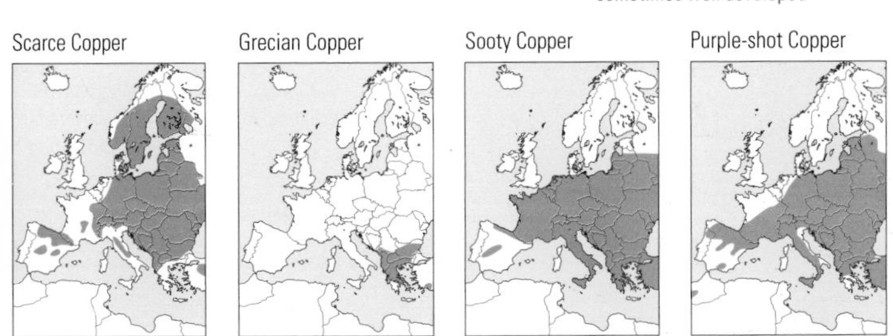

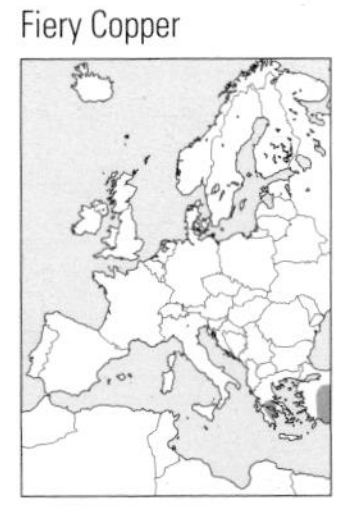

Lesser Fiery Copper *Lycaena thersamon*

RANGE Italy, E and SE Europe, Israel, Lebanon, Turkey, Iraq, Iran, Afghanistan, Ukraine, S Urals, Altai.
L. thersamon Esper 1784 TL: Sarepta, S Russia.
DISTRIBUTION Widespread, generally very local. Central peninsular Italy: E and SE Europe from about 50°N to N Peloponnesos and E Aegean islands of Thassos, Kos and Rhodes. 0-1600m. In Greece, distribution correlates closely with that of *L. ottomana*.
VARIATION Sometimes with filamentous 'tail' on hw at v2 (f. *omphale* Klug): in Greece, 'tailed' individuals occur sporadically in first brood, more commonly in subsequent broods.
FLIGHT-PERIOD Polyvoltine. Mid April/October according to locality and altitude.
HABITAT Dry grassy, flowery meadows or scrub clearings; sometimes very hot, dry, rocky places.
LIFE-HISTORY LHP Polygonum aviculare. Ova laid on leaves, stems and flowers. Larvae feed on leaves and flowers. Captive females refuse to oviposit on *Polygonum persicaria*, *P. hydropipe*r or *Rumex acetosella*: captive larvae reject these, as well as *R. acetosa* and *Cytisus scoparius* (Fabaceae) and *Chamaecytisus hirsutus* (Fabaceae). The widely quoted use of *Rumex* and *Sarothamnus* [=*Cytisus*] appears to originate from mis-quotation of an early literature reference (Malicky 1969). On Cyprus, distribution of butterfly is said to correlate with that of '*Polygonum bellardi*' [=*P. patulum* or *P.* (?)*rurivagum*]
BEHAVIOUR Both sexes greatly attracted to blossom of *Thymus* and *Sambucus ebulus*. Frequently, a colony may reveal its existence by the appearance of only one or two specimens.

Moroccan Copper *Lycaena phoebus*

RANGE Morocco.
L. phoebus Blachier 1908 TL: High Atlas, Morocco.
DISTRIBUTION Very local but common. W Morocco: region of Marrakech (Asni; El-Kelaa-des-Srarhna; Nid de Cigogne; 400-2200m); High Atlas (Toubkal massif); Anti-Atlas (Tafraoute; Tizi-n-Taraktine; Ida-Ougnidf; Tizi-n-Taghatine; 1000-1800m). Records for Algeria and Tunisia have been discredited.
FLIGHT-PERIOD Voltinism uncertain, possibly regionally variable: district of Marrakech, late April/late September in at least two broods: in hot, dry, barren localities, March/May: at higher altitudes in High Atlas, late August/September.
HABITAT Grassy flowery places especially with *Thymus*; margins (drainage ditches) of cultivation; dry, barren places in Anti-Atlas.
LIFE-HISTORY LHPs: High Atlas, possibly *Polygonum aviculare*: Anti-Atlas, *P. equisetiforme*. Reputed use of *Rumex* requires confirmation: field-observations indicate that, where opportunities exist, neither *R. papilio* nor *R. vesicarius*, are exploited by ovipositing females.

Purple-edged Copper *Lycaena hippothoe*

RANGE Europe, C and S Siberia, S Urals, Altai.
L. hippothoe hippothoe Linnaeus 1761 TL: S Sweden.
DISTRIBUTION N Spain: Cantabrian Mts.; S. de la Demanda; S. Mancilla; S. Moncayo. From Pyrenees eastwards through much of Europe to about 62°N in Fennoscandia. Absent from Britain, NW France, coastal S France, N Holland, S Italy, S Balkans and Greece. 400-1800m.
DESCRIPTION AND VARIATION Male ups with striking purple flush: female upf orange discal area variable; uph orange submarginal markings prominent; unf orange discal flush variable. In central E Europe, *sumadiensis* Szabo: resembles nominate form closely: bivoltine.
FLIGHT-PERIOD Univoltine in W and N Europe (including NW Hungary), June/late July: bivoltine in central E Europe (including S and E Hungary), May and late July/August.
HABITAT Marshy meadows, hillside bogs.
LIFE-HISTORY LHPs *Polygonum bistorta*; *Rumex acetosa*. Hibernates as a small larva.
L. hippothoe eurydame Hoffmannsegg 1806 TL: Mts near Geneva.
syn: *eurybia* Ochsenheimer 1808.
DISTRIBUTION Alps of France, Switzerland, Italy, Austria: also, Apuane Alps and C Appennines. 1500-2500m. Altitudinal range overlaps that of nominate form but not on same mountains.
DESCRIPTION Male ups without purple flush: female ups uniform brown, sometimes with vestigial orange submarginal markings; unf without orange flush.
FLIGHT-PERIOD Univoltine. July/mid September according to altitude.
HABITAT Damp alpine meadows.
LIFE-HISTORY LHPs *Polygonum bistorta*; *Rumex acetosa*. Hibernates as a small larva.
L. hippothoe stiberi Gerhard 1853 TL: Lapland.
DISTRIBUTION Fennoscandia from about 62°N (Dovrefjeld) to North Cape. 0-400m.
DESCRIPTION Male ups gc lighter golden-red; unf orange discoidal flush and unh orange band distinct: female upf discoidal area orange extending towards outer margin. In both sexes, unh gc colour light greyish-buff; ups and unh submarginal bands well developed.
FLIGHT-PERIOD Univoltine. Late June/July.
HABITAT Grassy places, often near shoreline on Norwegian coast.
LIFE-HISTORY LHP *Rumex acetosa*. Hibernates as an ovum.

LESSER FIERY COPPER

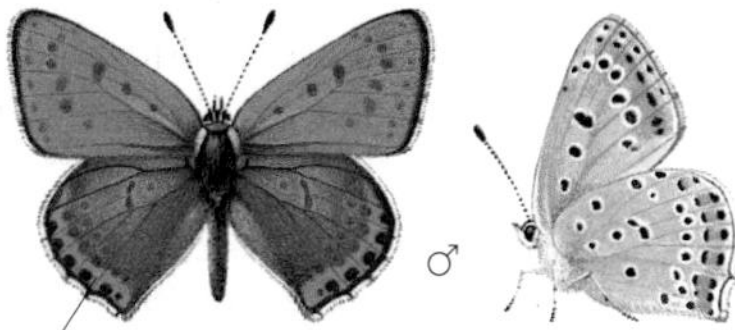

♂

♀

Hw with grey suffusion leaving narrow orange submarginal border

MOROCCAN COPPER

♂

♀

Restricted to Morocco

PURPLE-EDGED COPPER

Upf regular series of submarginal and pd spots characteristic

le flush
picuous
w costa
below
on hw

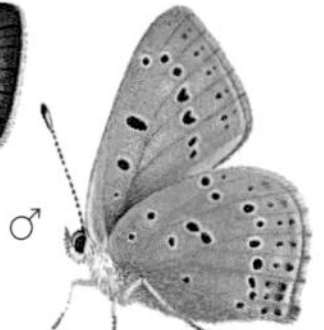

♂

♀

L. h. hippothoe

♂

♀

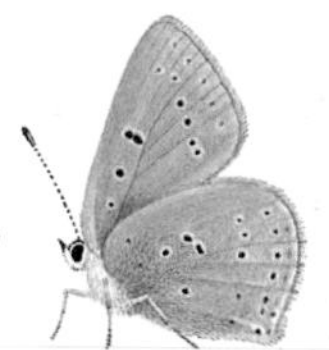

Ups lacking purple flush

L. h. eurydame
(Alps)

Lesser Fiery Copper

Moroccan Copper

Purple-edged Copper

♂

♀

L. h. stiberi
(Fennoscandia)

Balkan Copper *Lycaena candens*

RANGE S Balkans, Greece, Turkey.
L. candens Herrich-Schäffer 1844 TL: Turkey.
DISTRIBUTION Locally common. Republic of Macedonia. S Serbia. Albania. Bulgaria. N and C Greece: Varnous Mts.; Voras Mts.; Rhodopi Mts.; Pindos Mts.; Mt. Olympos. 900-2000m.
DESCRIPTION Resembles nominate form of *L. hippothoe* closely: larger; male genitalia distinctive.
FLIGHT-PERIOD Univoltine. Mid June/late July.
HABITAT Hillside bogs, in beech or pine woodland clearings, containing many distinctive plants, especially *Geum coccineum* and *Silene asterias*; less often exposed, dry, grassy places above tree-line.
LIFE-HISTORY LHP *Rumex* sp. near polymorphic *R. acetosa*. Hibernating larvae are often inundated in early spring.

Long-tailed Blue *Lampides boeticus*

RANGE Worldwide temperate zones.
L. boeticus Linnaeus 1767 TL: Algeria.
DISTRIBUTION Canary Islands, NW Africa, Mediterranean islands and Europe to about 54°N (N Germany). Generally widespread and common in southern areas. Occasionally common in Channel Islands. Rare in S England and generally scarcer in northern range, where appearance probably depends solely on migration: residency uncertain in most regions, including S Europe (see below). 0-2700m.
FLIGHT-PERIOD Polyvoltine. Canary Islands, throughout year in several, overlapping broods. In N Africa and Europe, February/November according to locality.
HABITAT Diverse. Hot, dry, flowery places; cultivated ground.
LIFE-HISTORY LHPs many genera of Fabaceae upon which larvae feed mainly on developing seeds: Canary Islands, *Cassia didymobotrya*; *Pisum sativum*; *Chamaecytisus palmensis*: N Africa and Europe, commonly *Colutea arborescens*: also in N Africa, *Helianthemum helianthemoides*. Sometimes a serious pest on cultivated *Pisum sativum* (Garden Pea) and *Phaseolus vulgaris* (Broad Bean). Whilst captively reared larvae appear willing to accept the seeds or flowers of an extraordinary range of Fabaceae, the natural exploitation of *Cercis siliquastrum* (Judas Tree) and *Robinia pseudacacia* (False Acacia), common Mediterranean species with large seed-capsules, does not appear to have been observed. Life-cycle in captivity 4-6 weeks, according to temperature. Apparent absent of a diapause stage suggests residency is possible only in warmer parts of the Mediterranean where continuity of larval food source is maintained (cf. *D. chrysippus*). Larvae attended by *Lasius niger*; *Camponotus compressus*; *C. cruetatus*; *C. sylvaticus*; *C. foreli*; *Prenolepis clandestina*; *Plagiolepis* sp.; *Tapinoma melanocephalum*.

Geranium Bronze *Cacyreus marshalli*

RANGE S Africa: introduced to S Spain.
C. marshalli Butler 1898 TL: S Africa.
The immature stages of this South African species are believed to have been accidentally introduced to the Balearic Islands, Spain, through the importation of *Pelargonium* cultivars. First reported in 1990 on Mallorca, the species quickly became a pest throughout this island. It has since extended its range to other Balearic Islands as well as the Spanish mainland: two specimens were captured near Logrono in 1992, another in Granada city-centre in 1995. In 1991, a male specimen was captured in a Brussels garden containing *Pelargonium* and several colonies were noted in the vicinity of Rome in 1996. The widespread popularity of *Pelargonium* as ornamental plants would seem conducive to further dispersion. In South Africa, this continuously brooded insect also feeds on *Geranium* spp. and its establishment in the wild in the warmer parts of the Mediterranean region would seem possible. In captivity, life-cycle occupies about one month at 25°C. Whilst a preference is shown for flowers and flower-buds, larvae attack all aerial components of *Pelargonium*. Larva is pale green with red markings and long, stiffish white hairs: pupa; similarly coloured and ornamented.

Lang's Short-tailed Blue *Leptotes pirithous*

RANGE N Africa, S and C Europe, Turkey, Middle East, Saudi Arabia, C Asia, India.
L. pirithous Linnaeus 1767 TL: Algeria.
syn: *telicanus* Lang 1789.
DISTRIBUTION Widespread and common. N Africa. Mediterranean Europe, including islands. Iberian peninsula. SW France: Pyrenees. SW Balkans. Greece. Less common in C Europe to about 48°N as a migrant: residency in most regions unconfirmed (see below). 0-1200m. Not recorded from Atlantic islands.
FLIGHT-PERIOD Polyvoltine. February/October.
HABITAT Diverse. Hot, dry scrubland; cultivated areas, especially Lucerne fields (*Medicago sativa*).
LIFE-HISTORY LHPs: many genera of Fabaceae: also, Lythraceae (*Lythrum salicaria*); Plumbaginaceae; Rosaceae; Ericaceae (*Calluna vulgaris*): in Greece, oviposition has been observed on *Sambucus ebulus* (Caprifoliaceae) and a *Jasminum* cultivar (Oleaceae) (captive larvae accept flower-buds of *J. nudiflorum*). Reported use of *Quercus suber* (Fagaceae) requires confirmation. Ovum stage usually 3 days, sometimes 6 days at same temperature. Life-cycle in captivity 4-8 weeks, depending on temperature. Larvae polymorphic: in Greece, larvae of various colours from pure white to dark green have been recorded on flowers of *Galega officinalis* (Fabaceae). Diapause stage – if any – unknown: attempts to induce diapause in captivity have been unsuccessful. Resident status in N and E Mediterranean uncertain: occurrence in S Europe may depend on early season migration from N Africa.

BALKAN COPPER

Purple flush conspicuous on fw costa and below cell on hw

LONG-TAILED BLUE

Steely violet-blue, browner towards margins, hw black spots near anal angle, boldest in s2

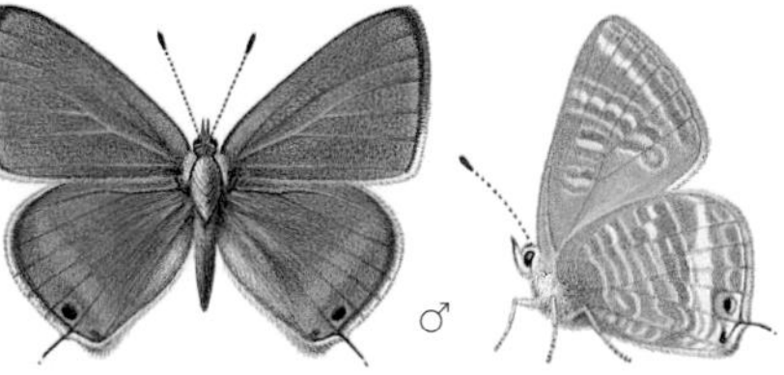

GERANIUM BRONZE

LANG'S SHORT-TAILED BLUE

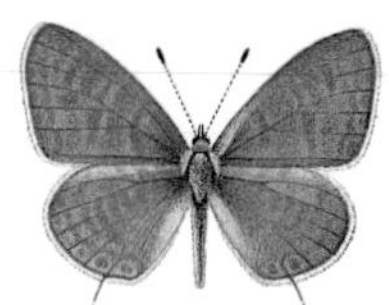

Balkan Copper

Long-tailed Blue

Lang's Short-tailed Blue

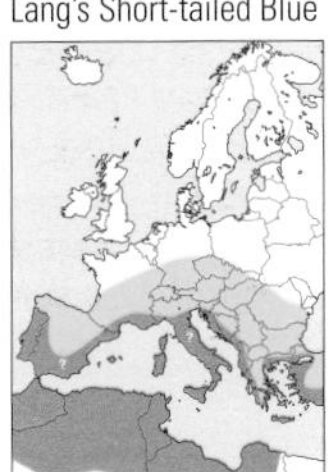

Canary Blue *Cyclyrius webbianus*

RANGE Canary Islands.
C. webbianus Brullé 1839 TL: Canary Islands.
DISTRIBUTION Restricted to Canary Islands: Gomera; La Palma; Tenerife; Gran Canaria. Generally 200-2500m – recorded above this range near summit of Mt. Teide, Tenerife (3500m). A single record for Hierro requires confirmation.
FLIGHT-PERIOD Polyvoltine. Throughout the year in a succession of several overlapping broods at lower altitudes: not recorded between early October and early May above 2000m on Tenerife (Cañadas Plateau).
HABITAT Rocky places amongst scrub at low altitudes; sometimes waste-ground close to human habitation; sheltered hollows with sparse vegetation on Mt. Teide, 2000-3000m.
LIFE-HISTORY LHPs Fabaceae, including *Cytisus canariensis*; *Spartocytisus rubigenus*; *Lotus sessilifolius*; *L. hillebrandii*; *L. glaucus*; *Adenocarpus viscosus*; *Teline stenopetala*. Captive larvae readily accept leaves and flowers of *Lotus corniculatus*, *L. uliginosus* and *Onobrychis viciifolia* and the flowers of *Lathyrus pratensis*, *Ulex europaeus*, *Cytisus scoparius* and *C. sessilifolius*. Diapause stage/winter survival strategy at high altitude on Tenerife unknown.
BEHAVIOUR Adults attracted to nectar of *Pterocephalus lasiospermum*; *Dittrichia viscosa*; *Micromeria* sp.
NOTE Closest known relative, *C. mandersi* Druce 1907, endemic in Mauritius and believed to be extinct.

Common Tiger Blue *Tarucus theophrastus*

RANGE N Africa, S Spain, Tropical Africa north of equator, SW Arabia.
T. theophrastus Fabricius 1793 TL: Morocco.
DISTRIBUTION Mainly coastal districts. Morocco: Anti-Atlas; High Atlas; Middle Atlas. Algeria. Tunisia. Generally 0-1400m – a single female recorded at 2600m near Oukaïmedan, High Atlas. S Spain: provinces of Cádiz; Almeria; Murcia. 25-250m. Reports from NW Sicily and Aspromonte require confirmation.
DESCRIPTION Uns black pd line disrupted by veins on both wings (cf. *T. rosaceus* and *T. balkanicus*).
FLIGHT-PERIOD Polyvoltine. NW Africa, April/November (recorded in all months in southern deserts): Spain, mid April/September: first brood often very scarce.
HABITAT Hot, dry, open scrubland usually dominated by large bushes of LHP, often in cultivated areas.
LIFE-HISTORY LHPs: Spain, *Ziziphus lotus*: NW Africa, *Ziziphus lotus*; *Z. jujuba* [=*Z. vulgaris*; *Z. sativa*] (cultivated in Mediterranean Europe, naturalized in some areas) and *Paliurus spina-christi* [=*Ziziphus spina-christi*]. (*Z. jujuba* and *P. spina-christi* occur in S Spain: *Z. lotus* occurs in Sicily: *Z. jujuba* is naturalized in S Italy). Ova laid on stems, usually at the base of a thorn. Larvae feed in systematic fashion, excavating adjacent furrows in lower cuticle of leaves, resulting in a characteristic pattern of elongate, parallel, translucent 'windows' on unbroken upper cuticle. In Spain, larvae attended by *Crematogastor fuentei*. Hibernates as a pupa. In captivity, pupae from first brood may remain in diapause until following spring.
BEHAVIOUR During most of the day, adults fly amongst branches or rest on leaves of LHP: in early evening, large numbers may sometimes gather at the tops of grass-stems near base of LHP.

Mediterranean Blue *Tarucus rosaceus*

RANGE N Africa, Egypt, Israel, Jordan, Lebanon, Saudi Arabia, Iraq, S Iran, NW India.
T. rosaceus Austaut 1885 TL: Algeria.
syn: *mediterraneae* Bethune-Baker 1917.
DISTRIBUTION Morocco. Algeria. Tunisia. 0-1400m.
DESCRIPTION Unf black pd line unbroken except at v6. Examination of genitalia advisable to confirm identification, owing to variation in wing-characters and possible confusion with *T. theophrastus* and *T. balkanicus*.
FLIGHT-PERIOD Polyvoltine. March/September.
HABITAT Hot, dry ground. Habitats usually shared with *T. theophrastus*.
LIFE-HISTORY LHP *Paliurus spina-christi*. In Saudi Arabia, *Ziziphus*. Larvae attended by *Plagiolepis pygmaea*; *Camponotus sicheli*; *Monomorium salomonis*.

Little Tiger Blue *Tarucus balkanicus*

RANGE NW Africa, Sudan, S Balkans, Greece, Turkey, Israel, Lebanon, Iran, Iraq, Saudi Arabia, Transcaucasus, C Asia.
T. balkanicus Freyer 1845 TL: 'Turkey'.
DISTRIBUTION Very sporadic and local. Morocco. Algeria. Tunisia. S Dalmatian coast. Albania. Republic of Macedonia. Bulgaria: Kresna; NE coast. N and C Greece; Corfu. A record for Samothraki requires confirmation. European Turkey. 50-850m.
DESCRIPTION Resembles *T. rosaceus* and *T. theophrastus* but males usually separable by:- upf large, prominent black discal and pd spots; uns dark pd spots usually confluent: male genitalia distinct.
FLIGHT-PERIOD Polyvoltine. Mid April/October. First brood often very scarce, population density increases rapidly in summer.
HABITAT Hot, dry, open scrubland, often dominated by the distinctive bushes of LHP.
LIFE-HISTORY LHP: Europe and N Africa, *Paliurus spina-christi*: also in N Africa, *Ziziphus lotus*. Ova laid on stems, usually at the base of a thorn. Larval feeding behaviour as for *T. theophrastus*. Larvae attended by ants. Hibernates as a pupa. In captivity, pupae from first brood may remain in diapause until following spring.
BEHAVIOUR Both sexes warm themselves in the early morning by sitting on rocks, usually with wings closed. In Greece, a small, purple-flowered *Micromeria* species is a frequently used nectar-source.

CANARY BLUE

Restricted to Canary Islands

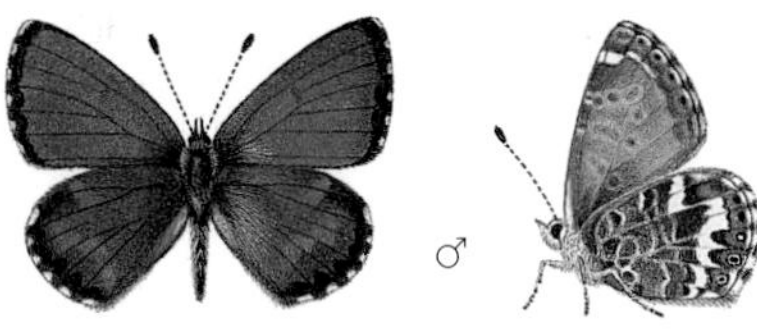

COMMON TIGER BLUE

Ups violet-blue: fw discoidal spot oblong

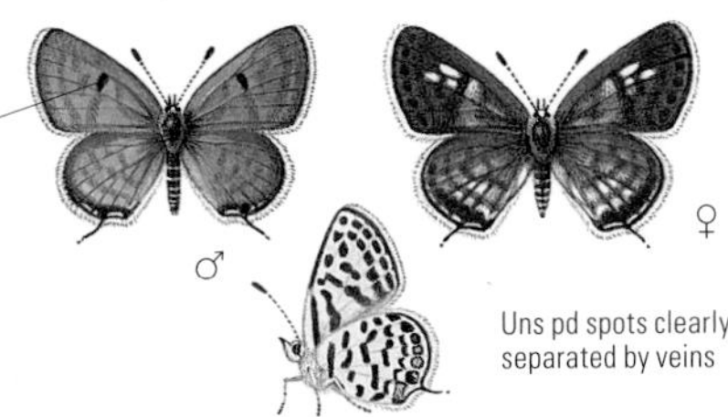

MEDITERRANEAN BLUE

Restricted to N Africa

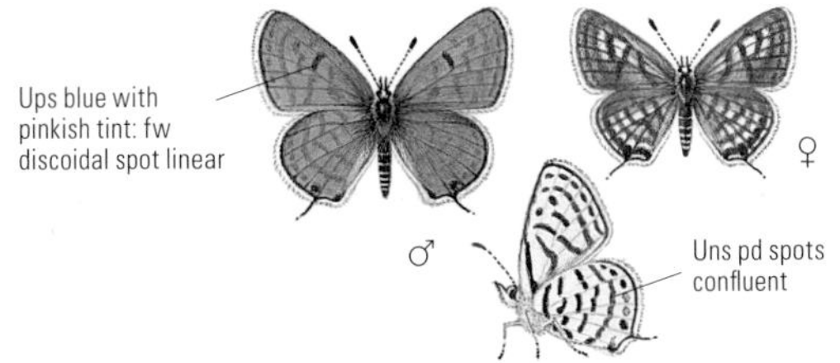

LITTLE TIGER BLUE

Uns pd spots confluent

♀ ups lacking white spots

Common Tiger Blue

Mediterranean Blue

Little Tiger Blue

Desert Babul Blue *Azanus ubaldus*

RANGE Gran Canaria, N and Tropical Africa, Egypt, Jordan, Israel, Saudi Arabia, S Asia.
A. ubaldus Stoll 1782 TL: Sri Lanka
DISTRIBUTION Canary Islands: Gran Canaria (recorded from Playa del Inglés (1982) and Maspalomas (1992)). S Morocco: 400-1000m. (Also reported from S Algeria (to at least 1500m) and S Tunisia).
DESCRIPTION Resembles *A. jesous*: both sexes: smaller; unf without cell-spot – almost always present in *A. jesous*. Male ups pale blue; dark marginal borders very narrow; upf with well-defined slightly darker blue androconial patch – a useful diagnostic feature; androconial scales very narrow, length variable; uph marginal spots in s1c and s2 small, obscure; uns gc pale greyish-brown, with transverse whitish striae; unh with two conspicuous round spots on costa and two larger marginal spots in s1c and s2, basal spots smaller, variable, often indistinct: female ups brown, often with obscure, blue basal suffusion; uns whitish striae better developed, other markings as for male.
FLIGHT-PERIOD Voltinism uncertain: probably polyvoltine. Records for Gran Canaria relate to late January and late April: records for Morocco span March/late summer: possibly continuously brooded in both regions – no diapause stage reported from elsewhere in range.
HABITAT Restricted to immediate vicinity of LHP – *Acacia* trees growing in very hot, dry places.
LIFE-HISTORY LHPs: Gran Canaria, not recorded – probably *Acacia* sp.: Morocco, *Acacia raddiana*; *A. seyal*. Larvae attended by *Camponotus* sp.; *Prenolepis* sp.
BEHAVIOUR Adults fly rapidly amongst branches of LHP, exploiting its flowers as a nectar-source. An entire colony may restrict itself to a single *Acacia* tree, despite the presence of others nearby. Both sexes take water from damp ground.
NOTE In Saudi Arabia, apparently subject to very marked seasonal fluctuations in population density (cf. apparent sporadic occurrence on Gran Canaria).

African Babul Blue *Azanus jesous*

RANGE Africa, Egypt, Israel, Lebanon, Syria, Saudi Arabia, Yemen, Oman.
A. jesous Guérin 1849 TL: Abyssinia.
DISTRIBUTION S and W Morocco: widespread on plains north of Marrakech: more sporadic and local on southern slopes of High Atlas and Anti-Atlas. 200-(?)1000m, most frequent 400-800m: single specimens have been recorded at 1800m on Toubkal massif. (Known to occur at 2000m in Oman).
DESCRIPTION Resembles *A. ubaldus*: both sexes: larger; unf black cell-spot distinct, very rarely absent – a useful diagnostic character. Male ups pale lilac-blue; brown marginal borders narrow, proximally diffuse; upf with dark spot at cell-end; androconial patch inconspicuous; androconial scales short, wide, coarsely striated; uph marginal spots in s1c and s2 small, obscure; uns gc greyish-brown, transverse whitish striae conspicuous; unf with small dark marginal spots in s2-6; unh spots as for *A. ubaldus* but larger, with an additional, large marginal spot in s6 and two indistinct spots in s4 and s5: female ups gc pale brown, sometimes with blue suffusion; upf dark discoidal spot often enclosed by pale suffusion, usually extending to inner margin; uns markings as for male.
FLIGHT-PERIOD At least trivoltine: February throughout summer in overlapping broods.
HABITAT As for *A. ubaldus*.
LIFE-HISTORY LHP *Acacia gummifera*: elsewhere in range, commonly *Acacia* spp.; also, *Prosopis farcta* (Sinai Peninsula); *Medicago* sp.; *Entada* sp. In Yemen, large numbers of pupae recorded under stones at base of host-tree (*Acacia etbaica*).
BEHAVIOUR As for *A. ubaldus*. (Displays migratory/dispersive tendency in Saudi Arabia).

African Grass Blue *Zizeeria knysna*

RANGE Canary Islands, N Africa, S Portugal, S Spain, Egypt, Israel, Lebanon, Syria, Iraq, E Saudi Arabia, Turkey, Cyprus, S Asia, Australia.
Z. knysna knysna Trimen 1862 TL: South Africa.
syn: *lysimon* Hübner 1805 (invalid homonym)
DISTRIBUTION Canary Islands: local in coastal districts: La Palma; Tenerife; Gran Canaria: very few records for Gomera; Hierro; Lanzarote: a record for Fuerteventura requires confirmation. 0-100m. Morocco. W Algeria. 0-1500m. S Portugal. Spain: mainly coastal valleys in Provinces of Cádiz; Málaga; Granada; Almeria: also recorded in river valleys on northern slopes of Sierra Nevada and elsewhere in similar inland sites. Recorded from districts of Madrid, Santandar and Benidorm. Apparently extinct in Rio Guadalaviar (S. de Albarracin, Teruel). 25-800m.
VARIATION Male ups, width of black marginal borders variable: female ups gc brown, sometimes with blue scaling at wing-bases extending into discal area: both sexes, uns markings variable.
FLIGHT-PERIOD Polyvoltine. Canary Islands: throughout the year in overlapping broods: NW Africa and Spain, February/October.
HABITAT Damp places in hot, coastal gullies; damp, sunny clearings in densely wooded river valleys; desert oases.
LIFE-HISTORY LHPs: Gran Canaria, *Amaranthus* sp. (Amaranthaceae): NW Africa, *Medicago sativa*; *M. tribuloides*; *Acanthyllis* sp.; *Melilotus messanensis* (Fabaceae); *Polygonum equisetiforme* (Polygonaceae); *Armeria delicatula* (Plumbaginaceae); *Tribulus terrestris* (Zygophyllaceae): S Spain, *Medicago minima*; *M. lupulina*; *M. sativa* (Fabaceae). Elsewhere in range, use of Oxalidaceae, Malvaceae and Euphorbiaceae has been reported. Captive larvae (Canary Islands) readily accept leaves and flowers of *Lotus corniculatus*, *L. uliginosus*, *Trifolium pratense*, *T. repens*, *Coronilla varia* and flowers of *Ulex europaeus*, *Cytisus scoparius* and *C. sessilifolius*. Captive larvae (Malta) are said to reject *Oxalis* and *Medicago* spp. but accept *Polygonum aviculare*. For some LHPs, larval coloration depends upon particular plant parts ingested. Ants attending larvae: *Tapinoma melanocephalum*; *Pheidole* sp. Ova parasitized by Chalcididae. On Gran Canaria, larvae parasitized by *Cotesia cupreus* (Braconidae).

DESERT BABUL BLUE

AFRICAN BABUL BLUE

AFRICAN GRASS BLUE

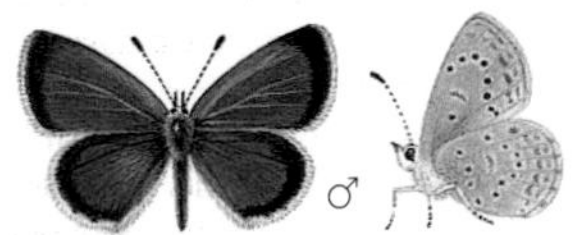

Desert Babul Blue

Z. knysna karsandra Moore 1865 TL: India.

DISTRIBUTION Widespread in E Algeria and Tunisia. 0-1500m. Malta. Sicily. Reports from Rhodes and Crete unconfirmed. Distributional relationship with nominate form in E Algeria unclear.

DESCRIPTION AND VARIATION Resembles nominate form closely: distinguished by small difference in male genitalia: both sexes, uns markings extremely variable: female ups blue suffusion variable.

FLIGHT-PERIOD Polyvoltine. Late February/October.

HABITAT As for nominate form.

LIFE-HISTORY LHPs: NW Africa, *Melilotus indica*; *Medicago sativa*.

African Babul Blue

African Grass Blue

Short-tailed Blue *Everes argiades*

RANGE N Spain, C, S and E Europe, Asia, Japan.
E. argiades Pallas 1771 TL: Samara, S Russia (April).
DISTRIBUTION N Spain (Cantabrian Mts.; S. de la Demanda; Pyrenees) through France, C Germany (very local in Bavaria), Switzerland (sporadic) N and western C Italy, NE Sicily to Gotland, Lithuania, Latvia, Balkans, European Turkey (Gelibolu) and N Greece (very local). A rare migrant in S England, more frequent in Belgium, Holland, N Germany, S Sweden (resident only on Gotland), Estonia and S Finland. 0-1000m.
DESCRIPTION Male ups violet-blue in first brood, less violet and darker in second brood; uph sometimes with small, black antemarginal spots in s1b-s4; unh orange spots in s1c and s2; hw 'tail' at v2 variable: female ups greyish-brown, often with blue discal and basal suffusion on fw and posterior submargin and disc of hw.
FLIGHT-PERIOD Bivoltine. Late April/mid June and July/August.
HABITAT Flowery bushy places, grassy banks, woodland clearings.
LIFE-HISTORY LHPs *Lotus corniculatus*; *L. uliginosus*; *Coronilla varia*; *Medicago sativa*; *M. lupulina*; *Trifolium pratense*; *Astragalus glycyphyllos*. Larvae cannibalistic.

Eastern Short-tailed Blue *Everes decoloratus*

RANGE SE Europe, (?)Turkey.
E. decoloratus Staudinger 1886 TL: Vienna, Hungary, Bulgaria.
syn: *sebrus* Hübner 1824 (name rejected by ICZN Op. 970)
DISTRIBUTION S Austria. Hungary. Slovenia. Romania. Republic of Macedonia. Albania. Bulgaria. N Greece: very local: known only from Phalakron massif and foothills of Rhodopi Mts. 250-1000m.
DESCRIPTION Male ups dusky-blue, scales are easily lost, giving somewhat dull appearance even in fairly fresh specimens; black outer marginal borders narrow, indenting along veins; upf with small black discoidal spot (cf. *E. alcetas* and *E. argiades*): female ups dark chocolate brown.
FLIGHT-PERIOD Trivoltine. May/June, July/August and September.
HABITAT Flowery, bushy places; sunny clearings in light deciduous woodland.
LIFE-HISTORY LHPs *Medicago lupulina*; *M. sativa*. Ova laid on flowers upon which larvae feed. Hibernates as a full-grown larva.

Provençal Short-tailed Blue *Everes alcetas*

RANGE Spain, S Europe, Balkans, Turkey, S Siberia, Urals, Altai.
E. alcetas Hoffmannsegg 1804 TL: Austria.
DISTRIBUTION Generally sporadic and local. Spain: Pyrenees. S France. Corsica. N and C Italy. S Austria. S Poland. (?)Slovakia. Hungary. Slovenia. Bosnia-Herzegovina. (?)Albania. Romania. Bulgaria. N Greece. 50-1200m.
DESCRIPTION AND VARIATION Male ups with very narrow black borders; hw 'tail' at v2 often vestigial; upf without black discoidal spot (cf. *E decoloratus*): female ups dark greyish-brown. In N Greece, unh orange mark in anal angle often reduced or absent.
FLIGHT-PERIOD Trivoltine. Late May/June, July/August and late September.
HABITAT Clearings in light deciduous woodland. In N Greece, all known habitats are associated with rivers, ditches or springs – favourable to the establishment of the LHP, *Galega officinalis*.
LIFE-HISTORY LHPs *Coronilla varia*; *Galega officinalis*. Ova laid on leaves. Larva feeds on leaves and flowers. Larvae attended by *Formica* (?)*cinerea* group.

Holly Blue *Celastrina argiolus*

RANGE N Africa, Europe, Turkey to C Asia (40-67°N), Japan, N America.
C. argiolus Linnaeus 1758 TL: England (Verity 1943).
DISTRIBUTION Widespread and common in NW Africa (0-2600m) and most of Europe (0-1900m). Sporadic in Ireland and N Scandinavia: generally absent from Scotland, where records appear to relate to dispersal from N England or accidental introduction: widespread on Mediterranean islands.
VARIATION Female seasonally dimorphic: second brood, upf black borders wider, blue basal flush, darker violet-blue; uph black costal margin wider.
FLIGHT-PERIOD Bivoltine. NW Africa, March/May and mid June/August (occasional fresh specimens September/October may represent a third brood or delayed emergence): Europe, early April/June and July/August.
HABITAT Diverse. Dry or damp bushy places, usually associated with woodland clearings/margins.
LIFE-HISTORY LHPs comprise a wide range of plant families:- *Rubus fruticosus; R. idaeus; R. discolore; Filipendula ulmaria; Discolores* sp.; *Pyracantha coccinea* (Rosaceae): *Ulex europaeus*; *Genisa tinctoria*; *Spartium junceum*; *Dorycnium pentaphyllum* (?)*germanicum*; *Astragalus glycyphyllos*; *Medicago sativa*; *Melilotus alba*; *M. officinalis*; *Galega officinalis*; *Colutea arborescens*; *Robinia pseudacacia* (Fabaceae): *Euonymus europaeus* (Celastraceae): (?)*Clematis vitalba* (Ranunculaceae); *Rhamnus cartharticus*; *Frangula alnus* [=*Rhamnus frangula*] (Rhamnaceae): *Humulus lupulus* (Cannabaceae): *Calluna vulgaris*; *Erica arborea*; *Arbutus unedo* (Ericaceae): *Escallonia macrantha* (Escalloniaceae): *Lingustrum vulgare*; *Syringa vulgaris* (Oleaceae): *Ilex aquifolium* (Aquifoliaceae): *Cornus sanguinea* (Cornaceae): *Hedera helix* (Araliaceae): *Lythrum salicaria* (Lytheraceae); (?)*Alnus glutinosa* (Betulaceae). Ova laid on calyx or stem of flower-buds or developing seeds: larvae feed on these components, less often on young, succulent leaves. In some woodland habitats, LHPs comprise *I. aquifolium* (Holly) and *H. helix* (Ivy) in first and second broods respectively. Larvae attended by *Lasius niger*; *L. alienus*; *L. fuliginosus*; *Camponotus japonicus*; *C. nearcticus*; *Formica subsericea*; *F. truncorum*; *Myrmica* sp. Hibernates as a pupa. Cyclical variation in inter-seasonal abundance has been attributed to larval parasitism.

SHORT-TAILED BLUE

♂ upf lacking discoidal spot

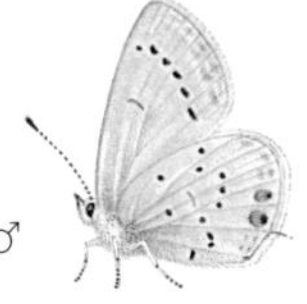
♂

Unh orange marginal spots distinctive

♀

EASTERN SHORT-TAILED BLUE

♂ upf dark discoidal spot characterisitc

♂

♀

PROVENÇAL SHORT-TAILED BLUE

Ups black marginal border very narrow, well defined: upf lacking discoidal spot

♂

♀

HOLLY BLUE

♀ with broad, black marginal borders

♂

♀

1st brood

♀

2nd brood

Short-tailed Blue

Eastern Short-tailed Blue

Provençal Short-tailed Blue

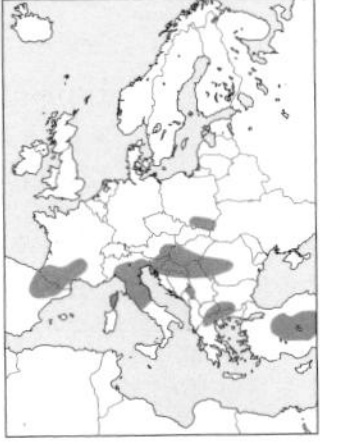

Holly Blue

Little Blue *Cupido minimus*

RANGE N and C Spain, through Europe, Asia and Mongolia to Amur.

C. minimus minimus Fuessly 1775 TL: Switzerland.
syn: *alsus* Denis and Schiffermüller 1775.

DISTRIBUTION Widespread and common. From Spain (Cantabrian Mts.; Montes Universales; Catalonia; Pyrenees) to Ireland, Britain, S and W Norway to 69°N, S and E Sweden, S Finland, Baltic states, Balkans and Greece, including Corfu and Kos. 50-2800m.

VARIATION Male ups pale blue scaling subject to variation, sometimes absent.

FLIGHT-PERIOD Univoltine (April/July) or bivoltine (April/June and late July/September) according to altitude and locality: in very hot conditions, desiccation of LHP may delay or even preclude a second brood.

HABITAT Diverse. Open grassy places; dry, rocky slopes and gullies; forest clearings. Restricted to calcareous soils.

LIFE-HISTORY LHP *Anthyllis vulneraria*. Ova laid on flowers, usually at base of calyx. Whitish larva feeds on developing seed through hole at base of calyx. Aligned with the similarly coloured calyx-tube, the larva is well-camouflaged when feeding, resting or during skin-changes (cf. *C. carswelli* and *C. lorquinii*). Hibernates as a full-grown larva. In captivity, pupation appears to be induced by contact with fresh, spring leaves of LHP. Larva may remain in diapause for 15 months. Larvae attended by *Lasius alienus*; *L. niger*; *Formica fusca*; *F. rufibarbis*; *Plagiolepis vindobonensis*; *Myrmica rubra*. Pupates in loose soil at base of LHP.

C. minimus trinacriae Verity 1919 TL: Palermo, Sicily.

DISTRIBUTION Sicily. 100-1500m.

DESCRIPTION Resembles nominate form: smaller; ups gc black; lacking blue scales. A similar form (*noguerae* Haig-Thomas) occurs in Montes Universales, E Spain.

FLIGHT-PERIOD Univoltine. April/May. Absence of second brood is possibly due to loss of aerial components of LHP through desiccation in summer months (cf. *C. m. minimus*).

HABITAT Dry limestone rocks.

LIFE-HISTORY LHP *Anthyllis vulneraria*.

Carswell's Little Blue *Cupido carswelli*

RANGE S Spain.

C. carswelli Stempffer 1927 TL: Sierra de Espuña, Spain.

DISTRIBUTION Restricted to mountains of S and SE Spain. S. de Tejeda; S. de Cazorla; S. de la Sagra; S. Segura; S. de Alcaraz; S. de Espuña. 1000-1800m. (*C. lorquinii* occurs in S. de Tejeda below 850m.).

DESCRIPTION Resembles *C. minimus*, except male ups have a small patch of purple scales at the base which may extend along some veins of the hw. Regarded by some authors as a form/ssp. of *C. minimus*.

FLIGHT-PERIOD Univoltine. Late April/early June. As in the case of *C. minimus*, desiccation of LHP in early/mid summer may inhibit larval development, precluding a second brood in late summer.

HABITAT Limestone rocks or dry grassland, often amongst open scrub.

LIFE-HISTORY LHP *Anthyllis vulneraria*. Oviposition and larval development parallels that of *C. minimus*: however, LHP is a colour variant in which upper part of calyx tube is sparsely mottled with the same dark reddish hue of the flowers. Similar mottling occurs on the posterior segments of the adult larva, apparently, for the purpose of mimicking the calyx tube, along which, like the larva of *C. minimus*, it aligns itself when feeding or resting. The yellow-flowered form of *A. vulneraria*, which has a pure white calyx, is apparently absent in the range of *C. carswelli*.

Osiris Blue *Cupido osiris*

RANGE Spain, S Europe, Turkey, C Asia.

C. osiris Meigen 1829 TL: not stated
syn: *sebrus* auct. Name rejected by ICZN OP. 970.

DISTRIBUTION N, S and E Spain. S France. W Switzerland. NW coastal and central peninsular Italy. (?)Slovakia. Austria. Hungary. Balkans. Greece, including Limnos. European Turkey. 500-1800m.

DESCRIPTION Male ups violet-blue with sharply defined very narrow black marginal borders: female ups dark brown; upf with occasional blue basal flush.

FLIGHT-PERIOD Univoltine (late May/July) or bivoltine (late April/late June and late July/early September) according to locality and altitude: second brood sometimes partial or may fail to appear in exceptionally dry conditions – LHP desiccation (cf. *C. minimus*).

HABITAT Open grassy, flowery places.

LIFE-HISTORY LHPs *Onobrychis* spp., including *O. viciifolia*; *O. montana*; *O. arenaria*. Ova laid on flowers upon which larvae feed. Hibernates as a larva. Larvae of first brood may enter and remain in diapause until following spring. Larvae attended by *Lasius alienus*.

Lorquin's Blue *Cupido lorquinii*

RANGE Morocco, Algeria, S Portugal, S Spain.

C. lorquinii Herrich-Schäffer 1851 TL: Spain.

DISTRIBUTION Morocco. Algeria. 1400-2700m. S Portugal: Serra de Monchique. S Spain: provinces of Cádiz and Málaga (Sierras of Tejeda, Almijara, Mijas, Blanca, Ronda, Bermeja, Crestellina and Grazalema); Granada (Sierra Nevada; S. de Alfacar); Jaen (S. de Jabalcuz). 100-2000m. (*C. carswelli* occurs above 1000m in S. de Tejeda).

DESCRIPTION Male ups violet-blue with broad black marginal borders: female ups dark greyish brown, occasionally with a few, blue, basal scales.

FLIGHT-PERIOD Univoltine. Generally mid April/mid June, sometimes emerging mid February in Anti-Atlas.

HABITAT Similar to that of *C. carswelli*.

LIFE-HISTORY LHP *Anthyllis vulneraria*. Ovipositing behaviour, larval development and adaptation to LHP, similar to that of *C. carswelli*. Larvae attended by *Plagiolepis pygmaea*; *Tapinoma nigerrimum*. Hibernates as a pupa.

LITTLE BLUE

♂ ups usually with basal dusting of silvery-blue scales, sometimes absent

CARSWELL'S LITTLE BLUE

♂ ups usually with basal dusting of purple scales, sometimes absent

Restricted to S & SE Spain

OSIRIS BLUE

LORQUIN'S BLUE

♂ ups dark marginal borders wide, indenting along veins

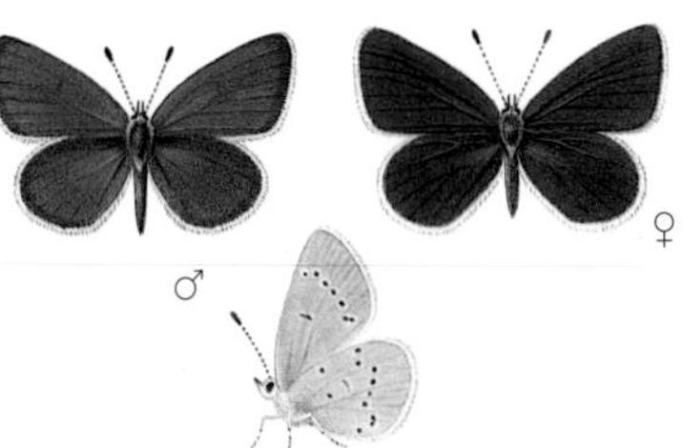

Little Blue

Carswell's Little Blue

Osiris Blue

Lorquin's Blue

Green-underside Blue *Glaucopsyche alexis*

RANGE Algeria, Tunisia, Europe, C Asia, Amur.
G. alexis Poda 1761 TL: Graz, Austria.
syn: *cyllarus* Rottembur 1775.

DISTRIBUTION Algeria: scarce and local: Saida; Aflou; Batna; Khenchela; Coverdo; Col de Ben-Chiacao; Lambessa. Tunisia: Hammamet. 500-1300m. Widespread and common in much of Europe, including S Fennoscandia, Corsica, Sicily and many Greek islands including Corfu. Absent from Atlantic Islands; Portugal; W Spain; Britain; N Belgium, Holland, N Germany; Denmark; Baltic states; Balearic Islands; Sardinia; Crete. 25-1500m.

DESCRIPTION AND VARIATION Male ups dark borders sometimes wide and suffuse; uns light grey, without marginal markings; unf pd spots may be greatly reduced: female ups blue basal suffusion variable. In some populations, in both sexes, unh greenish-blue flush may extend almost to margin e.g., Dijon, S France. In Scandinavia, unh black pd spots greatly reduced. In N Africa, *melanoposmater* Verity, male uns pd spots and blue basal flush reduced; female ups usually with blue basal suffusion: similar forms occur in Europe.

FLIGHT-PERIOD Univoltine. April/early July. Whilst the typical form occurs in N Greece in April, males with wide, ups dark borders have been reported in the same localities in early July: a similar form, emerging early June, occurs in Taygetos Mts. (1400-1600m) .

HABITAT Diverse. Flowery banks, open scrub, damp meadows, woodland clearings.

LIFE-HISTORY LHPs: several genera of Fabaceae including, *Astragalus onobrychis*; *A. glycyphyllos*; *Galega officinalis*; *Vicia* spp.; *Coronilla varia*; *Calicotome villosa*; *Spartium junceum*; *Medicago* spp.; *Melilotus alba*; *Onobrychis* spp.; *Cytisus* spp.; *Colutea arborescens*. Ova laid on flowers upon which larvae feed. Larvae are usually greenish or dusky-pink, with brownish variegations, but sometimes pure, bright yellow if reared on the similarly coloured flowers of *Spartium junceum*: all larvae tend towards a whitish colour prior to pupation. Larvae attended by *Lasius alienus*; *Formica pratensis*; *F. selysi*; *F. fusca*; *F. cinerea*; *F. nemoralis*; *F. subrufa*; *Camponotus aethiops*; *C. maxiliensis*; *Myrmica scabrinodis*; *Crematogaster auberti*; *Tapinoma erraticum*. Hibernates as a pupa. In captivity, pupa may remain in diapause for two winters.

Black-eyed Blue *Glaucopsyche melanops*

RANGE N Africa and SW Europe.
G. melanops melanops Boisduval 1828 TL: Aix-en-Provence.

DISTRIBUTION France: Haute Garonne and Pyrénées-Orientales to Ardèche and Basses Alpes. Italy: W Ligurian Alps. 100-800m

DESCRIPTION Uns pale greyish-brown with faint marginal markings (cf. G. alexis): female ups blue suffusion variable, may be absent or extend to outer margin.

FLIGHT-PERIOD Univoltine. Mid April/May.

HABITAT Scrub or open woodland, often containing *Erica arborea* and *Spartium junceum*.

LIFE-HISTORY LHPs: *Dorycnium decumbens*; *D. suffruticosum*; *Genista* sp.; *Lotus hispidus*; *Anthyllis cytisoides*. Ova laid on flowers upon which larvae feed. Larvae attended by *Camponotus foreli*; *C. cruentatus*; *C. micans*; *C. sylvaticus*. Hibernates as a pupa. In captivity, pupa may remain in diapause for two seasonal cycles.
G. melanops algirica Heyne 1895 TL: Nemours.

DISTRIBUTION Morocco. Algeria: Algiers; Lambessa. Tunisia. 600-2600m. N Portugal. Spain. 600-1100m.

DESCRIPTION AND VARIATION Male ups marginal borders 2-3mm wide; uns marginal markings bolder; unh with faint grey marginal and antemarginal spots: female ups basal blue suffusion reduced or absent. Transitional to nominate form in Catalonia. In High Atlas (up to 2600m), *alluaudi* Oberthür: male ups tinged violet; dark, marginal borders usually wider; female ups blue suffusion reduced, often vestigial or absent.

FLIGHT-PERIOD Univoltine. February/June. Report of a second brood in Tunisia (September/October) requires confirmation.

HABITAT Dry scrub containing a tall Broom (?*Cytisus*).

LIFE-HISTORY LHPs: *Ononis atlantica*; *Adenocarpus anagyrifolius*; *Hedysarum flexuosum*.

Odd-spot Blue *Turanana endymion*

RANGE Greece, Turkey, Turkestan.
T. endymion taygetica Rebel 1902 TL: Mt. Taygetos, Greece.
syn: *panagaea* Herrich-Schäffer 1851 (invalid homonym)

DISTRIBUTION S Greece: Mt. Chelmos; Mt. Taygetos. 1500-2300m.

DESCRIPTION AND VARIATION Male ups dull blue; black marginal borders 2mm wide; upf cell-end marked by fine black, often crescent-shaped mark; uns gc greyish; unf black pd spots large – that in s3 conspicuously displaced distad; unh with dull yellow-buff submarginal spot in s2 (usually vague, sometimes absent in majority of specimens – (?)seasonally variable): female ups brown; uns gc greyish-brown. Mt. Chelmos: male uns gc distinctly browner; unh submarginal spot in s2 orange, usually conspicuous, but sometimes absent even in female. Male genitalia of Mt. Chelmos and Mt. Taygetos populations structurally identical, but different from that of nominate form (TL: Amasya, Turkey).

FLIGHT-PERIOD Univoltine. Late May/mid July in prolonged emergence.

HABITAT Exposed, dry limestone rocks, supporting low-growing, mostly cushion-forming shrubs. Colonies are generally very small, sometimes limited to a few hundred square metres. All known habitats shared with *Lycaena thetis*.

LIFE-HISTORY LHP *Acantholimon androsaceum* (Plumbaginaceae). Ova laid on calyx of flowers, within which the newly-hatched larva feeds. Hibernates as a pupa. Apparently highly adapted to LHP, which it shares with *Lycaena thetis* in the same habitats; however, competition between the two species appears to be negligible. Association with ants does appear to have been observed in Europe.

BEHAVIOUR Males sometimes stray considerably from LHP

GREEN-UNDERSIDE BLUE

BLACK-EYED BLUE

ODD-SPOT BLUE

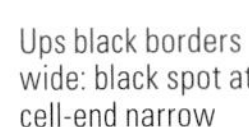

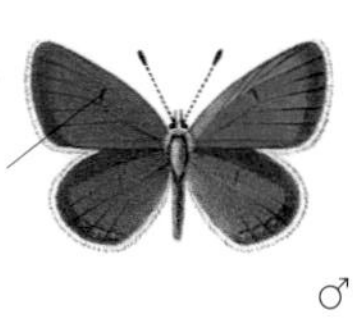

♀ brown with blue flush

♀

T. e. taygetica

Green-underside Blue

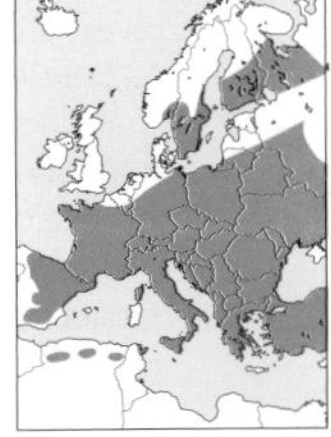

Black-eyed Blue

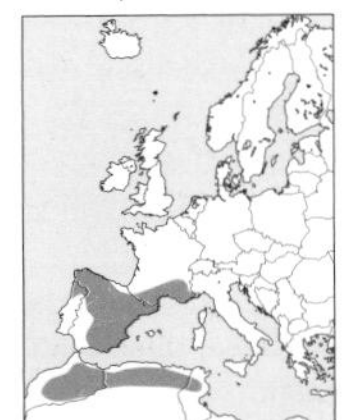

Odd-spot Blue

in search of water and have been noted on damp patches at 1150m. In warm windless conditions, adults sometimes assemble in large numbers on bushes of *Crataegus pycnoloba* to bask in late afternoon sun. Attracted to the flowers of *Thymus*.

CONSERVATION On Mt. Chelmos, human activity poses a serious threat to this species as well as *Lycaena thetis*.

Alcon Blue *Maculinea alcon*

RANGE N Spain, C and E Europe, Denmark, S Sweden, Turkey, Caucasus, Siberia, C and S Urals, Kazakhstan, Mongolia, Altai.
M. alcon Denis and Schiffermüller 1775 TL: Vienna.
DISTRIBUTION Very local, sporadic in most regions. N Spain: Province of Santander (Herrera 50m). France. NE Belgium. Germany. SW Sweden and W Denmark. N Italy. Switzerland, Austria through (?)Slovakia and Hungary to Poland and Lithuania. Distribution uncertain in some regions owing to possible confusion with *M. rebeli* (below). 0-1000m. **DESCRIPTION** Male ups gc dull dusty-blue. **FLIGHT-PERIOD** Univoltine. Mid June/mid August according to locality and season: peak emergence normally late July. **HABITAT** Marsh meadows, usually associated with flood-plains of rivers or lakes. **LIFE-HISTORY** LHPs *Gentiana pneumonanthe*; *G. asclepiadea*; (?)*G. cruciata*. Ova laid singly but often in large numbers, mainly on flower-buds. Small larvae feed and live within the calyces of flowers until late summer, thereafter in symbiotic relationship with *Myrmica ruginodis*, *M. rubra*, or *M. scabrinodis* ants. Further larval development, hibernation and pupation occurs within nest of adoptive ant species. **CONSERVATION** As for all wetland species, land-drainage at sites well-removed from habitats may be no less consequential than direct interference, which, if coincident with periods of prolonged drought, poses a serious threat to ecologically sensitive species – adverse climatic events are probable rather than possible, and most marshland insects are already disadvantaged by the small size of most of their habitats. **NOTE** That the reputedly distinctive features of ecology and altitudinal range of *M. alcon* and *M. rebeli* (below) are not infrequently at variance with wing morphology, has given rise to uncertainties in identification and distribution. Intermediate forms of the two taxa, reported as *M. rebeli*, occur at low altitude in the environs of Paris. In S Scandinavia, (?)*M. alcon* occurs at low altitudes and utilizes *Gentiana pneumonanthe* as a LHP, but wing-characters are reported to correspond to those of *M. rebeli*. The only two, known colonies of *M. alcon* in Belgium occur approximately at sea-level in damp/wet habitats and both utilize *G. pneumonanthe*: reports of *M. rebeli* in Belgium appear to be unsubstantiated. The ground-water level of some habitats of *M. rebeli* in N Italy and N Greece is more typical of those of *M. alcon*. A taxon resembling *M. alcon* but utilizing *Gentiana cruciata* as a LHP in habitat approximating to that of *M. rebeli* has been reported from Croatia. In Bakony Mts. (W Hungary), altitudinal separation of *M. alcon* and *M. rebeli* may be as little as 200m. Possibly, *M. alcon* and *M. rebeli* are conspecific, with adaptive wing-morphology corresponding to marked ecological diversity. Within the genus, *M. arion* displays a wide range of altitudinal variation in wing morphology: additional, lesser variation, apparently of ecological origin but unrelated to altitude, is also apparent.

Mountain Alcon Blue *Maculinea rebeli*

RANGE N Spain, SC, E and SE Europe.
M. rebeli Hirschke 1904 TL: Austria.
DISTRIBUTION Very sporadic and very local. N Spain: Picos de Europa; S. de la Demanda; provinces of Soria; Santander; Huesca (Ordessa); Gerona; (?)Teurel. France: E Pyrenees; Massif Central; Basses and Hautes Alps. Italy: C Apennines; Dolomites; Apuane Alps; C Apennines. Switzerland. S Germany, Czech Republic, Slovakia and S Poland to S Balkans and N Greece (Pindos Mts.; Mt. Phalakron; Rhodope Mts.; Mt. Cholomon). 600-2250m. **DESCRIPTION AND VARIATION** Resembles *M. alcon* closely: male ups gc brighter blue, lacking violet overtones. In Bakony Mts. (W Hungary), *xerophila* Berger: resembles nominate form: both sexes larger; female ups gc very dark grey. **FLIGHT-PERIOD** Univoltine. Mid June/July. **HABITAT** Typically, damp or wet meadows, also in drier situations. In N Greece, occurs in boggy woodland clearings in Rhodope Mts. (1500m), but in dry, grassy, gullies above tree-line on Mt. Phalakron (1450-1850m). **LIFE-HISTORY** LHP principally *Gentiana cruciata*: also, *G. germanica*; *G. asclepiadea*. Oviposition and life-cycle similar to *M. alcon*: adoptive ant species *Myrmica scabrinodis*, *M. sabuleti*, *M. schenki* or *M. sulcinodis*. **CONSERVATION** Many colonies are vulnerable in consequence of small habitat-size: damage to LHPs from grazing, trampling and, in populated areas, flower-picking, poses a significant threat.

Scarce Large Blue *Maculinea telejus*

RANGE Pyrenees, C Europe, Caucasus, C and S Urals, Siberia, Kazakhstan, Mongolia, N China, Korea, Japan.
M. telejus Bergsträsser 1779 TL: Hanau, W Germany.
syn: *euphemus* Hübner 1800.
DISTRIBUTION Very scarce and local. France: Gers; Gironde; Dordogne; Charante; Isère; Savoie; Haut-Rhin. N Switzerland: very local. N Italy: Piedmont; Trieste. C and S Germany. Austria. Hungary. Slovakia. S Poland. SW Latvia: a single known colony. Extinct in Belgium. Reports from Spain (Valle d'Aran) require confirmation. 700-1600m. Often occurs with *M. nausithous*. **FLIGHT-PERIOD** Univoltine. Mid June/mid August. **HABITAT** Marsh meadows, containing an abundance of LHP. **LIFE-HISTORY** LHP *Sanguisorba officinalis*. Ova laid on flowers. Life-cycle similar to that for *M. alcon*: Larvae/pupae attended by *Myrmica sabuleti*, *M. rubra*, *M. scabrinodis* or *M. vandeli*.

Dusky Large Blue *Maculinea nausithous*

RANGE N Spain, E France, C Europe to 52°N, Turkey, Caucasus, C and S Urals, Altai.
M. nausithous Bergsträsser 1779 TL: Hanau, W Germany.
syn: *arcas* Rottemburg 1775 (invalid homonym).
DISTRIBUTION Very scarce and local. N Spain: Picos de Europa; Soria; S. de la Demanda. E France: Savoie; Isère; Ain; Côte-d'Or; Haut-Rhin; Vosges. N Switzerland. C and S Germany. Austria (absent from Tirol). Czech Republic. Slovakia. Hungary. 700-1600m. Often occurs with *M. telejus*. **FLIGHT-PERIOD** Univoltine. Mid June/mid August according to locality.

ALCON BLUE

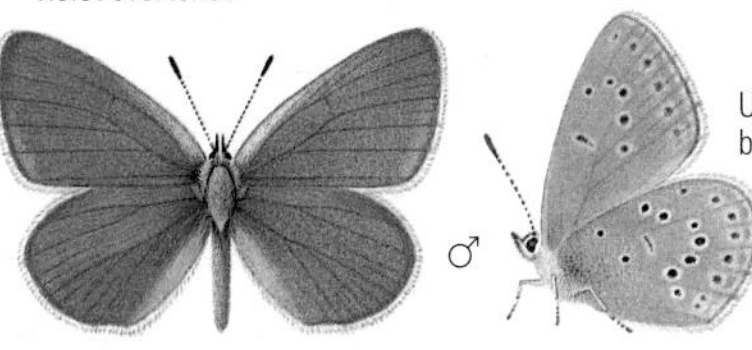

MOUNTAIN ALCON BLUE

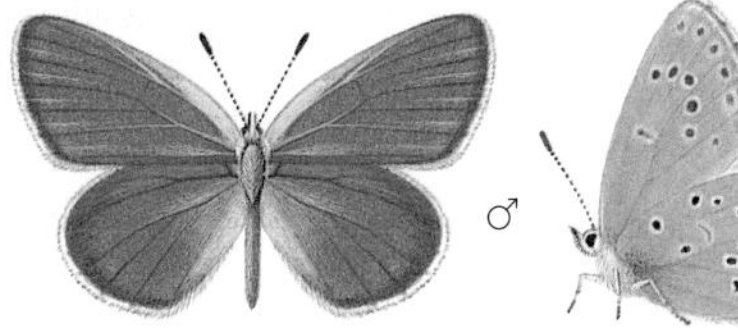

SCARCE LARGE BLUE

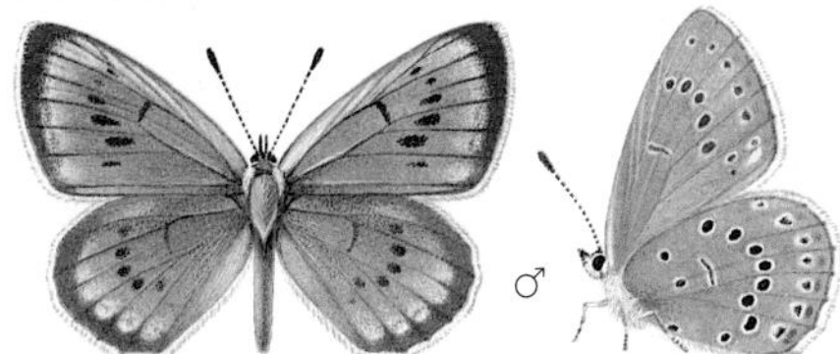

DUSKY LARGE BLUE

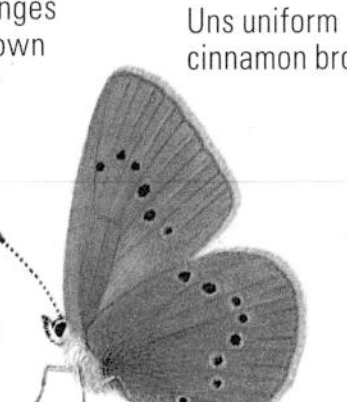

Alcon Blue

Mountain Alcon Blue

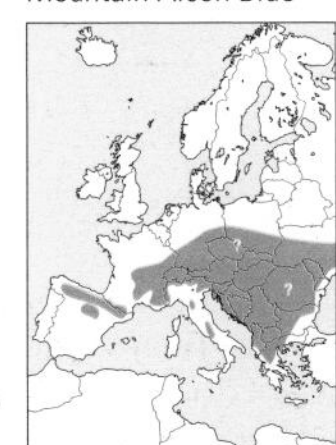

Scarce Large Blue

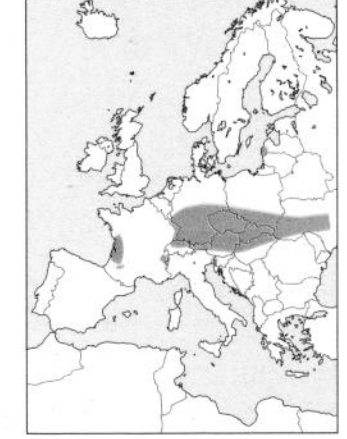

Dusky Large Blue

HABITAT Marsh meadows, containing an abundance of LHP – habitat as for *M. telejus*, but with some preference for drier margins. **LIFE-HISTORY** LHP *Sanguisorba officinalis*. Ova laid on flowers. Life-cycle similar to that for *M. alcon*: Larvae/pupae attended by *Myrmica rubra* or *M. scabrinodis*.

Large Blue *Maculinea arion*

RANGE Europe, Turkey, Russia, W Siberia, S Urals, N Kazakhstan, Mongolia, China, Japan.

M. arion Linnaeus 1758 TL: Nuremberg, Germany (Fruhstorfer).

DISTRIBUTION N and C Spain, Italy, N and C Greece and European Turkey to S Sweden, Lithuania, Latvia (rare and local), (?)Estonia and S Finland. Absent from Portugal, N Belgium, N Holland, N Germany and Mediterranean islands except Corsica. 50-2000m. Indigenous British population extinct.

VARIATION Coastal regions of SE France, NW Italy and Corsica, f. *ligurica* Wagner ups black markings well developed – similar and transitional forms occur in most lowland populations. Above 1500m in C Alps, Balkans and Greece, *obscura* Christ: ups pd areas greyish; black pd markings largely obscured; basal flush dull blue with violet overtone: a closely related, but well-characterised form occurs at 1000-1400m in SE Switzerland and Greece: ups brighter blue flush extending to submargin; black marginal borders and pd markings clearly defined: transitional forms are common in Greece. Progressive ups darkening with increasing altitude would appear to be a clinal adaptation, possibly relating to a compensatory need to absorb solar energy more rapidly in prevailing cooler conditions.

FLIGHT-PERIOD Univoltine. Late May/July according to altitude and locality.

HABITAT Dry, grassy, bushy places; woodland clearings.

LIFE-HISTORY LHPs *Thymus* spp., including *T. serpyllum* and *T. praecox*. Ova laid on flowers. Life-cycle similar to that for *M. alcon*: larvae/pupae attended by *Myrmica sabuleti* or *M. scabrinodis*.

Iolas Blue *Iolana iolas*

RANGE Morocco, Algeria, C Spain, SC and SE Europe, Turkey, Iran.

I. iolas Ochsenheimer 1816 TL: Hungary.

DISTRIBUTION Widespread, usually very local. Morocco: very local: High Atlas (Tizi-n-Test): possibly now extinct in Col de Jerada, E Morocco. Algeria: Medea; Berrouaghia; Blida; Aflou; El Bayadh; Djelfa; Batna. 800-1600m. S and E Spain: Sierra Nevada; Montes Universales; Catalonia. S France: E Pyrenees to Provence and Savoie. Switzerland: restricted to Rhône Valley. N and C Italy. Austria and Hungary to Balkans and Greece. 100-1700m.

VARIATION In NW Africa, uns marginal markings indistinct in both sexes; male ups more violet-blue; female ups bluish suffusion extensive (*debilitata* Schultz): similar forms occur in Spain. Taxon *debilitata* accorded specific rank by some authors, with or without further differentiation in recognition of local forms: Montes Universales, *thomasi* Hemming; Catalonia, *farriolsi* de Sagarra.

FLIGHT-PERIOD Univoltine, May/early July: single or very small numbers of fresh specimens have been recorded in August/September, indicating a partial second brood or possibly delayed emergence due to exceptional weather conditions: state of development of LHP is an important consideration in respect to either possibility – an absence of seed-capsules would necessitate a profound departure from normal, larval feeding regime (see below).

HABITAT Dry, bushy places, usually on calcareous soils.

LIFE-HISTORY LHPs principally *Colutea arborescens*: NE Greece, *C. cilicica*. Ova laid on seed-capsules or inside calyx. Larvae feed exclusively on seeds, sometimes in company with larvae of other lycaenids (*L. boeticus*; *P. argus*; *C. argiolus*; *G. alexis*; *L. pirithous*). Larvae strongly myrmecophilous: attended by *Tapinoma erraticum*. Pupates under stones. Hibernates as a pupa. In captivity, diapause may extend over two seasonal cycles.

BEHAVIOUR Single males have been recorded several kilometres from areas containing known LHP.

Vogel's Blue *Maurus vogelii*

RANGE Morocco.

M. vogelii vogelii Oberthür 1920 TL: Tizi-n-Taghzeft, Morocco.

DISTRIBUTION Very local. Morocco: Taghzeft Pass; district of Timhadit and Itzer. 1900-2200m.

FLIGHT-PERIOD Univoltine. Mid August/mid September.

HABITAT Dry, stony places with very sparse vegetation.

LIFE-HISTORY LHP *Erodium petraeum crispum* [=*Erodium cheilanthifolium*].

M. vogelii insperatus Tennent 1994 TL: Tizi-n-Test, High Atlas, Morocco.

DISTRIBUTION Morocco: High Atlas (Tizi-n-Test). 2400-2880m.

DESCRIPTION Resembles nominate form closely. Male uns gc browner, tinged yellow; submarginal orange markings paler, with proximal whitish markings vestigial or absent; white rings enclosing discal and pd spots slightly reduced.

FLIGHT-PERIOD Probably univoltine: data very limited: late May/June.

HABITAT Steep, stony slopes.

LIFE-HISTORY LHP *Erodium petraeum crispum* [=*Erodium cheilanthifolium*]. Larvae feed at night, resting at base of LHP during the day. Larvae attended by ants.

Large Blue

Iolas Blue

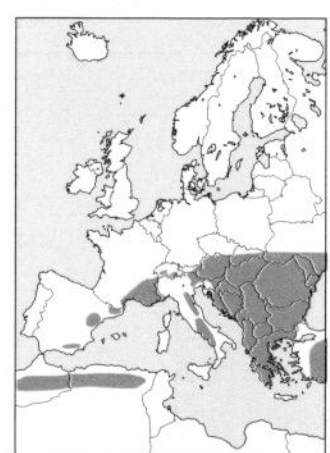

LARGE BLUE

M. a. arion

M. a.* f. *obscura

Extent and colour of ups bluish flush dependent upon altitude

IOLAS BLUE

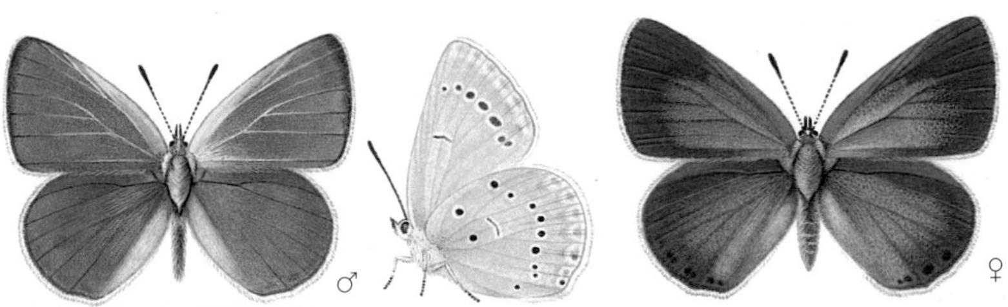

VOGEL'S BLUE

Ups discoidal spot prominent. Fringes strongly chequered

Restricted to Morocco

Vogel's Blue

Chequered Blue *Scolitantides orion*

RANGE Spain, S France, N Italy, E and SE Europe, S Fennoscandia, Turkey, C Asia, Japan.

S. orion orion Pallas 1771 TL: E Russia.

DISTRIBUTION Very local in coastal areas. S Norway, S Sweden and S Finland. Absent from Baltic states. 0-300m.

DESCRIPTION Male ups extensive bright silvery- or violet-blue, somewhat disrupted by black veins; upf black marginal spots with proximal whitish/silvery-greyish band, somewhat broken and striated; uph black marginal spots faintly ringed pale blue or white: female ups gc very dark greyish-brown, blue flush vestigial, variable but rarely absent.

FLIGHT-PERIOD Univoltine. Mid May/June.

HABITAT Rocky slopes/rock ledges largely devoid of vegetation except LHP.

LIFE-HISTORY LHP *Sedum album*. Hibernates as a pupa.

S. orion lariana Frühstorfer 1910 TL: Lake Como.

DISTRIBUTION Very local and sporadic. Spain: S. de Espuna; Montes Universales; Alicante to Catalonia; Huesca. S France: Gironde; Lot-et-Garonne; Massif Central; E Pyrenees to Basses Alps; Corsica. N Italy and S Switzerland to S Poland, Hungary, Balkans and N Greece: Mt. Orvilos; Phalakron massif; Rhodopi massif; Askion Mts.; Mt. Olympus. European Turkey. 200-1100m.

DESCRIPTION Male ups darker blue markings less extensive, rarely extending beyond discoidal spot: female ups very dark greyish-brown, almost black, usually without blue basal flush.

VARIATION Subject to marked local and regional variation. In Republic of Macedonia (Treska Valley) and NW Greece (Askion Mts.): resembles nominate form closely.

FLIGHT-PERIOD Generally univoltine (late May/June), bivoltine in some areas of Switzerland (April/May and July /August).

HABITAT Dry, often very hot, stony slopes/soil-banks/gullies, often amongst scrub; sometimes grassy, rocky clearings in light deciduous woodland: usually on calcareous substrates.

LIFE-HISTORY LHPs *Sedum album*; *S. telephium*; *S. hispanicum*; *S. maximum*. Ova laid at base of leaves, upon which larvae feed. Captive larvae accept many *Sedum* species. Larvae attended by *Camponotes vagus*; *C. aethiops*; *Tapinoma erraticum*. Hibernates as a pupa under stones or sometimes in small hollows in loose sandy soil near base of LHP.

Bavius Blue *Pseudophilotes bavius*

RANGE Morocco, Algeria, SE Europe, Turkey, Caucasus, Crimea, S Urals.

P. bavius bavius Eversmann 1832 TL: S Urals.

DISTRIBUTION Widely separated colonies. Romania: districts of Cluj and Bistrita Nasaud (Transylvania). Republic of Macedonia: Skopje (Treska Valley); Gradsko. NW Greece: Askion Mts. 700-1200m. S Greece: Mt. Chelmos and environs (Kalavrita, Zachlorou), southwards to Sparta. Turkey in Europe. 600-1200m.

VARIATION In Romania, *hungaricus* Doiszeghy 1913 [TL: Vita, Bistrita Nasaud]: male ups silvery-blue. In Republic of Macedonia, *macedonicus* Schultze: male ups dull, somewhat greyish-blue; uph usual submarginal spots absent except for small, pale orange mark in anal angle. In Peloponnesos *casimiri* Hemming: male ups bright blue; uph orange submarginal spots well developed. In Askion Mts., resembles *casimiri* but variable – in same colony, some individuals closely correspond to *macedonicus*.

FLIGHT-PERIOD Univoltine. Mid May/June.

HABITAT Dry, sheltered rocky slopes, gullies or small clearings amongst scrub on calcareous soils.

LIFE-HISTORY LHPs Salvia spp.: Romania, *S. nutans*; NW Greece, *S. officinalis*; S Greece, *S. verbenaca*. In S Greece, ova laid on tips of developing flower-stems, upperside of young basal leaves and at base of stem-leaves. Larvae feed on flowers, less often on leaves and stems. Most larvae are green but a pinkish form appears to correspond to those feeding exclusively on flowers. Captive larvae readily accept *Salvia argentea*, *S. aethiopis*, *S. sclarea*, *S. nemorosa* and *S. verticillata*. In Romania, larvae are susceptible to heavy parasitization (>95%) by *Apanteles lycaenae* (Diptera). Hibernates as a pupa: in nature, a single example has been recorded under basal leaf of *S. sclarea*. Larvae of *hungaricus* attended by ants (sp. not determined).

CONSERVATION In S Greece, most known habitats appear to be threatened by grazing – sheep and goats are very partial to the flower-stems of *S. verbenaca*.

P. bavius fatma Oberthür 1890 TL: Lambessa, Algeria.

DISTRIBUTION Very local. Morocco: Middle Atlas (Anosseur; Ifrane; Azrou; Immouzer). Algeria: Aures Mts. (Lambessa; Col de Telmet). 1500-1800m.

DESCRIPTION Male uph prominent submarginal orange spots extends to s7. Female ups blue flush generally more extensive.

FLIGHT-PERIOD Univoltine. Late April/early June.

HABITAT Dry scrub; flowery meadows; clearings in light woodland.

LIFE-HISTORY LHP *Salvia argentea*.

BEHAVIOUR Adults often rest on basal leaves of LHP.

Sardinian Blue *Pseudophilotes barbagiae*

RANGE Sardinia.

P. barbagiae de Prins and van der Poorten 1982 TL: Sardinia.

DISTRIBUTION Sardinia: Monti del Gennargentu (Fonni; Lanusei; Desulo). 800-1500m. Reports from Monte Limbara require confirmation.

DESCRIPTION Male ups darkish, somewhat greyish-brown; intensity of blue basal flush diminishing progressively towards pd area; black discoidal spot small or vestigial; uns gc darker than for *P. baton*; unh submarginal orange markings poorly developed, usually vestigial: female similar; ups uniform dark brown. Separable from closely allied taxa by distinctive characters in male genitalia.

FLIGHT-PERIOD Univoltine. May/June.

HABITAT Dry rocky, scrub clearings and slopes.

LIFE-HISTORY LHP *Thymus* (?)*herba-barona*.

CHEQUERED BLUE

Fringes heavily chequered

S. o. lariana

colour variants

Uns markings
well developed.

BAVIUS BLUE

Uph orange submarginal
lunules distinctive

P. b. casimiri

P. b. macedonicus

P. b. fatma
(Morocco and Algeria)

Unh orange submarginal
band prominent

SARDINIAN BLUE

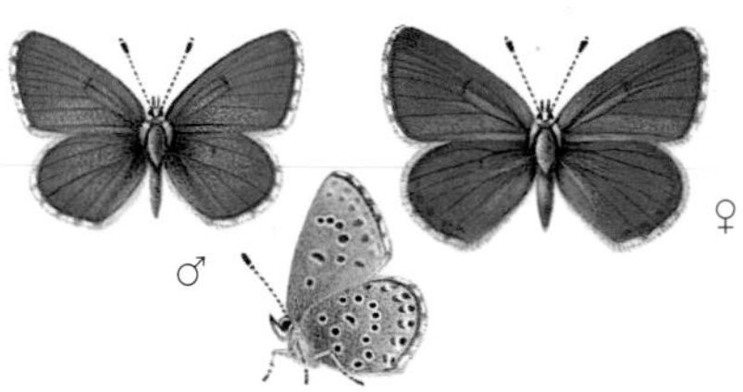

Restricted to
Sardinia

Chequered Blue

Bavius Blue

Sardinian Blue

Baton Blue *Pseudophilotes baton*

RANGE N Portugal, N Spain, France, S and C Europe.
P. baton Bergsträsser 1779 TL: Hanau, Germany.
DISTRIBUTION N Portugal. N Spain. France to 49°N. Corsica. Switzerland. Italy. Sicily. S Germany. W Czech Republic. Poland. W Austria. 200-2000m.
FLIGHT-PERIOD Generally bivoltine, April/June and late July/early September: univoltine in some localities at higher altitudes, June/July.
HABITAT Dry grassy and flowery places; sheltered slopes; rocky gullies.
LIFE-HISTORY LHPs *Thymus serpyllum*; *T. vulgaris*; *T. nitens*; *T. praecox* (?)*polytrichus*; *Satureja montana*; *S. hortensis*; *Lavendula staechas*; *L. angustifolia*; *L. latifolia*; *Mentha suaveolens*; *M. longifolia*; *M. rotunda*; *Calamintha nepeta*. Ova laid on flowers, sometimes on leaf stems. Larvae feed on flowers and developing seeds. Like other European members of this genus, captively reared larvae appear to require direct sunlight and high temperatures for healthy development. Larvae attended by *Lasius alienus*; *Myrmica scabrinodis*. Hibernates as a pupa.

Eastern Baton Blue *Pseudophilotes vicrama*

RANGE E Europe, Balkans, Greece, Turkey, C Asia, Tian Shan, China.
P. vicrama schiffermuelleri Hemming 1929 TL: Dom Altenberg, Austria.
DISTRIBUTION S Finland. Baltic states. Poland. SE Germany. Czech Republic. Slovakia. Austria. NE Italy: Trentino-Alto Adige (western limit). Hungary. Balkans and Greece, including Corfu, Kithira, Crete, Skyros, Andros, Paros, Sifnos, Limnos, Lesbos, Chios, Ikaria, Samos, Karpathos, Rhodes and Kos. European Turkey. 0-1900m.
VARIATION Resembles *P. baton*. Appreciably larger, especially female: unh orange submarginal spots well developed in s1b-5. Readily separable from *P. baton* by distinctive character of valve in male genitalia (individually and regionally variable).
FLIGHT-PERIOD Bivoltine. April/early June and July/August according to altitude and location.
HABITAT Dry scrubland; grassy banks; rocky gullies; woodland clearings.
LIFE-HISTORY LHPs *Thymus longicaulis chaubardii*; *T. glabresens*; *T.* (?)*comptus*; *T. ocheus*; *T. striatus* or *atticus*; *Saturja montana*; *S. thymbra*. Oviposition, early development and hibernation as for *P. baton*. Larvae strongly myrmecophilous: attending ant species not determined: captive larvae appear reluctant to pupate, possibly due to absence of ants.

Panoptes Blue *Pseudophilotes panoptes*

RANGE Portugal, Spain.
P. panoptes Hübner 1813 TL: Spain.
syn: *P. baton panoptes* auct.
DISTRIBUTION Portugal and Spain south of Cantabrian Mts. and Pyrenees: widespread and common. 600-1900m.
DESCRIPTION Resembles *P. baton*. Male unh pale orange or yellow submarginal spots vestigal or absent.
FLIGHT-PERIOD Bivoltine. Late March/June and July/August.
HABITAT As for *P. baton*.
LIFE-HISTORY LHP *Thymus mastichina*; *T. villosus*; *Saturja montana*.
NOTE Justification for separation from *P. baton* at species level unclear.

False Baton Blue *Pseudophilotes abencerragus*

RANGE Morocco, Algeria, Tunisia, Portugal, Spain, Egypt, Israel, Jordan, W Arabia.
P. abencerragus Pierret 1837 TL: Province of Oran, Algeria.
DISTRIBUTION Widespread but local. Morocco. Algeria. Tunisia. 100-2500m. S Portugal: S. da Estrêla, Alemtejo, Algarve. C and S Spain: Provinces of Madrid (Arganda; Camporeal; Loeches; Aranjuez); Extremadura (Alcácer do Sal); Cuenca (S. de Cuenca); Jaen (S. de Jabalcuz; S. de la Pandera); Málaga (Antequera; Rhonda; Foljambe). 100-1500m.
VARIATION In N Africa, uns paler than Iberian populations, sometimes yellowish-grey.
FLIGHT-PERIOD Univoltine in Iberian peninsula, April/May (early April at 100m in Algarve). Bivoltine in High Atlas, late March/early June and August/September (occasionally, fresh specimens have been recorded in July).
HABITAT Dry flowery places usually associated with light scub.
LIFE-HISTORY LHPs: NW Africa, *Thymus hirtus*; *T. fontanesii*; *Salvia taraxicifolia*; *Medicago* (?)*turbinata*: Spain, *Cleonia lusitanica*. Ova laid on underside of leaves of *C. lusitanica* but larvae live entirely within flower-heads, refusing to eat leaves in captivity. Larval colouring differs appreciably from that of *P. baton*, *P. panoptes* and *P. vicrama*.

Baton Blue

Eastern Baton Blue

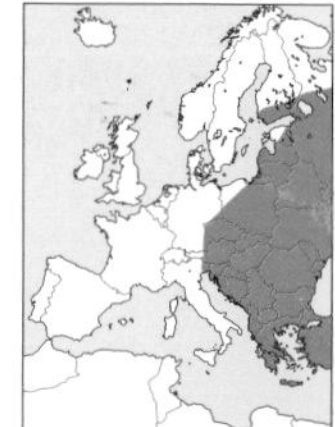

Panoptes Blue

False Baton Blue

BATON BLUE

♂
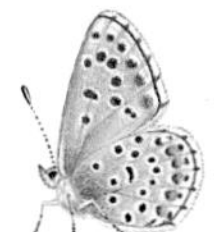

♀

EASTERN BATON BLUE

Ups variable

♂

♀

PANOPTES BLUE

♂

♀

Unh pale orange submarginal spots poorly developed

FALSE BATON BLUE

♂ ups deep lustrous blue

♂

♀

Unh submarginal orange band absent or vestigial

Grass Jewel *Chilades trochylus*

RANGE Greece, Turkey, Egypt, Middle East, Iran, Afghanistan, C Africa.

C. trochylus Freyer 1844 TL: Turkey.

DISTRIBUTION Very local and sporadic. Greece: Lake Vegoritis; Olympus massif; Mt. Hymettus; Pastra Mts; Mt. Parnassos; Delphi; N Peloponnesos (Xilocastro); Evia; Samos; Chios; Rhodes; Crete. 25-900m.

VARIATION Ups discoidal spots sometimes faintly ringed white.

FLIGHT-PERIOD Polyvoltine. Late March/late October.

HABITAT Hot, dry, stony places; sometimes on disturbed soils in areas of cultivation. Some habitats are extremely small – 200m^2.

LIFE-HISTORY LHP on Mt. Parnassos massif, *Andrachne telephioides* (Euphorbiaceae): natural use of *Heliotropium hirsutissimum* (Boraginaceae) in Europe not confirmed, although both plant species are exploited in Israel and Sinai peninsula. Captive larvae feed readily on flowers and leaves of *Heliotropium hirsutissimum*. Hibernates as a pupa. On Mt. Parnassos, larvae attended by *Acantholepis* near *caucasica*: outside of Europe, *Pheidole quadrispinosa*; *Prenolepis* sp.; *Iridomyrmex* sp.

Martin's Blue *Plebejus martini*

RANGE E Morocco, N Algeria.

P. martini martini Allard 1867 TL: Algeria.

DISTRIBUTION Algeria: Batna; Lambessa; Khenchela; Oran; Algiers; Kabylie; Tlemcen Mts. 1400-1900m.

FLIGHT-PERIOD Univoltine. Mid May/early July according to locality.

HABITAT Dry, stony, flowery places with some scrub, e.g., *Quercus ilex*; *Chamaerops humilis*; *Thymus*.

LIFE-HISTORY LHPs *Astragalus massiliensis*; *Acanthyllis numidia*. Larvae attended by *Crematogaster* sp.

P. martini ungemachi Rothschild 1926 TL: Aselda (High Atlas), Aghbalu Larbi, Taghzeft Pass (Middle Atlas, Morocco).

DISTRIBUTION Morocco: widespread but local: High Atlas (Tizi-n-Talremt; Imilchil; Reraya Valley); Middle Atlas (Boulemane; Sefrou; Tizi-bou-Zabel). 1400-2200m.

DESCRIPTION Resembles nominate form closely. Uns white rings, enclosing black discal and pd spots, better defined; female ups submarginal orange spots usually larger but variable; uns gc greyer.

FLIGHT-PERIOD Univoltine. Mid May/June.

HABITAT Stony, flowery places.

LIFE-HISTORY LHP *Astragalus incanus incurvus*.

P. martini regularis Tennent 1995 TL: Dj. Lakraa, Morocco.

DISTRIBUTION Morocco: W Rif Mts. (Dj. Lakraa). 1900-2100m.

DESCRIPTION Resembles nominate form: male ups slightly darker blue; upf and uph lacking black cell-spots.

FLIGHT-PERIOD Univoltine. Late June/July.

HABITAT Open, stony slopes.

LIFE-HISTORY LHP *Astragalus armatus*.

Allard's Blue *Plebejus allardi*

RANGE Morocco, Algeria, Tunisia, W Libya, Israel.

P. allardi Oberthür 1874 TL: Sebdou, W Algeria.

DISTRIBUTION Widely scattered and local. Morocco: Anti-Atlas. 1300-1500m. Algeria: Sebdou (Tlemcen Mts.) 900m. Tunisia: Isle of Jerba 10-25m; Zriba 480m.

DESCRIPTION Resembles *P. martini*. Ups black veins more prominent near outer margin; uns gc darker, greyish-brown; uns markings better developed.

FLIGHT-PERIOD Univoltine. Mid April/mid May according to altitude.

HABITAT Hot, dry, rocky slopes or sandy ground with sparse, low-growing vegetation.

LIFE-HISTORY LHP *Astragalus caprinus*. Ova laid on underside of developing leaves.

BEHAVIOUR Both sexes fond of resting on LHP.

Loew's Blue *Plebejus loewii*

RANGE Greece (E Aegean Islands), Turkey, Iraq, Iran, Afghanistan, Pakistan.

P. loewii Zeller 1847 TL: Turkey.

DISTRIBUTION Aegean Islands: Kos; Patmos; Kalimnos; Tilos; Rhodes. 0-800m.

FLIGHT-PERIOD Voltinism uncertain: only one brood (late May/late June) observed on Rhodes. Reportedly univoltine in Turkey.

HABITAT Dry rocky places.

LIFE-HISTORY LHP unknown in Europe and Turkey. (Saudi Arabia, *Astragalus spinosus*; *A. sieberi*).

Grass Jewel

Martin's Blue

Allard's Blue

GRASS JEWEL

Unh with black marginal spots with silvery-green crescents

MARTIN'S BLUE

Restricted to Morocco and Algeria

Unh markings usually poorly developed

♀ dark brown with blue flush, hind-wing with black spots bordered with orange

ALLARD'S BLUE

Restricted to Morocco, Algeria and Tunisia

Unh markings usually well developed

LOEW'S BLUE

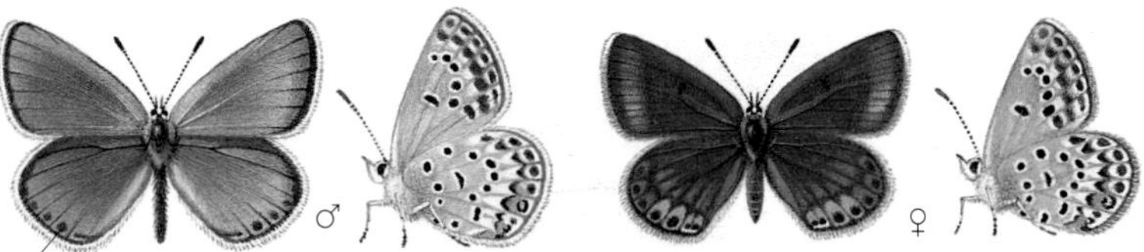

Uph antemarginal black spots prominent

Zephyr Blue *Plebejus pylaon*

RANGE Spain, Switzerland, Italy, Balkans, Greece, Turkey, Middle East, N Iran, SW Russia.

P. pylaon sephirus Frivaldsky 1835 TL: Slivno, Bulgaria.

DISTRIBUTION Generally sporadic, often locally common. Hungary. Serbia. (?)Albania. Republic of Macedonia. Romania. Bulgaria: Pirin Mts. NW and C Greece: Varnous Mts.; Vernon Mts; Askion Mts.; Mt. Parnis; Pindos Mts. S Greece: Mt. Chelmos; Mt. Menalon. European Turkey. Records for Taygetos Mts. require confirmation. 500-2050m.

DESCRIPTION AND VARIATION Male ups violet-blue; unh antemarginal black spots without silvery-bluish/greenish scales. In Republic of Macedonia and Greece, f. *brethertoni* Brown: resembles nominate ssp. closely (probably synonomous): size variable, usually large; male uph sometimes with reddish spots in anal angle: female ups submarginal orange spots variable in colour, size and number, sometimes confluent, rarely with obscure, proximal, ray-like projections on fw.

FLIGHT-PERIOD Univoltine. Mid May/July according to locality and altitude.

HABITAT Usually open dry, grassy, sometimes sandy places containing an abundance of LHP: exceptionally, damp woodland clearings: on calcareous soils.

LIFE-HISTORY LHPs: Hungary, *Astragalus exscapus*; *A. dasyanthus*: Greece, *A. exscapus* (Smolikas massif: extremely local); *A. parnassi cyllenus* (S Pindos Mts., Mt. Chelmos); *A. angustifolius* (Askion Mts.; Mt. Menelon); *Astracantha rumelica* [=*Astragalus creticus rumelicus*] (Sarantaporus Valley, Pindos Mts.). Ova laid on leaves, upon which larvae feed. Hibernates as a small larva. Pupates at base of LHP, often at entrances to galleries of ants'nest. Larvae attended by *Bothriomyrmex gallicus*; *Tapinoma simrothi*; *Lasius niger*; *Lasius near alienus*; *Camponotus* (?)*aethiops*; *C.* (?)*laconicus*; *Tetramorium* near *caespitum*; *Formica pratensis*.

BEHAVIOUR Males often assemble in large numbers on damp ground.

P. pylaon trappi Verity 1927 TL: Simplon.

syn: *lycidas* Trapp 1863 (invalid homonym)

DISTRIBUTION (?)SE France: Savoie (Val d'Isère). S Switzerland: Bernese Alps (Gemmi Pass); Pennine Alps (Simplonpass; Saastal; Zermatt). N Italy: Piedmont (Val di Cogne; Val d'Ossola); Venosta Alps (Schlandrounertal; Val Passiria). 1000-2000m.

DESCRIPTION AND VARIATION Male ups darker violet-blue; black marginal borders slightly wider: female ups dark brown, often with blue basal suffusion; uph dark orange spots in anal angle vestigial or absent, often replaced by black dots. In Piedmont, f. *augustini* Mentzer: slightly smaller. In S Tirol, f. *delattini* Junge: slightly larger.

FLIGHT-PERIOD Univoltine. Late June/early August according to season and altitude.

HABITAT Sheltered grassy places; small, pinewood clearings.

LIFE-HISTORY LHP *Astragalus exscapus*. Early-stage development as for *L. p. sephirus*. Larvae attended by *Formica lugubris*; *F. lemani*.

P. pylaon hespericus Rambur 1839 TL: Sierra de Alfacar, Andalusia.

DISTRIBUTION Spain: Teruel (S. de Albarracin 1000-1500m); Madrid (Loeches; Camporeal; Arganda; 700-800m); Toledo (La Mata 700-800m); Granada (Sierra Nevada; S. de Alfacar; 1150-1300m). Most colonies extremely local.

DESCRIPTION AND VARIATION Male ups bright turquoise blue; uph black antemarginal spots sometimes faintly ringed pinkish-violet; uph, ochreous mark sometimes present in s1a: female ups medium brown; uph with 2-4 submarginal orange spots in anal angle, variable, sometimes absent. In provinces of Madrid and Toledo: averagely slightly larger; male ups slightly brighter.

FLIGHT-PERIOD Univoltine. Mid May/June.

HABITAT Dry, rocky gullies, often amongst scrub; dry grassy places in woodland clearings. LHPs usually extremely local.

LIFE-HISTORY LHPs: S. de Albarracin, *Astragalus turolensis* [=*A. aragonensis*]; *A. sempervirens muticus*: Madrid and Toledo, *A. alopecuroides* [=*A. narbonensis*]: Granada, *A. clusii* [=*A. tumidus*]. Oviposition and development as for *sephirus*. Larvae/pupae attended by *Formica cinerea*; *F. subrufa*; *Plagiolepis pygmaea*; *P. schmitzi*; *Camponotus* near *aethiops*; *C. cruentatus*; *C. foreli*; *C. sylvaticus*; *Crematogaster auberti*. Pupates near base of LHP, often at entrances to galleries of ants'nest.

CONSERVATION Most colonies appear to be vulnerable, particularly those in close proximity to areas of cultivation: at least two colonies have been eradicated in Sierra Nevada in last two decades by urban expansion.

Reverdin's Blue *Plebejus argyrognomon*

RANGE France, C, E and SE Europe, Turkey.

P. argyrognomon Bergsträsser 1779 TL: Hanau, Germany.

syn: *ismenias* Meigen 1829 (invalid homonym); *aegus* Chapman 1917

DISTRIBUTION France: Dordogne; Charante; Vienne; Isère and Haute Savoie to Paris and Aisne. NW Switzerland. Italy. Germany to S Norway (including Oslofiord island of Borøya), S Sweden, E Latvia (very local), Balkans and N Greece (very local). Records for Mt. Parnassos require confirmation. 200-1500m.

DESCRIPTION Resembles *P. idas*: individual wing-characters not diagnostic but overall appearance usually sufficient for identification. Male genitalia distinctive.

VARIATION In Scandinavia, *norvegica* Nordstrom: female ups bright, shiny blue. In Balkans and Greece: often large; female ups invariably brown. In France, Germany and Austria, female ups blue suffusion variable within and between populations but usually limited to wing-bases. Geographical variation in degree and incidence of female ups blue suffusion suggests a clinal change, possibly associated with climatic conditions (cf. *P. amanda*).

FLIGHT-PERIOD Generally bivoltine, mid May/June and late June/July: univoltine in Scandinavia, late June/late August according to season.

ZEPHYR BLUE

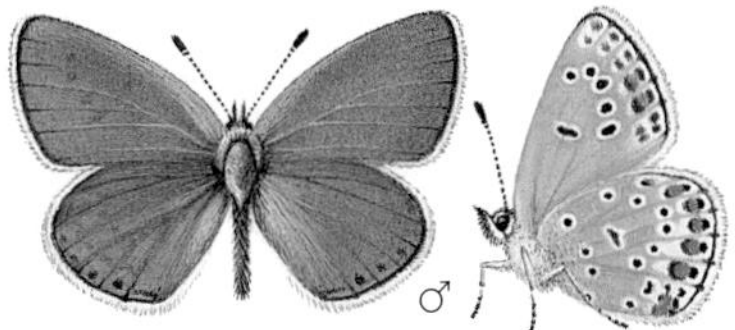

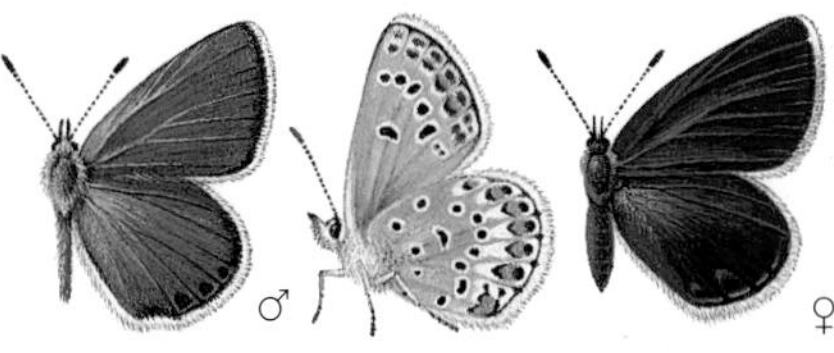

P. p. trappi
(Alps)

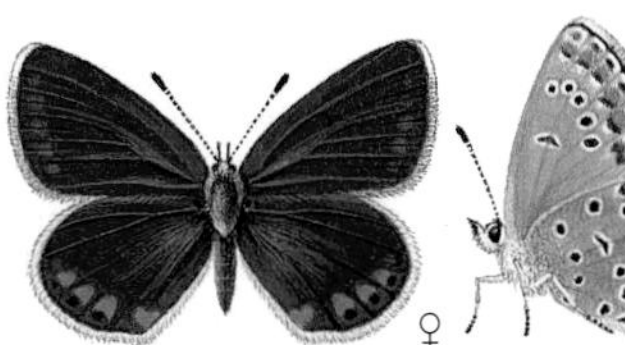

P. p. sephirus

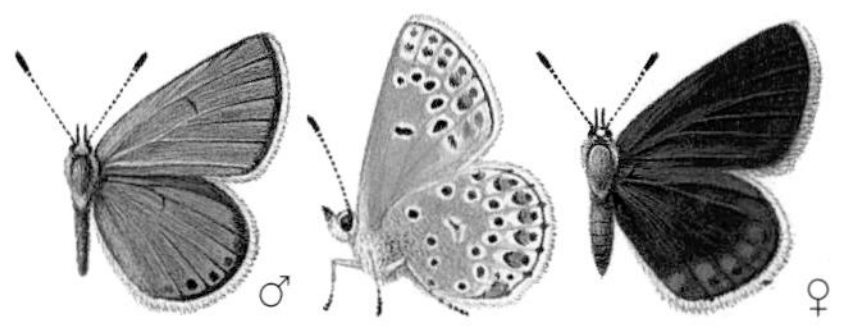

P. p. hespericus
(Spain)

REVERDIN'S BLUE

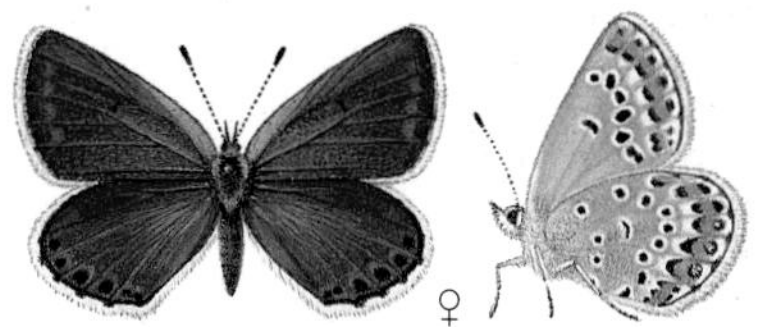

HABITAT Grassy, flowery, bushy, dry or damp places.
LIFE-HISTORY LHPs *Coronilla varia*, *Astragalus glycyphyllos*. In Scandinavia, *A. glycyphyllos* is the sole LHP, also apparently in Greece – despite presence of *C. varia* in all known habitats. Ova laid on either surface of leaves. Hibernates as an ovum or small larva. In Greece, hibernated larvae feed on developing leaves below base of LHP. Larvae attended by *Lasius niger*; *L. alienus*; *Myrmica scabrinodis*; *M. sabuleti*; *Camponotus vagus*.

Zephyr Blue

Reverdin's Blue

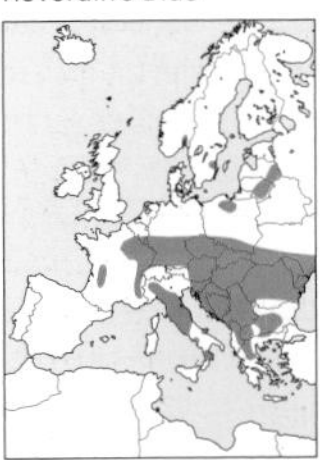

Silver-studded Blue *Plebejus argus*

RANGE Europe, Turkey, temperate Asia, N China, Japan.

P. argus argus Linnaeus 1758 TL: S Sweden (Verity 1943). syn: aegon Denis and Schiffermüller 1775.

DISTRIBUTION Widespread, locally common. From N and E Spain to 69°N in Fennoscandia, Balkans, Greece (including Corfu and Thassos) and European Turkey. 0-1500m. A record for Kykladian island of Tenos requires confirmation. Absent from Ireland and Scotland.

DESCRIPTION Male fore-tibia with spine (cf. *Plebejus idas*).

VARIATION Numerous ssp./forms have been described to account for minor variation in size; development of markings; ups and uns gc, especially female ups blue suffusion. Generally, uns gc correlates with character of habitat: darker forms occur on dark, acidic soils (heaths, bogs etc.), paler forms on limestone. In S Greece, males with reddish marginal spots in s1-3 uph occur rarely. On Mt. Erimanthos (NW Peloponnesos) above 1500m: large; male ups black borders exceptionally narrow – uph black submarginal spots largely obscured by gc; uns gc whitish, markings well developed: female ups brown: in E Spain, *montesiai* de Sagarra: male ups and uns closely similar: female ups extensively suffused bright blue.

FLIGHT-PERIOD Bivoltine. May/June and July/August.

HABITAT Diverse. Most habitat types in altitudinal range: in very damp to very dry conditions.

LIFE-HISTORY LHPs: Fabaceae, spp. of the genera:- *Lotus*; *Ulex*; *Cytisus*; *Genista*; *Colutea*; *Astragalus*; *Ononis*; *Medicago*; *Hippocrepis*; *Coronilla*; *Galega*: Cistaceae, *Helianthemum*: Ericaceae, *Calluna vulgaris*; (?)*Erica* sp. In northern Europe, hibernates as a fully-formed larva within ovum-case: in one example in Greece, a second instar larva was found hibernating within its exuvium attached to the underside of a stone. Larvae strongly myrmecophilous. Ova laid on plants in close proximity to ants' nests. Larvae attended by *Lasius niger*; *L. alienus*; (?)*Formica cinerea*. Adult larvae pupate in ants' nest into which they are ushered by attending ants. Without ants, captive adult larvae become very 'agitated' and usually die (cf. *Tomares ballus*).

P. argus caernensis Thompson 1941 TL: Great Ormes Head, N Wales.

DISTRIBUTION N Wales: coastal areas: Great Ormes peninsula. 10-100m.

DESCRIPTION AND VARIATION Small. Male ups, bright blue; uns white with pale blue, basal suffusion: female upf and uph usually suffused blue to submargin; ups orange submarginal spots usually well developed, especially hw. A similar but larger race, *cretaceae* Tutt, appears to be close to extinction on the chalk-grassland of SE England: a related form, occurring on coastal limestone of central S England (Dorset), appears less vulnerable.

FLIGHT-PERIOD Univoltine. Mid June/late August. Emerges 2-4 weeks earlier than other British populations.

HABITAT Dry, sheltered, grassy places on limestone.

LIFE-HISTORY LHP *Helianthemum nummularium*. Development as for nominate form.

P. argus aegidion Meisner 1818 TL: Grimsel Pass, Switzerland.

DISTRIBUTION Central Alps. 1500-2000m.

DESCRIPTION AND VARIATION Resembles nominate form. Male ups black marginal borders 2-3mm wide; uns greyish: female ups orange submarginal spots reduced, confined to hw. Transitional to nominate form below 1500m.

FLIGHT-PERIOD Univoltine. Early July/August.

HABITAT Alpine grassland.

P. argus hypochionus Rambur 1858 TL: Andalucia.

DISTRIBUTION N Portugal. S and C Spain. Not reported from Gibraltar. 600-2400m.

DESCRIPTION AND VARIATION Larger; male ups brighter blue; uns chalky-white: female ups orange submarginal spots well developed, usually in complete series on fw and hw. Transitional forms and geographical/altitudinal overlap with other races, presents a complex and poorly understood distributional pattern in Iberian Peninsula.

FLIGHT-PERIOD Univoltine. Early June/late July.

HABITAT Flowery, grassy places; rocky gullies.

P. argus corsicus Bellier 1862 TL: Corsica.

DISTRIBUTION Corsica. 500-1000m. Very local. (A tentative record from the island of St. Maria (within political boundary of Sardinia, 15km SE of Corsica) merits investigation – possibly arises from confusion with *P. idas*).

DESCRIPTION AND VARIATION Resembles nominate form: male uns gc yellowish or brownish grey; markings ill-defined; unh submarginal spots yellowish or pale orange: female ups usually with blue suffusion, especially hw. On St. Maria, smaller; male ups and uns gc and uns markings said to be identical to that of nominate form: female ups blue suffusion extensive.

FLIGHT-PERIOD Univoltine. July.

HABITAT Grassy, woodland clearings.

LIFE-HISTORY LHP yellow-flowered (?)*Genista* sp.

Cranberry Blue *Vacciniina optilete*

RANGE Central Alps, NE Europe, Republic of Macedonia, Japan, N America.

V. optilete Knoch 1781 TL: Braunschweig, Germany.

DISTRIBUTION Central Alps of SE France (Hautes-Alpes; Haute-Savoie), N Italy, Switzerland and W Austria (Gross Glockner). 1500-2800m. S and C Germany to Czech Republic, Slovakia, Poland, Baltic states and Fennoscandia. 100-1400m. Republic of Macedonia: Sar Pl.; Vraca Pl.; Pelister massif. Above 2000m.

FLIGHT-PERIOD Univoltine. Late June/August according to latitude and altitude.

HABITAT Heaths; moors; raised bogs; dry or damp forest clearings on acidic soils.

LIFE-HISTORY LHPs: Central Alps, *Vaccinium uliginosum*: Fennoscandia, *V. uliginosum*; *V. myrtillus*; *V. oxycoccus*; *Erica tetralix*. Ova laid on various plant parts including stems. Larvae feed on leaves and flowers. Hibernates as a small larva, sometimes on dead, fallen leaves of LHP.

SILVER-STUDDED BLUE

Ups black marginal borders wide

♀ brown sometimes with blue basal suffusion

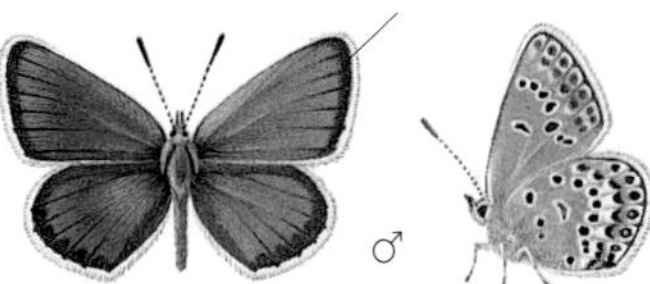

P. a. argus

Unh marginal black spots with silvery blue-green pupils

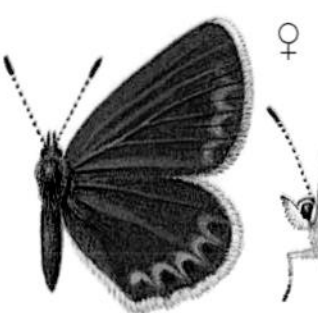

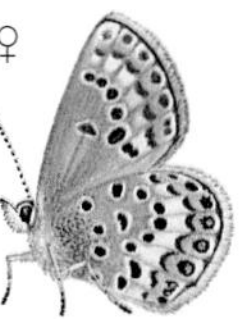

P. a. hypochionus
(N Portugal, S & C Spain)

Uns markings poorly defined

P. a. aegidon
(Central Alps)

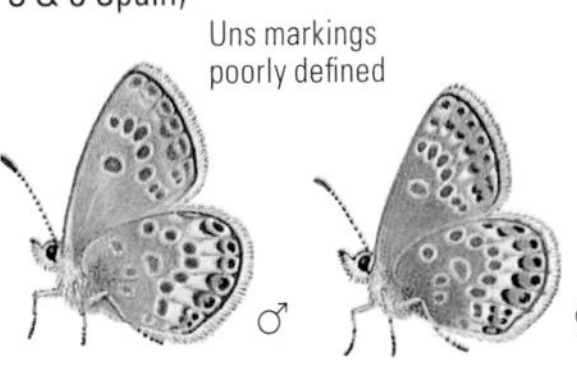

P. a. corsicus
(Corsica)

CRANBERRY BLUE

Unh s2 with prominent orange-red spot, containing black spot with silvery-blue centre

Silver-studded Blue

Cranberry Blue

Idas Blue *Plebejus idas*

RANGE Europe, Turkey, Middle East, Asia, N America.
P. idas Linnaeus 1761 TL: Sweden

DISTRIBUTION Spain: local in Sierra Nevada; Montes Universales; Soria; Burgos; Cantabrian Mts.; Pyrenees; Catalonia. France, eastwards throughout most of Europe. 200-2100m. Absent from Britain; S Greece; Mediterranean islands.

DESCRIPTION AND VARIATION Male fore-tibia lacking spine (cf. *P. argus*). Range/character of variation broadly similar to that of *P. argus*: many forms/ssp. have been described to account for local/regional variation. Above 1800m in central Alps, *haefelfingeri* Beuret: small; male ups bluer; uns, greyish-buff. Below 1000m in Alps and Pyrenees, *opulentus* Verity: large; uns well marked. At 1000-1500m in Alps and Pyrenees, *alpinus* Berce: transitional to *opulentus*. In N Scandinavia, *lapponicus* Gerhard: resembles *haefelfingeri*: small; uns discal and pd spots small; female ups gc brown, often suffused blue; uph orange spots vestigial. Above 1800m in Sierra Nevada, S Spain, *nevadensis* Oberthür: resembles *magnagraeca* (below) but averagely smaller.

FLIGHT-PERIOD Univoltine (late June/August) or bivoltine (late May/June and July/August) according to altitude and locality.

HABITAT Bushy places; grassy woodland clearings; heaths, in dry or damp situations; sheltered grassy banks and hollows at highest levels.

LIFE-HISTORY LHPs *Cytisus scoparius; Genista pilosa; Lotus corniculatus; Melilotus alba; Anthyllus vulneraria; Calluna vulgaris*. Hibernates as an ovum. Larvae are strongly myrmecophilous and pupate within an ants' nest. Larvae/pupae attended by *Lasius niger*; *Formica cinerea*; *F. selysi*; *F. exsecta*; *F. lemani*; *F. pressilabris*; *F. lugubris*; *F. cunicularia*; *F. lefrancoisi*; *F.* (?)*fusca*.

P. idas calliopis Boisduval 1832 TL: Grenoble.

DISTRIBUTION France: Basses Alpes; Haut Alpes. 500-1000m.

DESCRIPTION Male uns discal and pd spots reduced: female ups dark brown, often with blue basal suffusion.

FLIGHT-PERIOD Univoltine. July/early August.

HABITAT Habitats dominated by bushes of LHP.

LIFE-HISTORY LHP *Hippophae rhamnoides* (Elaeagnaceae). Adult activity confined largely to proximity of LHP. Larvae attended by *Formica* spp. patrolling LHP.

P. idas magnagraeca Verity 1936 TL: Mt. Olympus, Greece.

DISTRIBUTION Republic of Macedonia. Bulgaria. N and C Greece. Widespread but local. 500-1800m.

DESCRIPTION Large: male ups black borders 2-3mm wide; ups gc generally darker blue, sometimes with purplish tint; black veins usually prominent: female ups brown; uph submarginal orange spots usually well developed, sometimes extending to fw in a complete series: both sexes, uns markings bold.

VARIATION Somewhat variable in all characters. Above about 1500m on Mt. Pangeon, Mt. Timphristos and Mt. Parnassos: smaller; male ups paler blue; black borders narrower; veins less conspicuous – resembles *nevadensis* Oberthür.

FLIGHT-PERIOD Univoltine. June/July.

HABITAT Grassy, flowery clearings in scrub or light woodland: above 1500m, dry gravelly slopes on acidic soils or dry grassy banks on limestone.

LIFE-HISTORY LHPs: Vernon Mts., *Genista depressa*; Rhodopi Mts., *Cytisus villosus*. Pupates amongst leaf-litter or on leaves of LHP. Larvae/pupae attended by *Formica pratensis*.

P. idas bellieri Oberthür 1910 TL: Bastelica, Corsica.

DISTRIBUTION Corsica. Sardinia. 0-1400m.

DESCRIPTION AND VARIATION Male ups black marginal borders, 1-2mm (Corsica) or 2-3mm (Sardinia); uns gc yellowish or brownish-grey, markings very prominent in both sexes: female ups darkish brown with extensive blue basal flush, especially hw.

FLIGHT-PERIOD Univoltine. Late June/July.

HABITAT Scrub and woodland clearings.

Geranium Argus *Eumedonia eumedon*

RANGE Europe, Turkey, Urals, Mongolia, Tian Shan, Altai.
E. eumedon Esper 1780 TL: Erlangen, W Germany.
syn: *chiron* Rottemburg 1775 (invalid homonym).

DISTRIBUTION Spain: S. de Maria; S. de Tejeda; Cantabrian Mts.; S. de la Demanda; S. de Cuenca; Pyrenees. France: Pyrenees; Massif Central; Provence to Jura. Italy: very sporadic. N Sicily. Commoner in NE range: Switzerland to N Fennoscandia (including Öland and Gotland) and Romania. Sporadic and local in W Croatia, Republic of Macedonia, Bulgaria and N and C Greece. Absent from NW Europe, Denmark and N Norway. In C and S Europe, 750-2400m: in Fennoscandia, 0-1300m: generally below 900m.

VARIATION At lower altitudes and in S Europe: generally larger; uns markings better developed. In N Fennoscandia and at higher altitudes in C Alps: small; uns greyish; uns markings reduced; male unf pd spots often very small, sometimes absent. In Balkans and Greece: generally much larger; uns gc light golden-brown, all markings bold, especially orange submarginal spots. Throughout range, uph submarginal spots variable in both sexes, better developed in female. On Mt. Parnassos, unh white stripe usually absent.

FLIGHT-PERIOD Univoltine. Mid May/mid August according to altitude, latitude and locality.

HABITAT Warm, sheltered, flowery, woodland or scrub clearings; sheltered alpine meadows. In dry or damp situations on calcareous or acidic soils.

LIFE-HISTORY LHPs *Geranium sanguineum*; *G. sylvaticum*; *G. tuberosum*; *G. palustre*; *G. pratense*; *G. cinereum*. Ova laid at base of stamens. Before hibernation, larvae feed almost exclusively on developing fruits. Hibernates as a small larva. Hibernated larvae feed on developing leaves. Larvae attended by *Lasius alienus*; *Myrmica* sp.; *Tapinoma* sp. In captive rearing, a second brood is easily induced.

BEHAVIOUR Adult activity confined largely to vicinity of LHP.

IDAS BLUE

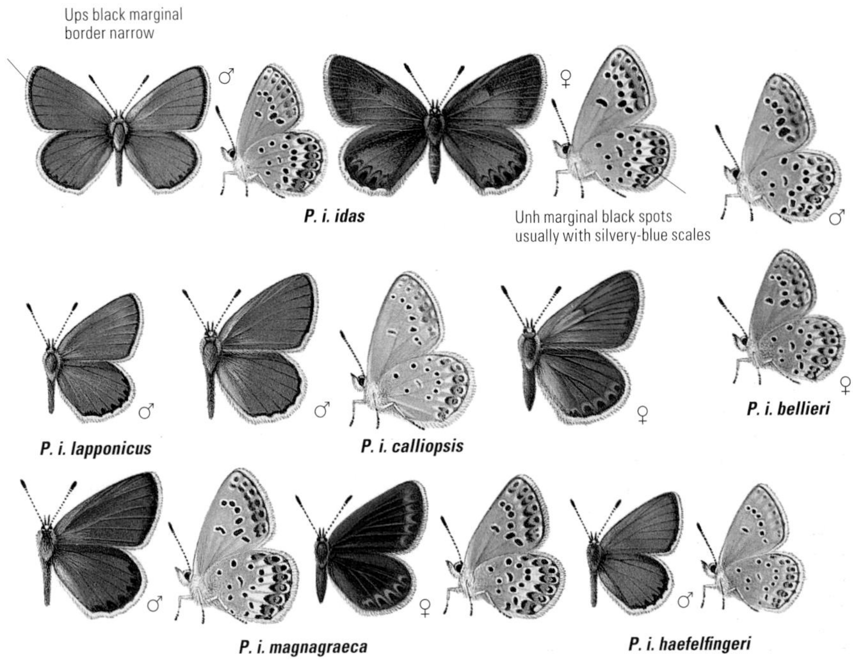

Ups black marginal border narrow

♂ ♀ ♂

P. i. idas

Unh marginal black spots usually with silvery-blue scales

♂ ♂ ♀ ♀

P. i. lapponicus

P. i. calliopsis

P. i. bellieri

♂ ♀ ♂

P. i. magnagraeca

P. i. haefelfingeri

GERANIUM ARGUS

Ups white fringes conspicuous – contrasting with dark gc of wings

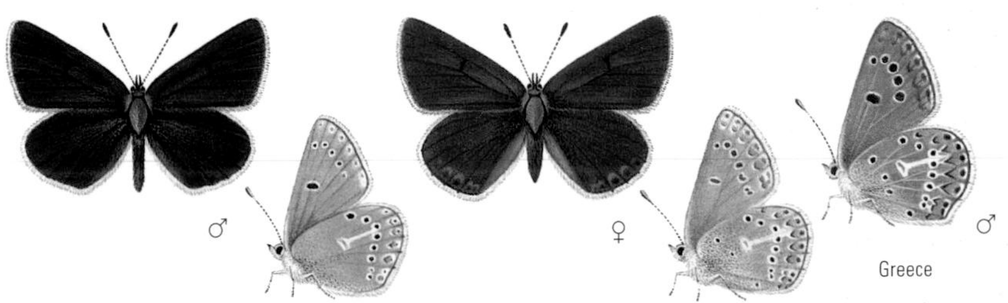

Uns pd spots variable in size, sometimes vestigial or absent on unf

Idas Blue

Geranium Argus

Cretan Argus *Kretania psylorita*

RANGE Crete.

K. psylorita Freyer 1845 TL: Mt. Ida, Crete.

DISTRIBUTION Restricted to Crete: Psyloritis Mts. (Mt. Ida); Dikti Mts. 1300-2000m. Locally abundant.

FLIGHT-PERIOD Univoltine. June/July.

HABITAT Rocky ground, dominated by LHP.

LIFE-HISTORY LHP *Astragalus* or *Astracantha*, not reliably determined at sp. level (cf. *K. eurypilus*).

BEHAVIOUR Flight very low, maintaining close proximity to LHP, seemingly to minimize danger of windswept terrain.

CONSERVATION Habitats reportedly threatened by increasing human activity.

Eastern Brown Argus *Kretania eurypilus*

RANGE Greece, Turkey, Middle East, Iran, S Russia.

K. eurypilus eurypilus Freyer 1851 TL: Amasya, Turkey.

DISTRIBUTION Greece: Samos (Mt. Kerketefs 1000-1450m). Two records (1901 and 1968) of female specimens from Mt. Chelmos are generally presumed to have arisen from confusion with closely similar female *Plebejus pylaon*.

VARIATION Female ups submarginal orange-red spots variable in number and size, sometimes large and in complete series on fw and hw, sometimes entirely absent.

FLIGHT-PERIOD Univoltine. June/late July.

HABITAT Open rocky limestone slopes/gullies/hollows, with sparse low-growing vegetation: above tree-line.

K. eurypilus pelopides van der Poorten 1984 TL: 'S Peloponesos'[Taygetos Mts.].

DISTRIBUTION S Greece: Taygetos Mts. 1400-2200m.

DESCRIPTION Resembles nominate form. Male ups gc greyer, lighter brown; submarginal orange spots paler; uph sometimes with slight greyish suffusion, broken by veins; uns gc greyer, brighter; submarginal and pd spots interposed with whitish band, broken by veins: female similar; fw outer margin more rounded; ups orange submarginal spots better developed; uph greyish suffusion apparent in about 50% of specimens.

FLIGHT-PERIOD Univoltine. Early June/late July in prolonged emergence.

HABITAT Sheltered gullies/hollows on limestone or metamorphic rocks, generally above tree-line.

LIFE-HISTORY LHP *Astracantha rumelica* [=*Astragalus creticus rumelicus*]. (In Lebanon, *Astracantha gummifera*). Ova laid on upperside of leaves. Hibernates as a small larva. Hibernated larva generally feeds in a concealed position by boring laterally into stem, just below new season's growth, and then axially downwards into stem: newly developed leaves are left intact, concealing posterior segments of larva. Larvae attended by *Camponotus kiesenwetteri*; *C. universitatus*. A high proportion of larvae are parasitized.

Brown Argus *Aricia agestis*

RANGE N Africa, S and C Europe, Turkey, Middle East, Iran, Tian Shan, Siberia, Amur.

A. agestis agestis Denis and Schiffermüller 1775 TL: Vienna, Austria.

syn: *astrache* Bergsträsse 1779; *medon* Hufnagel 1776 (invalid homonym)

DISTRIBUTION Widespread and common. N Spain, eastwards through S Britain to Denmark (including Fyen, Sjælland, Lolland, Falster and Bornholm) and S Sweden. Lithuania: rare and very local. Recorded from most Mediterranean islands. Absent from Balearic Islands (replaced by *A. a. cramera* (below)), Ireland, Scotland, W Denmark, Latvia and Estonia. 0-1700m.

DESCRIPTION AND VARIATION First brood uns gc grey; second brood sandy to rusty-brown. In S Europe, including Mediterranean islands, *calida* Bellier: ups and uns submarginal orange spots well developed.

FLIGHT-PERIOD Generally bivoltine in N and C Europe, May/June and July/September: possibly univoltine in Lithuania, June/July: trivoltine at lower altitudes in S Europe, April/October.

HABITAT Dry or damp, grassy, flowery places in diverse range of climatic conditions: on calcareous soils.

LIFE-HISTORY LHPs, *Helianthemum nummularium*; *Erodium cicutarium*; *E. ciconium*; *Geranium tuberosum*; *G. asphodeloides*; *G. sanguineum*. Ova laid on upperside of leaves upon which larvae feed. Hibernates as a small larva. Larvae attended by *Lasius niger*; *L. alienus*; *L. flavus*; *Myrmica sabuleti*.

NOTE Sympatric with *A. artaxerxes allous* in Lithuania.

A. agestis cramera Eschscholtz 1821 TL: Canary Islands.

syn: *canariensis* Blachier 1889.

DISTRIBUTION Canary Islands: Gomera; Hierro; La Palma; Tenerife; Gran Canaria. 300-1600m. Morocco. Algeria. Tunisia. 0-2500m. Portugal. Spain, south of the Cantabrian Mts. and Pyrenees. Balearic Islands: Ibiza; Mallorca; Menorca. 0-1900m.

DESCRIPTION AND VARIATION Resembles nominate form. Ups submarginal orange spots strongly developed, often forming a continuous band disrupted by veins. Uns gc variation as for nominate form. Male genitalia distinctive: accorded specific rank by some authors.

FLIGHT-PERIOD Polyvoltine in Canary Islands, recorded in all months, broods partially overlapping: bivoltine or trivoltine in NW Africa and S Europe (April/October), according to altitude.

HABITAT Dry, usually rocky, flowery places on calcareous soils.

LIFE-HISTORY LHPs: Tenerife, *Tuberaria guttata*; *Helianthemum nummularium*: Spain and NW Africa, *Helianthemum*; *Erodium*; *Geranium*. Ova laid mainly on upper surface of leaves. Larvae feed on leaves. Larvae are polymorphic: attended by *Lasius* sp.; *Myrmica* sp. Captive larvae accept many species of *Erodium* and *Geranium*.

CRETAN ARGUS

Unf lacking black spot in cell

Restricted to Crete

♂

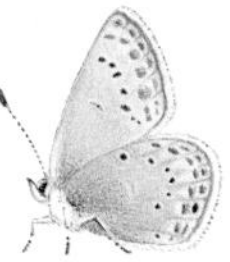

♀

EASTERN BROWN ARGUS

Unh gc and pattern of markings distinctive: unh black spot in s2 with silvery blue-green scales

Restricted to S Greece and Samos

♂

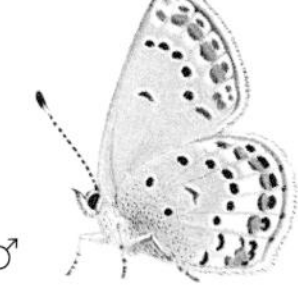

♀

K. e. pelopides

BROWN ARGUS

Unf lacking cell-spot

♂

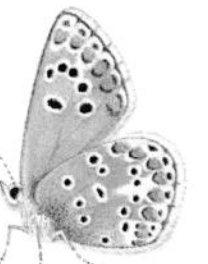

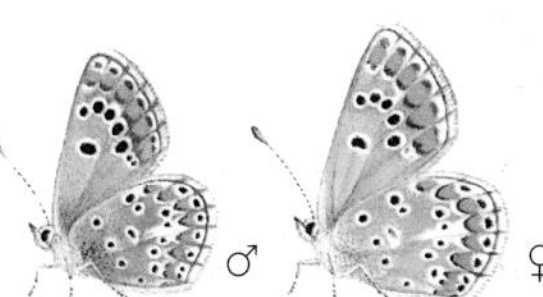
♂ ♀

Unh pd spot in s6 displaced towards wing base

1st brood
A. a. agestis

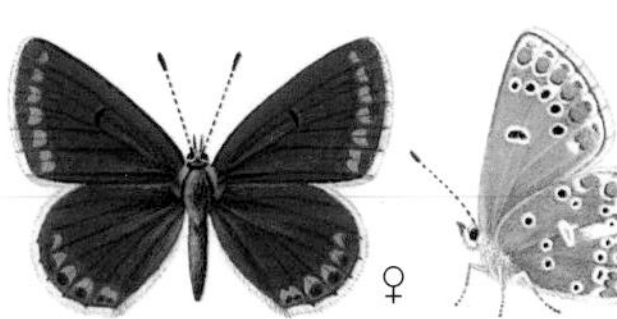
♀

A. a. agestis

♂

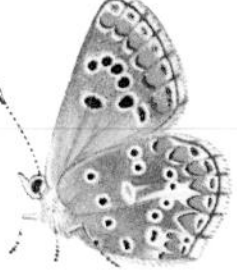

♀

2nd brood
A. a. cramera

Cretan Argus

Eastern Brown Argus

Brown Argus

Mountain Argus

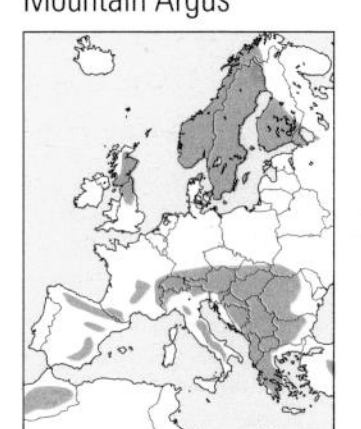

Spanish Argus

Mountain Argus *Aricia artaxerxes*

RANGE N Africa, Europe, Turkey, eastwards to Altai Mts.

A. artaxerxes artaxerxes Fabricius 1793 TL: Scotland.

DISTRIBUTION Scotland. N England. 0-350m.

DESCRIPTION AND VARIATION In Scotland, upf discoidal spot invariably white: in N England, this distinctive feature comprises only about 5-10% of specimens – more usually black, sometimes faintly ringed white (*salmacis* Stephens); in Scotland, unh ocelli often reduced to black points, rarely absent, better developed in *salmacis*, transitional in some colonies in S Scotland. In all populations, ups orange submarginal spots variable, often reduced to obscure markings in s1 and s2 uph, rarely absent. **FLIGHT-PERIOD** Univoltine. Mid June/late July according to locality and season. **HABITAT** Mostly, sunny south-facing slopes with short grass; usually on limestone but always on calcareous soils. Many habitats occur on coastal cliffs. **LIFE-HISTORY** LHP principally *Helianthemum nummularium*; use of *Erodium* and *Geranium* are suspected alternatives in some localities. On *Helianthemum*, ova laid on ups surface of leaves, upon which small larvae feed on the lower cuticle. Hibernates as a small larva amongst leaf litter at base of LHP. Larvae attended by *Lasius* sp.

A. artaxerxes allous Geyer 1837 TL: Alps of Provence.

syn: *inhonora* Jachontov 1909.

DISTRIBUTION Pyrenees. Alps of central Europe. Sicily (above 2000m). S Germany. S Poland. Czech Republic. Slovakia. Hungary. Baltic countries (very local and rare). Fennoscandia to 70°N. Republic of Macedonia: Sar Pl. Bulgaria. Greece. Absent from Tatra and Carpathian Mts. 1400-2200m in S Europe, progressively lower altitudes north of C Alps, sea-level in S Fennoscandia. **DESCRIPTION AND VARIATION** Generally small; ups dark brown; fw apex pointed, especially in male; ups orange submarginal spots usually confined to hw, often reduced to obscure patch in anal angle; fringes poorly chequered. Female markings generally better developed. Development of markings appears to be clinal, with smaller, darker and poorly marked forms predominating in colder conditions – higher altitudes and latitudes. The affinity of *A. a. artaxerxes* and *A. a. allous* is indicated by characters of the former (upf white discoidal spot; uns reduced ocelli) arising, sporadically, in populations of the latter: such forms occur in Sweden: forms resembling *salmacis* have been recorded in NW Greece. **FLIGHT-PERIOD** Univoltine. Early June/Mid August; emergence dependent on locality. **HABITAT** Sheltered, flowery slopes, generally with short grass; on calcareous soils, including base-rich sand dunes in Scandinavia. **LIFE-HISTORY** LHPs *Helianthemum nummularium*; *Geranium sanguineum*; *G. sylvaticum*; *G. asphodeloides*; *G. cinereum subcaulescens*; *Erodium cicutarium*. In NW Greece, oviposition has been observed on *Potentilla recta*. Ova usually laid on ups surface of leaves, upon which larvae feed. In some localities, oviposition on *H. nummularium* is confined largely to plant specimens growing in heavy shade of other plants, such as *Verbascum*. Hibernates as a small larva amongst leaf-litter or moss at base of LHP. Larvae attended by *Lasius* sp. **NOTE** Sympatric with *A. agestis* in Lithuania.

A. artaxerxes montensis Verity 1928 TL: Andalusia.

syn: *montana* Heyne 1895 (invalid homonym); *nevadensis* Oberthür 1910 (invalid homonym).

DISTRIBUTION Morocco: Anti-Atlas (scarce); High Atlas; Middle Atlas; 900-2800m. Spain. S France: Massif Central; Vosges; Jura; Basses Alpes. Italy. Sicily. Balkans. S Greece. 1000-2200m. **DESCRIPTION AND VARIATION** Generally large; fw pointed; uns gc creamy-grey to light, creamy-brown; orange spots well developed. Forms with upf white markings do not appear to have been reported. In some regions, small specimens may be difficult to distinguish from *A. a. allous*. Balkan and Greek populations, sometimes referred to as *macedonicus* Verity, appear to fall within the range of variation of *A. a. allous*. **FLIGHT-PERIOD** Univoltine. Late June/September according to altitude and locality. **HABITAT** Warm, flowery, grassy or rocky places on calcareous soils. **LIFE-HISTORY** LHPs *Helianthemum*; *Erodium*. **NOTE** Distributional relationship (geographical/altitudinal) of *A. a. montensis* and *A. a. allous* is not well understood. Generally, *A. a. montensis* frequents warmer and drier terrain at lower altitudes in Mediterranean region: often sympatric and synchronous with *A. agestis*. In N and C Greece, and on Mt. Erimanthos (NW Peloponnesos), populations closely resembling *A. a. allous* occur at 1500m and above: in Taygetos Mts. (S Peloponnesos), *A. a. montensis* occurs from 1000m to at least 1600m. *A. a. montensis* is accorded specific rank by some authors.

Spanish Argus *Aricia morronensis*

RANGE Spain, France (E Pyrenees).

A. morronensis morronensis Ribbe 1910 TL: Mt. Morron, S. de Espuña, Murcia.

syn: *idas* Rambur 1840 (invalid homonym); *ramburi* Verity 1929.

DISTRIBUTION Very sporadic and very local. Spain: S. de Maria; S. de Cazorla; S. de Segura; S. de Espuña; S. de Gredos; S. de Guadarrama; Picos de Europa; S. de Prieta; S. de Andia; Pyrenees (Ordesa). France: E Pyrenees (Col du Tourmalet). 900-2200m. **VARIATION** Size and development of markings variable between populations. Ups black discoidal spot sometimes faintly ringed white; upf apex with some white scaling. **FLIGHT-PERIOD** Voltinism unconfirmed for all populations: univoltine above 1800m, July/August. **HABITAT** Sparsely vegetated, sometimes dry, rocky ground. **LIFE-HISTORY** LHPs *Erodium cicutarium*; *E. ciconium*; *E. malacoides*. Ova laid on leaves upon which larvae feed. Hibernates as a small larva. Larvae attended by *Lasius niger*; *Crematogastor auberti*; *Tapinoma erraticum*; *T. nigerrimum*.

A. morronensis ramburi Verity 1913 TL: Sierra Nevada, Granada.

DISTRIBUTION Spain: Sierra Nevada, Granada. 2050-3000m. **DESCRIPTION** Small; ups gc medium brown; submarginal orange spots absent; upf discoidal spot, small, black; uns gc café-au-laît; unh pale yellow-orange submarginal spots inconspicuous, sometimes absent.

Maps on p. 129

MOUNTAIN ARGUS

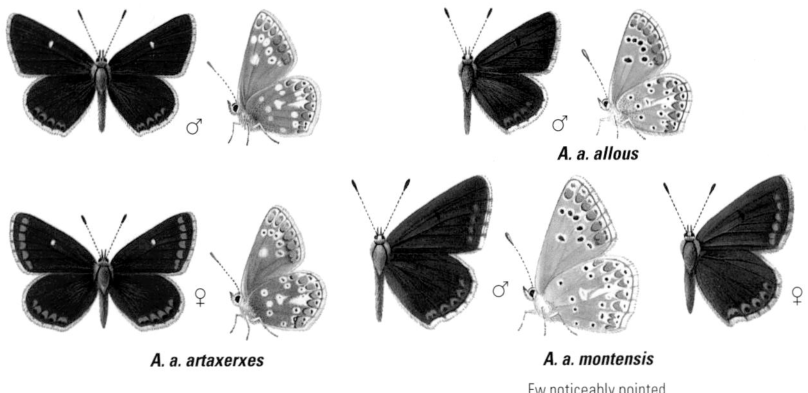

SPANISH ARGUS

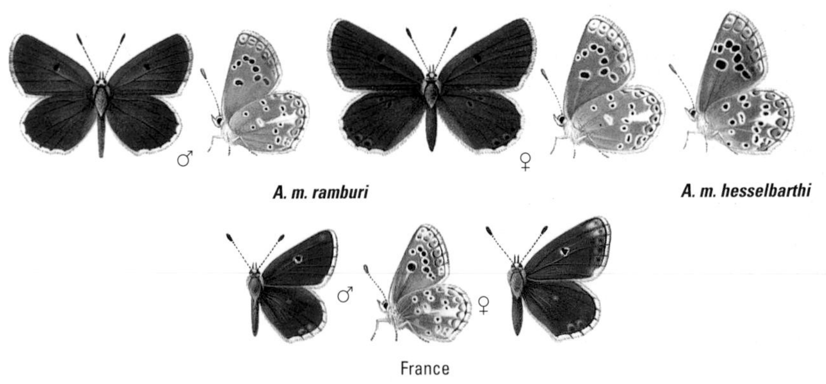

FLIGHT-PERIOD Univoltine. Late June/July. **HABITAT** Exposed, extensively rocky, usually flattish terrain with sparse, low-growing vegetation locally dominated by LHP: on dark-coloured slates (carboniferous schists). Colonies widely dispersed: usually very small. **LIFE-HISTORY** LHP *Erodium petraeum crispum* [=*Erodium cheilanthifolium*]. Larvae feed on leaves. Hibernates as a small larva: attended by *Tapinoma* sp. **BEHAVIOUR** Flight very fast and low. In very hot or windy conditions, shelter usually sought amongst or under small, broken slates: roosts in similar positions. Rapid heating of dark, slaty rock by early morning sun is exploited by both sexes; after basking with fully opened wings, full activity is achieved within 15-20 minutes, even with air (shade) temperature of 9-12°C.

A. morronensis hesselbarthi Manley 1970 TL: Abejar, Soria.

DISTRIBUTION Spain: known only from environs of Abejar, Province of Soria. 950-1100m. **DESCRIPTION** Both sexes: large; ups dark brown; uph with orange submarginal spots in anal angle; uns gc darker than nominate form; uns markings well developed. **FLIGHT-PERIOD** Bivoltine. Late May/June and July/August. **HABITAT** Flowery meadows. **LIFE-HISTORY** LHP *Erodium cicutarium cicutarium* [=*Erodium primulaceum*]. Larvae feed on leaves. Hibernates as a small larva: attended by ants. **CONSERVATION** Possibly threatened with extinction from local development and exploitation of habitat for agricultural purposes: a significant proportion of known habitat has been destroyed in recent years.

Blue Argus *Ultraaricia anteros*

RANGE Balkans, Greece, Turkey, Iran.

U. anteros Freyer 1838 TL: Constantinople.

DISTRIBUTION Croatia: Velebit Mts. SW Serbia: Sinjajevica Pl.; Komovi Pl. Republic of Macedonia: Sar Pl.; Jakupica; Galicica Pl. Albania. S Romania. Bulgaria: Rila Mts.; Rhodope Mts. Greece: widespread, locally common: Vernon Mts.; Varnous Mts.; Voras Mts.; Mt. Orvilos; Rhodope Mts; Phalakron massif; Mt. Pangeon; Mt. Olympus; Grammos massif; Epano Arena; Pindos Mts.; Mt. Chelmos. (Records from E Thrace and Taygetos Mts. require confirmation.) European Turkey. 550-2000m.

DESCRIPTION AND VARIATION Male upf with small, black discoidal spot; unf basal spot absent in about 30% of individuals. Male ups gc variation appears to relate to density or disposition of blue scales: some specimens are shiny, bright blue, others appearing dull and relatively non-reflective even in fresh condition. First brood, unh gc greyish or buff; subsequent broods, unh gc rich, ochreous-tan, especially female.

FLIGHT-PERIOD Voltinism dependent on altitude: possibly univoltine (late June/July) at 2000m: bivoltine or trivoltine (early May/September) at lower altitudes.

HABITAT Generally open grassy, flowery places; sometimes bushy places or clearings in light woodland: usually on limestone.

LIFE-HISTORY LHPs *Geranium asphodeloides* or *G. sanguineum* at lower altitudes; *G. macrorrhizum* or *G. cinereum subcaulescens* above 1600m. Ova laid on underside of basal leaves (cf. *A. artaxerxes*), upon which larvae feed (cf. *E. eumedon*). A third generation is produced consistently from captive rearing of ova obtained from second brood.

Silvery Argus *Pseudaricia nicias*

RANGE Pyrenees, Alps of C Europe, Fennoscandia, Russia, W and S Siberia.

P. nicias nicias Meigen 1830 TL: Rhetian Alps (Verity 1943).

syn: *donzelii* Boisduval 1832.

DISTRIBUTION Spain: Pyrenees; Pto. de la Bonaigua; Valle de Arán. Andorra. France: Pyrenees; Basses Alps. NW Italy. S and E Switzerland (Valais; Engadine). 1000-2300m.

FLIGHT-PERIOD Univoltine. Early July/early September according to altitude.

HABITAT Warm, sheltered, often damp places with an abundance of flowers and long grasses: typically, luxuriant meadows/hayfields bordered by woodland.

LIFE-HISTORY LHPs *Geranium sylvaticum; G. pratense*. Ova laid on flowers. Small larvae feed on flowers and developing seeds before hibernation, developing leaves and flower-buds after hibernation. Larvae attended by ants.

P. nicias scandica Wahlgren 1930 TL: Sweden.

DISTRIBUTION Eastern central Sweden from 60°N to 66°N. S Finland except W coast. 0-300m.

DESCRIPTION Male ups brighter pale blue, sometimes with greenish tinge; marginal borders greyer, narrower, well defined.

FLIGHT-PERIOD Univoltine. Early July/Mid August.

HABITAT Grassy slopes, flowery meadows or large forest clearings with a SW aspect; bushy, low-lying coastal districts, including beaches.

LIFE-HISTORY LHP *Geranium pratense*.

Alpine Blue *Albulina orbitulus*

RANGE C European Alps, Norway, S Urals.

A. orbitulus de Prunner 1798 TL: Piedmont, N Italy.

syn: pheretes Hübner 1805.

DISTRIBUTION Central European Alps of France, Italy, S and E Switzerland and Austria. 1000-2700m. Mountains of Norway and Sweden from 61°N to 64°N. 800-1200m.

VARIATION Female ups blue basal suffusion variable, sometimes extensive, especially on hw.

FLIGHT-PERIOD Univoltine. July/August in Alps; June/July in Scandinavia.

HABITAT At lower altitudes: flowery, often damp places: at higher altitudes: exposed, sometimes steep but well-consolidated flowery slopes with short grass; habitats are often small 'islands' amongst screes or extensive rocky outcrops.

LIFE-HISTORY LHP *Astragalus alpinus*. Hibernates as a small larva.

Pontic Blue *Neolysandra coelestina*

RANGE S Greece, Turkey, S Urals.

N. coelestina hera Eckweiler and Schurian 1980 TL: Mt. Chelmos, S Greece.

DISTRIBUTION S Greece: Aroánian Mts. (Chelmos massif) and mountains to NW of Kalavrita. 700-1800m.

VARIATION Male unh sometimes with pale orange spots in s1-3: female ups rarely with blue basal suffusion.

FLIGHT-PERIOD Univoltine. Late May/mid June. At upper limit of altitudinal range, fresh specimens occur sporadically early/mid July .

HABITAT Woodland clearings at lower altitudes; open grassy gullies; sheltered hollows above the tree-line; screes: on calcareous substrates.

LIFE-HISTORY LHP *Vicia cracca stenophylla* [=*Vicia dalmatica*]: other *Vicia* sp., present in some habitats, do not appear to be exploited. Ova laid on stems and stipules. Captive larvae accept many *Vicia* sp., but neither flowers nor leaves of *Anthyllis vulneraria*. In S England, larvae hibernated in second instar from late August to mid March. Habitat and LHP often shared with *A. amanda*.

BLUE ARGUS

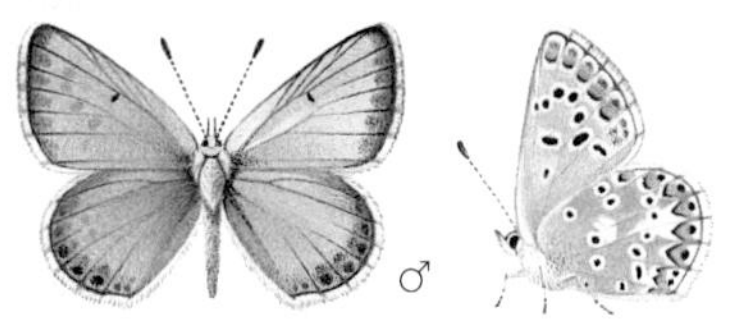

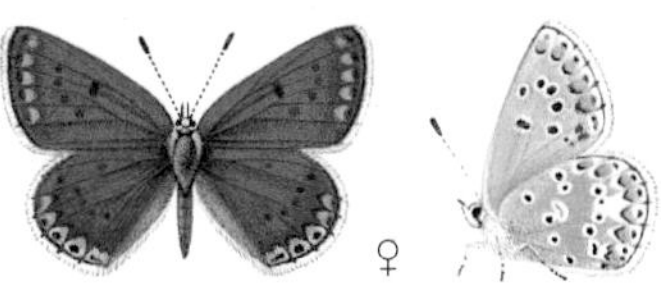

SILVERY ARGUS

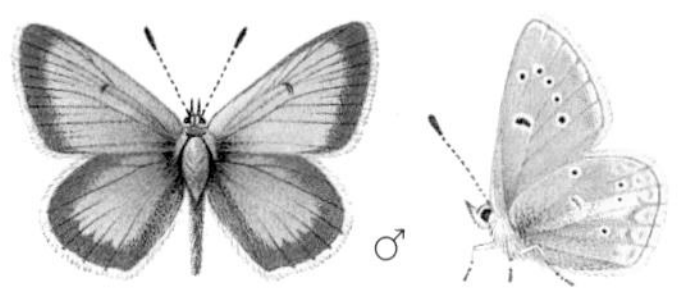

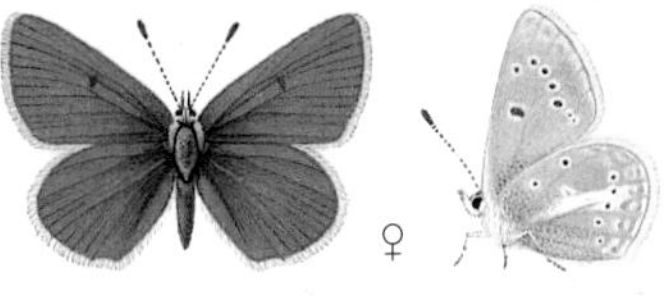

ALPINE BLUE

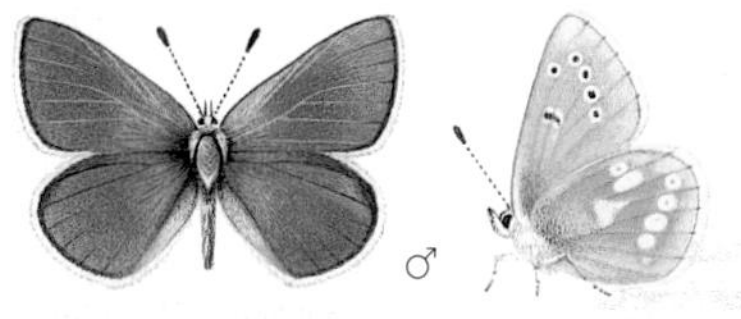

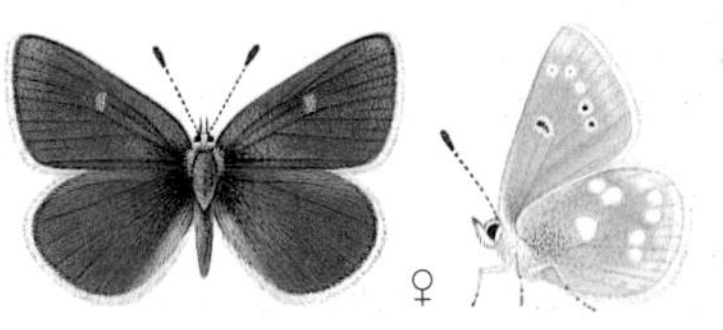

PONTIC BLUE

(Mt Chelmos, S Greece)

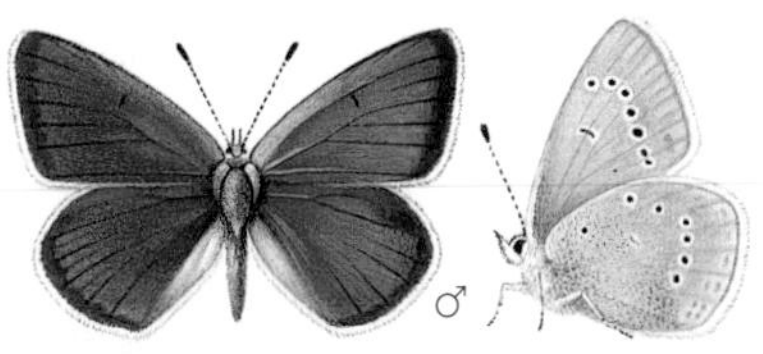

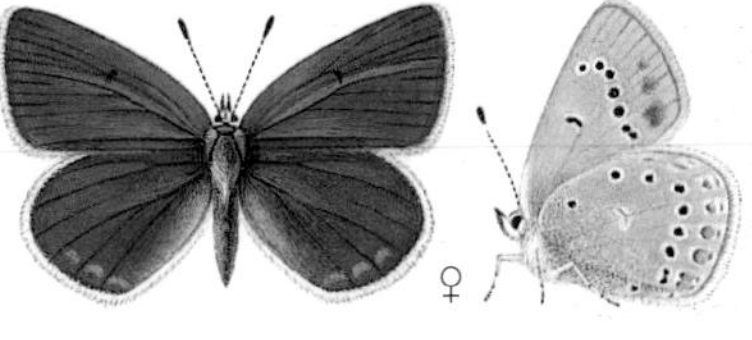

Blue Argus

Silvery Argus

Alpine Blue

Pontic Blue

Glandon Blue *Agriades glandon*

RANGE S Spain (Sierra Nevada), Pyrenees, Alps of C Europe, N Fennoscandia, Arctic Asia, Siberia, Arctic Urals, Arctic N America.

A. glandon glandon de Prunner 1798 TL: W Alps.
syn: *orbitulus* Esper 1800 (invalid homonym).

DISTRIBUTION France: Pyrenees; Basses Alpes. Alps of S and E Switzerland, Italy, Germany and Austria. 1800-2700m. **VARIATION** Male ups silvery-blue often diffuse towards margin; upf and uph discoidal spots sometimes small, rarely absent; uns black pupils in white spots sometimes reduced to minute points, occasionally, white spots absent except on costa (*albocellatus* Osthelder); unh orange spots variable, rarely absent: both sexes, ups discoidal spots sometimes ringed white, especially in female. **FLIGHT-PERIOD** Univoltine. Early July/Late August. **HABITAT** Rocky ground with short grass, often sparsely vegetated rocky outcrops. Colonies often extremely small, sometimes apparently quite isolated. Often sympatric with *A. orbitulus* at higher altitudes. **LIFE-HISTORY** LHP *Vitaliana primuliflora* [=*Androsace vitaliana*] or *Androsace obtusifolia* on acidic substrates; *A. chamaejasme* on acidic or calcareous substrates. Ova laid on various plant parts, including dead leaves. Larvae feed on flowers, developing seeds and leaves. Hibernates as a small larva. Larvae not attended by ants. **BEHAVIOUR** Males may wander a considerable distant from breeding ground to drink from damp patches. Flight is fast and low. Uses the cover of small stones to shelter from strong winds.

A. glandon zullichi Hemming 1933 TL: Sierra Nevada.
syn: *nevadensis* Zullich 1928 (invalid homonym).

DISTRIBUTION S Spain: confined to Sierra Nevada, Granada. 2500-3000m. **DESCRIPTION** Resembles nominate form: male ups silvery pale blue suffusion variable, sometimes extending to outer margin. **FLIGHT-PERIOD** Univoltine. Late June/August. **HABITAT** Shallow depressions or small gullies on otherwise exposed, wind-swept and barren greyish-brown soils supporting sparse, low-growing, vegetation dominated by LHP. Colonies mostly widely dispersed and usually extremely small. **LIFE-HISTORY AND BEHAVIOUR** LHP *Vitaliana primuliflora* [=*Androsace vitaliana*]. Development as for nominate form. Even in close proximity to fallen snow and at low air temperatures (diurnal range, +5°C to -10°C), hibernated larvae begin feeding in early spring – activity resulting, apparently, from rapid solar heating of LHP and surrounding soil/rocks. Pupal colouring slightly variable, generally darker than that of nominate from.

A. glandon aquilo Boisduval 1832 TL: North Cape.

DISTRIBUTION Norway: 66°N to North Cape: Nordland; Troms; Finnmark. Sweden: Lycksele Lappmark; Torne Lappmark (Björkliden; Jieprenjokk). NW Finland: Kilpisjärvi. 50-900m. **DESCRIPTION** Resembles nominate form: smaller; male ups pale silvery or greyish-blue; marginal borders narrow; unh white marginal spots confluent, generally lacking ocelli: female upf pale submarginal spots elongate, sometimes with an incomplete series of similar pd markings. **FLIGHT-PERIOD** Univoltine. Late June/early August, according to season. **HABITAT** Short, grass turf associated with slate or shale rocks, especially eroded ledges with south-eastern exposure: also relating barren, rocky places, including consolidated areas of steep, screes where vegetation can establish itself. **LIFE-HISTORY** LHP *Saxifraga aizoides*; *S. oppositifolia*. Ova laid on underside of leaves. On *S. aizoides*, small larvae feed on flower-buds, but principally on leaves by excavating soft tissue between cuticles. Reported use of *Astragalus alpinus* requires confirmation: butterfly is known to occur in habitats devoid of this plant, which is also rejected by captive larvae. Hibernates as a small larva. **BEHAVIOUR** Flies very fast and low, often resting on or between stones. Large numbers may sometimes congregate on flat rocks.

Chelmos Blue *Agrodiaetus iphigenia*

RANGE S Greece, Turkey, Transcaucasus.

A. iphigenia nonacriensis Brown 1977 TL: Mt. Chelmos, Greece.

DISTRIBUTION Scarce and local. Confined to Mt. Chelmos and environs. 1100-1750m. **DESCRIPTION** Female may be readily distinguished from other sympatric *Agrodiaetus* by its dark chocolate brown ups; distinctive white fringes; greyish uns gc; small diffuse, orange-brown submarginal spots in s1a-4: other markings in normal pattern. **FLIGHT-PERIOD** Univoltine. Mid June/late July, according to season and altitude. **HABITAT** Mostly dry, open treeless ground, usually with low scrub; always on a calcareous substrate, but not exclusively limestone. Some colonies occur in small clearings amongst tall scrub, or, more rarely, woodland. **LIFE-HISTORY** LHP *Onobrychis alba*. Hibernates as small larvae on underside of stones. Larvae attended by *Lasius alienus*. **BEHAVIOUR** Males occasionally wander considerable distances to visit damp ground. Females rarely leave the confines of their breeding ground. Both sexes bask with partially open wings early morning and late afternoon. Males (?)invariably feed with closed wings. **CONSERVATION** Intensive grazing of habitat appears to pose a significant threat. It is evident that much of the LHP owes its survival to the protective, browse-deterring, spiny plants, such as *Astragalus parnassi*, amongst which it is mostly to be found.

Damon Blue *Agrodiaetus damon*

RANGE Spain, S, C and E Europe, Turkey, S and C Urals, Mongolia, Altai.

A. damon Denis and Schiffermüeller 1775 TL: Vienna.

DISTRIBUTION Sporadic, locally common. N and E Spain: provinces of Cuenca; Teruel; Palencia; Santander; Burgos; Huesca; Lérida; Gerona; Barcelona. France: C Pyrenees; Cevennes; Haute-Savoie; Jura Mts. N and central peninsular Italy. Switzerland. S Germany. Czech Republic. Slovakia. Hungary. S Poland. Estonia. SE Latvia (a single known colony). S Croatia. Bosnia-Herzegovina. SW Serbia. Republic of Macedonia. NW Greece (Grammos massif to Mt. Timphristos). 1000-2100m. **VARIATION** In Estonia and (?)Latvia, *ultramarina* Schawerda: large; male ups deeper blue; wing veins prominent. In Montes Universales (Teruel, Spain), *noguerae* de Sagarra: resembles nominate form closely. **FLIGHT-PERIOD** Univoltine. Mid July/August. **HABITAT** At lower altitudes, dry scrub or open

GLANDON BLUE

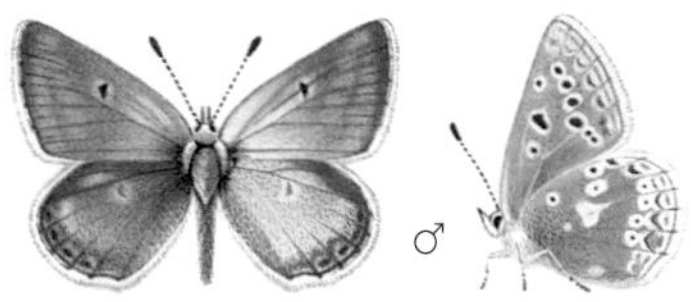
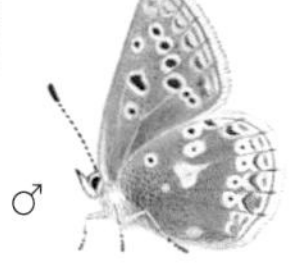

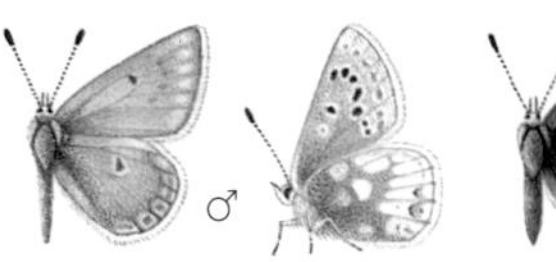

Upf and uph discoidal spot usually white-winged

Unh orange spot in s2 usually prominent

A. g. aquilo
(Arctic Fennoscandia)

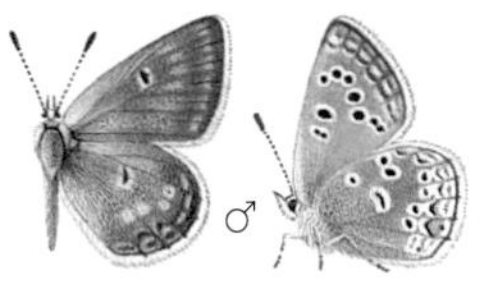

A. g. glandon

♀ brown with faint pale submarginal markings, discoidal spots often ringed white

A. g. zullichi
(S Spain)

CHELMOS BLUE

White fringes conspicuous

(Mt Chelmos, S Greece)

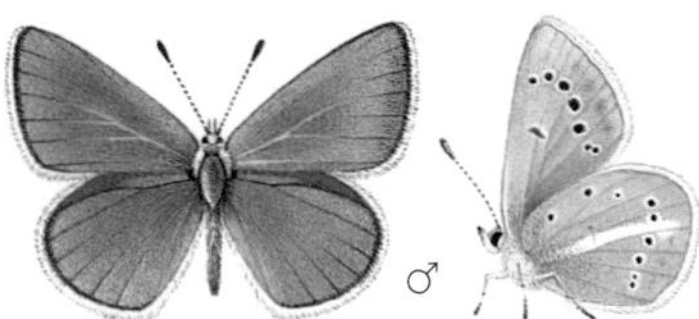

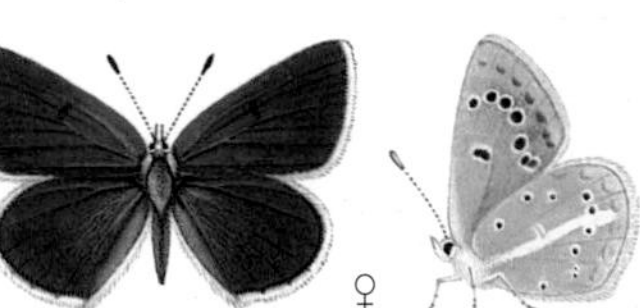

DAMON BLUE

Ups dark marginal wide, diffuse: veins prominent

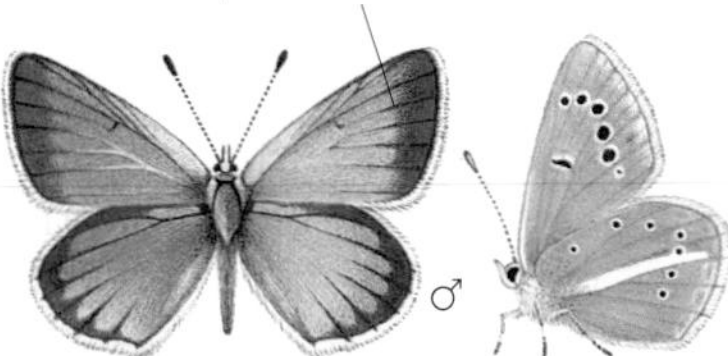

woodland: at highest altitudes, sheltered gullies/hollows on open grassy slopes. **LIFE-HISTORY** LHPs *Onobrychis* spp., including *O. montana*; *O. alba*. Hibernated larvae feed in characteristic and systematic manner on upper cuticle of leaflets by removing soft tissue between veins. Larvae attended by *Lasius niger*; *L. alienus*; *Formica pratensis*. Hibernates as an ovum or first instar larva in C Europe; as second instar larva on Mt. Tymphristos, Greece (2000m).

Glandon Blue

Chelmos Blue

Damon Blue

Gavarnie Blue *Agriades pyrenaicus*

RANGE N Spain (Picos de Europa and Pyrenees), France (Pyrenees), Balkans, Greece, Turkey, Transcaucasus.

A. pyrenaicus pyrenaicus Boisduval 1840 TL: Pyrenees.

DISTRIBUTION Spain: Gerona (La Molina). France. Hautes-Pyrénées: Gavarnie, Cauterets, Col du Tourmalet. 1800-2200m.

VARIATION Male ups submarginal white markings subject to slight individual variation, sometimes transitional to *A. p. asturiensis* (below).

FLIGHT-PERIOD Univoltine. June/July.

HABITAT At lower altitudes, short turf on well consolidated ground: at higher level, south-facing, barren outcrops of limestone rocks or craggy cliff-faces supporting often very isolated LHP specimens on small ledges or in crevices.

LIFE-HISTORY LHP *Androsace villosa*. Hibernated larvae feed on developing leaves and flowers. Larvae not attended by ants.

A. pyrenaicus asturiensis Oberthür 1910 TL: Picos de Europa.

DISTRIBUTION N Spain: Picos de Europa. 1550-2100. Locally common in widely scattered colonies.

DESCRIPTION Resembles nominate form. Male ups brighter, more silvery-blue; submarginal obscure white markings extending to fw in a continuous narrow band broken by veins: female ups slightly paler brown, with obscure whitish striae submarginal white markings disrupted, often obscure; dark discoidal spots usually ringed white.

FLIGHT-PERIOD Univoltine. Mid June/early August.

HABITAT AND LIFE-HISTORY As for nominate form.

A. pyrenaicus dardanus Freyer 1844 TL: Turkey [(?) Balkans].

DISTRIBUTION Bosnia-Herzegovina: Vran Pl.; Cvrsnica. SW Serbia (Montenegro): Mt. Durmitor. Republic of Macedonia: Sar Pl.; Jakupica Pl. Bulgaria: Mt. Alibotus. N Greece: Mt. Orvilos (the southernmost extension of Alibotus massif). 1500-2300m.

DESCRIPTION Similar to nominate form. Smaller.

FLIGHT-PERIOD Univoltine. June/July.

HABITAT Exposed, expansive, grassy slopes on dry calcareous soils.

LIFE-HISTORY LHP *Androsace villosa*. Hibernated larvae feed on developing leaves and flowers.

Mazarine Blue *Cyaniris semiargus*

RANGE Morocco, Europe, Turkey, Middle East, C Asia, N China, Korea.

C. semiargus semiargus Rottemburgh 1775 TL: Saxony, Germany.

syn: *acis* Denis and Schiffermüller 1775.

DISTRIBUTION Morocco: Anti-Atlas; High Atlas 2300-2700m; Middle Atlas 1600m. N Portugal. N and E Spain: Cantabrian Mts.; Pyrenees. S and C Spain: S. de Alfacar; Sierra Nevada; S. de Segura; S. de Espuña; Montes Universales; S. de Guadarrama; S. de la Demanda; province of Soria (Abejar). Pyrenees to N Fennoscandia (rare and local north of Arctic Circle), N Greece and European Turkey. Absent from Peloponnesos and Mediterranean islands except Sicily. Extinct in Britain. 0-2200m.

VARIATION In Morocco, and occasionally in S Spain, female ups basal areas extensively blue. In NW Greece, female unh often with brown or dark grey spot in anal angle, sometimes replaced by orange. In C Greece, Mt. Timphristos and Mt. Parnassos, nominate form replaced by *parnassia* Staudinger: small; male ups brighter blue; black marginal borders narrower, better defined; unh rarely with orange spot in anal angle: female uph occasionally with one or two orange spots in anal angle, unh orange spotting in anal angle more frequent. A similar form has been reported from Mt. Parnis and Athens basin.

FLIGHT-PERIOD Generally univoltine (NW Africa and Europe), early May/early August according to altitude and locality: reportedly bivoltine or trivoltine in Switzerland, May/October.

HABITAT Grassy, flowery, often damp places; meadows; hayfields; scrub or woodland clearings.

LIFE-HISTORY LHP *Trifolium pratense*. Confirmation of natural use of other, frequently quoted Fabaceae appears to be lacking: however, in C Greece, opportunistic use of *T. physodes*, growing amongst an abundance of *T. pratense* has been recorded. Ova laid on flowers, upon which larvae feed prior to hibernation. Hibernated larvae feed on developing leaves. Striking similarity of colour/colour-pattern of larva and various plants parts upon which it feeds, rests and hibernates, suggests a close adaptation to *T. pratense*. Larvae attended by *Lasius* sp.

C. semiargus helena Staudinger 1862 TL: Mt. Taygetos, S Greece.

DISTRIBUTION Greece. Restricted to the Peloponnesos: Mt. Panakhaikon; Mt. Chelmos; Mt. Menalon; Mt. Oligirtos; Mt. Taygetos. 650-1800m.

VARIATION Submarginal orange markings variable, especially in female. In respect to development of female ups blue suffusion and orange markings, gradation of *C. semiargus* forms in Europe (especially Greece), Turkey and Middle East, is suggestive of a cline: within this range, male genitalia appear to be sensibly constant, chromosome numbers identical.

FLIGHT-PERIOD Univoltine. Late April/late June according to altitude.

HABITAT Grassy, flowery, often damp places, usually amongst open scrub and scattered trees: LHP usually abundant.

LIFE-HISTORY LHP *Trifolium physodes*. Ova laid amongst flowers. Before hibernation in third instar, larvae feed entirely within the swollen calyces of the developing flowers. Larvae hibernate on underside of stones near LHP and/or ants'nests. Hibernated larvae feed on developing leaves. Usually pupates at the entrance to ant galleries in close proximity to LHPs. Larvae/pupae attended by *Camponotus vagus*; *C. aethiops*. Captive larvae accept many *Trifolium* species: in nature, where density of larvae may be very high, opportunistic use of isolated plants of *T. purpureum*, growing in a carpet of *T. physodes*, has been observed.

BEHAVIOUR In calm, warm conditions, adults often assemble in large numbers on grass stems to bask in late afternoon sun.

GAVARNIE BLUE

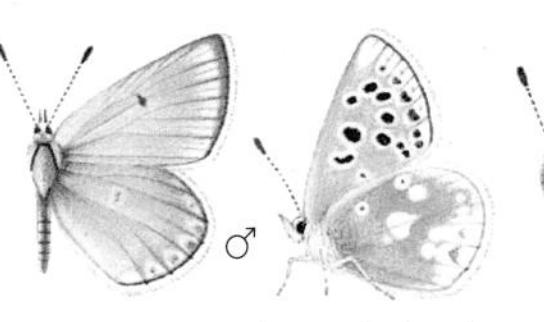

A. p. asturiensis
(N Spain)

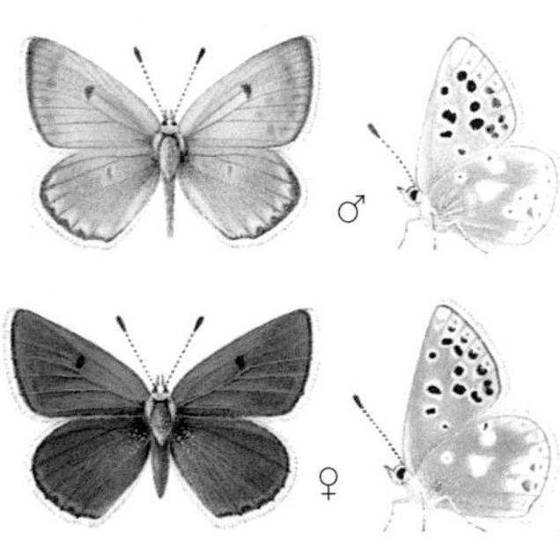

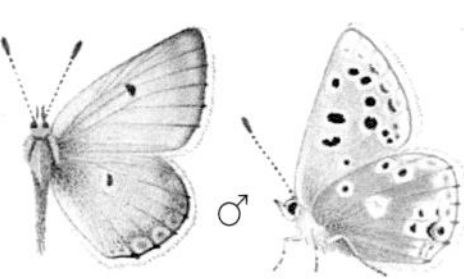

A. p. pyrenaicus

♀ grey-brown, discoidal spot sometimes large and diffuse or faintly ringed white, hw sometimes with faint white marginal lunules

A. p. dardanus
(Balkans)

MAZARINE BLUE

C. s. semiargus

C. s. parnassia
(C Greece)

Gavarnie Blue Mazarine Blue

C. s. helena
(Peloponnesos)

Furry Blue *Agrodiaetus dolus*

RANGE SW Europe, Italy.

A. dolus dolus Hübner 1823 TL: Maritime Alps (Verity 1943).

DISTRIBUTION Spain: provinces of Santander; Navarra; Burgos; Alava; Longono; Huesca; Lérida; Gerona; Barcelona. S France: Bouches-du-Rhône; Vacluse; Drôme; Var; Alpes-de-Haute-Provence; Alpes-Maritimes. NW Italy: Maritime Alps: very local. 600-1500m.

DESCRIPTION AND VARIATION Male upf brown basal androconial patch with slightly roughened appearance. Unh white stripe absent or vestigial in both sexes. In Catalonia, *fulgens* de Sagarra: resembles nominate form closely: slightly larger; male uns gc somewhat greyer: female ups darker brown. Chromosome number, 123-125: cf. *A. ainsea*, CN=108.

FLIGHT-PERIOD Univoltine. Mid July/August.

HABITAT Flowery, grassy places amongst scrub; untended margins of cultivated ground.

LIFE-HISTORY LHP *Onobrychis viciifolia*. Ova laid on flowers. Hibernates as a small larva.

A. dolus vittatus Oberthür 1892 TL: Lozère, France.

DISTRIBUTION S France: Aveyron; Hérault; Gard; Lozère. 500-1000m.

DESCRIPTION Male ups gc whitish or pale bluish grey, basal area with bluish suffusion; brownish veins well defined: female ups appreciably darker brown than nominate form.

FLIGHT-PERIOD, HABITAT AND LIFE-HISTORY As for nominate form.

A. dolus virgilius Oberthür 1910 TL: Sulmona, Abruzzi.

DISTRIBUTION Peninsular Italy: from Emilia-Romagna (Bologna) to Calabria (Monte Pollino) in widely dispersed colonies. 600-1100m.

DESCRIPTION Male ups gc white, narrow marginal border, internally somewhat diffused, especially along veins; upf with pale blue basal suffusion, brown androconial patch rough: female ups darker brown than nominate form.

FLIGHT-PERIOD, HABITAT AND LIFE-HISTORY As for nominate form.

Forster's Furry Blue *Agrodiaetus ainsae*

RANGE N Spain.

A. ainsae Forster 1961 TL: Ainsa, N Spain.

DISTRIBUTION N Spain: Burgos (Villasur; Pto. de Paramo de Masa; Villanueva de Argaño; Peñahorada; Monasterio de Rodilla; Sotopalacios; Briviesca; Monasterio de Fresdelva); Alava (S. de Urbasa); Huesca (Ainsa; S. de la Peña; Jaca). Locally common. 950-1200m.

VARIATION Populations in the province of Burgos (*pseudovirgilius* de Lesse) differ slightly, in wing markings and size, from nominate form in Huesca: chromosome numbers identical (CN=108) (cf. *A. dolus*).

FLIGHT-PERIOD Univoltine. July/August.

HABITAT Dry, grassy, bushy places; clearings in light deciduous or pine woodland.

LIFE-HISTORY LHP *Onobrychis* (?)*viciifolia*.

Escher's Blue *Agrodiaetus escheri*

RANGE Morocco, Europe.

A. escheri escheri Hübner 1823 TL: Var, S France (Verity 1943) syn: *agestor* Godart 1824.

DISTRIBUTION Spain: Sierra Nevada to Cantabrian Mts. and Pyrenees. Sporadic, locally common. France (Massif Central; Bouche du Rhône; Basses Alps). Switzerland (Rhône Valley; Simplon; Graubunden). N Italy (Ortler Alps; Dolomites). Records for N Portugal require confirmation. 500-2000m.

DESCRIPTION Male ups black borders very narrow; uph marginal border vaguely undulate: female ups submarginal orange spots variable, ranging from 2 or 3 diffuse spots in anal angle hw, to a continuous band hw and fw: both sexes, unf without cell-spot; all markings bold (cf. *Polyommatus icarus*).

FLIGHT-PERIOD Univoltine. Late May/August according to locality and altitude.

HABITAT Flowery, rocky places.

LIFE-HISTORY LHPs: principally, *Astragalus monspessulanus*; also, *A. sempervirens*; *A. exscapus*; *A. incanus*. Ova laid on underside of leaves. Hibernates as a small larva. Hibernated larvae feed below plant-crown on developing leaves. Larvae attended by *Myrmica specioides*; *Formica cinerea*.

A. escheri splendens Stefanelli 1904 TL: Florence.

DISTRIBUTION N Italy: Liguria; Tuscany; Emilia-Romagna to Campania: very sporadic. 300-1000m.

DESCRIPTION AND VARIATION Generally smaller; male ups paler blue; black borders slightly wider; uns gc tending to white; uns markings slightly reduced: female ups submarginal spots well developed. Individual specimens closely resembling or transitional to nominate form reputedly not uncommon.

FLIGHT-PERIOD Univoltine. Early June/July.

HABITAT Flowery rocky places, usually amongst low scrub.

A. escheri dalmaticus Speyer 1882 TL: Dalmatia.

syn: *olympena* Verity 1936.

DISTRIBUTION Slovenia. SW Croatia. S Bosnia-Herzegovina. SW Serbia. Republic of Macedonia. Bulgaria. Albania. Greece. Reports from Taygetos Mts. require confirmation. 500-1500m.

DESCRIPTION Male ups silvery-blue sometimes with greenish reflections; marginal black borders 1-2mm (cf. nominate form): female ups resembles nominate form: uns markings prominent in both sexes.

FLIGHT-PERIOD Univoltine. Mid May/late June.

HABITAT Dry, flowery, often rocky places amongst sparse vegetation; damp woodland clearings above 1000m.

LIFE-HISTORY LHPs principally *Astragalus monspessulanus*; also *A. spuneri*. Ova laid on underside of leaves. Hibernates as a larva. Hibernated larvae feed on developing leaves below plant-crown. Larvae attended by *Plagiolepis* sp.

A. escheri ahmar Le Cerf 1932 TL: Djebel Ahmar, Morocco.

DISTRIBUTION Morocco: Anti-Atlas (Dj. Ahmar; no recent reports from Tizi-n-Tiskine); Middle Atlas (Dj. Bou-Iblane). 1750-2000m. Very local – rarely reported.

DESCRIPTION Resembles nominate form. Smaller; male ups dull blue; female ups submarginal spots yellow. Uns markings less prominent in both sexes.

FLIGHT-PERIOD Univoltine. June.

HABITAT Flowery slopes.

FURRY BLUE

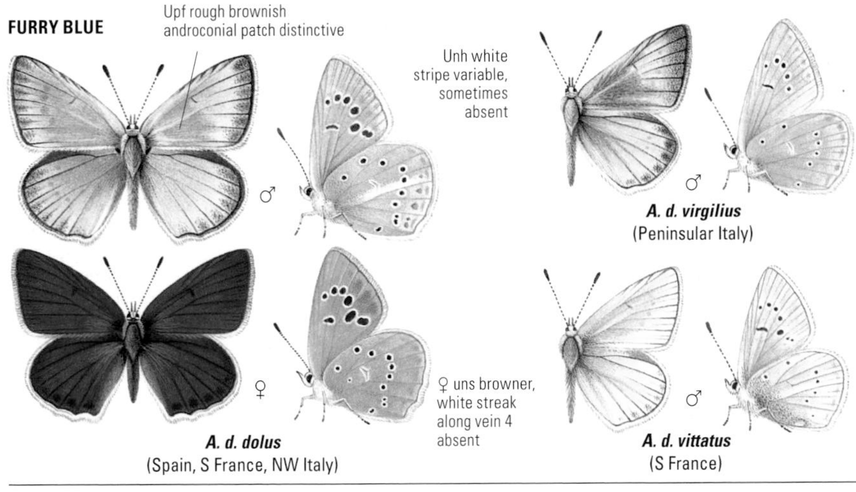

FORSTER'S FURRY BLUE

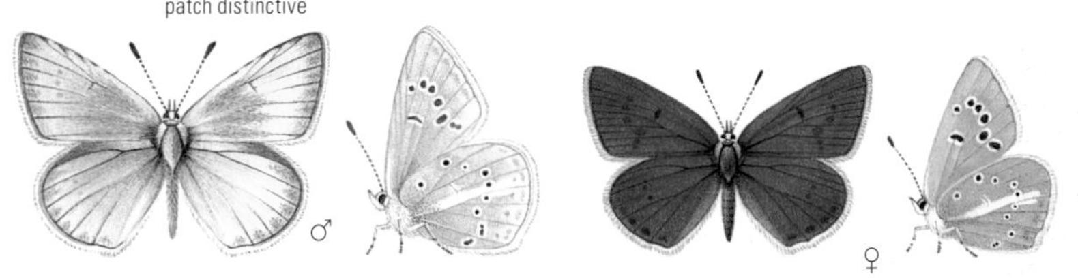

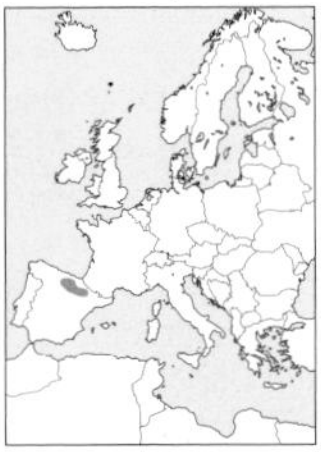

ESCHER'S BLUE

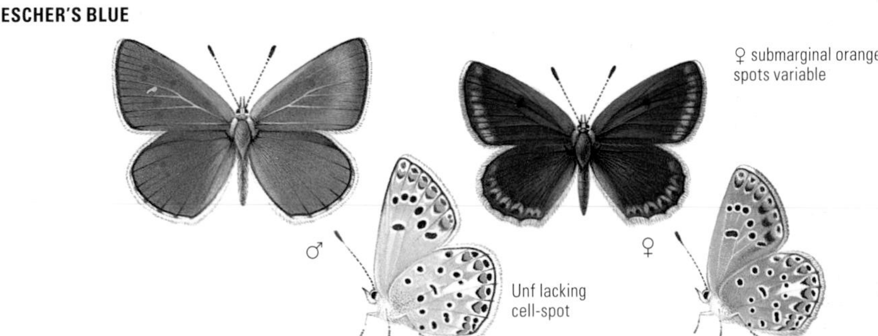

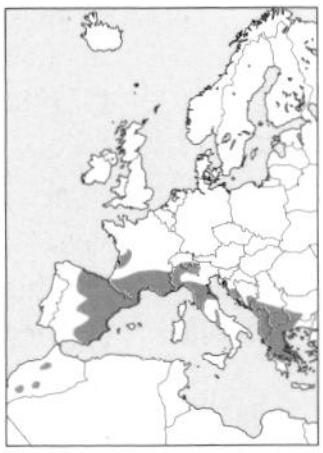

Ups marginal border wide, distinctive

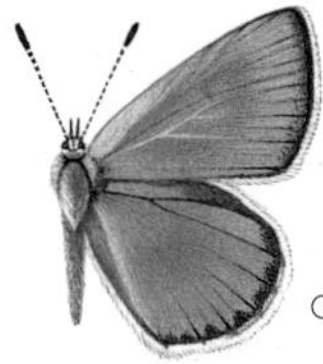

♂

A. e. dalmaticus
(SE Europe)

Furry Blue

Forster's Furry Blue

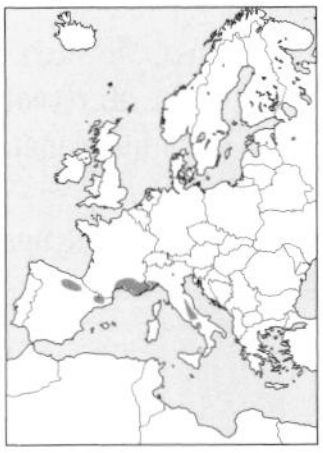

Escher's Blue

Amanda's Blue *Agrodiaetus amanda*

RANGE N Africa, Spain, Europe, Turkey, W Asia Iran.
A. amanda amanda Schneider 1792 TL: S Sweden.
syn: *icarius* Esper (after 1792)
DISTRIBUTION Spain (Sierra Nevada; Montes Universales; S. de la Demanda; Cantabrian Mts.; Pyrenees) through S France, Italy, C Switzerland and E Germany to S Fennoscandia, Balkans, Greece and European Turkey. Largely absent from coastal districts of Italy: absent from Mediterranean islands except NE Sicily and Lesbos. 100-2000m.
VARIATION Male ups fuscous borders variable in width. In Scandinavia, female ups often suffused blue (*isias* Frühstorfer).
FLIGHT-PERIOD Univoltine. Late May/July according to locality.
HABITAT Warm grassy, often damp places containing an abundance of LHP, usually associated with bushes or light woodland; sheltered gullies above tree-line.
LIFE-HISTORY LHPs *Vicia* spp., including *V. c. cracca*; *V. c. stenofolia*; *V. villosa*; *V. onobrychioides*; *V. terasperma*; *V. incana*; *V. sibthorpii*; *V. cassubica*. Ova laid on both surfaces of leaves. Hibernates as a small larva amongst leaf-litter at base of LHP. Hibernated larvae feed on developing leaves. In NW Greece, larvae attended by *Tapinoma simrothi*; *Lasius alienus*: elsewhere, *L. niger*; *Myrmica specioides*; *Formica cinerea*.
A. amanda abdelaziz Blachier 1908 TL: Atlas Mts., Morocco.
DISTRIBUTION Morocco: High Atlas (Oukaïmeden; Dj. Ahmar). Middle Atlas (Azrou). Rif Mts. (Dj. Lakraa; Ketama). Algeria: Djurdjura Mts. 1300-2600m.
DESCRIPTION Male ups paler silvery-blue; uns markings reduced; unh orange spots in anal angle vestigial or absent: female ups brown, sometimes with a few, blue basal scales; yellowish-orange submarginal spots well developed, sometimes forming continuous band on hw and fw; upf sometimes with faint orange, somewhat striated suffusion.
VARIATION Female ups sometimes extensively suffused blue (*cyanea* Aigner): proportion of brown to blue females seasonally variable, suggesting influence of climatic factors (temperature/humidity) on form: possibly, cooler and/or damper conditions in larval/pupal development favour the blue form (cf. *isias* in Scandinavia).
FLIGHT-PERIOD Univoltine. Late May/mid July.
HABITAT Flowery, grassy places, especially alpine meadows.
LIFE-HISTORY LHPs *Vicia ononbychioides*; *V. atlantica*.

Chapman's Blue *Agrodiaetus thersites*

RANGE Morocco, S Europe, Turkey, Middle East, Iran, Caucasus, S Urals, Tian Shan.
A. thersites Cantener 1834 TL: Vosges, NE France.
DISTRIBUTION Morocco: Middle Atlas 1500-2000m. S Portugal. Spain. France (Pyrenees), north-eastwards to 51°N in Germany. E and SE Europe. Absent from Mediterranean islands except Sicily, Samos, Kos and Rhodes. European Turkey. 0-1500m.
DESCRIPTION AND VARIATION Male upf androconial patch conspicuous at oblique angles. Spring brood: both sexes, unh gc grey: female ups blue suffusion often extending to outer margins. Summer brood: both sexes unh sandy-brown; female ups brown; unf yellowish-grey. Both sexes, unf without cell-spot (cf. *Polyommatus icarus*).
FLIGHT-PERIOD Bivoltine. April/June and June/August: emergence of summer brood possibly depending on weather conditions (see below).
HABITAT Warm dry, rocky, bushy places; grassy clearings in scrubland; meadows; areas of neglected cultivation.
LIFE-HISTORY LHPs *Onobrychis caput-galli*; *O. viciifolia*; *O. peduncularis* (Morocco). Ova laid on leaves. Larva feeds on leaf cuticles, leaving major veins intact. In drier habitats where *O. caput-galli*, an annual, is the only *Onobrychis* sp. available, aestivation as an ovum or undeveloped larva is possibly required pending germination of LHP seeds arising from spring flowering. In Greece, females of first brood (April) have been observed to oviposit freely on *O. caput-galli*, whilst, in the same habitat, ova of the second brood (June) are laid on dried grass stems, in total absence of LHPs – except the distinctive seeds of *O. caput-galli*. In absence of alternative LHPs, observed variance in flight-time of summer brood may relate to absence of rain required for seed germination. Hibernates as small larva. Larvae attended by *Lasius alienus*; *Myrmica scabrinodis*; *Tapinoma erraticum*.

Anomalous Blue *Agrodiaetus admetus*

RANGE Central E and SE Europe, Turkey.
A. admetus Esper 1785 TL: Hungary.
DISTRIBUTION Hungary. Croatia. W Bosnia-Herzegovina. SW Serbia. W Republic of Macedonia. Albania. Bulgaria. Greece. European Turkey. Sporadic, locally common. 50-1500m.
DESCRIPTION Male unh white stripe poorly developed; female uns marginal and submarginal markings prominent, white chevron along v4 often reduced or absent.
FLIGHT-PERIOD Univoltine. Mid June/July.
HABITAT Hot dry, grassy, flowery scrubland.
LIFE-HISTORY LHPs *Onobrychis viciifolia*; *O. caput-galli*. Oviposition observed on flowers of both plant species, by same female in same habitat. Larvae attended by *Camponotus gestroi*; *Crematogaster sordidula*; *C. sordidula* var. *mayri*. Hibernates under stones as a small larva.

Amanda's Blue

Chapman's Blue

AMANDA'S BLUE

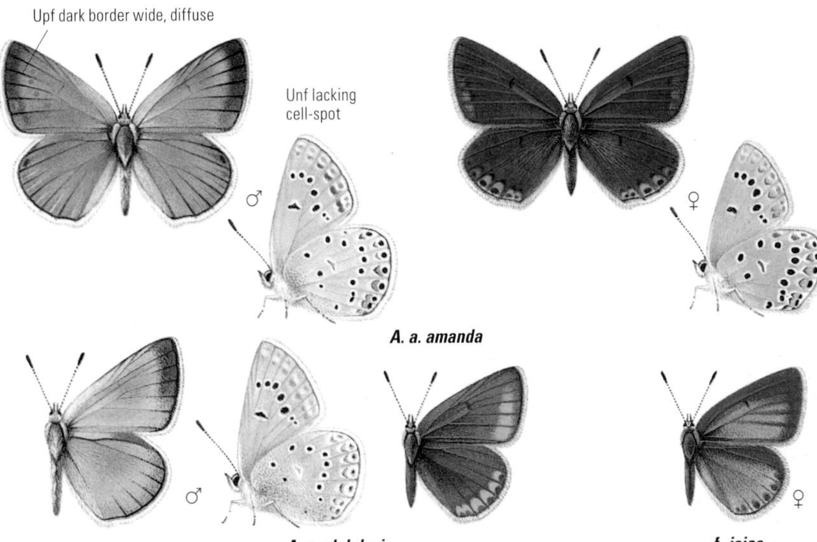

A. a. abdelaziz
(Morocco)

f. *isias*
(Scandinavia)

CHAPMAN'S BLUE

Upf androconial patch distinctive

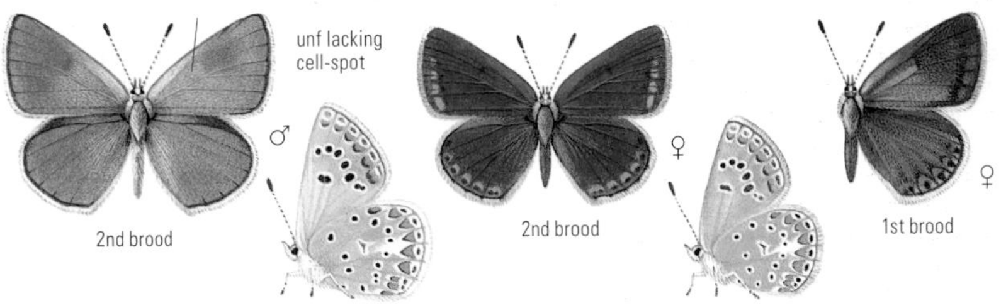

ANOMALOUS BLUE

Anomalous Blue

Oberthür's Anomalous Blue *Agrodiaetus fabressei*

RANGE Spain.

A. fabressei Oberthür 1910 TL: Albarracin, C Spain.

DISTRIBUTION N and E Spain: provinces of Teruel (S. de Albarracin), Cuenca (Serrania de Cuenca), Soria (Abejar) and Burgos (Peñahorada; Sotopalacios). 900-1500m.

DESCRIPTION Male unh without white stripe along v4: female unh small white chevron sometimes present on v4. Both sexes: uns marginal and submarginal markings vestigial or absent.

FLIGHT-PERIOD Univoltine. Late June/August.

HABITAT Rocky gullies with scrub; dry grassy slopes.

LIFE-HISTORY LHP *Onobrychis viciifolia*; Ova laid on flowers. Hibernates as a small larva. Larvae attended by ants.

Agenjo's Anomalous Blue *Agrodiaetus agenjoi*

RANGE NE Spain.

A. agenjoi Forster 1965 TL: Spain (Catalonia).

DISTRIBUTION NE Spain: provinces of Gerona, Barcelona and Lérida. 700-1500m.

DESCRIPTION Resembles *A. fabressei* closely. Male ups dark brown; unh without white stripe along v4.

FLIGHT-PERIOD Univoltine. July/August.

HABITAT As for *A. fabressei*.

NOTE Taxonomic status uncertain: perhaps better regarded a local variant of *A. fabressei*.

Piedmont Anomalous Blue *Agrodiaetus humedasae*

RANGE N Italy.

A. humedasae Toso and Balleto 1979 TL: Cogne, N Italy.

DISTRIBUTION NW Italy: known only from Valle d'Aosta (Cogne Valley). 800-950m.

DESCRIPTION Male uns gc pale creamy-brown, somewhat darker than *A. violetae* (below); unh without white stripe.

FLIGHT-PERIOD Univoltine. Mid July/August.

HABITAT Flowery slopes amongst scrub and small trees.

LIFE-HISTORY LHP *Onobrychis viciifolia*. Ova laid on flowers, upon which larvae feed. Hibernates as a small larva. Hibernated larvae attended by ants.

CONSERVATION Known habitat very restricted and in close proximity to human habitation and areas of cultivation.

Andalusian Anomalous Blue *Agrodiaetus violetae*

RANGE S Spain.

A. violetae Gomez Bustillo and Borrego 1979 TL: Sierra de Almijara, Andalusia.

DISTRIBUTION S Spain: Málaga (S. de Tejeda); Granada (S. de Almijara; S. de La Losa); Jaen (S. de Segura; S. de Cazorla); Albacete (S. de Alcaraz). 1200-1750m.

DESCRIPTION Resembles *A. ripartii* closely. Male uns gc pale creamy-brown (less grey than *A. ripartii*); unh white stripe prominent.

FLIGHT-PERIOD Univoltine. Late June/early August.

HABITAT Grassy, flowery places.

LIFE-HISTORY LHPs *Onobrychis viciifolia*; *O. peduncularis*. Ova laid on flowers, upon which larvae feed. Hibernates as a small larva. Hibernated larvae attended by *Camponotus piceus*.

NOTE Taxonomic status uncertain: possibly conspecific with *A. ripartii*.

Oberthür's Anomalous Blue

Agenjo's Anomalous Blue

Piedmont Anomalous Blue

Andalusian Anomalous Blue

OBERTHÜR'S ANOMALOUS BLUE

(N and E Spain)

♀ uns white stripe obscure

AGENJO'S ANOMALOUS BLUE

Restricted to NE Spain

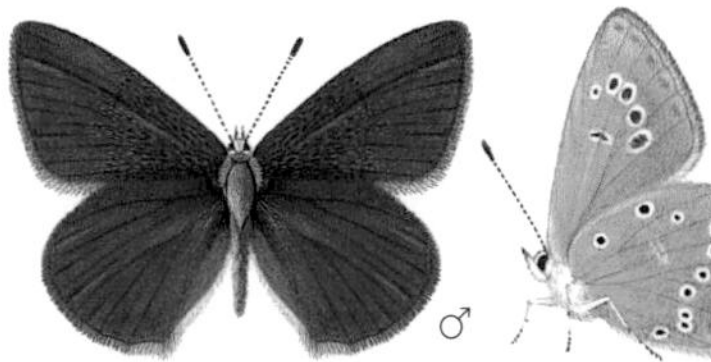

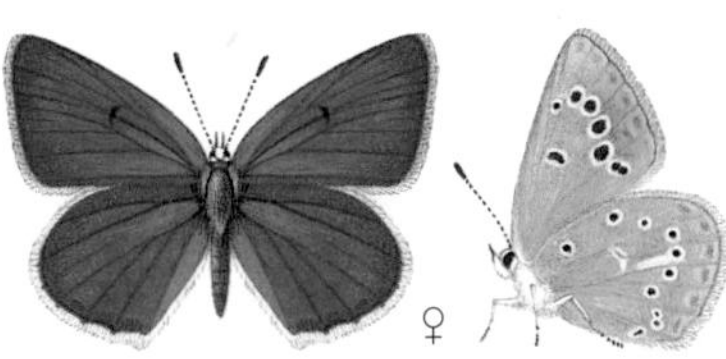

Unh white stripe, short, often absent

PIEDMONT ANOMALOUS BLUE

Restricted to NW Italy

Unh white stripe lacking

ANDALUSIAN ANOMALOUS BLUE

Restricted to S Spain

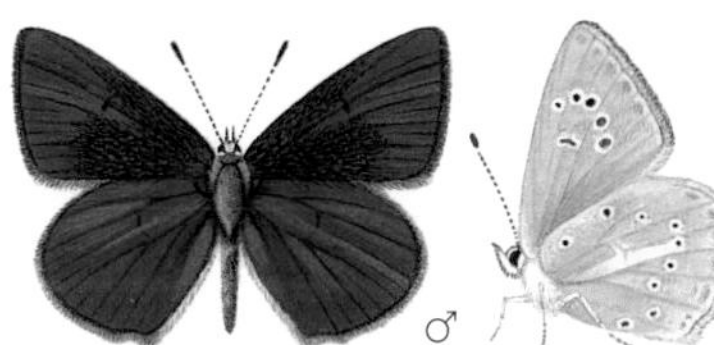

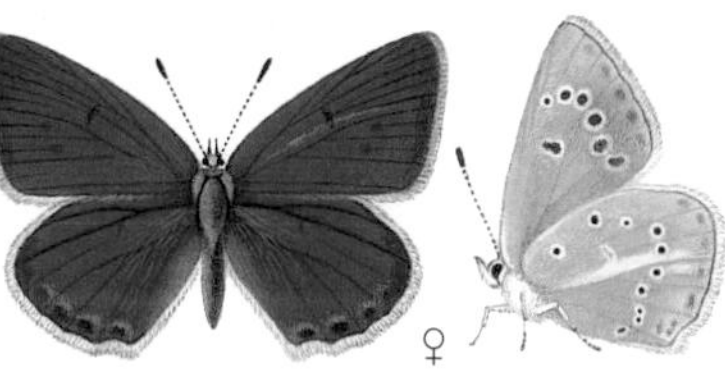

Grecian Anomalous Blue *Agrodiaetus aroaniensis*

RANGE Greece.

A. aroaniensis Brown 1976 TL: Mt. Chelmos, Greece.

DISTRIBUTION Greece: Phalakron massif; Vernon Mts.; Smolikas massif; Mt. Timphristos; Parnassos massif; Panakhaikon Mts.; Chelmos massif; Menalon Mts; Taygetos Mts. Widespread but generally very local. 800-1550m.

DESCRIPTION Uns gc distinctive, uniform yellowish-grey; unh lacking white stripe on v4.

FLIGHT-PERIOD Univoltine. July/early August.

HABITAT Dry bushy or rocky places; sometimes in light woodland.

LIFE-HISTORY LHP *Onobrychis arenaria*. Ova laid on flowers upon which larvae feed. Larvae attended by *Camponotus gestroi*; *Crematogaster sordidula* var. *mayri*. Hibernates as a small larva.

Ripart's Anomalous Blue *Agrodiaetus ripartii*

RANGE Spain, S and SE Europe, Poland, Turkey, S Ural, S Siberia, Tian Shan, Altai.

A. ripartii Freyer 1830 TL: Spain.

DISTRIBUTION N and E Spain: Cuenca; Teruel (Montes Universales); Segovia; Logrono; Burgos (Peñahorada; Sotopalacios); Huesca (S. de la Peña; Jaca; Ainsa; Toila). France: Var; Alpes-Maritimes; Vacluse; Alpes-de-Haute-Provençe; Ardèche; Drôme; Hautes-Alpes. NW Italy: Maritimes Alps: very local. S Poland. Republic of Macedonia. Bulgaria. Albania. Greece. European Turkey. 50-1800m.

DESCRIPTION Unh white stripe along v4 prominent.

VARIATION In Greece, *pelopi* Brown: unh white stripe often narrower, less conspicuous.

FLIGHT-PERIOD Univoltine. Late June/early August.

HABITAT Dry bushy places, often grassy; sometimes in light woodland.

LIFE-HISTORY LHPs *Onobrychis viciifolia*; *O. arenaria*; *O. saxatilis*; *O. alba*; *O. montana*. Ova laid on flowers upon which larvae feed. In Greece, larvae attended by *Crematogaster sordidula*; *C. sordidula* var. *mayri*; *Camponotus gestroi*; *Lasius alienus*. Hibernates as a small larva.

Higgins' Anomalous Blue *Agrodiaetus nephohiptamenos*

RANGE N Greece, Bulgaria.

A. nephohiptamenos Brown and Coutsis 1978 TL: NE Greece.

DISTRIBUTION N Greece: Mt. Pangeon; Mt. Phalakron; Mt. Orvilos. Bulgaria: Mt. Alibotush (the northerly extension of Mt. Orvilos in Greece). 1500-2000m.

DESCRIPTION Male hw fringes conspicuously white.

FLIGHT-PERIOD Univoltine. Mid July/late August: emergence time very dependent upon local weather conditions.

HABITAT Open grassy, flowery slopes above tree-line on limestone.

LIFE-HISTORY LHP *Onobrychis montana scardica* – a distinctive ssp. confined to Balkan peninsula. This plant has not been noted below the lower altitude limit of the butterfly: biotopes do not appear to contain other *Onobrychis* species. Hibernates as a small larva. Hibernated larvae feed on leaves at base of LHP. Larvae attended by ants.

BEHAVIOUR Whilst *A. nephohiptamenos* is essentially an allopatric member of its group, males have been recorded drinking on damp ground in company with *A. admetus*, *A. pelopi* and *A. aroaniensis* at lower limit of altitudinal range.

Grecian Anomalous Blue

Ripart's Anomalous Blue

Higgin's Anomalous Blue

GRECIAN ANOMALOUS BLUE

Restricted to Greece

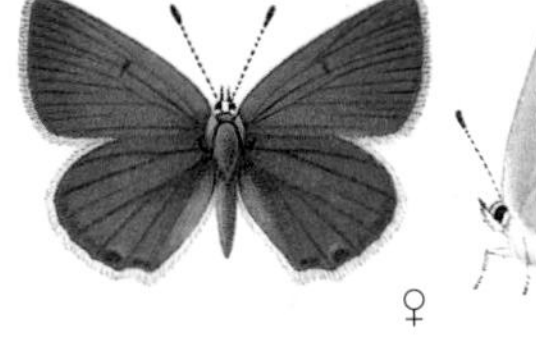

♂ ♀

Uns uniform yellowish-grey, hw white stripe along vein 4 faint or absent

RIPART'S ANOMALOUS BLUE

Unh white stripe well developed

♂ ♀

A. r. ripartii

♂ ♀

A. r. pelopi
(S & C Greece)

HIGGIN'S ANOMALOUS BLUE

(N Greece and Bulgaria)

Uph fringes white

♂ ♀

Gallo's Anomalous Blue *Agrodiaetus galloi*

RANGE S Italy.
A. galloi Bolleto and Toso 1979 TL: Monte Pollino, Reggio Calabria.
DISTRIBUTION S Italy: Reggio Calabria; Mt. Pollino, Piano de Ruggio, Serra del Prete, Vallone di Malvento, Campo Tenese, Orsomarso Mts. (Piano di Campolungo). 1100-2200m, most abundant at 1750-1900m.
DESCRIPTION Male ups gc chestnut brown with olive tones; fringes brown; upf sex-brand conspicuous; uns gc sandy-brown; antemarginal markings vestigial, obscure; fringes cream-white; unh white stripe on v4 conspicuous: female ups gc slightly browner, tinged reddish; fw less pointed; uns black spots conspicuously ringed white; ups and uns fringes creamy-white.
FLIGHT-PERIOD Univoltine. July/August.
HABITAT Grassy slopes; beechwood clearings; screes at highest altitudes.

Turquoise Blue *Plebicula dorylas*

RANGE S and C Europe, Turkey, Transcaucasus.
P. dorylas Denis and Schiffermüler 1775 TL: Vienna.
syn: *argester* Bergsträsser 1779; *hylas* Esper 1793 (invalid homonym)
DISTRIBUTION N and C Spain (Montes Universales, S. de la Demanda, Cantabrian Mts., Pyrenees). NW Pyrenees to S Sweden (including Öland and Gotland) and Lithuania (very rare and local). E Europe, Balkans and Greece. Probably extinct in Latvia. Records from Sicily require confirmation. Records for Corfu, Tenos and Syra probably arise from nomenclatural confusion. 75-2300m.
DESCRIPTION AND VARIATION In C Spain, males ups gc and wing shape varies appreciably: female ups sometimes with blue basal flush; wing bases always with a few blue scales (cf. female *P. nivescens*).
FLIGHT-PERIOD Bivoltine at lower altitudes, May/June and late July/August; univoltine at high altitude, late June/August.
HABITAT Grassy, flowery places, usually amongst scrub at lower altitudes; sheltered hollows on open grassy slopes on high mountains: on calcareous soils.
LIFE-HISTORY LHP *Anthyllis vulneraria*. Ova laid on leaves, upon which larvae feed. Hibernates as a small larva beneath the crown of LHP: post-hibernated larvae feed below crown of plant exclusively on leaves. Larvae attended by *Lasius alienus*; *Myrmica scabrinodis*; *Formica cinerea*.
NOTE Although *C. minimus* shares *Anthyllis vulneraria* with *P. dorylas* in most habitats in S Europe, competitive feeding is avoided by the exploitation of different plant components – *C. minimus* feeds exclusively on seeds (captive larvae accept leaves if offered no alternative).

Nevada Blue *Plebicula golgus*

RANGE S Spain.
P. golgus golgus Hübner 1813 TL: Sierra Nevada, S Spain.
DISTRIBUTION S Spain: confined to Sierra Nevada. 2400-3000m. Locally abundant.
FLIGHT-PERIOD Univoltine. Late June/Late July.
HABITAT Exposed slopes, with low-growing, often with very sparse vegetation on greyish/brownish substrate, often strewn with dark, slaty rock – carboniferous schists.
LIFE-HISTORY LHP *Anthyllis vulneraria arundana*. Ova laid singly on either leaf-surface near midrib. Larvae hibernate beneath crown of LHP. Larvae attended by *Tapinoma nigerrimum*.
NOTE At peak emergence, both sexes observed in roughly equal abundance (cf. *P. dorylas*; *P. nivescens*; *P. atlantica*).
P. golgus sagratrox Aistleitner 1984 TL: Sierra de la Sagra, S Spain.
DISTRIBUTION S Spain: S. de la Sagra (Province of Granada). 1900-2350m. Locally abundant.
DESCRIPTION Both sexes readily distinguishable from nominate form by overall brighter appearance. Male ups paler blue; uns gc white: female ups paler brown; ups often with orange submarginal spots, better developed on uph; uph often with blue scales at wing-base and along veins; uns gc paler, tending to white. Male genitalia as for nominate form (See Note 1).
FLIGHT-PERIOD Univoltine. Late June/late July.
HABITAT Steep, dry slopes with sparse, low-growing vegetation on limestone.
LIFE-HISTORY LHP *Anthyllis vulneraria arundana*. Ova laid singly on either leaf-surface near midrib. Limited observations indicate that larvae feed exclusively on leaves in nature: captive larvae readily accept leaves and flowers of several varieties/subspecies of *A. vulneraria* and other (undetermined) *Anthyllis* spp. Hibernates as a small larva beneath crown of LHP. Larvae attended by *Lasius niger*.
NOTE ONE Taxon erected to species level on basis of geographical isolation and phenotypic distinction from *P. g. golgus*: however, specific separation remains unsubstantiated. That geographical/ecological isolation of a species does not guarantee evolutionary divergence is exemplified by the taxonomic inseparability of respective LHPs. The principal superficial difference in the two taxa (colour tone) may be attributed to widely differing geological character (slate grey-brown in the case of nominate form, white limestone in the case of *sagratrox*) of the terrain in which each form needs to survive and to which, therefore, each may be expected to adapt. Equivalent adaptation to geological substrate coloration is apparent for many European butterflies.
NOTE TWO As for nominate form, both sexes observed in roughly equal abundance at peak emergence (cf. *P. dorylas*; *P. nivescens*; *P. atlantica*).

GALLO'S ANOMALOUS BLUE

Restricted to S Italy

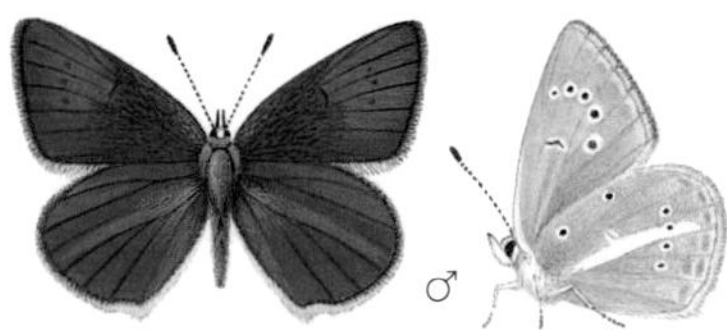

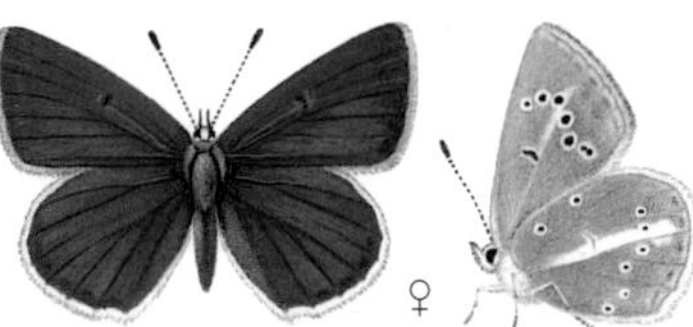

TURQUOISE BLUE

Uns pattern of markings and gc distinctive

NEVADA BLUE

Restricted to Sierra Nevada, S Spain

A. g. golgus

Restricted to Sierra de la Sagra, S Spain

A. g. sagratrox

Gallo's Anomalous Blue

Turquoise Blue

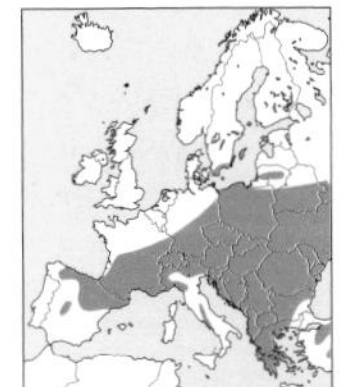

Nevada Blue

Mother-of-pearl Blue *Plebicula nivescens*

RANGE Spain.

P. nivescens Keferstein 1851 TL: Sierra de Alfacar, Granada.

DISTRIBUTION SW Spain to S Cantabrian Mts. and S Pyrenees. Widespread, generally very local. 1000-1900m.

FLIGHT-PERIOD Univoltine. Late May/early August in prolonged emergence.

HABITAT Hot, dry, limestone rocks, usually amongst scrub.

LIFE-HISTORY LHP *Anthyllis vulneraria*. Ova laid on either leaf-surface near midrib; a small leaf on a small plant is most often selected. Small larvae hibernate beneath crown of LHP. Larvae attended by *Tapinoma nigerrimum*.

NOTE Females generally not commonly observed (cf. *P. dorylas*; *P. golgus*; *P. atlantica*).

Atlas Blue *Plebicula atlantica*

RANGE Morocco, Algeria.

P. atlantica Elwes 1905 TL: High Atlas, Morocco.

DISTRIBUTION Widespread, generally very local. Morocco: High Atlas (1700-2700m); Middle Atlas (Tizi-n-Taghzeft; Col du Zad; Dj. bou Iblane; 1300-2100m); W Rif Mts. (Dj. Lakraa; Dj. Tissouka; Ketama; 1300-2100m). Algeria (Aures Mts.; Djurdjura Mts.; 1700-2500m).

VARIATION Male uph black submarginal spots sometimes with proximal pinkish-orange scales (*rosea* Tennent). In all populations, female ups submarginal orange markings sometimes forming a wide band with proximal ray-like projections extending to fw cell. In Middle Atlas and W Rif Mts., *weissi* Dujardin: generally smaller; female upf submarginal orange spots reduced, with those in s6-8 sometimes absent. In Algeria, *barraguei* Dujardin: male ups white marginal markings better developed; uns orange spots and unh discal and pd markings reduced or absent; female uph blue basal scaling usually well developed.

FLIGHT-PERIOD Bivoltine. Late May/July and August/September.

HABITAT Flowery places; dry, stony slopes with scrub.

LIFE-HISTORY LHP *Anthyllis vulneraria*: reputed use of *Vicia tenuifolia* requires confirmation. Ova laid singly near midrib on upperside of leaf.

NOTE Females generally very uncommon (cf. *P. dorylas*; *P. nivescens*).

Meleager's Blue *Meleageria daphnis*

RANGE S Europe, Turkey, Lebanon, Syria, Iran, Transcaucasus, S Urals.

M. daphnis Denis and Schiffermüller 1775 TL: Vienna.

syn: *meleager* Esper 1779.

DISTRIBUTION Spain: very local and uncommon: province of Madrid; Burgos; Cuenca and Teruel (Montes Universales); Logrono (S. de la Demanda); foothills of Pyrenees (Huesca to Gerona). S France: Pyrénées-Orientales to Massif Central, Savoie and Alpes-Maritimes. Switzerland: Valais (Rhône Valley); NE Engadine. Italy. Sicily. S Germany (Tauberland; Baulandes) through S Poland to Balkans, European Turkey and Greece (widespread, locally common), including SE Aegean island of Simi. 200-1700m.

VARIATION Female f. *steeveni* Treitschkes: ups gc greyish-brown; markings outlined by whitish or greyish suffusion, sometimes extending along veins: (?) exclusive form in Spain: intermediate forms occur in N and C Greece: in S Greece, f. *steeveni* (often with ups white scaling reduced) predominant.

FLIGHT-PERIOD Univoltine. Mid June/August according on locality.

HABITAT Grassy or bushy places, usually on limestone/base-rich substrates.

LIFE-HISTORY LHP *Coronilla varia*. Ova laid on leaves upon which larvae feed. In hot, dry situations, plants heavily shaded by rocks or bushes are usually preferred for oviposition. Hibernates as an ovum or small larva: attended by *Lasius alienus*; *Formica pratensis*; *Tapinoma erraticum*.

Mother-of-pearl Blue

Atlas Blue

Meleager's Blue

MOTHER-OF-PEARL BLUE

Restricted to Spain

ATLAS BLUE

Ups and uns pattern of markings distinctive

Restricted to Morocco and Algeria

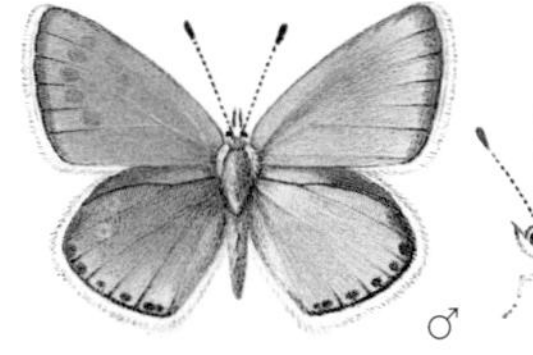

MELEAGER'S BLUE

Hw scalloped

f. *steeveni*

Chalk-hill Blue *Lysandra coridon*

RANGE Europe, Ukraine, S Urals.

From Spain to Bulgaria, chromosome numbers (CN=87-92) appear to be roughly clinal, with higher counts predominating in E Europe. It should perhaps be mentioned that a narrow range of variance in chromosome number is not indicative of speciation: experiment demonstrates that cross-pairing of individuals from populations having slightly different chromosome number occurs easily and produces viable offspring: the process of fertilization (fusion of gamete cells – ovum and sperm) involves pairing of chromosomal elements, with functional exclusion of supernumerate components. Although it would appear that some genetic information is necessarily lost in this process, chromosomal pairing during fertilization is probably not – if at all – entirely random, suggesting that such loss as occurs, is selective and of little or no material consequence – indeed, a possibility implied by the viability of progeny. For many species, including our own, it is known that many genes carried on chromosomes are essentially redundant, persisting only as a legacy of evolutionary history.

Spanish races of *L. coridon* present a complex distributional and taxonomic problem. Theoretically, the problem may, at least in part, relate to the sympatric occurrence of the allied taxon, *L. albicans*, itself subject to considerable local/regional variation. That the two species share the same LHP in many habitats and, in the larval stage, may even compete for the same species of attending ant, represents, in effect, mutual ecological pressure which, so it may be surmised, has induced adaptive responses from both species. In some habitats, further complication may arise from the presence of *L. hispania*. Such influences, if applicable, are almost exclusive to Spain where the greatest range of phenotypic variation in *L. coridon* is to be found. In the limiting case, adaptation may lead to speciation and, indeed, some Spanish *Lysandra* taxa described here below species level are accorded specific rank by some authors. However, whilst many taxonomically relevant questions remain unanswered, the following provisional assignments are considered appropriate pending acquisition of definitive biological data.

L. coridon coridon Poda 1761 TL: Graz, Austria.

DISTRIBUTION From N Spain (Pyrenees: very local on southern slopes: 1200-2000m), eastwards through most of Europe, including S England, to Lithuania, Balkans and Greece. Absent from Fennoscandia, S Peloponnesos and Mediterranean islands. A record for European Turkey requires confirmation. 100-2000m.

VARIATION Male ups gc locally/regionally variable. In Julian Alps: male ups distinctly bluer than nominate form, and without yellowish reflections. In Greece, *graeca* Rühl: male ups duller, greyish-blue with yellowish reflections: a similar form occurs in Apennines. Uns gc colour and development of markings also varies geographically, with paler and less well-marked forms predominant in Mediterranean regions. Female ups with various degrees of blue suffusion are very rare in most populations but frequent in others: in f. *syngrapha* Keferstein, ups heavy blue suffusion extends to submargin: a dominant form in some localities in SW France.

FLIGHT-PERIOD Univoltine. Late June/early October according to altitude and locality. Univoltine in most of Slovakia (late June/early August), consistently bivoltine (May/June and August/September) in one small area – details lacking.

HABITAT Dry, bushy, flowery places, usually associated with short grass: restricted to calcareous soils.

LIFE-HISTORY LHP *Hippocrepis comosa*. Ova laid on leaves of LHP and other substrates, including dead grass-stems and stones. In N and C Europe, hibernates as an ovum: in Greece, as a second instar larva on underside of a stone covering an entrance to an ants'gallery. Larvae attended by *Lasius niger*; *L. alienus*; *L. flavus*; *L.* (?)*fuliginosus*; *Plagiolepis vindobonensis*; *Formica rufa*; *Myrmica scabrinodis*; *M. sabuleti*; *M. schencki*; *Tetramorium caespitum*.

NOTE ONE Males which appear to be hybrids of *L. coridon* and *L. bellargus* (f. *polonus* Zeller), appear regularly and not uncommonly on Mt. Chelmos, Peloponnesos: rare elsewhere in Europe.

L. coridon caelestissima Verity 1921 TL: C Spain, Albarracin.

DISTRIBUTION E Spain: provinces of Teruel and Cuenca (Montes Universales). Locally abundant. 1050-1800m.

DESCRIPTION AND VARIATION Male ups gleaming sky-blue: female ups usually brown, very rarely silvery sky-blue (f. *deliciosa* de Sagarra – cf. *L. c. coridon* f. *syngrapha*): both sexes, variation in ups and uns markings, including that relating to common aberrations, parallels that of nominate form.

FLIGHT-PERIOD Univoltine. July/August.

HABITAT Sheltered slopes/gullies/hollows in pinewood clearings on short grassy turf: restricted to limestone/calcareous substrates of Montes Universales. (Reported occurrence on exclusively non-calcareous substrates is untenable: upper strata of Montes Universales consists almost exclusively of limestone; at lowest altitudinal range, soils of non-calcareous rocks are base-rich in consequence of ground-water alkalinity – run-off from higher levels).

LIFE-HISTORY LHP *Hippocrepis comosa*. Ova laid on leaves. In captivity, hibernates as an ovum or unfed larva.

NOTE Males with very pale blue ups, f. *caerulescens* Tutt, are presumed to be hybrids of *L. c. caelestissima* and *L. albicans arragonensis*. Overlap in altitudinal range of these taxa is apparently quite limited; *L. a. arragonensis* appears to be very local and sporadic above 1400m.

L. coridon asturiensis de Sagarra 1924 TL: Puerto de Pajares (Cantabrian Mts.)

DISTRIBUTION N Spain: provinces of Oviedo; Leon; Palencia; Santander; Burgos; Logrono; Alava; Guipúzcoa; Vitoria; Huesca. Locally abundant. 600-1950m.

DESCRIPTION AND VARIATION Male ups gc shiny, silvery-blue, lacking yellowish reflections – blue shade locally/regionally variable: size, regionally variable: female indistinguishable from nominate form or pale silvery-blue (f. *syngraphoides* de Sagarra – cf. *L. c. coridon* f. *syngrapha*); proportion of blue females regionally variable:- Pto. de Pajares (Oviedo), 50%; Picos de Europa (Leon and Santander), 0%: Huesca 80-95%. In Huesca (S. de la Peña and environs of Jaca), f. *manleyi* de

CHALK-HILL BLUE

♂ ups faint yellowish reflections distinctive

L. c. coridon

L. c. caelestissima (E Spain)

f. *deliciosa*

f. *syngrapha*

♂ ups lacking yellowish tint

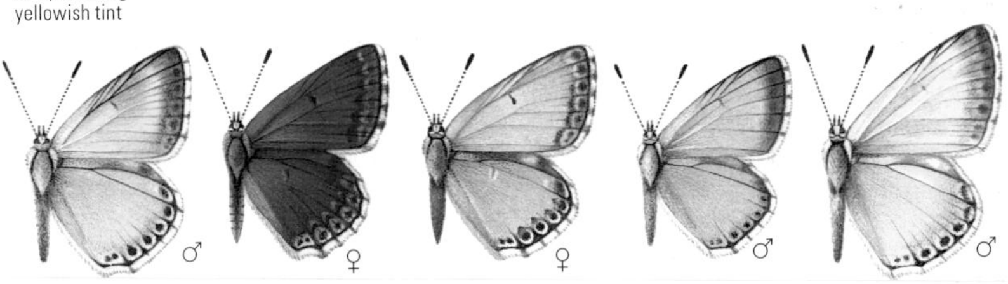

♂ ♀ ♀ ♂ ♂

L. c. asturiensis (N Spain)

f. *syngraphoides*

L. c. graeca x *L. bellargus* (f. *polonus*)

L. c. caelestissima x *L. a. arragonensis* (f. *caerulescens*)

Lesse: resembles nominate ssp. closely: both sexes slightly larger: male ups gc slightly paler blue; upf dark marginal border wide: female f. *syngraphoides* closely similar to that of nominate ssp. Near Peñahorada (Burgos), f. *burgalesa* Agenjo: males averagely very small; upf dark marginal border wide: female, normal size; ups gc brown in (?)all specimens.

FLIGHT-PERIOD Univoltine. July/August.

HABITAT As for nominate form: restricted to calcareous soils. (Reported presumed occurrence on acidic, 'red'soils is probably erroneous: in consequence of a high iron content, limestone soils are often ochreous: LHP not (?) known on acidic soils).

LIFE-HISTORY LHP *Hippocrepis comosa*. Ova laid on leaves. In captivity, hibernates as an ovum or unfed larva.

Chalk-hill Blue

NOTE Males with pale blue ups, reported from Burgos, are presumed to be hybrids of *L. c. asturiensis* and *L. albicans arragonensis*.

L. coridon gennargenti Leigheb 1987 TL: Barbagia Seulo [Sardinia]

DISTRIBUTION Sardinia. Very local and uncommon. 800-1300m.

DESCRIPTION Male ups gc shiny, pale blue, without yellowish reflections (cf. nominate form): female ups light blue (cf. *L. c. coridon* f. *syngrapha*, *L. c. asturiensis* f. *syngraphoides* and *L. c. caelestissima* f. *deliciosa*): both sexes, uns as for nominate.

FLIGHT-PERIOD Univoltine. July/August.

HABITAT As for nominate form: restricted to calcareous soils.

NOTE Recent DNA studies indicate significant genetic departure from nominate form.

L. coridon nufrellensis Schurian 1977 TL: Mufrella Hauptkamm [Corsica]

DISTRIBUTION Corsica: apparently known only from type-locality. 1900-2200m.

DESCRIPTION Resembles nominate form.

FLIGHT-PERIOD Available data very limited: presumed to be univoltine: type-series acquired 23-27th July 1975.

NOTE Disparity in spelling of taxon and toponym is a *lapsus calami*.

Macedonian Chalk-hill Blue *Lysandra philippi*

RANGE N Greece.

L. philippi Brown and Coutsis 1978 TL: mountains of NE Greece.

DISTRIBUTION N Greece: Mt. Pangeon; Mt. Phalakron. 600-1900m.

DESCRIPTION AND VARIATION Resembles *L. coridon* closely: differentiated by much lower chromosome number (CN=20-26, *L. coridon*, CN=84-92). Male ups pale silvery-blue, lacking yellowish reflections: female resembles *L. coridon*. On Mt. Pangeon, female ups with extensive blue suffusion in about 50% of specimens: equivalent forms not reported from Mt. Phalakron. Male ups gc very rarely pale, sky-blue, intermediate between *L. philippi* and *L. bellargus* suggesting possible hybridization.

FLIGHT-PERIOD Univoltine. Early July/August.

HABITAT Dry, open scrub at lower altitude; grassy slopes at higher levels: always on limestone.

LIFE-HISTORY LHP *Hippocrepis comosa*. Ova laid on leaves. Hibernates as a second instar larva on underside of a stone covering an entrance to an ants' gallery. Larvae attended by ants.

Macedonian Chalk-hill Blue

Provence Chalk-hill Blue

Spanish Chalk-hill Blue

Provence Chalk-hill Blue *Lysandra hispana*

RANGE E Spain, SE France, N Italy.

L. hispana Herrich-Schäffer 1852 TL: Spain

syn: *rezneciki* Bartel 1905

DISTRIBUTION Spain: Jaén; Granada; Albacete; Murcia; Alicante; Valencia; Castellon; Tarragona; Barcelona; Gerona; Lérida; Huesca; Navarra. France: Pyrénées-Orientales; Aude; Hérault; Ardèche; Drôme; Basses Alpes; Var; Alpes-Maritimes. Italy: Liguria; N Tuscany. 400-1000m.

DESCRIPTION Male ups somewhat dull, bluish-grey with silvery-yellowish reflections; unh somewhat darker and greyer than *L. coridon*, with which it flies in most localities in the second brood. Female indistinguishable from *L. coridon*.

FLIGHT-PERIOD Bivoltine. Mid April/late June and August/early October.

HABITAT Dry flowery, usually grassy places, often amongst scrub: on calcareous soils.

LIFE-HISTORY LHP *Hippocrepis comosa*; (?)*Anthyllis gerardi*. Ova laid on leaves. Larvae attended by *Plagiolepis pygmaea*; *Crematogaster sordidula*.

NOTE Hybridizes with *L. bellargus*.

Spanish Chalk-hill Blue *Lysandra albicans*

RANGE Morocco, Spain.

L. albicans Herrich-Schäffer 1851 TL: Spain.

DISTRIBUTION Morocco: Middle Atlas (Boulemane; Dj. bou Iblane; 900-1700m); W Rif Mts. (Dj. Bouhalla; Dj. Lakraa; 1300-1800m). Spain, except Cantabrian Mts., western provinces, Catalonia and eastern coastal districts. 500-1500m.

VARIATION Several races have been described to account for local/regional variation. Individual variation in some colonies is often appreciable. In Middle Atlas Mts., *berber* Le Cerf: small; male ups pale greyish-blue, marginal borders well defined. In W Rif Mts., *dujardini* Barragué: resembles berber closely: both sexes, markings reduced; male unf discal and basal spots often absent. In S Spain: large; male ups generally very pale, almost white. In E and N Spain, *arragonensis* Gerhard: both sexes very variable in all wing-characters: male ups gc silvery blue-grey; upf border variable in width and colour – very pale grey to black: forms transitional to nominate form occur between Sierra Nevada and Montes Universales. In provinces of Madrid and Toledo, *bolivari* Romei: male ups gc almost white; submarginal markings usually well defined. In Spain, variation appears to be roughly clinal, with larger, paler forms with reduced uns markings predominating in the south. Taxa *arragonensis* and *bolivari* accorded specific rank by some authors: chromosome number of *arragonensis* (Estepar, province of Burgos) and nominate form 82.

FLIGHT-PERIOD Univoltine. Mid June/August according to locality.

HABITAT Dry rocky places, often with sparse vegetation.

LIFE-HISTORY LHP *Hippocrepis comosa*; (?)*H. multisilquosa*. Ova laid on upperside of leaves. Larvae attended by ants.

MACEDONIAN CHALK-HILL BLUE

Restricted to N Greece

PROVENCE CHALK-HILL BLUE

SPANISH CHALK-HILL BLUE

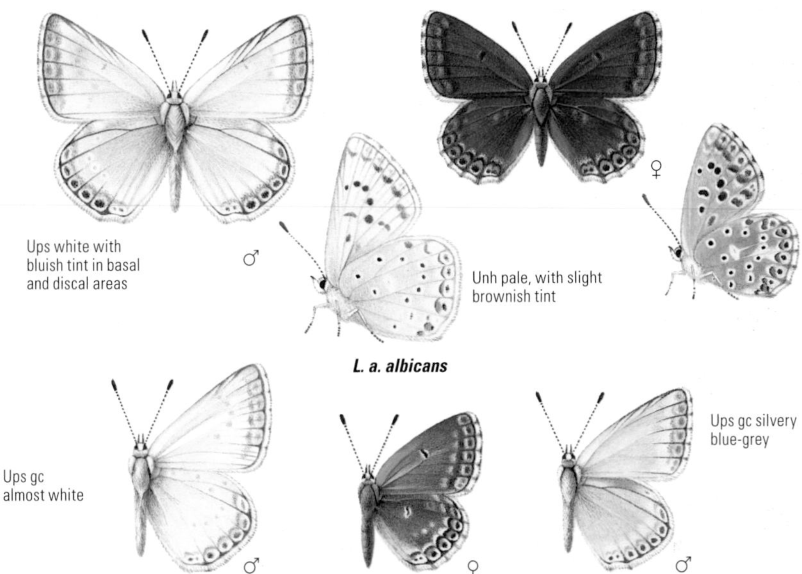

L. a. bolivari
(Madrid and Toledo)

L. a. arragonensis
(E & N Spain)

Adonis Blue *Lysandra bellargus*

RANGE Europe, Turkey, Iraq, Iran, Caucasus, Transcaucasus.
L. bellargus Rottemburg 1775 TL: W Germany.
syn: *adonis* Denis and Schiffermüller 1775.

DISTRIBUTION Most of Europe from Mediterranean coast, European Turkey to S England and Lithuania. Absent from N Belgium, Holland, N Germany, S peninsular Italy, S Peloponnesos and Mediterranean islands except Mallorca. Extinct in Latvia. 100-2000m. A solitary record for NW Africa (Dj. Lakraa, Rif Mts.) merits investigation.

VARIATION Male ups gc somewhat variable, sometimes with greenish reflections; upf rarely with a few black submarginal spots; uph very rarely with orange spots in anal angle: females ups blue suffusion, sometimes extending to outer margins (*ceronus* Esper) – frequent in some localities in C Spain; uph submarginal orange spots variable, sometimes in a complete series on hw and fw. In both sexes, larger and more boldly marked forms are commoner in S Europe.

FLIGHT-PERIOD Bivoltine. Mid May/June and late July/mid September. Reputedly univoltine on Mt. Chelmos and elsewhere S Greece.

HABITAT Generally dry grassy places, often amongst scrub: on calcareous soils.

LIFE-HISTORY LHPs Hippocrepis comosa; Coronilla varia: in Greece, both LHPs are exploited, but not, apparently, in the same habitat. Ova laid on leaves. Hibernates as a small larva. Larvae attended by *Lasius alienus*; *L. niger*; *Plagiolepis pygmaea*; *Myrmica sabuleti*; *M. scabrinodis*; *Tapinoma erraticum*. Often pupates under a stone or amongst leaf-litter/moss at an entrance to an ants'nest.

NOTE Known to hybridize with *L. coridon* (f. *polonus* Zeller): such specimens have intermediate but variable chromosome numbers: cf. *L. c. coridon*. Hybridizes with *L. hispana*. Pale blue male *Lysandra* specimens occur in circumstances suggesting hybridization of *L. bellargus* and *L. philippi*. Hybrids with *L. albicans* appear to be unknown.

Spotted Adonis Blue *Lysandra punctifera*

RANGE Morocco, Algeria, Tunisia.
L. punctifera Oberthür 1876 TL: Lambessa, Algeria.

DISTRIBUTION Widespread, locally common. Morocco. Algeria. Tunisia. 700-2800m.

DESCRIPTION AND VARIATION Male uph black submarginal spots prominent, sometimes with proximal reddish marks (*rubromaculata* Oberthür); uns markings well developed; white fringes boldly chequered: female ups blue suffusion shows a marked altitudinal cline, with bluest forms predominating at higher altitudes (cf. blue female forms of other lycaenids occurring in generally cooler/damper habitats at higher latitudes).

FLIGHT-PERIOD Bivoltine. Generally May/June and late August/September: emergence much dependent on altitude and locality; recorded in March in Anti-Atlas Mts. and late October in Tunisia.

HABITAT Flowery places; grassy hollows; dry slopes.

LIFE-HISTORY LHPs *Hippocrepis scabra*; (?)*Onobrychis* sp. Larvae attended by *Monomorium salomonis*; *Crematogaster scutellaris*.

NOTE In S Spain, male *L. bellargus* specimens sometimes resembles *L. punctifera* very closely: chromosome number of *L. bellargus* (CN=45) differs significantly from that of *L. punctifera* (CN=24): male genitalia distinctive. The close integral proportionality in chromosome numbers suggests the theoretical possibility of polyploidy (cf. *G. pumilio*): cross-pairing experiments would seem especially worthwhile.

Phalakron Blue *Polyommatus andronicus*

RANGE N Greece.
P. andronicus Coutsis and Chavalas 1995 TL: Mt. Phalakron (N Greece)

DISTRIBUTION SW Bulgaria Mt. Alibotus 1400m. N Greece. Mt. Orvilos; Menikion Mts.; Phalakron Mts. 1000-1800m.

DESCRIPTION Resembles *P. icarus* closely: both sexes larger; male ups gc slightly darker and shinier: female ups largely devoid of blue basal scales: compared to *P. icarus*, male genitalia disproportionately larger, elements of female genitalia similarly distinctive. Cross-pairing experiments with *P. icarus* would be of value in the further investigation of this taxon.

FLIGHT-PERIOD Univoltine. Late June/early July. Flies with second brood *P. icarus*.

HABITAT Sheltered grassy or rocky slopes.

Adonis Blue

Spotted Adonis Blue

Phalakron Blue

ADONIS BLUE

f. *ceronus*

SPOTTED ADONIS BLUE

colour variant

Common Blue *Polyommatus icarus*

RANGE Canary Islands, temperate N Africa, Turkey, Middle East, temperate Asia.

P. icarus Rottemburg 1775 TL: Saxony, Germany.

DISTRIBUTION Canary Islands: very local: Fuerteventura; Lanzarote; Tenerife (Punta Hidalgo – recently confirmed). Records for La Palma and Gran Canaria require confirmation. Widespread and very common in NW Africa (0-2700m) and Europe, including all major and most smaller Mediterranean islands. Absent from Madeira and Azores. 0-2900m. **DESCRIPTION** Male upf without androconial patch (cf. male *A. thersites*): male and female unf with black cell-spot – rarely absent (cf. male and female *A. thersites*): female ups gc brown often with blue basal and discal shading. **VARIATION** In both sexes, appreciable local, regional, inter-seasonal and intra-seasonal variation in size and wing-markings appears largely attributable to the extraordinary ecological adaptability of this, the most widespread of the European lycaenids. In N and W Ireland and NW Scotland, *mariscolore* Kane: univoltine: large; male fw more pointed; ups gc brighter blue; uns gc pale, markings conspicuous: female ups bright blue suffusion extending to all wing-margins. (Larvae of Scottish populations captively reared in S England retain univoltine character, but produce females devoid of ups blue scaling, indicating ecological control of blue suffusion, the extent of which, more generally, appears to correlate positively with cooler and/or damper conditions during larval/pupal development). Some populations of S Norway above 500m, resemble *mariscolore* closely: in N Fennoscandia, generally more typical of nominate form. In N Spain (provinces of Oviedo and Burgos), f. *boalensis* Verhulst and Verhulst: size regionally/seasonally variable; male ups slightly darker blue, black marginal borders slightly wider: female ups gc brown: both sexes, uns gc darker, all markings conspicuously bolder – in overall appearance, quite distinctive: in Burgos, *boalensis* occurs on acidic bogs in close proximity (within 200m) to nominate form flying synchronously on a calcareous substrate – a combination of circumstances indicative of ecological adaptation. In adaptive response to unusually acidic conditions, alteration of wing-characters, especially gc, is not uncommon for some species; in the present example, the sympatric and synchronous *C. glycerion iphioides*, *C. euphrosyne* and *C. selene* are abnormally dark on all wing-surfaces. In Sardinia and Corsica, f. *sardoa* Wagner: female upf submarginal orange spots well developed, often confluent, sometimes with ray-like projections towards cell, or with faint orange suffusion in discal and pd areas. In S Europe and NW Africa, f. *celina* Austaut: male ups black marginal borders slightly wider; uph with black marginal dots (variable in number and size), sometimes extending to fw: a recurrent form in some localities. **FLIGHT-PERIOD** Voltinism dependent on locality and altitude. Univoltine (June/July) in colder climates – at higher latitudes (N Ireland, Scotland and Lapland) and altitudes (Sierra Nevada above 2700m): bivoltine/trivoltine (May/early October) in S Britain and C Europe: at least trivoltine at sea-level in S Europe (late March/early November). In Canary Islands, recorded in all months, less commonly in summer – possibly aestivating in ovum or larval stage in hottest periods. **HABITAT** Very diverse. Occurs in almost all habitat-types. **LIFE-HISTORY** LHPs: many genera/species of Fabaceae, including: *Galega*; *Ononis*; *Lotus*; *Medicago*; *Trifolium*; *Melilotus*; *Genista*; *Astragalus*; *Astracantha*; *Onobrychis*; *Anthyllis*; *Coronilla* in most of Europe, commonly *Lotus corniculatus* and *Medicago lupulina*: Lanzarote and Fuerteventura, *Lotus lancerottensis*. Larvae attended by *Lasius alienus*; *L. flavus*; *L. niger*; *Formica subrufa*; *F.* (?)*cinerea*; *Plagiolepis pygmaea*; *Myrmica sabuleti*; *M. lobicornis* var. *alpestris*. **NOTE** *Polyommatus abdon* Aistleitner and Aistleitner 1994, described from mountains of SE Spain, appears to be conspecific with *Polyommatus icarus*: minor differences reported in male ups gc and genitalia appear to fall within the range of variation of the latter taxon.

False Eros Blue *Polyommatus eroides*

RANGE E and SE Europe, Turkey, Urals, N Kazakhstan, W Siberia.

P. eroides Frivaldsky 1835 TL: Balkans.

DISTRIBUTION Slovakia. Poland. (?)Albania. Republic of Macedonia. Bulgaria: Pirin Mts. Greece: Grammos Massif; Varnous Mts.; Vernon Mts.; Voras Mts.; Rhodope Mts.; Mt. Pieria. 950-2100m. **DESCRIPTION** Male ups black marginal borders 1-2mm wide; uns gc uniform dove grey: both sexes, uns markings well developed: female ups gc uniform medium brown, sometimes with very faint greyish tint, lacking blue basal suffusion. **FLIGHT-PERIOD** Univoltine. Mid June/late July according to altitude. **HABITAT** Open flowery banks or slopes with short grass, often amongst rocks above treeline: (?)always on acidic substrates, especially granite: parts of habitat are often damp or wet, but LHP appears to favour well-drained, dry, often gravelly banks/slopes with short vegetation. **LIFE-HISTORY** LHP *Genista depressa*. Ova laid on leaves. Small larvae feed on leaves: hibernated larvae feed on flowers. Larvae attended by *Tapinoma* sp. **BEHAVIOUR** Males often gather in large numbers on damp ground.

Eros Blue *Polyommatus eros*

RANGE Spain (Pyrenees), France, European Alps, Italy (Apennines), Balkans, Turkey, NW and C Asia.

P. eros Ochsenheimer 1808 TL: Alps of Tyrol and Switzerland.

DISTRIBUTION Spain: Pyrenees; Pto. de Bielsa; Pto. de Viella; Pto. de La Bonaigua; La Molina. France: C and E Pyrenees; Massif Central (Cantal); Central European Alps of France, Italy, S Switzerland and W Austria (Gross Glockner). Italy: C Apennines. Bosnia-Herzegovina: Prenj Pl.; Jahorina Pl. SW Serbia: Mt. Durmitor. Republic of Macedonia: Placenska Pl.; Baba Pl. (Mt. Pelister). 1200-2700m, generally above 1800m. **FLIGHT-PERIOD** Univoltine. July/September according to altitude. **HABITAT** Grassy, flowery slopes on limestone, usually with short turf. **LIFE-HISTORY** LHPs *Oxytropis halleri*; *O. campestris*. Ova laid on leaves upon which larvae feed. Hibernates as a small larva. Larvae attended by *Formica lemani*; *Myrmica gallienii*. **BEHAVIOUR** Males often gather in large numbers on damp ground.

COMMON BLUE

♂ upf lacking androconial patch; cell-spot rarely absent

♀ blue flush ranges from a few basal scales to blue suffusion extending to wing margins

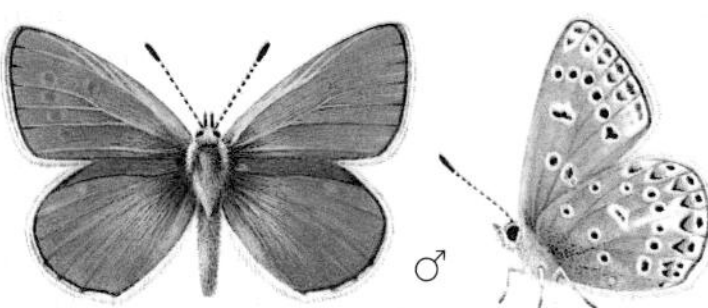

P. i. icarus

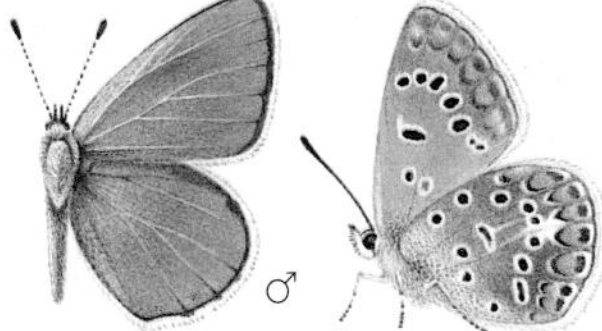

f. ***boalensis***

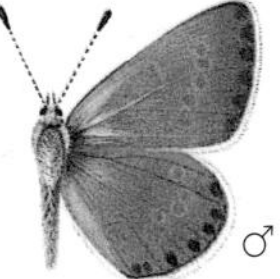

f. ***celina***
(C Europe, NW Africa)

colour variant

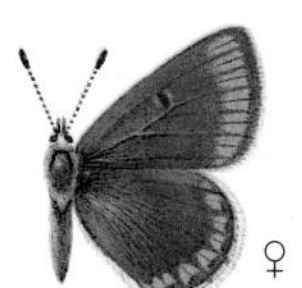

f. ***sardoa***
(Sardinia and Corsica)

FALSE EROS BLUE

Ups black marginal border wide, distinctive

Unf cell-spot usually present

Ups blue basal flush

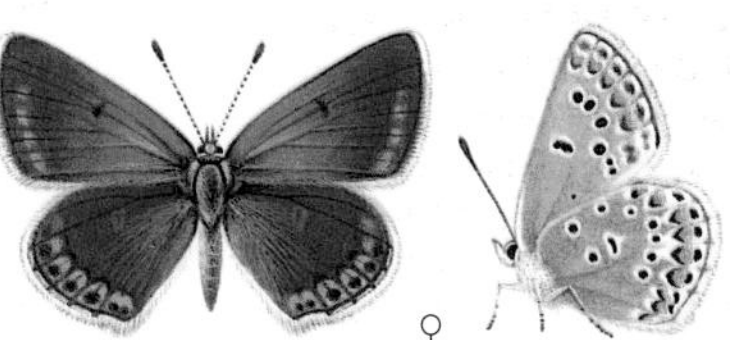

EROS BLUE

Unf cell-spot usually present

Common Blue

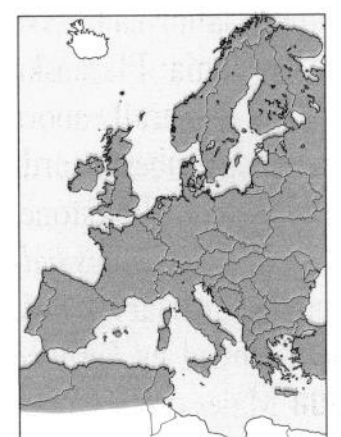

False Eros Blue

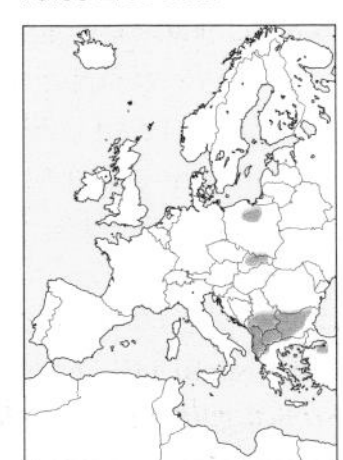

Eros Blue

Taygetos Blue *Polyommatus menelaos*

RANGE S Greece.
P. menelaos Brown, 1976 TL: Langhanda Pass, Taygetos Mts.
DISTRIBUTION Greece: known only from Taygetos Mts. 1250-2000m.
DESCRIPTION Resembles *P. eros*. Both sexes, larger, uns gc paler, tending to white.
FLIGHT-PERIOD Univoltine. Early June/late July according to season.
LIFE-HISTORY LHP *Astragalus taygeteus* – endemic to Taygetos Mts. Ova laid on leaves, upon which small larvae feed. Hibernated larvae feed on flower-buds. Larvae attended by *Camponotus aethiops*.
HABITAT Sheltered gullies and hollows, generally above the treeline, on limestone or metamorphic rocks. Often occurs with *K. eurypilus*.
BEHAVIOUR In hot conditions, males gather in large numbers on damp ground.

RIODINIDAE Grote 1895

Closely related to the Lycaenidae. A large family whose distribution centres on tropical America. A few genera occur in the eastern Palearctic region, as well as tropical Asia and Africa. Represented in Europe by a single species.

Duke of Burgundy Fritillary *Hamearis lucina*

RANGE From N and C Spain eastwards throughout S and C Europe, European Turkey, Urals.
H. lucina Linnaeus 1758 TL: England (Verity 1943).
DISTRIBUTION N and C Spain, eastwards through most of Europe (including England: very local) to SE Sweden and Latvia (a single known colony). N and C Greece: very local: not reported east of Rhodope Mts. or south of Mt. Timphristos. Absent from N Germany, Denmark, Finland, S Italy and Mediterranean islands except N Sicily. 50-1600m.
VARIATION S Europe, usually larger. Second brood: ups dark markings more extensive, sometimes obscuring orange uph gc.
FLIGHT-PERIOD Univoltine (May/June) or bivoltine (April/June and July/September) according to altitude, latitude and local conditions – univoltine in hot Mediterranean localities where LHP may become desiccated in summer.
HABITAT Grassy, flowery clearings in woodland or scrub.
LIFE-HISTORY LHPs *Primula vulgaris*; *P. veris*; *P. elatior*. Ova usually laid singly or in pairs, less often 3-6, on underside of leaves. Larvae feed on leaves. Hibernates as a pupa.

LIBYTHEIDAE Boisduval 1833

Related to the Nymphalidae. Represented in the Palearctic region by three species, of which one occurs in Europe. The conspicuous palpi are over three times the length of the head.

Nettle-tree Butterfly *Libythea celtis*

RANGE Algeria, Tunisia, S Europe, Turkey, C and NW Asia, N India, Siberia, China, Taiwan, Japan.
L. celtis Laicharting 1782 TL: Bolzano, S Tirol.
DISTRIBUTION N Algeria and NW Tunisia: local and uncommon. Portugal and Spain: very sporadic and generally rare, more frequent in Pyrenees. Andorra: locally common. S France (Pyrénées-Orientales to Ardèche and Alpes-Maritimes) through Italy, SE Switzerland (extremely local) to S Slovakia (very occasional – residency in doubt), Hungary, Balkans, Greece (widespread, locally common) and European Turkey: generally sporadic and very local in northern range: reported from Corsica, Elba, Sardinia, Sicily, Lipari Islands, Malta, Crete and Lesbos. 400-1500m.
DESCRIPTION Male unh greyish: female unh light brown, with buff or pinkish tints in fresh specimens.
FLIGHT-PERIOD Univoltine. June/August: reappearing after hibernation, late March/late April.
HABITAT Mostly open, bushy areas with scattered, generally small, deciduous trees.
LIFE-HISTORY LHP *Celtis australis*. Ova laid close to leaf-buds. Larvae feed on leaves. When disturbed, larvae descend 2-3m from LHP on silken threads. Adults sometimes enter hibernation as early as August. In SE European, where *C. australis* appears to be uncommon, the possible alternative use of other *Celtis* species is suggested by the reported utilization of *C. caucasica* in NW Asia. Captive larvae accept *Ulmus* (?)*minor* and *Ulmus glabra* reluctantly.
BEHAVIOUR Disperses over a wide area in mid or late summer, vagrant specimens having been recorded as high as 2300m. Dispersion appears to be confined largely within established residential range: in terms of survival strategy, behaviour therefore differs fundamentally from that of migrant species (cf. *C. cardui*). Freshly emerged adults often congregate in large numbers to drink on damp ground.

TAYGETOS BLUE

Rrestricted to Taygetos Mts. S Greece

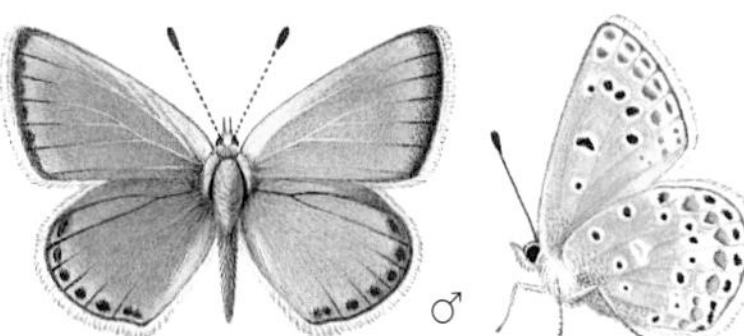

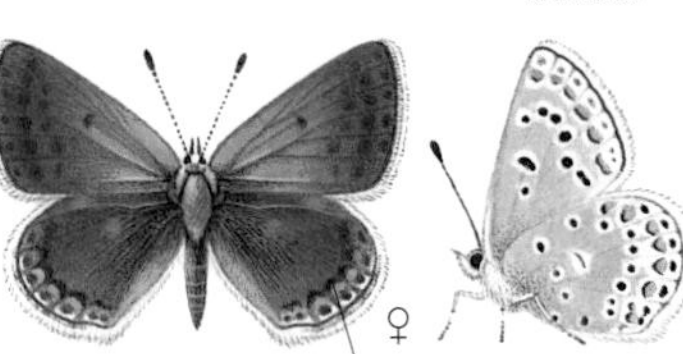

♀ ups gc brown with distinct greyish tint; uph submarginal orange spots often internally bordered black

DUKE OF BURGUNDY FRITILLARY

NETTLE-TREE BUTTERFLY

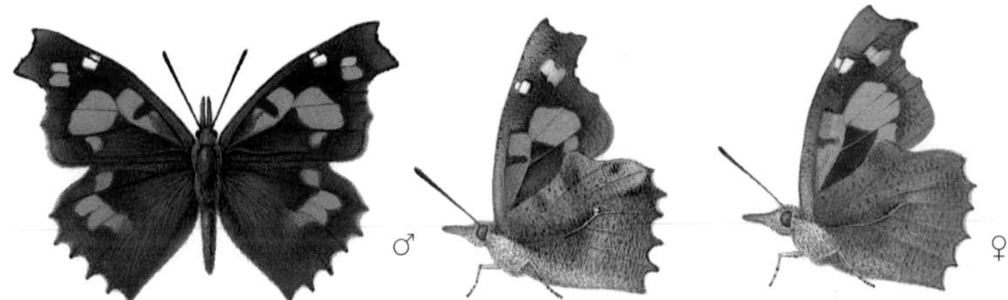

Taygetos Blue

Duke of Burgandy Fritillary

Nettle-tree Butterfly

DANAIDAE Boisduval 1933

This large family of large butterflies is confined mostly to tropical zones. Two of the eight species recorded in the Palearctic region occur, somewhat sporadically in Europe. Both are well-known migrants whose brightly coloured, conspicuous larvae feed on plants from which toxic substances are assimilated, rendering larva, pupa and adult butterfly generally unpalatable to birds: in fact, the harmful chemicals are concentrated in the wings and abdomen, and, in North America, some birds species have exploited this disparity by feeding only on the thoracic segments: for one bird species, known to be immune to the poison, adult *Danaus plexippus* butterflies provides the main part of its diet.

Milkweed or Monarch *Danaus plexippus*

RANGE Azores, Canary Islands, S Portugal, S Spain, Mauritius, India, Papua New Guinea and other E Indian islands, Australia, New Zealand, Hawaii, S Peru to Canada.

D. plexippus Linnaeus 1758 TL: Pennsylvania.

DISTRIBUTION Resident in coastal districts of Canary Islands (except Lanzarote) and S Spain (province of Málaga): resident below 100m: occasional as vagrants/migrants to 400m. Occasional as migrants in Azores, Lanzarote, S and W Portugal, Gibraltar, more rarely, Ireland, SW England and S France.

DESCRIPTION Male uph with black sex-brand on v2: female similar but lacking sex-brand.

FLIGHT-PERIOD Polyvoltine in Canary Islands: continuously brooded: recorded in all months. (Hibernates as an adult in Mexico and SW U.S.A.).

HABITAT Hot, dry places: in Canary Islands, coastal areas, including parks and gardens: in S Spain, coastal gullies, almost invariably in close proximity to cultivated areas.

LIFE-HISTORY LHPs: Mediterranean region, *Asclepias curassavica*: Canary Islands, *A. curassavica* and *Gomphocarpus fruticosus* – neither of which are native species; other Asclepiadaceae, including native *Periploca laevigata*, endemic *Ceropegia* spp. and non-native *Calotropis procera* are apparently not exploited. In Canary Islands, larvae recorded in all months.

BEHAVIOUR This well-known, C and N American migrant is known to have greatly extended its range since the middle of 19th century, colonizing New Zealand in 1840, Australia in 1870 and Canary Islands in 1880: first noted as a resident of Spain in 1980: reported from S France, Corsica and Mauritius in 1983. (In N America, migrates northwards from over-wintering quarters in spring and summer, returning in autumn.)

CONSERVATION In S Spain, the use of herbicides/insecticides, weed-burning and rubbish-disposal threatens extinction of resident colonies, most of which are small and isolated.

♀

MILKWEED OR MONARCH

Milkweed or Monarch

Plain Tiger *Danaus chrysippus*

RANGE Canary Islands, Africa, sporadic in coastal Mediterranean regions, central E Turkey, Saudi Arabia, tropical Asia, Australia.

D. chrysippus Linnaeus 1758 TL: S China.

DISTRIBUTION Canary Islands: resident on La Palma; Gomera; Fuerteventura (very local); 0-600m: probably no longer resident on Tenerife and Gran Canaria, but recorded as an occasional migrant. N Africa: resident and locally common in W Morocco (Sous Valley), N Algeria (Gharddia and Touggourt) and Tunisia (Douz; Sfax; Gabes; Sousse): more widely observed as single, migrant specimens. Recorded from mainly coastal districts of S Spain (Málaga and Almeria), S France, Corsica, Sardinia, Sicily, W Italy, Montenegro, Albania, Corfu, W and S Greece and Crete: temporary/(?)permanent breeding populations appear to have become established in some localities.

DESCRIPTION Male ups gc variable, light orange-brown to Chestnut-brown; upf apex dark brown, enclosing transverse white spots, sometimes coalescing into a band broken by veins; uph with black sex-brand on v2: female similar but lacking sex-brand.

VARIATION Polymorphism marked: f. *alcippus* Cramer, uph tawny-brown gc replaced by white: f. *alcippoides* Moore, white area less extensive, transitional to nominate form: incidence of both forms regionally and seasonally variable.

FLIGHT-PERIOD Polyvoltine. Canary Islands: continuously brooded: recorded in all months: N Africa, March/November: N and E Mediterranean region, May/October.

HABITAT Bushy, rocky places; hot, coastal gullies, usually in close proximity to cultivated areas; gardens.

LIFE-HISTORY LHPs: Canary Islands: *Asclepias curassavica*; *Gomphocarpus fruticosus*; *Caralluma burchardii* (Fuerteventura); possibly also *Ceropegia hians* and *Calotropis procera* on La Palma and Gran Canaria respectively: Morocco and S Europe, *A. curassavica atropurpurea*; *C. procera*: Algeria and Tunisia, *Pergularia tomentosa*; *Cynanchum acutum*: S Europe, *A. curassavica*. Reported use of *Calystegia sepium* (Convolvulaceae) requires confirmation. Larvae recorded in all months in Canary Islands. Life-cycle in tropical Africa approximately one month. For a species having no diapause stage, winter residence in the often very cold eastern Mediterranean region seems unlikely; the impression of persistence in particular habitats more probably due to recurring early spring migration and subsequent establishment of temporary colonies which survive until onset of cold weather (cf. *C. cardui*; *C. crocea*; *L. boeticus*).

BEHAVIOUR A powerful and wide-ranging migrant. In northern Corfu, in late September 1989, large numbers were observed, apparently migrating southwards.

CONSERVATION As in the case of *D. plexippus*, human activity poses a significant threat to resident colonies in S Spain.

NYMPHALIDAE Swainson 1827

This large family, well represented in Europe, contains many well-known, common and widespread species. A few colourful and conspicuous species such as the Peacock, Small Tortoiseshell, Painted Lady and Red Admiral are often to be found in gardens and parks, even in large cities: this group comprises the so-called 'vanessids'. A few are migrants, capable of extending their range throughout most of the subcontinent during summer months. The largest group, the fritillaries, are to be found throughout the region. Some species occur well within the Arctic Circle, whilst a few inhabit the equally inhospitable semi-deserts of N Africa. Larvae are often conspicuously coloured and spectacularly adorned with spiny protruberances: these 'warning colours' and unappetising structural features serve to discourage the predatory attention of birds. Small larvae of the genera *Melitaea*, *Mellicta*, *Hypodryas* and *Eurodryas* feed and hibernate gregariously in silk-webs, dispersing in later instars after hibernation to feed singly or in small companies: pupae are suspended on plant-stems, often of robust grasses, the underside of leaves or sometimes on stones.

Two-tailed Pasha *Charaxes jasius*

RANGE Mainly coastal Mediterranean region. Represented by two subspecies in Ethiopia and equatorial Africa.

C. jasius Linnaeus 1767 TL: Barbaria (Algeria).

DISTRIBUTION Locally common in coastal districts of Morocco, Algeria, Tunisia, W Portugal and elsewhere in Mediterranean region, including Balearic Islands, Corsica, Sardinia, Sicily, Corfu, Crete, Samos, Ikaria, Chios and Rhodes: also, in isolated inland regions of Spain (Huelva and Málaga to Salamanca and Madrid) and France (Provence to Ayeron, Lozère and Ardèche). Absent from N Adriatic coast (central peninsular Italy to Istria). Generally 0-1200m but recorded sporadically to 2400m in High Atlas.

FLIGHT-PERIOD Bivoltine. May/June and mid August/mid October.

HABITAT Hot, dry, often dense, mixed scrub containing an abundance of LHP: often on hillsides.

LIFE-HISTORY LHP principally *Arbutus unedo*: the structure, colour-pattern and behaviour of the larva suggests a high-level of adaptation to *A. unedo*. In Gibraltar, oviposition has been reported on *Osyris quadripartita* (restricted to S Iberian peninsula and Balearic Islands). Ova/larvae have been recorded on *Nicotiana glauca* on Samos and *Citrus nobilis* and *C. sinensis* in N Africa. Captive rearing of larvae on *Rhamnus* sp. merits confirmation. Hibernates as a larva.

BEHAVIOUR Exhibits marked territorial and 'hilltopping' behaviour. Both sexes greatly attracted to fermenting fruit; ethanol appears to be the key attractant – wine and other alcoholic beverages are potent baits.

PLAIN TIGER

TWO-TAILED PASHA

Plain Tiger

Two-tailed Pasha

Purple Emperor *Apatura iris*

RANGE Europe, NW Kazakhstan, S Urals, Amur, NE China, Korea.

A. iris Linnaeus 1758 TL: Germany and England.

DISTRIBUTION N Portugal: Minho. N Spain: scattered colonies: S. de Guadarrama; S. de la Demanda; Cantabrian Mts; Pyrenees, Valle de Aran. Eastwards from Pyrenees through S England, N Italy to Denmark (including Fyen, Sjælland, Lolland, Falster and Bornholm), S Sweden (Skåne: first noted 1985), Baltic states, Balkans and NW Greece Varnous Mts.; Vernon Mts.; Pindos Mts. (Grammos massif to district of Trikala). 50-1500m.

DESCRIPTION AND VARIATION Upf dark spot in s2 obscured by gc; uph inner edge of white discal band linear (cf. *A. ilia*). Rarely, ups white markings greatly reduced or absent (f. *iole* Denis and Schiffermüller).

FLIGHT-PERIOD Univoltine. Mid June/mid August.

HABITAT Mature, deciduous woodland, with small clearings or tracks bordered by LHP.

LIFE-HISTORY LHPs, *Salix caprea*; *S. cinerea*; *S. alba*; *S.* (?)*atrocinerea*. Ova laid on upperside of leaves in the shaded, interior parts of the tree, most frequently 1-2m above ground-level. Larva feeds near leaf-tip, producing a characteristic symmetrical pattern, leaving main rib and tissue at leaf-tip intact. Hibernates as a small larva in a stem-fork on LHP.

BEHAVIOUR Males strongly attracted to carnivore excrement, human perspiration, hot road-tar and fumes of petroleum spirit. Both sexes often rest on leaves of trees (commonly oak) several metres above the ground.

NOTE *A. iris* and *A. ilia* often share same habitat and sometimes the same LHP (*Salix alba*).

Freyer's Purple Emperor *Apatura metis*

RANGE E and SE Europe, European Turkey, SW Russia, Kazakhstan, W Siberia, Amur, NE China, Korea, Japan.

A. metis Freyer 1829 TL: Pecs (Fünfkirchen), Hungary.

DISTRIBUTION Associated largely with river systems in:- Austria (Danube), Hungary (Danube; Drava), Slovenia (Sava), N Serbia (Danube), Bulgaria (widespread but local in river valleys), N Greece (Thiamis; Voidomátis; Strimonas; Nestos; Evros; Lake Doirani) and European Turkey (Evros Valley; Balli; Inecik). Not reported from Republic of Macedonia. 0-650m.

DESCRIPTION AND VARIATION Resembles *A. ilia*: generally smaller; ups brighter; upf orange pd band expanded at apex; uph dark pd spots obscured by dark background; uph outer edge of pale discal band well marked by discontinuity at v4 – component of band in s4, large, sharply angular (diamond-shaped). Polymorphism unknown. (Cf. *A. ilia*).

FLIGHT-PERIOD Bivoltine. Late May/June and mid July/August.

HABITAT Wooded river margins containing mature specimens of LHP.

LIFE-HISTORY LHP *Salix alba*. Ova laid on upperside of leaves. Hibernation as for *A. ilia*.

BEHAVIOUR In very hot conditions, adults may rest for several hours on leaves in higher branches of LHP. Males are attracted to carnivore excrement and often take water from riverside sand-bars: both sexes sometimes assemble on LHP to take sap issuing from wounded bark.

NOTE In N Greece, *A. metis* and *A. ilia* are sympatric in the region of Lake Doirani: sympatry not known in the interconnected Sarantàporos and Voidomátis river systems, where both species occur with no obvious ecological separation.

Purple Emperor

Freyer's Purple Emperor

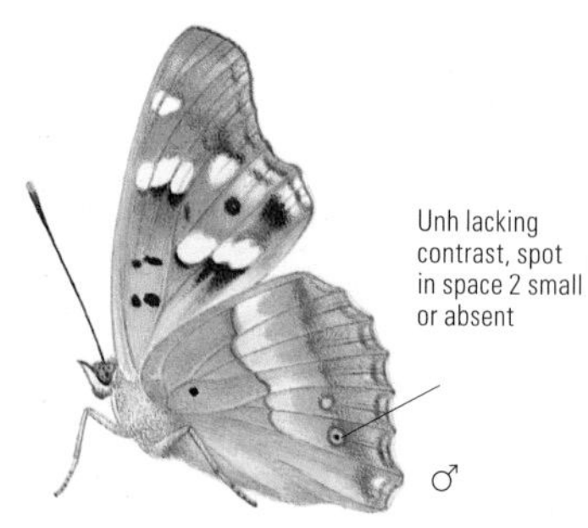

A. metis

PURPLE EMPEROR

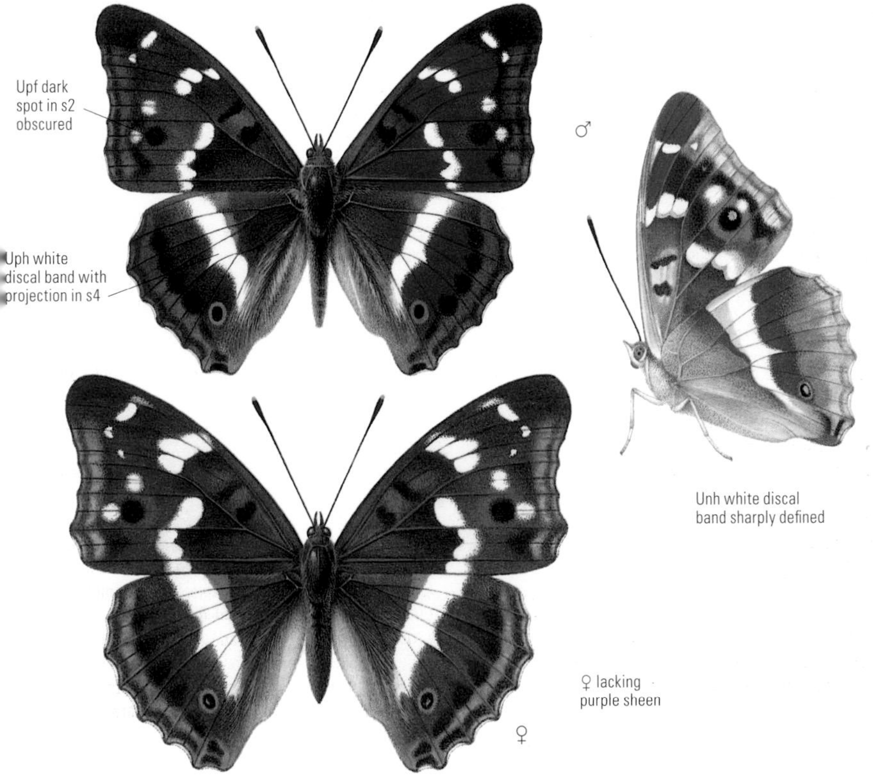
Upf dark
spot in s2
obscured
Uph white
discal band with
projection in s4
♂
Unh white discal
band sharply defined
♀ lacking
purple sheen
♀

FREYER'S PURPLE EMPEROR

♂ and ♀ uph dark pd markings
confluent, forming a distinctive band
Upf dark
spot in
s2 small
♂
♀
♂ and ♀ ups dark pd distinctive
♂ and ♀ uph discal band well
marked by discontinuity at v4

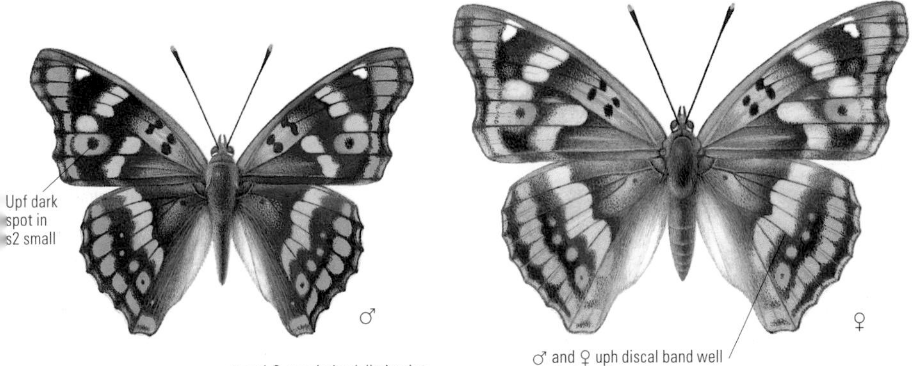

Lesser Purple Emperor *Apatura ilia*

RANGE C and S Europe, Caucasus, S Urals, NW Kazakhstan, NE China.

A. ilia Denis and Schiffermüller 1775 TL: Vienna.

DISTRIBUTION N Portugal: Minho. N Spain: Cantabrian Mts.; provinces of Huesca and Catalonia. From Pyrenees eastwards to Latvia, Balkans and NW Greece. Absent from Britain, Holland, N Germany, Poland, Fennoscandia and S Italy. 300-1300m.

DESCRIPTION AND VARIATION Upf dark spot in s2 well defined, ringed orange; uph inner edge of pale discal band non-linear (cf. *A. iris*); pd spots rounded, sometimes confluent, conspicuous against orange background (cf. *A. metis*). Both sexes polymorphic: f. *clytie* Denis and Schiffermüller: ups yellow to orange-brown; ups white markings, except apical spots, replaced by yellow: characters and incidence regionally variable. In Catalonia, f. *barcina* Verity: ups and uns all white markings well developed; discal band wide; pale submarginal markings usually present; uns gc colour paler: polymorphism rare: a similar form occurs in W peninsular Italy.

FLIGHT-PERIOD Univoltine (late May/July) or bivoltine (June and August/September).

HABITAT Deciduous woodland clearings, tracks etc., bordered by LHP; wooded river valleys, especially river banks where LHPs, often *Salix alba*, occur in abundance.

LIFE-HISTORY LHPs *Populus tremulae*; *P. alba*; *P. nigra*; *Salix alba*: also, NE Spain, *S.* (?)*atrocinerea catalaunica*. Ova laid on upperside of leaves. Hibernates as a small larva.

BEHAVIOUR As for *A. iris*.

Thaleropis ionia

RANGE (?)Greece (Kastellorizo), Turkey, NE Iraq, NW Iran, Caucasus.

T. ionia Eversmann 1851 TL: Amasya

The sole European record relates to a male, noted by Mr J. G. Coutsis, in the Goulandris Museum, Athens: the site of capture is given as Kastellorizo, a small island 120km east of Rhodes. Known on nearby Turkish mainland. In overall appearance, bears a slight superficial resemblance to *A. metis*, but readily separable by upf and unf white spots in s3-s5, in addition to several other distinctive wing-characters. LHP in Armenia, *Salix* sp.

False Plain Tiger *Hypolimnas misippus*

RANGE Egypt, Lebanon, central S Turkey, Saudi Arabia, Tropical Africa and Asia, C America, Australia.

H. misippus Linnaeus 1764 TL: America.

DISTRIBUTION This powerful migrant was first reported from the Canary Islands (Tenerife) in 1895. Since 1987, appears to have become resident on Gomera, although the persistence of some colonies is in doubt. Vagrant specimens have been noted in the Azores. Absent from N Africa.

DESCRIPTION Large; fw length 30mm; male ups very dark brown or black; large, white, round discal spots, fw and hw, and upf apex white oval spot with brilliant violet reflections at distal borders; uns gc brownish with ups pattern of white spots repeated. Sexual dimorphism striking: except for absence of hw black discal spots, the female is a close mimic of both white and orange forms of female *Danaus chrysippus*.

FLIGHT-PERIOD Polyvoltine. All confirmed records relate to October/February, suggesting that colonies may be temporary and due only to recurring late-season migration from Tropical Africa.

HABITAT The few extant records relate to gardens in coastal regions.

LIFE-HISTORY LHP on Gomera unknown: elsewhere in range, species of:- *Portulaca*; *Talinum*; *Ficus*; *Ipomoea*; *Amaranthus*; *Hibiscus*; *Sedum*: species of at least the latter four genera occur on Gomera. Larvae are gregarious.

Lesser Purple Emperor

LESSER PURPLE EMPEROR

Poplar Admiral *Limenitis populi*

RANGE C and E Europe, C and S Urals, W and S Siberia, Mongolia, NE China, Japan.

L. populi Linnaeus 1758 TL: Sweden (Verity 1950).

DISTRIBUTION N and E France (very local in Brittany; local in Drôme and Vacluse (Rhône Valley)), Switzerland, N Italy, eastwards to 66°N in Fennoscandia (including Gotland), Republic of Macedonia, Bulgaria and N Greece (Rhodopi Mts.). Absent from SW France, Britain, N Holland, N Germany and W Norway. Extinct in Denmark. 200-1500m.

VARIATION Male ups gc somewhat variable, dark brown to dark slate-grey with bluish overtone; white discal markings sometimes reduced or absent (f. *tremulae* Esper), common in some populations.

FLIGHT-PERIOD Univoltine. Late May/late July: emergence seasonally variable in some localities. Flight-time short, usually 8-12 days.

HABITAT Mixed deciduous woodland, with clearings, roads etc. bordered by LHP.

LIFE-HISTORY LHP *Populus tremula*. Ova laid on upperside of leaves. Larva feeds in a similar fashion to *A. iris* except that tissue at leaf-tip is also consumed. For hibernation, the small larva forms a hibernaculum from a partly consumed leaf, bound to its adjacent stem with silk. Pupates on upperside of LHP leaf.

BEHAVIOUR Males attracted to carnivore excrement, human perspiration, hot road-tar, petroleum spirit and damp wood-ash.

Southern White Admiral *Limenitis reducta*

RANGE S and C Europe, Turkey, Middle East, W Iran, Caucasus.

L. reducta Staudinger 1901 TL: Hankynda.

syn: *camilla* Denis and Schiffermüller 1775 auct.: *anonyma* Lewis 1872 auct.: *rivularis* Stichel 1908 auct.

DISTRIBUTION N Portugal. N and EC Spain. NW and S France (Brittany and Normandy: very local) eastwards through S Germany, Slovakia, Balkans, Greece and European Turkey, including Mediterranean islands of Corsica, Sardinia, Elba, Sicily, Corfu, Lefkas, Kefalonia, Zakynthos, Kithira, Kea, Thassos, Limnos, Lesbos, Chios, Ikaria, Samos, Kos, Nissiros and Rhodes. 0-1650m. Absent from Balearic Islands and Crete.

FLIGHT-PERIOD Univoltine in northern range (mid June/early August); bivoltine in Mediterranean region (mid May/June and mid July/August).

HABITAT Dry, rocky or grassy places amongst scrub; sheltered, dry or damp woodland clearings.

LIFE-HISTORY LHPs *Lonicera periclymenum*; *L. etrusca*; *L. implexa*; *L. xylosteum*; *L. alpigena*; *L. nummulariifolia*; *L. caprifolium*. Ova laid singly on upperside of leaves, upon which larve feed. Larval colouring variable: bright green and reddish in C Europe, dull green and greyish-violet in Mediterranean region. Hibernates as a small larva within a hibernaculum formed from a leaf secured to LHP stem with silk.

Poplar Admiral

Southern White Admiral

POPLAR ADMIRAL

♂

♀

SOUTHERN WHITE ADMIRAL

White Admiral *Limenitis camilla*

RANGE C Europe, Turkey, Urals, NW Kazakhstan, Amur, NE China, Korea, Japan.
L. camilla Linnaeus 1763 TL: Germany
syn: *sibilla* Linnaeus 1767
DISTRIBUTION N Spain: Cantabrian Mts.; Pyrenees. Eastwards from Pyrenees through S England, E Denmark (including Fyen, Sjælland, Lolland, Falster and Bornholm) to Baltic states, Balkans, N Greece (Rhodopi Mts.: extremely local) and European Turkey. Sporadic in SE France, absent from S and E peninsular Italy and Mediterranean islands. 0-1500m. No recent records from S Sweden (Skåne).
FLIGHT-PERIOD Univoltine. Mid June/mid August.
HABITAT Sunny clearings in large deciduous woodlands, often in damp, humid situations; conifer plantations and pine forests with deciduous wooded margins.
LIFE-HISTORY LHPs *Lonicera periclymenum*; *L. caprifolium*; *L. xylosteum*; *Symphoricarpus racemosa*. Ova laid singly on upper surface of leaves of shaded plants. Larva feeds from leaf-tip towards the stem, leaving mid-rib intact, along which it rests. Hibernates as a small larva within a hibernaculum formed from a leaf secured to LHP stem with silk.
BEHAVIOUR Adults greatly attracted to bramble blossom.

Common Glider *Neptis sappho*

RANGE SE Europe, C and SE Asia, N China, Taiwan, Korea, Japan.
N. sappho Pallas 1771 TL: Volga, S Russia.
syn: *aceris* Esper 1783; *hylas* auct.
DISTRIBUTION NE Italy (Gorizia). Slovenia. Slovakia. Hungary. NE Croatia. N Serbia. Romania. Republic of Macedonia (Treska Valley, Skopje district). Bulgaria. N Greece (Rhodopi Mts. and southern foothills). Very local in many regions. Extinct in Austria. 200-1550m.
FLIGHT-PERIOD Bivoltine. Mid May/late June and July/August.
HABITAT Damp deciduous woodland, usually associated with river valleys: in Hungary, predominantly associated with (?)'Acacia' trees.
LIFE-HISTORY LHPs *Lathyrus vernus*; *L. niger*. Hibernates as a small larva. Pupa mimics a dead leaf attached to stem of LHP. One locality in N Greece, in which *L. vernus* and *L. niger* appear to be absent, is dominated by *Robinia pseudacacia*, reportedly a LHP in Japan: cf. habitat character in Hungary.
BEHAVIOUR Characteristic gliding flight is confined mostly to dappled shade of woodland canopy, where both sexes also rest or bask with outspread wings.
NOTE Often associated with *L. morsei* in northern range.

Hungarian Glider *Neptis rivularis*

RANGE S European Alps, E Europe, Turkey, Caucasus, C Asia, S Siberia, Mongolia, N China, Taiwan, Korea, Japan.
N. rivularis Scopoli 1763 TL: Graz, Austria.
syn: *lucilla* Schiffermüller 1775.
DISTRIBUTION SE Switzerland. N Italy. Slovenia. E Austria. Slovakia. Hungary. S Poland. W Croatia (Dalmatian coast) through C Serbia, Bosnia-Herzegovina to E Romania: very sporadic and local in S Balkans; Republic of Macedonia (Galicica Pl.; Treska Valley), SW Bulgaria and N Greece (Rhodopi Mts.: very local). 500-1600m.
FLIGHT-PERIOD Univoltine. Late May/early August.
HABITAT Open deciduous, more rarely, coniferous woodland.
LIFE-HISTORY LHPs *Spiraea chamaedryfolia*; *S. salicifolia*; *Aruncus dioecus*; *Filipendula ulmaria*. Ova laid on leaf-edge, mostly at tip coincident with medial vein; about 25% are deposited a short distance from this point. Young larva feeds from below leaf-tip towards stem, leaving mid-rib intact: rests and sometimes hibernates in a tube formed from terminal leaf-remnant. Captive larvae accept *S. bumalda*. Pupa mimics a dead leaf attached to stem of LHP.

White Admiral

Common Glider

Hungarian Glider

WHITE ADMIRAL

COMMON GLIDER

HUNGARIAN GLIDER

Camberwell Beauty *Nymphalis antiopa*

RANGE Europe, Turkey, throughout temperate Asia and most of N America.

N. antiopa Linnaeus 1758 TL: Sweden (Verity 1950).

DISTRIBUTION Occasional in N Portugal. N Spain (S. de Guadarrama; S. de la Demanda; Cantabrian Mts.; Pyrenees) eastwards through most of Europe to N Fennoscandia, S Greece and European Turkey. Demarcation of residency and migration uncertain in some northern areas, perhaps seasonally variable. Progressively less frequent towards NW Europe; a rare migrant in Britain. Reported from Mallorca ((?)migrant): not recorded from other Mediterranean islands. Generally 0-2000m: occasional as migrants/vagrants in barren terrain above 2600m.

FLIGHT-PERIOD Univoltine. S Europe, mid June/July; Scandinavia, August/September. Hibernated specimens appear March/June according to locality.

HABITAT Diverse. Sunny woodland glades; river valleys; dry rocky gullies; sand dunes; parks; suburban gardens. Hibernated butterflies are usually found in sites with an abundance of LHP: fresh specimens may appear almost anywhere in summer.

LIFE-HISTORY LHPs *Salix alba*; *S. cinerea*; *S. atrocinerea*; *S. caprea*; *S. aurita*; *S. viminalis*; *Populus tremula*; *P. nigra*; *P. alba*. Ova laid in large batches around circumference of a stem in upper part of LHP. Larvae feed gregariously in a silken web in early instars – singly towards maturity. Pupation sites include bushes and trees, but not usually the plant upon which larvae have fed. Hibernates as an adult in cool dark places, e.g., hollow trees, wood-stacks, road-drains.

BEHAVIOUR A powerful migrant, dispersing from its breeding grounds soon after emergence. Usually encountered in very small numbers or singly. Attracted to fermenting fruit, the sap of wounded trees and nectar-rich plants: hibernated specimens are fond of *Salix* blossom. Recorded taking nectar from *Urtica dioica* in largely barren terrain at 2300m and moisture from snow at 2200m.

Peacock Butterfly *Inachis io*

RANGE Europe, Turkey, throughout temperate Asia to Japan.

I. io Linnaeus 1758 TL: Sweden (Verity 1950)

DISTRIBUTION Widespread and common in most of Europe south of 64°N to northern half of Iberian peninsula, Sierra Nevada, N central Greece, European Turkey and Mediterranean islands of Sicily, Corsica, Sardinia (above 400m), Corfu, Samos and Simi. Reported only once from NW Africa (Algiers, 1961). Records for N Scotland appear to relate to migration. 0-2500m.

FLIGHT-PERIOD Univoltine. Normally June/August but enter diapause between late July and early October according to weather conditions. Hibernated specimens appear March/May.

HABITAT Open, sunny places in woodland; wooded riverbanks; damp meadows; fallow fields or disturbed ground; sheltered rocky gullies with bushes/small trees at upper limit of altitudinal range. LHP usually in great abundance.

LIFE-HISTORY LHPs: mainland Europe, *Urtica dioica*: Samos (where *U. dioica* is not indigenous) *Parietaria officinalis*. Larvae feed in companies until almost full-grown. At low altitude (150m) in NW Greece, mature larvae have been recorded in late August. Hibernates as an adult in cool, dark places: hollow trees, dense vegetation, wood-stacks, outhouses, rock-crevices, stone walls etc.

BEHAVIOUR Hibernated adults feed on *Salix* blossom in spring. Common on the blossom of *Buddleia davidii* in summer.

Small Tortoiseshell *Aglais urticae*

RANGE Europe, eastwards to Pacific coast.

A. urticae urticae Linnaeus 1758 TL: Sweden (Verity 1950).

DISTRIBUTION Common throughout Europe. Absent from Atlantic Islands, NW Africa and Mediterranean Islands except Sicily (replaced by *A. u. ichnusa* on Corsica and Sardinia). 0-3000m.

VARIATION At high altitude: generally larger; ups gc brighter. In Lapland, generally smaller; ups gc slightly darker.

FLIGHT-PERIOD Univoltine in colder regions in N Europe and at high altitudes in S Europe, late May/August according to season and locality: bivoltine or trivoltine in warm localities, May/October. Hibernated specimens appear March/April.

HABITAT AND LIFE-HISTORY Diverse. Occurs in almost all sites containing LHP *Urtica dioica*. Especially common in areas of human habitation and heavily grazed pasture where soil enrichment favours establishment of LHP. Natural use of *U. urens* as a LHP requires confirmation. Ova laid in large batches on underside of leaf. Small larvae feed on leaves in companies in silken webs, singly or in small groups as development proceeds. Hibernates as an adult, often in human dwellings, out-houses, etc. In common with many other 'vanessids', a high proportion of larvae are lost to dipterous parasites.

BEHAVIOUR Commonly observed at mountain summits –'hilltopping'. Fond of basking on walls, paths etc. Hibernated specimens are fond of *Salix* blossom: attracted to *Buddleia davidii*, *Sedum spectabilis* and *Aster novi-belgii* in summer. Hibernation sometimes interrupted on warm days in late winter.

A. urticae ichnusa Hübner 1824. TL: not stated.

DISTRIBUTION Corsica. Sardinia. 700-2500m.

DESCRIPTION Ups brighter; upf black spots in s2 and s3 absent or vestigial.

FLIGHT-PERIOD Bivoltine. May/October, reappearing March/April after hibernation.

HABITAT As for nominate form but restricted to mountainous areas.

LIFE-HISTORY LHP (?)*Urtica dioica*. Captively reared *ichnusa* is said to produce imagines identical to or resembling nominate form.

BEHAVIOUR Often 'hilltops'.

CAMBERWELL BEAUTY

PEACOCK BUTTERFLY

SMALL TORTOISESHELL

Camberwell Beauty

Peacock Butterfly

Small Tortoiseshell

A. u. ichnusa
(Corsica and Sardinia)

Large Tortoiseshell *Nymphalis polychloros*

RANGE N Africa, S and C Europe, Turkey, S Russia, C and S Urals, Kazakhstan, Himalayas.

N. polychloros Linnaeus 1758 TL: Sweden (Verity 1950).

DISTRIBUTION Morocco. Algeria. Tunisia. 200-2600m. From Iberian peninsula through most of Europe, including S England (very rare and local, extinct in many areas) to Baltic states, SE Sweden (including Bornholm and Öland) to Balkans, Greece and European Turkey. Occasional in Denmark, S Norway and S Finland as a migrant. Reported from Sicily, Corsica, Sardinia, Elba, Corfu, Crete, Lesbos, Ikaria, Samos, Kos and Rhodes. 0-1700m. Not reported from Balearic Islands.

DESCRIPTION Ups gc rusty-orange; inner margin well defined; legs and palpi dark brown, nearly black (cf. *N. xanthomelas*).

VARIATION In N Africa, *erythromelas* Austaut: ups gc brighter: transitional to nominate form in S Spain.

FLIGHT-PERIOD Univoltine. Late June/August. Hibernated specimens appear March/April.

HABITAT Diverse. Mature deciduous woodland with warm, sunny clearings; light, open woodland, often in hot, dry areas in Mediterranean region.

LIFE-HISTORY LHPs *Ulmus procera*; *U. glabra*; *U. campestris*; *U. americana*; *Salix caprea*; *S. alba*; *S. pedicellata*; *S. viminalis*; *Prunus avium*; *P. domestica*; *P. padus*; *Pyrus communis*; *Malus domestica*; *Populus tremula*; *P. nigra*; *P. alba*; *Sorbus tormilis*; *Crataegus monogyna*. Ova laid in a single batch around circumference of a stem, usually sited in upper part of LHP. Larvae feed gregariously in a silken web in early instars, singly towards maturity. Pupates frequently on branches of LHP. Hibernates as an adult in cool dark places, e.g., hollow trees, wood-stacks, road-drains.

BEHAVIOUR Migrant. Appears to disperse quickly following its emergence. Fond of basking in late afternoon sun.

NOTE Has become increasingly uncommon in NW Europe in recent decades.

Yellow-legged Tortoiseshell *Nymphalis xanthomelas*

RANGE E Europe, Turkey, C Asia, China, Korea, Japan.

N. xanthomelas Esper 1781 TL: Germany, Austria.

DISTRIBUTION Probably resident in E Slovakia, SE Poland, E Hungary and Romania: possibly resident in W Republic of Macedonia and NW Greece (very local and rare): occurrence in S Fennoscandia, Baltic states and most of S Balkans possibly dependent on migration, with perhaps establishment of temporary colonies. In Bulgaria, common and widespread in the 1920's, now possibly extinct as a resident species: becoming increasingly uncommon in other parts of European range. 0-2000m.

DESCRIPTION Resembles *N. polychloros*: ups gc reddish-orange, brighter; inner edge of dark submarginal borders suffused – indistinct; legs and palpi light brown or buff.

FLIGHT-PERIOD Univoltine. July/September. Hibernated specimens appear in May.

HABITAT Damp deciduous woodland, especially in river valleys.

LIFE-HISTORY LHPs *Salix* spp.; *Populus* spp. Oviposition, development and hibernation as for *N. polychloros*.

BEHAVIOUR Migrant.

False Comma *Nymphalis vaualbum*

RANGE E Europe, Turkey, C Asia, NE China, Korea, Japan, S Canada and northern U.S.A.

N. vaualbum Denis and Schiffermüller 1775 TL: Vienna.
syn: *l-album* Esper 1781.

DISTRIBUTION Reported from S Finland, Baltic states, Poland, Czech Republic, Slovakia, E Austria, Hungary, Romania, W Balkans (last reported 1972 in Bosnia-Herzegovina) and Bulgaria (a single record, 1942). Distinction between permanent populations, migration and temporary colonies established through migration difficult to establish: occurrence in W, N and S limits of European range most probably relate to migration. Becoming increasingly uncommon in European range. 0-(?)1500m.

DESCRIPTION White markings near upf apex and uph costa prominent (cf. *N. polychloros* and *N. xanthomelas*).

FLIGHT-PERIOD Univoltine. June/July. Hibernated specimens appear in March/April.

HABITAT Clearings in deciduous woods.

LIFE-HISTORY LHPs *Salix* spp.; *Populus* spp.; *Ulmus* spp. Small larvae live in silken webs.

BEHAVIOUR Migrant.

Large Tortoiseshell

Yellow-legged Tortoiseshell

False Comma

LARGE TORTOISESHELL

YELLOW-LEGGED TORTOISESHELL

FALSE COMMA

Red Admiral *Vanessa atalanta*

RANGE Azores, Canary Islands, N Africa, Europe, Turkey, Iran. N America to Guatemala. Haiti and New Zealand.
V. atalanta Linnaeus 1758 TL: Sweden (Verity 1950).
DISTRIBUTION Azores. Canary Islands. Morocco. Algeria. Tunisia. Throughout Europe, including all larger and many smaller Mediterranean islands, as a resident or migrant: in northernmost range, Ireland, Britain and most of Fennoscandia, appearance probably depends largely on migration. 0-2500m.
FLIGHT-PERIOD Univoltine. June/October: hibernated specimens usually appear in March/April; has been recorded on warm days in winter months near Mediterranean coast.
HABITAT Diverse. Occurs in many habitats other than those containing its LHPs.
LIFE-HISTORY LHPs: Canary Islands, *Urtica urens*; rarely *Parietaria* sp.: NW Africa, *Urtica membranacea*, *U. pilulifera*; *U. urens*; *Parietaria officinalis*: Europe, *U. dioica*; (?)*U. urens*; *P. officinalis*; *P. diffusa*; *P. debilis*. Ova laid usually near tip of leaves of plants growing in open sunny positions. Larvae feed singly in rolled-up leaves. Larvae are polymorphic. Pupates on LHP stems. Hibernates as an adult, sometimes successfully in Britain.
BEHAVIOUR Migrant. Often basks on walls, rock faces etc. Greatly attracted to nectar-rich plants, e.g., *Rubus fruticosus*, *Eupatorium cannabinum*, *Hedera helix*, *Sedum spectabilis* and *Buddleia davidii*.

Indian Red Admiral *Vanessa indica*

RANGE Canary Islands, Madeira, India, China, Japan, Korea.
V. indica vulcania Godart 1819 TL: Canary Islands (Kirby 1904)
syn: *callirhoe* Millière 1867; *occidentalis* Felder 1862.
DISTRIBUTION Madeira; occasional on nearby island of Porto Santo. Canary Islands: Gran Canaria; Tenerife; Gomera; La Palma; Hierro. Occasional (?) migrant on Fuerteventura. Not recorded from Lanzarote – suitable habitat appears to be absent. Absent from Azores, N Africa and European mainland. 0-1500m.
FLIGHT-PERIOD Polyvoltine. Occurs throughout the year, apparently without diapause.
HABITAT AND BEHAVIOUR Laurel forests where LHP grows as an undershrub. Often found outside of natural habitat, in gardens, parks etc., where it visits nectar-rich plants. On Tenerife often found on laurel blossom.
LIFE-HISTORY LHPs *Urtica morifolia*; *Parietaria* sp. On *U. morifolia*, ova laid singly, more rarely in pairs, on terminal leaves of shaded plants (cf. *V. atalanta*). Larva feeds within a rolled-up leaf in which it also pupates.
NOTE No populations are known between Atlantic islands and India.

Map Butterfly *Araschnia levana*

RANGE N Spain, C and E Europe, Caucasus, C Asia to NE China, Korea and Japan.
A. levana Linnaeus 1758 TL: Germany.
DISTRIBUTION N Spain (E Pyrenees: very local) eastwards through N and C France, Switzerland to E Denmark (including Fyen, Sjælland, Lolland and Falster), S Sweden (SW Skåne – first recorded in 1992); Baltic states, Bulgaria and N Greece (Nestos and Evros river systems). Absent from S France, Italy, Dalmatian coast, (?)Albania and Republic of Macedonia. 0-1400m. Reports for Portugal require confirmation.
DESCRIPTION AND VARIATION Seasonal dimorphism well marked. First brood (f. *levana*): ups gc dusky-orange with black markings. Second brood (f. *prorsa* Linnaeus): ups gc dark brown; creamy-yellow or white discal band disrupted at v4 upf. Intermediate forms (f. *porima* Ochsenheimer) are not uncommon.
FLIGHT-PERIOD Generally bivoltine. May/June and July/August: sometimes a partial third brood in favourable localities/seasons.
HABITAT Deciduous woodland clearings or bushy margins.
LIFE-HISTORY LHPs *Urtica dioica*; *U. urens*. Ova laid in chains suspended from underside of leaf – closely resembles character of flowers/flower-buds. Small larvae live in companies, dispersing towards maturity. Hibernates as a pupa.

Red Admiral

Map Butterfly

RED ADMIRAL

INDIAN RED ADMIRAL

Restricted to Canary Islands and Madeira

MAP BUTTERFLY

Painted Lady *Vanessa cardui*

RANGE Cosmopolitan, except S America.
C. cardui Linnaeus 1758 TL: Europe, Africa.
DISTRIBUTION Most of the region as a migrant, progressing northwards from N Africa in early spring, extending its range to within the Arctic Circle during summer months. Permanent resident of N Africa, Canary Islands, Madeira and some warmer Mediterranean areas: possibly semi-permanent in other, southerly localities in a succession of favourable seasons. Relatively rare in Ireland and Scotland. Reported occasionally from Iceland, which has no indigenous butterflies. Generally 0-3000m: migrants often occur at higher altitudes.
FLIGHT-PERIOD Polyvoltine. Has no diapause stage; flies in all months in areas of permanent residence. In northern Europe, migrants usually appear May/June: breeding and further dispersal persists until onset of cold weather.
HABITAT Virtually any site containing LHPs, most commonly areas containing an abundance of thistles.
LIFE-HISTORY Worldwide, LHPs comprise an extraordinary range of plant families of which Cucurbitaceae; Asteraceae; Fabaceae; Vitaceae; Malvaceae; Brassicaceae; Boraginaceae have been recorded for N Africa and/or Europe: *Cirsium*, *Carduus* (thistles), *Echium* and *Malva* (especially *M. sylvestris*) appear to be most commonly used. Larvae have been recorded on cultivated *Glycine max* (Soya Beans) in Germany. Ova laid singly, usually on upperside of leaves upon which larvae feed. Ovum stage may be as short as 3 days in S Europe: life-cycle 5-8 weeks according to conditions. Larvae are polymorphic. On Fuerteventura (LHP commonly *Malva parviflora*), larvae often parasitized by *Cotesia vanessae* (Braconidae).
BEHAVIOUR Thistles serve a dual purpose as rich nectar-sources and LHPs. A common summer visitor to *Buddleia davidii* bushes in gardens and parks.

American Painted Lady *Vanessa virginiensis*

RANGE Madeira, Canary Islands, S Canada, N America to Venezuela, Guatemala: occasional in Hawaii.
V. virginiensis Drury 1773 TL: New York.
syn: *huntera* Fabricius 1775.
DISTRIBUTION Canary islands: Tenerife; apparently extinct on Gomera and La Palma. Occasional migrant in W and S Portugal (especially Algarve), Azores, more rarely in Spain (including Huesca), very rarely in SW Ireland, W Wales and S England. Not reported from N Africa or (?)Madeira. 0-1500m.
FLIGHT-PERIOD Polyvoltine. Recorded in all months on Tenerife except February and November.
HABITAT Flowery places.
LIFE-HISTORY LHP on Tenerife unknown: in N America, several genera of Asteraceae; Fabaceae; Malvaceae; Boraginaceae; Urticaceae; Balsaminaceae; Scrophulariaceae. Suspected of entering diapause in winter months as an adult: diapause may be disrupted temporarily during warm periods.

Queen of Spain Fritillary *Issoria lathonia*

RANGE Madeira, Canary Islands, N Africa, Europe, Turkey, Middle East, W and C Asia to N India, Mongolia.
I. lathonia Linnaeus 1758 TL: Sweden (Verity 1950).
DISTRIBUTION Madeira and Canary Islands (Gran Canaria; Tenerife; Gomera; La Palma) as migrants only. Morocco. Algeria. Tunisia. Most of Europe to 63°N in Fennoscandia as a resident, and 66°N as a migrant in W Finland. Resident on Corsica, Sardinia and Sicily: not reported from eastern Mediterranean islands. Rare as a migrant in S England. 0-2700m: vagrants/migrants occur at higher altitudes. Commoner in summer months as populations expand and disperse. In S Europe in late summer, relatively greater abundance at higher altitudes is possibly due to superior condition of LHPs which are less likely to have become desiccated.
FLIGHT-PERIOD Trivoltine. March/October.
HABITAT Diverse. Almost all habitat-types.
LIFE-HISTORY LHPs: *Viola* spp. belonging principally to the distinctive, but taxonomically unseparated group recognizable as 'pansies' – *Viola tricolor*; *V. arvensis*; *V. aetolica*; *V. lutea*; *V. biflora*; *V. calcarata*; *V. corsica*; *V. odorata*. Reliable data regarding widespread, natural use of 'violets' appear to be lacking – species of this group are occasionally rejected by captive larva. Ova laid singly on leaves of LHP, where growing in dry conditions amongst sparse vegetation: in damp conditions, ova are often deposited on low, soft herbage other than LHP. In captivity, newly-hatched larvae from early broods, as well as small wild larvae, often wander – apparently aimlessly – amongst the leaves of 'pansies' and/or 'violets' for several days before dying without attempting to feed. In nature, small or large larvae often rest in exposed positions on stones, fallen wood-bark and a variety of plants. Pupates near ground-level, suspended from plant-stems or underside of leaves. Pupal colouring variable: shiny, uniform greyish-green or brownish with white dorsal patch, in either case, resembling a bird-dropping. Reputedly hibernates as an ovum, small larva, pupa or adult.
BEHAVIOUR A well-known migrant. In late afternoon sun, adults often bask on hot paths, walls, etc.

Painted Lady

Queen of Spain Fritillary

PAINTED LADY

AMERCIAN PAINTED LADY

QUEEN OF SPAIN FRITILLARY

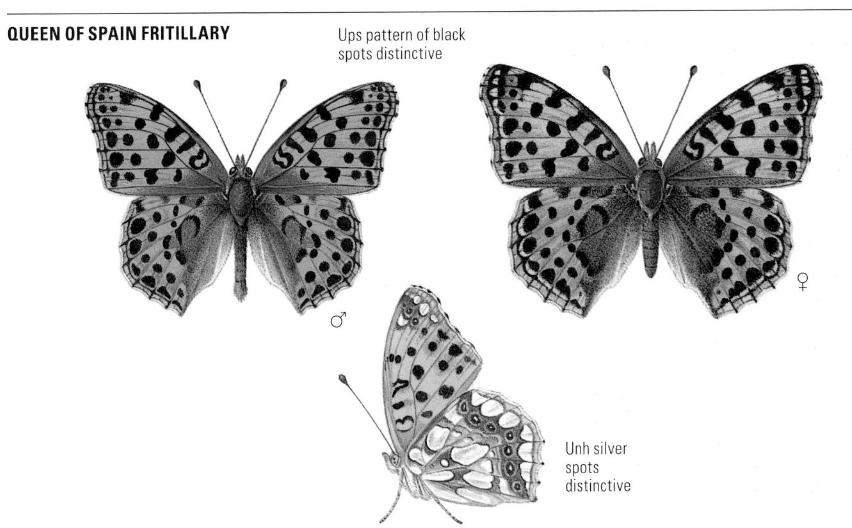

Comma Butterfly *Polygonia c-album*

RANGE N Africa, Europe, Turkey, C Asia, N China, Korea, Japan.

P. c-album Linnaeus 1758 TL: Sweden

DISTRIBUTION Morocco. Algeria. Tunisia. 500-2700m. Most of Europe, including England, Wales, Fennoscandia to 68°N and European Turkey. Absent from SW Iberian peninsula, Ireland and Mediterranean islands except Sicily, Corsica, Sardinia and Corfu. Occasional in N Holland, N Germany and Denmark. Apparently extinct in Scotland. 0-2000m.

DESCRIPTION Unh cell-end with white 'comma', variable. In summer broods – those which do not enter winter diapause – uns gc yellowish-brown with bright, variegated pattern (f. *hutchinsoni* Robson). Specimens destined for hibernation in late summer or autumn, uns dark brown with obscure, dark greenish marbling; this cryptic pattern, appropriate for hibernating adults, appears to arise from photo-period influence on larval/pupal development.

FLIGHT-PERIOD Bivoltine in most of Europe, late May/June and July/August, reappearing March/April after hibernation: usually univoltine in Scandinavia, June/August: trivoltine in warmest areas of S Balkans and Greece, May/October.

HABITAT Woodland clearings, often in damp places.

LIFE-HISTORY LHPs: NW Africa, *Ribes grossularia*; *R. uva-crispa*: Europe, *Urtica dioica*; *Salix caprea*; *S. alba*; *Humulus lupulus*; *R. uva-crispa*; *R. nigrum*; *R. rubrum*; *Corylus avellana*; *Ulmus glabra*; *U. minor*; *U. procera*; *U. laevis*. Captive larvae accept *Parietaria officinalis*. Ova laid singly on upperside of leaves. Hibernates as an adult amongst dense vegetation, tree roots, overhanging banks, road-drains, out-houses, etc.

BEHAVIOUR Hibernation sometimes disrupted briefly on warm days in late winter. Adults often feed on *Salix* blossom in early spring.

NOTE Declined rapidly in Britain about the turn of the century, but has recovered much of its former range since 1920/1930: now common and widespread in S England and Wales (cf. *L. camilla*). Short/medium term residency in areas close to limit of range possibly relate to erratic or periodic increases in adjacent, permanent populations accompanied by dispersion.

Southern Comma *Polygonia egea*

RANGE SE France, Italy, S Balkans, Greece, Turkey, Middle East, Iran to N India.

P. egea Cramer 1775 TL: Istanbul and Izmir.

DISTRIBUTION SE France. Corsica. NW coastal and peninsular Italy. Sicily. Dalmatian coast. Albania. Republic of Macedonia. Bulgaria. Greece, including Corfu, Crete and many other Aegean Islands. European Turkey. Absent from Sardinia and Rhodes. 0-1700m: uncommon above 1100m.

DESCRIPTION First brood: ups yellowish-brown with dark brown markings, variable in size and number; uns yellowish with complex pattern of variegation; unh with small, white 'y'-shaped mark at cell-end. Summer brood(s): ups and uns usually slightly darker.

FLIGHT-PERIOD Bivoltine or trivoltine. May/October. Hibernated specimens reappear late March.

HABITAT Hot, dry, steep rocky places: often common in villages where old walls provide a foot-hold for LHP.

LIFE-HISTORY LHP *Parietaria officinalis*. Captive larvae reluctantly accept *Urtica dioica* but reject *Salix caprea* and *Ulmus glabra*. Hibernates as an adult.

BEHAVIOUR Fond of basking on rock faces, walls, hot paths, etc.

Comma Butterfly

Southern Comma

COMMA BUTTERFLY

Ups black markings bold, extensive

♂

Unh with white 'C'-shaped mark at cell-end

♂

♀

2nd brood

1st brood

f. *hutchinsoni*

SOUTHERN COMMA

Ups black markings sparse

Unh with small white 'Y'-shaped mark at cell-end

♂

2nd brood

♂

♀

1st brood

Cardinal Fritillary *Argynnis pandora*

RANGE Canary Islands, N Africa, S Europe, Turkey, Middle East, Iraq, Iran, S Russia, Kazakhstan, Afghanistan, N Pakistan, N India.

A. pandora Denis and Schiffermüller 1775 TL: Vienna.
syn: *maja* Cramer 1776.

DISTRIBUTION Canary Islands: La Palma; Gomera; Hierro; Tenerife. 500-1500m. Morocco. Algeria. Tunisia. 200-2600m. Portugal. Spain. Balearic Islands. W and S France. Corsica. Sporadic in N Italy, widespread in S Italy. Sardinia. Elba. Sicily. S Switzerland, Austria. Czech Republic. Slovakia. Hungary. Balkans. Greece, including Corfu, Crete, Thassos, Limnos and Samos. European Turkey. 50-1650m.

VARIATION Aberrant form *maruxa* Agenjo, uns normal greenish gc replaced by pinkish-buff: reputedly recurrent in some localities of C Spain.

FLIGHT-PERIOD Univoltine in much of Europe, generally mid May/early July: bivoltine in NW Africa, May/June and August/late September: possibly bivoltine in parts of S Europe (univoltine in Sardinia, mid June/late August): in Canary Islands, late May/mid September with no apparent discontinuity.

HABITAT AND BEHAVIOUR Open clearings, bordered by bushes, in deciduous or open pine woodland. Habitats invariably contain, or are in proximity to an abundance of robust, nectar-rich plants, *Carduus*, *Cirsium*, *Centaureae* etc., upon which both sexes are avid feeders.

LIFE-HISTORY LHPs *Viola* spp., including *V. cheiranthifolia* (Tenerife). Ova laid on dead vegetation, less often on LHP in shade of dense undergrowth. Hibernates as a small larva.

Pallas's Fritillary *Argynnis laodice*

RANGE Central E Europe, C and S Urals, S and W Siberia, NW Kazakhstan, Amur, Japan.

A. laodice Pallas 1771 TL: S Russia.

DISTRIBUTION Latvia. Lithuania. E Poland. Slovakia. E Hungary. Romania. An occasional migrant in Estonia, SE Sweden (including Gotland) and S Finland.

VARIATION Ups dark markings and black suffusion variable.

FLIGHT-PERIOD Univoltine. July/August.

HABITAT Damp, flowery meadows in open woodland at low altitudes.

LIFE-HISTORY LHP *Viola palustris.*

BEHAVIOUR Both sexes attracted to bramble blossom.

Cardinal

Pallas's Fritillary

♀ upf white subapical spot distinctive

CARDINAL

h olive-green
ffusion often
tensive

♂

♀

PALLAS'S FRITILLARY

♀ upf sex-brands
on v1 and 2
Inconspicuous

♂

Silver-washed Fritillary *Argynnis paphia*

RANGE Algeria, Europe, Turkey, temperate Asia to Yakutia. *A. paphia* Linnaeus 1758 TL: Sweden.

DISTRIBUTION Algeria (Blida; Djurdjura massif; Lambessa; Batna; Dj. Aures; Collo; S'Gag; 800-1600m). Generally widespread and common from N Portugal, N and E Spain (including S. de Cazorla and S. de Segura: sporadic) through Ireland and S Britain to S Fennoscandia (including Fyen, Sjælland, Lolland, Falster, Bornholm and Gotland), Greece and European Turkey: recorded from Sicily, Corsica, Sardinia, Elba, Crete, Lesbos, Samos, Ikaria and Andros. 0-1500m.

VARIATION Unh gc and 'silver-wash' subject to appreciable variation, especially in Mediterranean region. In Algeria, *dives* Oberthür: ups black markings well developed; unh 'silver-wash' generally obsolete, replaced by yellowish-green. In Corsica and Sardinia, f. *immaculata* Bellier: unh 'silver-wash' replaced by extensive silvery-golden suffusion: forms transitional to nominate form not uncommon in Mediterranean region. In Spain, Italy and occasionally in S Greece, *anargyria* Staudinger: uns gc yellowish; 'silver-wash' replaced by pale, diffuse discal band. In NW Africa and S Europe, unh silver-white markings sometimes well developed, prominent (*argyrea* Oberthür). Female dimorphic: f. *valesina* Esper: ups suffused greyish-green or greenish-brown; usual black markings replaced by dark brown: recurrent form in most European populations, but unknown in N Africa and Sardinia.

FLIGHT-PERIOD Univoltine. Late May/September according to locality.

HABITAT Sunny, woodland clearings with bushy margins, usually containing bramble or other nectar-rich plants.

LIFE-HISTORY LHPs: *Viola* spp.: Algeria, *V.* (?)*mumbyana*: Europe, *V. reichenbachiana*; *V. canina*; *V. odorata*; *V. riviniana*. Ova laid in crevices in tree-bark, where newly-hatched larvae hibernate: deciduous trees, less often conifers, sited near an abundance of well-shaded LHP, are usually selected.

Silver-washed Fritillary

SILVER-WASHED FRITILLARY

f. ***valezina***

f. ***immaculata***
(Corsica and Sardinia)

f. ***argyrea***

Dark Green Fritillary *Argynnis aglaja*

RANGE Morocco, Europe, Turkey, Asia, China, Japan.
A. aglaja Linnaeus 1758 TL: Sweden (Verity 1950).
syn: *charlotta* Haworth 1802.

DISTRIBUTION Morocco: Middle Atlas (Ain Leuth; Azrou; Ifrane; 1500-1800m); Rif Mts. (Bab-Berred; Dj. Lakraa; Ketama; 1200-1500m). Widespread and common in most of Europe, including Britain, Ireland, Orkney Islands and European Turkey: absent from Mediterranean islands except Sicily. 0-2200m.

VARIATION In Middle Atlas, *lyauteyi* Oberthür: large; male ups gc dusky orange-buff; black markings well developed; unf with pale pinkish-orange basal flush; unh green suffusion brighter, more extensive: female ups pale yellowish-buff, with greyish-green suffusion. In Rif Mts., *excelsior* Rothschild: resembles *lyauteyi*: ups gc brighter; unf basal flush deeper pink. In colder climates, e.g., Scotland, ups black markings are often heavy.

FLIGHT-PERIOD Univoltine. June/August, according to locality and altitude.

HABITAT Open grassy, flowery slopes; clearings in light woodland; damp meadows; heaths; moorlands. Most frequent on calcareous soils.

LIFE-HISTORY LHPs *Viola hirta*; *V. tricolor*; *V. palustris*. Ova laid on both surfaces of leaves. At rest, small larvae often secrete themselves in the smaller, furled leaves of LHP. Hibernates as an unfed larva amongst leaf-litter or in bark-crevices at base of small shrubs or trees. Pupates on robust plant-stems near ground-level.

Corsican Fritillary *Argynnis elisa*

RANGE Corsica, Sardinia.
A. elisa Godart 1823 TL: Corsica and Sardinia.

DISTRIBUTION Corsica. Sardinia. 800-1500m.

FLIGHT-PERIOD Univoltine. Late June/mid August.

HABITAT Dry, open heaths; bushy places; light woodland.

LIFE-HISTORY LHP *Viola corsica*. Hibernates as a fully formed larva within ovum-case.

Dark Green Fritillary

Corsican Fritillary

High Brown Fritillary

Niobe Fritillary

CORSICAN FRITILLARY

DARK GREEN FRITILLARY

Pd spots absent

♂

♀

A. a. aglaja

A. a. lyauteyi
(Morocco)

A. a. aglaja
(Scotland)

High Brown Fritillary *Argynnis adippe*

RANGE NW Africa, Europe, Turkey, temperate Asia.
A. adippe adippe Denis and Schiffermüller 1775 TL: Vienna.
syn: *cydippe* Linnaeus 1761
DISTRIBUTION Most of Europe, including England and Wales, to 66°N in Fennoscandia (including Fyen, Sjælland, Lolland, Falster, Bornholm, Öland and Gotland), Greece and European Turkey. Absent from Mediterranean islands except Sicily. 0-2100m.
DESCRIPTION Male upf sex-brands on v2 and v3 conspicuous; uph with hair-fringe along v7.
VARIATION F. *cleodoxa* Ochsenheimer: unh gc buff or yellowish, without green basal suffusion; all markings reduced; silver spots obsolete except as pupils of pd reddish-brown spots: very rare in N Europe, progressively more frequent through central S Europe to Balkans, preponderating south of central Alps and replacing nominate form in Greece: nominate form occurs only rarely in S Balkans and has once been reported from N Greece. F. *cleodoxa* is common in Pyrenees, occurring with nominate form and the intermediate f. *cleodippe* Staudinger: these three forms become rapidly less common south of Pyrenees where they are replaced by f. *chlorodippe* Herrich-Schäffer: unh suffused olive-green; silver spots fully developed; series of reddish pd spots complete.
FLIGHT-PERIOD Univoltine. Late May/August according to locality and altitude.
HABITAT Generally dry, grassy bushy places; clearings in light woodland.
LIFE-HISTORY LHPs *Viola* spp., including *V. canina*; *V. odorata*; *V. hirta*. Ova laid on leaves. Hibernates as a fully formed larva within ovum-case. Pupates on robust plant-stems near ground-level.
NOTE In decline in Britain.
A. adippe auresiana Früstorfer 1908 TL: Djebel Aures, Algeria.
DISTRIBUTION Morocco: Anti-Atlas (Tizi-n-Melloul); High Atlas (Tizi-n-Talrhemt; Tizi-n-Test; Oukaïmeden; Dj. Aourach; 1750-2800m); Middle Atlas (Ifrane; Tizi-Tarhzeft; Azrou; 1300-1700m); Rif Mts. (Bab-Berred; Dj. Lakraa; Ketama; Taghsut; 1000-1800m). Algeria: Dj. Aures; Kabylie; 1300-1700m.
DESCRIPTION AND VARIATION Resembles *chlorodippe* closely: unh green suffusion darker; basal silver spots often smaller or absent. Male ups sex-brand vestigial; uph hair-fringe on v7 sparse. In High Atlas, f. *astrifera* Higgins: smaller; paler; black markings reduced. In Rif Mts., f. *hassani* Weiss: resembles *auresiana* closely: slightly larger; ups gc brighter; black markings heavier; unh green suffusion more extensive. All forms of *auresiana* appear to lack unh rounded, black-pupilled yellow/silver spot near cell-base – characteristic of *A. niobe*.
FLIGHT-PERIOD Univoltine. June/early August according to locality.
HABITAT Open, dry, bushy places; grassy, flowery slopes; rocky slopes with sparse vegetation; open woodland.
NOTE Regarded as specifically distinct by some authors, and as a ssp. of *A. niobe* by others. In the absence of definitive biological data, present provisional taxonomic assignment, based on close superficial similarity to *A. adippe* populations of S Spain, seems appropriate.

Niobe Fritillary *Argynnis niobe*

RANGE Europe, Turkey, Middle East, Iran, C Asia, Mongolia, Amur.
A. niobe Linnaeus 1758 TL: Sweden (Verty 1950).
DISTRIBUTION Most of Europe to 62°N in Fennoscandia (including Sjælland, Falster, Bornholm, Öland and Gotland) and European Turkey. Absent from NW Africa, SW coastal district of Iberian peninsula, central N Italy, most coastal areas of peninsular Italy, Ireland, Britain and Mediterranean islands except N Sicily. 0-2400m.
DESCRIPTION AND VARIATION Male ups resembles *A. adippe*: upf sex-brand on v2 and v3 narrow – often greatly reduced or absent in C and S Spain; unh usually with small, roughly circular, yellow or silver spot, often with black pupil or thin black ring, near cell-base – a useful distinguishing character (cf. *A. adippe* and *A. aglaja*) F. *eris* Meigen: unh silver spots absent, but usual positions outlined black; gc variable, pale greenish-yellow to yellowish-buff: a wide variety of transitional forms are not uncommon in Fennoscandia and some localities of C Europe. F. *eris* appears to be present in all C European populations, in widely varying ratios to nominate form, replacing the latter entirely in Iberian peninsula, S Balkans and Greece (reports of nominate form from Sierra Nevada and Portugal require confirmation). In some localities of Massif Central and in C Apeninnes, nominate form preponderates. In (?)much of Spain, f. *altonevadensis* Reisser: a variant of f. *eris*: both sexes smaller, ups gc paler: female ups and uns black markings reduced.
FLIGHT-PERIOD Univoltine. Late May/August according to locality and altitude.
HABITAT Open grassy places often amongst scrub; rocky gullies with sparse vegetation; woodland clearings.
LIFE-HISTORY LHPs *Viola* (?)*canina*; *V. odorata*; *V. hirta*; *V. palustris*. Ova laid on dead vegetation near LHP. Hibernates as a fully-formed larva within its ovum-case. Large larvae often rest in full sun on pieces of fallen tree-bark or dead wood.

Maps on p. 186

♀ markings and grey suffusion variable, may be heavy

HIGH BROWN FRITILLARY

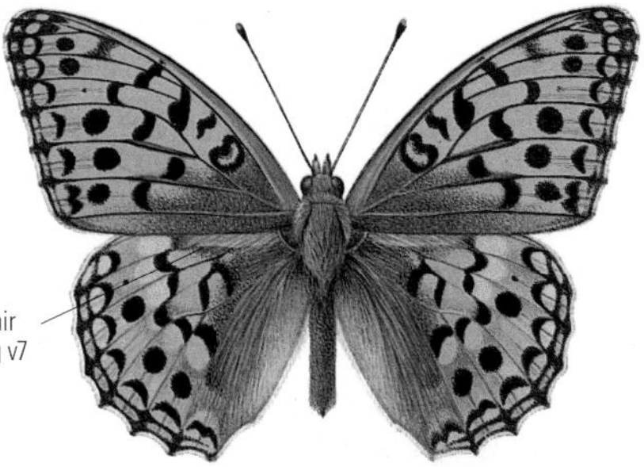

Upf sex-brands on v2 and 3 prominent
Uph with hair fringe along v7

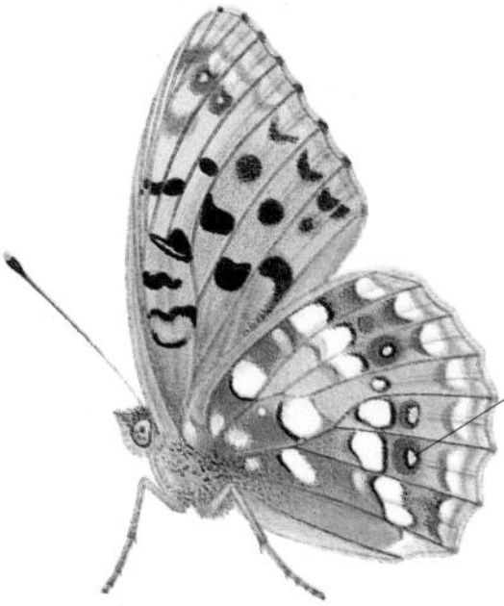

♂
Unh white-pupilled, reddish-brown pd spots distinctive

♀

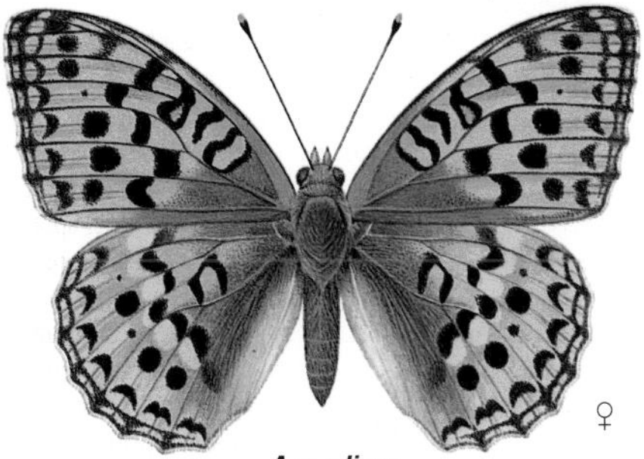

A. a. adippe

♂

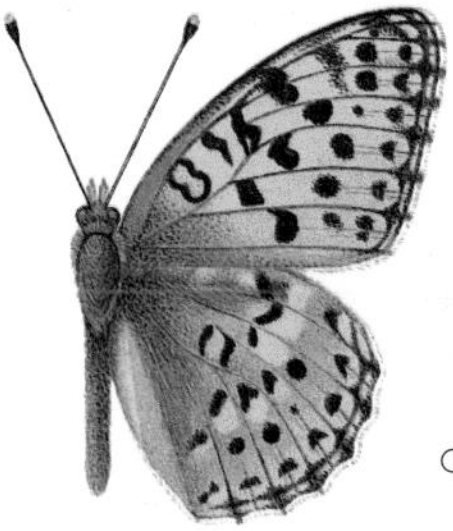

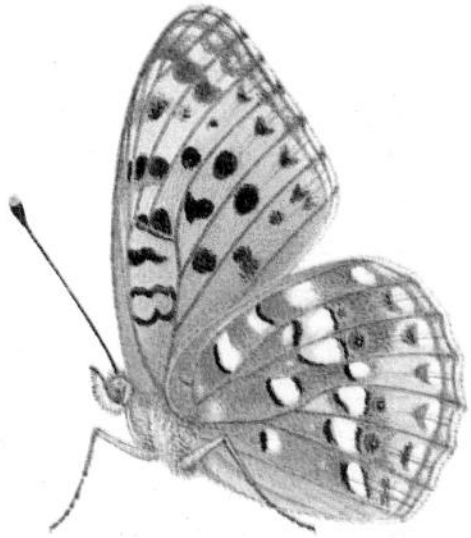

A. a. auresianna* f. *astrifera (High Atlas)

♂

f. *chlorodippe*

♂

f. *cleodippe*

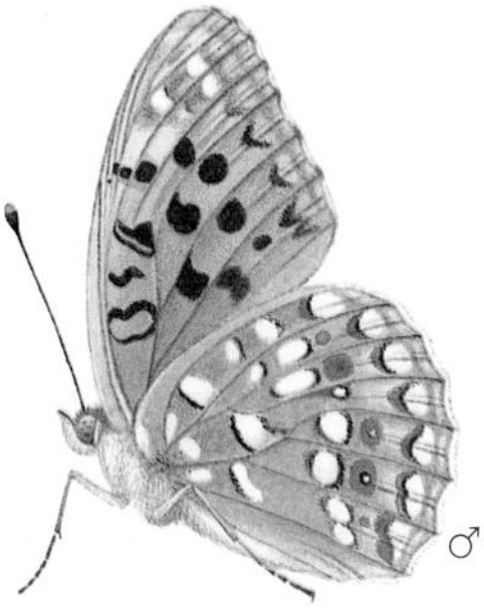

Unh silver spots absent
♂

f. *cleodoxa*

A. a. adippe

NIOBE FRITILLARY

pf sex-brand
n v2 and
narrow,
conspicuous,
ometimes
bsent
Uph without hair fringe along v7

♂
Unh veins black; small yellow spot near cell-base, usually black-pupilled characteristic

♂

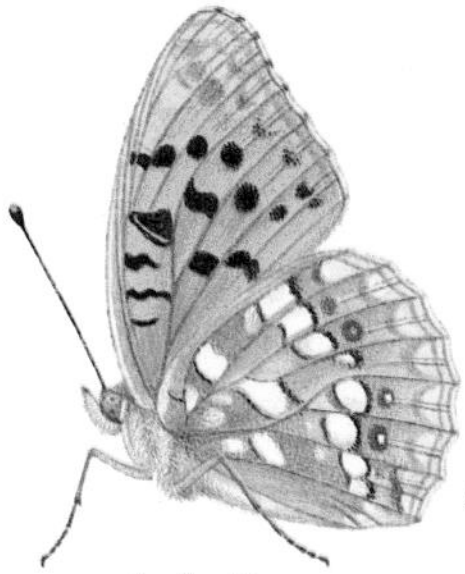

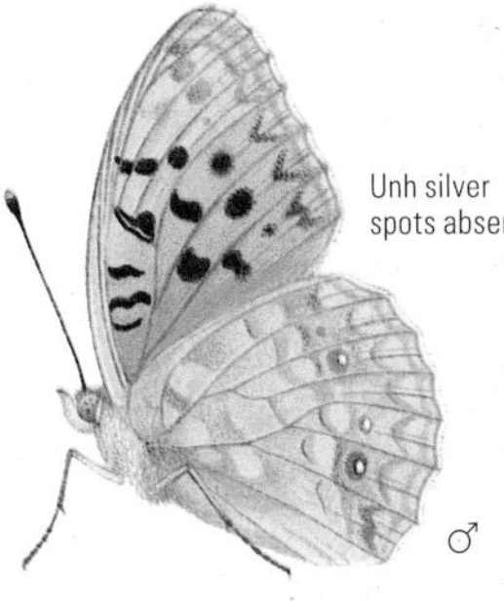

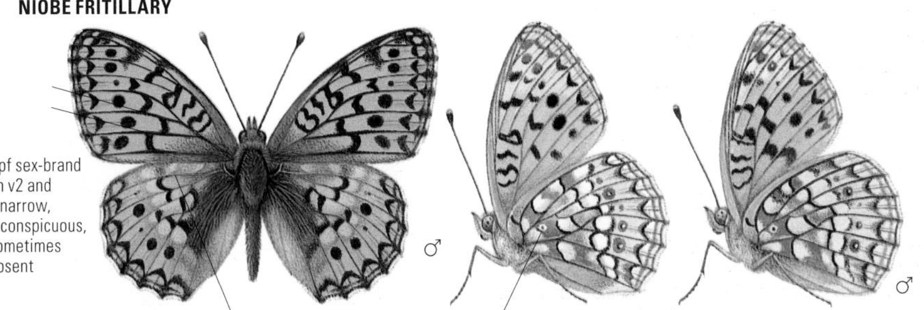

f. *eris*

Twin-spot Fritillary *Brenthis hecate*

RANGE S Europe, Turkey, Iran, C Asia, Altai.
B. hecate Denis and Schiffermüller 1775 TL: Vienna.
DISTRIBUTION Spain: scattered colonies: Sierra Nevada; S. de Segura; Montes Universales; S. de la Demanda; Cantabrian Mts.; Soria; Huesca; Catalonia. S France: very local in Provence; Basses Alpes. N Italy. Commoner in E Europe: Czech Republic and Slovakia to Balkans, N and C Greece and European Turkey. 25-1500m.
DESCRIPTION AND VARIATION Ups pd spots of uniform size (cf. *B. daphne*). In E Europe, unh markings darker.
FLIGHT-PERIOD Univoltine. Generally late May/late July: Bulgaria and NE Greece, late April/early May in favourable seasons.
HABITAT Flowery, grassy meadows, usually sheltered by bushes or light woodland.
LIFE-HISTORY LHP principally *Filipendula ulmaria*.

Marbled Fritillary *Brenthis daphne*

RANGE S Europe, NE Turkey, Iraq, Iran, S Urals, NW Kazakhstan, S Siberia, Mongolia, China, Japan.
B. daphne Denis and Schiffermüller 1775 TL: Vienna
DISTRIBUTION Spain: S. de Guadarrama; Montes Universales; Cantabrian Mts.; Pyrenees; Catalonia. Local in S France. Italy. Switzerland and S Germany to S Poland, Balkans, N and C Greece and European Turkey. Absent from Mediterranean islands except N Sicily and Samos. 75-1750m.
DESCRIPTION Ups pd spots irregular in size (cf. *B. hecate* and *B. ino*): both sexes, unh base of s4 (adjacent to cell-end) yellow, partly shaded or striated orange-brown (cf. *B. ino*).
FLIGHT-PERIOD Univoltine. Late May/early August.
HABITAT Bushy, flowery places, often in woodland clearings.
LIFE-HISTORY LHPs *Rubus fruticosus*; *R. idaeus*. Ova laid on upperside of leaves. Larvae often rest on upperside of leaves of LHP. Hibernates as an ovum or small larva.

Lesser Marbled Fritillary *Brenthis ino*

RANGE Europe, Turkey, throughout temperate Asia, Polar Urals, Yakutia, Japan.
B. ino Rottemburg 1775 TL: Halle, Germany.
DISTRIBUTION Spain: Cantabrian Mts.; Province of Burgos; S. de la Demanda; Pyrenees. From E Pyrenees to 66°N in Fennoscandia and Balkans. In Italy, restricted to foothills of S Alps and Calabria. Absent from Portugal, Britain, N France, N Belgium, N Holland, Greece, European Turkey and Mediterranean islands. 0-2000m.
DESCRIPTION AND VARIATION Both sexes: unh base of s4 (adjacent to cell-end) wholly yellow – apparent as a discrete, rectilinear spot separating cell and dark pd area (cf. *B. daphne*): ups black markings and dark suffusion very variable.
FLIGHT-PERIOD Univoltine. In C and S Europe, early June/late July: in Scandinavia, late June/mid August according to season, altitude and latitude.
HABITAT Damp flowery places, sheltered by bushes or light woodland, usually near rivers or marshes; also hillside bogs.
LIFE-HISTORY LHP principally *Filipendula ulmaria*: also, *F. petalata*; *Rubus chamaemorus*; *R. idaeus*; *Aruncus dioicus*; *Sanguisorba officinalis*. Reported use of *S. minor* (?)*minor* and *S. minor muricata* in Spain requires confirmation. On *F. ulmaria*, ova laid singly or in pairs mostly amongst flower-buds which they closely resemble. Small larvae feed on flowers and leaves. Hibernates as an ovum or small larva.

Twin-spot Fritillary

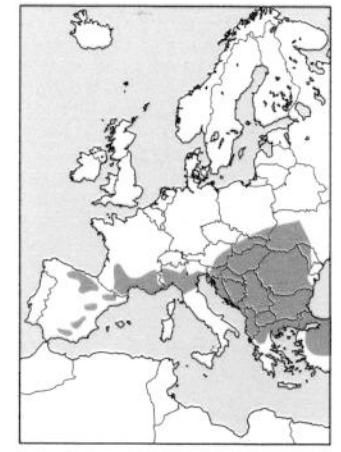

Marbled Fritillary

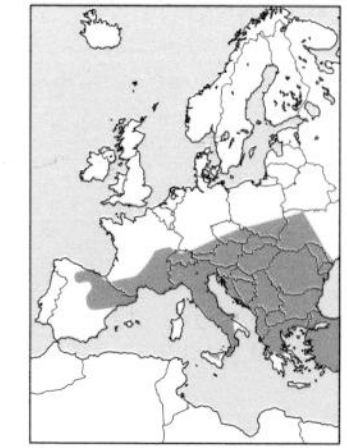

Lesser Marbled Fritillary

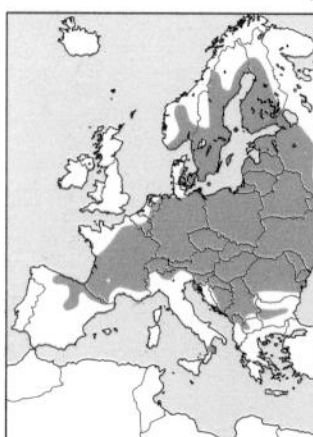

TWIN-SPOT FRITILLARY

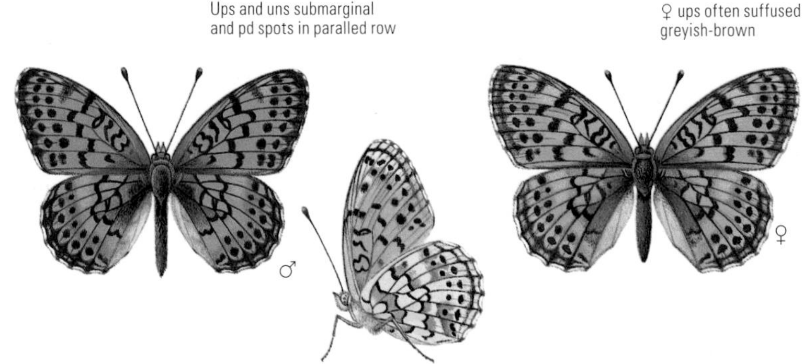

MARBLED FRITILLARY

LESSER MARBLED FRITILLARY

Shepherd's Fritillary *Boloria pales*

RANGE Alpine and subalpine levels in S Europe.
B. pales pales Denis and Schiffermüller 1775 TL: Vienna.
DISTRIBUTION Eastern Alps of Bavaria and N and E Tirol. Dolomites. Julian Alps. Tatra Mts. Carpathian Mts. 2200-2700m.
DESCRIPTION Upf black discal markings bold, macular (cf. *B. napaea*); unf markings obscure – 'ghosted'; unh basal and pd areas reddish. F. *tatrensis* Crosson du Cormier (Tatra Mts.) and f. *carpathomeridionalis* Crosson and Popescu-Gorj (S Carpathian Mts.) superficially indistinguishable from nominate form.
FLIGHT-PERIOD Univoltine. Late June/early September.
HABITAT AND LIFE-HISTORY Flowery alpine meadows. LHP *Viola calcarata*.
B. pales palustris Frühstorfer 1909 TL: Zermatt, Switzerland.
DISTRIBUTION Alpes-Maritimes, through S Alps to SW Tirol. Local in C Appenines. Bosnia-Herzegovina: Prenj Pl. SW Serbia: Mt. Durmitor. Albania. Republic of Macedonia; Sar Pl.; Mt. Pelister. Bulgaria: Rila Mts.; Pirin Mts. Generally 1500-2800m, occasionally at 1200m.
DESCRIPTION Smaller; ups paler; upf discal markings thinner; unh reddish coloration more extensive. F. *contempta* Rebel and Zerny (SW Serbia and Republic of Macedonia) and f. *rilaensis* Varga (Rila Mts.) superficially indistinguishable from *B. p. palustris*.
FLIGHT-PERIOD Univoltine. Mid July/mid August.
HABITAT Flowery alpine/subalpine meadows.
LIFE-HISTORY As for nominate form.
B. pales pyrenesmiscens Verity 1932 TL: Gèdre, Haute-Pyrénées.
DISTRIBUTION Cantabrian Mts.; Pyrenees. 1500-2100m.
DESCRIPTION Both sexes: larger; ups gc slightly paler; uph black basal suffusion reduced, not encroaching cell: female ups sometimes suffused greyish-violet.
FLIGHT-PERIOD Univoltine. Late June/August.
HABITAT AND LIFE-HISTORY As for nominate form.

Mountain Fritillary *Boloria napaea*

RANGE E Pyrenees, Central Alps, Fennoscandia, S Siberia, Altai, Amur, Alaska, Wyoming.
B. napaea Hoffmannsegg 1804 TL: Alps of Tirol.
DISTRIBUTION Spain and France: very local: E Pyrenees (Gerona; Puy de Puymorens; Val d'Eyne; Cambre d'Aze; Pic du Carlit). Andorra. Alps of France, S Switzerland, Italy and Austria. 1500-2500m. Norway and W Sweden from 60°N to North Cape. 0-1100m. A report for Cantabrian Mts. (Pto. de San Glorio 1600m) requires confirmation.
DESCRIPTION Resembles *B. pales*. Male ups paler; upf black discal markings thin – not macular; unh paler: female ups suffused grey, often with strong violet reflections and greenish basal overtones, most noticeable in fresh specimens.
FLIGHT-PERIOD Univoltine. Late June/August.
HABITAT In S Europe, flowery alpine/subalpine meadows: habitat-character similar in Scandinavia, but at lower altitudes – sometimes on shoreline in N Norway.
LIFE-HISTORY LHPs *Viola* spp. including *Viola biflora*; *Polygonum viviparum*. Ova laid on leaves of LHP or other nearby soft herbage. Hibernates as a small larva. At higher altitudes and latitudes, larval development occupies two seasonal cycles.

Cranberry Fritillary *Boloria aquilonaris*

RANGE C Europe, Fennoscandia, Arctic Russia, S Urals, W Siberia, Altai.
B. aquilonaris Stichel 1908 TL: Gellivare, Sweden.
syn: *arsilache* Knoch 1781 (invalid homonym)
DISTRIBUTION Small, widely scattered colonies in S Belgium (Ardennes), France (Massif Central; Orne; Eure; Seine-Maritime; Nièvre; Jura; Doubs; Haute-Saône; Haute-Rhin; Vosges) and Switzerland (Jura Mts.; Prealps; Engadine). Progressively less sporadic from Bavaria and Austria, through Czech Republic, Slovakia, Poland to Baltic states. Widespread, locally common in Fennoscandia, including Sjælland. 100-2000m.
DESCRIPTION AND VARIATION Male ups bright fiery-red; ups and unf black basal and discal spots well developed; upf spots in s1b v-shaped, arranged horizontally thus > < or, less often, joined at apices or connected by a short streak (cf. *B. napaea*). In S Fennoscandia and C Europe, usually larger (f. *alethea* Hemming).
FLIGHT-PERIOD Univoltine. Mid June/August.
HABITAT Raised peat bogs or wet heaths, often sheltered by light woodland and usually in close proximity to permanent water.
LIFE-HISTORY LHP *Vaccinium oxycoccos* [=*Oxycoccus quadripetalus*; *O. palustris*]. Ova laid on stems and leaves. Hibernates as a small larva. Development may occupy two seasonal cycles in northernmost range.
BEHAVIOUR Despite their exceptional brilliance, males have a remarkable ability to 'vanish' in flight.
CONSERVATION As with all other wetland species, habitats are especially vulnerable to drainage in adjacent areas.

Shepherd's Fritillary

Mountain Fritillary

SHEPHERD'S FRITILLARY

MOUNTAIN FRITILLARY

CRANBERRY FRITILLARY

Balkan Fritillary *Boloria graeca*

RANGE SW Alps, Balkans, Greece.

B. graeca Staudinger 1870 TL: Mt. Veluchi [Timphristos], Greece.

DISTRIBUTION SW Alps of France and Italy. Bosnia-Hercegovina: Prenj Pl. SW Serbia: Mt. Durmitor. Republic of Macedonia: Mt. Pelister; Placenska Pl.; Galicica Pl.; Sar Pl.; Kozuf Pl. Bulgaria: Rila Mts.; Pirin Mts.; Rhodopi Mts.; Slavayanka Mts. Greece: Varnous Mts.; Vernon Mts.; Voras Mts.; Mt. Orvilos; Pindos Mts. (Epano Arena and Grammos massifs to Mt. Ghiona). 1450-2600m.

VARIATION In Bosnia-Herzegovina and Rila Mts., f. *balcanica* Rebel: slightly smaller, otherwise closely similar to nominate form – no ecological barriers are apparent between Greek and Balkan populations where these share the same mountain massives at political boundaries. In SW Alps, f. *tendensis* Higgins: unh ocellated pd spots generally better developed.

FLIGHT-PERIOD Univoltine. Mid June/early August.

HABITAT Open grassland, often containing *Juniperus communis nana*. On calcareous or acidic soils.

LIFE-HISTORY LHP *Viola* sp.; *V.* (?)*tricolor macedonica*. Ova laid on leaves of LHP, as well as other plants, e.g., *Teucrium chamaedrys* and *Juniperus communis nana*. Hibernates as a small larva.

Bog Fritillary *Proclossiana eunomia*

RANGE Europe, Russia, Mongolia, NE China, Sakhalin, N America.

P. eunomia eunomia Esper 1799 TL: Prussia.

syn: *aphrape* Hübner 1799/80.

DISTRIBUTION Very sporadic and local in W Europe. N Spain: E Cantabrian Mts. Andorra. France: Pyrénées-Orientales; Vosges; Ardennes. S Belgium: Ardennes. N Italy: Val Venosta. S Germany. Austria. Czech Republic. Slovakia. Poland. 300-1500m. Bulgaria: Stara Pl. 1600-1900m. Absent from Ireland, Britain, Holland, Denmark and Hungary.

DESCRIPTION Both sexes: unh series of dark brown or black pd rings with pale yellow or white centres; basal, discal and pd spots yellow.

FLIGHT-PERIOD Univoltine. Late May/early July.

HABITAT Marsh meadows by rivers or lakes; raised peat bogs.

LIFE-HISTORY LHP *Polygonum bistorta*. Ova laid on underside of leaves, singly or in small clusters. Hibernates as a small larva.

CONSERVATION Most habitats are extremely small and correspondingly vulnerable; many have been destroyed by drainage and afforestation: commercial forestry activity continues to pose a threat in S Belgium.

P. eunomia ossiana Herbst 1800 TL: Not stated.

DISTRIBUTION Norway, Sweden and Finland: widespread and common. Baltic states: sporadic but locally common. 50-900m. Absent from Denmark.

DESCRIPTION AND VARIATION Resembles nominate form, sometimes very closely. Both sexes: generally smaller; ups and uns markings well defined; unh basal, discal and pd spots white or silver; ups often with dark suffusion, especially in female. Slight regional variation in size, ups gc and markings, often obscured by significant individual variation.

FLIGHT-PERIOD Mid June/mid July: emergence date subject to seasonal conditions.

HABITAT AND LIFE-HISTORY LHPs *Polygonum viviparum*; *Viola palustris*. Hibernates as a larva. Larval development may occupy two seasonal cycles.

Titania's Fritillary *Clossiana titania*

RANGE Central Alps of Europe, Poland, S Finland, Latvia, Balkans, Urals, Siberia, Transbaikal, Mongolia, Amur, Sakhalin, N Korea, N America, Canada.

C. titania titania Esper 1793 TL: 'Sardinia' [Piedmont].

DISTRIBUTION France: Massif Central; Hautes-Alps; Isère. Italy: Cottian Alps. 300-1800m.

DESCRIPTION Male ups brownish-orange; black markings fine: unh marbled yellow and brown with greenish or violet tints: female ups and uns paler.

FLIGHT-PERIOD Univoltine. Mid June/late August.

HABITAT Flowery meadows in woodland clearings.

LIFE-HISTORY LHP *Polygonum bistorta*. Hibernates as a fully-formed larva within ovum case. Pupates on plant-stems near ground-level.

C. titania cypris Meigen 1828 TL: Bavaria and Switzerland.

syn: *amathusia* Esper 1784 (invalid homonym)

DISTRIBUTION Alps of E Italy, S and C Switzerland (also Jura Mts.), Bavaria and Austria. Poland. (?)Hungary. Latvia. Estonia. S Finland. (?)NW Croatia. Bosnia-Herzegovina: Vranica Pl.; Jahorina Pl.; Zelengora Pl. SW Serbia: Mt. Durmitor; Sinjajevina Pl. (?)Albania. Romania: Transsylvania. 800-1600m.

DESCRIPTION Male ups reddish; all black markings heavy: unh darker, with complex marbling – brown, purple, maroon, pale violet and yellow: female ups gc paler.

FLIGHT-PERIOD, HABITAT AND LIFE-HISTORY As for nominate form.

Balkan Fritillary

Bog Fritillary

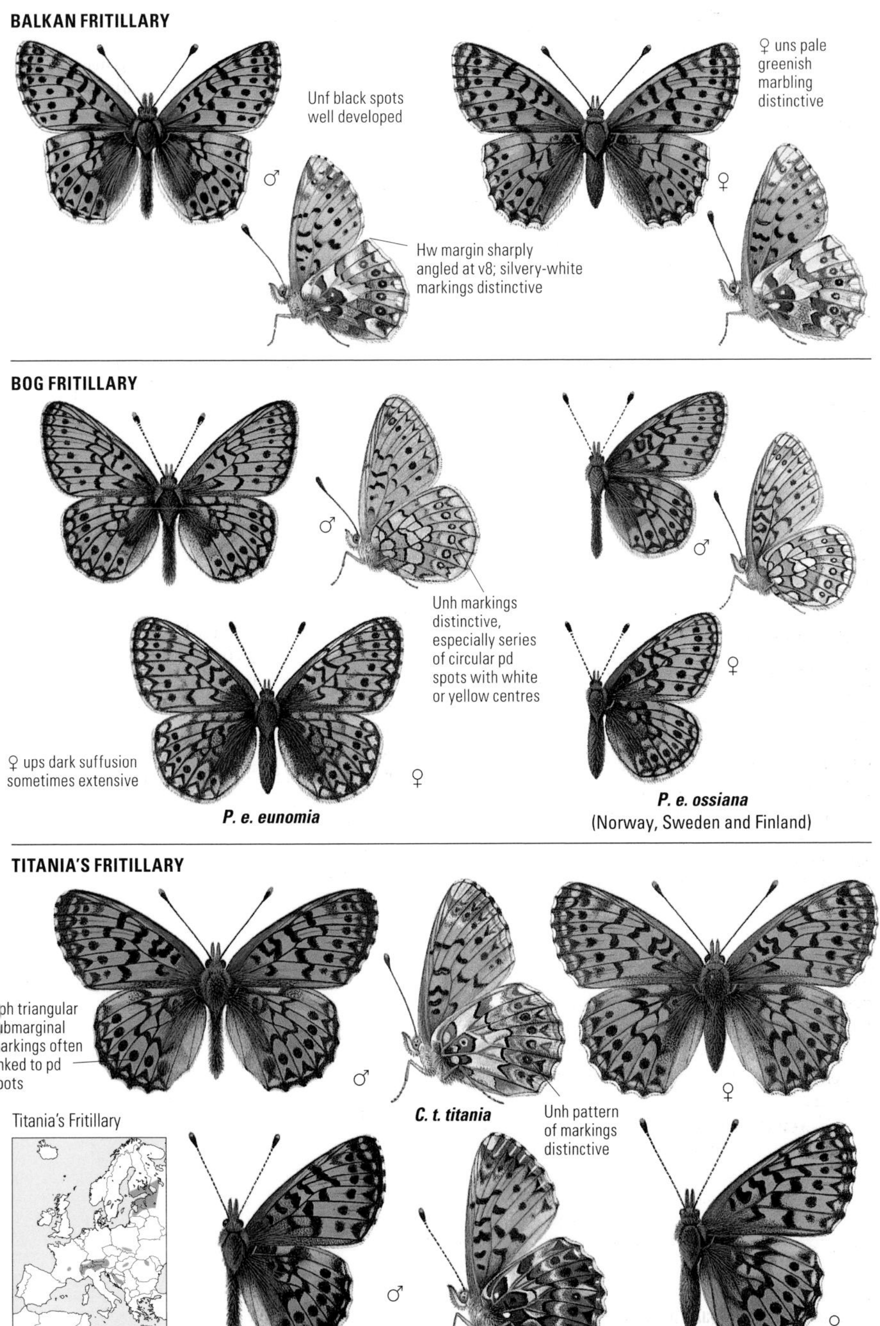
BALKAN FRITILLARY
Unf black spots well developed
♂
Hw margin sharply angled at v8; silvery-white markings distinctive
♀ uns pale greenish marbling distinctive
♀
BOG FRITILLARY
♂
Unh markings distinctive, especially series of circular pd spots with white or yellow centres
♂
♀
♀ ups dark suffusion sometimes extensive
♀
P. e. eunomia
P. e. ossiana
(Norway, Sweden and Finland)
TITANIA'S FRITILLARY
h triangular
bmarginal
arkings often
ked to pd
ots
♂
♀
Titania's Fritillary
C. t. titania
Unh pattern of markings distinctive
♂
♀
Unh purple, violet and yellow markings distinctive
C. t. cypris

Pearl-bordered Fritillary *Clossiana euphrosyne*

RANGE Europe, Turkey, Russia, N Kazakhstan.
C. euphrosyne Linnaeus 1758 TL: Sweden (Verity 1950).
DISTRIBUTION Widespread, locally common. N Spain, eastwards through most of Europe, including Britain and central W Ireland, to North Cape and S Greece (Mt. Chelmos and Taygetos Mts.). Absent from W and C Denmark, E Italy and Mediterranean islands except N Sicily. 0-1900m. Records for N Portugal require confirmation.
DESCRIPTION Unh cell-base reddish; chevrons enclosing marginal silver spots proximally blunt, often obscure (cf. *C. selene*).
VARIATION In Fennoscandia: generally smaller; ups markings with variable dark suffusion, sometimes obscuring gc, especially in female: relationship of named forms, e.g. f. *fingal* Herbst, f. *lapponica* Esper, f. *septentrionalis* Nordström, largely obscured by individual and local variation.
FLIGHT-PERIOD Univoltine in N Europe and at high altitudes in S Europe, late May/July: elsewhere, a partial second brood may occur, April/June and July/September.
HABITAT Deciduous or coniferous woodland clearings.
LIFE-HISTORY LHPs *Viola* spp., including *V. reichenbachiana*; *V. canina*; *V. palustris*; *V. odorata*; *V. riviniana*; *V.* (?)*rhodopeia*; *V. hirta*. Ova laid on low herbage as well as LHP. Hibernates as a half-grown larva.

Small Pearl-bordered Fritillary *Clossiana selene*

RANGE Europe, Russia, Mongolia, Sakhalin, Korea, N America.
C. selene Denis and Schiffermüller 1775 TL: Vienna.
DISTRIBUTION N Portugal. Spain: S. de Guadarrama; S. de la Demanda; Cantabrian Mts.; Pyrenees. France, eastwards through most of N and C Europe (including Britain), Baltic Islands to North Cape, N Balkans and SW Bulgaria. Sporadic in S France. Absent from Ireland, Ligurian Alps and peninsular Italy. 0-2200m.
DESCRIPTION Unh cell-base yellow; chevrons enclosing marginal silver spots, well developed, sharply angled at proximal apex; size of dark pd spots irregular – large in s2, largest in s5 (cf. *C. euphrosyne*).
VARIATION In Fennoscandia, f. *hela* Staudinger: generally smaller with variable dark ups suffusion. Inter-seasonal variation has been attributed to the influence of temperature on larval/pupal development.
FLIGHT-PERIOD Univoltine at higher latitudes and altitudes, mid May/early July: bivoltine in warmer regions, early May/late June and mid July/early September: second brood appears to be partial in some parts of C Europe.
HABITAT Forest clearings, often in damp places; meadows in wooded river valleys; moorland; marshy areas near lakes.
LIFE-HISTORY LHPs *Viola canina*; *V. palustris*; *V. riviniana*; *V. hirta*. Ova laid on low herbage as well as LHP. Hibernates as a half-grown larva or sometimes as a pupa in Scandinavia.

Arctic Fritillary *Clossiana chariclea*

RANGE Arctic Fennoscandia, Arctic Siberia, Greenland, Labrador, Arctic America.
C. chariclea Schneider 1794 TL: Lapland.
DISTRIBUTION N Fennoscandia north of 68°. Sweden, mountains north and south of Lake Torneträsk (Pallentjåkka; Nissuntjårro; Snurijåkkåtan; Pessivare; Vilgesgierdu). Norway: mountains north of Swedish border to Gargia and Porsanger. Mountains of NW Finland (Saana; Malla; Kilpisjärvi; Enontekiö). 100-1400m.
FLIGHT-PERIOD Univoltine. Usually emerges late June/early July, flying for about two weeks: emergence may be delayed until early August in adverse seasonal conditions.
HABITAT Open, windswept, dry, rocky tundra with small grassy hollows, patches of Dwarf Birch (*Betula nana*) and other low shrubs.
LIFE-HISTORY LHP not reported: ova are sometimes laid on dead vegetation – twigs and grasses.
BEHAVIOUR Even in overcast conditions, often rests with outspread wings in shelter of stones or shrubs.
NOTE In N America, treated as a ssp. of *C. titania* by some authors.

Pearl-bordered Fritillary

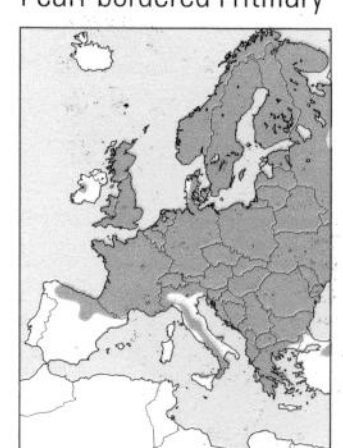

Small Pearl-bordered Fritillary

Arctic Fritillary

PEARL-BORDERED FRITILLARY

SMALL PEARL-BORDERED FRITILLARY

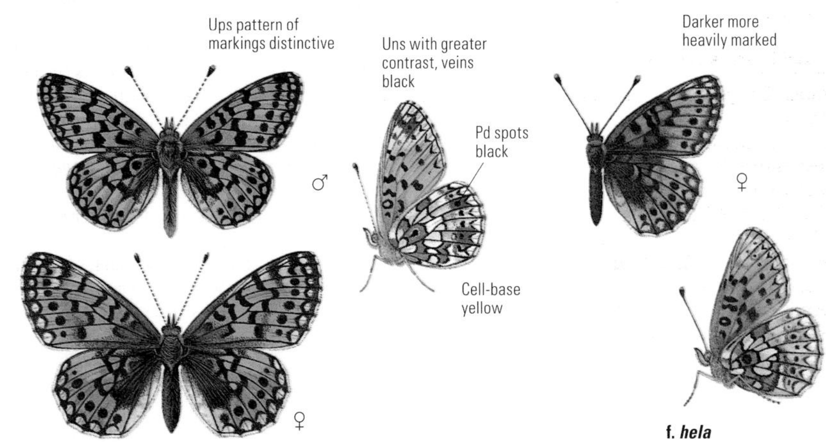

ARCTIC FRITILLARY

Frejya's Fritillary *Clossiana freija*

RANGE Scandinavia, Baltic countries, Arctic and S Siberia, Transbaikal, Mongolia, Yakutia, Khamchatka, Japan, N America including scattered colonies in Rocky Mts. to 35°N.

C. freija Thunberg 1791 TL: Sweden.

DISTRIBUTION Norway, Sweden and Finland: widespread, generally common. NE Latvia: very rare and local – last recorded in 1980. (?)Estonia. Absent from Denmark, coastal areas of Norway, Sweden south of 59°N and Lithuania. 200-1000m.

DESCRIPTION Unh with distinctive 'zig-zag' discal line in s1b-s3.

FLIGHT-PERIOD Univoltine. Generally late May/late June: fresh specimens may appear in late July/early August in retarded seasons.

HABITAT Dry grassy/rocky slopes/hollows with scattered, low-growing shrubs; marshes/peat bogs with *Vaccinium uliginosum* and *Rubus chamaemorus*, often sheltered by trees.

LIFE-HISTORY LHPs *Vaccinium uliginosum*; *Rubus chamaemorus*; *Arctostaphylos alpina*; *A. uva-ursi*; *Empetrum nigrum*: (In Japan, *Rhododendron aureum* – *R. lapponicum* is widespread in Lapland). Ova laid on leaves.

Weaver's Fritillary *Clossiana dia*

RANGE Europe, Turkey, Caucasus, Transcaucasus, Russia, N Kazakhstan, Mongolia.

C. dia Linnaeus 1767 TL: Austria.

DISTRIBUTION Spain: Cantabrian Mts.; provinces of Burgos, Soria, Huesca, Gerona and Barcelona. From Pyrenees, eastwards through much of C and E Europe to Baltic states, Balkans, European Turkey and Greece: Varnous Mts.; Phalakron massif; Mt. Olympus; Pindos Mts. (Grammos massif to Mt. Timphristos). Absent from SW France, N Germany, S Italy, Britain, Fennoscandia and Mediterranean islands except N Sicily. 500-1550m.

DESCRIPTION Resembles *C. titania cypris*. Smaller; ups gc paler; hw more sharply angled at v8; unh variegated yellow, brown, purple and violet, variable, sometimes very pale; discal and marginal spots silvery-white.

FLIGHT-PERIOD Bivoltine or trivoltine, late April/early September.

HABITAT Dry or damp, bushy, grassy and flowery clearings in light woodland or mature forests.

LIFE-HISTORY LHPs *Viola* spp., including, *V. odorata*; *V. hirta*; *V. canina*; *V. reichenbachiana*; *V. tricolor*. Ova laid on leaves of well-shaded LHPs. Hibernates as a half-grown larva.

Polar Fritillary *Clossiana polaris*

RANGE Circumpolar: Arctic regions of Europe north of 68°N, Asia, Greenland, N America.

C. polaris Boisduval 1828 TL: North Cape.

DISTRIBUTION Generally very local and uncommon. Sweden: Torne Lappmark; mountains north of Lake Torneträsk. 1000-1400m. Norway: E Troms; Finnmark; Gargia (Grönnasen); Porsanger; Varanger. 100-1400m. Finland: Pallastunturi; Kilpisjärvi (Mt. Saana); Karigasniemi (Mt. Ailigas). 600-1000m.

FLIGHT-PERIOD Univoltine. Late May/early August; normally appears early July but emergence much dependent on seasonal conditions.

HABITAT Open tundra. Females particularly, tend to associate closely with small, dry, south or west-facing rock-ledges or gentle slopes, characterised by an abundance of *Dryas octopetala*, *Cassiope tetragona* and *Astragalus alpinus* and the absence of low shrubs; the base of such slopes are damp and carpeted by *Betula nana* (Dwarf Birch), usually with some inclusion of *Salix* spp. and *Vaccinium uliginosum*.

LIFE-HISTORY LHP(s) unconfirmed in Europe: in N America, *Dryas integrifolia*; *D. octopetala*; *Vaccinium uliginosum*. In N America, hibernates as a newly-hatched or large (third or fourth instar) larva.

BEHAVIOUR Similar to that of *C. chariclea*.

Frigga's Fritillary *Clossiana frigga*

RANGE Fennoscandia, Baltic states, N Asia, Mongolia, Amur, Kamchatka, N America, including isolated colonies in Rocky Mts. to Colorado.

C. frigga Thunberg 1791 TL: Lapland.

DISTRIBUTION Norway and Sweden (60-71°N): generally local and uncommon, more widespread in the far north; absent from coastal districts of Norway south of 66°N. Widespread in Finland. Baltic states: very rare and local (last recorded in Latvia in 1987). 100-450m.

VARIATION Ups gc and black markings variable; basal, discal and pd spots sometimes confluent; veins often with dark suffusion; unh basal and discal gc pale reddish-brown to maroon with pinkish or violet overtones.

FLIGHT-PERIOD Univoltine. Late June/late July according to season.

HABITAT Marshes, peat bogs and wet heaths in vicinity of birch and willow scrub, usually bordering permanent water.

LIFE-HISTORY LHP *Rubus chamaemorus*. Ova laid singly on leaves. Hibernates as a larva. Newly-hatched captive larvae sometimes refuse *R. chamaemorus* but accept *Polygonum viviparum*, and, in later instars, *Rubus fruticosus*.

Frejya's Fritillary

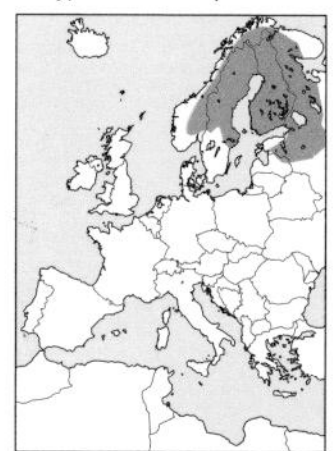

Weaver's Fritillary

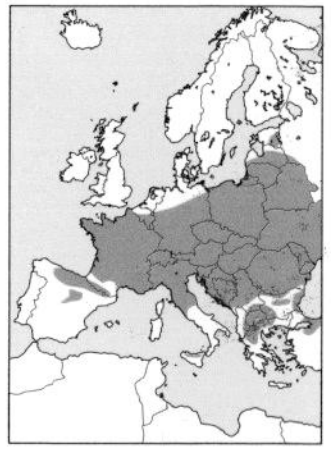

FREJYA'S FRITILLARY

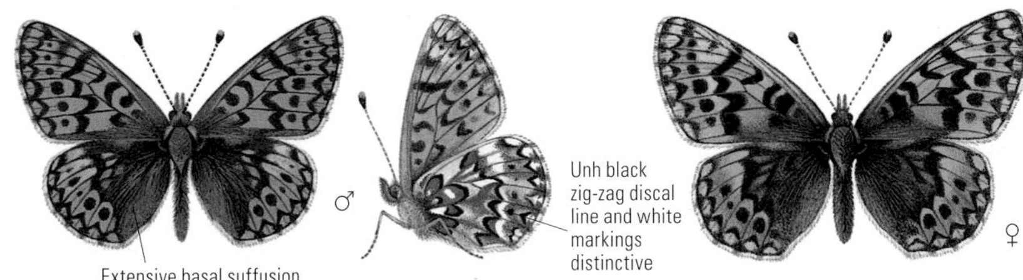

WEAVER'S FRITILLARY

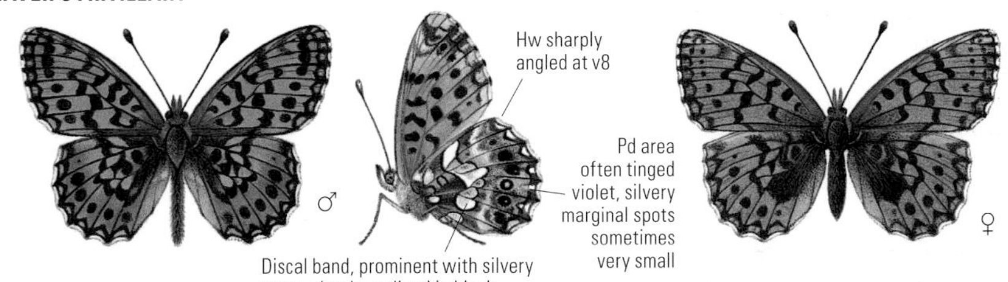

POLAR FRITILLARY

(Arctic Fennoscandia)

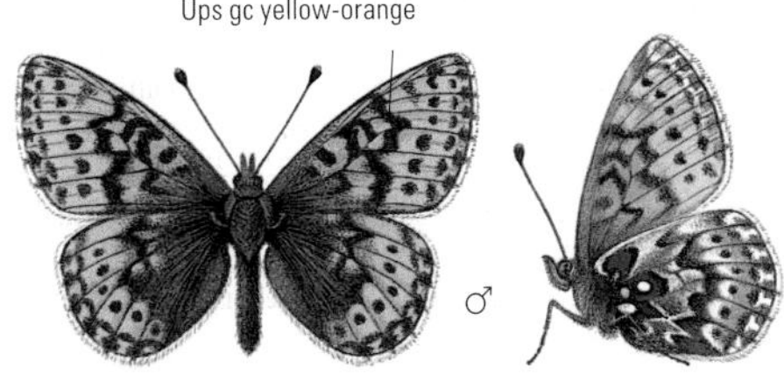

FRIGGA'S FRITILLARY

Thor's Fritillary *Clossiana thore*

RANGE Central European Alps, NE Europe, Russia, Sakhalin, Mongolia, NE China, N Korea, Japan.

C. thore Hübner 1803 TL: Alps of Tyrol

DISTRIBUTION Sporadic and local. Alps of Switzerland, (local north of Rhône Valley; Engadine), Bavaria and Austria. Italy: Dolomites; Carinthian Mts. 800-1800m. Norway, W Sweden (62°-70°N) and NW Finland. 300-1000m.

DESCRIPTION AND VARIATION Ups black markings heavy; uph margin wide, obscuring large submarginal spots; unh dark with pale discal and marginal spots. In N Scandinavia, *borealis* Staudinger: ups gc slightly paler; ups black markings much reduced; unh paler, pale discal and marginal spots obscure: individuals with ups dark markings closely resembling nominate form recur in most Lapland colonies. In S Fennoscandia, *carelia* Valle: transitional to nominate form.

FLIGHT-PERIOD Univoltine. C Alps Mid June/early August: Lapland, late June/early August according to locality and season. Records of a (?)partial second brood in Austria require confirmation.

HABITAT AND BEHAVIOUR In central Alps, shaded clearings in deciduous or coniferous woodland. In Lapland, damp wooded margins of rivers or small mountain streams, characterised by *Geranium sylvaticum*, *Trollius europaeus* and an abundance of *Viola biflora*: both sexes frequent areas of dappled sunlight, often basking on leaves of *G. sylvaticum*.

LIFE-HISTORY LHPs *Viola* spp., including *V. biflora*. In central Alps, possibly also in Lapland, larval development occupies two seasonal cycles, giving rise to relatively greater abundance in alternate years.

Dusky-winged Fritillary *Clossiana improba*

RANGE N Fennoscandia, Novaya Zemlya, Arctic Urals, Yamal and Gydan Peninsulas, Arctic Siberia, Chukotka, Arctic America.

C. improba improbula Brykner 1920 TL: Lapland.

DISTRIBUTION Fennoscandia north of 68°N. From Mt. Nuolja and mountains north of Lake Torneträsk (Torne Lappmark, Sweden) to Rosta Ankerlia, Norway. NW Finland: Kilpisjärvi. 600-1050m. Local population density subject to very marked seasonal variation – can occur in great abundance.

FLIGHT-PERIOD Univoltine. Late June/early August according season.

HABITAT Open, flat, grassy terrain or gentle slopes with SE aspect providing shelter from prevailing NW winds.

LIFE-HISTORY LHP(s) unknown: oviposition on *Polygonum viviparum* reported, but natural use as LHP apparently not confirmed. In N America, adults associate closely with *Salix* spp. of which *S. arctica* and *S. reticulata* are confirmed LHPs: oviposition, but not larval feeding, has also been observed (rarely) on *P. viviparum*: early-stages occupy two seasonal cycles. In Lapland, *S. reticulata* and other arctic *Salix* spp. occur within distribution of butterfly.

BEHAVIOUR Flies fast and very close to the ground when disturbed. Well-camouflaged when settled with outspread wings on similarly coloured patches of bare ground. Both sexes are especially fond of the nectar of *Silene acaulis*: males sometimes take moisture from damp peaty soil.

Glanville Fritillary *Melitaea cinxia*

RANGE Morocco, W. Algeria, Europe, Turkey, Lebanon, Russia, N Kazakhstan, Mongolia.

M. cinxia Linnaeus 1758 TL: Sweden.

DISTRIBUTION Morocco: W High Atlas (Toubkal massif 2000-2600m); Middle Atlas (Azrou; Ifrane; Col du Zad; Tizi-n-Tretten; 1500-2000m). W Algeria. N Portugal. Spain: S. de Guadarrama; Montes Universales; Cantabrian Mts. to Pyrenees and Catalonia. Extending eastwards through most of Europe, including S England (restricted to Isle of Wight), Channel Islands, Italy to S Fennoscandia, Greece and European Turkey. Absent from Mediterranean islands except Sicily and Corfu. 0-2000m.

VARIATION In S Europe, female ups gc uniform sandy-buff with variable dark or greyish suffusion. In High Atlas, *atlantis* le Cerf: ups gc paler; black markings heavy but lacking dark suffusion.

FLIGHT-PERIOD Generally univoltine: NW Africa, late April/June; N, C and W Europe, early May/mid July; SE Europe, late April/early August in prolonged emergence: bivoltine in some regions of NE Spain, France, Switzerland and Italy, May/June and August/September.

HABITAT Diverse. Grassy, flowery places: open hillsides; scrub/woodland clearings; areas/margins of cultivation.

LIFE-HISTORY LHPs: Middle Atlas, *Centaurea pullata*; *Scorzonera pygmaea*: Europe, *Plantago lanceolata*; *P. subulata*; *P. bellardii deflexa*; *P. argentea*; *P. cynops*; *P. major*; *P. media*; *Centaureae* (?)*graeca*; *Centaureae* sp.; *Veronica teucrium*. Ova laid in large batches on underside of leaf. Small larvae feed and hibernate in a silken web, dispersing in late instars. Pupates near ground on grass or other plant-stems.

Thor's Fritillary

Dusky-winged Fritillary

THOR'S FRITILLARY

C. t. thore

C. t. borealis
(N Scandinavia)

DUSKY-WINGED FRITILLARY

(N Fennoscandia)

Ups smoky suffusion characteristic

Unh smoky reddish-brown; costa narrowly edged white; white marks in s4 and 7 distinct

GLANVILLE FRITILLARY

Uph pd black spots distinctive

Glanville Fritillary

♀ ups gc ranges from sandy-buff to fulvous, dark markings often heavy

Freyer's Fritillary *Melitaea arduinna*

RANGE SE Balkans, Greece, Turkey, Israel, Iraq, Iran, N Afghanistan, Caucasus, Volga, S Urals, (?)Uzbekistan, E Kazakhstan, Kyrgyzstan, Altai.

M. arduinna rhodopensis Freyer 1836 TL: 'European Turkey' [Bulgaria].

DISTRIBUTION Republic of Macedonia: Mt. Pelister; Prilep; Vardar Valley. Bulgaria: Ludogorie; Sboryanovo; Burgas; Kula; Vrushka Tchuka. Romania: Tultscha. Greece: Varnous Mts.; Vernon Mts.; N and C Pindos Mts. Very local, often common. 500-1500m.

VARIATION Female ups often with dark suffusion.

FLIGHT-PERIOD Univoltine. Late May/early August: peak emergence, usually late June.

HABITAT Grassy, flowery banks in sheltered, bushy woodland clearings.

LIFE-HISTORY LHP *Centaurea* (?)*graeca*. Ova laid in large batches on underside of leaf. Small larvae feed on leaves and stem cuticle (stem leaves are small and sparse) in silken web where they also hibernate: after hibernation, larger larvae disperse. Small larvae ((?)second instar) are unusual for having a decidedly greenish appearance. Mature larvae superficially very similar to Spanish *M. phoebe*. Pupates on robust plant stems near ground-level. Captive larvae accept many *Centaurea* spp., but reject *Plantago lanceolata* and *P. bellardii deflexa* (cf. *M. cinxia*).

Knapweed Fritillary *Melitaea phoebe*

RANGE N Africa, Europe, Turkey, Middle East, C Asia, Mongolia, N China.

M. phoebe Denis and Schiffermüller 1775 TL: Austria.

DISTRIBUTION Morocco. Algeria. 900-2700m. Portugal and Spain, through C and S France, Italy, C Germany to SE Latvia, Balkans, European Turkey and Greece. Common and widespread in much of S and C Europe: often sporadic in northern range: not reported recently from Lithuania or Estonia. Absent from Britain, northern C Europe, Fennoscandia, N and C Switzerland, much of Bavaria and Mediterranean islands except Sicily, Chios and Lesbos. 0-1900m.

VARIATION Geographical, seasonal and altitudinal variation marked, especially in Spain. Nominate form occurs in most regions from Pyrenees eastwards, north of C Alps to Balkans and Greece. South of Alps, also in Bavaria, f. *alternans* Seitz: ups contrasting areas of pale and darker orange-fulvous gc well delineated by heavy black markings. In Iberian Peninsula, *occitanica* Staudinger: resembles *alternans*: ups colour contrast similar, black markings generally less intense, characters better developed in summer brood. Late summer broods in S Europe, often small; ups pale, black markings reduced; unh gc pale (f. *pauper* Verity): reduced size possibly due to retarded larval development arising from desiccation of LHPs. In hot/dry localities in NW Africa, *punica* Oberthür: small; ups yellowish with some variegation on hw; upf black discal markings well developed; uns gc white: a larger, well-marked form (f. *gaisericus* Hemming) occurs in Morocco (Middle and High Atlas) and is said to resemble that of S Europe.

FLIGHT-PERIOD Largely bivoltine, Mid April/mid June and late June/early September. Voltinism uncertain at higher altitudes: emergence prolonged.

HABITAT Diverse. Dry, open flowery and grassy places, often amongst scrub or light woodland.

LIFE-HISTORY LHPs *Centaurea* spp., including *C. jacea*; *C. montana*; *C. graeca*; *C. scabiosa*; *C. nigrescens*; *C. alba*; *C. columbaria*: NW Africa, also, possibly *Leuzea acaule* [=*Rhaponticum acaule*]: natural use of *Plantago* spp. requires confirmation. Ova laid in batches on underside of leaf. Small larvae live in a silken web before and after hibernation, feeding on leaves. Larvae tend to disperse in final instar. Pupates near ground on plant stems or at base of stones. Colouring of mature larvae regionally variable in S Europe: in Spain, resembles that of *M. arduinna*: dorsum black with inconspicuous white marks (variable); sides rusty-orange, spiny tubercles whitish/pale grey: in central S Europe and Greece; gc black with conspicuous white speckling; spiny tubercles pale orange.

NOTE F. *punica* considered specifically distinct by some authors: a single male specimen has been reported recently from Bulgaria.

Freyer's Fritillary

Knapweed Fritillary

Aetherie Fritillary

False Heath Fritillary

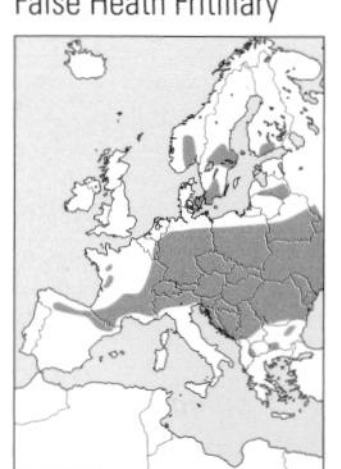

Desert Fritillary

FREYER'S FRITILLARY

Ups and uns pattern
of markings distinctive
♀ ups often heavily
suffused grey
♂
♀

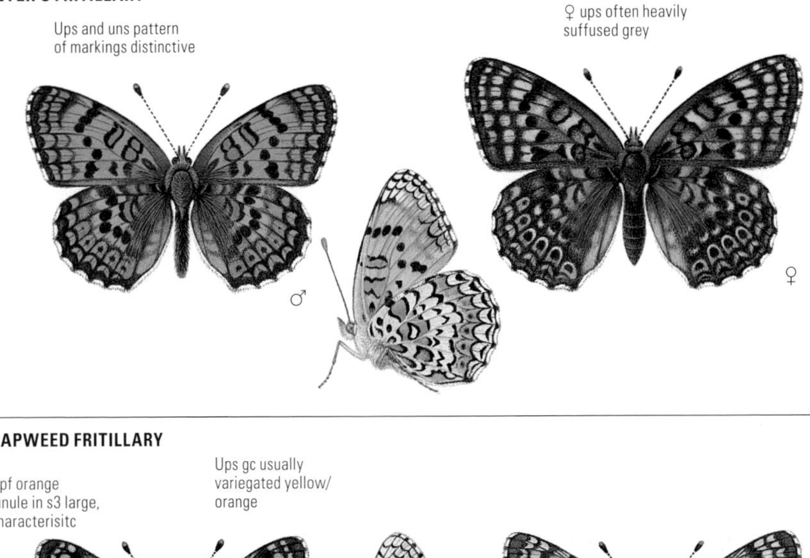

KNAPWEED FRITILLARY

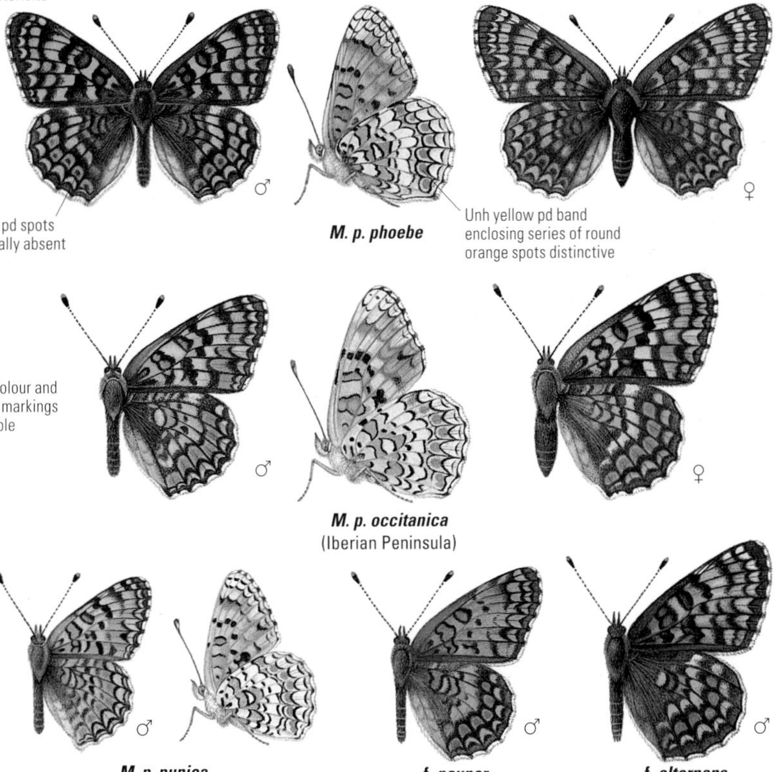

Upf orange
lunule in s3 large,
characterisitc
Ups gc usually
variegated yellow/
orange
♂
♀
Upf pd spots
usually absent
Unh yellow pd band
enclosing series of round
orange spots distinctive
Ups colour and
black markings
variable
♂
♀
♂
♂
♂

M. p. phoebe

M. p. occitanica
(Iberian Peninsula)

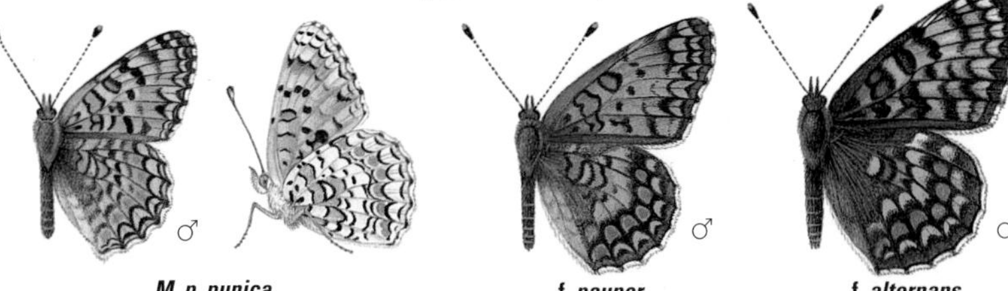

M. p. punica
(NW Africa)

f. ***pauper***
(S Europe)

f. ***alternans***
(S Alps)

Aetherie Fritillary *Melitaea aetherie*

RANGE NW Africa, S Portugal, S Spain, Sicily.
M. aetherie Hübner 1826 TL: Spain
DISTRIBUTION Very sporadic and local. Morocco: Middle Atlas (Azrou; Taghzeft Pass; Aghbala Larbi; Meknes; Ifrane; Oulmes; Dj. bou Iblane; 1300-1800m); High Atlas (Oukaïmeden; Asif-n-Ait-Iren; Toubkal massif; 2000-2800m). Algeria: Kabylie; Aures Mts.; Oran; Teniet-el-Had; Tlemcen; Col du Ben-Chicao; Algiers; Ain-Draham; Sebou; Lambessa; Bainen; Khenchela; 1200-1800m. Tunisia: Kroumerie; Tunis. S Portugal: Algarve; 25-250m. S Spain: provinces of (?)Huelva; Cádiz; Málaga; Jaen; 50-800m. NW Sicily: Petralia; La Madonie; Ficuzza; Lupo; 800-1100m.
VARIATION In NW Africa, *algirica* Rühl: resembles nominate form: unf black discal spots well developed: female ups gc pale orange usually with upf and uph posterior area suffused greyish. In Sicily, *perlinii* Turati: very similar: smaller; female ups suffusion slightly accentuated (cf. *M. didyma meridionalis*).
FLIGHT-PERIOD Univoltine in Iberian Peninsula (mid April/May) and NW Africa (May/July, according to altitude): reportedly bivoltine in Sicily, May/June and September.
HABITAT Hot, dry, grassy, flowery places: scrub clearings; marginal/neglected areas of cultivation.
LIFE-HISTORY LHPs: Spain, *Centaurea calcitrapa*; *C. carratracensis*; *Cynara cardunculus*: suspected use of *Centrophyllum coeruleum* (?)unconfirmed. Ova laid in batches on underside of leaf. Hibernates as a small larva. Captive larvae accept leaves of *Cynara scolymus* (Globe Artichoke).
CONSERVATION In Iberian Peninsula, close proximity to cultivated areas or human habitation poses a serious threat to residual habitats: coastal development in S Portugal (Algarve) is directly responsible for extinction of many colonies.

False Heath Fritillary *Melitaea diamina*

RANGE N Spain, C, E and SE Europe, NE Turkey, S and NW Russia, S Siberia, Transbaikal, Amur, Mongolia, NE China, Korea, Japan.
M. diamina Lang 1789 TL: Augsburg.
syn: *dictynna* Esper 1779 (invalid homonym)
DISTRIBUTION N Spain: Cantabrian Mts.; Pyrenees; Catalonia. SW, central W and E France. N Italy to S Belgium, S Holland, through Poland to Republic of Macedonia (Jablanica Pl.; Galicica Pl.) and Bulgaria (Rila Mts.; Rhodopi Mts; Musala massif). S Norway, Sweden (including Öland) and Finland to 62°N. Denmark: restricted to Sjælland: formerly very rare – no recent records. Latvia: sporadic, locally common. Absent from Britain, N and C France, S coastal areas of France, N Germany, N Poland, Lithuania, Estonia, peninsular Italy, Greece and European Turkey. 100-2000m.
DESCRIPTION AND VARIATION Male ups gc orange-fulvous on disc, pale yellow or white near outer margins; black markings extensive, obscuring much of gc, especially near outer margins; uns gc very pale; marginal yellowish band bordered by fine black lines: female ups gc paler. In N Italy, generally at lower altitudes, *wheeleri* Chapman: ups dark suffusion absent, markings clearly defined; upf with dumb-bell shaped discal mark in s1b. In N Spain (E Pyrenees and Cantabrian Mts.), *vernetensis* Rondou: resembles *wheeleri*: unh coloration more uniform, averagely paler. In Catalonia, *codinai* de Sagarra: resembles *vernetensis*; slightly larger; ups black markings further reduced; upf dumb-bell shaped mark prominent in s1b. These and related variants, occur regularly in most populations in S Alps: development of ups dark suffusion follows an altitudinal cline, with darkest forms preponderating at higher level.
FLIGHT-PERIOD Univoltine at higher latitude and altitude, May/July; bivoltine at low level in S Alps and Spain, May/July and August/September.
HABITAT Damp, grassy, flowery places, sometimes associated with woodland.
LIFE-HISTORY LHPs *Valeriana officinalis*; *V. officinalis* (?)*collina* [=*V. wallrothii*]; *V. dioica*; *V.* (?)*repens*; *V.* (?)*pratensis*. Natural use of *Plantago lanceolata*; *Filipendula ulmaria*; *Melampyrum nemorosum*; *M. pratense*; *Veronica chamaedrys*; *Polygonum bistorta* requires confirmation. Captive larvae accept *Centranthus ruber* and reject *Plantago lanceolata*. Ova laid in batches on leaves. Small larvae feed and hibernate in silken web, dispersing shortly after hibernation. Pupates near ground on plants. In one captive rearing experiment, a proportion of larvae from Monte Baldo required two seasonal cycles for full development.

Desert Fritillary *Melitaea deserticola*

RANGE Morocco, Algeria, Tunisia, Libya, Egypt, Jordan, Israel, Lebanon, Syria, Saudi Arabia, Yemen.
M. deserticola Oberthür 1876 TL: Algeria.
DISTRIBUTION Morocco: Anti-Atlas: Tafraoute. High Atlas (Ourika; Amizmiz; Dades and Todra gorges); Middle Atlas. Algeria: Biskra; Mecheria; Laghout; Aflou. Tunisia: Tamerzad. 400-1800m.
DESCRIPTION Resembles *M. didyma* closely: separable on basis of following characters: unh black chequering restricted to distal half (extending to wing margin in *didyma* – especially noticeable near veins): ventral surface of terminal one-third of antennal shaft orange, dorsal surface black (both surfaces black in *didyma*): antennal club entirely black (club-tip ringed orange in *didyma*): ventral surface of abdomen sandy-yellow/orange (white in *didyma*).
FLIGHT-PERIOD Voltinism uncertain in all regions: generally bivoltine, February/April and June: in some localities, apparently univoltine, April/May. (In eastern range, voltinism (one to four broods) appears to vary according to seasonal conditions: time of appearance of later broods vary, possibly due to aestivation.
HABITAT Hot, dry gullies; sandy places; rocky slopes.
LIFE-HISTORY LHPs: principally *Linaria aegyptiaca*: natural use of *Plantago media* and *Anarrhinum fruticosum* requires confirmation. Larva black, almost unicolorous. Circumstantial evidence suggests larvae aestivate in unfavourably hot conditions possibly due to desiccation of LHP.

Maps on p. 202

AETHERIE FRITILLARY

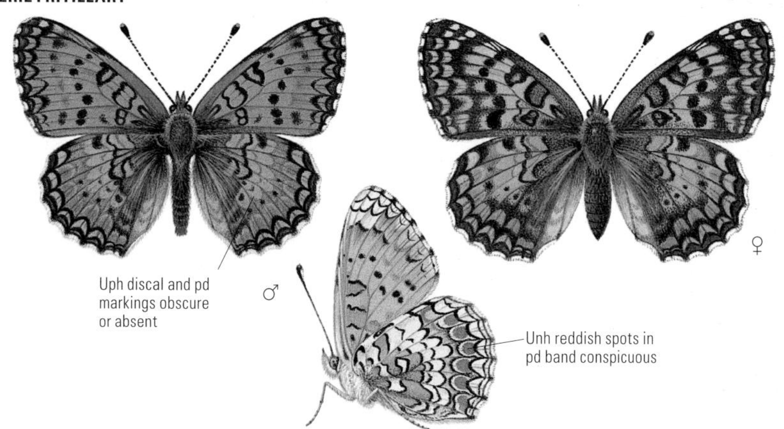

FALSE HEATH FRITILLARY

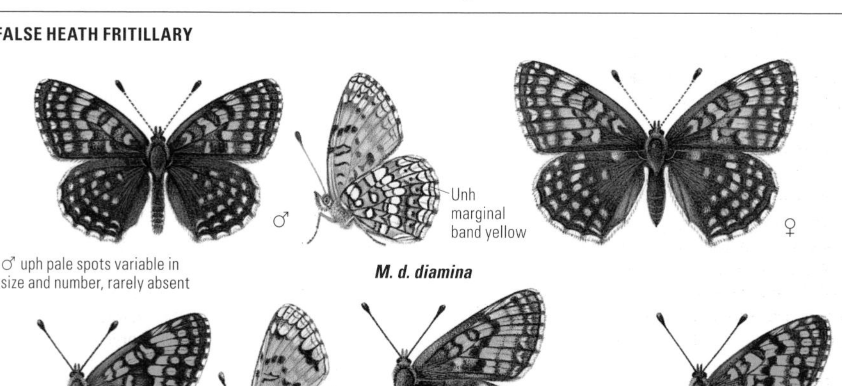

DESERT FRITILLARY

Spotted Fritillary *Melitaea didyma*

RANGE NW Africa, S and E Europe, Turkey, Middle East, N Iran, Afganistan, N Pakistan, Kazakhstan, Russia, Mongolia, W China.

M. didyma Esper 1779 TL: Bavaria.

DISTRIBUTION Widespread and common. Morocco: Anti-Atlas; High Atlas; Middle Atlas. Algeria. Tunisia. 0-2700m. Most of S and C Europe to S Belgium, Harz Mts., Lithuania and SE Latvia (locally common): Mediterranean islands of Sicily, Elba, Corfu, Levkas, Evia, Thassos, Limnos, Lesbos, Chios and Samos. 0-2300m. Absent from Britain, Holland, N Germany, N Poland, Estonia and Fennoscandia.

DESCRIPTION AND VARIATION Several forms have been described in recognition of considerable individual, local and geographical variation. From NW France, N of Alps to central E Europe (0-750m), nominate form: male ups fulvous-red; black markings variable; unh orange basal band usually continuous; black marginal spots rounded (cf. *M. trivia*): female ups gc paler, usually with some greyish suffusion. From N Spain, through southern slopes of C Alps to SE Europe (500-1700m), *meridionalis* Staudinger: male ups fiery orange-red; pd spots vestigial: female ups gc paler; upf and uph posterior area with variable greyish suffusion, less pronounced at lowest altitudes. In N Africa, S Iberian peninsula, Mediterranean region, Balkans and Greece (800-2300m), *occidentalis* Staudinger: ups gc pale fulvous or buff; black markings reduced; pd spots usually absent; unh basal orange band disrupted: female ups grey suffusion usually absent. A consideration of geographical, altitudinal, intra-seasonal, inter-seasonal variation, and the results of captive rearing under varied conditions, suggests diversity of form is at least partly attributable to ecological factors, the most influential of which are possibly those of temperature and/or humidity on larval/pupal development. Generally, extent of female ups dark suffusion appears to follow an altitudinal cline, with darkest females occurring at higher altitudes, that is, at lower average ambient temperature. First brood in S Greece, above 900m, corresponds to *meridionalis*, whereas second brood (larval/pupal development at relatively higher temperature) fits description of *occidentalis*: at sea-level in Greece, *occidentalis* occurs in spring and summer broods. Small, pale and lightly marked forms, e.g., *dalmatina* Staudinger, occur in late summer broods throughout Mediterranean region, especially at low altitude: reduced size is possibly the consequence of poor nutritional quality of desiccated LHPs.

FLIGHT-PERIOD Bivoltine or trivoltine. NW Africa, March/October: Europe, Mid April/September.

HABITAT Diverse. Dry flowery places; woodland or scrub clearings; meadows; dry rocky gullies; neglected and marginal areas of cultivation.

LIFE-HISTORY LHPs include *Linaria vulgaris*; *L. peloponnesiaca*; *L. alpina*; *Antirrhinum brevifolium*; *Misopates orontium* [=*Antirrhinum orontium*]; *Plantago subulata*; *P. amplexicaulis*; *P. bellardi deflexa*; *P. lanceolata*; *P. major*; *Veronica teucrium*; *V. chamaedrys*; *Digitalis grandiflora*; *D. pupurea*; *Stachys recta*; *Valeriana officinalis*; *V. montana*; *V. persica*; *Verbascum thapsus*. Ova laid in batches. Hibernates gregariously as small larvae, often in the shelter provided by leaves or bracts of dead flower-heads of LHP. Large larvae roost singly at the tops of grass stems. Dry grass stems and stones are favoured pupation sites.

NOTE Parallel between female *M. didyma meridionalis* and *M. aetherie algirica* is striking: ups pattern of greyish suffusion similar: both forms occur at higher altitudes, suggesting equivalent or similar factors ((?)temperature/humidity) of ecological control of phenotypes.

Lesser Spotted Fritillary *Melitaea trivia*

RANGE S Europe, Turkey, Middle East, Iran, Afghanistan, S Russia, Kazakhstan, N Pakistan, N India.

M. trivia trivia Denis and Schiffermüller 1775 TL: Vienna.
syn: *fascelis* Esper 1784

DISTRIBUTION N Italy (Turin; Lake Garda; Bolzano); S Apennines (Mte. Pollino): very sporadic and local. Slovenia to Slovakia, Balkans, Greece and European Turkey. Absent from Mediterranean islands except Thassos, Lesbos, Chios, Samos, Ikaria and Kos. Widespread and common in SE range. 0-1700m.

DESCRIPTION AND VARIATION Unh marginal spots somewhat triangular, usually not round; discocellular vein present in hw (cf. *M. didyma*). Second brood: often small; ups gc paler, black markings reduced. In Italy, transitional to *ignasiti* de Sagarra (below).

FLIGHT-PERIOD Bivoltine. Mid April/early May and June/August.

HABITAT Usually hot, dry, flowery places, often amongst scrub; neglected cultivated ground.

LIFE-HISTORY LHPs *Verbascum thapsus*; *V. densiflorum*; *V. longifolium*; *V. speciosum*; *V. delpicum*. Small larvae feed and hibernate in a silken web. Large larvae tend to live in loose companies, resting on upperside of LHP leaves. Captive larvae accept *Buddleia davidii*. Often pupates on grass stems, sometimes at base of stones.

M. trivia ignasiti de Sagarra 1926 TL: Portugal.

DISTRIBUTION N and C Portugal: Provinces of Beira Baixa; Beira Alta; Beira Litoral; Tràs-os-Montes. Spain: Cantabrian Mts.; S. de Guadarrama; S. de la Demanda; Huesca; Catalonia; Montes Universales; S. de Gádor. (?)500-1200m. Very local, generally uncommon. Detailed distribution uncertain owing to possible confusion with *M. didyma*.

DESCRIPTION AND VARIATION Ups gc uniform pale yellow-orange; black markings clearly defined. In S. de Gádor, f. *augustini* Augustin: similar.

FLIGHT-PERIOD AND HABITAT As for nominate form.

LIFE-HISTORY LHP *Verbascum thapsus*. Development as for nominate form.

SPOTTED FRITILLARY

Submarginal spots flattened or slightly concave rarely running down veins

Ups bright fulvous red, black markings variable

♂ ♂

Orange discal band usually unbroken

Unh submarginal spots rounded

M. d. dalmatina

♀ black marking less clearly defined

Unh discoidal vein absent from cell end

♀ ♀

M. d. didyma

dark form
M. d. meridionalis

♂ ♀ ♂ ♀

M. d. meridionalis ***M. d. occidentalis***

LESSER SPOTTED FRITILLARY

Spotted Fritillary

Ups bright fulvous orange, black markings variable

Submarginal spots crescent-shaped

Unh submarginal spots triangular

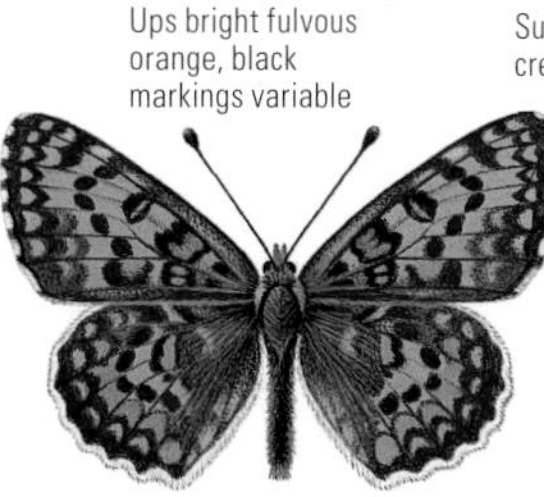

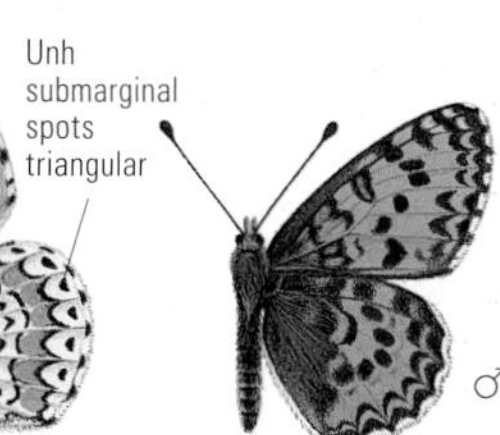

♂ ♂

Unh orange discal band irregular, often broken

Lesser Spotted Fritillary

♀ ♀

M. t. trivia ***M. t. ignasti***

Heath Fritillary *Mellicta athalia*

RANGE Europe, Turkey, throughout temperate Asia to Japan.

M. athalia athalia Rottemburg 1775 TL: Paris.
syn: *neglecta* Pfau 1945.

DISTRIBUTION Common and widespread. Most of N and E Europe, including S England (very local) and European Turkey from a line connecting NW Pyrenees, N Alps and W Slovenia: SW of this region, replaced by *M. athalia celadussa* (below). Absent from Mediterranean islands and S Greece. 0-2200m.

DESCRIPTION Unf pale marginal spots in s2 and s3 usually with conspicuous black internal borders, sometimes including s1b and s4, more rarely reduced to a black mark or thick line bordering s2: this character, and overall appearance, usually allows separation from other members of the genus. Male genitalia distinct.

VARIATION Many forms/ssp. have been described, reflecting appreciable local and regional variation: most are perhaps better regarded as ecological variants or segments of geographical or altitudinal clines. In Bulgaria (Stara Pl.), f. *boris* Früstorfer: ups dark marginal borders heavy: reportedly does not represent the average Bulgarian population which corresponds more closely to nominate form.

FLIGHT-PERIOD Generally univoltine in a prolonged emergence (mid May/mid August): a partial second brood (mid to late August/September) has been reported in favourable localities/seasons.

HABITAT Diverse. Dry or damp, grassy, flowery places, often amongst bushes or in woodland clearings.

LIFE-HISTORY LHPs include *Plantago lanceolata*; *P. alpina*; *Veronica chamaedryas*; *V. montana*; *V. officinalis*; *Melampyrum pratense*; *M. sylvaticum*; *Digitalis purpurea*; *D. ferruginea*; *D. lutea*; *Linaria vulgaris*. Ova laid in batches on underside of leaf. Larvae feed and hibernate in silken webs. Larger larvae disperse after hibernation, feeding singly or in small groups, sometimes switching to alternative LHPs. Pupates on plant stems or leaves near ground.

M. athalia norvegica Aurivillius 1888 TL: Dovrefjeld, Norway.

DISTRIBUTION Fennoscandia: 62-70°N. 0-800m.

DESCRIPTION AND VARIATION Small; ups markings regular, well defined; unf pale marginal spots in s2 and s3 absent, replaced by gc, but dark proximal border retained. In C Sweden and Finland, f. *lachares* Frühstorfer: ups black markings finer, creating wider fulvous discal and pd bands: transitional forms occur in low-lying districts of S Sweden.

FLIGHT-PERIOD Univoltine. June/July according to season.

HABITAT Grassy, flowery places with bushes and small trees (400-800m). In S Fennoscandia, flowery woodland clearings, usually on dry, sandy heaths (0-300m).

LIFE-HISTORY LHPs *Plantago* sp., *Veronica* sp., *Melampyrum* sp. Development as for nominate form.

M. athalia celadussa Frühstorfer 1910 TL: Maritime Alps.
syn: *pseudathalia* Reverdin 1921.

DISTRIBUTION N Portugal. N Spain and Sierra Nevada. S France. S Switzerland. Italy and Sicily – complementing distribution of nominate form. 0-2600m.

DESCRIPTION AND VARIATION Resembles nominate form. Male genitalia distinct: male ups markings generally finer; female ups dark suffusion uncommon. Interface with nominate form wide, extending to over 150km in parts, populated by intermediate forms. In Portugal and NW Spain, f. *biedermanni* Querci: large; ups submarginal and pd black lines fine, discal line thicker: transitional forms occur in central W Spain. In Sierra Nevada (S Spain), f. *nevadensis* Verity: univoltine: ups golden-yellow; black markings fine. In S Europe, late broods usually small with ups black markings reduced (f. *tenuicola* Verity).

FLIGHT-PERIOD Univoltine at higher altitudes, June/July; bivoltine below subalpine level, May/June and late July/August.

HABITAT AND LIFE-HISTORY As for nominate form.

Grisons Fritillary *Mellicta varia*

RANGE European Alps, Apennines.

M. varia Meyer-Dür 1851 TL: Graubünden Alps.

DISTRIBUTION France: Alpes-Maritimes, through Drôme to Haute-Savoie (not W of Rhône Valley). 1500-2500m. Switzerland: Valais (Alpes Valaisannes; Bernese Alps); Grisons (mountains bordering Engadine Valley). Austria: Tirol. Italy: Maritime Alps; S Alps including Ortler; 2000-2650m; C Apennines (Monte Livata; Monte Sibillini; Gran Sasso; Abruzzi; 1200-2600m).

DESCRIPTION AND VARIATION Upf pd line often thin and broken; discal mark in s1b variable, often dumb-bell, sigma or club-shaped, repeated on unf with conspicuous adjoining black basal bar: female ups usually with extensive greyish suffusion. Development of ups black markings, and dark suffusion in female, subject to marked individual/local variation. In Ligurian Alps 1800m, *piana* Higgins: larger.

FLIGHT-PERIOD Univoltine. Late June/late August according to altitude

HABITAT Sheltered flowery slopes and hollows with short grass.

LIFE-HISTORY LHPs *Plantago alpina*; *Gentiana verna*; *G. acaulis*. Ova laid in batches on leaves. Larvae hibernate in groups, dispersing after hibernation.

Heath Fritillary

Grisons Fritillary

HEATH FRITILLARY

Unf black mark in s2 (often in s3 but smaller) characterisitic

♂ ♀

M. a. athalia

♂ ♀ ♂ ♂

dark

f. *biedermanni*

f. *nevadensis*

M. a. celadussa
(N Portugal, N Spain, Sierra Nevada)

♂ ♂

M. a. norvegica
(Fennoscandia)

M. a. athalia* f. *boris
(Bulgaria)

GRISON'S FRITILLARY

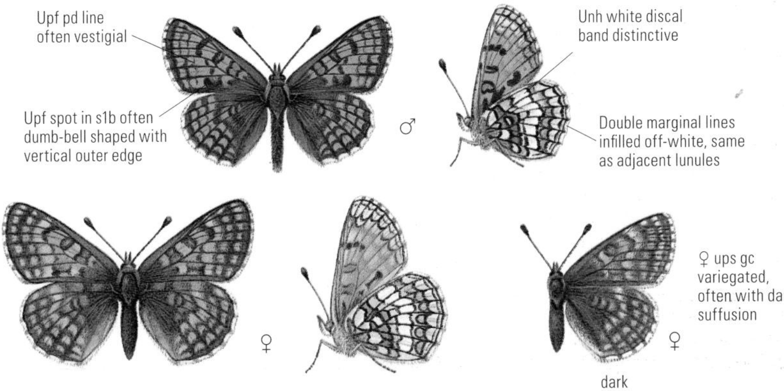

Upf pd line often vestigial

Upf spot in s1b often dumb-bell shaped with vertical outer edge

♂

Unh white discal band distinctive

Double marginal lines infilled off-white, same as adjacent lunules

♀ ♀

♀ ups gc variegated, often with dark suffusion

dark

Provençal Fritillary *Mellicta deione*

RANGE N Morocco, W Algeria, SW Europe.

M. deione deione Geyer 1832 TL: Aix-en-Provence.

DISTRIBUTION Widespread in Spain except central W and NW districts. S France: C and E Pyrenees to Massif Central and Hautes-Alps. N Italy: very sporadic: Maritime Alps; Cottian Alps; Val d'Aosta to Dolomites. 200-1600m.

DESCRIPTION AND VARIATION Male ups gc uniform yellow-orange; black markings fine; ups black discal mark in s1b heavy, usually dumb-bell, bell or club-shaped; unf dark proximal shading of marginal spots in s1b-s4 vestigial or absent (cf. nominate form of *M. athalia*); uns gc pale; unh submarginal and discal bands bright, uniform yellow-orange; submarginal band with distinctive rounded orange spots in each space: female ups gc paler, usually with distinctly paler shade in fw pd area. Nominate form is prevalent in S France and C Spain. In S and SE Spain (?)1000-1600m (*magna* Seitz) and E Pyrenees 1500m ((?)*praestantior* Verity; (?)*mirabilis* Rutimeyer): first brood: larger; ups brighter. In Cantabrian Mts. 1500m, S. de la Demanda and Montseny Mts., (*signata* de Sagarra) and C Pyrenees (*rondoui* Oberthür), (?)1000-1600m: smaller; ups darker. In N Italy (200-1500m), *vesubiana* Verity, *tessinorum* Frühstorfer and *phaisana* Frühstorfer: larger; ups black markings heavier – transitional to *berisalii* (below). In all regions, expected altitudinal clines, that is, with larger, brighter forms at low level, replaced progressively by smaller, darker races at higher altitudes, are generally not apparent.

FLIGHT-PERIOD Bivoltine. Mid May/June and mid August/ early September.

HABITAT Open, flowery meadows; grassy, flowery woodland margins; bushy places.

LIFE-HISTORY LHPs *Linaria vulgaris*; *L. alpina*; (?)*Antirrhinum sempervirens*; *A. hispanicum*; *Chaenorhinum minus* [=*Linaria minor*]; (?)*Digitalis lutea*; (?)*Cymbalaria muralis*. Ova laid in batches on underside of leaves. Larvae feed and hibernate gregariously.

M. deione berisalii Rühl 1891 TL: 'Simplon' [in error].

DISTRIBUTION Switzerland: apparently restricted to Rhône Valley (Saillon; Martigny; Folly; Varen). 300-1200m.

DESCRIPTION AND VARIATION Male ups dark fulvous; black markings heavy, marginal borders wide: female ups gc more uniform.

FLIGHT-PERIOD Univoltine. Mid May/mid July.

HABITAT Dry, bushy places, often near cultivated areas.

LIFE-HISTORY LHPs *Linaria vulgaris*; *L. alpina*; *Chaenorhinum minus* [=*Linaria minor*]; (?)*Antirrhinum latifolium*; (?)*Digitalis lutea*. Development as for nominate form. Captive larvae accept *Antirrhinum majus* and *Linaria purpurea*.

M. deione rosinae Rebel 1910/1911 TL: Cintra [S Portugal].
syn: *philomena* Frühstorfer 1917

DISTRIBUTION S Portugal: widespread but local: Minho to Algarve (S. de Monchique; Serra do Caldeirão). 100-400m.

DESCRIPTION Male ups gc dark fulvous; black markings heavy; unf pale marginal spots with proximal dark line in s2 and s3 – not as thick as in *M. athalia*; unf discal spot in s1b heavy, irregular in shape: female ups dark suffusion more intense and extensive; uns orange-red markings prominent.

FLIGHT-PERIOD Bivoltine. Early April/May and July.

HABITAT Dry, flowery, bushy places.

LIFE-HISTORY LHPs *Linaria vulgaris*; *L.* (?)*micrantha*. Development as for nominate form. Captive larvae accept *Antirrhinum majus*.

M. deione nitida Oberthür 1909 TL: Tlemcen, Sebdou (Algeria).

DISTRIBUTION N Morocco: W Rif Mts. (Dj. Lakraa; Dj. Kelaa; Izlan). W Algeria: Sebou; Tlemcen. 900-1800m.

DESCRIPTION AND VARIATION In both sexes, fw outer margin strongly convex in most specimens; ups paler, yellowish-orange; ups black markings fine, marginal lines very narrow, sometimes paired; unh discal markings reduced; unh pale discal band usually unmarked: female similar. Male genitalia conform to nominate form. In W Rif Mts.: in July, smaller, with female ups gc more uniform (lacking usual contrastive colour bands) than specimens from same locality in late April/May.

FLIGHT-PERIOD Voltinism uncertain: possibly bivoltine (cf. seasonal variation) in Rif Mts. (mid April/early August) and univoltine in Algeria (May/June).

HABITAT Dry, flowery valleys; open grassy slopes; *Quercus* scrub.

Meadow Fritillary *Mellicta parthenoides*

RANGE SW Europe.

M. parthenoides Keferstein 1851 TL: Soucy, France.
syn: *parthenie* Godart 1819 (invalid homonym).

DISTRIBUTION Widespread in Iberian Peninsula. France, except NE. Very local in S Germany, Switzerland (Jura; Schaffhausen), NW Italy (Ligurian and Cottian Alps). 400-2400m.

DESCRIPTION AND VARIATION Male ups bright fulvous-orange, hw discal field usually clear of black markings; upf marginal and submarginal black lines of uniform thickness; pd line fine, often disrupted in s4; black discal markings heavy; upf discal mark in s1b variable in thickness but distinctly oblique (cf. *M. varia*). Regionally and locally very variable: in Spain, ups markings generally better defined, contrasting sharply with clear, bright gc.

FLIGHT-PERIOD Univoltine at higher altitudes, early June/July; bivoltine at lower levels, May/June and August/September.

HABITAT Open, flowery, grassy places bordering woodland.

LIFE-HISTORY LHPs *Plantago lanceolata*; *P. alpina*; *P. media*. Ova laid in batches on underside of leaves. Larvae feed and hibernate in companies, dispersing in later instars.

Provençal Fritillary

Meadow Fritillary

PROVENÇAL FRITILLARY

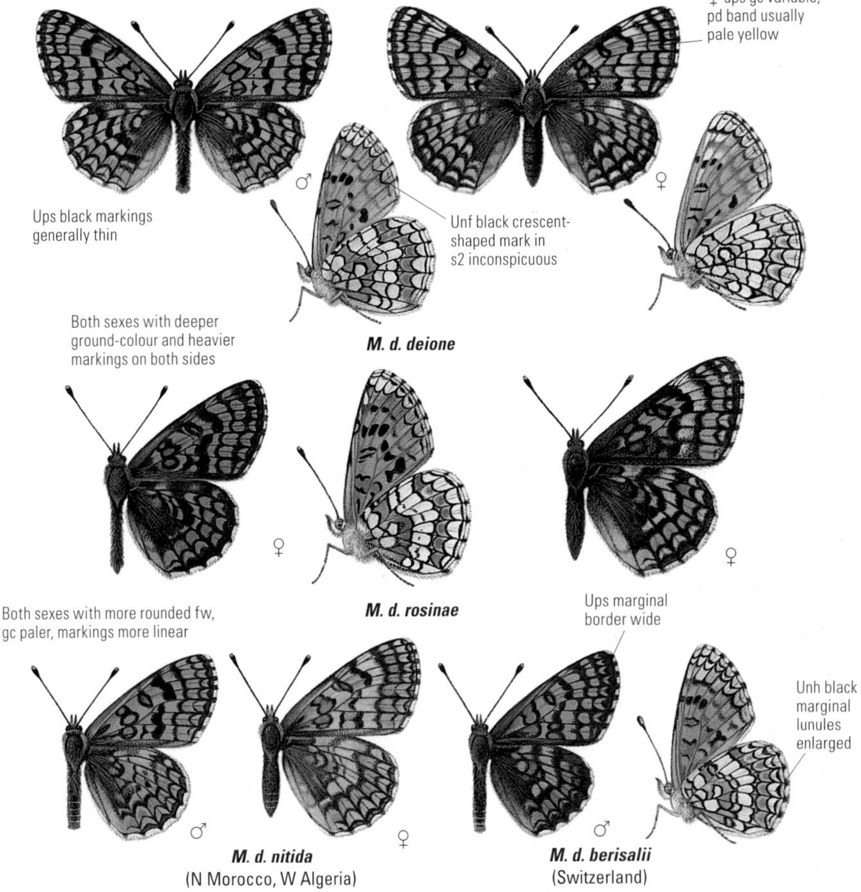

♀ ups gc variable, pd band usually pale yellow

♂

♀

Ups black markings generally thin

Unf black crescent-shaped mark in s2 inconspicuous

Both sexes with deeper ground-colour and heavier markings on both sides

M. d. deione

♀

♀

Both sexes with more rounded fw, gc paler, markings more linear

M. d. rosinae

Ups marginal border wide

Unh black marginal lunules enlarged

♂

♀

♂

M. d. nitida
(N Morocco, W Algeria)

M. d. berisalii
(Switzerland)

MEADOW FRITILLARY

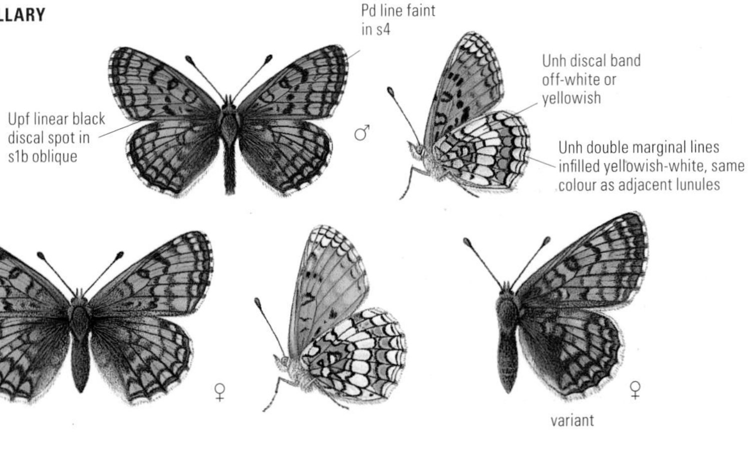

Pd line faint in s4

Unh discal band off-white or yellowish

Upf linear black discal spot in s1b oblique

♂

Unh double marginal lines infilled yellowish-white, same colour as adjacent lunules

♀

♀

variant

Nickerl's Fritillary *Mellicta aurelia*

RANGE C and E Europe, Turkey, Transcaucasus, S Urals, N Kazakhstan, W Siberia, Tian Shan.
M. aurelia Nickerl 1850 TL: Erlangen, Germany.
syn: *parthenie* Borkhausen 1788 (invalid homonym).
DISTRIBUTION W France to Latvia, Balkans and N Greece (Vernon Mts.; Rhodopi Mts.: very local). Absent from Britain, NW and SW France, N Belgium, Holland, Fennoscandia, C and S Italy and Republic of Macedonia. Reports from S Sweden unconfirmed. 100-1500m.
DESCRIPTION AND VARIATION Male ups black markings often suffused greyish; upf marginal pd line complete (cf. *M. parthenoides*); spacing of marginal, submarginal, pd and discal lines roughly even, creating a uniform macular gc pattern (cf. *M. parthenoides*); unh double marginal lines infilled yellow, slightly darker than adjacent spots: female ups gc generally somewhat paler. Darker forms often occur on damp peaty soils.
FLIGHT-PERIOD Univoltine. Early June/late July, in prolonged emergence in some southern localities.
HABITAT Open, grassy and flowery places, with sparse bushes or small trees; damp peat mosses; heaths.
LIFE-HISTORY LHP *Plantago lanceolata*. Ova laid in batches on underside leaves. Larvae feed and hibernate in companies, dispersing in later instars.

Assmann's Fritillary *Mellicta britomartis*

RANGE C Europe, C Asia, Transbaical, Mongolia, NE China, Korea.
M. britomartis Assmann 1847 TL: Breslau, Germany.
DISTRIBUTION Central E Germany to NE Poland and SE Sweden. N Italy: very local: Val d'Aosta; Val di Susa; Turin; Lake Maggiore; Lake Guarda; Friuli-Venezia. Slovenia. Hungary. N Serbia. Romania. Bulgaria: very local: Stara Pl. (Sliven); Burgas. Reported presence in NE Switzerland relates to one male and two female specimens taken on separate occasions from same, general locality. 300-900m.
DESCRIPTION AND VARIATION Male ups resembles *M. aurelia*. Larger; male ups gc darker, black markings heavier, lacking dusky suffusion; unh submarginal spots often with chocolate brown proximal border; double marginal lines infilled dusky-orange or brown – distinctly darker tone than adjacent yellow spots (cf. *M. aurelia*). In some cases, examination of male genitalia may be necessary to effect separation from *M. aurelia*: larval and pupal stages readily separable.
FLIGHT-PERIOD Univoltine in most localities, late May/early August: reportedly bivoltine in NW Italy (Ticino Valley), May/June and late July/early August.
HABITAT Warm, sheltered grassy and bushy places at woodland margins.
LIFE-HISTORY LHPs *Plantago lanceolata*; *Veronica teucrium*; *Rhianthus minor*. Ova laid in batches on underside of leaves. Larvae feed and hibernate in a silken web.

Little Fritillary *Mellicta asteria*

RANGE Central European E Alps.
M. asteria Freyer 1828 TL: Chur, Switzerland.
DISTRIBUTION Very local. E Switzerland: Grisons, high mountains bordering Engadine Valley. Italy: C and E Alps, including Ortler. Austria: Tirol to Gross Glockner; Gurktaler Alps. 2000-2700m.
DESCRIPTION Small; ups often heavily suffused greyish in both sexes.
FLIGHT-PERIOD Univoltine. Early July/late August.
HABITAT Confined to alpine tundra: open valleys and slopes with short grass.
LIFE-HISTORY LHP *Plantago alpina*. Ova laid in clumps on underside of leaves. Larval development occupies two seasonal cycles.

Scarce Fritillary *Hypodryas maturna*

RANGE C and E Europe, Caucasus, Urals, E Kazakhstan, S and W Siberia, Transbaikal, Mongolia.
H. maturna Linnaeus 1758 TL: Not stated.
DISTRIBUTION Generally very local: colonies widely dispersed. France: Oise; Seine-et-Marne; Yonne; Nièvre; Allier; Saône-et-Loire; Côte-d'Or; Haute-Marne; Haute-Saône. Germany. Czech Republic. Slovakia. Poland. SE Sweden: Uppland; Dalarne; Västmanland. Baltic states. S Finland. Austria. Hungary. Romania. Slovenia. Croatia. Serbia. Bosnia-Herzegovina. Albania. W Republic of Macedonia: Sar Pl.; Radika Valley. Bulgaria: Ludogorie Hills. 200-1000m.
FLIGHT-PERIOD Univoltine. Late May/early July according to locality and season.
HABITAT Small, bushy clearings containing young Ash or Aspen trees in mixed deciduous woodland, often in limestone valleys, sometimes in damp situations.
LIFE-HISTORY LHPs (before hibernation) *Fraxinus excelsior*; *Populus tremula*; (?)*Salix caprea*. Ova laid usually in a single large batch on underside of leaf of a small specimen (<6m) of LHP. Larvae feed and hibernate gregariously in a silken web which, in autumn, falls to the ground along with dead leaves. After hibernation, larvae disperse and feed singly on *F. excelsior*, *P. tremula*, *Plantago lanceolata*, *Veronica chamaedrys*, *Lonicera periclymenum* or *Succisa pratensis*. In captivity, a proportion of larvae require two seasonal cycles to achieve maturity (cf. *H. intermedia*).
BEHAVIOUR Adults rest and roost in trees and seem to prefer the nectar of shrubs, e.g., *Ligustrum vulgare* and *Viburnum lantana*, to that of low-growing herbs.
CONSERVATION Decline in many regions (N France; Bavaria; S Sweden) has been attributed to forestry management, land drainage and habitat destruction for agricultural purposes.

NICKERL'S FRITILLARY

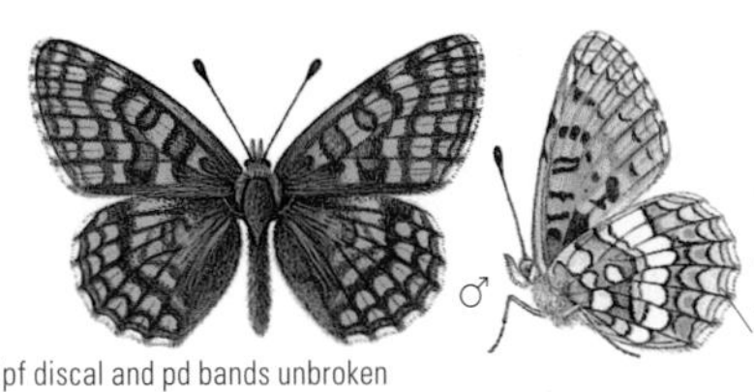

Upf discal and pd bands unbroken

Unh marginal lines infilled yellowish, slightly darker than adjacent lunules

♀ ups, gc paler, sometimes variegated

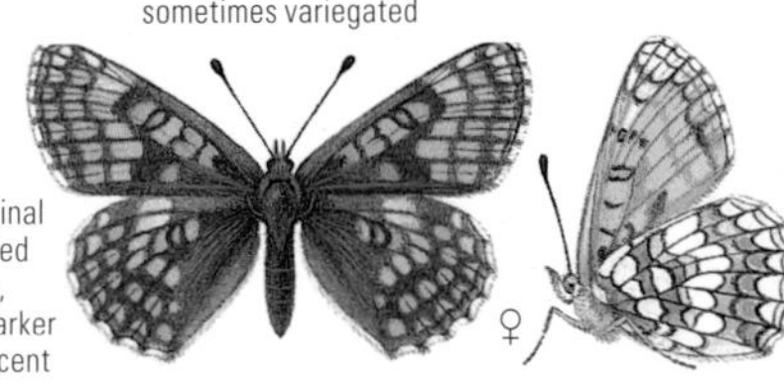

ASSMANN'S FRITILLARY

Upf pd line unbroken

Unh orange submarginal orange spots often with dark brown internal border

Unh marginal lines infilled yellowish-brown, darker than adjacent lunules

LITTLE FRITILLARY

Restricted to Central Alps

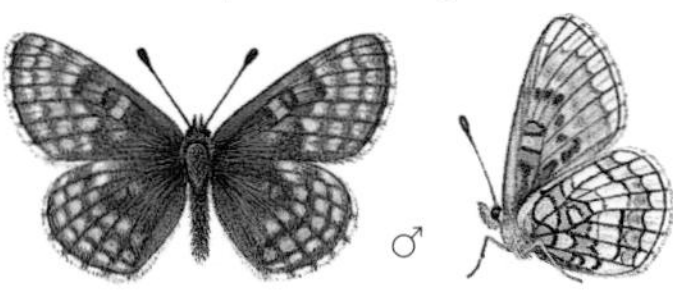

SCARCE FRITILLARY

Ups and uns colouring and pattern of markings distinctive

Nickerl's Fritillary

Assmann's Fritillary

Little Fritillary

Scarce Fritillary

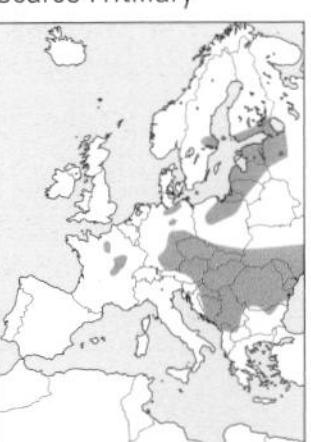

Asian Fritillary *Hypodryas intermedia*

RANGE C European Alps, S and C Urals, S and W Siberia, Transbaikal, Mongolia, Amur, NE China, Sakhalin, Korea.
H. intermedia wolfensbergeri Frey 1880 TL: Maloja Pass, Engadine.
DISTRIBUTION France: Haute-Savoie; Savoie; Izère; Hautes-Alpes. Switzerland: Valais (S of Rhône Valley) to Engadine. Italy: N Cottian Alps; Ortler Alps; Dolomites; Karinthian Mts. Slovenia: Julian Alps (Triglav Massif). 1500-2400m – more often 1700-2000m. **DESCRIPTION** Unh pale discal band with medial thin black line, often broken (cf. *H. cynthia*). **FLIGHT-PERIOD** Univoltine. Late June/early August. **HABITAT** Small clearings in light coniferous woodland, often associated with small streams and low-growing shrubs, e.g., *Juniperous communis nana*, *Rhododendron ferrugineum* and *Alnus viridis*. **LIFE-HISTORY** LHP *Lonicera caerulea*. Ova laid in batches on underside of leaves. Hibernates as a larva, the full larval development of which occupies two seasonal cycles. **NOTE** Sympatric with *H. maturna* in some parts of E Palearctic range (Kentei Mts.).

Cynthia's Fritillary *Hypodryas cynthia*

RANGE European Alps, Bulgaria.
H. cynthia Denis and Schiffermüller 1775 TL: Vienna.
DISTRIBUTION France: Alpes-Maritimes to Haute-Savoie. Switzerland: Valais to St. Gallen and Engadine. Italy: W Ligurian Alps, S Alps, Ortler Alps to Dolomites. Austria: W Tirol to Niedere Tauern. 900-3000m. Bulgaria: Pirin Mts. 2200-2700m; Rila Mts. 2000-2800m. Records for Bavarian Alps require confirmation. **DESCRIPTION AND VARIATION** Male ups white discal and basal markings definitive: female resembles female *H. intermedia*, but lacking unh black line in pale discal band and with black points in each space of uph and unh red pd band. Above 1800m, west of Hohe Tauern, *alpicola* Galvagni: smaller; ups black suffusion more extensive, almost obscuring pale submarginal band; red markings reduced, sometimes absent on fw. In E Austria, sporadic occurrence of transitional forms at high and intermediate altitudes (east of Brenner), and larger, brighter forms than nominate form at lowest altitudes, suggests ecological modification with the combined characters of geographical and altitudinal clines. In Bulgaria, *leonardi* Frühstorfer (Rila Mts.) and *drenowskii* Röber (Pirin Mts.): large; brightly marked. **FLIGHT-PERIOD** Univoltine. Late June/early August. **HABITAT** Open, grassy slopes dominated by low shrubs, which often include *Juniperous communis nana* (Central Alps) or *J. sibirica* (Bulgaria). **LIFE-HISTORY** LHPs *Plantago alpina*; *Viola calcarata*. Ova laid in batches on underside of leaves. Hibernates as a larva, the full larval development of which occupies two seasonal cycles.

Lapland Fritillary *Hypodryas iduna*

RANGE N Fennoscandia, E Turkey, Kola Peninsula, Caucasus, Polar and Subpolar Urals, NE and S Siberia, Yakutskaya, Mongolia, Altai.
H. iduna Dalman 1816 TL: Sweden.
DISTRIBUTION N Fennoscandia from Arctic Circle to Arctic Sea. In Finland, restricted to a few sites close to Norwegian border. Sporadic and very local in some regions. 300-700m. **FLIGHT-PERIOD** Univoltine. Late June/mid July: date of emergence dependent on local/regional weather conditions. **HABITAT** Damp heathland with sparse scrub, often in close proximity to marshes with small open areas of standing water; hillside bogs; drier rocky terrain at highest altitudes. **LIFE-HISTORY** LHPs *Veronica alpina*; *V. fructicans*; *Plantago*; *Vaccinium*. Ova laid in small batches on leaf. Larvae feed and hibernate gregariously in small groups in a silken web. **BEHAVIOUR** In rapid flight close to the ground, males appear surprisingly grey and bear a striking resemblance to a large *Pyrgus* sp. Adults often bask or seek shelter from strong winds amongst Dwarf Birch (*Betula nana*). **NOTE** Although predominantly an arctic species, occurs in lower latitudes where equivalent ecological conditions are provided, evidently, by the compensating influence of high altitude; e.g., Mt. Ararat, 40°N, 4000m (*H. i. inexpectata* Sheljuzhko) and in the Altai Mts., 50°N, 1800-2700m (*H. i. sajana* Higgins) where further compensation derives from the more general, cooler conditions of a subarctic zone.

Spanish Fritillary *Eurodryas desfontainii*

RANGE Morocco, Algeria, Iberian peninsula.
E. desfontainii desfontainii Godart 1819 TL: Algeria.
DISTRIBUTION Morocco: Middle Atlas (Azrou; Annoceur; Tizi-n-Tretten; Ifrane; Mrassine; Douar de Garde; Mischliffen; Timhadit; Zehroun Massif; 500-2100m); High Atlas (Dades Valley; Tilmi; Djebel Siroua; Col du Kerdous; 2800m); Rif Mts. (Chechaouen); Algeria: (Sebdou; Daya; El Hacaiba; Tlemcen Mts.; 1500-1800m). **DESCRIPTION AND VARIATION** Fw outer margin curvature slightly irregular near v6; unf discal area pale rose-red; black markings prominent (cf. *E. aurinia*). *F. gibrati* Oberthür, ups gc brighter, appears to fall within range of variation of nominate form. **FLIGHT-PERIOD** Univoltine. Mid April/early June. **HABITAT** Dry, rocky or grassy gullies/slopes, often amongst scrub; grassy/flowery meadows. **LIFE-HISTORY** LHP *Knautia arvensis*. Larvae feed and hibernate in silken webs, which have been found on plants other than the LHP. Larvae are said to aestivate in summer heat, becoming active with the onset of autumn rain.
E. desfontainii baetica Rambur 1858 TL: Andalusia.
DISTRIBUTION S Portugal: Algarve. Spain: Province of Burgos, W Pyrenees and Catalonia through Madrid to Andalusia. France: Pyrénées-Orientales (Sournia: very local). Absent from Cantabrian Mts. Sporadic and generally very local. 50-1800m. **DESCRIPTION AND VARIATION** Unf discal area yellow but variable – individuals indistinguishable from nominate form occur in Teruel and Andalusia. In provinces of Teruel, Alicante and Huesca, uns markings often better defined (*zapateri* Higgins). In S Portugal (Algarve 100-200m): very large, especially female; ups pale spots in marginal band vestigial; female ups gc pattern less contrastive. **FLIGHT-PERIOD** Univoltine. Mid April/early June according to altitude. **HABITAT** Hot, dry, grassy scrubland; rocky gullies; dry stream beds; neglected areas of cultivation. **Continued on p. 350**

ASIAN FRITILLARY

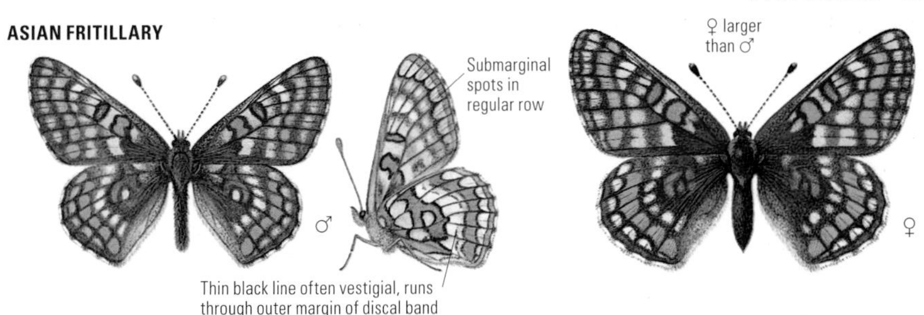

CYNTHIA'S FRITILLARY

LAPLAND FRITILLARY

♂ and ♀ ups colouring and pattern of marking distinctive

(N Fennoscandia)

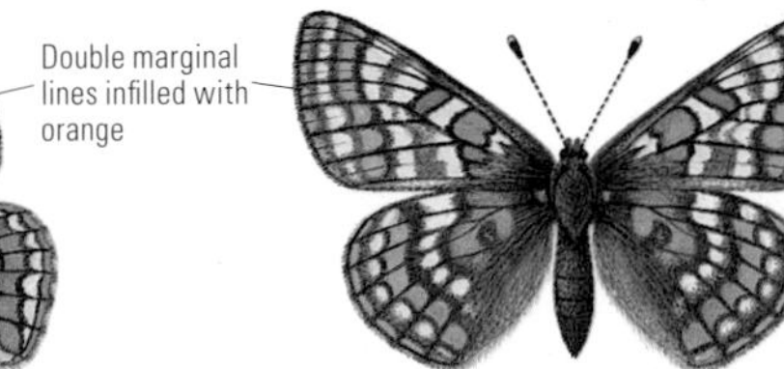

SPANISH FRITILLARY

Maps on p. 217

Marsh Fritillary *Eurodryas aurinia*

RANGE Morocco, Algeria, Europe, Turkey, temperate Asia, Korea.

E. aurinia aurinia Rottemburg 1775 TL: Paris.

DISTRIBUTION From Pyrenees, through most of Europe, including Britain, to 62°N in Fennoscandia, including Öland and Gotland. 0-2200m. Absent from C and S Greece, Mediterranean islands and peninsular Italy, except Monti Aurunci and Monti del Matese. 0-1950m.

VARIATION Ups gc and black markings subject to considerable individual, local and regional variation. Divergence within a colony and between isolated colonies, even within a small area of distribution, is often appreciable. To a lesser extent, significant inter-seasonal differences are also apparent, indicating an ecological origin for at least some of the observed variation. Whilst a large number of subspecies have been described to accommodate regional differences, difficulties of taxonomic classification are compounded by the widespread occurrence of transitional forms, interspersed with distinctive, local ecological variants. In the absence of a biological basis for distinction, the greater proportion of descriptions at subspecies level lack justification, thereby creating, in some instances, a false impression of genetically distinct and geographically restricted populations. Subspecific assignments to S Balkan and N Greek races (*balcanica* Schawerda and *bulgarica* Frühstorfer), for example, is confounded by the sporadic occurrence, in the same region, of mountain populations indistinguishable from those of NW and C Europe. Similarly, *kricheldorffi* Collier (Asturia Mts., N Spain), shares much of the character of *scotica* Robson (W Scotland) and *hibernica* Birchall (Ireland): these forms, characterised by extensive ups dark suffusion and orange pd bands/cellular spots contrasting with yellowish discal markings, appear to be ecological modifications arising from damp and/or cold conditions: in warmer/drier conditions of central S and SE Europe, tendency towards bicoloured forms with dark markings is largely reversed. Distinctive forms/sspp. occupying substantial geographical areas are described below.

FLIGHT-PERIOD Univoltine. Mid April/mid July, according to altitude.

HABITAT Diverse. Damp or dry flowery, grassy places; deciduous or coniferous woodland margins or clearings on calcareous or acidic soils; damp, open heathland; sheltered places on exposed mountain slopes.

LIFE-HISTORY LHPs include, *Succisa pratensis* (N and C Europe); *Scabiosa columbaria*; *S.* (?)*ochroleuca* (NW Greece); *Lonicera periclymenum*; *L. implexa*; *Gentiana lutea* (Switzerland); (?)*Digitalis* sp. (Slovenia). Reported use of *Plantago* spp. in Slovakia requires confirmation. Ova laid in batches on underside of leaves. Larvae feed and hibernate in a silken web.

E. aurinia provincialis Boisduval 1828 TL: Provence, France.

DISTRIBUTION SE France: Bouches-du-Rhône; Var; Alps-Maritimes; Alpes-de-Haute-Provençe; Hautes-Alpes; Isère. N Italy. 300-1000m – exceptionally to 2250m.

DESCRIPTION AND VARIATION Ups gc almost unicolorous pale orange, pd bands slightly darker; black markings fine; uns very pale sandy-orange. F. *comacina* Turati; smaller and paler, very local near Lake Como and Lake Lugano at 900m. West of Rhône Valley to Catalonia, transitional to *beckeri* Herrich-Schäffer (below). At higher altitudes in Piedmont, transitional to nominate form. In Croatia, *rotunda* Röber: resembles *provincialis*: averagely larger: transitional to nominate form in parts of Bosnia-Herzegovina and W Serbia.

FLIGHT-PERIOD Univoltine. May/June.

HABITAT Dry, flowery clearings in light woodland or scrub.

LIFE-HISTORY LHPs *Succisa pratensis*; *Scabiosa columbaria*; *Cephalaria leucantha*; *Knautia arvensis*.

E. aurinia beckeri Herrich-Schäffer 1851 TL: Cádiz.

DISTRIBUTION Morocco: very local: Middle Atlas; Rif Mts; 300-1800m. C Algeria: very local: Blida; Col de Ben-Chicao; Berrouaghi; 1000-1200m. Portugal. Spain: Pyrenees and Cantabrian Mts. to Andalusia. 10-1700m.

VARIATION At lowest altitudes in Algarve (10-100m), very large; gc tone averagely darker on both surfaces; ups black markings heavier; unh pale rings enclosing black points in marginal band reduced or absent. Transitional to nominate form in foothills of Cantabrian Mts. and Pyrenees. In C Algeria, *barraguei* Betz: upf and uph mediodiscal bands and upf pd band yellow – contrasting with orange gc; uns gc paler, unh orange pd paler.

FLIGHT-PERIOD Univoltine. NW Africa April/June according to locality: S Portugal (Algarve, 10-100m), early April/late May: Spain, late May/late June.

HABITAT Hot, dry, flowery places, often amongst rocks and open scrub: in NW Africa, flowery, grassy slopes, often on damp or marshy ground; clearings in dense or light woodland.

LIFE-HISTORY LHPs: Spain, *Lonicera periclymenum*; *L. implexa*; *L. etrusca*; *Scabiosa columbaria*; *S. atropurpurea*; (?)*Knautia arvensis*: Morocco, *L. implexa*; (?)*L. biflora*; (?)*L. etrusca*; (?)*L. periclymenum*.

E. aurinia debilis Oberthür 1909 TL: E Pyrenees.

syn: *merope* de Prunner (invalid homonym)

DISTRIBUTION Andorra. France: Ariège; Pyrénées-Orientales; Alpes-de-Haute-Provençe to Haute-Savoie. Switzerland. Germany: Allgäuer Alps. Austria: Tirol; Carnic Alps. 1500-2600m: rarely below 1800m.

VARIATION At high altitudes in Central Alps, *glaciegenita* Verity: male ups pale dusky-yellow, heavily suffused grey, variable; reddish-orange submarginal and cellular markings reduced. Clinal variation in wing-markings is apparent, with brighter forms occurring at lower altitudes in S and W Alps: expected accompanying clinal variation in size is, however, reversed with larger forms occurring in N and E Alps – possibly explained by a two year life-cycle at highest altitudes, thus providing more time for larval development.

FLIGHT-PERIOD Univoltine. Late June/late August according to altitude.

HABITAT Open grassy slopes; damp alpine meadows: on calcareous or non-calcareous soils.

BEHAVIOUR Flight fast and low.

LIFE-HISTORY LHPs *Gentiana verna*; *G. acaulis*; *G. clusii*; *G. alpina*; *Primula viscosa*. Ova laid in clusters on underside of leaves. Larvae feed on flowers. Hibernates as a small larva.

MARSH FRITILLARY

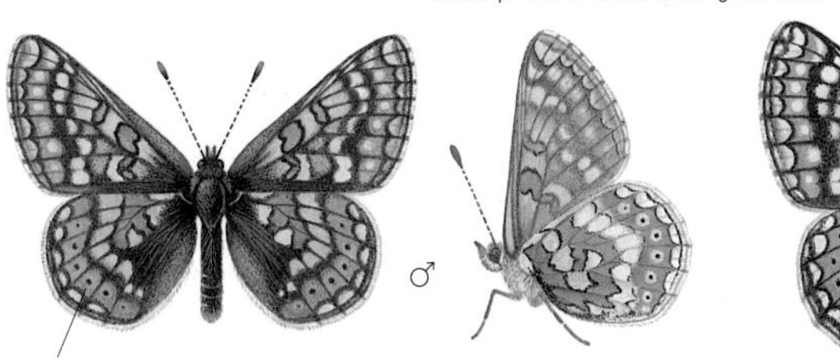

E. a. debilis
(C Alps, Pyrenees)

E. a. bulgarica
(S Balkans, N Greece)

E. a. beckeri
(Spain, Portugal, N Africa)

Marsh Fritillary

Asian Fritillary

Cynthia's Fritillary

Lapland Fritillary

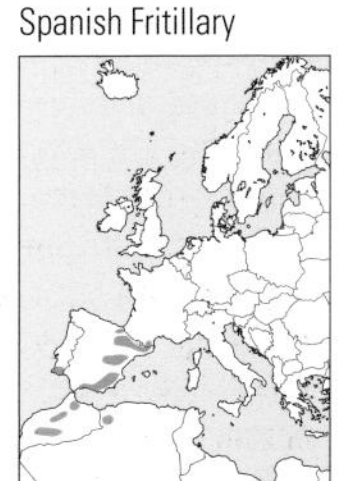
Spanish Fritillary

SATYRIDAE Boisduval 1833

A very extensive family of small, medium and large butterflies comprising about one-third of European species. Most are some shade of brown, usually with distinctive ocelli on the underside of the hind-wing and one or more prominent ocelli in the apical region of the upper and underside fore-wing: as observation shows, these ocelli – so-called 'eye-spots' – tend to divert the point of attack of a predatory bird or lizard from the more vital parts of the insect. An atypical group are the 'marbled whites', so-called because of their white ground-colour and intricate pattern of black markings. The genus *Erebia* comprise a large and distinctive group of mostly small or medium-sized insects, easily recognizable by their very dark brown, sometimes almost jet black ground-colour: these are mostly inhabitants of mountains, with some species occurring at altitudes as high as 3000m. Of the many endemic European *Erebia* species, more than a dozen are confined to the Central Alps. Amongst several other endemic species, having equally or even more restricted distributions, some are found only on the Atlantic islands. As far as is known, larvae of all European satyrid butterflies feed on grasses (Poaceae), mostly during the hours of darkness (this information is not repeated in the following account of species). Grasses are low in proteins and larval development is greatly protracted, often requiring several months. Most species hibernate as immature larvae (where confirmed for individual species, this information has been omitted from the general account). Although larval shape varies appreciably according to the relative proportions of component structures, the larvae of most species are quite distinctive and characterized by a smooth taper originating in the thorax or abdomen and terminating in twin 'tails' in the last abdominal segment. Larvae are generally quite sensitive to any form of disturbance and, if touched, will usually drop immediately from their feeding station and burrow into the base of the larval host-plant; the same reaction is sometimes induced by bright, artificial light. Pupae are suspended from plant-stems or secreted within or below the compact base of the larval host-plant, or amongst moss or in small hollows under stones.

Marbled White *Melanargia galathea*

RANGE NW Africa, Europe, Turkey, Transcaucasus.

M. galathea galathea Linnaeus 1758 TL: Germany (Verity 1953).

DISTRIBUTION N Spain (Cantabrian Mts. to W and C Pyrenees), eastwards through most of Europe, including S England and Sicily, to Lithuania, C Greece and European Turkey. 0-1750m. Absent from N Holland, N Germany and Peloponnesos. Last reported from Latvia in 1950. Generally widespread and common, but absent from substantial areas within main region of distribution. Largely replaced by *M. lachesis* (below) in Pyrénées-Orientales; Aude; Hérault; Gard: intermediate forms, believed to be hybrids, are frequent in areas of contact.

DESCRIPTION Upf cell without medial transverse black bar (cf. *M. russiae*); upf basal and distal areas of cell black; unf distal one-third of cell grey, separated from white area by irregular transverse black line; cell-base with limited dark suffusion. (Cf. *M. lachesis*).

VARIATION Ups black suffusion variable: in C and S Italy, S Balkans and Greece, dark forms predonderate (f. *procida* Herbst): in NE Italy (f. *magdalenae* Reichl), black markings further extended, totally obscuring white gc in extreme examples. Ups and uns gc sometimes yellow, commonly associated with f. *procida*, in which ups female costa is often conspicuously buff. F. *leucomelas* Esper: unh uniformly white, unmarked – a recurrent form, commoner in the south. F. *galene* Ochsenheimer: unh pd ocelli absent.

FLIGHT-PERIOD Univoltine. Generally June/July, exceptionally late May/early September.

HABITAT Diverse. Grassy, flowery, bushy places.

BEHAVIOUR Adults are especially fond of the nectar of *Centaurea*, *Scabiosa*, *Cirsium* and *Carduus* spp.

LIFE-HISTORY LHPs include *Brachypodium pinnatum*; *B. sylvaticum*; *Bromus erectus*; *Poa trivialis*; *Phleum pratense*; *Agrostis capillaris*; *Dactylis glomerata*; *Molinia caerulea*; *Avena pubsecens*; *Festuca rubra*. Ova are ejected amongst grasses during flight. Mature larvae are polymorphic.

M. galathea lucasi Rambur 1858 TL: Bougie, Algeria.

DISTRIBUTION Morocco. Algeria. Tunisia. 800-2600m. Common and widespread.

DESCRIPTION Ups black marginal markings averagely more extensive; distal part of cell greyish, closed by transverse black bar near cell-end: female unh pd ocelli with blue pupils.

VARIATION Development of ups black marginal markings appear to follow an east-west cline, with darkest forms (f. *fumata* Mokhles) prevalent in Morocco. Variants equivalent to f. *leucomelas* Esper not reported.

FLIGHT-PERIOD Univoltine. Mid May/July at lower altitudes; June/early September at highest altitude.

HABITAT As for nominate form.

Iberian Marbled White *Melanargia lachesis*

RANGE Portugal, Spain, S France.

M. lachesis Hübner 1790 TL: Languedoc [S France].

DISTRIBUTION Portugal and Spain: widespread and common. France: Pyrénées-Orientales; Aude; Hérault; Gard (not reported east of Rhône Valley). 0-1600m.

DESCRIPTION Upf cell white except for black suffusion at distal extremity (cf. *M. g. galathea*), lacking medial transverse black bar (cf. *M. russiae*).

VARIATION Ups dark suffusion variable in extent and colour (brownish to black); uns gc whitish or yellowish. F. *cataleuca* Staudinger: unh uniformly white – equivalent to *M. galathea* f. *leucomelas* Esper.

FLIGHT-PERIOD Univoltine. Early June/early August.

HABITAT Dry, grassy, bushy, flowery places.

MARBLED WHITE

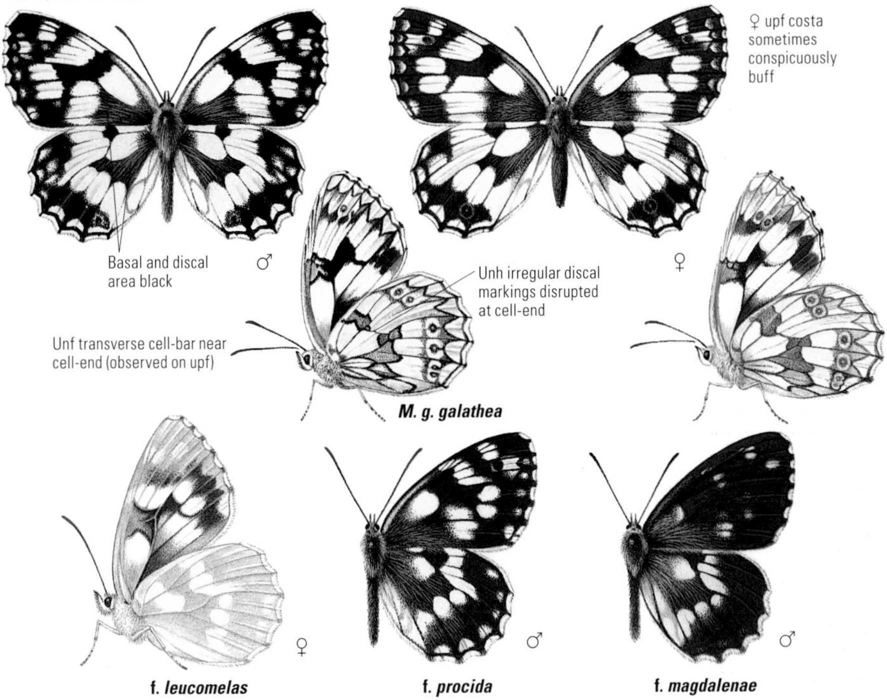

♀ upf costa sometimes conspicuously buff

Basal and discal area black

♂

Unh irregular discal markings disrupted at cell-end

♀

Unf transverse cell-bar near cell-end (observed on upf)

M. g. galathea

♀

♂

♂

f. ***leucomelas***

f. ***procida***

f. ***magdalenae***

IBERIAN MARBLED WHITE

Upf and unf cell white, terminating in sharp point at cell-end

Uph basal and discal black markings vestigial or absent

♂

♀

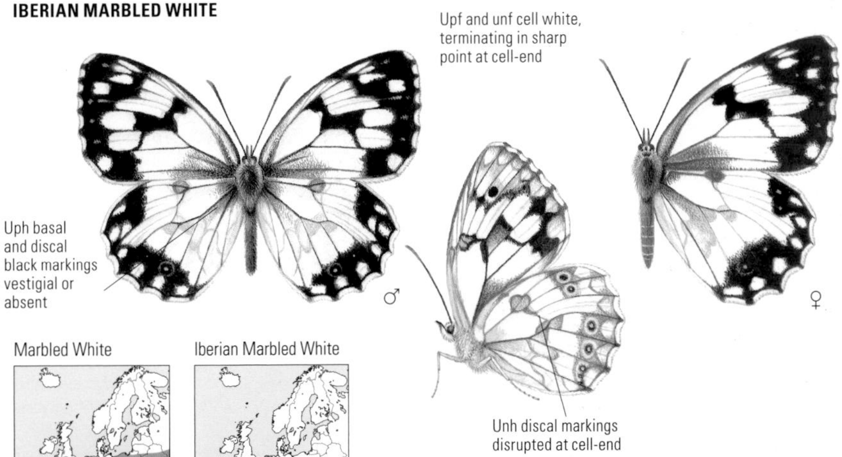

Marbled White

Iberian Marbled White

Unh discal markings disrupted at cell-end

Esper's Marbled White *Melanargia russiae*

RANGE SW and SE Europe, Italy, E Turkey, Transcaucasus, S Russia to W Siberia, E Kazakhstan.

M. russiae russiae Esper 1783 TL: S Russia

DISTRIBUTION Occurred formerly in Hungary, now presumed extinct in Europe: extant in Caucasus, S Urals Mts., Tien Shan and Altai Mts.

DESCRIPTION Ups marginal and subapical markings clearly defined, associated dark suffusion minimal.

M. russiae cleanthe Boisduval 1833 TL: Basses Alpes.

DISTRIBUTION N Portugal: Serra da Estrêla. N, C and E Spain. S France: E Pyrenees; S Massif Central; Vaucluse; Alpes-de-Haute-Provençe; Drôme; Hautes-Alpes. 600-1650m.

DESCRIPTION Upf cell with medial transverse irregular black bar, often diffuse or partly obscured by greyish or fuscous cellular suffusion (cf. *M. galathea*; *M. lachesis*; *M. larissa*).

VARIATION Ups dark suffusion variable in extent and colour – dark brownish to black. Lightly marked specimens resembling nominate form are not uncommon. A female form equivalent to *M. galathea* f. *leucomelas* has been recorded from Burgos, N Spain.

FLIGHT-PERIOD Univoltine. Late June/mid August.

HABITAT Dry, grassy places, often in bushy clearings in sparse pinewood.

M. russiae japygia Cyrillo 1787 TL: S Italy.

DISTRIBUTION Italy: Apennines (Florence to Avellino); Apulia; Calabria; N Sicily (Madonie; Monte Nebrodi; Monti Peloritani). 1000-1450m. Albania: Jablanica Pl. W Republic of Macedonia: Bistra Pl.; Jablanica Pl.; Placenska Pl.; Mt. Pelister. NW Greece: Vernon Mts.; Varnous Mts.; Voras Mts.; Timfi Mts.; Mitsikeli Mts. 1300-2100m.

DESCRIPTION AND VARIATION Ups dark suffusion more extensive, especially in Italy, but variable. In Italy and Greece, lightly marked forms, closely resembling nominate form, occur commonly, preponderant in some colonies.

FLIGHT-PERIOD Univoltine. Late June/mid August.

HABITAT Dry, rocky limestone slopes and open gullies dominated by grasses: less often, dry, gravelly slopes with short grasses on non-calcareous substrates.

LIFE-HISTORY LHPs *Stipa pennata*; *Aegilops geniculata*; *Brachypodium pinnatum*; *B. sylvaticum*. In Greece, mature larvae are usually entirely green, but a small proportion have green bodies and light brown heads.

Esper's Marbled White

Balkan Marbled White

Balkan Marbled White *Melanargia larissa*

RANGE SE Europe, Turkey, Transcaucasus, N Iran.

M. larissa Geyer 1828 TL: Cres (Cherso Is.), Croatia (Hemming 1937).

DISTRIBUTION Croatia: Dalmatian coastal region. S Serbia. Albania. Republic of Macedonia. S Bulgaria: Pirin Mts.; Rhodopi Mts. Greece, including Corfu, Levkas, Limnos, Lesbos and Siros. European Turkey. 0-2150m – usually below 1500m.

DESCRIPTION AND VARIATION Upf, distal one-third of cell closed by dark line (cf. *M. russiae*), basal area of cell largely suffused fuscous-grey; ups basal areas extensively suffused fuscous-grey, often obscuring uph cell completely (cf. *M. russiae*). In some localities, especially S Dalmatia, ups marginal and pd dark suffusion greatly reduced (*herta* Geyer): intermediate forms not uncommon. Female forms with unh light buff or whitish occur in Greece (cf. *M. galathea* f. *leucomelas*). On Limnos and Lesbos, *lesbina* Wagener: ups dark suffusion extensive, partly or largely obscuring white marginal chevrons.

FLIGHT-PERIOD Univoltine. Late May/early August according to locality.

HABITAT Warm, dry, grassy, flowery, places; often amongst bushes and rocks in open woodland.

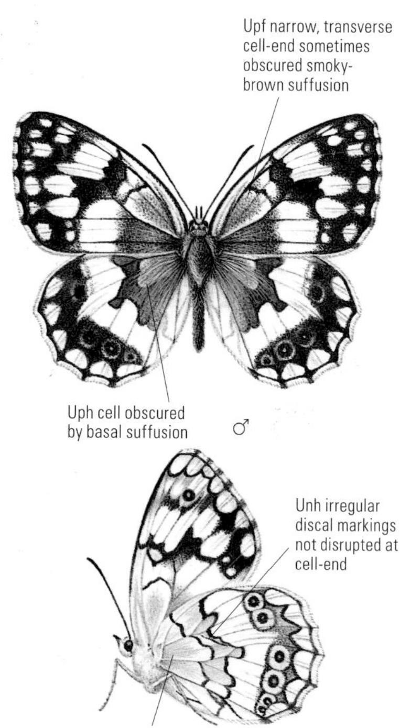

ESPER'S MARBLED WHITE

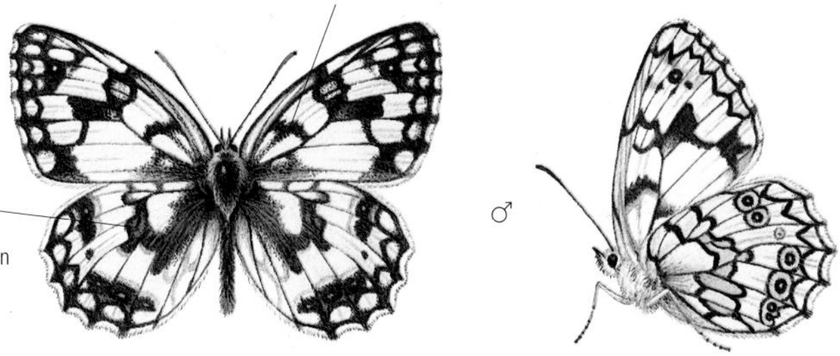

Upf and unf medial cell-bar irregular

Uph cell white, not obscured by dark suffusion

♂

Unh gc yellowish-brown markings

♀

M. r. cleanthe

Ups dark markings extensive, butvariable

♂

M. r. japygia

BALKAN MARBLED WHITE

Upf and unf medial transverse cell-bar very narrow, irregular

f. *herta*

Ups basal area heavily suffused smoky-brown

Western Marbled White *Melanargia occitanica*

RANGE NW Africa, SW Europe.

M. occitanica occitanica Esper 1793 TL: Toulouse.

syn: *psyche* Hubner 1800; *syllius* Herbst.

DISTRIBUTION N and C Portugal. Spain: widespread but local: absent from NW, NC and extreme SW. France: E Pyrenees to Ardèche and Provence. Italy: Maritime Alps: very local. 0-1500m. A record for Corsica requires confirmation.

DESCRIPTION Unh veins brownish – overall pattern very distinctive; curved longitudinal brownish line in s1b linked at both ends to v1b.

FLIGHT-PERIOD Univoltine. Late April/late June, according to locality.

HABITAT Hot, dry, grassy, rocky places.

LIFE-HISTORY LHPs *Brachypodium pinnatum*; *Dactylis glomerata*; *Lygeum spartum*. In captivity, newly-hatched larvae have been observed to enter and remain in diapause for 15 months.

M. occitanica pelagia Oberthür 1911 TL: Sebdou, Algeria.

DISTRIBUTION Morocco: Middle Atlas; High Atlas. W Algeria. Widespread but local. 500-2000m. Not recorded from E Algeria or Tunisia.

DESCRIPTION AND VARIATION Upf base of s3 always white – transverse black cellular bar clearly separated from discal markings (cf. nominate form). Moroccan populations resemble nominate form closely, those of Algeria show closer affinity to those of Sicily (cf. *M. o. pherusa* (below)).

FLIGHT-PERIOD Univoltine. Mid May/June.

HABITAT As for nominate form.

M. occitanica pherusa Boisduval 1833 TL: Sicily.

DISTRIBUTION NW Sicily: very local: mountains south of Palermo. 600-1000m.

DESCRIPTION AND VARIATION Ups black markings reduced, especially uph discal area; upf, base of s3 always white; uph and unh ocelli, smaller, sometimes absent (f. *plesaura* Bellier); unh veins brown, finer.

FLIGHT-PERIOD AND HABITAT As for nominate form.

NOTE Clinal variation in wing-markings from Iberian Peninsula through N Africa to Sicily is clearly evident. The disjunctive distributional relationship with the closely similar, but allopatric *M. arge* (below) is striking: it would appear that *M. arge* is the evolutionary culmination of a once uninterrupted cline of *M. occitanica* extending to southern Italian mainland: a small, but constant difference is apparent in valve of male genitalia; chromosome numbers unknown.

Italian Marbled White *Melanargia arge*

RANGE Peninsular Italy.

M. arge Sulzer 1776 TL: Kingdom of Sicily [included C Appenines in 1776].

DISTRIBUTION NE Sicily (Monte Nebrodi; Monti Peloritani): W and C Italian mainland: Monti di Tolfa; Monti della Laga to S Calabria. Absent from E Italy, except Gargano and Salentina Peninsulas. 350-1500m.

DESCRIPTION AND VARIATION Resembles *M. occitanica pherusa*. Ups and uns black markings reduced; upf posterior extremity of cell-bar tapered to a fine line, not quite reaching median vein; black oval/circular mark at cell-end often enclosing bluish scales; base of s3 usually with some dark suffusion; unh veins black; dark longitudinal curved line in s1b linked at both ends to v1b (cf. *M. ines*). In E Italy, f. *couzzana* Stauder: unh markings reduced: intermediate forms (f. *turati* Rostagno) occur in SW Italy (Aspromonte).

FLIGHT-PERIOD Univoltine. Early May/mid June.

HABITAT Dry, rocky and grassy places.

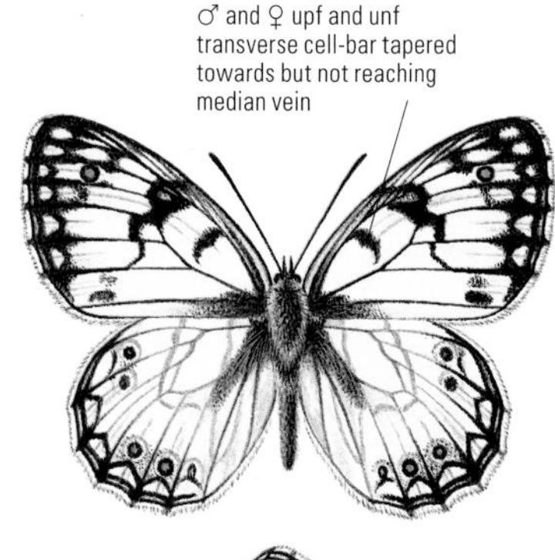

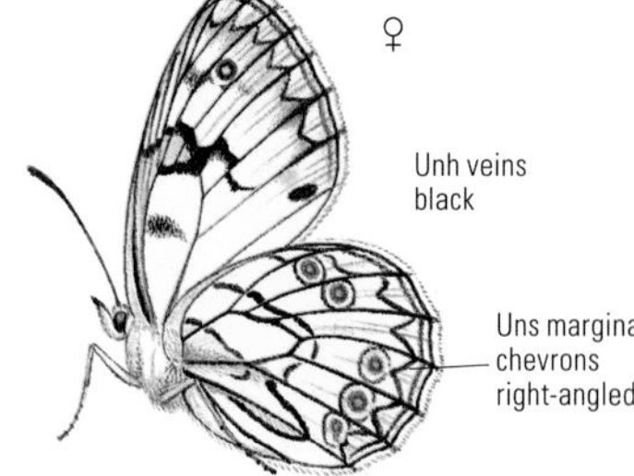

Western Marbled White

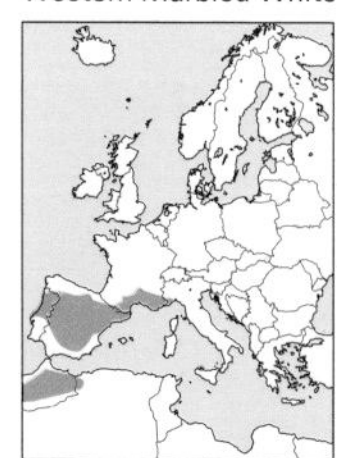

Italian Marbled White

WESTERN MARBLED WHITE

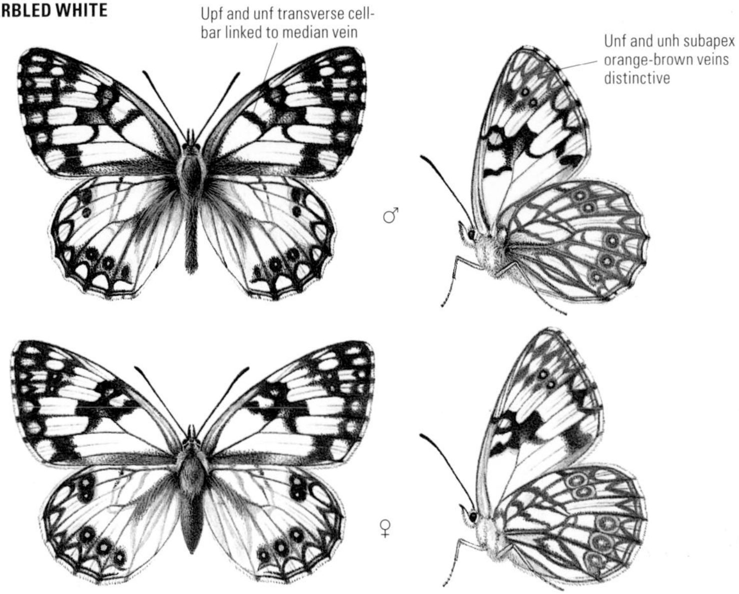

Upf and unf transverse cell-bar linked to median vein

Unf and unh subapex orange-brown veins distinctive

♂

♀

M. o. occitanica

♂

M. o. pelagica
(Morocco, Algeria)

♂

M. o. pherusa
(NW Sicily)

ITALIAN MARBLED WHITE

Upf blue-centred ocelli in s4 and 5 distinctive

Restricted to S Italy and NE Sicily

♂

Spanish Marbled White *Melanargia ines*

RANGE Morocco, Algeria, Tunisia, Portugal, Spain, N Libya.

M. ines Hoffmannsegg 1804 TL: Spain.

DISTRIBUTION Morocco. Algeria. Tunisia. 300-2600m. Portugal. Spain: south of Cantabrian Mts. and Pyrenees. Widespread, locally common. 50-1500m.

VARIATION Fairly constant in Europe. At high altitudes in Morocco, ups black markings often heavier (f. *jehandezi* Oberthür).

FLIGHT-PERIOD Univoltine. Late March/late June according to locality.

HABITAT Dry, grassy and rocky places: habitats often shared with *M. occitanica*.

BEHAVIOUR Males recorded 'hilltopping' at 2788m in High Atlas.

LIFE-HISTORY LHP: in S Spain, *Brachypodium pinnatum*. In dry conditions in captivity, newly-hatched larvae enter diapause without feeding.

Eastern Rock Grayling *Hipparchia syriaca*

RANGE SE Europe, Turkey, Transcaucasus, Lebanon, Syria, Iran.

H. syriaca Staudinger 1871 TL: Syria, Cyprus.

DISTRIBUTION Croatia: Dalmatian coast. SW Serbia (Montenegro). Albania. Republic of Macedonia. Bulgaria. Greece, including Corfu, Kefalonia, Thassos, Lesbos, Chios, Samos and Rhodes. 0-1300m.

DESCRIPTION AND VARIATION See *H. fagi*. Male ups pale pd band variable, often partly obscured by dark suffusion: on Rhodes, *ghigii* Turati: ups pd band largely obscured by dark suffusion.

FLIGHT-PERIOD Univoltine. Generally June/August, records span early May/mid September suggesting possibility of aestivation.

HABITAT Hot, dry, bushy places in woodland, most often open pinewoods; hot, dry oak forests in Bulgaria; hot, dry, deciduous or pine woodland in NE Greece; very small clearings in dense pine forests reported for some colonies on Rhodes.

BEHAVIOUR Males rest on stones, more often on tree trunks; several may assemble on a single tree.

Spanish Marbled White

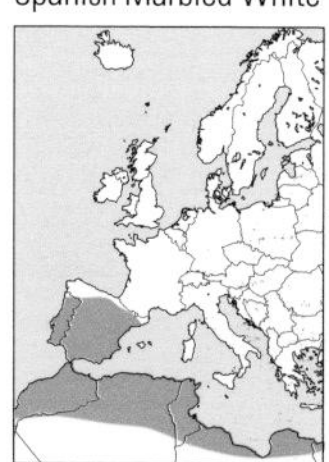

Eastern Rock Grayling

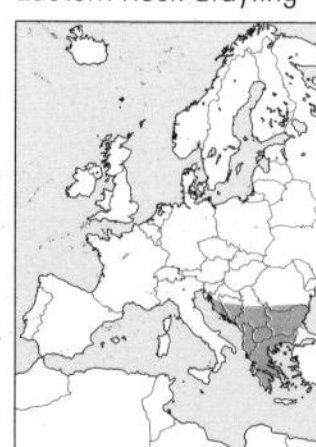

SPANISH MARBLED WHITE

Ups and uns markings distinctive

EASTERN ROCK GRAYLING

Restricted to SE Europe

Ups pale pd band often obscured by dusky suffusion

♂

♀

Woodland Grayling *Hipparchia fagi*

RANGE N Spain, S and C Europe, N Caucasus, Volga, S Urals, W Kazakhstan.
H. fagi Scopoli 1763 TL: Krain, Yugoslavia.
syn: *hermione* Linnaeus 1764
DISTRIBUTION N Spain (Aragon; Catalonia), through C, S and E France (sporadic in central regions, commonest in SE), C Germany (sporadic and local in Bavaria), S Poland, Italy to Balkans and S Greece. Absent from N France, Belgium, (?)S Holland, N Germany, European Turkey and Mediterranean islands except Sicily and Levkas. Records for Portugal, Corfu and Lithuania require confirmation. 50-1800m, usually below 1000m.
DESCRIPTION Resembles *H. alcyone* and *H. syriaca* very closely: reliable separation probably impossible without reference to male/female genitalia.
FLIGHT-PERIOD Univoltine. Early June/mid September according to locality.
HABITAT Bushy, grassy, woodland clearings; margins of pine forests.
LIFE-HISTORY LHPs *Bromus erectus*; *Festuca rubra*; *Brachypodium pinnatum*.
BEHAVIOUR Often rests, sometimes in assembly, in shade on tree-trunks or interior of bushes.

Rock Grayling *Hipparchia alcyone*

RANGE Morocco, SW, C and E Europe, S Norway, Ukraine.
H. alcyone alcyone Denis and Schiffermüller 1775 TL: Vienna, Austria.
syn: *aelia* Hoffmannsegg 1804.
DISTRIBUTION Spain. France: mainly in E and W Pyrenees; S Massif Central; Basses Alpes; Yonne; Saône-et-Loire; Jura. Italy: Liguria; C Apennines; Aspromonte. Switzerland (Jura; Valais; Tessin) to Austria, Hungary, Poland, S Norway (Telemarken; Augder) and SE Latvia. Local and generally scarce in northern range. 0-1600m: usually above 500m. Distribution uncertain in many regions owing to confusion with *H. fagi*.
DESCRIPTION AND VARIATION See *H. fagi*. Ups and uns gc, coloration of ups pd band (white to yellowish) and development of markings subject to marked variation.
FLIGHT-PERIOD Univoltine. Late June/mid August.
HABITAT Bushy, grassy, rocky woodland clearings/margins; in Norway, extensive, glacial rock-formations, with sparse, low-growing vegetation and scattered pine trees.
LIFE-HISTORY LHPs *Brachypodium pinnatum*; *B. sylvaticum*; *Festuca ovina*.
H. alcyone caroli Rothschild 1933 (June) TL: Morocco.
syn: *natasha* Hemming 1933 (December).
DISTRIBUTION Morocco: Middle Atlas (Azrou; Ifrane; Mischliffen; Aïn Leuh; Taghzeft; Zad; Aïn Kola; Rae El-Ma; Tizi-n-Treken; Timhadit; Daiet-Achlef; Dj. Hebri); Rif Mts. (Chefchaoune; Dj. Lakraa; Ketama). 1000-2000m.
DESCRIPTION Differs from nominate form by small differences in genitalia; character of Julian organ regionally variable.
FLIGHT-PERIOD Univoltine. Late June/early October.
HABITAT Steep, rocky slopes; open woodland.

Woodland Grayling

Rock Grayling

♀

WOODLAND GRAYLING

♂

♀

ROCK GRAYLING

♂

Algerian Grayling *Hipparchia ellena*

RANGE Algeria, Tunisia.
H. ellena Oberthür 1894 TL: Bône, Algeria.
DISTRIBUTION E Algeria: Bône; Lambessa; Yakouren; Bou Youseff; Blida; Batna; W Tunisia: Aïn Draham; Kroumirie. 1500-1800m. Locally common.
DESCRIPTION Ups white pd band well defined – devoid of dark suffusion (cf. *H. alcyone caroli*).
FLIGHT-PERIOD Univoltine. July/September.
HABITAT Oak forests (*Quercus mirbecki*).
LIFE-HISTORY LHP *Brachypodium ramosum*. Hibernation stage unconfirmed.

Delattin's Grayling *Hipparchia volgensis*

RANGE Albania, Republic of Macedonia, Bulgaria, Greece.
H. volgensis delattini Kudrna 1975 TL: Pristina [Republic of Macedonia].
DISTRIBUTION Albania. Republic of Macedonia: Vadar Valley and associated river systems. Bulgaria: mainly in southern region. Greece: NW Macedonia; W Thessaly; N Peloponnesos (Aroanian Mts.); Zakynthos. 700-1700m.
DESCRIPTION AND VARIATION Inseparable from *H. semele* without reference to male genitalia. Fertilized females possess a rudimentary sphragis (cf. *H. semele*, *H. christenseni* and *H. cretica*). On Mt. Chelmos (Aroanian Mts.) *muelleri* Kudrna: ups slightly darker; male genitalia differ slightly, but very variable – distinction possible only by quantified (statistical) evaluation.
FLIGHT-PERIOD Univoltine. Early June/August.
HABITAT Hot, dry, rocky gullies; screes; dry scrub; open pine woodland.

Algerian Grayling

Delattin's Grayling

ALGERIAN GRAYLING

Restricted to Algeria

♂

♀

DELATTIN'S GRAYLING

H. v. delattini
(SE Europe)

Grayling *Hipparchia semele*

RANGE Europe to 63°N in Fennoscandia: distribution uncertain E of Europe.

H. semele semele Linnaeus 1758 TL: Sweden (Verity 1953).

DISTRIBUTION Generally widespread and common. Most of Europe, from Portugal to S Fennoscandia (including Fyen, Sjælland, Lolland, Falster, Borholm, Öland, Gotland and Aland), S Serbia, S Romania and Bulgaria. In Britain, Scandinavia and Baltic states, shows marked preference for coastal margins. Absent from Albania, Republic of Macedonia, much of S Bulgaria and Mediterranean islands except N and E Sicily (1000-1800m). Records for N Greece require confirmation. 0-2000m. Distribution in E and SE Europe uncertain due to confusion with related taxa.

VARIATION Variation in size, gc and development of markings (especially unh) appears largely attributable to ecological adaptation. Darker forms tend to occur on peat-based soils, paler forms on limestone. Many forms have been described to account for local/regional character. In C and S Europe, f. *cadmus* Frühstorfer: larger: male ups yellow-orange pd band greatly reduced, often restricted to s2 and s5, enclosing ocelli; uph yellow-orange pd area and unh white pd band usually well developed: female upf pd better developed. In Sicily, *wilkinsoni* Kudrna: resembles nominate form closely: male genitalia structurally similar but disproportionately larger.

FLIGHT-PERIOD Univoltine. June/September according to locality.

HABITAT Diverse. Heathland; grassy, bushy places; open woodland; sand dunes; coastal cliffs; dry rocky slopes/gullies: on calcareous and non-calcareous soils.

LIFE-HISTORY LHPs *Festuca ovina*; *Koeleria pyramidata*; *Agrostis curtisii* [=*A. setacea*]; *Phleum phleoides*; *Ammophlia arenaria*; x *Ammocalamagrostis baltica* [=*Ammophlia arenaria* x *Calamgrostis epigejos* (=*Ammophlia arundinacea*)]; *Deschampsia cespitosa*; *Vulpia myuros*; *Aira praecox*; *Elymus repens* [=*Agropyron repens*]; *Bromus erectus*; *Briza media*; *Sesleria albicans*; *Lolium prenne*. In some habitats, ova are laid exclusively on dead vegetation. Distribution of the hybrid, x *A. baltica* ('marram' grass – an inhabitant of coastal margins) shows some correlation with that of the butterfly in its northern range.

H. semele leighebi Kudrna 1976 TL: Isola di Vulcano [Lipari Islands].

DISTRIBUTION Italy: Lipari [=Eolian] Islands (Volcano; Panarea). 0-500m. Widespread and very common.

DESCRIPTION Ups orange markings well developed, bright; male genitalia probably indistinguishable from nominate form but androconial scales 30% longer. Resembles *H. aristaeus blachieri* very closely: male genitalia distinct: reputedly, fw/hw size-ratio of *H. a. blachieri* comparatively greater.

FLIGHT-PERIOD Univoltine. Mid May/early August.

HABITAT Diverse. Rocky slopes; gullies; scrub; open pine woods; gardens.

Cretan Grayling *Hipparchia cretica*

RANGE Crete (Greece).

H. cretica Rebel 1916 TL: Crete.

DISTRIBUTION Crete: widespread and common. 100-1500m.

DESCRIPTION Resembles *H. semele* very closely: male genitalia larger; androconia differ slightly. Fertilized females possess a prominent sphragis (cf. *H. semele*, *H. christenseni* and *H. volgensis*).

FLIGHT-PERIOD Univoltine. Mid May/mid August.

HABITAT Dry, rocky slopes with bushes and sparse trees: olive groves.

LIFE-HISTORY Hibernation stage unconfirmed.

BEHAVIOUR Rests on shaded side of tree-trunks in very hot conditions.

Hipparchia christenseni

RANGE Karpathos (Greece).

H. christenseni Kudrna 1977 TL: Mt. Lastros, Karpathos.

DISTRIBUTION Karpathos; Mt. Lastros; Kali Limnos. Very local. 300-750m.

DESCRIPTION Resembles *H. semele* and *H. cretica* very closely: separable on basis of male genitalia and androconia. Fertilized females possess a rudimentary sphragis (cf. *H. semele*, *H. volgensis*, *H. cretica*, *H. mersina* and *H. pellucida* – taxonomic relationship to these species presently unclear).

FLIGHT-PERIOD Univoltine. Early June/late June.

HABITAT Dry, bushy, stony places; pinewood clearings.

LIFE-HISTORY Hibernation stage unconfirmed.

BEHAVIOUR Adults often rest on the trunks of pine trees; in treeless, bushy terrain, males often settle on stones.

Grayling

Cretan Grayling

GRAYLING

CRETAN GRAYLING

Restricted to Crete

Southern Grayling *Hipparchia aristaeus*

RANGE Madeira, NW Africa, Mediterranean Islands, S Balkans, Greece, Turkey.

H. aristaeus aristaeus Bonelli 1826 TL: Monti Gennargentu, Sardinia.

syn: *sardoa* Spuler 1902.

DISTRIBUTION France: Corsica (Evisa; Col du Lavezo; Vizzavona; Corte; Ajaccio).

Italy: widespread on islands: Sardinia; Capraia; Elba; Giglio; Ponza. 500-1800m.

DESCRIPTION Large; ups orange markings bright, well developed.

FLIGHT-PERIOD Univoltine. June/late August.

HABITAT Dry, rocky places with sparse scrub.

H. aristaeus senthes Frühstorfer 1908 TL: Taygetos Mts. [S Greece].

DISTRIBUTION Albania. Republic of Macedonia. S Bulgaria. Greece, including Levkas, Thassos, several islands of Cycladian Archipeligo and E Aegean chain: not reported from Crete, Karpathos or Rhodes. European Turkey. 50-1600m.

DESCRIPTION Ups orange/yellowish areas reduced, suffused greyish-brown. Resembles *H. s. semele* and *H. volgensis delattini*: male genitalia distinctive.

FLIGHT-PERIOD Univoltine. Late May/mid August according to locality.

HABITAT Dry, rocky and bushy places; bushy, woodland clearings.

H. aristaeus algirica Oberthür 1876 TL: Daya, Lambessa, Collo [Algeria].

DISTRIBUTION Morocco. Algeria. Tunisia. Widespread and common. 1200-2400m.

DESCRIPTION Resembles *H. a. senthes* and *H. s. semele*.

FLIGHT-PERIOD Voltinism uncertain: records span late April/October: reportedly univoltine at high altitudes (June/July); elsewhere, the possibility of prolonged emergence, aestivation and wide, regional and/or seasonal variation in emergence date may create false impression of bivoltinism.

HABITAT Dry, rocky slopes with sparse vegetation; grassy, flowery places.

LIFE-HISTORY LHP *Lygaeum spartum*.

H. aristaeus blachieri Früstorfer 1908 TL: Italy, Sicily.

syn: *siciliana* Oberthür 1915.

DISTRIBUTION Sicily: Puerta Antena; Messina; Palermo; Madonie; Mt. Elbei; Taormina; Isnello; Palazzolo Acreide; Ficuzza; Cefalu. 700-1900m.

DESCRIPTION Ups pd orange-fulvous areas extensive. Superficially inseparable from *H. semele leighebi* but male genitalia distinct.

FLIGHT-PERIOD Univoltine. Mid June/August.

HABITAT Dry, rocky slopes with sparse vegetation.

H. aristaeus maderensis Bethune-Baker 1891 TL: Madeira.

DISTRIBUTION Madeira: Aira de Serrado; Poiso; Pico Arieiro. Local and uncommon. 800-1800m.

DESCRIPTION Male ups markings largely obscured by dark brown suffusion; unh white discal band prominent: female ups markings better developed.

FLIGHT-PERIOD Univoltine. Late July/mid September.

HABITAT South-facing, steep rocky slopes in sparse deciduous or coniferous woodland.

LIFE-HISTORY LHPs *Holcus* sp.; *Agrostis* sp.

Southern Grayling

SOUTHERN GRAYLING

H. a. aristaeus
(Corsica, Sardinia, Capraia, Elba, Giglio)

H. a. algirica
(N Africa)

H. a. senthes
(S Balkans)

H. a. maderensis
(Madeira)

Azores Grayling *Hipparchia azorina*

RANGE Azores.

H. azorina Strecker 1899 TL: Azores

DISTRIBUTION Azores: Pico 600-2000m; Sao Jorge 480-720m; Faial 700-above 1000m; Terceira 1000m.

DESCRIPTION AND VARIATION Male upf sex-brand conspicuous. Three forms/sspp., corresponding to their islands of origin, have been described:- *picoensis* Le Cerf (Pico); *ohshimai* Esaki (Faial); *jorgense* Oehmig (Sao Jorge); *barbarensis* (Terceira): differentiated by systematic differences in imago size, wing-coloration, androconia, male genitalia and early-stage morphology.

FLIGHT-PERIOD Univoltine. June/October.

HABITAT Sheltered grassy slopes.

LIFE-HISTORY AND BEHAVIOUR LHP: Pico and Faial, *Festuca jubata*: Sao Jorge and Terceira, (?)*F. jubata*: circumstantial evidence indicates monophagacity. Ova laid exclusively on LHP. Hibernation stage unconfirmed. Sex of mature larvae of *ohshimai* ((?)*picoensis*; (?)*jorgense*; (?)*barbarensis*) is readily determined by the width of the head. Adults take nectar from *Rubus ulmifolius*, *R. hochstetteranum*, *Pontentilla erecta* and *P. anglica*. Despite the paucity of flowering plants on the Azores, *Vaccinium cylindraceum*, *Thymus caespititius* and *Daboecia azorica*, where available, do not appear to be exploited as nectar sources by *Hipparchia azorina*, *H. caldeirense* (below) or *H. miguelensis* (below).

Oehmig's Grayling *Hipparchia caldeirense*

RANGE Azores.

H. caldeirense Oehmig 1981 TL: Caldeira Seca, Flores.

DISTRIBUTION Azores: Flores (Caldeira Seca; Pico dos Sete Pes). Above 700m.

DESCRIPTION Male upf without androconial scales (cf. *H. azorina* and *H. miguelensis*).

FLIGHT-PERIOD Univoltine. June/late September.

HABITAT Grassy sheltered valleys on the slopes of the Caldeira Seca and Pico dos Sete Pes.

LIFE-HISTORY AND BEHAVIOUR LHP *Festuca jubata*: circumstantial evidence indicates monophagacity. Hibernation stage unconfirmed. Captive larvae reject *F. ovina* but accept *F. scoparia*. For both sexes, nectar sources as for *H. azorina*.

Le Cerf's Grayling *Hipparchia miguelensis*

RANGE Azores.

H. miguelensis Le Cerf 1935 TL: Sao Miguel.

DISTRIBUTION Azores: Sao Miguel. 600-1000m.

DESCRIPTION Male upf sex-brand conspicuous. Specific distinction from other *Hipparchia* species of the Azores based on adult and early-stage morphology.

FLIGHT-PERIOD Univoltine. Late June/late September.

HABITAT Sheltered, grassy hollows and small valleys.

LIFE-HISTORY AND BEHAVIOUR LHP *Festuca jubata*: circumstantial evidence indicates monophagacity. Hibernation stage unconfirmed. For both sexes, nectar sources as for *H. azorina*, in addition to *Calluna vulgaris*.

Samos Grayling *Hipparchia mersina*

RANGE Greece (E Aegean Islands), Turkey.

H. mersina Staudinger 1871 TL: Mersin, SW Turkey.

DISTRIBUTION Greece: Lesbos 150-600m; Samos 300-1150m.

DESCRIPTION Androconia scales long and slender. Fertilized females possess a rudimentary sphragis (cf. *H. pellucida* and *H. christenseni*).

FLIGHT-PERIOD Univoltine. Mid May/mid July.

HABITAT Dry, grassy clearings amongst rocks, sparse bushes and trees.

LIFE-HISTORY On Samos, very small larvae, together with full-grown examples have been recorded in April.

♂

AZORES GRAYLING

Restricted to
Azores: Pico, Sao Jorge,
Faial, Terceira

OEHMIG'S GRAYLING

Restricted to
Azores: Flores

SAMOS GRAYLING

Restricted to
Lesbos and Samos

Corsican Grayling *Hipparchia neomiris*

RANGE Corsica, Sardinia, Elba.
H. neomiris Godart 1824 TL: Corsica.
DISTRIBUTION Corsica: Soccia; Cap Corse; La Face; Haut Asco; Tattone; Col de Sorba; Vizzavona. 300-2000m. Sardinia: Monti di Alà; Monti del Gennargentu; Fonni; Lanusei; Seulo. 300-1800m. Capraia. Elba: Mte. Peronne; Mte. Maolo; Mte. Capanne. 300-1200m.
FLIGHT-PERIOD Univoltine. Mid June/August.
HABITAT Open, rocky slopes with low-growing vegetation and scrub, usually associated with pinewoods.

Eastern Grayling *Hipparchia pellucida*

RANGE Greece (E Aegean Islands), Turkey, Cyprus, N Iraq, N Iran, Crimea, Transcaucasus.
H. pellucida Stauder 1924 TL: Terter [Azerbaijan].
DISTRIBUTION Greece: Lesbos; Ikaria. 400-700m.
DESCRIPTION Fertilized females possess a prominent sphragis (cf. *H. mersina* and *H. christenseni*).
FLIGHT-PERIOD Univoltine. Late May/July (data limited).
HABITAT Dry, grassy, rocky slopes or screes with scattered bushes; dry, gently sloping, stony ground with sparse, low-growing vegetation and scattered pine trees.

Powell's Grayling *Neohipparchia powelli*

RANGE Algeria.
N. powelli Oberthür 1910 TL: Djebel Amour, Algeria.
DISTRIBUTION C and E Algeria: scarce and local: Aflou; Guelt-es-Stel; Dj. Senalba; Dj. Amour; El Bayadh. 1100-1200m.
DESCRIPTION Resembles *N. hansii*. In both sexes, fw apical angle distinctly sharper; male ups darker; ocelli obscure, faintly ringed yellow; upf sex-brand poorly defined; unf pd area brown, ocelli ringed yellow; unh whitish discal band narrow, diffuse on outer margin; veins greyish. Wing-characters constant in known range.
FLIGHT-PERIOD Univoltine. August/October.
HABITAT Hot, dry, rocky places with sparse vegetation.
LIFE-HISTORY LHP *Lygaeum spartum*. Hibernation stage unconfirmed.
NOTE Taxonomic and distributional relationship with *N. hansii* not clearly understood: male genitalia and androconia very similar.

Corsican Grayling

Powell's Grayling

POWELL'S GRAYLING

Ups markings poorly defined

Unh veins greyish

Restricted to C & E Algeria

CORSICAN GRAYLING

Restricted to Corsica, Sardinia, Capraia and Elba

EASTERN GRAYLING

(Lesbos and Ikaria)

♂

♀

Tree Grayling *Neohipparchia statilinus*

RANGE NW Africa, S and C Europe, Turkey.
N. statilinus Hufnagel 1766 TL: District of Berlin.
DISTRIBUTION Morocco. Algeria. Tunisia. 900-2500m. S Europe (including European Turkey, Sicily, Elba, Corfu and Thassos) to NW France, Poland and Lithuania (first recorded 1971): common and widespread in Portugal, Spain, SE France, C and S Italy, S Balkans and Greece: very local and sporadic in SW and C France, Czech Republic, Slovakia and Hungary: possibly extinct in Germany. Absent from Britain, NE France, Belgium, Holland, N Switzerland, Bavaria, NW Austria, Carpathian Mts. and Fennoscandia. 0-1400m.
DESCRIPTION AND VARIATION Unh submarginal line variable, often obscure (cf. *N. fatua*). Many forms have been described in recognition of marked regional and local variation, especially unh gc – dark greyish-brown, through medium grey, devoid of brownish tones, to light greyish-brown or pale grey; variation in submarginal, discal, mediobasal lines and irroration varies independently of gc. In N Africa, *sylvicola* Austaut: unh dark greyish-brown; antemarginal band darker brown: similar forms occur in S Spain.
FLIGHT-PERIOD Univoltine. Late June/October with peak emergence generally late July/early August in most southern localities.
HABITAT Hot, dry, rocky areas, often amongst scrub or in open pinewoods, less often, deciduous or mixed woodland.
LIFE-HISTORY LHPs include *Bromus erectus*; *B. sterilis*; *Bothriochola ischaemum*; *Stipa pennata*; *Lygaeum spartum*.

Freyer's Grayling *Neohipparchia fatua*

RANGE S Balkans, Greece, Turkey, Transcaucasus, Israel, Jordon, Lebanon, Syria.
N. fatua Freyer 1844 TL: Gediz, Province of Kütahya, W Turkey (Kudrna 1977).
syn: *allionii* Hübner 1824 (invalid homonym)
DISTRIBUTION Sporadic, locally common. S Croatia. S Bosnia-Herzegovina. SW Serbia. Republic of Macedonia. Albania. S Bulgaria. Greece, including Lefkas, Kithera, Thassos, Paros and most E Aegean islands. European Turkey. Not reported from Corfu or Crete. 0-600m.
DESCRIPTION Resembles *N. statilinus*: larger; male ups very dark; unh dark mediobasal, discal and submarginal lines well defined (cf. *N. statilinus*).
FLIGHT-PERIOD Univoltine. Late May/early October according to locality.
HABITAT Hot, dry, stony gullies and rocky slopes, often with bushes in sparse, usually coniferous woodland; olive groves; orchards.
LIFE-HISTORY Hibernated larvae recorded feeding only on well-shaded plants of a tall, robust, clump-forming grass.
BEHAVIOUR Often rests in shade on tree-trunks.

Tree Grayling

Freyer's Grayling

TREE GRAYLING

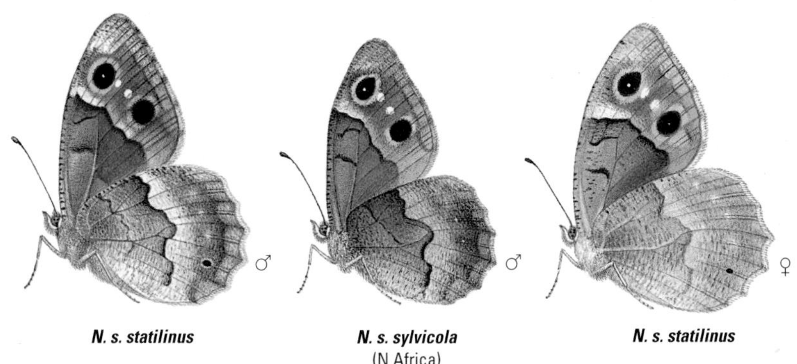

N. s. statilinus ***N. s. sylvicola*** (N Africa) ***N. s. statilinus***

FREYER'S GRAYLING

Austaut's Grayling *Neohipparchia hansii*

RANGE Morocco, Algeria, Tunisia, NW Libya.
N. hansii Austaut 1879 TL: Daya, Algeria.
DISTRIBUTION Morocco: Anti-Atlas; Middle Atlas (Tizi-Tanout-ou-Fillali; Azrou; Aïn Leuh; Tirhboula; Foum Khereg); High Atlas (Dj. Ayachi; Tizi-n-Talhremt; Tizi-n-Test). Algeria: El Mizab; Sebdou; Blida. Tunisia: Tunis; Korbous; Cap Bon. 1000-2100m.
DESCRIPTION AND VARIATION Resembles *N. statilinus* closely: upf sex-brand smaller. In both sexes, all wing-characters subject to marked variation: male genitalia and androconia allow reliable separation from *N. statilinus* with which it sometimes occurs.
FLIGHT-PERIOD Univoltine. Late August/November.
HABITAT Rocky, slopes with sparse vegetation.
LIFE-HISTORY Hibernation stage unconfirmed.

Canary Grayling *Pseudotergumia wyssii*

RANGE Canary Islands.
Distinction between following forms based on small morphological differences in wing-markings, male genitalia and, in some cases, size/structure of ova. Hibernation stage unconfirmed.
P. wyssii wyssii Christ 1889 TL: Tenerife, Canary Isles.
DISTRIBUTION Tenerife: widespread but local in central mountains. 1400-2000m.
FLIGHT-PERIOD Univoltine. Early June/early September according to altitude.
HABITAT Rocky gullies in pine forests.
P. wyssii bacchus Higgins 1967 TL: Hierro, Canary Isles.
DISTRIBUTION Hierro: confined to Frontera; Sabinosa. 300-1500m.
FLIGHT-PERIOD Univoltine. Mid July/late August.
HABITAT Very steep, grassy cliffs and associated vineyards at cliff-base.
P. wyssii gomera Higgins 1967 TL: Gomera, Canary Isles.
DISTRIBUTION N and W Gomera: known largely from coastal districts: Barranco de Argaga; Barranco de Arure; Vallehermoso; Hermigua; Agulo; 200-300m: recently recorded inland at higher (unspecified) altitude.
FLIGHT-PERIOD Univoltine. Late May/early September.
HABITAT Rocky gullies and slopes; steep grassy/bushy cliffs; vineyards; scrub margins of laurel forest.
P. wyssii tilosi Manil 1984 TL: Los Tilos, La Palma.
DISTRIBUTION NE La Palma: Barranco del Agua; Los Tilos; Santa Cruz; Barranco de la Rio de las Nieves; La Cumbrecita. 400-1300m.
FLIGHT-PERIOD Univoltine. Late July/early September.
HABITAT Rocky gullies in laurel or pine forests.
P. wyssii tamadabae Owen and Smith 1992 TL: Pinar de Tamadaba, Gran Canaria.
DISTRIBUTION Gran Canaria: Pinar de Tamadaba; Morgan; Pozo Nieves; Tiraiana; Maspalomas; Roque Nublo; Barranco de los Palmitos. 400-2000m
DESCRIPTION Distinguished from other forms by unf apical ocellus with white pupil in 50% of males, 100% in females.
FLIGHT-PERIOD Univoltine. Early April/early September according to altitude.
HABITAT Rocky gullies in pine forests.

Austaut's Grayling

AUSTAUT'S GRAYLING

Restricted to C & E Algeria

Upf discal area usually well delineated

CANARY GRAYLING

Restricted to Canary Islands

♂

P. w. wyssii

♀

P. w. wyssii

♀

P. w. bacchus (Hierro)

Striped Grayling *Pseudotergumia fidia*

RANGE NW Africa, SW Europe.

P. fidia Linnaeus 1767 TL: 'Barbarie' Algeria.

DISTRIBUTION Widespread but local. Morocco: Middle Atlas; High Atlas. Algeria. Tunisia. 1000-2200m. Iberian Peninsula, except W Pyrenees and N Spain. Mallorca. France: E Pyrenees to Ardèche and Provence. NW Italy: Maritime Alps: very local. 0-1400m.

VARIATION In NW Africa, unh veins conspicuously paler (f. *albovenosa* Austaut).

FLIGHT-PERIOD Univoltine. Europe, late June/late August according to locality: NW Africa, July/October.

HABITAT Hot, rocky slopes with scrub; dry soil-banks with bushes and sparse, low-growing vegetation; rocky places in light woodland.

LIFE-HISTORY LHPs include *Cynodon dactylon*; *Dactylus glomerata*; *Brachypodium* sp.; *Poa annua*; *P. pratensis*; *Milium multiflorum*; *Oryzopsis* sp.

The Hermit *Chazara briseis*

RANGE NW Africa, Spain, C Europe to 50°N, Turkey, Iran, Afghanistan to NW China.

C. briseis Linnaeus 1764 TL: Germany.

DISTRIBUTION Widespread. Morocco. Algeria. Tunisia. 0-2500m. From Spain (except extreme N and W), C Italy, S Greece and European Turkey to S Poland. 0-2000m. Absent from Portugal, NW and N France, Belgium, Holland, N Germany, S Italy, and Mediterranean islands except Sicily. In France, range has contracted considerably in recent decades, now largely confined to SE: also extinct in parts of Germany. Sporadic in Switzerland and N Italy.

VARIATION In S Europe, female ups white markings sometimes replaced by yellowish-buff or creamy-brown (f. *pirata* Esper – not known in N Africa). In SE Europe, female unh sometimes suffused pink.

FLIGHT-PERIOD Univoltine. Late May/October according to locality and altitude.

HABITAT Dry, often hot, stony places amongst scrub; dry, bushy grassland.

LIFE-HISTORY LHPs include *Bromus erectus*; *Festuca ovina*.

Striped Grayling

The Hermit

STRIPED GRAYLING

w fringes
learly
hequered

♀

♂

Unh pattern of markings and colourings distinctive

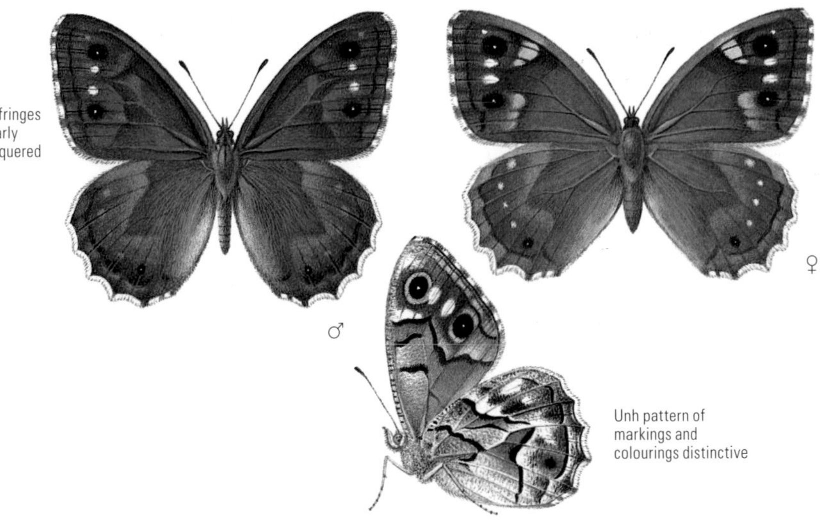

THE HERMIT

♂ and ♀ ups and uns pattern of markings distinctive

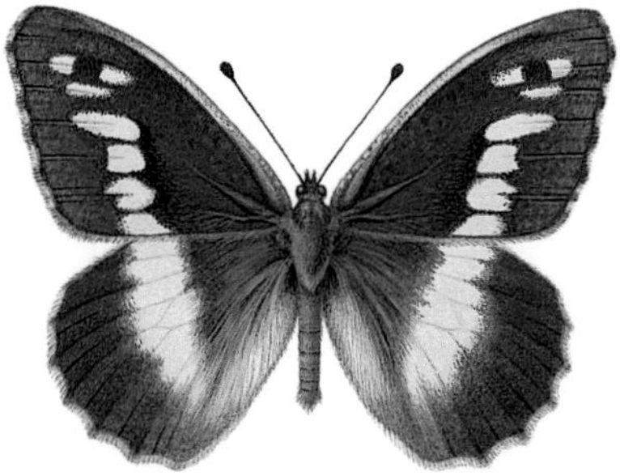

♂

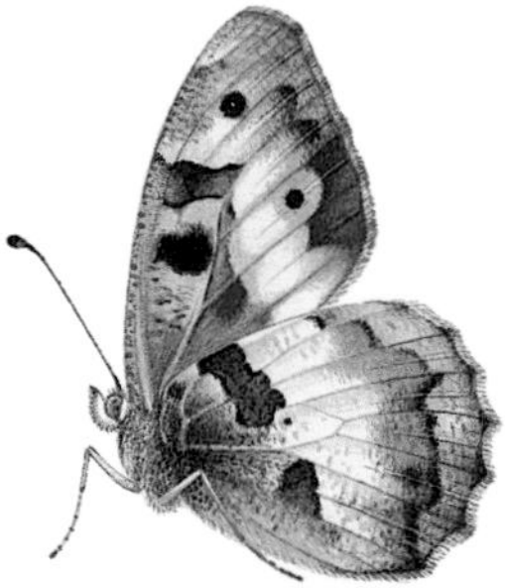

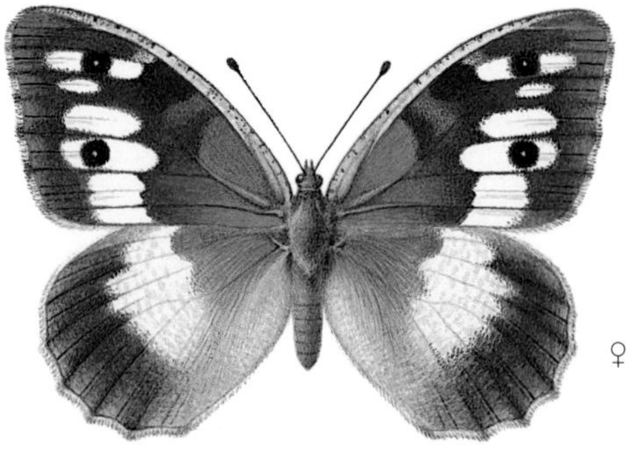

♀

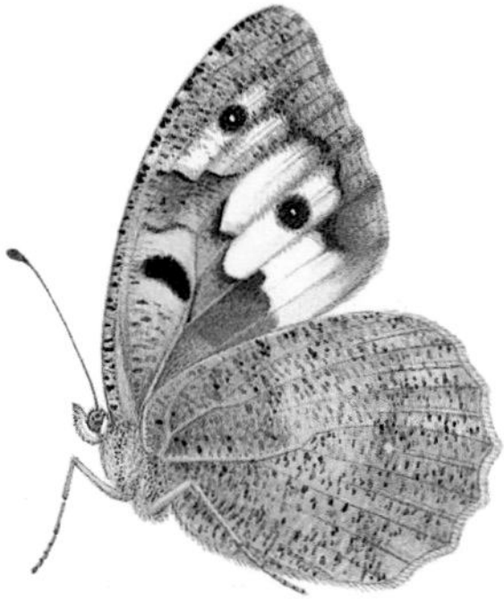

Southern Hermit *Chazara prieuri*

RANGE Spain, Morocco, Algeria.

C. prieuri Pierret 1837 TL: Bougi [Bejaïa], Algeria.

DISTRIBUTION Local and often very scarce. Morocco: Middle Atlas (Col du Zad); High Atlas (Tizi-n-Talrhemt; Aït Oumghar; Dj. Ayachi). Algeria: Sebdou; Télagh; Beni-Ounit; Sidi-bel-Abbes; Dj. Senalba; Dj. Metlili; El Bayadh; Aflou; Djelfa. 1200-2000m. Spain: provinces of Granada (S. de Baza; S. de La Sagra); Murcia (S. de Espuña); Teruel (Montes Universales); Madrid; Huesca; Zaragoza; Alicante. Mallorca. 900-1450m.

DESCRIPTION AND VARIATION Male upf with conspicuous buff patch in cell: in both sexes, unh veins conspicuously pale (cf. *C. briseis*). In Spain, female ups white markings replaced by fulvous in about 50% of specimens (f. *uhagonis* Oberthür): not reported from N Africa.

FLIGHT-PERIOD Univoltine. NW Africa, June/July: Spain, Mid July/mid August.

HABITAT Hot, dry, rocky gullies with scrub; dry, grassy, stony slopes in open coniferous woodland.

LIFE-HISTORY LHP *Lygeum spartum*: in captivity, larvae accept *Festuca ovina*; *Poa annua*.

Moroccan Grayling *Pseudochazara atlantis*

RANGE Morocco.

P. atlantis Austaut 1905 TL: High Atlas Mts., Morocco.

syn: *maroccana* Meade-Waldo 1906

DISTRIBUTION Morocco: Anti-Atlas (Tizi-n-Melloul; Tizi-n-Tieta); High Atlas (Tizi-n-Talrhemt; Imilchit; Oukaïmeden); Middle Atlas (Col du Tagzhzeft; Col du Zad; Tizi-Tarhzeft); W Rif (Bab Taza; Dj. Lakraa). 1600-3000m.

DESCRIPTION AND VARIATION Upf rounded white spots in s3 and s4, sometimes vestigial, occurs in about 50% of specimens from the High Atlas. Fringes not chequered or only weakly so. Androconial scales variable between individuals in the same colony; scale-base rounded or shouldered. Development of markings and gc locally variable: f. *benderi* Weiss and f. *colini* Wyatt, relating to minor differences in size and gc, fall within range of variation of nominate form.

FLIGHT-PERIOD Univoltine. Mid June/early August according to altitude.

HABITAT Barren, rocky slopes.

LIFE-HISTORY Hibernation stage unconfirmed.

Southern Hermit

Moroccan Grayling

♀

SOUTHERN HERMIT

♂ and ♀ ups and uns pattern of markings distinctive

Restricted to Spain, Morocco and Algeria

♂

♀

♀

f. *uhagonis*

MOROCCAN GRAYLING

Restricted to Morocco

♂

Grecian Grayling *Pseudochazara graeca*

RANGE Greece, Republic of Macedonia.
P. graeca Staudinger 1870 TL: Mt. Parnassos and Mt. Chelmos, Greece.
syn: *Satyrus mamurra* var. *graeca* Staudinger 1870
DISTRIBUTION Republic of Macedonia: Pelister massif. NW and C Greece: Mt. Olympus; Mt. D'rfis (1000-1745m). Pindos Mts. (Smolikas massif to Mt. Parnassos) 1200-2200m. S Greece: Mt. Chelmos; Mt. Panakhaikón; Mt. Ménalon; Mt. Taygetos. 1000-2200m. Not recorded from Varnous Mts. (NW Greece) – the southern extension of Pelister massif.
DESCRIPTION Upf white pd spots in s3 and s4 sometimes poorly represented. Androconial scale-base, rounded.
VARIATION Small but systematic local variation in size and coloration, especially unh, appears to be due to ecological adaptation to the geological character of habitat. Amongst several variants, described formally as ssp., *coutsisi* Brown [=*zagoriensis* Aussem] is the most distinctive: ups suffused smoky, greyish-brown; upf ocelli often lacking white pupils; uns darker: known only from N Smolikas massif, Timfi Mts. and Katara Pass 1200-1600m.
FLIGHT-PERIOD Univoltine. Mid July/late August.
HABITAT Mostly open, grassy places amongst limestone rocks above treeline: f. *coutsisi* occurs on dry, grassy slopes amongst scrub and light, mostly pine woodland; on Smolikas massif, on friable, greyish, metamorphic rocks.
LIFE-HISTORY On Mt. Timphristos, larvae feed on a pleasantly perfumed grass.
NOTE *P. graeca* appears to be closely related to *P. aurantiaca* Staudinger 1871 from N Iran (Elburz Mts.): minor differences in wing-markings are possibly attributable to ecological adaptation, but androconial scales of *P. aurantiaca* are wider at the base and almost double the length. In the absence of a full understanding of taxonomic significance of androconial morphology (cf. *P. atlantis*), the relationship of *P. graeca* and *P. aurantiaca* remains unclear.

Nevada Grayling *Pseudochazara hippolyte*

RANGE S Spain, eastwards with marked distributional disjunction to S Urals, Kazakhstan, Kyrgyzstan, S Siberia, Mongolia.
P. hippolyte williamsi Romei 1927 TL: Sierra Nevada, S Spain
DISTRIBUTION S Spain: Sierra Nevada 2000-2700m; S. de los Filabres 1850-2020m; S. de Gádor 2000-2200m; S. de Maria 1400-2040m; S. de Guillimona 1500-2000m. Records for S. de Espuña require confirmation.
DESCRIPTION AND VARIATION Fringes chequered. Upf without submarginal white spots in s3 and s4. Androconial scale-base shouldered. Two forms have been described to account for minor, local variation: S. de Maria, *aislada* Eitschberger and Steiniger: larger; paler: S. de Gádor, *augustini* Weiss: slightly smaller; uns gc slightly brown.
FLIGHT-PERIOD Univoltine. Late June/late July.
HABITAT Dry, grassy slopes, with patches of bare, stony soil: on greyish or greyish-brown non-calcareous rocks.
LIFE-HISTORY LHP *Festuca ovina*. Larvae, captively reared in S England, (cf. photo-period) hibernate in second instar.
NOTE Type locality of *P. hippolyte hippolyte* Esper 1784 lies in the Ural Mts. of S Russia, about 5000km from Spain: no intermediate populations are known. Nominate form replaced by *mercurius* Staudinger 1887 in SE limit of Palearctic range (Alexander Mts., Kyrgyzstan).

Grecian Grayling

Nevada Grayling

GRECIAN GRAYLING

Restricted to Republic of Macedonia and Greece

Uph orange pd band well defined

♀

♂

P. g. graeca

♂ ♀

P. g. graeca* f. *coutsisi

NEVADA GRAYLING

Restricted to S Spain

Grey Asian Grayling *Pseudochazara geyeri*

RANGE Albania, Republic of Macedonia, Greece, Turkey.
P. geyeri occidentalis Rebel and Zerny 1931 TL: Albania.
DISTRIBUTION Albania: mountains near Lake Ohrid. SW Republic of Macedonia: Galicica Pl.; Pelister massif. 1500-1700m. NW Greece: Mt. Malimadi; Triklarion Mts. 1450-1650m.
DESCRIPTION Fringes chequered. Upf without submarginal white pd spots in s3 and s4. Androconial scale-base bulbous.
FLIGHT-PERIOD Univoltine. Mid July/late August according to season.
HABITAT Dry, rocky and grassy limestone slopes above treeline.
LIFE-HISTORY Ova stage 10 days, hatching synchronously. Captive larvae accept *Festuca ovina*. Hibernation stage unconfirmed.
BEHAVIOUR Both sexes fond of sitting on stones or bare soil: attracted to nectar of purplish *Centaureae* sp.

Brown's Grayling *Pseudochazara mamurra*

RANGE NW Greece, Turkey.
P. mamurra amymone Brown 1976 TL: District of Ioannina, NW Greece.
DISTRIBUTION Reported only once from one area N of Ioannina, NW Greece.
DESCRIPTION Male upf and unf with small white spots in s3 and s4. Androconial scale-base bulbous, shouldered; similar to nominate form. Female known but not formally described (illustrated).
FLIGHT-PERIOD AND HABITAT The few specimens reported from Greece so far were captured 5-10th July 1975, on rocky ground at 650m just N of Ioannina.
LIFE-HISTORY Early-stages unknown.
NOTE In Turkey, *P. mamurra* is markedly variable; also, characteristically local and uncommon, a feature shared, evidently, with *amymone*: more usually, *Pseudochazara* spp. are abundant, if often local.

Macedonian Grayling *Pseudochazara cingovskii*

RANGE Republic of Macedonia.
P. cingovskii Gross 1973 TL: Prilep [Republic of Macedonia].
syn: *Satyrus (Pseudochazara) sintenisi cingovskii* Gross 1973
DISTRIBUTION Republic of Macedonia: known only from Pletvar massif, near Prilep, south of Skopje. 1000-1200m.
DESCRIPTION Upf and unf elongate white pd spots in s3 and s4 prominent. Fringes chequered. Androconial scale-base shouldered.
FLIGHT-PERIOD Univoltine. Late July/early August.
HABITAT Dry, white limestone rocks with sparse vegetation.
LIFE-HISTORY Hibernation stage unconfirmed.
NOTE Considerable confusion has persisted for many years in respect to taxonomy, nomenclature, morphology and distribution of *P. cingovskii* and *P. mniszechii tisiphone*: these taxa are superficially, at least, quite distinct and are not known to share the same habitats, nor indeed, the same countries.

Grey Asian Grayling

Brown's Grayling

Macedonian Grayling

GREY ASIAN GRAYLING

(SE Europe)

BROWN'S GRAYLING

Restricted to NW Greece

MACEDONIAN GRAYLING

Restricted to Republic of Macedonia

Dils' Grayling *Pseudochazara orestes*

RANGE Greece, Bulgaria.
P. orestes de Prins and van der Poorten 1981 TL: Drama, N Greece.
DISTRIBUTION N Greece: Phalakron massif 800-1650m; Menikion Mts. 800-1000m; Mt. Orvilos 1000-1800m. Bulgaria: Pirin Mts. 900m.
DESCRIPTION Upf and unf white spots in s3 and s4 usually prominent. Fringes chequered. Androconial scale-base shouldered.
FLIGHT-PERIOD Univoltine. Mid June/late July.
HABITAT Hot, dry, mostly south-facing limestone cliffs/steep rocky slopes; gentler slopes containing large areas of flat, naked rock amongst small, shrubby deciduous trees, principally *Carpinus*, *Quercus*, *Fraxinus* and *Ulmus*.
LIFE-HISTORY Ova laid in shade, on dead leaves of tufted-grasses lodged in crevices or under rock ledges. In captivity, life-cycle from ovum is completed without diapause in extended photo-period of S England. Captive larvae accept a variety of grasses, including *Agrostis stolonifera*.
BEHAVIOUR Both sexes retire to the shade and relative cool of rock crevices and ledges in exceptionally hot conditions. Occasional population 'explosions' are accompanied by dispersion to lower altitudes – recorded at 250m in 1987.

Dark Grayling *Pseudochazara mniszechii*

RANGE NW Greece, Turkey, N Iran, Armenia.
P. mniszechii tisiphone Brown 1980 TL: NW Greece.
DISTRIBUTION NW Greece: S Vernon Mts. 850-1100m; environs of Grammos Mt. 1000-1500m; N Smolikas massif 1000-1450m. Local, usually very common.
DESCRIPTION Upf and unf elongate white pd spots in s3 and s4 prominent. Fringes chequered. Androconial scale-base shouldered.
FLIGHT-PERIOD Univoltine. Mid July/late August.
HABITAT Dry, slopes comprising a greyish, friable, metaorphic rock supporting sparse, low-growing vegetation amongst light scrub and open woodland. All known habitats contain same species of a robust, purple-flowered thistle (?)*Carduus* sp. which appears to be an important nectar source for both sexes.
LIFE-HISTORY In captivity, life-cycle from ovum is completed without diapause in extended photo-period of S England. Captive larvae accept *Festuca ovina*: pupates 1-2cm below soil-level. Hibernation stage unconfirmed.
BEHAVIOUR At peak emergence, fresh males and females occur in approximately equal numbers. Both sexes show a marked preference for sitting on bare patches of soil, rather than stones. Roosts in well-concealed spaces, usually deep between large stones.

Dil's Grayling

Dark Grayling

DILS' GRAYLING

Restricted to N Greece, SW Bulgaria

Unh white pd band conspicuous

♂

Ups bright orange pd well delineated

♀

DARK GRAYLING

(NW Greece, S Albania)

Ups deep orange pd band distinctive

♂

♀

White-banded Grayling *Pseudochazara anthelea*

RANGE Albania, Republic of Macedonia, Bulgaria, Greece, Turkey, N Iraq.

P. anthelea anthelea Hübner 1825 TL: Turkey.

DISTRIBUTION Greece: in Europe, known only from E Aegean islands: Lesbos; Samos; Kos; Kalimnos; Chios; Rhodes. 550-1500m.

DESCRIPTION AND VARIATION Male ups sex-brand prominent and distinctive; androconial scales small, rounded at base; fringes strongly chequered. Sexual dimorphism very marked; female ups yellowish-brown. On Rhodes (Mt. Ataviros 500m), *atavirensis* Coutsis: female ups transitional to *amalthea* Frivaldsky (below).

FLIGHT-PERIOD Univoltine. Late May/early July.

HABITAT Dry, stony slopes and gullies, usually on limestone: at lower altitudes, often amongst sparse bushes and/or light pine or deciduous woodland.

BEHAVIOUR Males are very territorial, often taking up advantageous positions on rocks.

P. anthelea amalthea Frivaldsky 1845 TL: Crete.

DISTRIBUTION Albania. Republic of Macedonia: widespread. SW Bulgaria: very local: Struma Valley. NW, C and S Greece: local but widespread; local on Crete. 500-1800m.

DESCRIPTION AND VARIATION Male closely resembles nominate form: female ups yellowish-brown areas replaced by white – form unknown in Asia. On Smolikas massif, female upf often with white pd spots in s3 and s4.

FLIGHT-PERIOD, HABITAT AND BEHAVIOUR As for nominate form.

LIFE-HISTORY Ova are appreciably smaller than those of other European *Pseudochazara* spp.

NOTE Morphologically closely related to Asiatic *P. telephassa* Hübner 1827.

Alpine Grayling *Oeneis glacialis*

RANGE C European Alps.

O. glacialis Moll 1783 TL: Zillertal, Austria.

DISTRIBUTION Alps of France (Alpes-Maritimes to Haute-Savoie), Switzerland (Valais to Engadine), Italy (including Dolomites), Bavaria, Austria (including Carnic Alps). 1400-2900m.

DESCRIPTION AND VARIATION Unh veins white (cf. *O. norna*). Ups ocellation and male ups orange pd areas subject to marked variation.

FLIGHT-PERIOD Univoltine. Early June/mid August according to altitude.

HABITAT Dry, grassy places amongst rocks or scree.

LIFE-HISTORY LHP *Festuca ovina*. Larval development requires two seasonal cycles.

White-banded Grayling

Alpine Grayling

WHITE-BANDED GRAYLING

♂ and ♀ ups and uns pattern of markings and colouring distinctive

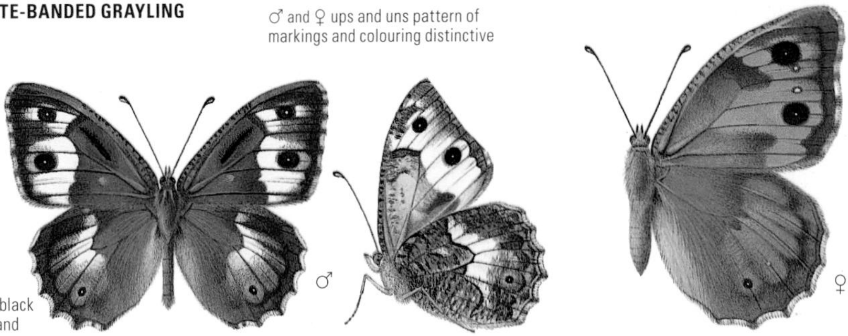

♂ upf black sex-brand conspicuous, distinctve

P. a. anthelea
(E Aegean islands)

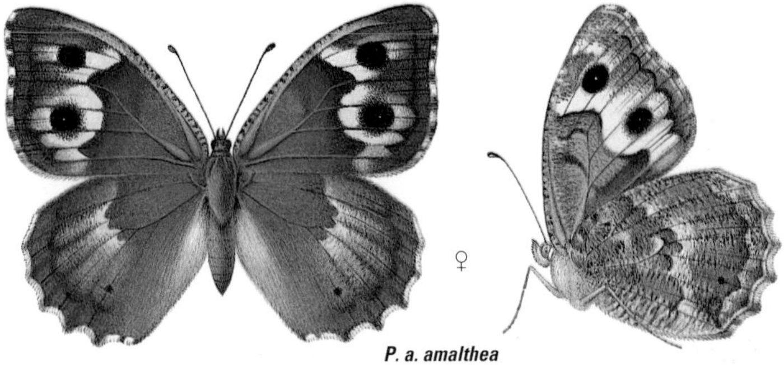

P. a. amalthea
(Balkan Peninsula, Crete)

ALPINE GRAYLING

Restricted to C Alps

Unh white veins conspicuous, distinctive

colour variant

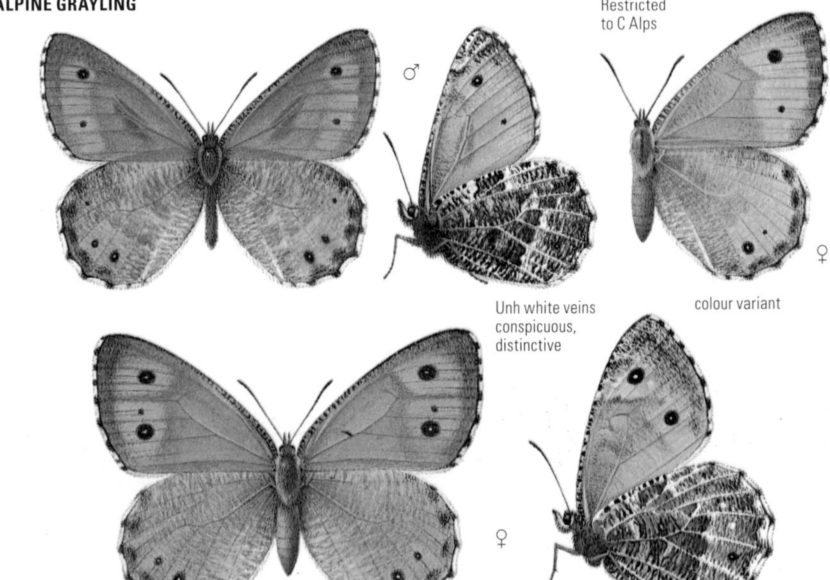

Norse Grayling *Oeneis norna*

RANGE Fennoscandia, Kola and Yamal Peninsulas, Urals, Siberia, Baikal, Japan.

O. norna Thunberg 1791 TL: Lapland.

DISTRIBUTION Norway: 62-70°N. W Sweden: Jämtland to Torne- Lappmark. NW Finland. Local, but widespread. 250-800m.

VARIATION Extremely variable in respect to all wing-characters including size and shape. Small, lightly marked specimens sometimes resemble *O. bore*, but ups are never quite as grey.

FLIGHT-PERIOD Univoltine. Mid June/mid July according to season.

HABITAT Heathy margins of bogs, often associated with open birch scrub; boggy and rocky slopes with scrub; damp grassy and mossy clearings in forests. Sympatric and synchronous with *O. jutta* in some habitats of C Sweden.

LIFE-HISTORY LHPs *Phleum pratense*; *Poa alpina*; *Carex* sp.; *Nardus* sp. Larval development requires two seasonal cycles: in captivity, newly-hatched larvae often die without attempting to feed.

Arctic Grayling *Oeneis bore*

RANGE N Fennoscandia, Kola Peninsula, Polar Urals, Polar Siberia, N America.

O. bore Schneider 1792 TL: Lapland.

DISTRIBUTION Very local. N Fennoscandia from 67°N to Arctic Sea. 100-1000m.

DESCRIPTION Ups gc with distinct greyish tone – lacking 'warmer', brownish tone of *O. norna*: upf and unf with small, round, very pale pd dot in s5, sometimes very obscure but usually present – absent in *O. norna*.

FLIGHT-PERIOD Univoltine. Mid June/late July according to season.

HABITAT Damp grassy/boggy places, characteristically dominated by small, slightly elevated areas of almost barren rock, which appear to be meeting places for males and females – (?)'hilltopping'.

LIFE-HISTORY LHP *Festuca ovina*. Larval development requires two seasonal cycles: in captivity, hibernates as an ovum in first winter.

BEHAVIOUR Both sexes sometimes rest on rocks for prolonged periods, even in bright sunshine: displays remarkable tenacity in clinging to exposed rock faces in strong winds.

Baltic Grayling *Oeneis jutta*

RANGE Fennoscandia, Kola Peninsula, Urals, Siberia, N Mongolia, Amur, Yakutia, Madagan, N America.

O. jutta Hübner 1806 TL: Lapland.

DISTRIBUTION Norway: 61-65°N except SW region. Sweden: locally common: 58-68°N. Finland. Baltic states: very local. NE Poland.

FLIGHT-PERIOD Univoltine. Early June/mid July according to latitude and season.

HABITAT Marshes dominated by grasses, especially *Carex* spp.; usually near open areas of water, invariably with scattered pine trees and often bordered by pine woodland.

LIFE-HISTORY Hibernation stage unconfirmed.

BEHAVIOUR Often rests on trunks of pine trees.

Norse Grayling

Arctic Grayling

Baltic Grayling

♀

NORSE GRAYLING

ARCTIC GRAYLING

Ocelli absent on all wing surfaces except for a very small dot in upf subapex

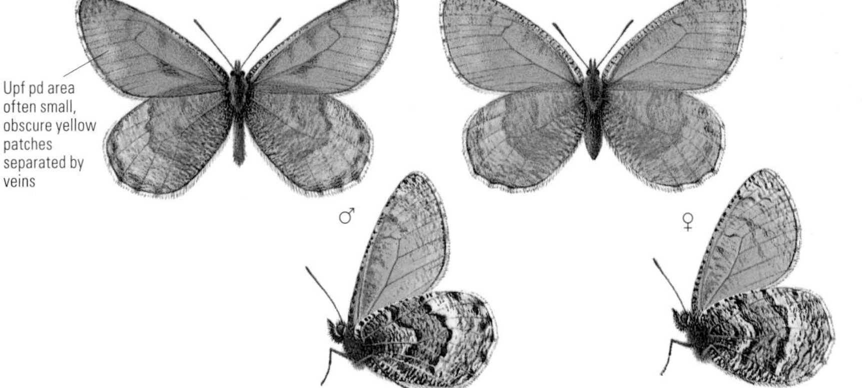

BALTIC GRAYLING

♂ and ♀ ups and uns pattern of markings and colouring distinctive

Black Satyr *Satyrus actaea*

RANGE SW Europe.

S. actaea Esper 1780 TL: S France.

DISTRIBUTION N Portugal: Serra da Estrêla. Spain: widespread, locally common. S France: E Pyrenees to Provence, northwards to Savoie and Puy-de-Dôme. NW Italy: Maritime Alps; Cottian Alps. 100-2000m.

DESCRIPTION Male upf with androconial patch in s1-3 (cf. *S. ferula*).

VARIATION Very marked in respect to all wing-markings, gc and size. Ups gc usually very dark brown or black, sometimes paler brown, especially in female: unh often very pale, but pale pd and discal bands remain conspicuous: female upf often with small white pd spots in s3 and s4.

FLIGHT-PERIOD Univoltine. Early June/late August according to locality and altitude.

HABITAT Dry, grassy, often rocky slopes; amongst rocks and scrub with scattered trees at lower altitudes.

NOTE Absent from Turkey, Middle East and W Asia: records from this region have been shown to relate to *S. ferula* (below).

Great Sooty Satyr *Satyrus ferula*

RANGE Morocco, S Europe, Turkey, Middle East, Iran, Transcaucasus, Ukraine, S Urals, Kazakhstan, SW Siberia, W China.

S. ferula ferula Fabricus 1793 TL: Italy.

syn: *bryce* Hübner 1800; *cordula* Fabricus 1793.

DISTRIBUTION Spain: province of Lérida (Val d'Aran; Rio Esera; Rio Noguera; 500-1400m). France: Pyrenees to Dordogne in small, widely dispersed colonies; more frequent in Massif Central, eastwards to Provence and Basses Alps (largely absent from Bouches-du Rhône and Var). Italy: foothills of C Alps; C Apennines; Calabria. S Switzerland (Valais; Tessin), eastwards to Balkans and Greece. 400-1800m.

DESCRIPTION Male upf without androconial patch (cf. *S. actaea*).

VARIATION Both sexes: ups and uns gc (very pale to very dark) and ocelli subject to considerable variation: female unh brightly marbled white/grey in some limestone localities.

FLIGHT-PERIOD Univoltine. Mid June/early August.

HABITAT Open, grassy and rocky slopes at higher altitudes; grassy, often bushy woodland clearings at lower altitudes.

LIFE-HISTORY LHP (Greece and Switzerland) *Festuca ovina*. A high proportion of larvae (up to 90%) have been found to be parasitized in some colonies. In cool, wet or overcast conditions, larvae recorded feeding in daylight hours.

S. ferula atlantea Verity 1927 (September) TL: Meknes, Morocco.

syn: *meknesensis* Strand 1927 (October).

DISTRIBUTION W Morocco: widespread but local. 1500-3000m. Reports from Rif Mts. require confirmation.

DESCRIPTION Male upf without androconial patch, otherwise resembles *S. actaea*.

FLIGHT-PERIOD Univoltine. Late June/mid September in prolonged emergence.

HABITAT Dry, grassy places or rocky slopes with sparse vegetation.

Black Satyr

Great Sooty Satyr

BLACK SATYR

♂ upf with sex-brand in s1-3
Upf black with white pupiled eye-spot in s5
♂
♀
Unh markings variable
Unh markings variable

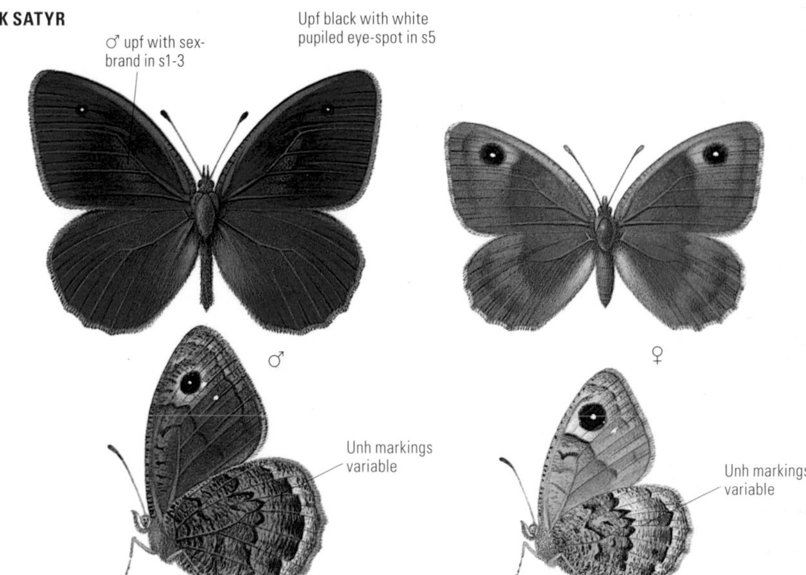

GREAT SOOTY SATYR

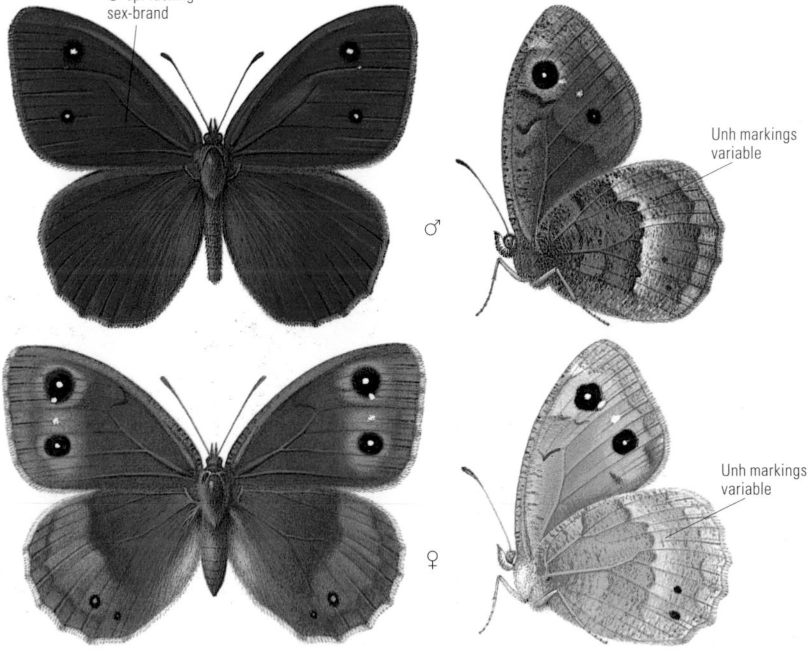
Black with white pupiled eye-spots in s2 and 5
♂ upf lacking sex-brand
Unh markings variable
♂
Unh markings variable
♀

Dryad *Minois dryas*

RANGE N Spain, C Europe, Turkey, W and C temperate Asia, Mongolia, Japan.
M. dryas Scopoli 1763 TL: Carniola.
syn: *phaedra* Linnaeus 1764.
DISTRIBUTION N Spain: very local: Cantabrian Mts.; Pyrenees. France (sporadic, commoner in E and SE), through N Italy, Switzerland, S Germany to N Poland, Balkans, N Greece (Rhodopi Mts.: very local) and European Turkey. 100-1600m.
VARIATION Female upf ocelli markedly variable in size.
FLIGHT-PERIOD Univoltine. Late June/early September according to locality.
HABITAT Grassy, bushy margins of mixed deciduous woodlands: often in damp places.

Great Banded Grayling *Kanetisa circe*

RANGE C and S Europe, Turkey, Iran to Himalayas.
K. circe Fabricus 1775 TL: Europe (Germany, Verity 1953).
syn: *proserpina* Denis and Schiffermüller 1775.
DISTRIBUTION Widespread and common. From Mediterranean, including Corsica, Sardinia, Sicily, Thassos, Lesbos and European Turkey, through most of C Europe to S Poland. 0-1650m.
FLIGHT-PERIOD Univoltine. Early June/mid September.
HABITAT Dry, grassy, bushy places; cultivated ground.
LIFE-HISTORY LHPs include *Festuca ovina*; *Bromus erectus*. Ova are ejected into low-growing vegetation during flight.

Dryad

Great Banded Grayling

♀

DRYAD

♂ and ♀ upf and unf blue-pupilled ocelli distinctive but variable

♂

Hw markings variable, sometimes obscured but dark submarginal band usually present

♀

GREAT BANDED GRAYLING

♂ and ♀ ups and uns markings distinctive

Giant Grayling *Berberia abdelkader*

RANGE Morocco, Algeria, Tunisia, NW Libya.
B. abdelkader Pierrett 1837 TL: Oran [Constantine] Province, Algeria.

DISTRIBUTION Morocco: High Atlas; Middle Atlas. N Algeria: Aures Mts. W Tunisia. 200-2300m.

DESCRIPTION Male ups gc medium to dark brown; upf subapical ocellus (s5), large, blue-pupilled; pd ocellus in s2, often small, sometimes vestigial, rarely absent; small, bluish pd spots in s3 and s4, sometimes also in s6; creamy-white, yellowish or creamy pale brown apical scaling extremely variable, sometimes extending to enclose ocellus in s2; unh brown mediobasal and discal lines prominent, angled at v4: female similar: markings better developed: upf outer margin often golden-brown; unh gc paler; whitish veins prominent.

VARIATION E Algeria (Bou-Saada to Dj. Metlili and Aures massif) to W Tunisia (700-1100m), *nelvai* Seitz [syn: *marteni* Chneour]: upf apex creamy-white, usually enclosing subapical ocellus, sometimes extending to pd ocellus (when present) in s2; uph pd ocelli in s2 and s5, when present, usually enclosed by pale or golden scales, sometimes extending to outer margin; uns resembles nominate form; unf subapical ocellus enclosed by whitish scales, sometimes extending to costa and outer margin to s2. In a restricted area of Middle Atlas, Morocco (1900-2300m), *taghzefti* Wyatt: characters intermediate of those of nominate form and *nelvai* Seitz. W Algeria (1200m), *saharae* Slaby: about 60% of males transitional to, or indistinguishable from *taghzefti*, the remainder resembling nominate form. Taxa *alfae* Slaby and *arvorum* Slaby appear to be synonymous with nominate form. The possibility that some, if not all of the above variants are examples of ecological adaptation or polymorphism has not been precluded: subspecificity of some taxa is, in any case, precluded by sympatry.

FLIGHT-PERIOD Univoltine. June/early November according to altitude and locality.

HABITAT Open rocky slopes and sandy places containing extensive stands of LHP.

LIFE-HISTORY LHP *Stipa tenacissima*: also, possibly *S. parviflora*. Hibernation stage unconfirmed.

BEHAVIOUR Both sexes take nectar from *Colchicum autumnale*.

Berberia lambessanus

RANGE Morocco, Algeria, Tunisia, (?)Libya.
B. lambessanus Staudinger 1901 TL: Lambessa, Algeria.

DISTRIBUTION Morocco: High Atlas; Middle Atlas; Rif Mts. N Algeria: Aures Mts. NE Tunisia: Cap Bon. 50-3160m.

DESCRIPTION Male ups gc very dark, tending to black; whitish apical suffusion entirely lacking; blue pd spots between ocelli (ups and unf) usually wedge-shaped and larger than those of *B. abdelkader*; uns gc very dark compared to *B. abdelkader*; veins not lined white: female very variable: sometimes resembling male: more generally, markings better developed with upf apical and marginal areas to s2 pale brown; unh veins conspicuously pale.

VARIATION Constant in known range: *romeii* Rothschild (W Rif Mts., Morocco) and *alexander* Chneour (Cap Bon, Tunisia) reportedly synonymous with nominate form.

FLIGHT-PERIOD Univoltine. April/November according to altitude and locality.

HABITAT Sometimes similar to that of *B. abdelkader*, but generally with more varied vegetation including light woodland.

LIFE-HISTORY LHP *Ampelodesmos tenax*: also, possibly *Stipa parviflora*. Ova laid mainly on dead leaves near base of LHP. A high proportion of ova have been found to be parasitized by a (?)hymenopteran which hibernates within ovum case.

NOTE *B. abdelkader* and *B. lambessanus* reportedly fly together at Lac Tislit, High Atlas Mts., Morocco, 2150-2250m.

Giant Grayling

Berberia lambessaus

GIANT GRAYLING

♂ upf pale subapex enclosing. Ocellus in s5 variable, sometimes extending to s2

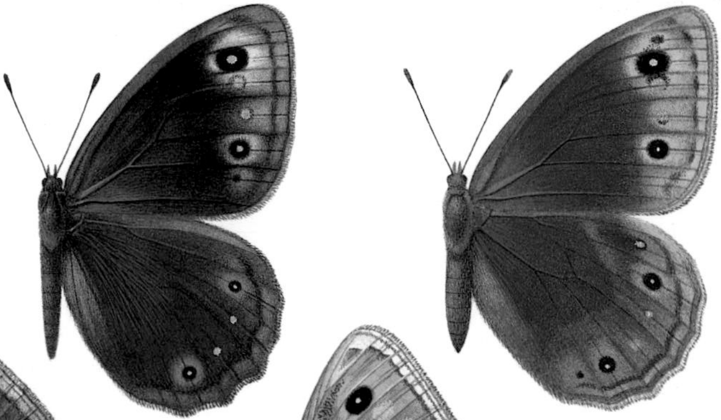

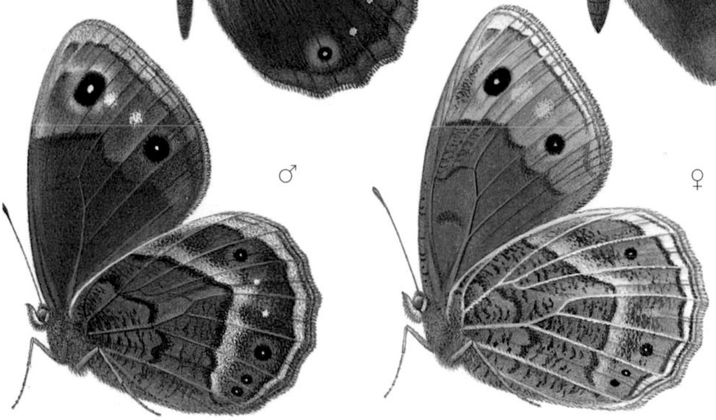

♂

♀

Berberia lambessanus

False Grayling *Arethusana arethusa*

RANGE Morocco, S Europe, Turkey to Tian Shan.

A. arethusa arethusa Denis and Schiffermüller 1775 TL: Vienna.

DISTRIBUTION From N Portugal, N and C Spain, France (Charante-Maritimes to Eure, Somme, Meurthe-et-Moselle and Haut-Rhin) to (?)NW Switzerland and S Germany (very local and rare), NE Italy, E Austria, Slovakia, Balkans, Greece and European Turkey. 0-2000m. Very sporadic in parts of C Europe and NW Balkans.

DESCRIPTION AND VARIATION Most wing-markings subject to marked local/individual variation. Ups orange pd markings often macular and obscure; unh gc brownish, cryptically irrorated; diffuse pale discal band variable.

FLIGHT-PERIOD Univoltine. Mid July/mid September according to locality. Grassy, bushy places; woodland borders; rocky gullies: on calcareous and non-calcareous soils.

A. arethusa dentata Staudinger 1871 TL: W France.

DISTRIBUTION W Morocco: High Atlas (Toubkal massif 2400-2700m: very local). Spain: Catalonia; (?)Granada. France: Pyrénées-Orientales to Ardèche and Provence. NW Italy (Maritime Alps: very local). 0-1000m.

DESCRIPTION AND VARIATION Ups orange pd bands well developed, but disrupted by veins; unf pd area with proximal brown line; unh paler, conspicuously irrorated; discal area bordered by diffuse whitish band; veins pale greyish or buff. In Morocco, *aksouali* Wyatt: resembles *dentata* closely: unh gc tending to yellowish-brown. In all regions, wing-markings subject to marked variation: closely similar forms have been recorded in Hungary and Greece.

FLIGHT-PERIOD AND HABITAT As for nominate form.

A. arethusa boabdil Rambur 1842 TL: Andalusia.

DISTRIBUTION S Spain: Andalusia (Sierra Nevada; S. de Alfarcar; S. de Almijara; S. de Los Filabres). 700-1700m.

DESCRIPTION Ups orange pd bands greatly reduced, often obscured by gc in male; unf pd area and apical ocellus with irregular proximal brown line; unh white discal band and white veins conspicuous.

FLIGHT-PERIOD Univoltine. Late June/August.

HABITAT Hot, dry, grassy places amongst scrub and limestone rocks.

NOTE Uncertainty in distributional relationship of above forms appears to relate to confusion arising from marked individual and local variation.

Arran Brown *Erebia ligea*

RANGE E Europe to Urals, Siberia, Altai, Transbaikal, Amur, Kamchatka, Japan.

E. ligea Linnaeus 1758 TL: Sweden (Verity 1953).

DISTRIBUTION France (Massif Central; Alpes-Maritimes to Vosges Mts.), through S Alps and Apennines to Czech Republic, S Poland, Balkans and N Greece (Varnous Mts.; Vernon Mts.; Rhodope Mts.). Fennoscandia, including Öland. Baltic states. Absent from C Switzerland, parts of Dalmatian coast, Denmark and S Lithuania. 0-1800m.

DESCRIPTION Male upf with sex-brand (cf. *E. euryale*).

VARIATION Ups reddish pd bands vary in colour and width; ocelli variable in size and number, sometimes small, lacking white pupils. In N Fennoscandia, f. *dovrensis* Strand: smaller; ups pd bands reduced; ocelli smaller, usually 'blind'; unh white pd band reduced, usually restricted to s5 and s6: transitional to nominate form in S Scandinavia.

FLIGHT-PERIOD Univoltine. Mid July/late August.

HABITAT AND BEHAVIOUR Sheltered, grassy, flowery, woodland/forest clearings, usually damp and humid, sometimes containing an abundance of bracken upon which adults often bask, even in warm, overcast conditions.

LIFE-HISTORY LHPs include *Carex sylvatica*; *C. strigosa*. Hibernates as an ovum or larvae. Larval development occupies two seasonal cycles in N Fennoscandia. Wing-characters of captively reared specimens of f. *dovrensis* reputedly approach those of nominate form.

False Grayling

Arran Brown

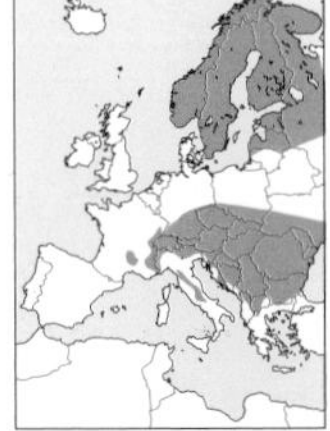

f. *dovrensis*
(N Fennoscandia)

FALSE GRAYLING

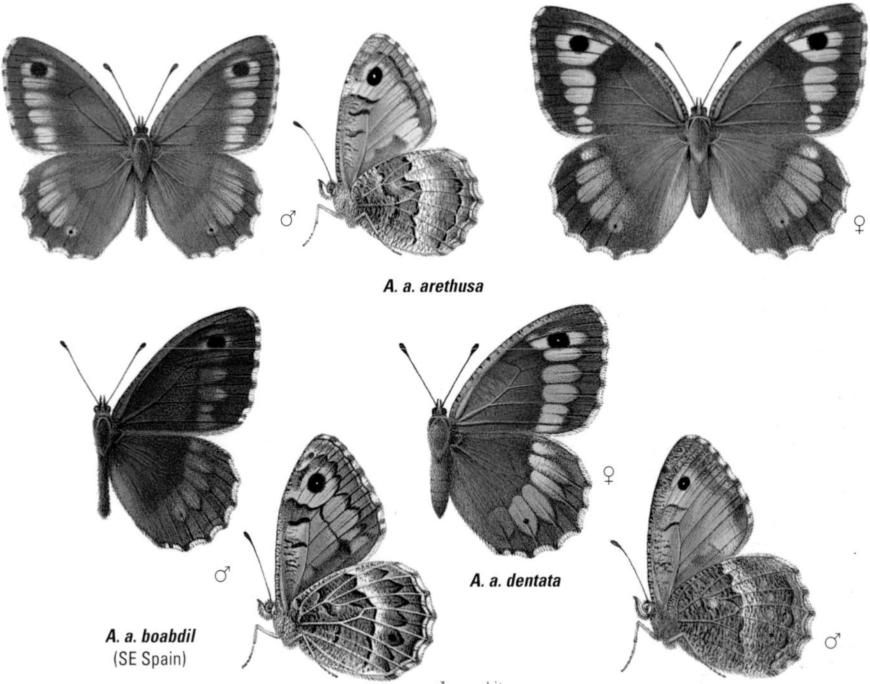
♂
♀
A. a. arethusa
♀
♂
A. a. dentata
A. a. boabdil
(SE Spain)
♂
♂ uns white
veins conspicuous,
distinctive
dark

ARRAN BROWN

♂ upf sex-brand
inconspicuous
Ups fringes
clearly chequered
♂
♀
Unh white
markings
distinctive

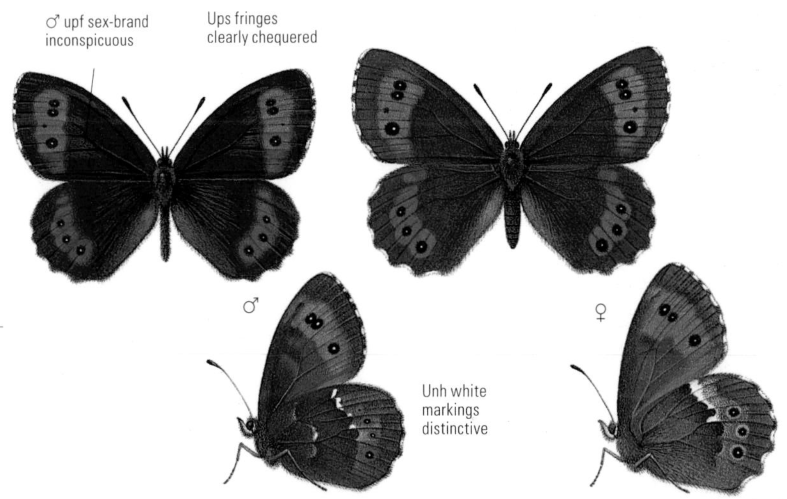

Large Ringlet *Erebia euryale*

RANGE Mountains of Europe from N Spain to Balkans, Urals, Kanin Peninsula.

E. euryale Esper 1805 TL: Riesengebirge.

DISTRIBUTION Widespread, locally common. Cantabrian Mts.; W and E Pyrenees; Massif Central; Jura Mts.; C European Alps; Bohemian Mts.; High Tatra Mts.; Carpathian Mts.; Ligurean Alps; C Apennines; Julian Alps; Dinaric Pl. to mountains of Albania, Republic of Macedonia, Bulgaria and N Greece (Varnous Mts.; Mt. Phalakron; Rhodope Mts.). 750-2500m, more generally 1200-2000m.

DESCRIPTION Male upf without sex-brand (cf. *E. ligea*). Male ups reddish pd bands or spots enclosing 'blind', usually elongate ocelli; uns ocelli usually white-pupilled; unh proximal edge of pd band sometimes with obscure, white tooth-like mark in s4, occasionally extending to costa as a narrow, obscure whitish band: female upf and unf ocelli sometimes with small white pupils; unh whitish or yellowish pd band broad, conspicuous.

VARIATION Very marked local and regional differences has given rise to many named forms, variants of which are common and often transitional to each other or to the nominate form. From Haute-Savoie, through W and C Switzerland to N Austrian Alps, Bohemian Mts., Tatra Mts. and NW Carpathian Mts., f. *isarica* Heyne: male ups elongate ocelli 'blind'; unh pd band variable, usually obscure: female uns markings similar to nominate form. In S Switzerland, f. *adyte* Hübner: ocelli usually white-pupilled: male unh darker; whitish, proximal pd markings similar to nominate form, generally less obscure but variable – tooth-like mark in s4 usually present: female unh pale pd band lightly irrorated with white scales, proximal border more regular, white markings in s4 to costa better developed. In SE Austria and Dolomites, f. *ocellaris* Staudinger: male ups markings reduced to small, red-ringed, 'blind' ocelli, sometimes absent: female ups markings generally better developed, but occasionally entirely absent: both sexes, unh markings similar to nominate form.

FLIGHT-PERIOD Univoltine. Late July/August.

HABITAT Grassy, flowery places in pinewood clearings; grassy slopes above treeline.

LIFE-HISTORY LHPs include *Sesleria varia*; *Festuca ovina*; *F. rubra*; *F. alpina*; *Poa nemoralis*; *Carex flacca*; *C. ferruginea*; *Calamagrostis varia*.

Eriphyle Ringlet *Erebia eriphyle*

RANGE C European Alps.

E. eriphyle Freyer 1839 TL: Grimsel Pass, Switzerland.

DISTRIBUTION Switzerland: Bernese Alps, Lepontine Alps to Alpstein and Engadine. Germany: Allgäuer Alps (Nebelhorn). Austria: Lechtaler Alps; Ötztaler Alps; Stubaier Alps; Hohe Tauern (Gross Glockner); Niedere Tauern; Sau Alp; Kor Alps. Italy: Ortler Alps; Dolomites. Widespread but very local. 1200-2250m.

DESCRIPTION Uph reddish spot in s4 constant, those in s2, s3 and s5 variable; unf often with reddish suffusion projecting from proximal border of paler pd band to wing-base; unh reddish-orange spots in s2-5 variable, lacking black pupils, spot in s4 larger, always present. (cf. *E. manto f. pyrrhula* and *E. melampus*).

VARIATION In E Alps, f. *tristis* Herrich-Schäffer: brighter, all markings better developed. Transitional to nominate form in E Switzerland and NW Tirol.

FLIGHT-PERIOD Univoltine. Late June/mid August according to locality and altitude.

HABITAT Damp, sheltered, herb-rich, alpine meadows, often associated with pinewoods; open areas amongst scrub in rocky gullies.

LIFE-HISTORY LHPs *Anthoxanthum odoratum*; *Deschampsia caespitosa*. Larval development occupies two seasonal cycles: in captivity, a proportion of larvae reportedly remain within ovum-case during first winter.

Large Ringlet

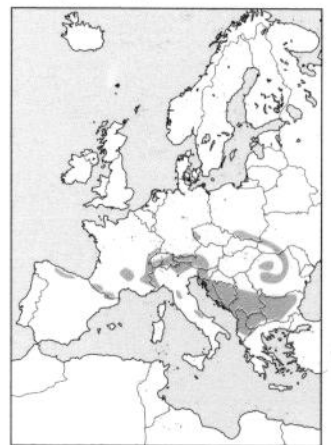

Eriphyle Ringlet

LARGE RINGLET

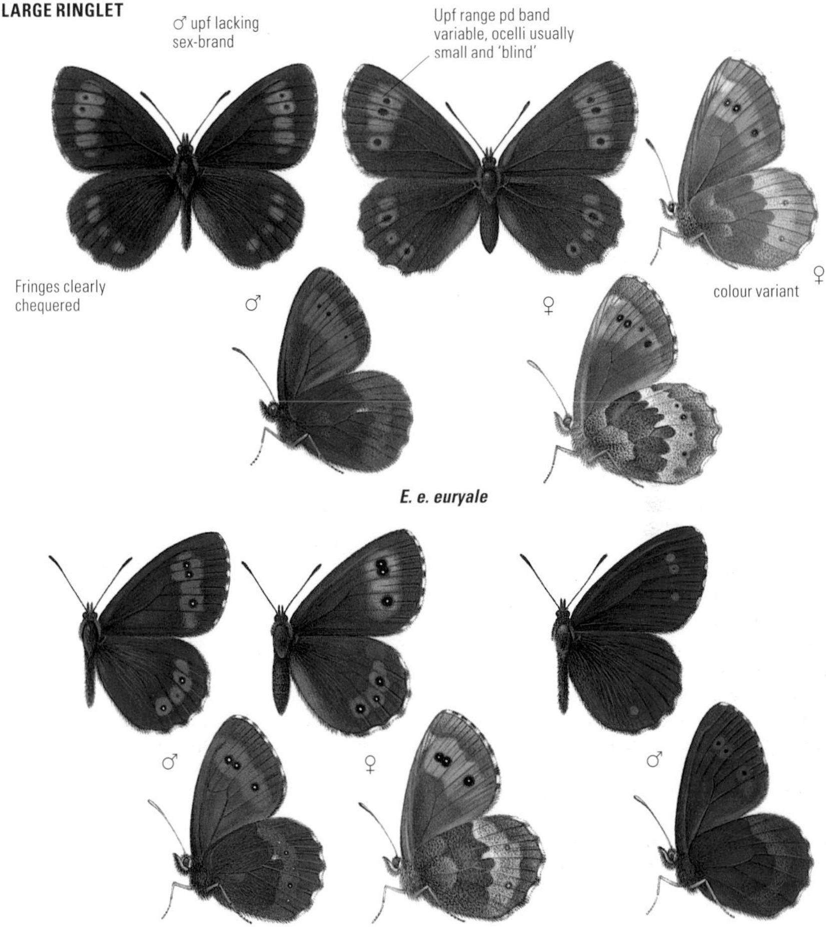

♂ upf lacking sex-brand
Upf range pd band variable, ocelli usually small and 'blind'
Fringes clearly chequered
♂
♀
colour variant
♀
E. e. euryale
♂
♀
♂
f. *adyte*
(S Switzerland)
f. *ocellaris*
(SE Austria, NE Italy)

ERIPHYLE RINGLET

Restricted to C Alps
Uph and unh pd orange-red spot large always lacking black pupil
♂
Unf red flush extending to wing base
♀
♂
f. *tristis*

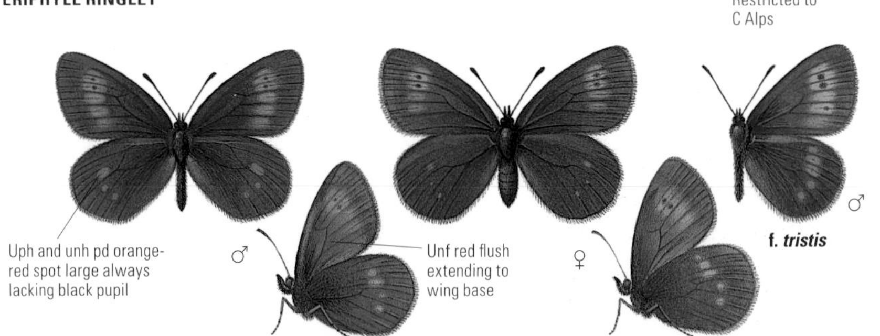

Yellow-spotted Ringlet *Erebia manto*

RANGE Europe.

E. manto manto Denis and Schiffermüller 1775 TL: Vienna.

DISTRIBUTION Alpes-Maritimes (very local); NE Isère to Haute-Savoie; Vosges Mts. C Alps to Julian Alps. Tatra Mts.; Carpathian Mts. Bosnia-Herzegovina: Vlasic Pl.; Vranica Pl.; Jahorina Pl. 1200-2500m.

VARIATION Many forms have been described in recognition of very marked individual, local and regional variation in size and development of pd and ocellular markings. Above 1800m in C Alps including Dolomites, f. *pyrrhula* Frey: very small; dark; all markings greatly reduced, sometimes absent. In Voges Mts., *vogesiaca* Christ: male larger; ups pd bands duller red, well developed; upf subapical black points vestigial or absent; unh pd band of more uniform width: female similar, but with unh markings variable in colour, pale yellow to bright orange-yellow, less often white (f. *bubastis* Meissner – a recurrent form in some localities in Switzerland).

FLIGHT-PERIOD Univoltine. Early July/early September.

HABITAT Damp, grassy, flowery meadows; woodland clearings; at high altitudes, slopes and pastures with grasses of moderate length.

LIFE-HISTORY LHP *Festuca rubra*. Early-stage development occupies two seasonal cycles: in captivity, proportion of ova reportedly hibernate in first winter.

E. manto constans Eiffinger 1908 TL: Hautes-Pyrénées.

DISTRIBUTION Spain: Picos de Europa. Above 1500m. Pyrenees (France and Spain): Pto. de Somport to Col du Tourmalet, Pto. de Beñasque and Pic Carlit. Massif Central (Plomb du Cantal; Mont Dore). 900-2300m.

DESCRIPTION Male ups and uns very dark, almost black; usual uns markings absent or vestigial: female paler; unh markings often vestigial.

FLIGHT-PERIOD AND HABITAT As for *E. m. manto*.

NOTE *E. serotina* Descimon and de Lesse 1953 described from Hautes-Pyrénées is believed to be a hybrid of *E. manto constans* and *E. epiphron fauveaui*. Only males have been recorded, flying in September on grassy slopes near Cauterets at about 1000m. The insect appears to be extremely rare. It resembles the local form of *E. epiphron* except that:- upf ocelli in s4 and s5 are white-pupilled; uph pd ocelli ringed red, sometimes white-pupilled; unf pd band well defined; unh dark brown with paler pd band; red-ringed pd ocelli small, lacking white pupils.

Yellow-banded Ringlet *Erebia flavofasciata*

RANGE S Switzerland, N Italy.

E. flavofasciata Heyne 1895 TL: Campolungo Pass, Tessin.

DISTRIBUTION N Italy: Val Formazza; Val di Dévero; Val Antigorio; Monte Castello; Val di Tóggia; Pso. di San Giácomo. S Switzerland: Tessin (Naret Pass; Sassello Pass; Campo di Torba; Campolungo Pass); Grisons (Val Calanca; San Bernardino Pass; Julierpass; Schafberg; Tscherva Glacier; Berninapass). Very local, usually common. 1800-2600m.

VARIATION In Engadine, f. *thiemei* Bartel: ups pd reddish spots smaller, often fewer; unh yellow pd band slightly narrower, rarely broken into ocellular rings.

FLIGHT-PERIOD Univoltine. Late June/mid August.

HABITAT Exposed, grass-covered or grassy and rocky slopes: grasses are usually of moderate length.

LIFE-HISTORY LHP *Festuca ovina*. Larval development occupies two seasonal cycles.

Yellow-spotted Ringlet

Yellow-banded Ringlet

YELLOW-SPOTTED RINGLET

♂

♀

Ups and uns pd bands lacking ocelli

E. m. manto

♂ and ♀ unh structure of pd band distinctive

♂

♀

E. m. vogesiaca

E. m. vogesiaca* f. *bubastis

♂

♀

♂

♀

E. m. manto* f. *pyrrhula

E. m. constans

YELLOW-BANDED RINGLET

Restricted to S Switzerland and N Italy

♂ and ♀ unf discal area dark red

♂

♀

Unh yellow band very distinctive

Mountain Ringlet *Erebia epiphron*

RANGE Mountains of Europe, excluding C and S Spain, Fennoscandia, C and S Greece and Mediterranean islands. Subject to considerable individual, local (ecological/altitudinal), regional as well as inter-seasonal variation in wing-markings, colour and, to a lesser degree, size. Considerable overlap in the variance of characters of geographically well-separated forms, coupled with confusion regarding descriptive accuracy (possibly due to non-rigorous sampling procedure), attaches some doubt to the taxonomic relevance of several named forms. Collectively, the following taxa probably embrace the full range of variation in wing-characters.

E. epiphron epiphron Knoch 1783 TL: Brocken, Harz Mts., W Germany.

DISTRIBUTION Believed to be extinct: formerly known only from Harz Mts. **DESCRIPTION** Characterised by well-developed markings and large size. Male upf pd rust-coloured band broad, usually complete, sometimes broken into discrete spots, enclosing black ocelli in s2-5; uph similar pd band enclosing black ocelli in s2-4; unh red-ringed ocelli distinctive: female markings better developed; unh reddish pd spots often confluent, forming a distinct band; ups and unh black ocelli sometimes enclosing minute white points.

E. epiphron mackeri Fuchs 1914 TL: Vosges Mts.
syn: *vogesiaca* Goltz 1914 (invalid homonym).

DISTRIBUTION France: Vosges Mts. 900-1100m. **DESCRIPTION** Resembles nominate form: smaller; upf rust-red pd bands narrower, usually broken into spots, variable; unh red-ringed ocelli reduced. **FLIGHT-PERIOD** Univoltine. Mid June/mid August according to season. **HABITAT** Sheltered gullies or hollows on open grass-covered slopes containing an abundance of grass species of moderate length: on granite rocks. **LIFE-HISTORY** LHP *Nardus stricta*. Captive larvae accept *Festuca ovina*; *F. rubra*.

E. epiphron mnemon Haworth 1812 TL: Scotland
syn: *scotica* Cooke 1943

DISTRIBUTION NW England: Cumbrian Mts. Scotland: Grampian Mts.; Ben Nevis; Ben Vain; Ben Lomond; Newtonmore. 350-1100m – more generally 500-800m. France: Massif Central: Cevennes (Aigoual massif); Auvergne (Monts du Cantal; Puy-de-Dôme). 900-1600m. Old records for Ireland have not been confirmed. **DESCRIPTION AND VARIATION** Resembles *mackeri*: smaller; gc darker; upf reddish pd bands usually more extensively broken into elongate, somewhat rectilinear spots; ups and uns ocelli variable in size and number, usually very small, sometimes absent; unh rarely with pd area distinctly paler. All wing-characters very variable. Variants (f. *cebennica* Leraut 1980 and f. *mixta* de Lesse 1951) described from Massif Central, appear to fall within range of variation of *mnemon*. **FLIGHT-PERIOD** Univoltine. Mid June/early August. **HABITAT** Damp, grassy, often marshy slopes or gullies. **LIFE-HISTORY** LHP, in Britain, *Nardus stricta*. Captive larvae accept *Poa annua*; *Festuca ovina*; *Deschampsia flexuosa*; *D. cespitosa*. **NOTE** Discovered in 1809 by T. S. Stothard near Ambleside, Cumbrian Mts., NW England: subsequently, type-locality erroneously given as 'Scotland'.

E. epiphron aetheria Esper 1805 TL: not stated [(?)Austria].

DISTRIBUTION C European Alps: Basses-Alpes and Hautes-Alpes to Bavarian Alps, Dolomites and Austrian Alps. Mountains of Slovenia, W Croatia, Bosnia-Herzegovina and SW Serbia. 1200-2700m. **DESCRIPTION** Resembles *mnemon*: all markings averagely poorly developed, variable; male upf red spot and ocellus in s3 often reduced: female upf pd ocelli sometimes with minute white pupils: both sexes, unh pd area paler – a feature better developed in habitats shared with *E. christi*. **VARIATION** At high altitudes in C Alps (prevalent in Engadine, W Austria and Dolomites above 1800-2000m), f. *nelamus* Boisduval 1828: small: male ups gc darker; all markings greatly reduced; upf reddish pd bands often obscure, enclosing two small subapical ocelli, often vestigial or absent; unh lacking ocelli. In Maritime Alps, Apuane Alps and C Apennines, *cydamus* Frühstorfer 1910: larger; resembles *mnemon* but markings variable. **FLIGHT-PERIOD** Univoltine. Late June/July according to altitude and locality. **HABITAT** Grass-covered slopes, usually with an abundance of grass species of moderate length: on calcareous or non-calcareous substrates. **LIFE-HISTORY** LHPs include *Nardus stricta*. At higher altitudes larval development occupies two seasonal cycles.

E. epiphron fauveaui de Lesse 1947 TL: E Pyrenees

DISTRIBUTION Spain and France: E Pyrenees (Andorra; Pic Carlit; Cambras d'Aze; Mt. Canigou). 1000-2300m. **DESCRIPTION** Resembles *mackeri*: larger; fw more pointed; upf pd band and elongate, 'blind' ocelli usually well developed. **VARIATION** Transitional to f. *pyrenaica* west of Andorra but variable: forms resembling *aetheria* are said to become increasingly common towards Luchon: at high altitudes in C Pyrenees, specimens sometimes indistinguishable from f. *nelamus*. **FLIGHT-PERIOD** Univoltine. Early June/July according to altitude and locality.

E. epiphron pyrenaica Herrich-Schäffer 1851 TL: Pic du Vignemale [W Pyrenees].

DISTRIBUTION Cantabrian Mts.; S. de la Demanda; S. de Cebollera; W Pyrenees (Basses-Pyrénées; Hautes-Pyrénées to Andorra). Above 1300m. **DESCRIPTION AND VARIATION** Distinction from *mackeri* and *fauveaui* difficult: markings averagely reduced but variable – individual specimens often indistinguishable from the aforementioned forms. In Asturian Mts., *valdeonica* Hospital 1948: upf pd bands well developed, ocelli small, sometimes absent; uph pd reddish spots and ocelli variable, sometimes absent. Present placement of recently discovered populations of S. de Cebollera and S. de la Demanda is provisional: available material inadequate for full evaluation of racial characters.

E. epiphron silesiana Meyer-Dür 1852 TL: Mt. Altvater [=Mt. Praded].

DISTRIBUTION Czech Republic: Silesian Mts. **DESCRIPTION** Resembles nominate form: size similar; all markings averagely reduced, especially unh pd reddish spots, very obscure or absent in male, not confluent in female.

E. epiphron transsylvanica Rebel 1908 TL: W Transylvanian Mts.

DISTRIBUTION N Slovakia and S Poland: Tatra Mts. Romania: Carpathian Mts.

MOUNTAIN RINGLET

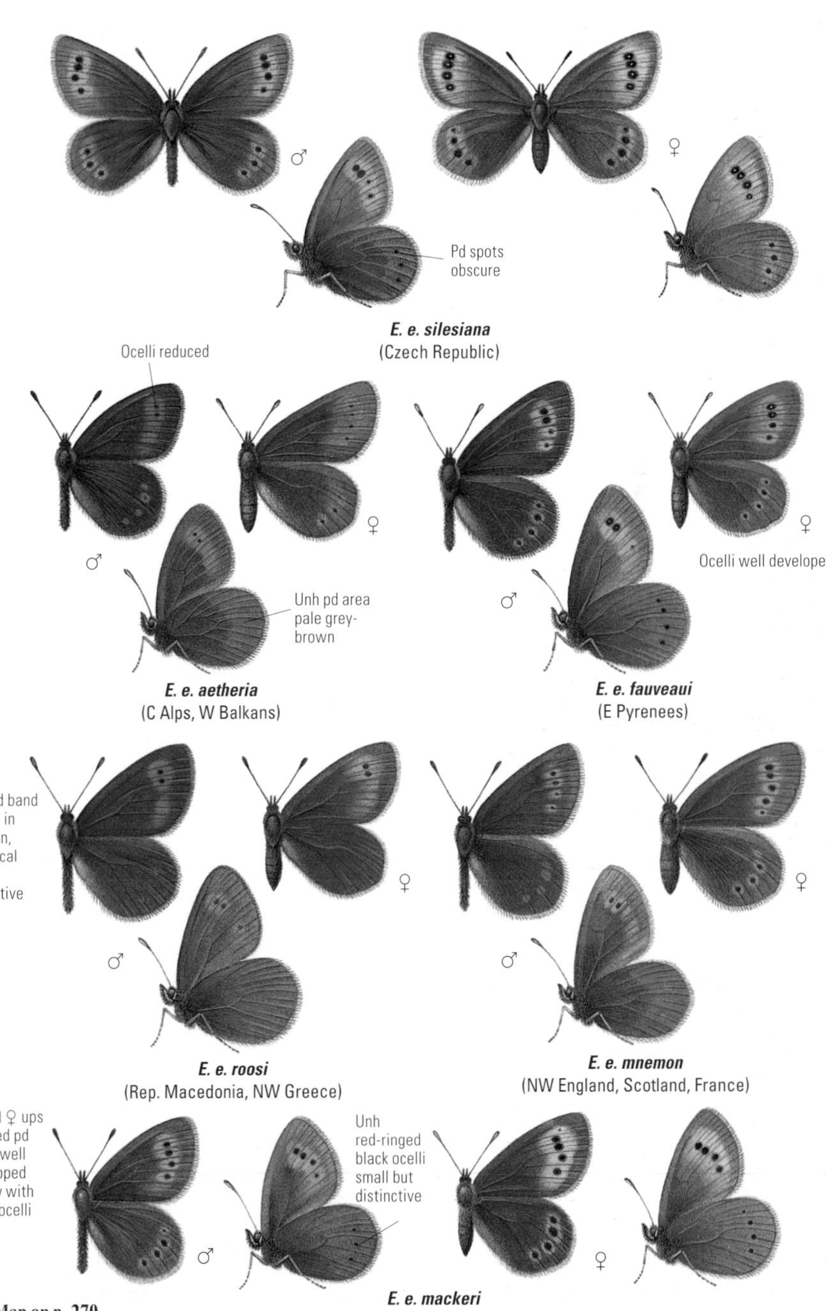

Map on p. 270

DESCRIPTION Resembles *silesiana*: upf pd well developed, broad, often extending below v1; ocelli small, variable in number, usually present in s4 and s5; uph red pd markings and enclosed ocelli usually well developed; unh pd ocelli ringed red.

E. epiphron retyezatensis Warren 1931 TL: Retezat Mts.

DISTRIBUTION SW Romania: Retezat Mts. (Reported occurrence in Bosnia-Herzegovina, Montenegro and Republic of Macedonia appears to be ill-founded). **DESCRIPTION AND VARIATION** Resembles *transsylvanica*: upf yellow-orange pd band broader near subapex (s4-6), sometimes with ray-like projections towards cell.

E. epiphron roosi **continued on p.350**

White Speck Ringlet *Erebia claudina*

RANGE E Alps of Austria.

E. claudina Borkhausen 1789 TL: Austria.

syn: *arete* Fabricus 1787 (Invalid homonym)

DISTRIBUTION Austria: Hohe Tauern (Mallnitz); Salzburg Alps (Weissbriachtal). Niedere Tauern; Seetal Alps (Zirbitzkogel); Sau Alp. 1800-2300m. **DESCRIPTION** Uph with 2 to 5 white pd points, usually 6 on unh. **FLIGHT-PERIOD** Univoltine. July/early August. In some localities, scarce or absent in alternate years. **HABITAT** Grassy slopes of somewhat variable character; usually above treeline. **LIFE-HISTORY** LHP uncertain: reputedly *Deschampsia cespitosa*. Relative abundance in alternate years suggests that two seasonal cycles are required for early-stage development.

Bulgarian Ringlet *Erebia orientalis*

RANGE Bulgaria.

E. orientalis Elwes 1900 TL: Rila Mts., Bulgaria.

DISTRIBUTION Bulgaria: Stara Pl. (Mt. Botev); Rila Mts. (Mt. Maljovica; Mt. Manchu; Kóstenets; Mt. Tcherni); Pirin Mts. (Mt. Vihren; Kameniti Dupki; Mt. Kamenica). Not recorded from Rhodopi Mts. 1800-2600m. **DESCRIPTION AND VARIATION** Fw narrow, pointed; male upf reddish pd spots slightly larger in s4 and s5, enclosing black points; uph and unh orange-red, black-pupilled pd spots almost circular, clearly defined: female ups gc brown, uns gc greyish-brown; yellow-orange pd bands and enclosed white-pupilled ocelli well developed; upf discal and basal areas suffused reddish-brown. In Pirin Mts., *infernalis* Varga: closely similar to nominate form. **FLIGHT-PERIOD** Univoltine. Generally late June/mid July: records span early June/early August. **HABITAT** Grassy areas near treeline. **LIFE-HISTORY** Hibernation stage unconfirmed.

Rätzer's Ringlet *Erebia christi*

RANGE SW Switzerland.

E. christi Rätzer 1890 TL: Laggintal, Simplon.

DISTRIBUTION SW Switzerland: south of Simplonpass: very local and uncommon: Rossbodental; Eggental; Laggintal; Zwischbergental. 1300-2100m. NW Italy: Piedmont (Véglia Alp 1700m). **DESCRIPTION** Upf 'blind' ocelli in s3-s6 co-linear (cf. *E. epiphron aetheria*). **FLIGHT-PERIOD** Univoltine. Late June/early August. **HABITAT** Steep, grassy, rocky slopes often with scattered trees and low bushes. **LIFE-HISTORY** LHP *Festuca ovina*. Larval development occupies two seasonal cycles. (Reportedly commoner in alternate years.) **CONSERVATION** In decline in some localities.

Lesser Mountain Ringlet *Erebia melampus*

RANGE C European Alps.

E. melampus Fuessli 1775 TL: Switzerland.

DISTRIBUTION Most of C European Alps from Maritime Alps to S Bavaria, E Austria and Dolomites. Widespread, generally common. 800-2400m. **DESCRIPTION AND VARIATION** Upf pd reddish/orange spots irregular, usually with small black points in s4 and s5, sometimes also in s2 and s3; uph usually with 4 pd spots, with or without black points, spot in s4 largest; uns pattern similar. (cf. *E. sudetica*). **FLIGHT-PERIOD** Univoltine. Early July/mid September according to altitude. **HABITAT** Damp or dry alpine meadows; grass-covered slopes; woodland clearings. **LIFE-HISTORY** LHPs *Anthoxanthum odoratum*; *Festuca ovina*; *Poa nemoralis*. In captive rearing from ovum, life-cycle is completed without diapause in extended photo-period of S England.

Mountain Ringlet

White Speck Ringlet

Bulgarian Ringlet

Rätzer's Ringlet

Lesser Mountain Ringlet

WHITE SPECK RINGLET

Restricted to Austrian Alps

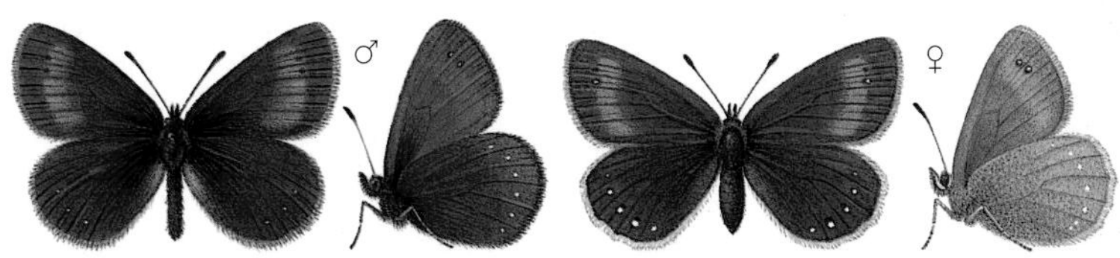

Uph and unh small white submarginal spots in regular series, distinctive

BULGARIAN RINGLET

Restricted to Bulgaria

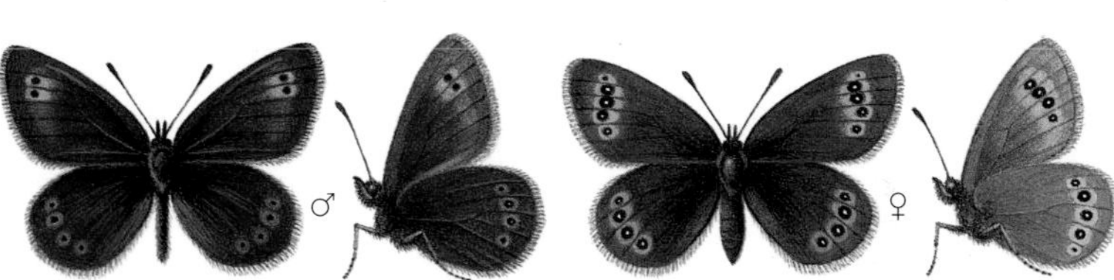

♂ and ♀ unh ocelli well developed

RÄTZER'S RINGLET

Restricted to SW Switzerland, NW Italy

Upf red pd band not constricted in s3: very small elongate black spots co-linear, distinctive

Uf discal area reddish

Unh pale pd area well delineated

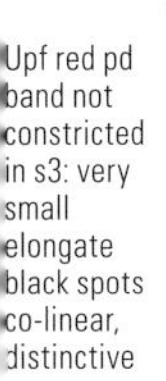

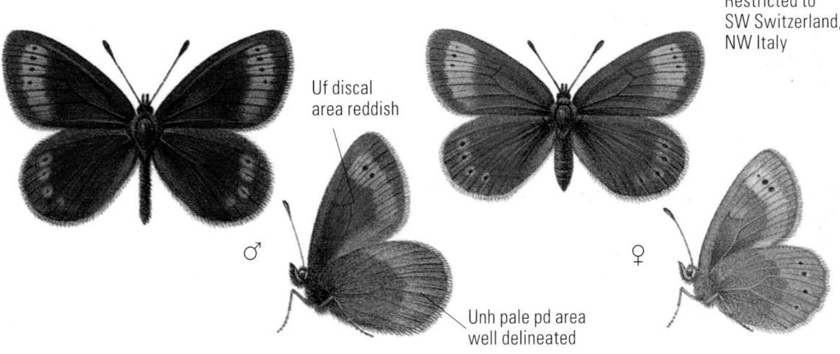

LESSER MOUNTAIN RINGLET

Restricted to C Alps

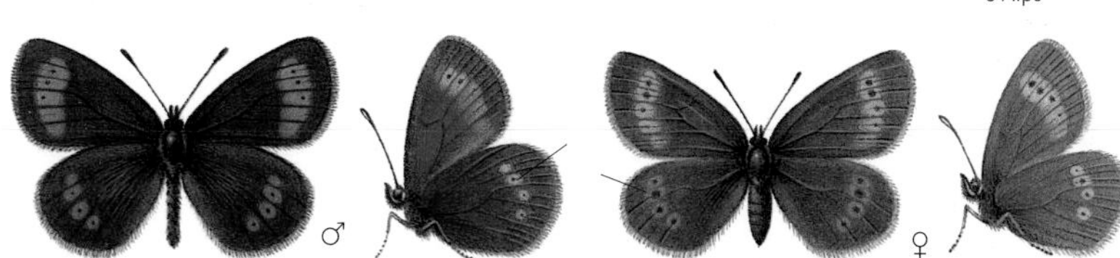

♂ and ♀ uph and unh series of pd spots in irregular series: spot s4 largest

Blind Ringlet *Erebia pharte*

RANGE C European Alps, Tatra Mts.

E. pharte Hübner 1804 TL: Alps of Switzerland.

DISTRIBUTION Central European Alps of France (N Alpes-Maritimes to Haute-Savoie: also Vosges Mts.), Switzerland, NW and NE Italy (Cottian Alps), SE Germany, Austria and W Slovenia (Julian Alps). S Poland and Slovakia: Tatra Mts. (?)Romania: Carpathian Mts. 1000-2500m, generally above 1400m.

DESCRIPTION Ups and uns orange-red pd markings always without ocelli or black points; upf and unf pd bands sharply defined – characteristically rectilinear.

VARIATION From W Tirol, eastwards, f. *eupompa* Frühstorfer: larger; pd bands brighter; upf pd band sometimes with ray-like, proximal extensions from s5 and s6. Above 1800m throughout range, f. *phartina* Staudinger: smaller; pd markings greatly reduced, rarely entirely absent. Occurs as an aberrant form below 1800m.

FLIGHT-PERIOD Univoltine. Early July/late August.

HABITAT Dry or damp alpine meadows; open grassy, flowery places in woodland at lower altitudes.

LIFE-HISTORY LHPs *Carex ferrunginea*; *C. flacca*; *Festuca ovina*; *F. quadriflora*; *F. rubra*; *Nardus stricta*. Larval development occupies two seasonal cycles.

Sudeten Ringlet *Erebia sudetica*

RANGE Europe.

E. sudetica sudetica Staudinger 1861 TL: Silesian Mts.

DISTRIBUTION Czech Republic: Mt. Praded [=Mt. Altvater]. Poland: Silesian Mts. Slovakia and Poland: Tatra Mts. Romania: Carpathian Mts., including Retezat Mts. and Radna Mts. 600-1200m.

DESCRIPTION AND VARIATION Ups and uns reddish, black-pupilled pd spots in a very regular series, forming continuous bands broken only by veins. (cf. *E. melampus*).

FLIGHT-PERIOD Univoltine. July/August.

E. sudetica liorana de Lesse 1947 TL: Cantal, C France.

DISTRIBUTION France: Monts du Cantal (Puy Mary; Le Lioran; Plomb du Cantal): E Isère; C Savoie. Switzerland: Bernese Alps (Grindelwald): very local. 1200-2000m.

DESCRIPTION AND VARIATION Resembles nominate form, but pd markings reduced: uph pd black-pupilled, reddish spots slightly smaller, usually restricted to s2-5.

FLIGHT-PERIOD Univoltine. Late June/mid August according to altitude.

HABITAT Damp, herb-rich meadows with long grasses, sheltered by woodland.

LIFE-HISTORY LHP *Anthoxanthum odoratum*.

Scotch Argus *Erebia aethiops*

RANGE C and E Europe, N Turkey, Transcaucasus, Urals, Altai, W Siberia.

E. aethiops Esper 1777 TL: S Germany.

DISTRIBUTION Scotland. NW England: very local. France: Massif Central; Cévennes; central E regions (sporadic in Allier, Cher, Nièvre, E Provence and Lorraine). Belgium to Latvia (very local), Switzerland, Balkans and N Greece (Rhodopi Mts.). N Italy: Apuane Alps; Ligurian Alps through Cottian Alps and main Alpine chain. Absent from N Germany and Fennoscandia. 0-2000m, generally 300-1500m.

DESCRIPTION Both sexes: upf reddish pd band usually constricted in s3. Male unh gc dark reddish-brown; basal area slightly paler, somewhat yellowish-brown; pd band silvery-grey, well defined, enclosing small white spots, sometimes narrowly ringed black, in s2-4: female unh gc brownish or yellowish-brown; basal and pd areas variable; pd band yellowish-buff in combination with basal area of similar but darker tone, or, pd band silvery-grey or violet-grey in combination with basal area of similar but darker tone; other markings as for male but better developed.

VARIATION Regionally/locally variable in size and development of pd markings. Often larger in southern range. In S Scotland, f. *caledonia* Verity: smaller; wings narrower; upf pd band narrower, often broken in s3, lacking ocellus in s3; unh markings often less distinct. On Monte Baldo, upf red pd band often reduced to narrow rings enclosing greatly reduced subapical ocelli; uph pd band and ocelli similarly reduced.

FLIGHT-PERIOD Univoltine. Late July/mid September.

HABITAT Sparsely wooded heathland; moorland; grassy marshland; open grassy, flowery woodland clearings and margins. On acidic and calcareous soils.

LIFE-HISTORY LHPs *Molinia caerulea*; *Sesleria caerulea*; *Carex sempervirens*; *Bromus erectus*; *Brachypodium pinnatum*; *Calamagrostis epigejos*; *Dactylis glomerata*; *Festuca ovina*; *Luzula nivea*; *Poa trivialis*; *Anthoxanthum odoratum*; *Briza media*.

Blind Ringlet

Sudeten Ringlet

Scotch Argus

BLIND RINGLET

SUDETEN RINGLET

SCOTCH ARGUS

♂ with sex-brand' pd band constricted in s3

Fringes weakly chequered

♂

♀

♀

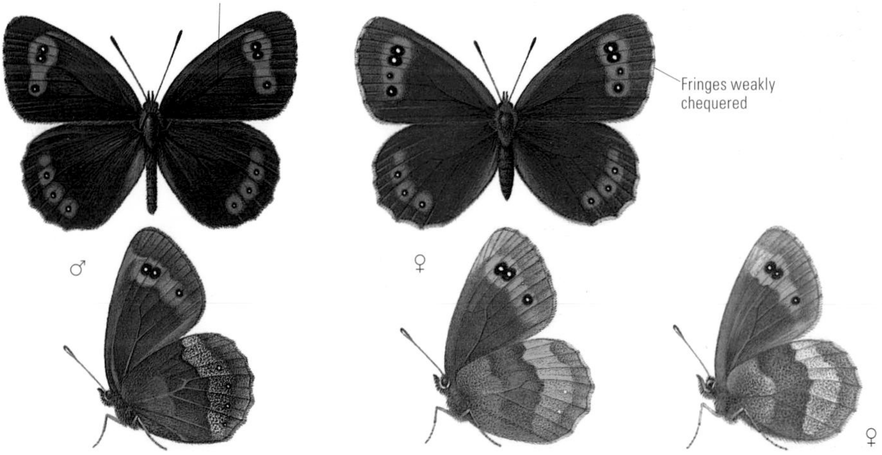

colour variant

de Prunner's Ringlet *Erebia triaria*

RANGE Europe.
E. triaria de Prunner 1798 TL: Exilles, Piedmont.
DISTRIBUTION N Portugal: Serra de Gerez. Spain: S. Madrona; Montes de Toledo; S. de Gredos; S. Guadarrama; Montes Universales; S. de la Demanda; S. de Cebollera; Cantabrian Mts.; W Pyrenees (Ordessa: very local). Andorra. France: Pyrenees; Alpes-Maritimes to Vaucluse, Isère and Savoie. Italy: Ligurian Alps through Cottian Alps to Trentino-Alto Adige. S and E Switzerland. S Austria. W Slovenia (Julian Alps). S Bosnia-Herzegovina. S Serbia. Albania. 400-2500m.
DESCRIPTION AND VARIATION Upf ocellus in s6 (nearly always present) almost co-linear with ocelli in s4 and s5; unh very dark, obscure irroration giving a slightly roughened appearance (cf. *E. meolans*). Upf pd band variable in colour and shape; usually enclosing 5 ocelli, but those in s3 and s6 sometimes reduced to black points, rarely absent. In Spain, *hispanica* Gumppenberg: regionally variable: smaller; ups pd bands averagely paler, tending to yellow-orange; upf pd band broader near apex – more tapered towards v2 relative to nominate form; unf pd reddish, darker than upf pd band: female ups gc paler brown.
FLIGHT-PERIOD Univoltine. Mid April/mid July according to altitude and season.
HABITAT Bushy and grassy woodland clearings in rocky places: in Spain, often small clearings in light pinewoods on limestone.
LIFE-HISTORY LHPs *Festuca ovina*; *Poa pratensis*; *P. alpina*; *Stipa pennata*.

Lapland Ringlet *Erebia embla*

RANGE NE Europe, NW Russia, Urals, Siberia, N and E Altai, Transbaikal, Yakutia, Mongolia, Kamchatka, Sakhalin, N Korea.
E. embla Thunberg 1791 TL: Västerbotton, Sweden.
DISTRIBUTION S and N Norway: Hedmark; Finnmark. Sweden: Dalarne to Torne Lappmark. Finland. NE Latvia: very local: last recorded in 1985. 100-400m.
FLIGHT-PERIOD Univoltine. Mid June/July according to season.
HABITAT Marshes with areas of permanent water, tussock grasses, sedge and willow, often in open pine or birch woodland.
LIFE-HISTORY LHPs: (?)*Carex* sp.; (?)*Deschampsia* sp. Hibernation stage unconfirmed.

Arctic Ringlet *Erebia disa*

RANGE Circumpolar. Arctic Europe, Kola, Yamal and Chukot Peninsulas, Polar and Subpolar Urals, N and W Siberia, Transbaikal, Mongolia, Yakutia, Magdan, Arctic N America.
E. disa Thunberg 1791 TL: Lapland.
DISTRIBUTION Fennoscandia from 65°N to Finnmark. 300-500m.
FLIGHT-PERIOD Univoltine. Early June/late July according to season and latitude.
HABITAT Bogs or marshes with drier, grassy areas or heaths, usually associated with scrub or small trees and small areas of permanent water.
LIFE-HISTORY Larval development occupies two seasonal cycles.

de Prunner's Ringlet

Lapland Ringlet

Arctic Ringlet

DE PRUNNER'S RINGLET

Red band tapers strongly towards anal angle

and ♀ upf
d unf subapical
elli almost
-linerar pd band
rongly tapered
wards inner
argin

♂ unh very dark, mottled with roughened appearance

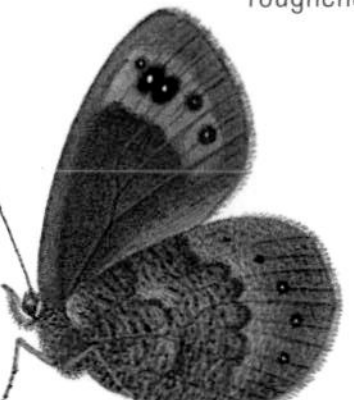

E. t. triaria ***E. t. hispanica***

LAPLAND RINGLET

♂ and ♀ ups and uns pattern of markings distinctive

ARCTIC RINGLET

♂ and ♀ ups and uns pattern of markings distinctive

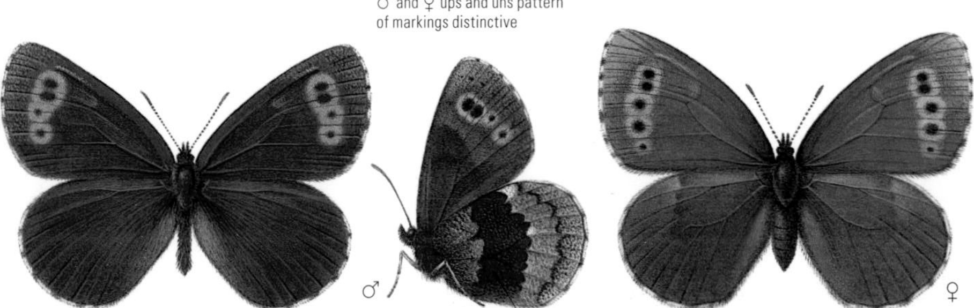

♂ and ♀ uph lacking ocelli

♂ and ♀ uph submarginal, pd and discal bands well delineated

Woodland Ringlet *Erebia medusa*

RANGE Europe, N Turkey, Transcaucasus, S Siberia, Mongolia, N China.

E. medusa Denis and Schiffermüller 1775 TL: Vienna.

DISTRIBUTION C and E France (Cher and Allier to Ardennes and Savoie) through S Belgium (Ardennes), N Italy (including Ligurian Alps) to N Germany (S of Hannover) N Poland, S Balkans, N Greece (S to Mt. Olympus and C Pindos Mts.) and European Turkey: also reported from Alpes-de-Haute-Provence. Widespread and locally common in SE range, sporadic elsewhere. 300-2300m.

DESCRIPTION Uns of antennal club-tip buff (cf. *E. oeme*).

VARIATION Geographical and altitudinal clines are evident in regard to size and wing-markings. In SE Europe, *psodea* Hübner [syn: *euphrasia* Frühstorfer; *botevi* Slaby]: larger; ups and uns yellow-orange pd spots brighter, larger, often confluent, especially in female; ocelli larger: intermediate forms occur in NW Balkans. Above about 1800m in E Central Alps, f. *hippomedusa* Ochsenheimer: small; all markings greatly reduced: transitional to nominate form at intermediate altitudes.

FLIGHT-PERIOD Univoltine. Early May/early August according to locality and altitude.

HABITAT Diverse. Damp, humid, grassy, flowery clearings in deciduous, coniferous or mixed woodland, often with an abundance of ferns; open grassy, flowery, woodland margins in dry or damp conditions; grassy slopes or gullies above treeline. On calcareous or non-calcareous soils.

LIFE-HISTORY LHPs include *Festuca ovina*; *F. rubra*; *Bromus erectus*; *Milium effusum*. At higher altitudes, larval development occupies two seasonal cycles. In captive rearing from ovum, life-cycle completed without diapause in photo-period of S England.

Arctic Woodland Ringlet *Erebia polaris*

RANGE Arctic Norway and Finland, Urals, N Siberia, Yakutia.

E. polaris Staudinger 1871 TL: Lapland.

DISTRIBUTION Arctic Norway and N Finland: mainly coastal districts from 69°N to Arctic Sea. 0-400m: generally below 200m.

DESCRIPTION Resembles *E. medusa*: ocelli smaller; unh with pale pd band, often obscure, sometimes absent.

FLIGHT-PERIOD Univoltine. Late June/late July according to season.

HABITAT Open, damp meadows; coastal river valleys; grassy clearings in light birch scrub.

LIFE-HISTORY Captive larvae accept *Festuca ovina*. In captive rearing from ovum, life-cycle completed without diapause in photo-period of S England. Hibernation stage unconfirmed.

NOTE Regarded as a form/ssp. of *E. medusa* by some authors.

Almond-eyed Ringlet *Erebia alberganus*

RANGE N Spain (Cantabrian Mts.), Central European Alps, Peninsular Italy, Bulgaria.

E. alberganus alberganus de Prunner 1798 TL: Piedmont. syn: *ceto* Hübner 1804.

DISTRIBUTION Spain: Cantabrian Mts. Main Alpine chain from Alpes-Maritimes through Isère, Cottian Alps, S and SE Switzerland (Pennine Alps, S Bernese Alps, Lepontine Alps, Upper and Lower Engadine) to Dolomites and Hohe Tauern. Peninsular Italy: E Ligurian Alps; Abruzzi. Republic of Macedonia: Korab Pl. 900-2200m.

VARIATION At high altitudes in E Central Alps, f. *caradjae* Caflisch: small; markings greatly reduced but lanceolate character of pd spots retained (cf. *E. medusa* f. *hippomedusa*). In W Alps, often large with well-developed markings (f. *tyrsus* Fruhstorfer). Intermediate forms are locally common.

FLIGHT-PERIOD Univoltine. Mid June/late August.

HABITAT Warm, flowery meadows often sheltered by woodland; grassy slopes, often south-facing.

LIFE-HISTORY LHPs *Festuca ovina*; *Anthoxanthum odoratum*.

E. alberganus phorcys Freyer 1836 TL: Bulgaria.

DISTRIBUTION Bulgaria: Stara Pl. 1000-2000m.

DESCRIPTION Resembles *E. a. alberganus*. All markings prominent; unh yellow pd lanceolate spots extended proximally; ocelli ringed orange.

FLIGHT-PERIOD Univoltine. July.

HABITAT Grassy slopes, often west-facing.

Woodland Ringlet

Arctic Woodland Ringlet

Almond-eyed Ringlet

WOODLAND RINGLET

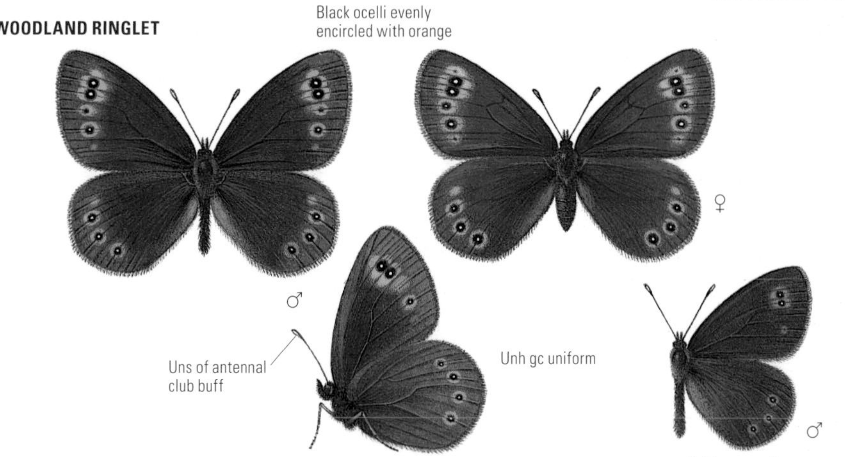

ARCTIC WOODLAND RINGLET

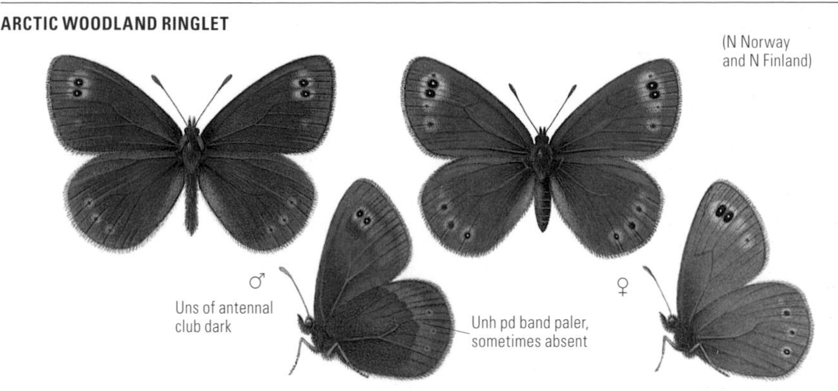

ALMOND-EYED RINGLET

♂ and ♀ usps and uns shape of pd spots distinctive

Sooty Ringlet *Erebia pluto*

RANGE Central European Alps, Peninsular Italy (C Apennines). A variable species, displaying a complex array of local, geographical and transitional forms. Populations whose wing-characters are sensibly constant over a substantial part of the range are described below.

E. pluto pluto de Prunner 1798 TL: Val Varodisiana, Piedmont.

DISTRIBUTION France and NW Italy: Alpes-Maritimes, through Basses and Hautes Alpes, Cottian Alps to Graian Alps. 1900-3000m.

DESCRIPTION Male ups gc uniform silky jet black; upf pd area with trace of dark brownish suffusion, otherwise unmarked: female ups gc variable, sometimes dark grey-yellow brown (khaki), generally with pale brownish pd spots, sometimes fused into a band on fw.

VARIATION In C Apennines (Gran Sasso), f. *belzebub* Costa: resembles nominate form: smallest race of the species: fw narrower; female unf copper-coloured pd area brighter.

FLIGHT-PERIOD Univoltine. Late June/late August according to altitude.

HABITAT Steep limestone screes; moraines.

BEHAVIOUR Activity of both sexes confined largely to rocky terrain which is often devoid of vegetation. Males sometimes drink from damp soil-patches. Adults may rest on rocks for prolonged periods with open wings in cool, overcast conditions.

E. pluto f. *alecto* Hübner 1804 TL: Lermoos [Austria].

DISTRIBUTION W Tirol to Kitzbühl Alps, Hohe Tauern, Ortler Alps, Dolomites, Carnic and Julian Alps. Subspecific characters best represented and reputedly most stable in Allgäuer, Lechtaler, Karwendel and Öetztaler Alps. 1900-2700m.

DESCRIPTION Male ups gc uniform silky dark brown or black; white-pupilled ocelli in s4 and s5 upf and s2-4 uph; unf pd area suffused reddish (cf. nominate form and f. *nicholli* (below). Female uph ocelli variable.

VARIATION In Ortler Alps, f. *velocissima* Frühstorfer: all markings generally better developed: in both sexes, ups pd band broad though usually indistinct; subapical ocelli usually conspicuous, but variable, sometimes absent: transitional to f. oreas (below) in E Switzerland. In Julian Alps, male unf red pd band more distinct (f. *triglavensis* Schawerda). In Dolomites, f. *dolomitana* Schawerda: extremely variable, locally transitional to nominate form or f. *nicholli* (below).

FLIGHT-PERIOD, HABITAT AND BEHAVIOUR As for nominate form.

E. pluto f. *nicholli* Oberthür 1896 TL: Campiglio, Brenta Alps.

DISTRIBUTION NE Italy: Brenta Alps; Monte Baldo. Above 2000m.

DESCRIPTION AND VARIATION Male ups and uns gc silky dark brown or black; upf white-pupilled ocelli in s2-5, of equal size in s4 and s5, smaller but of equal size in s2 and s3 and displaced slightly distad; uph ocelli in s2-4 of equal size: ups ocellular pattern repeated on uns: female ups gc dark brown; ocelli enclosed by narrow, obscure, reddish pd bands; unf discal area reddish-brown; unh brown, veins conspicuously darker. On Monte Baldo, f. *burmanni* Wolfsberger: markings slightly better developed and less variable.

FLIGHT-PERIOD AND HABITAT As for nominate form.

E. pluto f. *oreas* Warren 1933 TL: Chamonix, Savoie.
syn: *glacialis* Esper 1804 (invalid homonym).

DISTRIBUTION France: Haute Savoie. S and E Switzerland and N Italy: Pennine Alps through Lepontine Alps to E Engadine; Bernese Oberland to Glarner Alps and Alpstein. Austria: S and E Öetztaler Alps. 1800-3000m.

DESCRIPTION Male ups gc dark silky brown; upf with dark reddish pd band, variable, sometimes vestigial; uph sometimes with obscure reddish pd marks; unf reddish pd band with sharp proximal border, discal and basal areas suffused darker red.

VARIATION In E Engadine, transitional to f. *velocissima*. In Bernese Oberland, f. *anteborus* Frühstorfer: transitional to nominate form but variable.

FLIGHT-PERIOD, HABITAT AND BEHAVIOUR As for nominate form.

LIFE-HISTORY LHPs *Festuca quadriflora*; *F. alpina*; *Poa minor*. Ova usually laid on rocks or dead, woody plant stems, sometimes at an appreciable distance from nearest LHPs. Larvae may be found in grassy areas adjacent to screes. Larval development occupies two seasonal cycles.

Sooty Ringlet

SOOTY RINGLET

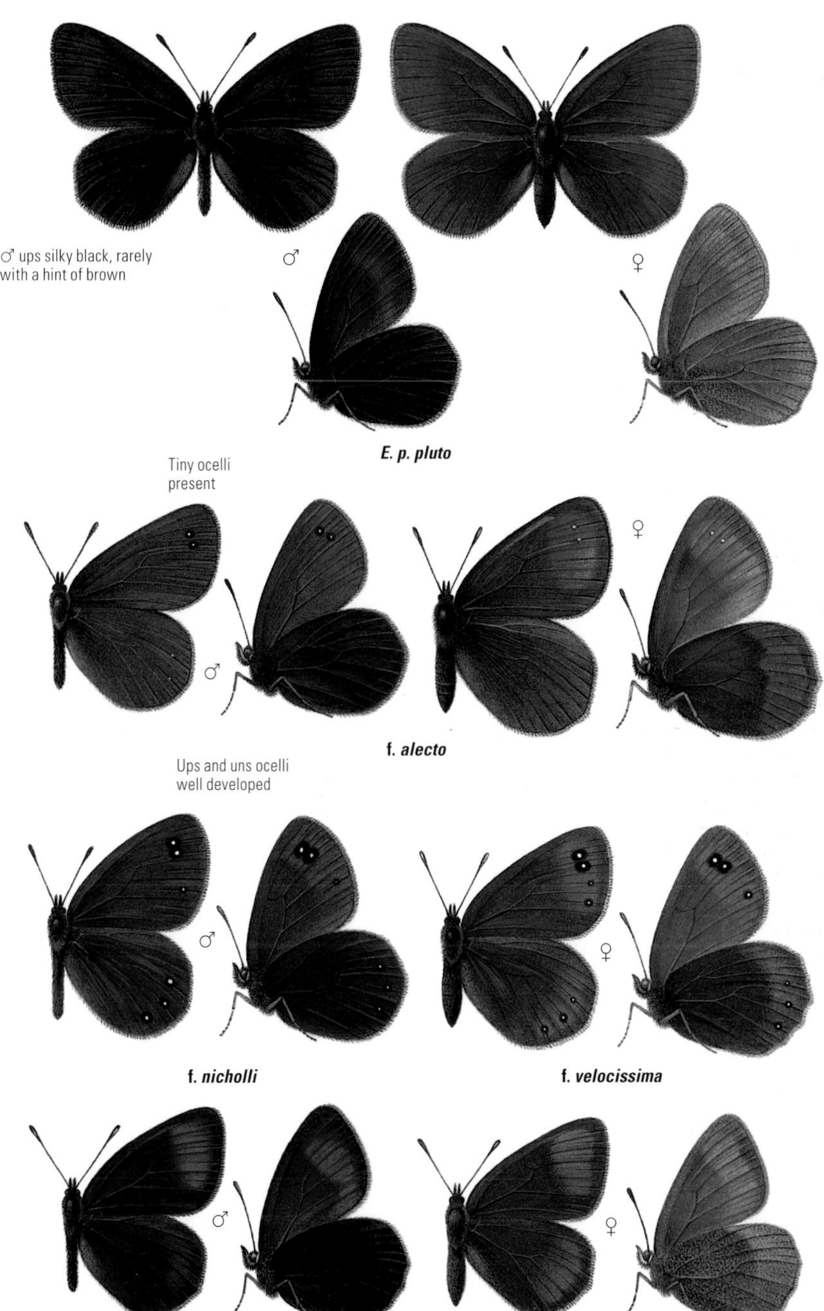

E. p. pluto

f. ***alecto***

f. ***nicholli***

f. ***velocissima***

f. ***oreas***

Silky Ringlet *Erebia gorge*

RANGE S Europe.

In central Alps, complexity of variation and distribution parallels closely that of *E. pluto* with which it shares many habitats. The development of pd bands and ocelli follows roughly the same geographical pattern – the least marked forms occurring in the Apeninnes and SW Alps, whilst maximum development is achieved in SE Switzerland and associated Italian massifs. The least stable populations of both species seem to occur in the Dolomites. The main forms, described below, often show transitional character where distributions overlap. Each form is liable to appear in almost any population as an occasional variant. Some colonies appear to be unstable, producing a wide variety of forms in roughly equal proportions.

E. gorge gorge Hübner 1804 TL: Switzerland and Tyrol.

DISTRIBUTION Alps of Savoie through Alps of S and C Switzerland and N Italy (except Ober Engadine, Bernina and Ortler Alps) to Bavarian and Austrian Alps: Dolomites; Julian Alps; Velebit Pl; Dinaric Alps; Rudoka Pl.; Pirin Mts.; Rila Mts.; Carpathian Mts.; Apunseni Mts.; Tatra Mts. 1800-3000m.

DESCRIPTION Male upf sex-brand inconspicuous; reddish pd band with distinct silky appearance; subapical twin ocelli white-pupilled, additional ocelli small when present; unh variegated dark grey/greyish-brown and light grey. Both sexes: hw outer margin irregular, usually with conspicuous 'bump' at v4 – a useful diagnostic character.

VARIATION Many populations of E Europe (Karawanken Alps, S Bosnia-Herzegovina, S Serbia and Carpathian Mts.) differ little from nominate form or appear transitional to f. *erynis* Esper (below): within this complex, upf pd band often extends to cell in s4 and s5 (*karwendeli* Zusanek; *hercegovinensis* Rebel; *vagana* Lorkovic; *rudkowskyi* Bang-Haas; *fredericikoenigi* Varga). At south-eastern limit of European range (Bulgaria), *pirinica* Buresch: larger, otherwise indistinguishable from nominate form.

FLIGHT-PERIOD Univoltine. Late June/late August according to altitude.

HABITAT Limestone screes; moraines.

LIFE-HISTORY LHPs *Poa minor*; *P. alpina*; *Sesleria varia*; *Festuca alpina*. Larval development occupies two seasonal cycles.

E. gorge f. *ramondi* Oberthür 1909 TL: Gavarnie, Hautes-Pyrénées.

DISTRIBUTION Spain: Cantabrian Mts.; Spain and France: Pyrenees: Ordessa and Pic du Midi d'Ossau to Pic du Midi de Bigorre and Mont Canigou. Above 1800m.

DESCRIPTION Resembles nominate form, but has 4 or 5 ocelli uph and unh. Specimens with additional ocellus in s6 upf resembles f. *triopes* Speyer (below). In Cantabrian Mts., often large (f. *gigantea* Oberthür).

FLIGHT-PERIOD AND HABITAT As for nominate form.

E. gorge f. *triopes* Speyer 1865 TL: Bernina Pass.

DISTRIBUTION Ober Engadine; Bernina Alps; Ortler Alps; Adamello Alps; Mte. Baldo. 1600-3000m. Reported as an occasional variant in Tatra Mts.

DESCRIPTION Resembles f. *ramondi*: all ocelli better developed: upf ocelli in s4-6 of equal size, contiguous and co-linear; ocelli in s2 and s3 smaller.

FLIGHT-PERIOD AND HABITAT As for nominate form.

E. gorge f. *erynis* Esper 1805 TL: Chamonix, Haute-Savoie.

DISTRIBUTION SE France and NW Italy: Basses and Hautes-Alpes to Savoie, Graian and Pennine Alps. Above 1900m. From Alpes-Maritimes to Savoie, Pennine and W Bernese Alps, an increasing proportion of f. *erynis* in each population is replaced by forms resembling f. *gorge*, the distinctive characters of which also develop progressively within same geographical transition.

DESCRIPTION Resembles f. *gorge*, but lacking ocelli.

VARIATION In Apuane Alps and C Apennines (Monti Sibillini; Abruzzi), f. *carboncina* Verity: smaller; gc darker; pd bands narrower; ocelli very small, often absent.

FLIGHT-PERIOD AND HABITAT As for nominate form.

E. gorge albanica Rebel 1917 TL: Gropa Strelit, Albania.

DISTRIBUTION S Albania: Tomor Mts. (?)S Serbia: Strelizt (SE Montenegro).

DESCRIPTION Male upf pd band narrow, short, somewhat diffuse; small white-pupilled ocelli only in s4 and s5, similar on unf; uph uniform black, unmarked; unh unicolorous dark brown with obscure, greyish antemarginal band.

False Mnestra Ringlet *Erebia aethiopella*

RANGE France, Italy.

E. aethiopella Hoffmannsegg 1806 TL: Piedmont [NW Italy].

syn: *gorgophone* Bellier 1863.

DISTRIBUTION Alps of SE France and NW Italy: Maritimes Alps to Hautes-Alpes and Cottian Alps: very local. 1800-2400m.

DESCRIPTION Male upf sex-brand conspicuous, extending from s1a-s4; pd band, extending to cell-end, usually with small white-pupilled ocelli in s4 and s5; uph pd band lacking ocelli (cf. *E. mnestra*).

FLIGHT-PERIOD Univoltine. Mid July/late August.

HABITAT Open, grassy slopes and valleys.

LIFE-HISTORY LHP *Festuca paniculata*: oviposition and post-hibernation larval feeding observed: local occurrence of butterfly and LHP appear highly correlated.

Silky Ringlet

False Mnestra Ringlet

SILKY RINGLET

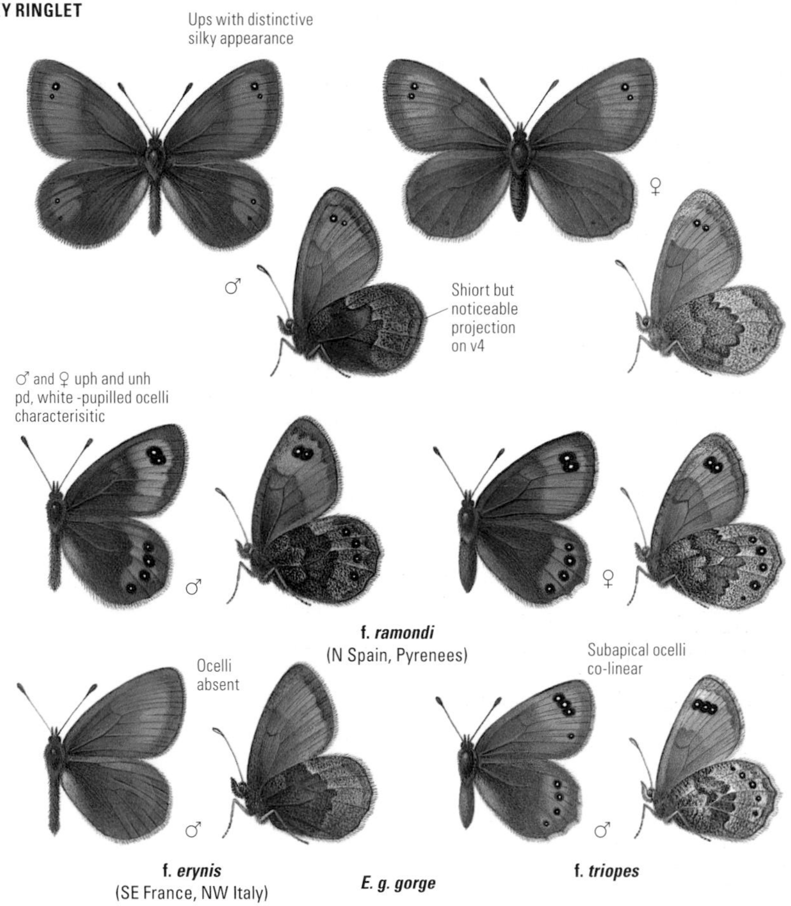

Ups with distinctive silky appearance
♂
♀
Shiort but noticeable projection on v4
♂ and ♀ uph and unh pd, white -pupilled ocelli characterisitic
♂
♀
f. ramondi
(N Spain, Pyrenees)
Ocelli absent
Subapical ocelli co-linear
♂
♂
f. erynis
(SE France, NW Italy)
E. g. gorge
f. triopes

FALSE MNESTRA RINGLET

Upf ♂ sex-brand conspicuous
Upf pd band projecting towards towards cell-end
Restricted to SE France, NW Italy
Uph pd band tapering toward inner margin; lackong ocelli
♂
♀

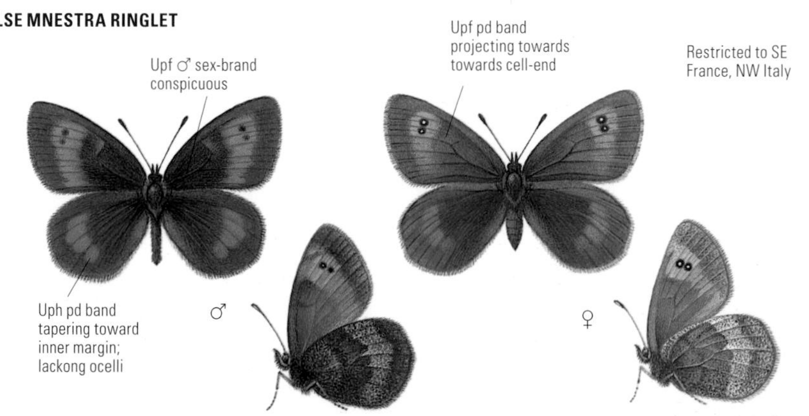

Nicholl's Ringlet *Erebia rhodopensis*

RANGE SE Europe.
E. rhodopensis Nicholl 1900 TL: Rila Mts., Bulgaria.
DISTRIBUTION Republic of Macedonia: Sar Pl. Bulgaria: Stara Pl.; Rila Mts.; Pirin Mts.; Rhodopi Mts. Greece: Grammos Mt. Very local. 1800-2600m.
DESCRIPTION AND VARIATION Resembles *E. aethiopella*: upf and unf white-pupilled subapical ocelli better developed; uph and unh pd ocelli with small white pupils. On Sar Pl., f. *sharsta* Higgins: unh brighter, gc greyish with white irroration.
FLIGHT-PERIOD Univoltine. July/August.
HABITAT Open grassy slopes, almost devoid of shrubs or trees.
LIFE-HISTORY LHP unknown: captive larvae accept *Poa* sp. in captivity. Hibernation stage unconfirmed.

Mnestra's Ringlet *Erebia mnestra*

RANGE Central European Alps.
E. mnestra Hübner 1804 TL: Swiss Alps.
DISTRIBUTION Alps of France (Isère; Hautes-Alpes; Savoie; Haute-Savoie), Italy (very local in Cottian Alps; Ortler Mts.; Adamello Mts.), S and SE Switerland (Valais to Engadine), Germany (Allgäuer Alps) and Austria (Oetztal Alps; Salzburg Alps; Karwendal Mts.). (?)High Tatra Mts. Generally very local, often scarce. 1500-2600m.
DESCRIPTION Male upf sex-brand inconspicuous; pd band extending to cell-end in s4 and s5; subapical ocelli absent or sometimes represented by two, small black points; uph pd band broken by veins, usually restricted to s3-5, lacking ocelli; unf brown marginal border well defined, discal and basal areas uniformly reddish, unmarked; unh uniformly brown, rarely with obscure pale pd band. (cf. *E. aethiopella*).
FLIGHT-PERIOD Univoltine. Early July/mid August.
HABITAT Steep slopes, dominated by grasses, including taller and coarser species.
LIFE-HISTORY LHPs *Festuca*; *Sesleria varia*. In some localities, larval development occupies two seasonal cycles.

Gavarnie Ringlet *Erebia gorgone*

RANGE Pyrenees.
E. gorgone Boisduval 1833 TL: Pyrenees.
DISTRIBUTION High Pyrenees. Spain: Balneario de Panticosa; Port de Beñasque; Port de la Picada; Tuc de Cabriols; Pic de l'Homme; Pto. de la Bonaigua. Andorra: Port d'Envalira (2450m). France: Col d'Aubisque; Cauterets; Cirque de Gavarnie; Col du Tourmalet. 1500-2450m.
DESCRIPTION Male ups gc dark brown; pd bands dark red, broken by dark veins; upf sex-brand in s1a-5 conspicuous: female unh pale veins conspicuous. (cf. *E. gorge* and *E. pronoe*).
FLIGHT-PERIOD Univoltine. Mid July/late August.
HABITAT Grassy places amongst rocks or small areas of scree; steep slopes, dominated by grasses including some taller species.

Spring Ringlet *Erebia epistygne*

RANGE Spain, France.
E. epistygne Hübner 1824 TL: not stated [Provence]
DISTRIBUTION Spain: Montes Universales (La Losilla; Calomarde; Moscardon; Frias de Albarracin; Griegos; Bronchales); Serrania de Cuenca (Castillia); S. de Javalambre; S. de Calderesos (Cubillejo de la Sierra; La Yunta); S. de Guadalajara (Cueva de la Hoz; Aguilar de Anguita; Guijo); Montseny Mts. 1000-1550m. Reports from S. de Moncayo (2300m: reported flight-period July) and C Pyrenees require confirmation. France: SW Cevennes; Provence (widespread but local). 450-1500m.
VARIATION In Spain, f. *viriathus* Sheldon: unh slightly greyer; marked individual/local variation of wing-characters overlaps that of nominate form.
FLIGHT-PERIOD Univoltine. Late March/late May according to season.
HABITAT Grassy and rocky clearings in open woodland. Limestone habitats of Montes Universales distinctive: dry, often flattish clearings, strewn with small rocks, in sparse pinewoods, with short grasses and sparse, low-growing shrubs.
LIFE-HISTORY LHP *Festuca ovina*. In captivity, life-cycle from ovum is completed without diapause in extended photoperiod of S England. Hibernation stage unconfirmed.

Nicholl's Ringlet

Mnestra's Ringlet

Gavarnie Ringlet

Spring Ringlet

NICHOLL'S RINGLET

♂ and ♀ ups ocelli usually present

Restricted to S Balkans

♂

♀

MNESTRA'S RINGLET

♂ upf subapical ocelli usually absent

Upf pd band projecting towards cell-end; uph pd band usually confined to s3-5

Sex-brand inconspicuous

Uph pd band reduced

♂

♀

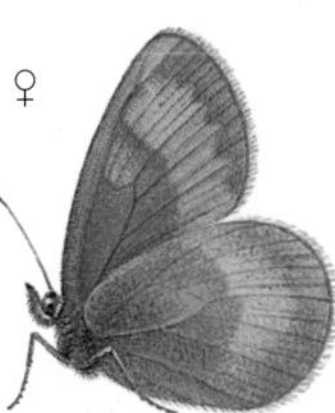

GAVARNIE RINGLET

♂ upf sex-brand conspicuous

Restricted to Pyrenees

♂

♀

SPRING RINGLET

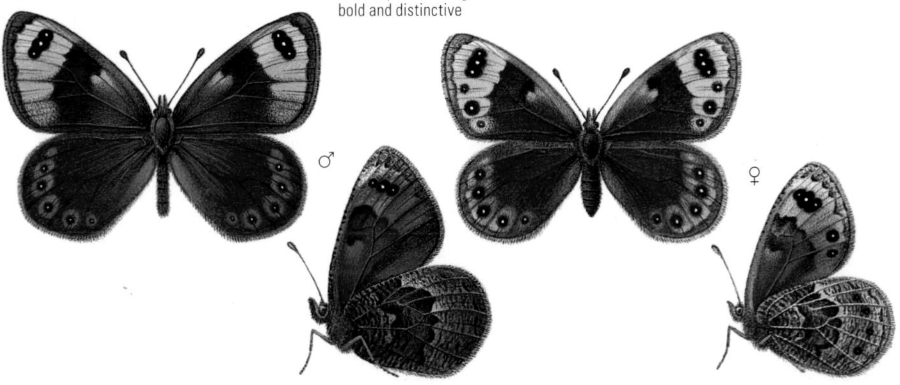

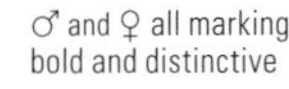

♂ and ♀ all markings bold and distinctive

♂

♀

The following six species comprise a closely related group for which external characters are often poorly differentiated and sometimes insufficient for reliable field identification. As far as is known, no two species of the group occupy the same habitats, and in instances of geographical overlap in distribution, altitudinal separation is usually clearly apparent. Distinctive characters in male genitalia allow ready separation. For *E. cassioides*, *E. hispania* and *E. ottomana*, at least, pupal colouring and shape are appreciably different for males and females: a difference in larval coloration is less obvious and generally more variable, but female larvae are noticeably greener.

Swiss Brassy Ringlet *Erebia tyndarus*

RANGE Central European Alps.

E. tyndarus Esper 1781 TL: Scheidegg, Switzerland.

DISTRIBUTION Pennine Alps (Col Ferret) and Berner Alps through Engadine, Ortler Alps, Allgäuer Alps to Brenner. 1200-2700m. Widespread and common. Reported occurrence in Hautes-Alpes (Col d'Izoard) requires confirmation.

DESCRIPTION AND VARIATION Male ups dark brown; upf with strong, brassy or greenish reflections, most apparent in fresh specimens; upf apex slightly rounded; subapical fulvous-red patch extending to cell in s4 and s5, usually enclosing twin, white-pupilled ocelli; uph sometimes with small, fulvous-red pd marks, lacking ocelli; unh grey gc and brown striae variable.

FLIGHT-PERIOD Univoltine. Generally early July/late August in prolonged emergence, sometimes extending to early October according to season and locality.

HABITAT Open, grassy clearings in pinewoods at lowest altitudes; grassy, stony and rocky areas above treeline.

LIFE-HISTORY LHPs include *Nardus stricta*; *Festuca ovina*.

Common Brassy Ringlet *Erebia cassioides*

RANGE N Spain, southern C Europe, S Balkans.

E. cassioides Hohenwarth 1793 TL: Heilegenblut, Austria.

DISTRIBUTION Spain: Cantabrian Mts.; Pyrenees. France: Pyrenees; Massif Central (Mont Dore; Mont Aigoual). Alps of France (Alpes-Maritimes to Isère and Haute-Savoie), NW Italy and W Switzerland (W Pennine Alps; Bernese Oberland to Faulhorn and Grindelwald). Peninsular and NE Italy: Apuane Alps; C Apennines; Monte Pollino; Dolomites. Austria: Hohe Tauern; Niedere Tauern. Romania: Retezat Mts. Albania. Republic of Macedonia: Sar Pl.; Osogovske Pl.; Placenska Pl. Bulgaria: Stara Pl.; Rila Mts.; Pirin Mts. 1600-2600m. Not reported from Greece.

DESCRIPTION Resembles *E. tyndarus*: male upf outer margin less convex; subapical fulvous-red patch usually not extending to cell or v3; twin, white-pupilled ocelli generally larger, contiguous; uph reddish pd marks and ocelli better developed. In Pyrenees, Massif Central and peninsular Italy, *arvernensis* Oberthür: resembles nominate form closely: upf twin subapical ocelli larger, white pupils conspicuous, especially in female, additional one or two ocelli or black points sometimes present in s2-4: female unh gc usually decidedly yellowish.

VARIATION Whilst many forms have been described, minor regional differences in size, gc and development of pd markings are largely obscured by individual and local variation.

FLIGHT-PERIOD Univoltine. Late June/early September according to locality.

HABITAT Grass-covered slopes; grassy places amongst rocks or screes.

LIFE-HISTORY LHPs include *Festuca ovina*. Differences in coloration are sufficient for sexual differentiation in larval and pupal stages.

Spanish Brassy Ringlet *Erebia hispania*

RANGE Spain (Pyrenees and Sierra Nevada), France (Pyrenees), Andorra.

E. hispania Butler 1868 TL: Spain [Sierra Nevada].

DISTRIBUTION Spain: Sierra Nevada 1800-2900m. Spain and France: W and C Pyrenees (Pto. de Portalet to Col du Tormalet and Pto. de Viella); E Pyrenees (Andorra to Mont Canigou). 1650-2300m

DESCRIPTION AND VARIATION Ups gc medium brown; all markings generally well developed, especially upf yellow-orange subapical patch and enclosed twin, white-pupilled ocelli (cf. *E. cassioides*). In Pyrenees, f. *rondoui* Oberthür: smaller; fw outer margin less rounded; ups markings better developed, especially in E Pyrenees (f. *goya* Frühstorfer).

FLIGHT-PERIOD Univoltine. In Sierra Nevada, mid June/late August according to season and altitude: in Pyrenees, early July/mid August.

HABITAT Open, grassy and rocky slopes: on calcareous and non-calcareous soils.

LIFE-HISTORY LHPs include *Festuca ovina*. Differences in coloration are sufficient for sexual differentiation in larval and pupal stages.

Swiss Brassy Ringlet

Common Brassy Ringlet

SWISS BRASSY RINGLET

♂ upf pd band
extending to s2 or 1b
Restricted
to C Alps
♂
♀
Unh greyish-brown,
variable

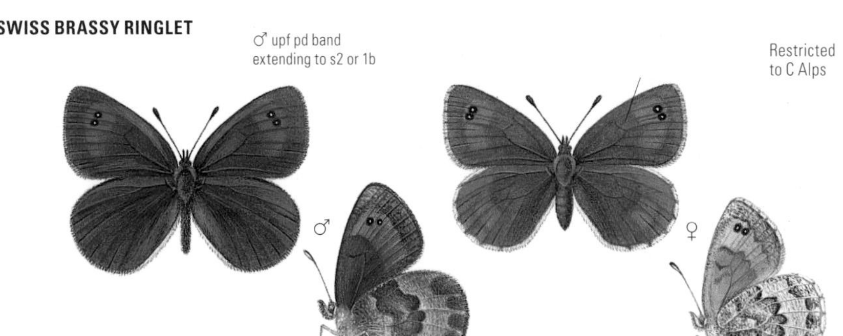

COMMON BRASSY RINGLET

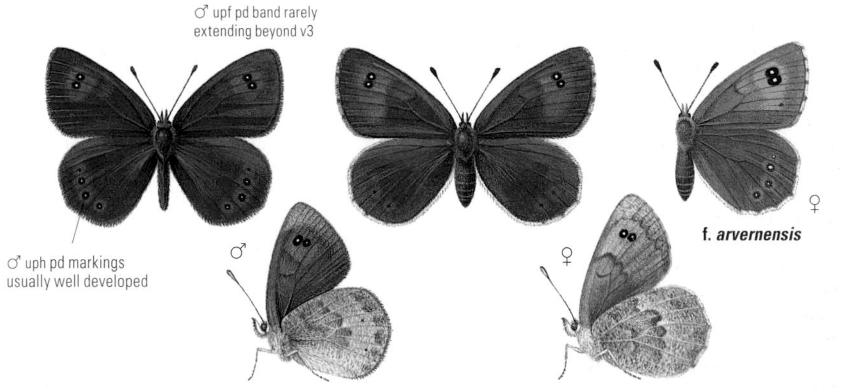

♂ upf pd band rarely
extending beyond v3
♀
f. *arvernensis*
♂ uph pd markings
usually well developed
♂
♀

SPANISH BRASSY RINGLET

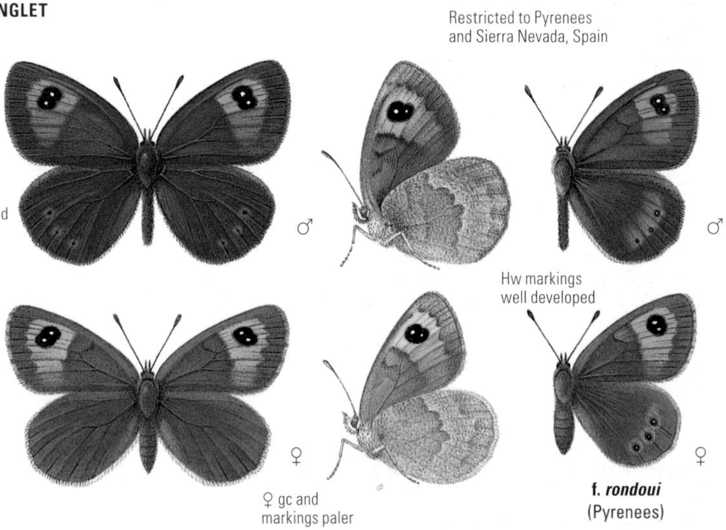

Restricted to Pyrenees
and Sierra Nevada, Spain
Upf pd band bright
yellow-orange,
tapering strongly
towards inner margin
Hw ocelli reduced
or absent
♂
♂
Hw markings
well developed
♀
♀
♀ gc and
markings paler
f. *rondoui*
(Pyrenees)

Spanish Brassy Ringlet

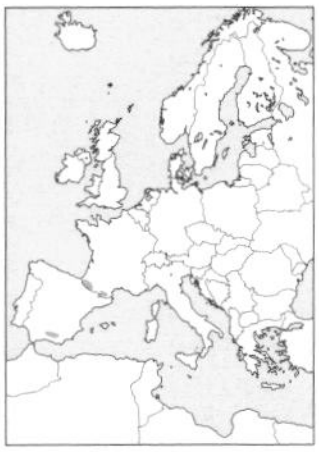

De Lesse's Brassy Ringlet *Erebia nivalis*

RANGE E Central European Alps.
E. nivalis Lorkovic and de Lesse 1954 TL: Gross Glockner.
DISTRIBUTION Switzerland: very restricted: Faulhorn; Grindelwald. 2250-2600m. NE Italy: Atesine Alps (Val di Vizze 2300-2450m). Austria: E of Öetztal: Brenner Pass; Stubaier Alps; Zillertaler Alps; Hohe Tauern; Niedere Tauern. 2100-2500m.
DESCRIPTION Male fw outer margin convex; upf subapical fulvous-red patch extending to cell in s4 and s5 and v3, enclosing small, twin, white-pupilled ocelli not contiguous; uph pd markings small or absent; unh gc lustrous bluish-grey.
FLIGHT-PERIOD Univoltine. Early July/late August.
HABITAT Grassy places, often small areas amongst limestone outcrops.
LIFE-HISTORY LHP *Festuca quadriflora*. Larval development occupies two seasonal cycles.
NOTE Geographically and/or altitudinally separated from *E. tyndarus* and *E. cassioides*.

Lorkovic's Brassy Ringlet *Erebia calcaria*

RANGE European Alps.
E. calcaria Lorkovic 1953 TL: Julian Alps.
DISTRIBUTION NE Italy: Piave di Cardore (Monte Cavallo; Mte. Santo): not reported from nearby Carnic Alps. W Slovenia: Karwanken Alps.; Julian Alps (Triglav). Above 1450m.
DESCRIPTION Resembles *E. tyndarus*: male ups darker brown; upf subapical white-pupilled ocelli usually very small; unh gc lighter, silvery-grey.
FLIGHT-PERIOD Univoltine. Mid July/late August.
HABITAT Grassy, rocky slopes.
LIFE-HISTORY LHPs include *Festuca ovina*. Hibernation stage unconfirmed.

Ottoman Brassy Ringlet *Erebia ottomana*

RANGE France (Massif Central), NE Italy, S Balkans, N and C Greece, N Turkey.
E. ottomana Herrich-Schäffer 1851 TL: not stated.
DISTRIBUTION France: Massif Central. NE Italy: Monte Baldo. S Croatia: Velebit Mts. S Bosnia-Herzegovina. S Serbia. Albania. Republic of Macedonia. Bulgaria. N and C Greece. Widespread, locally abundant. 850-2450m, more generally 1400-2000m.
DESCRIPTION AND VARIATION Ups pd markings usually well developed. All wing-characters, including fw-shape, subject to marked individual and local variation. Basis for regional differentiation of Balkan and Greek populations (referrable to *bulgarica* Drenowsky [=*bureschi* Warren], *drenowskyi* Varga, *durmitorensis* Warren, *balcanica* Rebel or nominate subspecies) is obscure; reputed regional differences appear to fall within the range attributable to individual, local and seasonal variation. In Massif Central, *tardenota* Praviel: small; male ups gc dark brown; upf ocelli small: both sexes, unh markings usually well developed. On Monte Baldo, *benacensis* Dannehl: male ups gc very dark brown; upf reddish pd markings reduced to thin ocellular rings enclosing very small subapical ocelli; uph pd reddish spots vestigial: both sexes, unh markings strongly developed: in overall character, a distinctive race.
FLIGHT-PERIOD Univoltine. Mid July/August according to altitude and season.
HABITAT Exposed, grass-covered slopes or plains at higher altitudes; below the treeline, small, damp grassy clearings in beech, coniferous or mixed forests.
LIFE-HISTORY LHPs include *Festuca ovina*. In extended photo-period of N Europe, captively reared larvae mature and pupate without entering diapause. Striking differences in larval colouring and pupal coloration/shape are sufficient for sexual differentiation.

De Lesse's Brassy Ringlet

Lorkovic's Brassy Ringlet

Ottoman Brassy Ringlet

DE LESSE'S BRASSY RINGLET

LORKOVIC'S BRASSY RINGLET

OTTOMAN BRASSY RINGLET

E. o. benacensis
(Monte Baldo)

Water Ringlet *Erebia pronoe*

RANGE Europe.

E. pronoe Esper 1780 TL: Styria.

DISTRIBUTION Pyrenees (Spain and France): Pto. de Arlas to Valle d'Arán and Andorra. E France: N Isère; N Savoie; Haute-Savoie; Jura; Doubs. Switzerland: Jura Mts; Bernese Oberland and Glarner Alps to Albula Alps; more local in Valais and Tessin. Italy: Cottian Alps; Orobic Alps to Dolomites. Bavarian Alps (absent from Allgäuer Alps). Widespread in Austrian Alps to Julian Alps. Local in Dinaric Alps. Republic of Macedonia: Sar Pl.; Vraca Pl.; Plackovica Pl. Bulgaria: Stara Pl.; Rila Mts. Slovakia and Poland: Tatra Mts. Romania: Carpathian Mts. 900-2800m.

DESCRIPTION AND VARIATION Male unh silvery-grey pd band with dark violet or purple reflections, contrasting with broad, brownish discal band; wing-base colour as for pd band but variable, sometimes obscure: female unh paler, bands more contrastive. In C Pyrenees, *glottis* Frühstorfer: ups reddish pd bands reduced; subapical ocelli well defined; male unh markings obscure. In Switzerland, *vergy* Ochsenheimer: upf reddish pd bands and ocelli much reduced, sometimes absent; unh markings less contrastive: in Balkans, *fruhstorferi* Warren: closely similar. In C Alps, transitional to nominate form in many areas.

FLIGHT-PERIOD Univoltine. Late June/late September according to altitude.

HABITAT Damp, grassy slopes or woodland clearings, often associated with small streams.

LIFE-HISTORY LHPs *Festuca ovina*; *F. quadriflora*.

Black Ringlet *Erebia melas*

RANGE SE Europe.

E. melas Herbst 1796 TL: Perzenieska, Romanian Banat.

DISTRIBUTION Widespread on mountains of SW Slovenia (Mt. Nanos); W Croatia (including Velebit Planina); Bosnia-Herzegovina; SW Serbia (Montenegro); N Albania. E Serbia (Rtanj Pl.). Romania: E Apuseni Mts. (Runc Gorge 500-700m); SW Carpathian Mts. (Cerna Valley 200-1400m); Retezat Mts. (1700-2200m); Haghimas Mts. (1500-1900m); central E Transylvanian Mts. (1000-1300m). Republic of Macedonia: Sar Pl.; Jablanica Pl.; Placenska Pl.; Kozuf Pl. Bulgaria: Stara Pl.; Rila Mts.; Pirin Mts. Greece: Mt. Phalakron; Mt. Olympus; Timfi Mts.; Mt. Timfristos; Mt. Parnassos. 900-2800m: usually above 1500m.

Water Ringlet

Black Ringlet

DESCRIPTION Male ups velvety-black or blackish-brown; upf with twin subapical white-pupilled black ocelli, often with ocellus in s2; uph usually with pd ocelli in s2-4; unf as upf; unh with obscure dark grey variegation and obscure pale antemarginal band: female slightly browner; upf and unf orange-red pd band enclosing subapical ocelli and ocellus in s2, usually constricted in s3; all ocelli larger; unh gc brownish, irrorated grey.

VARIATION In Apuseni Mts., *runcensis* König 1965: both sexes, all markings better developed: female upf bright orange-red pd band wider, extending to s1b; ocelli larger; uph large pd ocelli in s1b-4, enclosed by orange-red band; unf pd band extending into discal area; costa, apex and outer margin light grey; unh irrorated light grey; darker discal area bordered by irregular dark line; pd ocelli large; antemarginal band paler. In Haghimas Mts. (E Carpathian Mts.), *carpathicola* Popescu-Gorj and Alexinschi 1959: wing-characters intermediate of *melas* and *runcensis*. In SW Slovenia and Velebit Pl., *leonhardi* Frühstorfer 1918: slightly smaller, but variable: male resembles nominate form but unh almost uniform black: female dark greyish-brown; ocelli reduced; upf reddish pd band obscure or absent; unh brown, variegated darker brown. In S Balkans and Greece, *schawerdae* Frühstorfer 1918: male resembles *leonhardi* closely, uph ocelli reduced: female brownish, variable, sometimes pale greyish-brown; ocelli smaller; fw reddish pd band very obscure, more usually absent: some specimens in some populations of Greece and Bulgaria are indistinguishable from *leonhardi*: morphological and distributional relationship of *leonhardi* and *schawerdae* unclear. Other named forms appear to be synonymous with, or relate to minor variation of above forms.

FLIGHT-PERIOD Univoltine. Mid July/mid September according to altitude.

HABITAT Rocky slopes with sparse grass; grass-covered slopes.

LIFE-HISTORY LHP unknown: on Mt. Timfristos 1900m, hibernated larvae have been recorded feeding on a heavily perfumed grass. Captive larvae accept *Festuca ovina*.

NOTE Lower altitudinal range in Romania, relative to W and S Balkans and Greece, may reflect adaptive compensation for significant climatic transition between the two regions: Romania is characterised by averagely lower temperatures and severe winters (possibly of ecological relevance to larval/pupal development).

WATER RINGLET

♂ unh pattern of markings with purple reflections characterisitic

♂ upf very dark, dull reddish-brown postdiscal markings reduced

E. p. pronoe

E. p. vergy
(Switzerland)

BLACK RINGLET

♂ and ♀ ups and uns gc and markings distinctive

E. m. schanerdae

Lefèbvre's Ringlet *Erebia lefebvrei*

RANGE Pyrenees (Spain and France), Cantabrian Mts. (N Spain).

E. lefebvrei Boisduval 1828 TL: Pyrenees.

DISTRIBUTION Spain: Picos de Europa; S. de la Demanda; E Pyrenees (Pto. de Beñasque; Puigmal; Pico de Finestrelles). France: C Pyrenees (Pic d'Anie to Pic du Midi de Bigorre and Col de Portillon): E Pyrenees (Carlit massif; Canigou massif). 1700-2700m.

DESCRIPTION Male ups and uns gc jet black; upf reddish pd band diffuse, variable, sometimes absent; upf and uph with 3 to 5 submarginal, white-pupilled black ocelli; uns markings similar: female gc paler; all markings better developed.

VARIATION Subject to considerable individual and local variation. In E Pyrenees, *pyrenaea* Oberthür: for most specimens, all markings reduced in both sexes: male upf reddish pd bands generally absent, vestigial in female; male uph usually without ocelli but variable. In Picos de Europa, *astur* Oberthür: resembles *pyrenaea*; markings averagely further reduced, but sufficiently variable to render individual specimens of the two populations inseparable.

FLIGHT-PERIOD Univoltine. Generally late June/late August according to altitude, locality and (?)season.

HABITAT Steep, limestone screes, bordered by grassy areas; rocky slopes.

Larche Ringlet *Erebia scipio*

RANGE SE France, NW Italy.

E. scipio Boisduval 1832 TL: Basses Alpes.

DISTRIBUTION SE France: Alpes-Maritimes; Alpes-de-Haute-Provençe; Vaucluse; Drôme; Hautes-Alpes; Savoie. NW Italy: Maritime Alps. Very local. 1400-2500m.

FLIGHT-PERIOD Univoltine. Late July/late August.

HABITAT Steep, rocky slopes with sparse grass; screes; moraines. On limestone.

LIFE-HISTORY LHP *Helictotrichon sedenense* – a specialized grass whose geographical and local distribution appears as restricted as that of the butterfly. Most other members of the genus have similar ecological preferences; *H. setaceum*, for example, is endemic to SW Alps and mountains of Provence, and occurs in at least some habitats of *E. scipio* – not recorded as a LHP.

Lefèbvre's Ringlet

Larche Ringlet

LEFÈBVRE'S RINGLET

Restricted to Picos de Europa

All wing markings variable, including development of dark red pd in ♂, sometimes almost absent

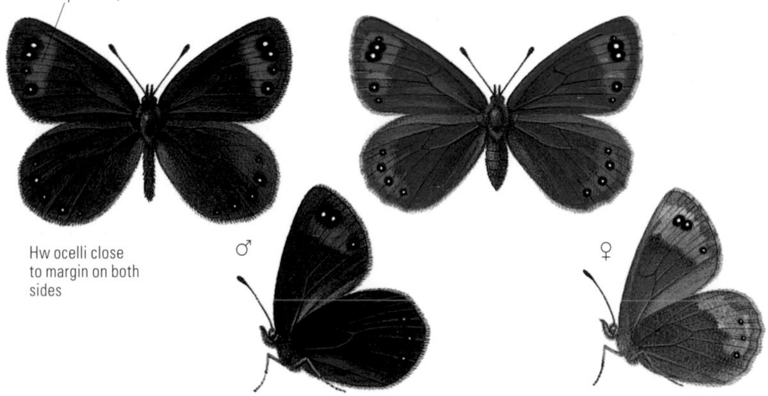

Hw ocelli close to margin on both sides

♂ ♀

E. l. lefebvrei

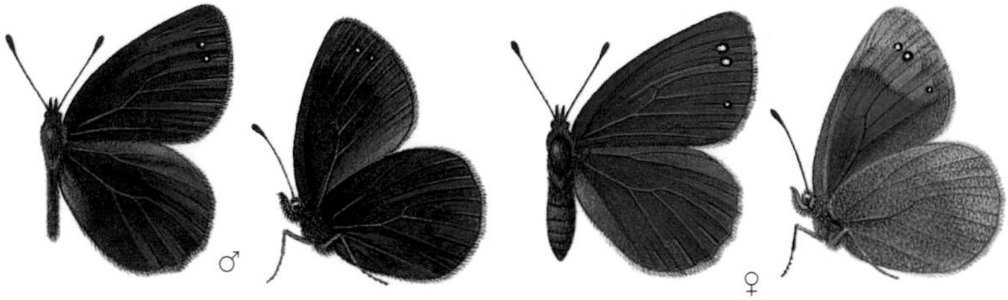

♂ ♀

♂ ups and uns, all markings reduced or absent

E. l. astur

LARCHE RINGLET

♂ and ♀ unh pd band lacking ocelli

♂ ♀

Unh gc smooth dark brown

Unh gc smooth pale grey

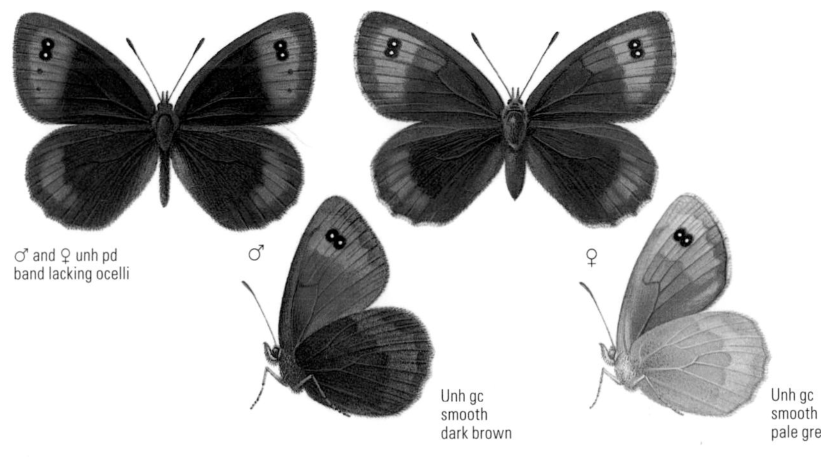

Styrian Ringlet *Erebia stirius*

RANGE SE European Alps (NE Italy, SE Austria, W Slovenia, NW Croatia).
E. stirius Godart 1824 TL: Klagenfurt, Carinthia.
syn: *nerine* Freyer 1831.

DISTRIBUTION From Monte Baldo through Brenta Alps, Dolomites, Karawanken Alps, Julian Alps to Kapela and Velebit Mts. 700-1800m.

DESCRIPTION AND VARIATION Resembles *E. styx*: unf brown marginal border slightly tapered towards s1b, without projection in s1b (distinction from *E. styx*); male unh more variegated, giving a slightly roughened appearance. At high altitudes in Dolomites, f. *morula* Speyer: smaller; all markings reduced: in some localities, transitional to nominate form.

FLIGHT-PERIOD Univoltine. Late July/early September, according to altitude.

HABITAT Rocky and grassy slopes usually on limestone.

LIFE-HISTORY LHP *Sesleria caerulea.*

Stygian Ringlet *Erebia styx*

RANGE SE Switzerland, N Italy, SE Germany, Austria, W Slovenia.
E. styx Freyer 1834 TL: not stated.
syn: *reichlini* Herrich-Schäffer 1860.

DISTRIBUTION Italy: Monte Generoso to Dolomites. Local in SE Switzerland: Tessin (Monte Generoso). Germany: Allgäuer Alps. Austria: Karwendel Mts. and Zillertal Alps to W Slovenia: Julian Alps (Trentadal; Mojstrovka Pass). 600-2200m. (Records for Vosges Mts. appear to have arisen from misidentification).

DESCRIPTION AND VARIATION Resembles *E. stirius*: unf brown marginal border of averagely uniform width with short, proximal cuspidal projection in s1b (a useful diagnostic character); male unh less variegated, appearing smoother. In Bergamasker Alps; Monte Generoso, *triglites* Frühstorfer: all markings better developed; upf pd band and subapical ocelli larger; unh ocelli sometimes absent. In Julian Alps, *trentae* Lorkovic: resembles *triglites* but markings further developed; ocelli large, pupils brilliant white: female uns gc variable.

FLIGHT-PERIOD Univoltine. Early July/early September according to locality.

HABITAT Warm, dry, rocky, often precipitous limestone slopes, usually with scattered bushes and trees.

LIFE-HISTORY LHP *Sesleria varia.* Larval development occupies two seasonal cycles in some localities at higher altitude.

Styrian Ringlet

Stygian Ringlet

STYRIAN RINGLET

♂
♀
♂ unf pd band prominent, dark marginal slightly tapered towards inner margin, without projection in s1b

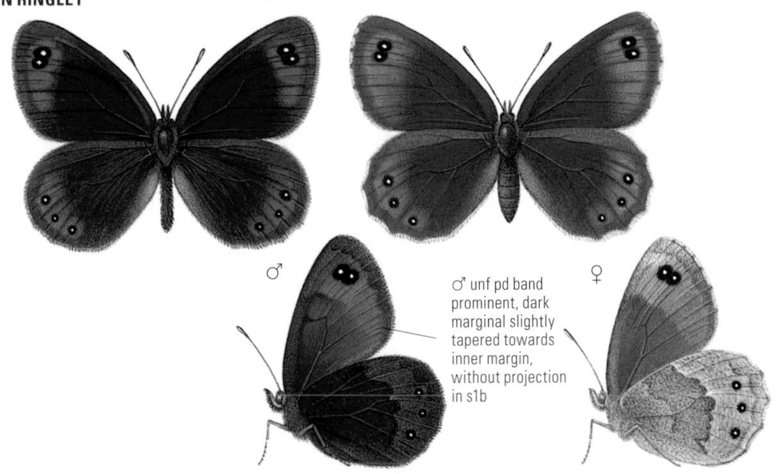

STYGIAN RINGLET

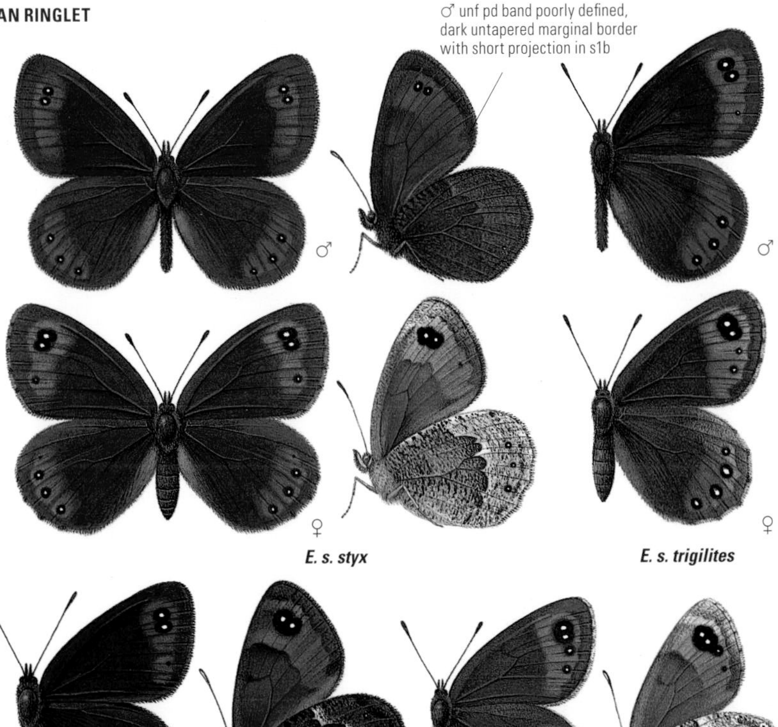
♂ unf pd band poorly defined, dark untapered marginal border with short projection in s1b
♂
♂
♀
♀

E. s. styx

E. s. trigilites

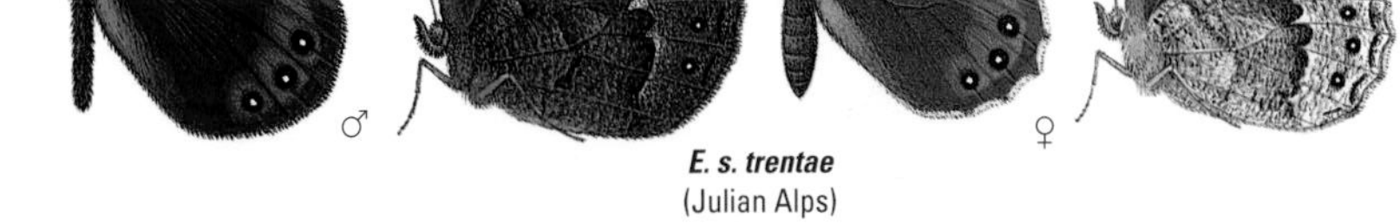
♂
♀

E. s. trentae
(Julian Alps)

Marbled Ringlet *Erebia montana*

RANGE C European Alps, Apennines.
E. montana de Prunner 1798 TL: Piedmont.
syn: *homole* Frühstorfer 1918.
DISTRIBUTION From Maritime Alps (France and Italy) through main Alpine chain to Allgäuer Alps, Öetztal Alps (Brenner Pass) and Dolomites. Generally widespread and common. Also Apuane Alps and C Apennines. 1100-2500m.
DESCRIPTION AND VARIATION Resembles *E. styx*: unf brown marginal border internally undulate, well defined. In E Alps, *goante* Esper: ups markings generally better developed; male unh gc darker but variable. In Apuane Alps (Mont Tambura), *vandellii* Casini: larger; unh darker.
FLIGHT-PERIOD Univoltine. Mid July/mid September according to altitude.
HABITAT Diverse. Grassy, flowery alpine and subalpine meadows; woodland clearings; rocky and grassy slopes; in dry or damp situations. Usually on limestone.
LIFE-HISTORY LHPs *Nardus stricta*; *Festuca alpina*; *F. ovina*.

Zapater's Ringlet *Erebia zapateri*

RANGE E Spain (Montes Universales).
E. zapateri Oberthür 1875 TL: Sierra de Albarracin.
DISTRIBUTION E Spain: Guadalajara (S. de Albarracin); Cuenca (Tragacete; Valdemeca; Ciudad Encantada; Valdecabras); Teruel (Albarracin; La Losilla; Colomarde; Moscardon; Griegos; Orihuela del Tremedel; Noguera; Bronchales; S. de Javalambre). 1050-1650m.
DESCRIPTION Male ups gc dark brown; upf bright yellow-orange pd band wide; uph reddish pd markings small or absent (cf. *E. neoridas*).
FLIGHT-PERIOD Univoltine. Late July/early September: first females emerge 10-12 days after first males (cf. *E. neoridas*).
HABITAT Open, grassy, sparsely bushy, pinewood clearings; very small, bushy openings with long grasses in pine and oak woodland; stony ground with short grasses in sparse pinewoods. On calcareous rocks, usually limestone.
LIFE-HISTORY LHP: hibernated larvae have been recorded on three species of Poaceae within a single colony. Posterior segment of larva blunt – almost without 'tails'.

Autumn Ringlet *Erebia neoridas*

RANGE NE Spain, S France, NW and C Italy.
E. neoridas Boisduval 1828 TL: Grenoble.
DISTRIBUTION Spain: Huesca (Valle d'Arazas); Lérida (S. di Cadi); Barcelona (S. del Montseny); Gerona (S. Gallabara). Andorra. France: C and E Pyrenees: Gavarnie; Col du Tourmalet; Pic Carlit; Mt. Canigou. Massif Central; Alpes-Maritimes to Vaucluse, Isère and Haute-Savoie. Italy: Maritime Alps to Susa Valley; Apuane Alps; C Apennines. 500-1600m.
DESCRIPTION Resembles *E. zapateri*: upf pd band dull, reddish-brown, slightly narrower near subapex, more tapered, extending to v1; twin, subapical ocelli better developed, white-pupilled ocellus in s2; uph pd orange-red spots often confluent, with ocelli in s2-4.
VARIATION Individual and local variation marked. On Monte Sibillini, *sibyllina* Verity: very small; ups pd bands mahogany-red, ocelli well developed; unh brightly marked.
FLIGHT-PERIOD Univoltine. Early August/early October: first females appear about two weeks after first males (cf. *E. zapateri*).
HABITAT Grassy, bushy places; open woodland.
LIFE-HISTORY LHPs *Digitaria sanguinalis*; *Poa annua*; *P. pratense*; *Festuca ovina*.

Marbled Ringlet

Zapater's Ringlet

Autumn Ringlet

MARBLED RINGLET

ZAPATER'S RINGLET

AUTUMN RINGLET

Bright-eyed Ringlet *Erebia oeme*

RANGE Europe.

E. oeme Hübner 1804 TL: Tirol.

DISTRIBUTION Pyrenees: Spain (Pto. de Beñasque; Valle d'Arán): France (Col d'Aubisque to Mt. Canigou): Andorra. France: Massif Central (colonies dispersed); Isère; Ain; Savoie; Haute-Savoie; Jura. Switzerland: S Jura; Bernese Alps to St. Gallen and Engadine. NW Italy: Ortler Alps; Dolomites. SE Germany (Bavarian Alps) through Austrian Alps to W Slovenia (Julian Alps), Croatia (Velebit Mts.), S Balkans and N Greece (Rhodopi Mts.). Reported from N Carpathian Mts. (Branyiszko, Slovakia). 900-2600m: more often 1500-2000m.

DESCRIPTION AND VARIATION Uns of antennal club-tip black (cf. *E. medusa*). Ups and unh reddish-orange markings and ocelli well defined, but variable, giving rise to several named local and regional forms. In Switzerland, *lugens* Staudinger: pd spots and ocelli smaller: transitional to nominate form in some areas of Allgäuer Alps and N Tirol. In E Austria, Balkans and Greece, *spodia* Staudinger: larger; all markings better developed: female unh pd yellowish spots often confluent, ocelli and ocellular white pupils large: the especially well-marked forms *pacula* Frühstorfer and *vetulonia* Frühstorfer represent the limit of development in wing-characters, but appear to have no racial significance.

FLIGHT-PERIOD Univoltine. Mid June/mid August according to altitude.

HABITAT Damp meadows, hillside bogs, stream margins etc., usually with an abundance of long grasses; in damp, bushy, woodland clearings at lower altitudes.

LIFE-HISTORY LHPs include *Poa alpina*; *P. pratensis*; *P. nemoralis*; *Festuca rubra*; *Carex flacca*; *C. sempervirens*; *Briza media*; *Molinia caerulea*. At high altitudes, larval development occupies two seasonal cycles.

Piedmont Ringlet *Erebia meolans*

RANGE Europe.

E. meolans de Prunner 1798 TL: Piedmont.

syn: *calaritas* Frühstorfer 1918.

DISTRIBUTION N and C Spain: S. de Bejar; S. de Gredos; S. de Guadarrama; S. de la Demanda; Cantabrian Mts.; Pyrenees. Andorra. France: Pyrenees; Massif Central; Alpes-Maritimes to Jura and Vosges. NW, C and S Switzerland. Italy: W Ligurian Alps to Cottian Alps, Pennine Alps, Tessin and Ortler Alps: Apuane Alps; C Apennines. Germany: south of Thuringer Wald. Austria: W Tirol; Hochschwab Mts. Records for Carpathian Mts. require confirmation. Absent from Dolomites. 600-2300m: generally below 1500m.

DESCRIPTION Upf small ocellus in s6 (when present) displaced distad, often conspicuously so relative to ocelli in s4 and s5; unh very dark, smooth in appearance. (Cf. *E. triaria*).

VARIATION Size and wing-markings markedly variable. In C Spain, *bejarensis* Chapman: larger; brighter; all markings well developed, upf with ocelli in s2-s6: progressively transitional to nominate form towards Cantabrian Mts. and Pyrenees. In Vosges Mts., Switzerland and E Alps, *stygne* Ochsenheimer: all markings averagely reduced but with marked local variation: in f. *valesiaca* Elwes, ups red pd markings vestigial or absent, sometimes reduced to narrow rings enclosing subapical twin ocelli on fw: prevalent in some localities in Pennine Alps.

FLIGHT-PERIOD Univoltine. Late May/mid August according to locality.

HABITAT Grassy, flowery woodland clearings

LIFE-HISTORY LHPs include *Agrostis capillaris*; *Deschampia flexuosa*; *Nardus stricta*; *Festuca ovina*.

Bright-eyed Ringlet

Piedmont Ringlet

BRIGHT-EYED RINGLET

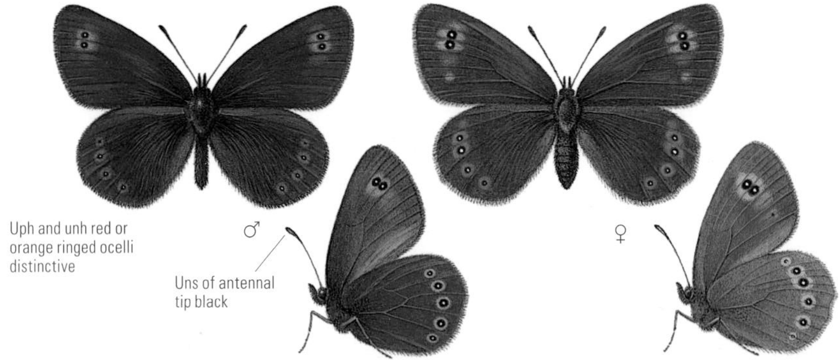

Uph and unh red or orange ringed ocelli distinctive

♂

Uns of antennal tip black

♀

E. o. oeme

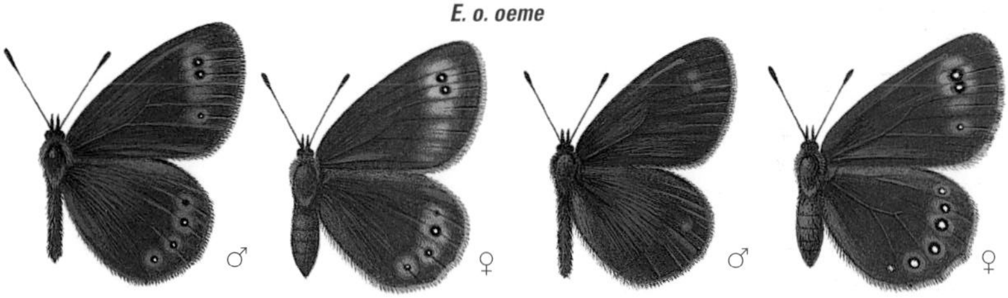

♂ ♀

E. o. spodia

♂

E. o. lugens

♀

E. o. spodia f. *pacula*

PIEDMONT RINGLET

♂

Unh very dark and smooth

♀

E. m. meolans

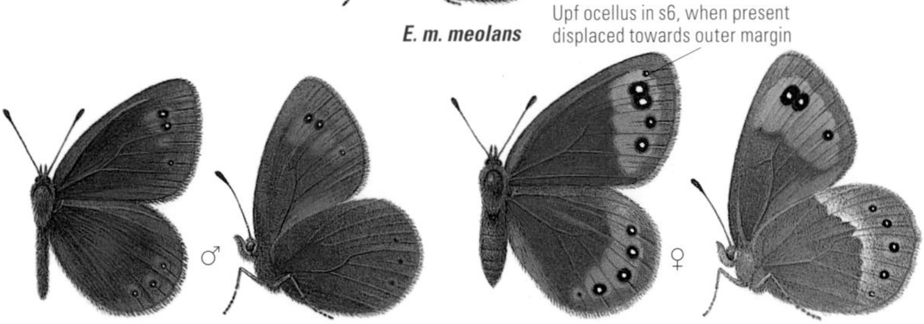

Upf ocellus in s6, when present displaced towards outer margin

♂

E. m. valesiaca

♀

E. m. bejarensis (C Spain)

Chapman's Ringlet *Erebia palarica*

RANGE NW Spain.
E. palarica Chapman 1905 TL: Pajares [Asturian Mts.].
DISTRIBUTION NW Spain: Cantabrian Mts. (provinces of Leon; Oviedo; Palencia; Santander). 1050-1650m.
DESCRIPTION Resembles *E. meolans*, but larger – the largest European member of the genus; unh with slightly roughened appearance.
FLIGHT-PERIOD Univoltine. Late May/late July according to season and altitude.
HABITAT Small, grassy, clearings amongst Broom ((?) *Cytisus*) or Mediterranean Heath (*Erica arborea*), in valleys and on slopes. On non-calcareous soils.
LIFE-HISTORY Hibernation stage unconfirmed.
BEHAVIOUR Females are secretive, spending much time amongst grasses growing within the cover of Broom or Heath.

Dewy Ringlet *Erebia pandrose*

RANGE Arctic and Alpine zones of Europe, Kola and Kanin Peninsulas, Polar Urals, Altai, Sajan, Mongolia.
E. pandrose Borkhausen 1788 TL: Styria.
syn: *lappona* Thunberg 1791.
DISTRIBUTION Spain: E Pyrenees (S. dels Canals). Andorra (El Serrat 2200m). France: E Pyrenees (Col de l'Artigue; Col de Puymorens to Canigou massif); Alpes-Maritimes to Haute-Savoie. Widespread and common throughout C European Alps. Italy: C Apennines: Monti della Laga. W Slovenia: Julian Alps. Romania: Carpathian Mts. Bosnia-Herzegovina: Vranica Pl.; Prenj Pl. S Serbia: Montenegro: Sinjajevina Pl. Republic of Macedonia: Sar Pl.; Jakupica Pl. 1600-3100m. Bulgaria: Rila Mts.; (?)Rhodopi Mts.; 2400-2900m. Fennoscandia (Norway, W Sweden and N Finland): 900-1200m in south: 500-1200m in N Sweden: near sea-level on Arctic coast.
DESCRIPTION (See *E. sthennyo*).
VARIATION Upf reddish pd markings often reduced, more rarely absent; ocelli in s4 and s5 sometimes absent or reduced to minute points; unh gc pale silvery-grey to dark grey or greyish-brown; mediobasal, discal and submarginal lines prominent or absent. Several sspp. have been described to account for minor, regional variation.
FLIGHT-PERIOD Univoltine. Early June/mid August according to locality and altitude: emerges about mid July in Lapland according to season.
HABITAT Slopes, open valleys with short grasses and rocky outcrops; damp or boggy, sloping areas with low bushes.
LIFE-HISTORY LHPs *Festuca*; *Poa*; *Sesleria*. Larval development occupies two seasonal cycles.

False Dewy Ringlet *Erebia sthennyo*

RANGE Pyrenees (Spain, France).
E. sthennyo Graslin 1850 TL: Bagnères de Bigorre, Pyrenees.
DISTRIBUTION Spain: C Pyrenees (Pto. de Portalet; Monte Perdido; Pto. de Beñasque). France: Pic du Midi d'Ossau to Pic du Midi de Bigorre and Luchon; Port de Salau to Andorra. Recorded just east of Andorra. Above 1800m.
DESCRIPTION Resembles *E. pandrose*, but differs in the following respects: upf ocelli closer to outer margin; dark discal line and cellular striae absent or vestigial; unf basal and discal dark striae absent; male unh pale, almost uniform grey, unmarked: female unh greyish-brown, markings vestigial or absent. Differences in male genitalia small but constant.
FLIGHT-PERIOD Univoltine. Late June/early August.
HABITAT Grass-covered slopes with rocky outcrops.
NOTE Occurs in close proximity to *E. pandrose* in some districts but not known to occupy same habitats.

Chapman's Ringlet

Dewy Ringlet

False Dewy Ringlet

Dalmatian Ringlet

Meadow Brown

Sardinian Meadow Brown

CHAPMAN'S RINGLET

DEWY RINGLET

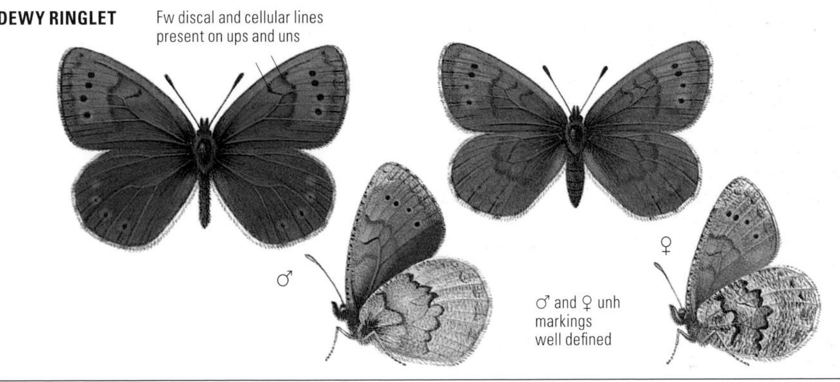

FALSE DEWY RINGLET

Dalmatian Ringlet *Proterebia afra*

RANGE Croatia (Dalmatia), NW Greece, Turkey, Crimea, Volga region, S Urals, NW and E Kazakhstan.
P. afra dalmata Godart 1824 TL: Sibenik, Dalmatia.
syn: *phegea* Borkhausen 1788
DISTRIBUTION Croatia: Dalmatian coastal districts (Zadar to Sibenik); island of Korcula. 150-500m. NW Greece: environs of Lake Vegoritis; Askion Mts.; Vourinos Mts. 550-1250m.
DESCRIPTION AND VARIATION Hw with precostal vein – cf. genus *Erebia*. Both sexes: ups and uns gc, size and number of ocelli and extent and colour of upf pale suffusion variable. In Greece, *pyramus* de Louker and Dils: wing-characters and male genitalia indistinguishable from *P. afra dalmata*.
FLIGHT-PERIOD Univoltine. Late April/late May.
HABITAT Dry, grassy, sparsely bushy limestone slopes, often gentle and undulating, strewn with small rocks. Habitats distinctive and often characterised by scattered Juniper bushes as the dominant shrub.
LIFE-HISTORY LHP *Fesctuca ovina*. The non-adhesive ova are sometimes ejected in small numbers into grass-tufts during hovering flight: a female may also use her recurved abdomen to guide two or three ova into the inverted conical base of a tuft of LHP whilst clinging to its outer stems. In extended photo-period of S England, development from ovum proceeds to completion (November/January) without diapause. Small differences in colouring of mature larvae allow separation of sexes: female larvae are slightly darker with greener tones. Hibernating stage in nature unknown. Pupa very dark, somewhat angular in shape – unlike that of genus *Erebia*.
BEHAVIOUR Females often visit flowers of *Globularia* and yellow Asteraceae.

Meadow Brown *Maniola jurtina*

RANGE Canary Islands, NW Africa, Europe, Turkey, N Iraq, N Iran to NW Kazakhstan, S and C Urals, W Siberia.
M. jurtina Linnaeus 1758 TL: Europe and Africa (Sweden Verity 1953).
DISTRIBUTION Widespread and common. Canary Islands: La Palma; Hierro; Gomera; N Tenerife; N Gran Canaria. NW Africa (0-2500m). Most of Europe south of 63°N, including Balearic Islands, Corsica, Sardinia, Capri, Sicily, Malta, Corfu, Levkas, Kithera, Crete, most W Aegean islands and E Aegean islands of Limnos and Psara. 0-1600m.
VARIATION In Canary Islands, NW Africa, Iberian Peninsula and SW France, *hispulla* Esper: larger; male resembles nominate form; unh size and number of ocelli variable: female ups yellow-orange areas extended; all uns markings bold, highly contrastive; dark basal area bordered by conspicuous yellow suffusion. Transitional to nominate form in S France, S Italy and S Greece. In Orkney Islands, NW Scotland, including Hebrides, Isle of Man, Ireland and Scilly Isles, *splendida* White: larger; male ups gc dark brown; upf orange-fulvous pd area often enclosing subapical ocellus and extending to s2, sometimes projecting to cell-end in s4 and s5: female upf yellow-orange pd band extending into discal area; uph pd area usually suffused orange. Ovum with 11-21 longitudinal ribs, regionally variable.
FLIGHT-PERIOD Univoltine. Late May/September with prolonged aestivation in southernmost range. In Scotland and Scandinavia, mid June/mid July according to season. In most of Greece, emergence date coincides with that of S England – first week of June. In S Portugal (Algarve), mid April/September. Canary Islands, late March/late September according to altitude.
HABITAT Diverse. Grassy, bushy, often flowery places with an abundance of taller grasses; cultivated ground; woodland clearings or margins; heaths. On calcareous or acidic soils in dry or damp conditions.
LIFE-HISTORY LHPs include *Poa pratensis*; *Lolium pratensis*; *Festuca rubra*; *F. arundinacea*; *Agrostis stolonifera*; *A. canina*; *Bromus erectus*; *Brachypodium pinnatum*; *Holcus lanatus*; *Avenula pubescens*; *Alopecurus pratensis*; *Anthoxanthum odoratum*. Pupal gc colour extremely variable – pale green to dark reddish-purple.
BEHAVIOUR In S Europe, adults retire to shade and relative cool of bushes in hottest part of the day.

Maniola megala

RANGE Greece (Aegean island of Lesbos), SW and S central Turkey.
M. megala Oberthür 1909 TL: Akbes, Province of Hatay.
DISTRIBUTION In Europe, known only from E Aegean island of Lesbos.
DESCRIPTION The following is based upon Turkish populations. Resembles *M. jurtina* in E Mediterranean region: appreciably larger; hw outer margin averagely more undulate: male unh pd ocelli larger, more numerous: female ups gc darker brown; all uns markings darker but sharply defined and highly contrastive. Ovum with 19-21 longitudinal ribs.
FLIGHT-PERIOD Data for Greece limited: univoltine in Turkey, early May/September, aestivating in summer.
NOTE Habitat similar to that of *M. telmessia* with which it is known to occur.

Sardinian Meadow Brown *Maniola nurag*

RANGE Sardinia.
M. nurag Ghiliani 1852 TL: Mt. Gennargentu, Sardinia.
DISTRIBUTION Sardinia. Above 500m.
DESCRIPTION Resembles *M. jurtina hispulla*. Both sexes: smaller, ups yellow-orange areas more extensive, especially in female. Male upf sex-brand conspicuous: female markings better developed, more sharply defined.
FLIGHT-PERIOD Univoltine. Late May/early August: females appear to aestivate.
HABITAT Grassy, flowery places amongst bushes and rocks.

Maps on p. 298

DALMATIAN RINGLET

♂ and ♀ overall pattern of markings and colouring distinctive

♂ and ♀ unh veins pale, conspicuous

MEADOW BROWN

♂ upf sex-brand conspicuous

♂

♀

Brighter, orange markings more extensive

Pd orange extends into cell-end

♀

♀

M. j. jurtina

M. j. hispulla

SARDINIAN MEADOW BROWN

♂ upf sex-brand prominent, distinctive

Restricted to Sardinia

Maniola chia

RANGE Greece (Aegean islands of Chios and Inousses).
M. chia Thomson 1987 TL: Chios,
DISTRIBUTION In Europe, known only from eastern Aegean islands of Chios and Inousses: widespread and common. 50-500m.
DESCRIPTION Individual specimens superficially indistinguishable from *M. jurtina* found in eastern Mediterranean region, but genitalia and biochemical differences distinct. Ovum has 13-14 longitudinal ribs. (No other *Maniola* species is known from Chios or Inousses).
FLIGHT-PERIOD Univoltine. Late May/late September, aestivating in summer.
HABITAT Grassy, rocky and bushy places; cultivated ground.

Maniola telmessia

RANGE Greece (Aegean Islands), Turkey, Jordan, Israel, Lebanon, Iraq, SW Iran.
M. telmessia Zeller 1847 TL: Marmaris, Province of Mugla (Olivier 1993).
DISTRIBUTION In Europe, known only from E Aegean islands: Lesbos; Samos; Ikaria; Fourni; Patmos; Leros; Telendos; Kalimnos; Pserimos; Kos; Tilos; Simi; Kassos; Rhodes; Karpathos; Kastellorizo. 0-1000m. A record for the island of Angistri, close to Peloponnesian coast, has been discredited.
DESCRIPTION AND VARIATION Resembles *M. jurtina*. Male upf pd yellow-orange band, often enclosing subapical ocellus, extending to v2 and projecting to cell-end or slightly beyond in s4 and s5. On Karpathos, male upf and female ups yellow-orange areas more extensive. (*M. jurtina* is absent from range of *M. telmessia* in E Aegean islands). Ovum has 14-16 longitudinal ribs.
FLIGHT-PERIOD Univoltine. Late May/late September, aestivating in summer.
HABITAT Grassy, rocky and bushy places; cultivated ground.

Maniola halicarnassus

RANGE SW Turkey, Greece (Aegean Island of Nissiros).
M. halicarnassus Thomson 1990 TL: Bodrum, Province of Mugla [SW Turkey].
DISTRIBUTION In Europe, known only from southern Aegean island of Nissiros. 50-100m.
DESCRIPTION The following is based upon Turkish populations: resembles *M. jurtina* but male upf sex-brand large, black, conspicuous, broad at inner margin, tapering towards cell – distinctly triangular: female superficially indistinguishable from *M. telmessisa*. Both sexes averagely larger than *M. telmessisa*. Male genitalia distinguishable from those of *M. megala*, *M. chia* and *M. jurtina*. Ovum has 18 longitudinal ribs.
FLIGHT-PERIOD AND HABITAT In Bodrum Peninsula, SW Turkey: univoltine, late May/early September, with prolonged aestivation: occurs in bushy, flowery places in company with *M. telmessisa* with which it is suspected of hybridizing.
NOTE Uniquely for genus *Maniola*, number of larval instars variable – five or six (cf. *M. telmessia*, five; *M. jurtina*, six).

Moroccan Meadow Brown *Hyponephele maroccana*

RANGE Morocco.
H. maroccana maroccana Blachier 1908 TL: High Atlas, Morocco.
DISTRIBUTION Morocco: High Atlas (Toubkal massif; Dj. Aourach). 1700-2800m.
DESCRIPTION Male upf orange pd patch often extending into basal area; apical ocellus large, white-pupilled; smaller ocellus usually in s2; sex-brand narrow, smoothly curved; unh greyish-brown.
FLIGHT-PERIOD Univoltine. June/August: females may emerge up to 14 days later than males.
HABITAT Rocky places with sparse vegetation.
LIFE-HISTORY Hibernation stage unconfirmed.
BEHAVIOUR Has been observed 'hilltopping' on summit of Adra-n-Guinnous (2788m).
H. maroccana nivellei Oberthür 1920 TL: Dj. Hebri, Tizi-n-Taghzeft, Middle Atlas.
DISTRIBUTION Morocco: Middle Atlas (Tizi-n-Taghzeft; Col du Zad; Dj. Hebri); Rif Mts. (Dj. Lakraa; Dj. Tidiquin). 1800-2200m.
DESCRIPTION Resembles nominate form: smaller; male upf orange pd area more restricted; apical ocellus small; ocellus in s2 vestigial or absent; unh gc paler greyish-brown: female ups ocelli averagely reduced.
FLIGHT-PERIOD, HABITAT AND LIFE-HISTORY As for nominate form.

Dusky Meadow Brown *Hyponephele lycaon*

RANGE Europe, Turkey, Israel, Lebanon to C Asia (Yenisey Valley) and Kyrgyzstan.
H. lycaon Kühn 1774 TL: Berlin.
DISTRIBUTION N Portugal, Spain (except SW), S France (except coastal areas) through N Italy, S Switzerland and Austria to S Finland, Balkans and Greece. Absent from NW Europe, Scandinavia, S peninsular Italy, European Turkey and Mediterranean islands except N Sicily. Widespread and locally common in SW and SE Europe: regionally sporadic, local and often scarce in C and NE districts. 0-2100m.
DESCRIPTION Male upf sex-brand narrow, disrupted by v2 and v3 (cf. *H. lupina*).
VARIATION Unh gc variable; generally greyish or greyish-brown, often whitish in limestone habitats.
FLIGHT-PERIOD Univoltine. June/August.
HABITAT Diverse. Bushy, grassy places, usually amongst rocks.
LIFE-HISTORY LHPs include *Festuca ovina*; *F. rubra*; *Bromus erectus*; *Stipa pennata:* two or more species may be used in a given habitat.
BEHAVIOUR In hot conditions, adults often seek shade of bushes, overhanging rocks or tree roots on earthen banks.

Maniola telmessia

Prominent sex-brand

♂ upf sex-brand prominent; orange pd extending towards cell

♂

Unh ocelli yellow ringed

Apical ocellus bold, sometimes with twin white pupils in female

♀

MOROCCAN MEADOW BROWN

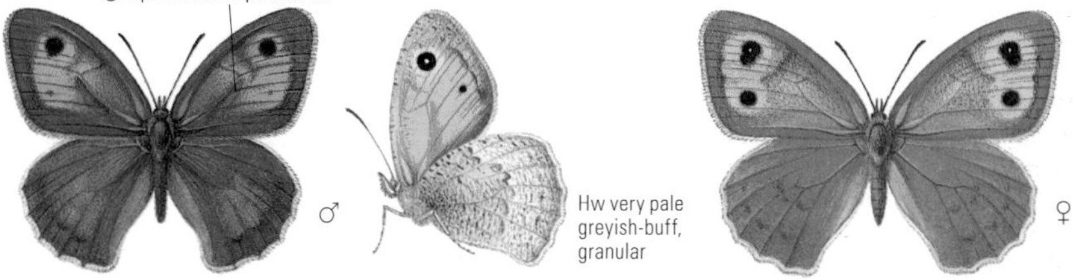

♂ upf sex-brand prominent

Hw virtually unmarked

Restricted to Morocco

♂

Hw very pale greyish-buff, granular

♀

DUSKY MEADOW BROWN

♂ upf sex-brand narrow, disrupted by veins; subapical ocellus 'blind'

♀ bold, dark ocelli 'blind'

♀ upf yellow discal area separate from pd band

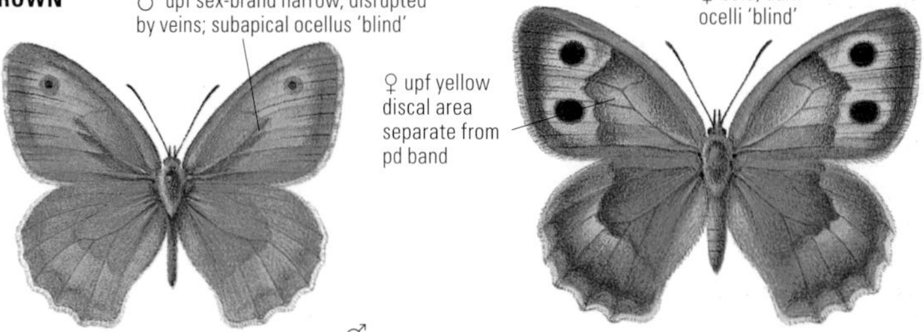

Moroccan Meadow Brown

Dusky Meadow Brown

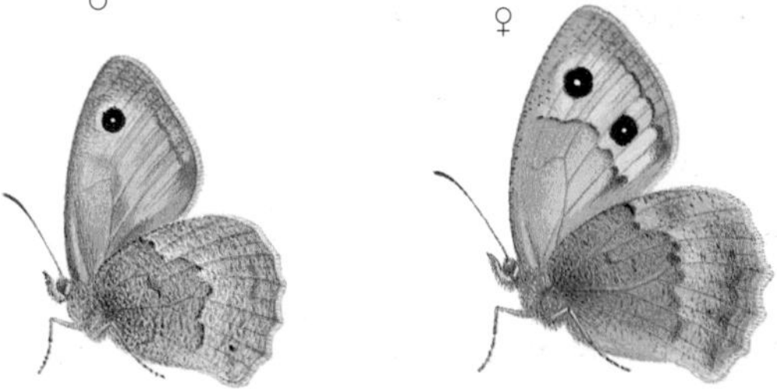

♂

♀

Oriental Meadow Brown *Hyponephele lupina*

RANGE NW Africa, S Europe, Turkey, Israel, Jordan, Lebanon, Iraq, N Iran to Tian Shan and Altai.
H. lupina Costa 1836 TL: Otranto [SE Italy].

DISTRIBUTION Morocco and Algeria: locally common. 500-2400m. N Portugal: Serra da Estrêla. S, C and NE Spain. France: very local: Aude to Hautes-Alpes and Alpes-Maritimes. Italy: N and C Apennines; Salentina Peninsula; Calabria (Aspromonte); N Sicily. Croatia: Dalmatian coast; Island of Krk. Hungary: Deliblat; Flamenda. SE Romania: Danube delta. S Serbia. Republic of Macedonia. S Bulgaria. Greece, including Lesbos, Chios, Kos, Rhodes and Crete. European Turkey. 0-2000m.

DESCRIPTION Male ups yellowish-brown with golden reflections; upf sex-brand broad, not broken by veins (cf. *H. lycaon*); hw undulate.

VARIATION Regionally/locally variable in size, male ups gc, length and width of sex-brand. In N Africa, Iberian Peninsula and SE France, *mauritanica* Oberthür: male ups dark greyish-brown, golden reflections inconspicuous: female ups slightly paler than nominate form. In Sicily, Balkans and Greece, *rhamnusia* Freyer: resembles nominate form: larger; male ups paler, more yellowish-brown in discal and pd areas; sex-brand conspicuous: female resembles nominate form closely.

FLIGHT-PERIOD Univoltine. Mid May/mid August according to locality: females aestivate mid summer.

HABITAT Hot, dry, grassy and bushy places.

Ringlet *Aphantopus hyperantus*

RANGE Europe, N Caucasus, S and C Urals, S and W Siberia, Mongolia, Amur, NE China, Korea.
A. hyperantus Linnaeus 1758 TL: Europe (Sweden Verity 1953).

DISTRIBUTION From N Spain (Cantabrian Mts. to E Pyrenees) through much of Europe, including Ireland, England, Wales and S Scotland, to 65°N in Fennoscandia, Balkans and N Greece (Macedonia; Thessaly: very local). 0-1600m. Absent from peninsular Italy and Mediterranean islands.

DESCRIPTION AND VARIATION Unh without pd and antemarginal metallic line; yellow-ringed ocelli in s5 and s6 displaced basad; s4 without ocellus (cf. *C. oedippus*). In N Britain: smaller; ups and uns gc tending to greyish yellow-brown; ocelli often small; unh ocelli sometimes replaced by small white dots (f. *arete* Mûller – sporadic in S England and C Europe): in SE Europe: large; all markings bold; uns gc brighter, with brassy golden reflections.

FLIGHT-PERIOD Univoltine. Mid June/late August.

HABITAT Grassy, bushy places; woodland clearings; in damp or dry situations.

LIFE-HISTORY LHPs include, *Brachypodium sylvaticum*; *B. pinnatum*; *Phleum pratense*; *Dactylis glomerata*; *Festuca rubra*; *Bromus erectus*; *B. hordeaceus*; *Cynosurus cristatus*; *Poa pratensis*; *P. nemoralis*; *Carex hirta*; *C. strigosa*; *C.* (?)*sylvatica*; *C. brizoides*; *C. panicea*; *Agrostis capillaris*; *Milium effusum*; *Elymus repens*; *Holcus mollis*; *H. lanatus*; *Deschampsia cespitosa*; *Molinia caerulea*; *Arrhenatherum elatius*; *Calamagrostis epigejos*. Two or more species/genera are often used in a single habitat. Non-adhesive ova are ejected during slow, low-level flight. Larvae feed on grass-plants well-shaded by vegetation, especially bramble.

False Meadow Brown *Pyronia janiroides*

RANGE C Algeria, W Tunisia.
P. janiroides Herrich-Schäffer 1851 TL: 'Spain' [in error for Algeria]

DISTRIBUTION Widespread, locally common. NE Algeria. W Tunisia. 500-1500m.

DESCRIPTION Male upf orange pd band proximally bordered by androconial patch; uph orange pd band wide; unh with 2-4 yellow pd ocelli in s2-s5, ocellus in s2 often with small, dark pupil. Both sexes, upf and unf subapical twin ocelli with white pupils (cf. *M. jurtina*).

FLIGHT-PERIOD Univoltine. July/early September.

HABITAT Dry, grassy, stony places amongst scrub.

LIFE-HISTORY LHP *Poa annua*. Hibernation stage unconfirmed.

Oriental Meadow Brown

Ringlet

False Meadow Brown

ORIENTAL MEADOW BROWN

H. l. lupina

RINGLET

FALSE MEADOW BROWN

Gatekeeper *Pyronia tithonus*

RANGE Morocco, Spain to S Britain, Balkans, Greece and W Turkey.

P. tithonus Linnaeus 1771 TL: Germany.

DISTRIBUTION Morocco: Rif Mts.; Ketama 1500m: very local. From Iberian peninsula through most of Europe, including S Ireland and England, to N Germany, C Poland, Balkans, Greece and European Turkey. Absent from S Italy and Mediterranean islands except S Corsica and Sardinia. Generally widespread and often abundant but distribution significantly disjunctive in many regions of C Europe. 0-1700m.

VARIATION In S Europe, especially hot localities, unh gc often yellowish-buff (*decolorata* Frühstorfer).

FLIGHT-PERIOD Univoltine. Early July/early September according to locality.

HABITAT Grassy, flowery, bushy, often in damp/humid places, usually associated with deciduous or pine woodland.

LIFE-HISTORY LHPs include, *Phleum pratense*; *Poa annua*; *P. nemoralis*; *P. trivialis*; *P. pratensis*; *Elymus repens*; *Agrostis capillaris*; *A. canina*; *Festuca ovina*; *F. rubra*; *F. pratensis*; *Lolium perenne*; *Dactylis glomerata*; *Milium effusum*. Non-adhesive ova sometimes deposited in grass-tufts or amongst other low-growing, bushy plants, but mostly ejected during low flight into grass-rich herbage. Larvae feed on well-shaded plants, often at margins of bramble patches or other dense shrubbery.

Southern Gatekeeper *Pyronia cecilia*

RANGE Morocco, Algeria, Tunisia, Libya, Spain, S France, Italy, SW Balkans, W Greece, NW Turkey.

P. cecilia Vallantin 1894 TL: Morocco.

syn: *ida* Esper 1785 (invalid homonym)

DISTRIBUTION Morocco. Algeria. Tunisia. 0-2200m. Portugal. Spain: S of Cantabrian Mts. and W Pyrenees; Balearic Islands. France: E Pyrenees to Ardèche and Alpes-Maritimes; Corsica. Sardinia. Records from S Switzerland require confirmation. Italy: very few, isolated colonies in northern districts, wide-spread S of Modena; Sardinia; Elba; Giglio; Sicily. Balkans: W coastal districts. (?) Albania. W and S Greece, including Corfu and Levkas: very local. European Turkey. 0-1200m.

DESCRIPTION Male upf androconial patch segmented.

VARIATION In western range: unh brightly marbled pale grey and white. In eastern range: duller grey with brownish tones.

FLIGHT-PERIOD Univoltine. Early June/mid August, according to locality.

HABITAT Hot, dry, sparsely grassy, rocky scrubland.

LIFE-HISTORY LHP(s) uncertain: reported use of *Deschampsia cespitosa* requires confirmation; distribution and ecology of *D. cespitosa* and recognized ssp. – inhabitants of wet/damp grassland – appear to correlate poorly with that of the butterfly. Captive larvae accept *Festuca ovina*, *Poa nemoralis*, *Brachypodium sylvaticum*, *Dactylis glomerata* and *Agrostis capillaris*.

Spanish Gatekeeper *Pyronia bathseba*

RANGE Morocco, Algeria, W Tunisia, SW Europe.

P. bathseba Fabricus 1793 TL: Morocco ('Barbaris')

syn: *pasiphae* Esper 1781 (invalid homonym)

DISTRIBUTION Widespread, locally common. Morocco. Algeria. W Tunisia. 700-1700m. Portugal. Spain: south of Cantabrian Mts.; absent from NW. France: Pyrénées-Orientales to Ardèche and Var. 300-1700m.

VARIATION In Europe, *pardilloi* Sagarra: generally larger; unh pale pd band wider; ocelli better developed. Intermediate forms occur throughout Spain.

FLIGHT-PERIOD Univoltine. Late April/July, according to locality.

HABITAT Grassy, bushy places; often in light woodland.

LIFE-HISTORY LHP *Brachypodium sylvaticum*.

Gatekeeper

Southern Gatekeeper

Spanish Gatekeeper

GATEKEEPER

SOUTHERN GATEKEEPER

SPANISH GATEKEEPER

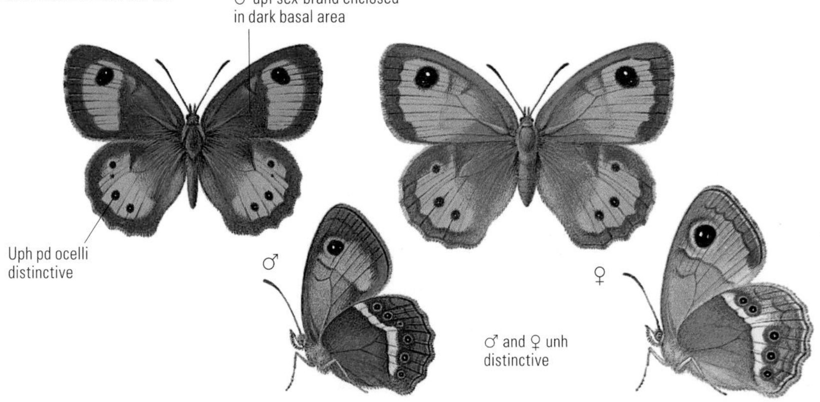

Large Heath *Coenonympha tullia*

RANGE N Europe, temperate Asia, N America.

Variation within and between colonies, even in small regions, may be quite marked: wing-characters most affected are:- ups gc, pale yellowish to ochreous-yellow or brownish; ups and unh ocelli, prominent, vestigial or absent; unh basal and discal coloration, light or darkish brown, less often greyish; unh whitish pd areas, extensive to vestigial. The following forms represent the overall range of variation. Flight-periods and habitats are similar for each form. LHPs given for *C. t. tullia* are widely used by other forms/sspp. In northern range, larval development reputedly occupies two seasonal cycles. Apart from direct interference, habitats are very sensitive to drainage/water extraction in adjoining areas: despite official protection afforded this butterfly, as recently as 1995/96, a colony in N Belgium (one of two known sites in this country) was reputedly eradicated by drainage of nearby land – designated as a human recreational facility.

C. tullia tullia Müller 1764 TL: Fridrichsdal, Denmark.
syn: *philoxenus* Esper 1780

DISTRIBUTION Small colonies generally widely dispersed in Ireland, Wales, NE England, SE Scotland and N Germany: widespread in Fennoscandia (including Baltic Islands) to 70°N. 0-500m.

VARIATION Transitional to *tiphon* Rottemburg (below) in some localities.

FLIGHT-PERIOD Univoltine. Mid June/early August according to locality.

HABITAT Peat bogs; raised bogs; blanket bogs; damp heaths bordering wetlands. Most habitats contain scattered trees (birch and pine), low shrubs (willow and bilberry) and are usually identifiable by the presence of cotton grass (*Eriophorum* sp.). Absent from alkaline or fertile soils.

LIFE-HISTORY LHPs include *Rhynochospora alba*; *Eriophorum vaginatum*; *E. angustifolia*; *Carex rostrata*.

C. tullia rothliebii Herrich-Schäffer 1851 TL: not stated.

DISTRIBUTION NW England: very local. N Belgium: a single colony known near Antwerp – possibly now extinct. A single colony is known from NE England (Yorkshire), within the range of nominate form. Very sporadic in Germany, perhaps elsewhere in C and E Europe.

C. tullia tiphon Rottemburg 1775 TL: Halle, W Germany.

DISTRIBUTION E and NE France: Savoie to Nièvre and Haut-Rhin; very restricted in Aisne and Ardennes. S Belgium: a single colony known in Ardennes. NW Switzerland: N of Rhône Valley to Jura Mts. Bavaria and N Austria to Baltic states and N Balkans: widespread and local. Below 1200m. Absent from Italy and S Austria.

VARIATION Transitional to *tullia* in some localities: specimens resembling *scotica* (below) occur as variants in Jura Mts.

C. tullia scotica Staudinger 1901 TL: Scotland.

DISTRIBUTION Scotland, including Hebrides and Orkney islands, north of a line from Glasgow to Aberdeen: transition to *tullia* in SE Scotland sharply delineated. Closely related forms occur in C Sweden. 0-800m.

VARIATION Ups gc very pale yellow in some localties; ocelli often vestigial or absent. Seasonally variable.

C. tullia demophile Freyer 1844 TL: Lapland.

DISTRIBUTION N Fennoscandia. C Norway above 200m. 0-500m.

DESCRIPTION Upf light yellowish-brown, with darker shading towards outer margin, uph uniformly darker; unh ocelli small, but usually present. Transitional to *tiphon* in S Finland and Baltic countries.

C. tullia lorkovici Sirajic and Cornalutti 1976.

DISTRIBUTION Bosnia-Herzegovina: district of Jaice.

DESCRIPTION Resembles *rothliebii*: averagely much larger – male fw length 18-23mm, female 18-25mm.

Eastern Large Heath *Coenonympha rhodopensis*

RANGE C Italy, S Balkans, N Greece.

C. rhodopensis Elwes 1900 TL: Rila Mts., Bulgaria.
syn: *occupata* Rebel 1903; *italica* Verity 1913.

DISTRIBUTION Italy: C Apennines (Monti Sibillini; Monte Terminillo; Abruzzi); Monte Baldo. W Croatia: Velebit Mts. Bosnia-Herzegovina: Vranica Pl; Jahorina Pl. S Serbia: Mokra Pl.; Hajia Pl. Republic of Macedonia: on all higher mountains. (?)Albania. Romania: Retezat Mts. Bulgaria: Stara Pl.; Osogovo Mts.; Vitosha Mts.; Slavyanka Mts.; Pirin Mts.; Rila Mts.; Rhodopi Mts. N Greece: Varnous Mts.; Voras Mts.; Mt. Orvilous; Vrontous Mts.; Mt. Phalakron; Rhodopi Mts. 1400-2200m.

DESCRIPTION AND VARIATION In both sexes, unf pale, anterior pd stripe absent (cf. *C. tullia*). Unh white mark in s3-5 always present; pd ocelli in s2, s3 and s6 present, sometimes small. In Italy and some mountains in Bulgaria and Greece, f. *italica* Verity: unh ocelli of equal size, in complete series.

FLIGHT-PERIOD Univoltine. Mid June/late July.

HABITAT Open, windswept, grassy plains or slopes above treeline; sometimes damp forest clearings, e.g., Rhodope Mts. (Greece) and Vitosha Mts. (Bulgaria).

LIFE-HISTORY In captivity, larvae pupate 'upside down' – with terminal posterior segment firmly attached to a stone or other rigid surface.

Large Heath

Eastern Large Heath

LARGE HEATH

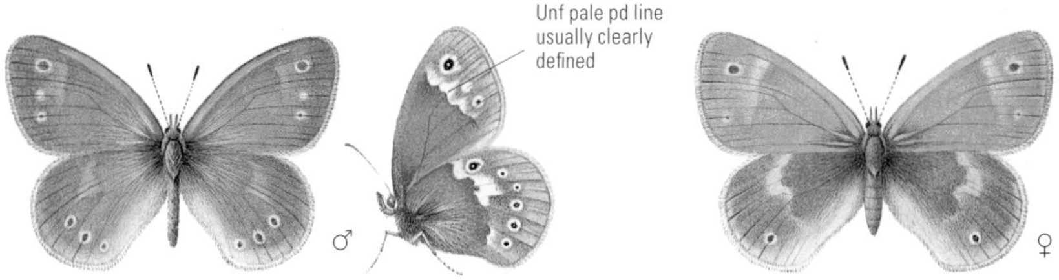

Unf pale pd line usually clearly defined
♂
♀

C. t. tullia

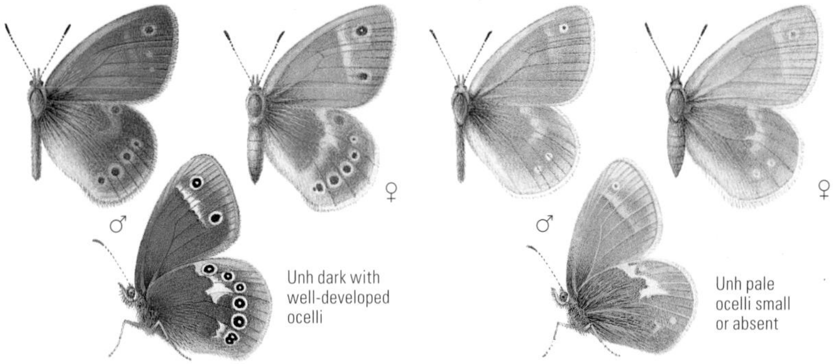

♂
♀
Unh dark with well-developed ocelli
♂
♀
Unh pale ocelli small or absent

C. t. rothliebii (NW England, N Belgium)

C. t. scotica (Scotland)

♂
♀

C. t. tiphon

EASTERN LARGE HEATH

Unf pd line absent or vestigial
♂
♂ and ♀ unh pale discal mark confined to s4 and 5
♀
♂ and ♀ unh series of pd spots usually complete

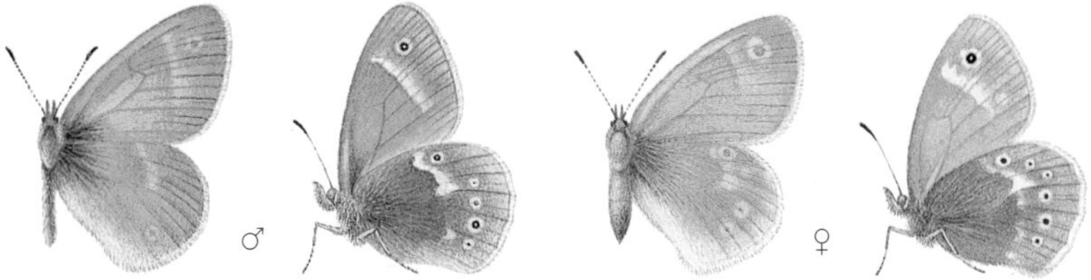

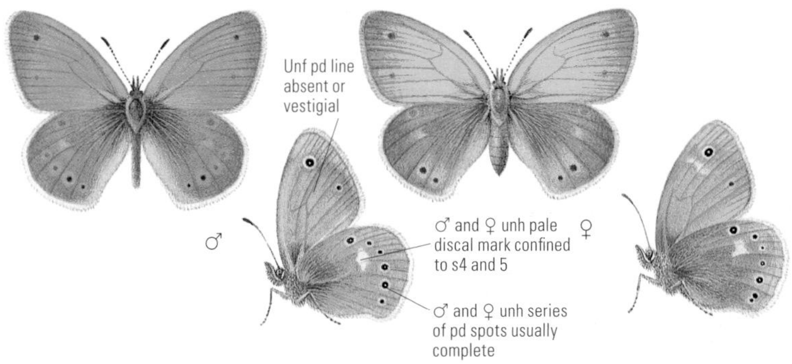

Small Heath *Coenonympha pamphilus*

RANGE N Africa, Europe, Turkey, Middle East, eastwards (40-60°N) to W Mongolia.

C. pamphilus Linnaeus 1758 TL: Sweden.

DISTRIBUTION NW Africa. 0-2700m. Throughout Europe including British Isles and most Mediterranean islands to 69°N in Fennoscandia. 0-1950m. Absent from Canary Islands, Azores, Madeira, Orkney Islands, Shetland Islands and Crete: not reported from SE Aegean Islands.

VARIATION Unh gc variable, grey to brownish; unh pd ocelli sometimes vestigial or absent. In some localities in S Europe, especially in summer broods, ups dark borders slightly wider (f. *marginata* Rühl). In NW Africa and SW Europe, f. *lyllus* Esper: ups submarginal dark borders wider; unf with diffuse black submarginal stripe in s1-5 and oblique reddish-brown pd bar in s2-6; unh basal and discal areas light sandy-brown, sometimes with well-defined, darker distal border; pd area pale creamy-buff; ocelli vestigial, often absent. All markings subject to appreciable variation: intermediate forms occur in Italy, S Balkans and Greece. In Sicily, *sicula* Zeller: resembles *C. thyrsis* Freyer (below).

FLIGHT-PERIOD Polyvoltine: number of broods and emergence of first brood greatly dependent on altitude and locality: February/November.

HABITAT Grassy places of very diverse character.

LIFE-HISTORY LHPs include *Festuca ovina*; *F. rubra*; *Poa annua*; *Anthoxanthum odoratum*; *Cynosurus cristatus*; *Dactylis glomerata*; *Nardus stricta*. Ova sometimes laid on plant-stems other than those of LHP. A proportion of larvae from early broods hibernate, in addition to those of final brood. Larvae polymorphic: greenish or reddish-brown.

Cretan Small Heath *Coenonympha thyrsis*

RANGE Crete.

C. thyrsis Freyer 1845 TL: Crete.

DISTRIBUTION Crete: widespread, locally common. 0-1800m.

VARIATION At higher altitudes: smaller; ups black marginal borders narrower; uns markings less prominent.

FLIGHT-PERIOD (?)Univoltine. Generally early May/early July according to altitude: recorded also in late July, August and early October (see Life-history).

HABITAT Grassy areas of diverse character, but reportedly showing preference for relatively damp areas, compared to those frequented by *C. pamphilus* on Greek mainland.

LIFE-HISTORY Larval polymorphism similar to that of *C. pamphilus*. In extended photo-period of S England, larval development of summer progeny is completed rapidly without diapause, suggesting partial/complete bivoltinism or possibly polyvoltinism in nature. Hibernation stage unconfirmed.

NOTE Apart from wing morphology and voltinism, genitalia and antennae differ significantly from those of *C. pamphilus*.

Corsican Heath *Coenonympha corinna*

RANGE Corsica, Sardinia.

C. corinna Hübner 1804 TL: Sardinia.

DISTRIBUTION Corsica. Island of Capraia (NE of Corsica). Sardinia: widespread, locally common. 0-2000m: generally below 1200m.

DESCRIPTION AND VARIATION Unh pale pd band irregular; ocelli vestigial or absent except in s3 and s6, when present, ocelli in s2-4 co-linear. In second and (?)subsequent broods: ups dark marginal borders wider, that of upf sometimes with internal cuspidal projection along v3. On Island of Capraia, f. *trettaui* Gross: transitional to *C. elbana*.

FLIGHT-PERIOD Polyvoltine. Mid May/August.

HABITAT Grassy, bushy and rocky places; open woodland; margins of cultivation.

Elban Heath *Coenonympha elbana*

RANGE W Italy (Elba, Giglo and nearby mainland).

C. elbana Staudinger 1901 TL: Elba.

DISTRIBUTION W Italy: Islands of Elba, Giglio and Giannutri; coastal area of Tuscany (Mte. Calvi; Mte. Massoncello; Mte. Ballone; Mte. della Uccellina; Mte. Argentario; Grosseto). 0-800m.

DESCRIPTION Unf dark antemarginal and submarginal lines prominent; unh pale pd band and proximal dark border almost linear in s2-s4; ocelli usually in complete series (cf. *C. corinna*).

FLIGHT-PERIOD Polyvoltine. Early May/September.

HABITAT Grassy, bushy places.

NOTE Specific status not established: perhaps better regarded as form/ssp. of *C. corinna*.

Small Heath

Cretan Small Heath

Corsican Heath

Elban Heath

SMALL HEATH

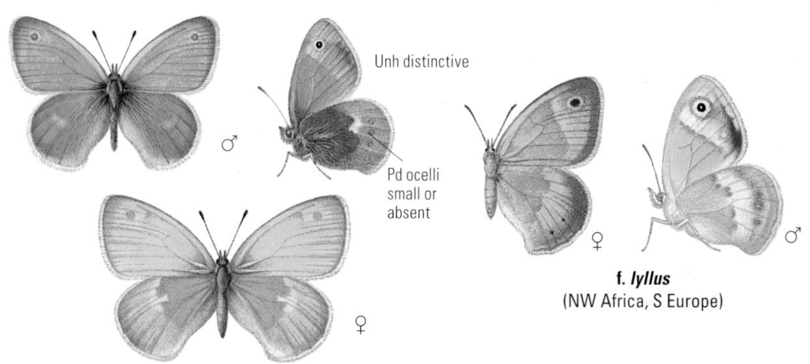

CRETAN SMALL HEATH

Ups and uns pattern of markings distinctive

Restricted to Crete

♂

♀

CORSICAN HEATH

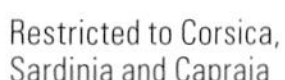

♂

♀

ELBAN HEATH

Ups and uns antemarginal lines distinctive

Rrestricted to Elba

♂

♀

Dusky Heath *Coenonympha dorus*

RANGE NW Africa, SW Europe to C Italy.

C. dorus dorus Esper 1782 TL: Toulouse, France.

DISTRIBUTION Portugal. Spain. France: Pyrénées-Orientales to Lozère, Haute-Alps and Alpes-Maritimes; (?)Lot. Italy: very local: Maritime Alps; N and C Apennines. 100-1700m.

DESCRIPTION Uph pd ocelli in s1c-4 in a proximally convex curved line – characteristic of nominate form and derivatives (cf. *C. vaucheri*).

VARIATION Ups coloration and uns markings subject to considerable regional, local and individual variation. In NW Spain and N Portugal, *bieli* Staudinger: male ups darker, smoky brown, ocelli vestigial; uns markings less contrastive, ocelli small: similar forms occur in E Spain and in some localities in S France. In C Italy, *aquilonia* Higgins: resembles *C. dorus*: male upf pd band, narrow, yellow-fulvous; unh pd ocelli small but series complete.

FLIGHT-PERIOD Univoltine. Early June/mid August.

HABITAT Dry, grassy and bushy places, often in woodland clearings; hot, dry rocky slopes and gullies, usually amongst scrub.

LIFE-HISTORY LHPs *Agrostis canina*; *A. alba*; *Festuca ovina*.

C. dorus fettigii Oberthür 1874 TL: Province of Oran [Telaghre] Algeria.

DISTRIBUTION Morocco: Middle Atlas; High Atlas; Rif Mts. Algeria. Tunisia. 800-2200m.

DESCRIPTION Male upf yellow-fulvous pd band sometimes extending into discal area; upf ocelli small or absent; unh discal area pale yellowish-grey, distal margin poorly defined except at anterior, paler pd area; ocelli very small, usually absent in s1, s4 and s5.

VARIATION Subject to marked individual and regional/altitudinal variation with some wing-characters more stable in some populations: distributional and ecological relationship of named forms/ssp. unclear. In C and E Algeria and W Tunisia (800-1600m), *nicholasi* Rothschild: male ups orange pd area more extensive; unh gc paler; anterior pale pd area averagely larger: female marginal brown borders narrower. In W Morocco (800-2200m), *inframaculata* Oberthür: resembles *fettigii* closely: variable, especially in Rif Mts.

FLIGHT-PERIOD Univoltine. Mid June/late August according to locality and altitude.

NOTE Accorded specific rank by some authors (see *C. dorus austauti* (below)).

C. dorus austauti Oberthür 1881 TL: Nemours, Algeria.

DISTRIBUTION NE Morocco: local: Beni-Snassen. W Algeria: Sounai; Nedroma; Maghnia; Lalla Marina; Zough-el-Beghal; Masser Mines. 600-900m.

DESCRIPTION Resembles nominate form. Upf apical ocellus dark, large, 'blind', clearly ringed orange; uph series of 'blind'pd ocelli usually complete; unh white-pupilled, orange ringed ocelli well developed; silver-grey antemarginal line conspicuous; proximal, central margin of pale discal band linear; antemarginal area of s1c-3 yellowish-buff. Similar forms occur in S Spain.

FLIGHT-PERIOD Univoltine. Mid June/early August.

HABITAT Dry, rocky places with sparse vegetation.

NOTE Often accorded specific rank: in absence of biological data, extensive range of superficial variation of above taxa precludes definitive evaluation.

Vaucher's Heath *Coenonympha vaucheri*

RANGE Morocco.

C. vaucheri vaucheri Blachier 1905 TL: High Atlas, Morocco.

DISTRIBUTION Morocco: High Atlas (Imilchil; Tizi-n-Test; Oukaïmeden; Tizi-n-Talremt; Amizmiz; Tizi-n-Melloul; Tizi-n-Tieta). 1800m to at least 3000m – a male was recorded at the summit of Dj. Toubkal (4167m) in June 1994.

DESCRIPTION Male ups gc orange, sometimes largely obscured by dark fuscous suffusion; upf subapical ocellus, large, dark, 'blind', usually ovoid bridging s4 and s5 – distinctive; uph series of 'blind'pd ocelli in s1c-4 almost linear (cf. *C. dorus*), occasional, smaller ocellus in s5 displaced basad; uns markings sharply defined; unf gc dusky-orange, contrasting with yellowish pd area; subapical ocellus with twin, silver-white pupils; unh dark, brownish basal area enclosing distinctive pale mark in cell; dark submarginal band enclosing small, white-pupilled ocelli in s1c-6; pale pd band distal edge irregular, with ray-like projections tending to penetrate submarginal band, especially along v4: female similar: larger; ups gc paler, generally lacking dark suffusion; markings better defined.

FLIGHT-PERIOD Univoltine. Late May/August or September according to season.

HABITAT Grassy slopes; more often, dry, rocky slopes with sparse vegetation.

LIFE-HISTORY Hibernation stage unconfirmed.

C. vaucheri annoceuri Wyatt 1952 TL: Annoceur, Middle Atlas.

DISTRIBUTION Morocco: Middle Atlas (Tizi-Tarhzeft; Tizi-n-Taghzeft; Col du Zad; Tizi-bou-Zabel; Annoceur). 1800-2300m.

DESCRIPTION Resembles nominate form. Usually smaller; ups brighter, lacking dark suffusion; ocelli smaller.

FLIGHT-PERIOD Univoltine. Late May/early August, according to season.

HABITAT AND LIFE-HISTORY As for nominate form.

C. vaucheri rifensis Weiss 1979 TL: Dj. Lakraa, Rif Mts.

DISTRIBUTION Morocco: W Rif Mts. 1900-2200m.

DESCRIPTION Resembles *annoceuri*. Small; ups and uns paler; upf subapical ocellus averagely smaller; unh submarginal band paler, contrasting poorly with pale pd band.

FLIGHT-PERIOD Univoltine. Late June/early August.

HABITAT AND LIFE-HISTORY As for nominate form.

C. vaucheri beraberensis Lay and Rose 1979 TL: Tizi-n' Ouguerd-Zegzaoune, Morocco.

DISTRIBUTION Morocco: High Atlas (Tizi-n'Ouguerd-Zegzaoune; Dj. Aourach; Imlil; Lake Tislit). 2150-3000m.

DESCRIPTION Resembles nominate form. Larger; ups pd areas sharply defined, paler, somewhat yellowish; marginal

DUSKY HEATH

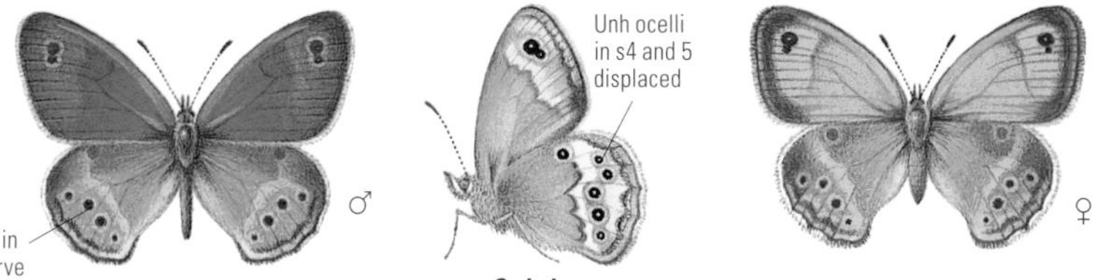

Unh ocelli in s4 and 5 displaced

♂

♀

Unh ocelli in convex curve towards basal area

C. d. dorus

♂

♀

♂

♀

C. d. bieli
(NW Spain, N Portugal)

C. d. fettigii
(Morocco, Algeria)

♂ upf subapical ocellus large, ringed orange

♂

♀

C. d. austauti
(NE Morocco, W Algeria)

VAUCHER'S HEATH

♂ and ♀ ups and uns pattern of markings distinctive

Restricted to Morocco

Dusky Heath

Vaucher's Heath

dark borders heavy; upf and unf subapical ocellus larger, prominent; unf pale yellow pd and orange basal areas well-delineated, contrastive; unh markings indistinguishable from those of nominate form.
FLIGHT-PERIOD Univoltine. Mid June/July.
HABITAT Hot valleys and rocky slopes.
LIFE-HISTORY Hibernation stage unconfirmed.
NOTE Taxonomic relationship of above forms not clearly understood: overall *known* variation in most wing-characters very marked (cf. *C. dorus*).

Pearly Heath *Coenonympha arcania*

RANGE W Europe, Turkey, Transcaucasus, S Russia, S and C Urals.
C. arcania Linnaeus 1761 TL: Sweden.
syn: *amyntas* Poda 1761.
DISTRIBUTION From N and C Spain through most of Europe (except Britain) to Norway (Oslo Fjord), S Sweden (S of Uppland, including Öland and Gotland), Balkans, N and C Greece and European Turkey. 50-1800m.
DESCRIPTION AND VARIATION Unh irregular, creamy-white pd band and ocelli conspicuous, ocellus in s6 proximal to pd band (cf. *C. darwiniana*). In E Spain, *chlorinda* de Sagarra: uph inner margin fulvous-orange, sometimes extending to anal angle, variable.
FLIGHT-PERIOD Univoltine. Mid May/mid August in a prolonged emergence.
HABITAT Grassy, flowery, bushy places; damp or dry woodland clearings.
LIFE-HISTORY LHPs *Poa pratensis*; *Melica ciliata*; *Holcus lanatus*.

Darwin's Heath *Coenonympha darwiniana*

RANGE Alps of France, S Switzerland and Italy .
C. darwiniana Staudinger 1871 TL: Switzerland (Valais).
DISTRIBUTION France: very local: Alpes-Maritimes; Alpes-de-Haute-Provençe. S Switzerland: restricted to southern alpine slopes (Valais to Graubunden). Italy: Venosta to Dolomites. 800-2100m.
DESCRIPTION Unh ocelli ringed yellow, ocellus in s6 contained within white pd band (cf. *C. arcania*).
FLIGHT-PERIOD Univoltine. Early June/August.
HABITAT Flowery, grassy places.

Alpine Heath *Coenonympha gardetta*

RANGE France, Italy, S Switzerland, Germany and Austria.
C gardetta de Prunner 1798 TL: Val Varaita, Alpes-Maritimes.
syn: *satyrion* Esper 1804; *philea* Hübner 1800 (invalid homonym); *neoclides* Hübner 1805.
DISTRIBUTION France: NE Massif Central; Alpes-Maritimes; Basses Alpes. Italy: Cottian Alps to Dolomites. S Switzerland: Valais to Engadine. Germany: Bavarian Alps. Austria: Tirol; Karawanken Mts. Reported from mountains of Bosnia-Herzegovenia, SW Serbia (Kopaonik Pl.) and Albania. 800-2900m: rarely below 1500m.
DESCRIPTION AND VARIATION Ups extensively or entirely greyish; unh ocelli not ringed yellow, usually enclosed in white pd band (cf. *C. darwiniana*). At lower altitudes, f. *macrophthamica* Stauder: upf basal area often with fulvous-orange flush; upf with small apical ocellus; unh ocelli larger.
FLIGHT-PERIOD Univoltine. Late June/mid September according to altitude.
HABITAT Exposed alpine meadows at higher altitude; grassy slopes with sparse bushes and trees at lower levels.

Moroccan Pearly Heath *Coenonympha arcanioides*

RANGE Morocco, N Algeria, N Tunisia.
C. arcanioides Pierret 1837 TL: Oran, Algeria.
DISTRIBUTION Morocco. N Algeria. N Tunisia. Local but widespread from coastal hills to northern slopes of Middle Atlas. 0-1800m.
DESCRIPTION Upf gc fulvous; dark fuscous outer marginal border and apex enclosing small, subapical 'blind' ocellus; uph dark fuscous with submarginal orange line in anal angle; unf discal area dusky orange, sharply divided from paler pd band; subapex, inner and outer margins greyish; subapical yellow-ringed, white-pupilled ocellus large, conspicuous; unh gc dark brown; irregular white pd band prominent; small, white-pupilled pd ocelli usually present in s1c-5; fw and hw with metallic antemarginal line: female similar: larger; ups paler.
FLIGHT-PERIOD Polyvoltine. April/September.
HABITAT AND BEHAVIOUR Dry, rocky, grassy places amongst scrub, often in gullies near oleander bushes and broom ((?)*Genista* sp.) amongst which adults often secrete themselves when disturbed.
LIFE-HISTORY Hibernation stage unconfirmed.

Pearly Heath

Darwin's Heath

Alpine Heath

Moroccan Pearly Heath

PEARLY HEATH

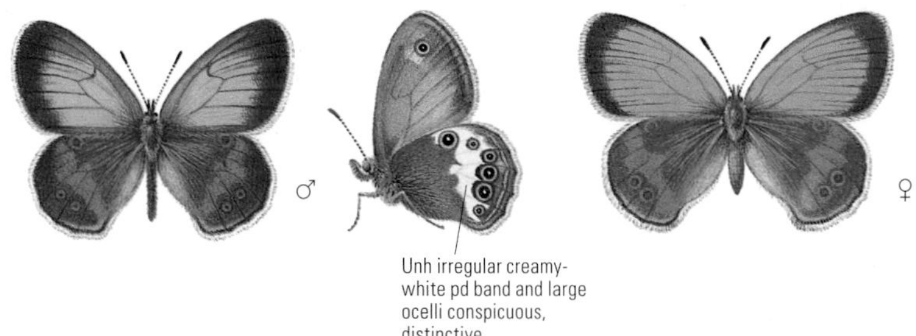

Unh irregular creamy-white pd band and large ocelli conspicuous, distinctive

---

DARWIN'S HEATH

Restricted to C Alps

Unh ocellus in s6

ALPINE HEATH

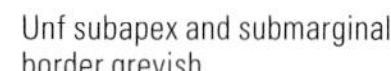
Unf subapex and submarginal border greyish

Unh white pd band enclosing complete series of ocelli distinctive

---

MOROCCAN PEARLY HEATH

Restricted to Morocco, N Algeria and N Tunisia

Unh white pd band distinctive

Russian Heath *Coenonympha leander*

RANGE S Balkans, N Greece, Turkey, NW Iran, Transcaucasus, S Urals.

C. leander Esper 1784 TL: Russia, Volga.

DISTRIBUTION Locally common. Romania: S Carpathian Mts. Republic of Macedonia. Bulgaria. N Greece: Varnous Mts.; Vernon Mts.; Askion Mts.; N Pindos Mts.; E Thrace. 350-1900m.

VARIATION In Pindos Mts. (Tzoumérka Mts. to Grammos Mt. 1000-1900m), *orientalis* Rebel: resembles nominate form except unh white ocellular rings confluent, extending proximally to form prominent pd band; variable, some individuals transitional to nominate form.

FLIGHT-PERIOD Univoltine. Generally mid May/early August according to altitude and locality: in NE Greece, mid April/May.

HABITAT Warm, grassy, flowery, bushy woodland margins/ clearings.

LIFE-HISTORY Captive larvae accept *Festuca ovina*; *Brachypodium sylvaticum*.

Chestnut Heath *Coenonympha glycerion*

RANGE Europe, Russia, N Kazakhstan, Mongolia.

C. glycerion glycerion Borkhausen 1788 TL: not stated.
syn: *iphis* Denis and Schiffermüller 1775 (invalid homonym)

DISTRIBUTION France: E Pyrenees; Massif Central; Provence to Ardennes. Italy: W Ligurian Alps to Cottian Alps; Venosta; C Apennines. Switzerland to S Finland, Balkans and N Greece (Rhodopi Mts.). 250-2100m, generally below 1800m.

DESCRIPTION Unh white discal marks in s1c and s4 distinctive; pd white-pupilled ocelli uneven in size, variable; orange antemarginal line in anal angle.

VARIATION Unh markings, size and number of ocelli subject to marked regional variation: unh ocelli sometimes absent (f. *bertolis* Prunner), especially at higher altitudes.

FLIGHT-PERIOD Univoltine. Early June/late August according to locality.

HABITAT Grassy, bushy places; woodland clearings: in damp or dry conditions.

LIFE-HISTORY LHPs *Brachypodium sylvaticum*; *Cynosurus cristatus*; *Briza media*; *Melica ciliata*; *Bromus erectus*; *B. hordeaceus*.

C. glycerion iphioides Staudinger 1870 TL: Castile, Spain.

DISTRIBUTION Spain: Cantabrian Mts. and Pyrenees to Montes Universales. 600-1600m. Not reported from Portugal.

DESCRIPTION Resembles *C. glycerion*: larger; upf apical ocellus absent; unh pd series of ocelli complete. Transitional to nominate form at higher altitudes in Pyrenees and Montes Universales (f. *pearsoni* Romei). Darker, somewhat greyish forms occur on damp acidic soils.

FLIGHT-PERIOD Univoltine. Late May/August.

HABITAT As for nominate form.

NOTE Considered specifically distinct by some authors.

Scarce Heath *Coenonympha hero*

RANGE NE France, S Scandinavia, C Europe, S and C Urals, Tobol River, W Siberia, Mongolia, Amur, Korea, Japan.

C. hero Linnaeus 1761 TL: S Sweden.

DISTRIBUTION Colonies generally very small, few in number and widely dispersed. France: Allier; Nièvre; Saône-et-Loire; Ain; Jura; Haut Rhin; Bas Rhin; Seine-et-Marne; Meuse; Moselle. NW, NE and C Switzerland. S and E Germany. N Austria. Poland to S Fennoscandia (Denmark, only on Sjælland) and Baltic states. 50-700m.

DESCRIPTION Ups very dark brown; uph ocelli prominent; unh ocellus in s6 not displaced basad; pd ocelli with irregular proximal pale band; antemarginal silver-grey and orange lines conspicuous (cf. *C. oedippus*).

FLIGHT-PERIOD Univoltine. Mid May/early July according to season and locality.

HABITAT Damp or wet meadows dominated by grasses, usually on infertile, peat-based soils; less often drier, grassy woodland clearings or herb-rich, flowery meadows.

LIFE-HISTORY LHPs *Leymus arenarius* [=*Elymus arenarius*]; *Hordeum marinum*; *Hordelymus europaeus*.

CONSERVATION One of the more seriously threatened of the European species: in rapid decline in many regions. Despite well-publicized European legislation to protect endangered European butterfly species, the essential, concomitant need to afford *equivalent* protection to habitats appears to have been largely or entirely ignored. In the case of *C. hero*, conversion of habitats to conifer or poplar plantations continues.

Russian Heath

Chestnut Heath

Scarce Heath

RUSSIAN HEATH

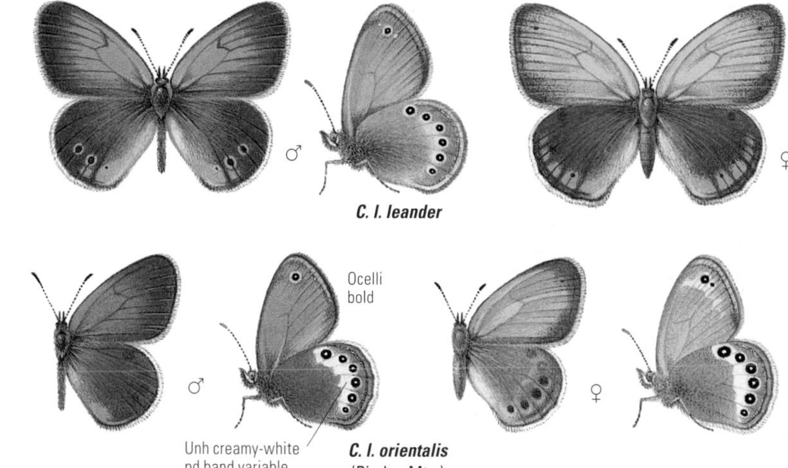

C. l. leander

C. l. orientalis
(Pindos Mts.)

CHESTNUT HEATH

C. g. glycerion

C. g. iphioides
(N Spain)

SCARCE HEATH

False Ringlet *Coenonympha oedippus*

RANGE Europe, W Russia, Urals, S and W Siberia, N Kazakhstan, Mongolia, China, Japan.

C. oedippus Fabricus 1787 TL: S Russia.

DISTRIBUTION Very sporadic, usually extremely local: Pyrénées-Atlantiques to Charante-Maritime and Charante; Sarthe; Seine-et-Marne; Savoie; Isère. Switzerland: Rhine Valley; Tessin. Italy: Varese; Treviso; Friuli-Venezia Giulia. Slovenia. Austria. Poland. Hungary. (?)Albania. No recent records from Germany or Bulgaria. Extinct in Belgium. Records for N Spain require confirmation. 150-500m.

DESCRIPTION AND VARIATION Unh ocellus in s6 displaced basad (cf. *C. hero*); ocellus in s5 (often very small) not displaced basad (cf. *A. hyperanthus*). Unh pale band proximal to pd ocelli variable, often absent. In some localities in Austria and Hungary, *hungarica* Rebel: ups and uns ocelli reduced, locally variable, rarely absent on female uph.

FLIGHT-PERIOD Univoltine. Early June/early August.

HABITAT Wet meadows and peripheral areas of damp, grassy, open scrubland, invariably associated with rivers or lakes.

LIFE-HISTORY LHPs *Poa palustris*; *P. pratensis*; *P. annua*. Conservation. A seriously threatened species – circumstances pertaining to *C. hero* apply equally to *C. oedippus*.

Speckled Wood *Pararge aegeria*

RANGE N Africa, Europe, Turkey, Israel, Syria, Transcaucasus, S and C Urals.

P. aegeria aegeria Linnaeus 1758 TL: S Europe and Algeria.
syn: *vulgaris* Zeller 1847.

DISTRIBUTION Widespread and common. NW Africa: northern coast to southern slopes of High Atlas. 0-2500m. Iberian Peninsula. Balearic Islands. SW and S France. S Switzerland. Italy. Corsica. Sardinia. Sicily. Aegean Islands of Crete, Lesbos, Samos, Kos and Karpathos. Not reported from Rhodes. First noted on Madeira in 1976, now widespread. 0-1500m.

DESCRIPTION In both sexes: gc orange; fw outer margin concave below subapex; (cf. *P. xiphioides* and *P. xiphia*).

VARIATION From NW France to Maritime Alps, eastwards into C France, transitional to *tircis* (below): intermediate forms also occur in SW Britain (Scilly Isles and Channel Islands), S Greece (Peloponnesos) and Samos. In exceptionally hot summers, specimens with gc corresponding to nominate form have been reported from C England. In NW Africa, unh gc pale buff to dark, reddish-brown.

FLIGHT-PERIOD Bivoltine or trivoltine, late February/early October according to locality and altitude.

HABITAT Deciduous, coniferous and mixed woodland. In hot localities of S Europe, often associated with tree-lined rivers or small streams.

BEHAVIOUR Prefers shady areas with dappled sunlight, where males often bask on sunlit leaves or woodland floor. Males are very territorial.

LIFE-HISTORY LHPs include *Brachypodium sylvaticum*; *B. pinnatum*; *Holcus lanatus*; *Cynodon dactylon*; *Agrostis gigantea*; *Dactylis glomerata*; *Elymus repens* [=*Triticum repens*; *Agropyron repens*; *Elytrigia repens*]. Madeira, *B. sylvaticum*. Hibernates as a larva or pupa.

P. aegeria tircis Butler 1867 TL: France.
syn: *egerides* Staudinger 1871.

DISTRIBUTION British Isles, C and E France, N and C Switzerland to 64°N in Fennoscandia (including Baltic Islands), Balkans and Greece, Corfu, Thassos, Lesbos. 0-1750m.

DESCRIPTION Resembles nominate form: in both sexes, gc yellow or creamy-white.

VARIATION In southern range, gc of late broods tends towards that of nominate form.

FLIGHT-PERIOD Bivoltine. Late March/mid June and late June/early October.

HABITAT AND LIFE-HISTORY As for nominate form.

NOTE Circumstances relating to variation in gc suggest strong ecological influence (temperature/humidity). Although phenotype of populations of Thassos and Lesbos (NE Aegean Islands) has not been reported, these islands fall within geographical range of *tircis* (widespread in N Turkey; recorded from Gelibolu Peninsula and some coastal sites in NW Turkey: replaced by nominate form in S Turkey).

Canary Speckled Wood *Pararge xiphioides*

RANGE Canary Islands.

P. xiphioides Staudinger 1871 TL: Canary Islands.

DISTRIBUTION Canary Islands: Gomera; La Palma; Tenerife; Gran Canaria. 200-2000m.

DESCRIPTION Fw outer margin linear: unh with white band extending from costa to cell (cf. *P. xiphia*).

FLIGHT-PERIOD Polyvoltine. Recorded throughout the year.

HABITAT Laurel and Chestnut forests; less often in Pine or other woodland.

LIFE-HISTORY LHPs: Tenerife, *Brachypodium sylvaticum*; *Carex divulsa*; *Agrostis tenuous*; *Luzula forsteri*; *Oryzopsis miliacea*; *Dactylis glomerata*: La Palma, *Brachypodium sylvaticum*; *B. pinnatum*. Hibernation stage unconfirmed.

False Ringlet

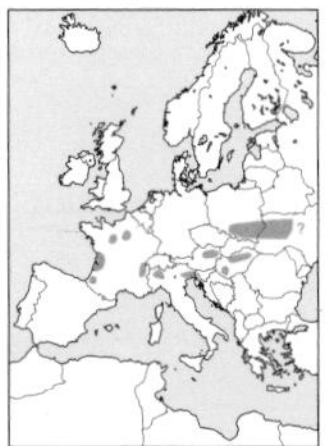

Speckled Wood

FALSE RINGLET

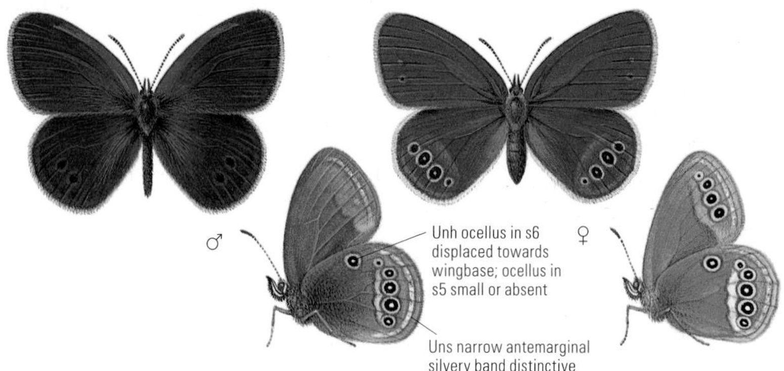

SPECKLED WOOD

P. a. aegeria

P. a. tircis

CANARY SPECKLED WOOD

Restricted to Canary Islands

Madeiran Speckled Wood *Pararge xiphia*

RANGE Madeira.

P. xiphia Fabricius 1775 TL: Madeira

DISTRIBUTION Madeira. 0-1000m.

DESCRIPTION Fw outer margin slightly convex: unh with small white mark on costa (cf. *P. xiphioides*).

FLIGHT-PERIOD Polyvoltine. Recorded in all months with no apparent discontinuity but with reduced abundance June/August.

HABITAT Laurel and chestnut forests.

LIFE-HISTORY LHPs *Brachypodium sylvaticum*; *Holcus lanatus*; *Agrostis gigantea*. Hibernation stage unconfirmed.

Wall Brown *Lasiommata megera*

RANGE N Africa, Europe, Turkey, Israel, Lebanon, Syria, Iraq, Iran, Transcaucasus, Turkmenistan.

L. megera Linnaeus 1767 TL: Austria and Denmark.

DISTRIBUTION Widespread and common. N Africa. 0-3000m. Most of Europe, from Ireland, S Scotland, S Scandinavia (including Baltic Islands), S Lithuania, S Latvia (possibly extinct) to Iberian peninsula, S Greece, European Turkey and most Mediterranean islands. Absent from N Denmark, Estonia and Finland. 0-2300m.

DESCRIPTION Upf with two, transverse cellular bars (cf. *L. maera*).

VARIATION Both sexes, unh gc brownish in N Europe, greyish in S Europe. On Corsica, Sardinia, Capraia, Montecristo and Balearic Islands, *paramegera* Hübner: resembles nominate form, but smaller; upf dark pd lines in s1b and s2 thinner or vestigial; uph irregular pd band absent. Transitional forms occur with nominate form in Balearic Islands and Sicily.

FLIGHT-PERIOD Bivoltine or trivoltine. Early April/October according to locality and altitude.

HABITAT Diverse. Grassy, rocky slopes/gullies; flowery meadows; woodland clearings associated with open stony ground, paths etc.

LIFE-HISTORY LHPs include *Dactylis glomerata*; *Agrostis tenuis*; *A. gigantea*; *A. capillaris*; *Deschampsia flexuosa*; *Holcus lanatus*; *Festuca ovina*; *Brachypodium sylvaticum*; *B. pinnatum*.

BEHAVIOUR Males are very alert and easily disturbed from paths, stones, rock faces or walls on which they often bask. Shelter provided by overhanging rocks are favoured roosting sites. Commonly found 'hilltopping': recorded near summit of Dj. Toubkal, High Atlas (4160m).

NOTE Population of Sardinia and (?)Corsica accorded specific status (*L. tigellius* Bonelli 1826) by some authors.

Northern Wall Brown *Lasiommata petropolitana*

RANGE Pyrenees, eastwards on most larger mountain massifs to Fennoscandia, N Turkey, N Siberia and Amur.

L. petropolitana Fabricius 1787 TL: Petrograd.

syn: *hiera* auct.

DISTRIBUTION Generally local. Higher mountain ranges of S Europe from Pyrenees, through Central Alps to Carpathian Mts., Balkans and N Greece. 500-2250m. Also, Norway, Sweden (including Gotland), Finland, Latvia and Estonia. 100-1200m. Absent from (?)Spain, Andorra, Massif Central, Denmark, Peninsular Italy, S Greece and Mediterranean islands.

DESCRIPTION Uph with irregular, transverse discal line (cf. *L. maera*).

FLIGHT-PERIOD Univoltine. Late April/early August according to altitude. Possibly a partial second brood at low altitudes in southern range.

HABITAT Grassy, stony, sandy or rocky banks and gullies in woodland clearings or margins.

LIFE-HISTORY LHPs include *Calamagrostis epigejos*; *Festuca ovina*; *Dactylis glomerata*. Hibernates as a larva or pupa.

BEHAVIOUR Adults often rest on bare ground or fallen tree-trunks. Shelter provided by overhanging rock-ledges or exposed tree-roots on earthen banks are favoured roosting/resting sites.

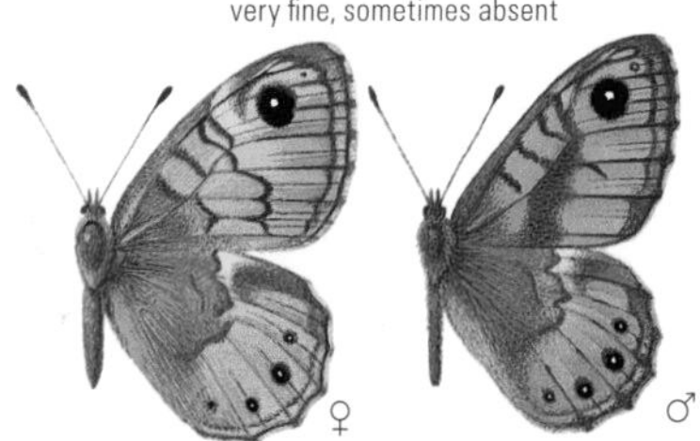

L. m. paramegera

Wall Brown

Northern Wall Brown

Large Wall Brown

Woodland Brown

MADEIRAN SPECKLED WOOD

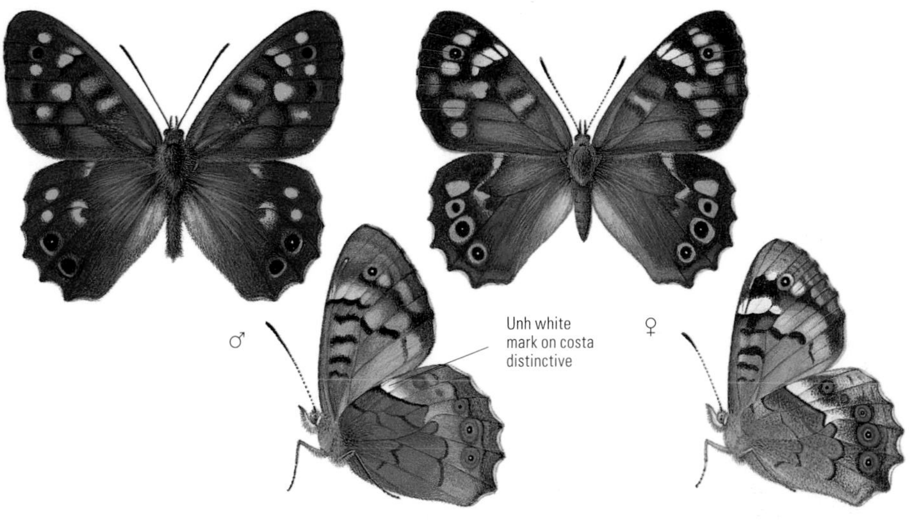

WALL BROWN

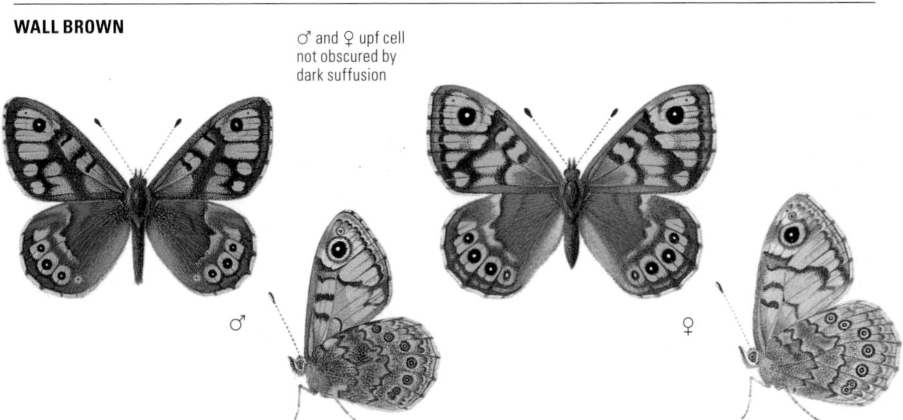

NORTHERN WALL BROWN

Large Wall Brown *Lasiommata maera*

RANGE N Africa and Europe to W Siberia and Tian Shan.
L. maera maera Linnaeus 1758 TL: Sweden (Verity 1953).
syn: *monotonia* Schilde 1885; *hiera* Fabricus 1777.
DISTRIBUTION Morocco. Middle Atlas; Rif Mts. Algeria: Djurdjura massif. Records for Tunisia require confirmation. 800-2500m. From Iberian Peninsula (except SW), Sicily, Greece and European Turkey (including many Ionian and Aegean Islands) through most of Europe to 68°N in Fennoscandia (including Öland). Absent from Britain, N Belgium, Holland, NW Germany, Denmark, N Finland, Balearic Islands, Corsica, Sardinia and Crete. 0-2000m.
DESCRIPTION AND VARIATION Upf with one transverse cellular bar (cf. *L. megera*); uph without transverse discal line (cf. *L. petropolitana*); unh gc variable, light grey to greyish-brown. In Fennoscandia, f. *borealis* Fuchs: smaller; ups dark suffusion more extensive, but upf subapical yellow/orange patch retained. In Iberian Peninsula and Mediterranean region, f. *adrasta* Illiger: female upf orange-fulvous pd area extended towards base: second brood smaller; ups orange markings more extensive.
FLIGHT-PERIOD Univoltine in north, mid June/late August; bivoltine in south, late April/June and June/late September. Reported trivoltinism in NW Africa requires confirmation.
HABITAT Dry, grassy, rocky or stony places, including steep slopes and screes.
LIFE-HISTORY LHPs include *Glyceria fluitans*; *Deschampsia flexuosa*; *Calamagrostis epigejos*; *C. arundinacea*; *C. varia*; *Nardus stricta*; *Hordeum marinum*; *Agrostis capillaris*; *Luzula luzuloides*; *Holcus mollis*; *Festuca rubra*; *F. ovina*.
BEHAVIOUR Recorded 'hilltopping' in Atlas Mts., and at 2900m in Sierra Nevada.
L. maera meadewaldoi Rothschild 1917 TL: Tizi Gourzá, Morocco.
syn: *alluaudi* Oberthür 1922.
DISTRIBUTION Morocco: High Atlas; known only from Toubkal massif (Tizi Gourzá; Oukaïmeden; Tizi-n-Test). 2100-3700m, more generally 2200-3200m.
DESCRIPTION Resembles nominate form: larger (male fw 27-30mm; female fw up to 32mm); male ups gc rusty-brown; unf gc dull yellow-orange with greyish tone; unh gc greyish-brown: female ups gc dull fulvous-orange; unf fulvous-orange; unh gc grey-brown: in both sexes, ups and uns ocellular white pupils prominent.
FLIGHT-PERIOD Voltinism uncertain: possibly univoltine. Generally mid June/August; records span late May/early September.
HABITAT Rocky slopes; cliffs; barren mountain ridges; steep grassy slopes – more usually, females frequent the latter habitat.
NOTE Regarded as specifically distinct by some authors. Known circumstances of occurrence suggest possible ecological influence on size, wing-markings and voltinism. Univoltinism, relating to cooler conditions prevalent at higher altitude, implies an extended period available for larval development, resulting in larger imagines relative to bivoltine forms at lower altitude. Adaptive alteration in wing-colour/pattern is also not unexpected: within the European range of the species, a correlation of phenotype and voltinism with climatic conditions is apparent.

Woodland Brown *Lopinga achine*

RANGE C Europe, Russia and NC Asia to Amur, Yssuri and Japan.
L. achine Scopoli 1763 TL: Carniola.
syn: *deianira* Linnaeus 1764.
DISTRIBUTION (?)N Spain: province of Vizcaya. France (C Pyrenees), through Switzerland (Jura; Valais; Tessin), N Italy (N of Po Valley to Julian Alps), Germany to SE Sweden (Östergötland; Gotland), Baltic states (including Dagö and Ösel), S Finland, N and E Balkans, (?)S Romania and (?)NE Bulgaria (first and last record 1902). Absent from Britain, Belgium, Holland, NW Germany and Denmark. 200-1500m. Generally very sporadic and local: reputedly in decline in France, Switzerland and N Italy.
VARIATION Uns pale band, proximal to pd spots, variable in width and colour.
FLIGHT-PERIOD Univoltine. Early June/late July.
HABITAT Grassy, bushy, often small clearings, in deciduous woodland; bushy margins of coniferous forests/plantations: in damp or dry conditions on calcareous and non-calcareous soils.
LIFE-HISTORY LHPs *Brachypodium sylvaticum*; *B. pinnatum*.

L. m. meadewaldoi (Morocco)

♂

Maps on p. 320

LARGE WALL BROWN

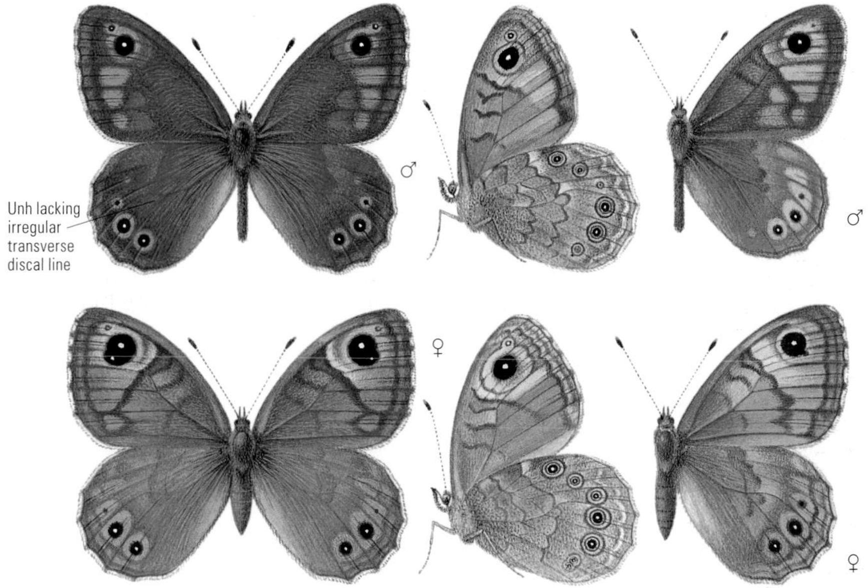
Unh lacking irregular transverse discal line
♂
♂
♀
♀

L. m. maera *L. m. maera* f. *adrasta*

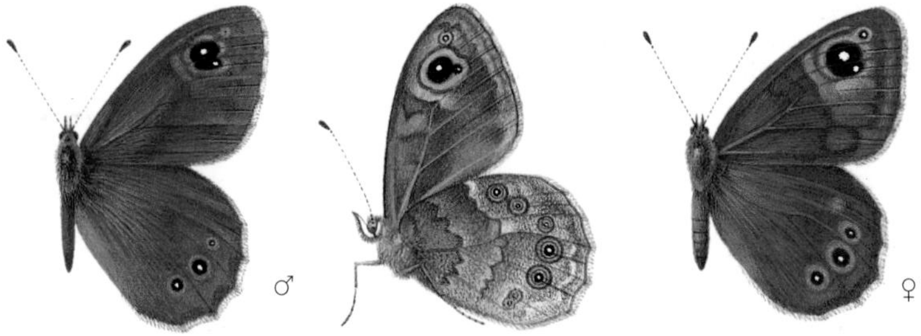
♂
♀

L. m. maera f. *borealis*
(Fennoscandia)

WOODLAND BROWN

Fw band yellow, hw white
♂
♀

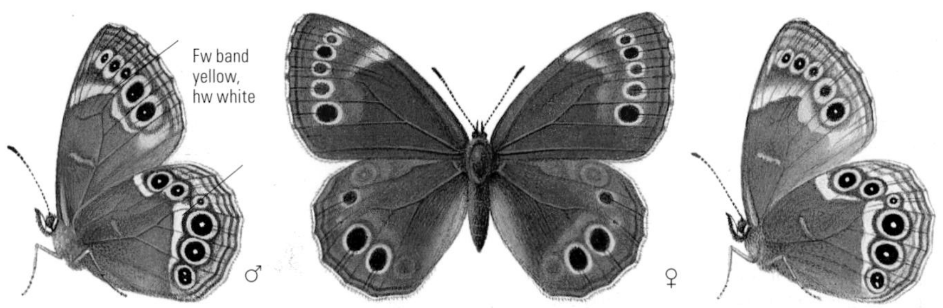

African Ringlet *Ypthima asterope*

RANGE Greece (Aegean Islands), Turkey, Middle East to India, Africa.
Y. asterope Klug 1832 TL: Syria and SW Saudi Arabia.
DISTRIBUTION Greece: known only from E Aegean Islands of Samos, Rhodes, Simi and Kastellorizo. 0-250m.
FLIGHT-PERIOD Polyvoltine. Early April/late October.
HABITAT Hot, stony, grassy places; dry stream-beds.
LIFE-HISTORY Captive larvae accept *Poa annua*.

Lattice Brown *Kirinia roxelana*

RANGE SE Europe, Turkey, Cyprus, Israel, Lebanon, Syria, N Iraq, W Iran.
K. roxelana Cramer 1777 TL: Istanbul.
DISTRIBUTION Widespread but local. SW Croatia (Dalmatian coast). S Bosnia-Herzegovina. Serbia. S Romania. Albania. Republic of Macedonia. Bulgaria. Greece, including Corfu, Levkas and most E Aegean islands. European Turkey. Not reported from Crete. 0-1750m.
FLIGHT-PERIOD Univoltine. Late April/September, according to locality. Fertilized females, along with a small number of males, appear to aestivate in hottest/driest summer months.
HABITAT Generally hot, dry bushy places, often in light, pine woodland: less often in cooler, damper conditions at higher altitudes.
LIFE-HISTORY Ova are laid in bark crevices on well-shaded bushes or trees. Unfed larvae sometimes enter brief diapause: feeding appears to be initiated by moisture and reduced temperature. Larvae, unusual and distinctive: long in proportion to width; pale green with paler, longitudinal stripes mimicking the veins and glossy reflections of grass-blades; posterior segment slender, with long 'tails'; head with two, lateral, slender, forward-projecting processes – resembling 'horns'. The small larva rests vertically in the fold of a wide grass-blade with the tips of its 'tails' and 'horns' splayed side-ways, coincident with leaf-edges: thus positioned, the larva closely resembles a small, green spider and is well camouflaged.
BEHAVIOUR Both sexes appear to spend much time in the interior, often deep shade of bushes, thickets or small trees: adults quickly retreat to such cover when disturbed. Males sometimes roost amongst rocks in exposed places, females more usually in bushes. In hot, calm conditions, both sexes sometimes gather at dusk in appreciable numbers on stony beds of dry watercourses, from which they are easily disturbed during early hours of darkness.

Lesser Lattice Brown *Kirinia climene*

RANGE SE Europe, Turkey, Ukraine, Caucasus, N Iran.
K. climene Esper 1783 TL: not stated.
DISTRIBUTION Very local and sporadic. (?)E Serbia. (?)SW Romania. (?)NE Albania. Republic of Macedonia: near Skopje, Gostivar, Lake Ochrid and Lake Prespa. NW Bulgaria: reported from Sliven (SE Stara Pl.) in 1896; presently known only from Vratsa (Gorna Kremena). NW Greece: N Pindos Mts.; Limni Mikri Préspa. 700-1600m. Records for district of Drama, N Greece require confirmation.
VARIATION Uph orange pd band variable, sometimes absent: female unh gc usually yellowish, less often greyish.
FLIGHT-PERIOD Univoltine. Mid June/late July.
HABITAT Grassy, bushy clearings in damp or dry mature deciduous or mixed woodland.
LIFE-HISTORY Larva closely resembles that of *K. roxelana*. Larvae feed on a robust, wide-stemmed grass. Larger larvae rest on stems opposite to a developing inflorescence: thus situated, a larva appears as an extension of the stem-node, rendering detection difficult.
BEHAVIOUR Adults often visit the forest canopy, where they roost on tree-trunks or underside of thicker tree-branches.

Lattice Brown

Lesser Lattice Brown

AFRICAN RINGLET

LATTICE BROWN

Upf sex-brand conspicuous, causing distortion of v1

♂

♀

LESSER LATTICE BROWN

HESPERIIDAE Latreille 1809

This ancient and cosmopolitan family is readily distinguished from other butterflies by several structural characters. The head of the adult insect is large, having similar proportions to the thorax, which itself is robust. The eyes are large and the distinctive antennae widely separated. Wing-veins are unbranched throughout their length. Males of the genera *Pyrgus*, *Muschampia* and *Carcharodus* have a costal fold on the fore-wing containing androconia. All species have a characteristic flight, some flying very fast and close to the ground. Some are known or suspected migrants. Larvae are usually cylindrical but in some genera tend to be bulbous in the posterior segments. The head is large. In some genera, a'collar'immediately behind the head may be marked with conspicuous white or yellow spots. In all European species for which the life-history is known, larvae live, feed and pupate in the security of shelters formed from leaves held in place by silk. Modification to the design of these structures may occur during larval development, a sequence of events well-illustrated by the genus *Pyrgus*, whose staple host-plants are species of *Potentilla* – plants with palmate, that is, three or five-lobed, leaves. Newly-hatched larvae feed singly on the concealed surfaces of overlapping leaves, drawn loosely together by a few strands of silk. Increasingly elaborate and secure constructions are employed in later instars. Half-grown larvae roll up individual leaves to form a tightly closed tubular tent, whereas larvae in their final instar adopt an entirely logical engineering strategy in which the outer edges of the three central lobes of a palmate leaf are drawn together, whilst the excess length of the central lobe is pulled down so as to form the lid of an irregular tetrahedron – a box. These structures are remarkably strong and difficult to tease open; situated on the more robust stems of the host-plant or concealed at its base amongst leaf litter, they also serve as hibernacula or pupation sites.

Grizzled Skipper *Pyrgus malvae*

RANGE Europe, NW Turkey, Tian Shan, Mongolia, N China, Korea.

P. malvae malvae Linnaeus 1758 TL: Aland Island, Finland. **DISTRIBUTION** From W France, Wales, S England, N and C Switzerland and N and E Austria to 65°N in Fennoscandia (including Baltic Islands), S Greece (including Lesbos) and European Turkey. Absent from Iberian peninsula, SW and S France and Italy – replaced by *P. malvae malvoides* (below). 0-1900m. **VARIATION** Aberrations with greatly extended and sometimes confluent white markings upf are not uncommon, especially in Greece. **FLIGHT-PERIOD** Univoltine (May/early July) or bivoltine (April/early June and late July/August) according to locality and altitude. Univoltine in N Europe, also in Greece and perhaps elsewhere in SE Europe. **HABITAT** Diverse. Grassy, flowery places. **LIFE-HISTORY** LHPs *Potentilla recta*; *P. sterilis*; *P. tabernaemontani*; *P. pedata*; *P. palustris*; *P. erecta*; *P. anglica*; *P. argentea*; *Fragaria vesca*; *Agrimonia eupatoria*; *Rubus fruticosus*. Hibernates as a pupa. In captivity, diapause may extend over two seasonal cycles.

P. malvae malvoides Elwes and Edwards 1897 TL: Biarritz. **DISTRIBUTION** Portugal. Spain. W and S France (Charante-Maritime through Massif Central to Haute-Savoie). SE Switzerland (S Engadine). SW Austria (S of Innsbruck). Italy, including Istria and Sicily. Absent from Balearic Islands, Corsica and Sardinia. 0-1800m. Exact distributional relationship with nominate form uncertain. **DESCRIPTION AND VARIATION** Wing-markings as for nominate form: male genitalia distinct. Interbreeds freely with nominate form in areas of distributional overlap, producing hybrids of intermediate character in male genitalia. In C Spain, ups white markings often reduced in second brood. **FLIGHT-PERIOD** Generally bivoltine, April/June and late July/August: univoltine at high altitudes, June/July. **HABITAT** As for nominate form. **LIFE-HISTORY** LHP: S Spain, *Potentilla pennsylvanica*. Hibernates as a pupa.

Pyrgus melotis

RANGE Turkey, Israel, Lebanon, Jordan, Syria, (?)N Iraq, Transcaucasus.

P. melotis Duponchel 1834. TL: Lebanon.

DISTRIBUTION According to *Guide des Papillons d'Europe* (Higgins and Riley, translated and adapted by Bourgoin 1988), this species occurs on the Kykladian island of Melos [= Milo or Milos]. Equivalent information is not given in any original, English edition of this field guide. Staudinger (1870), Seitz (1906) and de Jong (1972) refer to the presence of the species on Melos. Warren (1926) also mentions 'the island of Milo'in quoting Greece amongst... 'the only reliable records I can find for Europe'. Of the five, poorly labelled, Greek specimens extant in the collection of the Natural History Museum, London, none of the data-labels refer specifically to this island or give locality data more precise than 'Greece': a large and remotely located label referring to 'Is of Milo'is pinned in the case carrying these and many other specimens including those of other *Pyrgus* species. The most recent of the five specimens is a male taken by Elwes in 1962; the only reference to site of capture are the letters'GR'. A search for *P. melotis* on Melos by Mr J. G. Coutsis of Athens in May 1985 proved negative. **DESCRIPTION** Unh extensive white, somewhat striated suffusion is very striking, rendering this species quite unlike any other European member of the genus.

Large Grizzled Skipper *Pyrgus alveus*

RANGE N Africa, Spain, Europe, Turkey, Transcaucasus, S and W Siberia, Urals, Transbaikal, Mongolia, N China.

P. alveus alveus Hübner 1803 TL: Germany.

DISTRIBUTION From W and C France (Massif Central; Jura Mts.; Vosges Mts.: very local and sporadic in other regions) through S Belgium to 60°N in Norway, Sweden (including Öland and Gotland), Baltic states and Finland, Balkans and

GRIZZLED SKIPPER

LARGE GRIZZLED SKIPPER

P. a. alveus

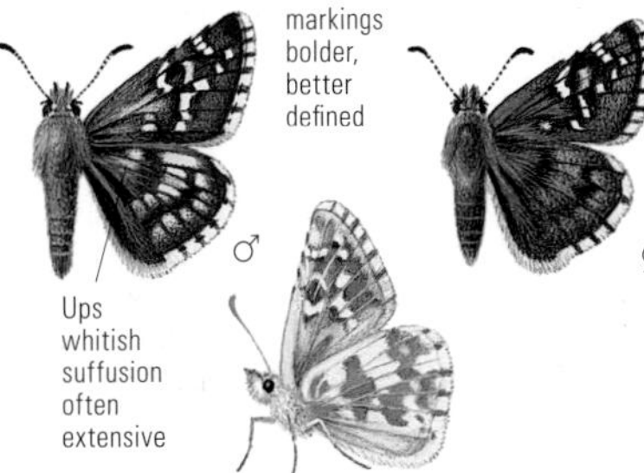

P. a. centralhispaniae
(N Portugal, Spain)

P. a. scandinavicus
(Norway, Sweden)

Grizzled Skipper   Large Grizzled Skipper

Greece (local but widespread in northern and central mountains: very local and scarce above 1400m on Mt. Chelmos). Absent from Britain, NW France, Holland, N Germany and Denmark. 800-2000m. **VARIATION** On Mt. Chelmos: large; both sexes, ups with striking whitish/yellowish suffusion (super-scaling). **FLIGHT-PERIOD** Univoltine. Late June/mid August according to locality and altitude. **HABITAT** Dry or damp grassy, flowery places: meadows; woodland clearings; sheltered gullies/hollows on subalpine slopes. **LIFE-HISTORY** LHPs *Potentilla sterilis*; *Helianthenum nummularium*. Ova laid on flowers of *Potentilla* or leaves of *Helianthemum*. Hibernates as a small larva.

P. alveus centralhispaniae Verity 1925 TL: Montes Universales, Spain.

DISTRIBUTION N Portugal and Spain: most mountainous areas including Sierra Nevada and S Pyrenees: widespread, often very local. S France: Pyrénées-Orientales sporadically through Cevennes, Massive Central to Côte-d'Or (S of Dijon); Haute-Savoie to Provence. Italy: Maritime Alps to Dolomites; C Apeninnes. 900-1800m. Exact distributional relationship with nominate form uncertain. Absent from Mediterranean islands: records for Sicily require confirmation. **VARIATION** Populations of Cantabrian Mts. (*accretus* Verity), S Spain (Sierra Nevada; S. de Segura; S. de la Sagra) and Apeninnes (*centralitaliae* Verity) differ in small characters in male genitalia. **FLIGHT-PERIOD** Univoltine. Early June/mid August.

continued on p. 350

Oberthür's Grizzled Skipper *Pyrgus armoricanus*

RANGE N Africa, Europe, Turkey, Transcaucasus, NW Asia, S Urals.

P. armoricanus Oberthür 1910 TL: Rennes, France.

DISTRIBUTION Morocco and Algeria: Middle Atlas. 1500-1800m. Iberian peninsula, Sardinia, Corsica, Sicily, through France (except NW and NE) to Denmark (restricted to Sjælland and Bornholm), S Sweden (restricted to S Skåne), Balkans, Greece (including Kithira and Crete) and European Turkey. 50-1700m.

DESCRIPTION Ups light coloration and bright yellowish unh characteristic and distinctive (cf. *P. alveus*).

VARIATION In NW Africa, *maroccanus* Picard: larger; all markings better developed. In S Greece, Kithira, Crete and European Turkey, *persicus* Reverdin: distinguished by small difference in male genitalia.

FLIGHT-PERIOD Generally bivoltine (May/June and July/late August): univoltine in northern range (late June/July). Has been reported from C Pyrenees late April: in Sardinia, most abundant in October.

HABITAT Grassy, rocky gullies/slopes, often hot, dry bushy places with an abundance of flowers.

LIFE-HISTORY LHPs *Potentilla tabernaemontani*; *P. reptans*; *P. arenaria*; *Fragaria vesca*; *Helianthemum nummularium*. Ova laid on flowers of *Potentilla* or leaves of *Helianthemum*.

BEHAVIOUR Attracted to flowers of *Thymus* and *Achillea*.

Foulquier's Grizzled Skipper *Pyrgus foulquieri*

RANGE NE Spain, S France, C Italy.

P. foulquieri Oberthür 1910 TL: Larche, Basses Alpes.

syn: *bellieri* Oberthür 1910.

DISTRIBUTION Spain: Catalonia: very local. S France: Massif Central; Aveyron to Bouches-du-Rhône, Var, Alpes-Maritimes, Isère and Savoie. Italy: Maritime Alps to Cottian Alps; Apennines (Mte. Sibillini; Abruzzi; Mte. Aurunci): very local. 500-1800m.

DESCRIPTION Resembles *P. alveus centralhispaniae*: uph pale markings better developed; pd spots larger; unh gc yellowish-brown.

VARIATION In C Italy, *picenus* Verity: smaller; ups paler; unh yellowish, slightly mottled yellowish-brown.

FLIGHT-PERIOD Univoltine. Mid July/August.

HABITAT Grassy flowery places.

LIFE-HISTORY LHP *Potentilla* sp.

Warren's Skipper *Pyrgus warrenensis*

RANGE E Central European Alps.

P. warrenensis Verity 1928 TL: Grisons, Switzerland.

syn: *alticola* Evans nec Rebel

DISTRIBUTION Widespread but very local in E Switzerland (Albulapass; Julier Pass; Bernina Pass). Italy: Ortler Alps (Pso. dello Stelvio); Dolomites (Pso. Falzarego; Pso. di Sella; Pso. di Pardoi) and Austria (Brenner Pass; Hohe Tauern). 1800-2600m.

DESCRIPTION Resembles *P. a. alveus*: smaller; markings less prominent.

FLIGHT-PERIOD Univoltine. July/August.

HABITAT Sheltered hollows, gullies and slopes with short turf and *Thymus*.

Olive Skipper *Pyrgus serratulae*

RANGE Spain, C Europe to Balkans and Greece, Turkey, Caucasus, S and C Siberia, Mongolia, Transbaikal.

P. serratulae Rambur 1839 TL: Spain.

DISTRIBUTION Spain: Sierra Nevada; S. de Segura; Cantabrian Mts.; S. de la Demanda; S. de Guadarrama; Serrania de Cuenca; Montes Universales; Pyrenees. C France through C Germany to S Lithuania, Latvia (very local and rare last reported in 1988), northern and peninsular Italy (C Apeninnes), Balkans, S Greece and European Turkey. Absent from Portugal, NW and NE France, Belgium, Holland and NW Germany. 50-2400m.

DESCRIPTION Both sexes: uns gc and markings distinctive and characteristic.

VARIATION In SE Europe, f. *major* Staudinger: consistently larger. Large forms occur sporadically in hot, low-lying localities elsewhere in S Europe.

FLIGHT-PERIOD Univoltine. Generally mid May/July: emergence prolonged at higher altitudes: reported from C Pyrenees late April.

HABITAT Open grassy, flowery places; damp woodland clearings; hot, dry scrubland at low altitudes.

LIFE-HISTORY LHPs *Potentilla recta*; *P. pedata*; *P. tabernaemontani*; *P. hirta*; *P. nevadensis*; *P. reptans*.

Oberthür's Grizzled Skipper

Foulquier's Grizzled Skipper

Warren's Skipper

Olive Skipper

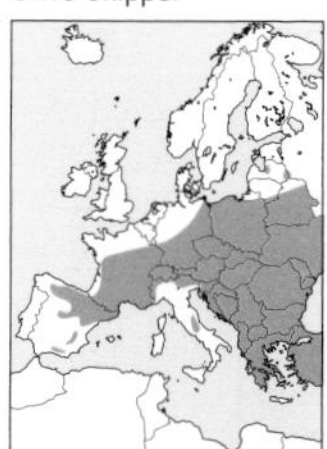

OBERTHÜR'S GRIZZLED SKIPPER

FOULQUIER'S GRIZZLED SKIPPER

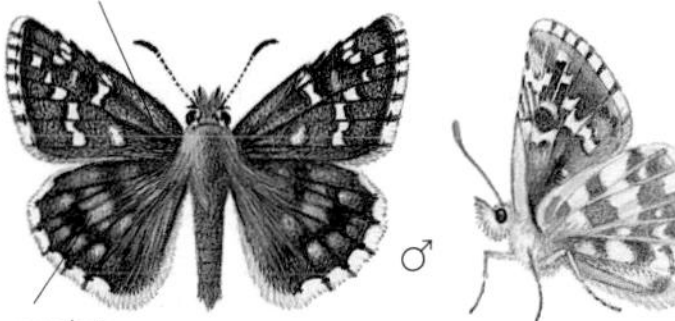

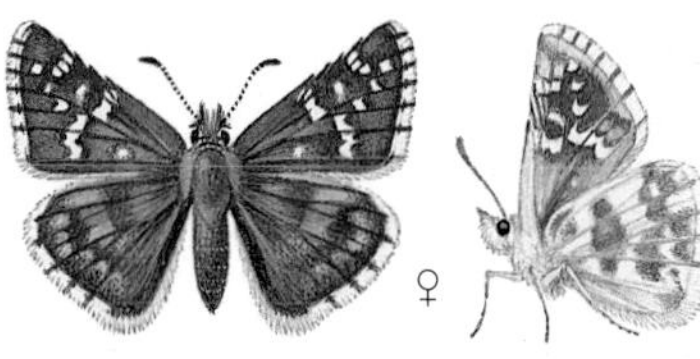

WARREN'S SKIPPER

Upf markings vestigial

Uph markings obscure

Restricted to C Alps

OLIVE SKIPPER

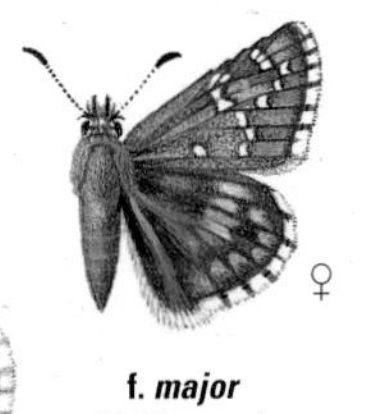

f. *major*
(SE Europe)

Carline Skipper

Rosy Grizzled Skipper

Sandy Grizzled Skipper

Yellow-banded Skipper

Carline Skipper *Pyrgus carlinae*

RANGE Portugal, Spain, S and C France, W and C Switzerland, S Germany, Austria, E Turkey, Armenia.

P. carlinae carlinae Rambur 1839 TL: Dalecarlia [in error].

DISTRIBUTION SE France and NW Italy (Maritime Alps to Savoie). SW Switzerland: Valais to Tessin (Campolungo Pass appears to be the most easterly location). A single record for Austria requires confirmation. Generally 1350-1900m: confirmed at 2900m on Col de Torrent and 950-1050m in various sites in France and Switzerland: records below this range require confirmation.

FLIGHT-PERIOD Univoltine. Late July/August.

HABITAT Open, flowery meadows; grassy, woodland clearings.

LIFE-HISTORY LHPs *Potentilla verna*; *P. reptans*; *P. hirta*; *P. tabernaemontani*.

P. carlinae cirsii Rambur 1839 TL: Fontainebleau, France. syn: *fritillum* Denis and Schiffermüller 1775

DISTRIBUTION Portugal and Spain: widespread and common. 800-1600m. S and C France. Switzerland: Vaud; Valais; Jura Mts. Very sporadic and local in S Germany, Austria and W Hungary. 300-1300m. Distributional relationship with nominate form uncertain. Records for NW Italy require confirmation.

DESCRIPTION Resembles nominate form: ups white markings better developed: male genitalia distinctive. Hybridizes with nominate form in areas of distributional overlap. Regarded as specifically distinct by some authors.

VARIATION Unh gc locally/regionally variable, yellow-brown to reddish-brown.

FLIGHT-PERIOD AND HABITAT As for nominate form.

LIFE-HISTORY LHPs *Potentilla reptans*; *P. erecta*; *P. verna*; *P. sterilis*; *P. cinerea* (Montes Universales).

Rosy Grizzled Skipper *Pyrgus onopordi*

RANGE Morocco, Algeria, SW Europe.

P. onopordi Rambur 1839 TL: Granada, Spain.

DISTRIBUTION Morocco and Algeria: Middle Atlas; High Atlas; Rif Mts. 0-2800m. Portugal and Spain: widespread. S France (Pyrénées-Orientales to about 46°N in Rhône Valley). Italy: generally widespread, sporadic in NE. 0-2000m.

DESCRIPTION Both sexes: unh large white anvil-shaped spots in s4 and s5 distinctive and characteristic.

FLIGHT-PERIOD Bivoltine or trivoltine. April/early October.

HABITAT Flowery meadows, sheltered streams and gullies in open grassland.

LIFE-HISTORY LHP: S Spain (Sierra Nevada), *Malva neglecta*. Ova laid on upperside of leaves. Captive larvae accept *Malope malachoides*.

Maps on p. 329

Sandy Grizzled Skipper *Pyrgus cinarae*

RANGE Central E Spain, S Balkans, Greece, Turkey, S Urals.

P. cinarae cinarae Rambur 1839 TL: Sarepta.

DISTRIBUTION Albania. Republic of Macedonia. Bulgaria. N Greece. European Turkey. Sporadic and local. 750-1600m.

FLIGHT-PERIOD Univoltine. Mid June/early August.

HABITAT Open, grassy, flowery places: also, dry, rocky terrain on calcareous and non-calcareous soils. Often occurs with *P. sidae*, *P. serratulae* and, in drier biotopes, *S. phlomides*.

LIFE-HISTORY LHP: Greece, *Potentilla recta*. Ova laid on flower-buds.

P. cinarae clorinda Warren 1927 TL: Cuenca, C Spain.

DISTRIBUTION C Spain: province of Cuenca (Montes Universales); very local. 900-1200m. Confirmed records include: Uña; Tragacete; Valdecabras; Huelamo; Ciudad Encantada. A tentative record from S. de Albarracin, pertaining to material collected by Querci in 1925, has not been confirmed.

DESCRIPTION Both sexes: ups and uns gc more yellowish, especially male unh.

FLIGHT-PERIOD Univoltine. Mid July/early September.

HABITAT Flowery, grassy, bushy pinewood clearings.

Yellow-banded Skipper *Pyrgus sidae*

RANGE W Spain, SE France, C Italy, Balkans, Turkey, Iran, Transcaucasus, NW Asia, S Urals, NW Kazakhstan, W Tian Shan.

P. sidae sidae Esper 1784 TL: Volga, S Russia.

DISTRIBUTION S Bosnia-Herzegovina. S Serbia. S Romania. Bulgaria. Albania. N Greece. European Turkey. 50-1750m, generally above 600m.

FLIGHT-PERIOD Univoltine. Generally mid May/late June; NE Greece, near sea-level, early April/May.

HABITAT Grassy, flowery banks/meadows, rocky gullies and slopes: most habitats contain an abundance of flowers, which often include *Vicia* and *Achillea* – much favoured nectar-sources.

LIFE-HISTORY LHP: Greece, *Potentilla recta*. Ova laid amongst flower-stamens. As an inhabitant of disturbed ground (areas of cultivation, roadsides, wasteland etc.), the ecological requirements of *Abutilon theophrasti* [=*A. avicennae*] (Malvaceae), a widely quoted LHP, do not appear compatible with those of the butterfly.

P. sidae occiduus Verity 1925 TL: Tuscany.

DISTRIBUTION W Spain: restricted to S. de Gredos. 700-1300m. SE France: Hérault; Bouches-du-Rhône; Var; Alpes-de-Haute-Provençe; Alpes-Maritimes. Italy: NW coastal district; Módena to Golfo di Gaeta; Belluno; Istria; 100-1400m.

DESCRIPTION Resembles nominate form: smaller; ups spotting less prominent; unh yellow discal band generally paler. Specimens of intermediate character are not uncommon.

FLIGHT-PERIOD Univoltine. Mid June/early July.

HABITAT Flowery grassland and scrub.

CARLINE SKIPPER

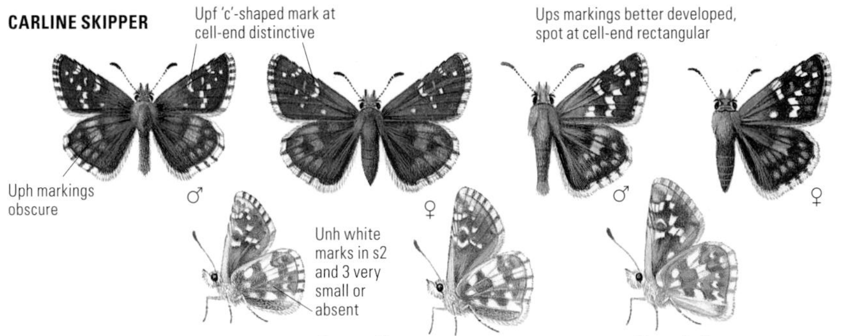

ROSY GRIZZLED SKIPPER

SANDY GRIZZLED SKIPPER

YELLOW-BANDED SKIPPER

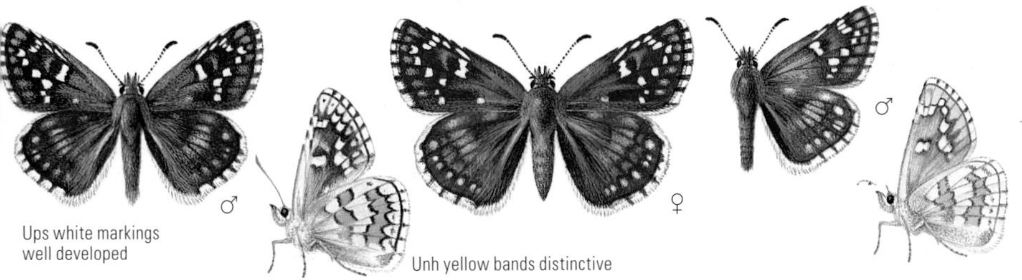

Safflower Skipper *Pyrgus carthami*

RANGE SW and C Europe, Balkans, N Greece, Turkey, Urals, S Russia, C Asia, Koptedagh.
P. carthami Hübner 1813 TL: Bavaria.
syn: *fritillarius* auct. nec Poda 1761.
DISTRIBUTION NE Portugal, Spain and peninsular Italy (C Apeninnes and Calabria) to S Lithuania, Balkans, N Greece (known only from Mt. Phalakron and Menikion Mts.) and European Turkey. Absent from W central Spain, Britain, N and W France, Belgium, Holland, N Germany and Mediterranean islands. Old records for Latvia appear to relate to misidentification. 600-1800m.
DESCRIPTION Male uph white, elongate submarginal markings usually prominent; unh white markings narrowly bordered pale grey, distinctive and characteristic.
VARIATION In S Spain, f. *nevadensis* Oberthür: ups white markings better developed; unh markings more sharply defined.
FLIGHT-PERIOD Univoltine. Late June/September in prolonged emergence.
HABITAT Sheltered gullies/hollows on open, grassy slopes; flowery meadows: often amongst rocks, bushes or in open woodland.
LIFE-HISTORY LHPs *Potentilla cinerea* (N Greece and Montes Universales); *P. arenaria*; *P. heterophylla*; *P. hirta*; *P. tabernaemontani*. Ova laid singly on upperside of leaf. Hibernates as a small larva.

Alpine Grizzled Skipper *Pyrgus andromedae*

RANGE Europe.
P. andromedae Wallengren 1853 TL: Dovre, Norway.
DISTRIBUTION Spain and France; Pyrenees. Alps of France, Italy, Switzerland, Germany and Austria. Slovenia: Julian Alps. Romania. Norway: Finnmark; Troms; Nordland; Nord-Trøndelag. Sweden: Torne Lappmark. 25-1000m. S Bosnia-Herzegovina. SW Serbia (Montenegro) and Republic of Macedonia: restricted to Sar Pl. 1200-3000m.
DESCRIPTION Unh prominent white spot and white streak in s1c gives a striking impression of an exclamation mark – useful diagnostic feature.
FLIGHT-PERIOD Univoltine. Scandinavia, mid June/July: C and SE Europe, generally July, records span mid May/late August.
HABITAT Sheltered, grassy places in open moorland, heaths and alpine grassland.
LIFE-HISTORY LHPs: Scandinavia, *Potentilla thuringiaca*; *Alchemilla glomerulans*; *Malva* sp.

Dusky Grizzled Skipper *Pyrgus cacaliae*

RANGE C and SE Europe.
P. cacaliae Rambur 1839 TL: 'Alps'.
DISTRIBUTION Alps of France, Italy, Switzerland, Germany and Austria. Bulgaria: Rila Mts., Stara Pl. Romania: Bucegi Mts. 1800-2800m. Records for Pyrenees, including Andorra (1978) require confirmation.
DESCRIPTION Ups white markings small in both sexes; uns markings indistinct, giving overall 'washed-out' appearance; unh gc extends to v1b; lacking basal spot in s2. (Cf. *P. andromedae*).
FLIGHT-PERIOD Univoltine. June/August.
HABITAT Sheltered hollows/gullies in open alpine grassland, often near low bushes or scrub.
LIFE-HISTORY LHPs *Potentilla* sp; *Sibbaldia* sp.

Northern Grizzled Skipper *Pyrgus centaureae*

RANGE N Fennoscandia, Arctic Russia, Altai Mts., Tchuja Mts., S and E Siberia, Mongolia, Transbaikal, Arctic N America southwards to Rocky Mts. and Appalachian Mts.
P. centaureae Rambur 1839 TL: Lapland.
DISTRIBUTION Norway, Sweden and Finland: 60°N-North Cape: widespread but generally absent from coastal regions. 0-950m.
DESCRIPTION Unh white veins prominent and distinctive.
FLIGHT-PERIOD Univoltine. Mid June/July according to season.
HABITAT AND LIFE-HISTORY Marshes, bogs and damp heath containing an abundance of LHP, *Rubus chamaemorus*.

Safflower Skipper

Alpine Grizzled Skipper
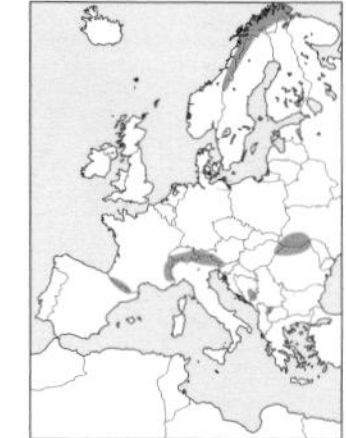

Dusky Grizzled Skipper

Northern Grizzled Skipper

SAFFLOWER SKIPPER

P. c. carthami

ALPINE GRIZZLED SKIPPER

DUSKY GRIZZLED SKIPPER

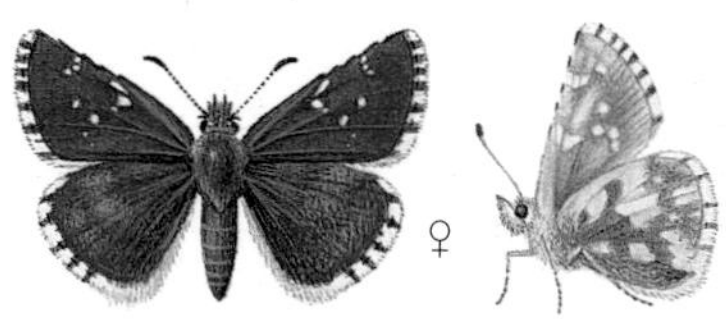

Unh lacking white spot at base of s2

NORTHERN GRIZZLED SKIPPER

Red Underwing Skipper *Spialia sertorius*

RANGE N Africa, S Europe. W Asia to Altai Mts., Tibet and Amur.

S. sertorius sertorius Hoffmannsegg 1804 TL: Germany.
syn: *hibiscae* Hemming 1936

DISTRIBUTION Portugal. Spain. France. S Belgium and NW Germany to W Czech Republic, Austria and Italy. Widespread and common. Reports from Corsica and Hungary require confirmation. 0-1650m.

DESCRIPTION First brood: unh gc creamy-yellow: second brood, unh gc reddish.

FLIGHT-PERIOD Bivoltine. April/June and mid July/August.

HABITAT Diverse. Hot, dry, flowery scrubland at sea-level: at higher altitudes, grassy slopes; flowery meadows; woodland clearings; bushy places.

LIFE-HISTORY LHPs: principally *Sanguisorba minor*: also (?)*Potentilla verna*; (?)*Rubus ideaus*. Oviposition, early-stage development/morphology appears to parallel that of *S. orbifer* (below).

S. sertorius therapne Rambur 1832 TL: Corsica.

DISTRIBUTION Corsica and Sardinia. 0-1500m.

DESCRIPTION AND VARIATION Resembles nominate form: smaller; upf cell-mark roughly square; unh gc reddish-brown, marginal markings reduced. Forms transitional to nominate form have been reported from Corsica.

FLIGHT-PERIOD Bivoltine. Late April/mid June and August/early September.

HABITAT Grassy, flowery places, often amongst low bushes and rocks.

S. sertorius ali Oberthür 1881 TL: Provinces of Oran and Constantine, Algeria.

DISTRIBUTION Morocco: Anti-Atlas; High Atlas; Middle Atlas; Rif Mts. Algeria. Tunisia. 500-2500m.

DESCRIPTION Ups gc colour paler, markings bolder, especially white discoidal spot; unh reddish-brown with darker striae; white discoidal spot conspicuous, white marginal spots elongate, veins pale brown.

FLIGHT-PERIOD Bivoltine (April/June and August/early September) or trivoltine (late February/October) according to locality and altitude.

HABITAT Rocky, flowery slopes and gullies; dry water courses.

LIFE-HISTORY LHP *Sanguisorba magnolii*.

Orbed Red Underwing Skipper *Spialia orbifer*

RANGE Sicily, E Europe, Balkans, Middle East, Afghanistan, S Russia, S Urals, Tian Shan.

S. orbifer Hübner 1823 TL: Hungary.

DISTRIBUTION Sicily. (?)E Czech Republic. Slovakia. S Poland. (?)SE Austria. Hungary. Balkans. Greece, including Corfu, Levkas, Kefalonia, Zakynthos, Kithera, Skopelos, Skyros, Limnos, Lesbos, Chios, Ikaria, Samos, Kos, Simi and Rhodes. European Turkey. Not reported from the Kykladian archipeligo, Crete or Karpathos. 0-2000m. Distributional relationship with *S. sertorius* unclear.

VARIATION Both sexes: first brood, unh gc creamy-yellow; second brood, unh reddish or rust-brown.

FLIGHT-PERIOD Bivoltine. Mid April/June and mid July/August: in Greece, emergence of first brood variable (mid April/late May) according to locality, altitude and season.

HABITAT As for *S. sertorius*.

LIFE-HISTORY LHP *Sanguisorba minor*. Ova laid singly amongst flower-buds. Initially, the small larva feeds entirely within the globular, compound flower: when too large to remain concealed, larva transfers to a leaf where it lives in a loose shelter gathered together with silk. In captivity, mature larvae of the first brood occasionally enter diapause, hibernating amongst dead leaves at base of LHP. Rolled-up stem-leaves serve as pupation sites.

Persian Skipper *Spialia phlomidis*

RANGE S Balkans, Greece, Turkey, N Israel, Lebanon, Syria, N Iran, S Russia, Transcaucasus.

S. phlomidis Herrich-Schäffer 1845 TL: Turkey.

DISTRIBUTION (?)S Croatia. SW Serbia. Albania. Republic of Macedonia. Bulgaria. Greece. Sporadic and usually very uncommon. 650-1650m, generally below 1000m.

FLIGHT-PERIOD Univoltine. Late May/June.

HABITAT Hot, dry, often rocky places; dry grassland with sparse, low-growing scrub. Usually on calcareous soils.

LIFE-HISTORY LHP not recorded for Europe: Lebanon, *Convolulus libanotica*: Greece, circumstantial evidence indicates *Convolulus* sp.

Aden Skipper *Spialia doris*

RANGE Morocco, Egypt, Arabia, Somalia, India.

S. doris daphne Evans 1949 TL: Ziz Valley, High Atlas, Morocco.

DISTRIBUTION Morocco: widespread but local: Anti-Atlas (Tizi-n-Bachkoum; El Drâà Valley; Tizi-n-Tinififft); High Atlas (Ziz Valley; Er Rachidia). 400-1750m.

FLIGHT-PERIOD Bivoltine. Late March/May and late August/September.

HABITAT Very hot, dry gullies with very sparse vegetation.

LIFE-HISTORY LHPs *Convolulus lanatus*; *C. caput-medusae*; *C. trabutianus*. (Sinai peninsula, *Ipomoea stolonifera* (also Convolulaceae)).

BEHAVIOUR Flight very fast and low.

Red Underwing Skipper

Orbed Red Underwing Skipper

RED UNDERWING SKIPPER

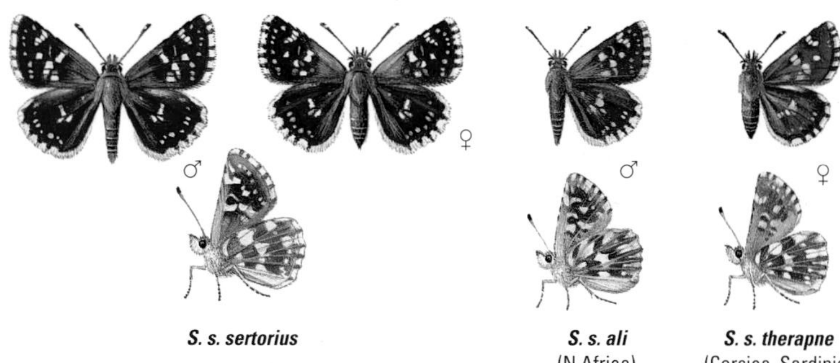

S. s. sertorius

S. s. ali (N Africa)

S. s. therapne (Corsica, Sardinia)

ORBED RED UNDERWING SKIPPER

Unh gc olive-green pale basal on costa usually round, discoidal spot round

1st brood

PERSIAN SKIPPER

Upf buff suffusion conspicuous

Unh discoidal spot bold, distinctive

Unh gc pale yellowish-grey, white discal band unbroken

Persian Skipper

Aden Skipper

ADEN SKIPPER

Restricted to Morocco

Unh spot in s7 well separated from large discoidal spot

Tessellated Skipper *Muschmpia tessellum*

RANGE SE Europe, Turkey, Middle East to S Siberia, Mongolia and N China.
M. tessellum Hübner 1803 TL: S Russia.
DISTRIBUTION Republic of Macedonia. Bulgaria. NW Greece: Vernon Mts.; Kerkeni Mts.; Askion Mts; Mt. Cholomon; Mt. Olympus. 800-1100m. Also, SE Aegean island of Simi 0-100m. European Turkey.
VARIATION Upf rarely with additional pair of obscure, elongate white spots in s1b (cf. *M. cribrellum*); unh gc yellowish, sometimes pale, delicate green.
FLIGHT-PERIOD Univoltine. Mid May/mid August in prolonged emergence: average peak emergence early June.
HABITAT AND BEHAVIOUR Open, grassy, sunny places with an abundance of flowers, especially *Vicia*, *Achillea* and *Thymus*, upon which both sexes are fond of resting and feeding.
LIFE-HISTORY LHP: NW Greece, *Phlomis samia*. Larva feeds within shelter of a small fold, secured by silk, near the edge and upper stem of a basal leaf. Hibernates as an immature larva. Prior to feeding, larger, post-hibernated larvae sever the leaf-stem vein sustaining that part of the leaf upon which they subsequently feed: possibly, this practice serves to counter the plant's chemical defences. (LHP in S Ural Mts., *Phlomis* (?)*tuberosa*: not confirmed as an European LHP although often quoted as such: apparently absent from *M. tessellum* habitats in N Greece).

Spinose Skipper *Muschampia cribrellum*

RANGE Balkans, Caucasus, S Siberia, S Urals, Kazakhstan, Altai, Mongolia, Amur, N and W China.
M. cribrellum Eversmann 1841 TL: S Russia.
DISTRIBUTION E Hungary. Romania: Cluj; Hunedoara. Republic of Macedonia: district of Skopje. 800-850m.
DESCRIPTION Resembles *M. tessellum*: smaller; ups and uns white markings more conspicuous; upf with two pairs of elongate white spots in s1b.
FLIGHT-PERIOD Univoltine. Mid May/mid June.
HABITAT Dry, flowery grassland with scattered bushes.
LIFE-HISTORY LHP(s) uncertain: reportedly *Potentilla* sp. (cf. *M. tessellum* and other members of the genus).

Sage Skipper *Muschampia proto*

RANGE NW Africa, Portugal, Spain, S Europe, Turkey.
M. proto Ochsenheimer 1808 TL: Portugal.
DISTRIBUTION Morocco: Middle Atlas. Algeria. 1200-1700m. Portugal. Spain. S France. Italy: Monte Gargano; Calabria; N Sicily. (?)Albania. Republic of Macedonia. Greece, including Kithira, Karpathos and Simi. 0-1600m.
VARIATION Uns gc seasonally variable, especially in female: greenish in spring emergence; brownish, orange or pinkish mid/late summer. In N Africa and occasionally in S Spain, f. *fulvosatura* Verity: large; markings well developed. Common features in male genitalia of *M. proto* from southern Aegean island of Simi and *M. mohammed* from N Africa have been reported.
FLIGHT-PERIOD Univoltine. April/October, emergence prolonged.
HABITAT Flowery places, often amongst mixed scrub on dry, rocky slopes or dry grassland: habitats often dominated by LHP.
LIFE-HISTORY LHPs: NW Africa, *Phlomis crinita*; *P. bovei*: Europe, *P. fruticosa*; *P. lychnitis*; *P. herba-venti*. Larva feeds, hibernates and pupates within a shelter formed usually from a single leaf.

Barbary Skipper *Muschampia mohammed*

RANGE Morocco, Algeria, (?)Tunisia.
M. mohammed Oberthür 1887 TL: Lambessa, Algeria.
DISTRIBUTION Morocco: Middle Atlas: very local (Azrou; Ifrane; Oulmès). Algeria: (Teniet-el-Haad; Sebdou; Tlemcen; Lambessa; Aures Mts.; Djurdjura Massif). 1500-1800m. A recent tentative record from Tunisia requires confirmation.
DESCRIPTION AND VARIATION Resembles *M. proto*. Hw outer margin distinctly undulate; veins brownish; unh discal spot, large, pale, nacreous: unh gc dark brown in first brood, reddish-brown in second brood.
FLIGHT-PERIOD Bivoltine or trivoltine. March/October according to locality and altitude.
HABITAT Rocky, flowery places.
LIFE-HISTORY LHPs *Phlomis crinita*; *P. bovei*.

Tessellated Skipper

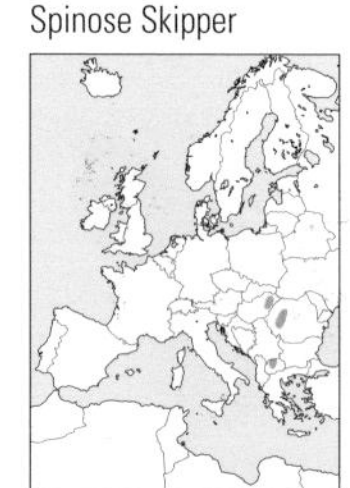

Spinose Skipper

Sage Skipper

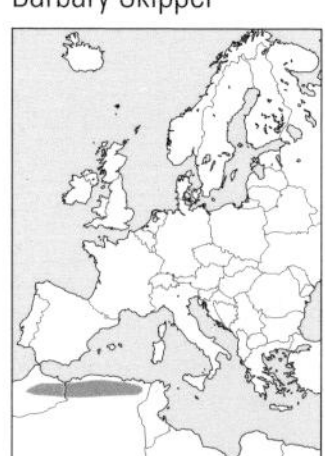

Barbary Skipper

TESSELLATED SKIPPER

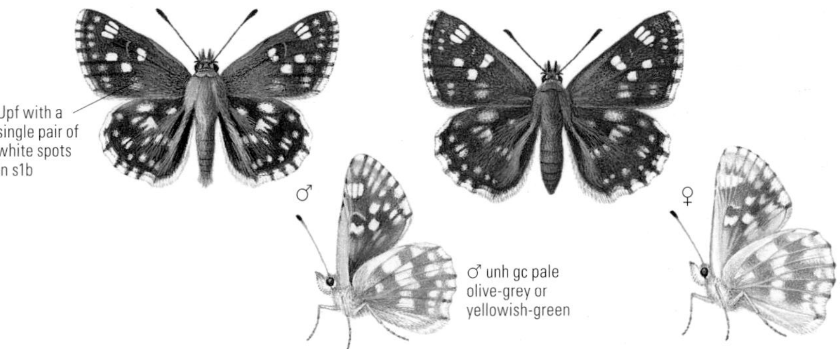

SPINOSE SKIPPER

SAGE SKIPPER

BARBARY SKIPPER

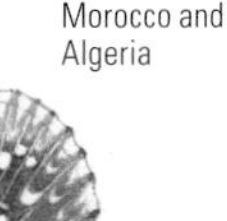

Algerian Grizzled Skipper *Muschampia leuzeae*

RANGE Algeria.

M. leuzeae Oberthür 1881 TL: Mascara, Algeria.

DISTRIBUTION Algeria: Blida; Chrea; Col de Ben-Chicao; Tenient-el-Had; Djurdjura Massif: local and uncommon. 1200-2000m.

DESCRIPTION Resembles *M. proto*. Ups gc dark grey; upf discoidal spot very large; unh pattern reticulate.

FLIGHT-PERIOD Univoltine. Mid May/July.

HABITAT Dry, flowery grassland.

LIFE-HISTORY LHP *Phlomis*.

Mallow Skipper *Carcharodus alceae*

RANGE S and C Europe, Turkey, Yemen, S and C Urals, W Kazakhstan, Turkestan, N Pakistan, N India, Altai, Tian Shan.

C. alceae Esper 1780 TL: Germany.

DISTRIBUTION In Europe, widespread and common south of 50°N including most Mediterranean islands. 0-2000m. Not confirmed in NW Africa. Presence in coastal district of SW Iberian peninsula from Lisbon to Cádiz not confirmed – apparently replaced entirely by *C. tripolinus* (below): distributional detail of the two species unknown in this region; only *C. alceae* has been confirmed in Málaga and Granada.

DESCRIPTION Male unf without hair-tuft. Indistinguishable from *C. tripolinus* by external characters: male genitalia distinct.

FLIGHT-PERIOD Polyvoltine. Early April/October in three or more broods.

HABITAT Diverse. Usually open flowery places, often with long grasses and light scrub, but well adapted to hot, dry, rocky terrain.

LIFE-HISTORY LHP principally *Malva sylvestris*: a common and widespread plant, adaptable to a wide range of conditions and remarkably resistant to grazing and trampling. Less commonly used LHPs include *M. neglecta*; *M. moschata*; *M. pusilla*; *Alcea rosea* [=*Althaea rosea*]. (Unexpected use of *Chrozophora hierosolymitana* (Euphorbiaceae) has been reported from E Palearctic range). Mature larva hibernates at base of LHP in a loose but strong structure formed from dead leaves held together by silk. Second brood larvae from Mediterranean region, captively reared below ambient temperature, often enter and remain in diapause until following spring.

BEHAVIOUR Under certain conditions which appear to relate to a reduction of light and/or temperature, males have the curious habit of lowering their wings below the plane of the thorax whilst recurving their abdomens in the opposite direction: captive specimens kept in darkness have been noted to retain this posture for several hours. This practice is exhibited by other members of the genus.

False Mallow Skipper *Carcharodus tripolinus*

RANGE Morocco, Algeria, Tunisia, Libya, SW Portugal, SW Spain.

C. tripolinus Verity 1925. TL: Garian plateau, Libya.

DISTRIBUTION Morocco. Algeria. Tunisia. Widespread from Sahara Desert to northern coast. 0-2500m. S Portugal and S Spain: confirmed in coastal districts from Lisbon (Estoril) to Cádiz. Exact distributional relationship with *C. alceae* unknown.

DESCRIPTION Unf without hair-tuft. Inseparable from *C. alceae* on basis of wing-characters: male genitalia distinct.

FLIGHT-PERIOD Polyvoltine. March/September.

HABITAT Hot, dry flowery and grassy places, rocky gullies and slopes.

LIFE-HISTORY LHP *Malva sylvestris*.

CONSERVATION Intense human activity on southern coast of Iberian peninsula poses a serious threat to habitat.

Marbled Skipper *Carcharodus lavatherae*

RANGE N Africa, Europe to 47°N, Turkey, Transcaucaus, S Urals.

C. lavatherae lavatherae Esper 1783 TL: S France.

DISTRIBUTION Morocco and Algeria: Middle Atlas: local and uncommon. Spain through S France (including Massif Central) S Switzerland, Italy (except northern central plains) to NE Balkans and N Greece. 200-1600m. N Greece appears to be limit of SE European range, where it occurs in isolated colonies interspersed with *C. lavatherae tauricus* (below).

DESCRIPTION Male unf without hair-tuft. Both sexes: ups greenish or yellowish-brown with darker marbling; upf inner margin often conspicuously reddish-brown or dull orange; unh whitish, usually tinged creamy-yellow; markings vague.

FLIGHT-PERIOD Univoltine. Mid May/late July. Reports of a second brood require confirmation.

HABITAT Hot, rocky gullies or dry grassy banks with sparse scrub: usually on limestone.

LIFE-HISTORY LHPs *Stachys recta*; *S. germanica*; *S. arvensis*. Ova laid on calyx. Small larvae feed between overlapping leaves loosely drawn together with silk.

BEHAVIOUR In very hot conditions, males may gather in large numbers to take moisture from damp soil: in intermittent sunshine, feeding insects appear to regulate their temperature by careful adjustment in wing-separation.

C. lavatherae tauricus Reverdin 1915 TL: Taurus Mts.

DISTRIBUTION Bosnia-Herzegovina. (?)S Serbia. (?)Albania. Republic of Macedonia. Romania. Bulgaria. NW Greece. European Turkey (Gelibolu). 500-1100m. Replaces nominate form in Turkey and elsewhere in eastern range.

DESCRIPTION Resembles nominate form: ups greenish/olive gc replaced with greyish or greyish-brown; uns gc chalky-white. In N Greece, nominate form and *tauricus* exist in small populations having no apparent ecological separation. Whilst male genitalia of the two forms are identical in shape, the uncus, tegumen and brachia of *tauricus* are consistently more robust – features readily apparent to the naked-eye.

FLIGHT-PERIOD Univoltine. Mid June/July.

HABITAT Grassy, flowery places with scrub and scattered trees.

LIFE-HISTORY LHP: NW Greece, *Stachys plumosa*. Ova laid

ALGERIAN GRIZZLED SKIPPER

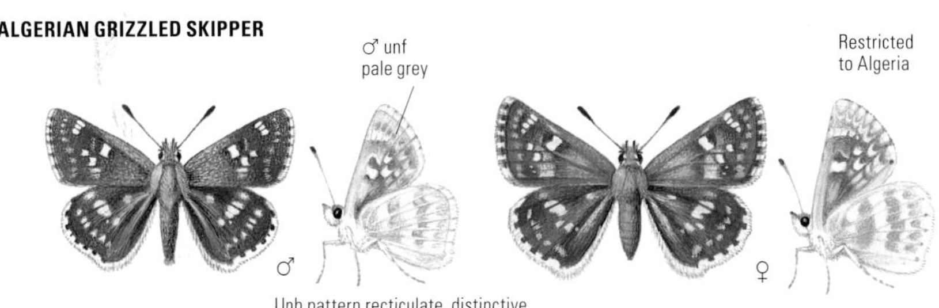

MALLOW SKIPPER

MARBLED SKIPPER

Algerian Grizzled Skipper

Mallow Skipper

False Mallow Skipper

Marbled Skipper

singly on calyx. Larger larvae feed in loosely rolled-up leaves. Mature larva dark grey, almost black, with extensive yellow mottling and fine, pale, long hairs. Small larvae hibernate in the shelter of dead leaves near base of host-plant. Pupates in final feeding station.

Southern Marbled Skipper *Carcharodus boeticus*

RANGE Iberian peninsula, S France, W Switzerland, NW and C peninsular Italy.
C. boeticus Rambur 1839 TL: Andalusia.
syn: *marrubii* Rambur 1840.
DISTRIBUTION N Portugal. Spain, south of Pyrenees. France: E Pyrenees; Cevennes; Provence. SW Switzerland; Valais. Italy: Piedmont; Appenines; Sicily. Progressively more dispersed in eastern range 500-1600m.
DESCRIPTION Male unf with hair-tuft. Both sexes: unh white markings arranged in a distinctive reticulate pattern.
VARIATION Ups gc becomes progressively paler in later broods, culminating in a light sandy-brown in late summer: colour of hair-tuft follows same trend and becomes smaller.
FLIGHT-PERIOD Voltinism dependent on locality: univoltine in Switzerland (July), trivoltine in S Spain (May, June/July and August/September).
HABITAT Hot, dry gullies, rocky slopes with sparse vegetation and scrub.
LIFE-HISTORY LHP (?)*Marrubium vulgare*. Hibernates as a small larva.

Eastern Marbled Skipper *Carcharodus stauderi*

RANGE N Africa, eastwards to Turkey, N Iran and Afghanistan.
C. stauderi Reverdin 1913 TL: El Kantara, Algeria.
DISTRIBUTION Morocco. Algeria. Tunisia. Widespread. 700-2400m. Greece: known only from E Aegean islands of Kos, Simi and Rhodes: near sea-level.
DESCRIPTION AND VARIATION Male unf with hair-tuft. Resembles *C. boeticus* closely: all markings extremely variable: male genitalia distinct.
FLIGHT-PERIOD Polyvoltine. NW Africa, records span March/October: Aegean Islands, May/June.
HABITAT Hot, dry, rocky, flowery places.
LIFE-HISTORY LHP: Morocco, *Marrubium vulgare*. Elsewhere in range, *Ballota hirsuta* (Hoggar Mts., S Algeria); *Phlomis floccusa* (Egypt); *Phlomis aurea* (Sinai peninsula).

Tufted Marbled Skipper *Carcharodus flocciferus*

RANGE Morocco, Spain, S and SE Europe, E Turkey, Transcaucasus, S Siberia, S Urals, Kazakhstan, Altai.
C. flocciferus Zeller 1847 TL: Sicily.
syn: *alchymillae* Hemming 1936
DISTRIBUTION Morocco: W Rif Mts.: very local and rare. 1500-2000m. Spain: sporadic, very local and generally uncommon: Cantabrian Mts.; S. de Gredos; S. de Guadarrama; S. de Segura; Montes Universales; S. de la Demanda; Pyrenees: records for Sierra Nevada require confirmation. S France: Massive Central. Central European Alps. Peninsular Italy and Sicily. S Poland. N Hungary. Slovenia: Julian Alps. Widespread but sporadic and local in C and S Balkans. Bosnia-Herzegovina: Vranica Pl.; Prenj Pl. SW Serbia: Orjen Pl.; Sinjajevita Pl. (?)Albania. Republic of Macedonia: Sar Pl.; Bistra Pl.; Placenska Pl.; Mt. Pelister. Romania: Carpathian Mts.. SW Bulgaria: Rila Mts.; Pirin Mts. Greece: Grammos Mt.; Pindos Mts.; Askion Mts.; Vourinos Mts.; Voras Mts.; Mt. Orvilos; Mt. Phalakron; Rhodope Mts.; Mt. Chelmos. Reports for Sardinia require confirmation. 1000-2000m.
DESCRIPTION Resembles *C. orientalis*: often larger; male unf dark hair-tuft prominent; ups gc darker grey; unh gc darker, often with bluish or violet tones in fresh specimens; whitish stripe and discoidal spot prominent.
FLIGHT-PERIOD Bivoltine in W and C Europe: late May/June and late July/August: apparently univoltine in Greece, early July/mid August.
HABITAT Grassy, flowery slopes or meadows, rocky gullies, sometimes in woodland clearings: often in damp places. Shows a marked preference for relatively cooler/damper conditions prevalent in upper-half of altitudinal range. Although usually separated by altitude and/or habitat-character from *C. orientalis* (below), which generally occurs in hotter and drier conditions below 1500m, the two species occur together very occasionally at about 1000m in Greece.
LIFE-HISTORY LHPs *Stachys recta*; *S. alpina*; *S. officinalis*; *S. germanica*; *S. palustris*; *S. sylvatica*; *S. scardica*. In last two instars, larva feeds in a fully enclosed tent fashioned from leaves at crown of LHP. Hibernates as a small larva near base of LHP. Larva and pupa closely similar to that of *C. orientalis*. Pupates in final feeding station.
BEHAVIOUR Both sexes fond of resting on tops of tall flower-stems, especially those of LHP (cf. *C. orientalis*).

Oriental Marbled Skipper *Carcharodus orientalis*

RANGE SE Europe, Turkey, Moravia, N Iran, S Urals.
C. orientalis Reverdin 1913 TL: S Greece.
DISTRIBUTION N Hungary. S Croatia: Dalmatian coast. S Serbia. (?)Albania. Republic of Macedonia. Bulgaria: Stara Pl. Greece, including Corfu, Kithera, Kea, Skyros, Limnos, Lesbos, Samos, Kos and Kalimnos. European Turkey. 25-1650m.
DESCRIPTION AND VARIATION Uns gc pale with obscure white markings (cf. *C. flocciferus*): male unf with prominent dark hair-tuft. Subject to marked individual variation in size and ups coloration.
FLIGHT-PERIOD Bivoltine or trivoltine (April/August) according to locality and altitude.
HABITAT Hot, dry, rocky, flowery slopes, gullies or grassland: often amongst sparse scrub or bushes. (See *C. flocciferus*).
LIFE-HISTORY LHP: S Greece, *Stachys* sp. Half-grown, post-hibernated larva feeds in rolled-up leaves.
BEHAVIOUR Males often sit on stones or soil in hot conditions (cf. *C. flocciferus*).

SOUTHERN MARBLED SKIPPER

Unh reticulate pattern distinctive

EASTERN MARBLED SKIPPER

♂ upf with
hair-tuft

TUFTED MARBLED SKIPPER

Ups purplish-grey, marbled with dark brown

♂ upf with hair-tuft prominent

Unh white discoidal spot and pale streak in s4 distinctive

ORIENTAL MARBLED SKIPPER

♂ upf with hair-tuft prominent

Southern Marbled Skipper

Eastern Marbled Skipper

Tufted Marbled Skipper

Oriental Marbled Skipper

Dingy Skipper *Erynnis tages*

RANGE Europe to 62°N, eastwards to Amur.
E. tages Linnaeus 1758 TL: Europe.
DISTRIBUTION Generally widespread and common from S Europe (including European Turkey) to Ireland, S Scotland, S Scandinavia (including Sjælland, Öland and Gotland) and (?)Estonia (including Dagö and Ösel). Possibly extinct in Latvia: very rare and local in Holland, N Belgium and Lithuania. In decline in Ireland and Britain. Absent from S Portugal, Gibraltar, SW Spain (Huelva) and Mediterranean islands except Corfu. A record for Kykladian island of Tinos requires confirmation. 50-2000m.
VARIATION Male upf with costal fold (cf. *E. marloyi*). Ups gc variable, pale brown (f. *brunnea* Tutt) to dark brown with dark, greyish-blue overtones (f. *clarus* Caradja). Ups markings variable, obscure to prominent. In W Ireland, *baynesi* Huggins: ups light brown; markings prominent. Darker forms appear to associate with cooler conditions at higher altitudes, e.g. Switzerland above 1500m.
FLIGHT-PERIOD Voltinism dependent on locality, altitude and season: usually univoltine in N and C Europe, late April/mid June: at least partially bivoltine in S Europe, early April/early June and late June/late August. A partial second brood may occur in N Europe in favourable seasons. From Mediterranean region, captively reared larvae from first brood often enter and remain in diapause until following spring.
HABITAT Diverse. Damp or dry grassy, flowery places.
LIFE-HISTORY LHPs principally *Lotus corniculatus*; *L. uliginosus*; *Hippocrepis comosa*. Conspicuous orange ova laid singly on upper surface of leaves. Larvae feed in an open but strong cage-like structure formed from leaves and silk. Full-grown larva hibernates amongst leaves of LHP bound together with silk. Pupates within hibernaculum in early spring.
BEHAVIOUR See *E. marloyi* (below).

Inky Skipper *Erynnis marloyi*

RANGE S Balkans, Turkey, Lebanon, Syria, N Iraq, N Iran, Transcaucasus.
E. marloyi Boisduval 1834 TL: Peloponnesos, S Greece.
DISTRIBUTION Albania. Republic of Macedonia. NW, C and S Greece, including Corfu, Lesbos, Chios and Samos. European Turkey. 600-2000m.
DESCRIPTION Male upf without costal fold (cf. *E. tages*).
FLIGHT-PERIOD Univoltine. Mid May/late June.
HABITAT Dry gullies; rocky slopes: on calcareous rocks, usually limestone.
BEHAVIOUR Females are fond of feeding on flowers of *Thymus*. 'Hilltopping', sometimes involving 20 or more male specimens, is a common occurrence. Especially wary and readily disturbed. Flash-assisted photographs taken in bright sunlight often record no trace of the butterfly, it having been startled by the flash or the noise of the camera-shutter mechanism and taken flight during the very short period of exposure. The exceptionally keen reflexes thus indicated may be related to the insect's common practice of sitting on white stones in the hot sun, for, in such positions, these almost black butterflies are very conspicuous and a clear target for the predatory and ubiquitous lizard. As it would appear that *E. marloyi*, like the lizard, benefits from the absorption of solar radiation in maintaining its activity, its dark colour is advantageous, possibly even necessary to ensure its survival. Similar responses have also been recorded for its similarly coloured cogener, *E. tages*.

Chequered Skipper *Carterocephalus palaemon*

RANGE C, N and E Europe, C and N Asia to Japan. N America.
C. palaemon Pallas 1771 TL: Russia.
DISTRIBUTION From N Pyrenees through C France, N Italy (common in Dolomites) to Arctic Circle, Balkans and N Greece (Rhodopi Mts.). Locally common in W Scotland. Extinct in England. Absent from Iberian peninsula except Val d'Aran (E Pyrenees), W and S France, Peninsular Italy, N Belgium, N Holland, Denmark, S Sweden, Albania, Republic of Macedonia and SE Bulgaria. 200-1600m.
DESCRIPTION Uns of antennal club-base dark in male, yellow in female.
FLIGHT-PERIOD Univoltine. Mid May/June at lower altitudes, July at 1600m.
HABITAT AND BEHAVIOUR Grassy, woodland clearings: often in damp places: on calcareous or acidic soils. Both sexes attracted to nectar of *Ajuga repans*; *A. pyramidalis*; *A. genevensis* (bugle) and *Endymion non-scriptus* (bluebell).
LIFE-HISTORY LHPs *Molinia caerulea*; *M. c. arundinacea*; *Calamagrostis epigejos*; *Brachypodium sylvaticum*; *B. pinnatum*; *Bromus ramosus*; *Dactylis glomerata*; *Alopecurus pratensis*; *Phleum pratense*. Ova laid singly on grass-blades. Larva feeds in a tube formed from a grass-blade by drawing together and securing edges with silk. Mature larva pale green, but assumes an adaptive straw or buff colour during hibernation amongst dead grass-blades bound together with silk. Pupates within hibernaculum in early spring.

Northern Chequered Skipper *Carterocephalus silvicolus*

RANGE NE Germany, N Poland, Baltic states, Fennoscandia to Siberia, Amur, Japan.
C. silvicolus Meigen 1829 TL: Brunswick, Germany.
syn: *sylvius* Knoch 1781 (invalid homonym).
DISTRIBUTION NE Germany: Helmstedt through Lüchow to Schwerin See. N Poland. Baltic countries: widespread and common. Denmark: restricted to Lolland. Norway: very sporadic from Telemark and Akerhaus through Nord-Trøndelag to Troms (69°N). Sweden: Skåne, Småland and Gotland; Närke, Söderland, Uppland and Dalarne to Arctic Circle. Finland: widespread and common. 0-(?)200m.
FLIGHT-PERIOD Univoltine. Late May/late June according to locality and season.
HABITAT Damp, sunny, sheltered, flowery woodland clearings.
LIFE-HISTORY LHPs *Bromus ramosus*; *Brachypodium sylvaticum*; (?)*Milium effusum*; *Cynosurus cristatus*.

DINGY SKIPPER

INKY SKIPPER

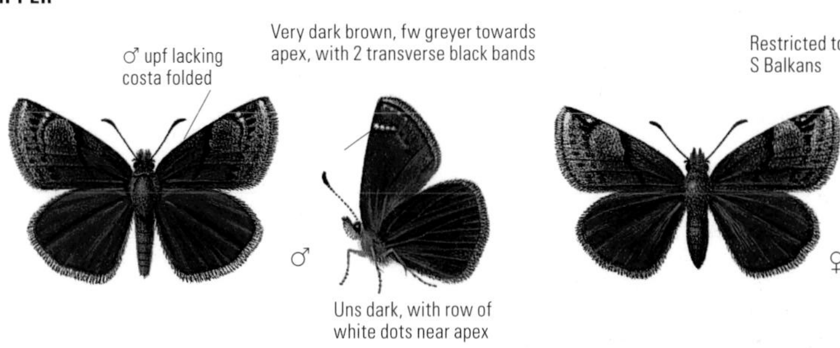

CHEQUERED SKIPPER

NORTHERN CHEQUERED SKIPPER

Dingy Skipper

Inky Skipper

Chequered Skipper

Northern Chequered Skipper

Large Chequered Skipper *Heteropterus morpheus*

RANGE N Spain, much of C Europe, Italy, Denmark, Sweden, Lithuania, Balkans, SE Bulgaria, NW Turkey, C Asia, Amur, Korea.

H. morpheus Pallas 1771 TL: Samara, S Russia.

syn: *steropes* Denis and Schiffermüller 1775.

DISTRIBUTION N Spain: Oviedo to San Sebastion. France: Pyrénées-Atlantiques through Nièvre (W and N of Massif Central) to Brittany and Somme (W of Somme Valley). Channel Islands: Jersey ((?)introduced). Very local in S Belgium, N Holland and NW Germany. Italy: Lazio; Piedmont through Dolomites to Trieste. Denmark: restricted to Lolland and Falster. Sweden: restricted to S Skåne. NE Germany to C and E Latvia (very local in C and S Lithuania), through E Czech Republic, E Austria to N Balkans, SE Bulgaria (Primorsko) and European Turkey. 0-1000m.

FLIGHT-PERIOD Univoltine. Late June/July.

HABITAT Woodland clearings with tall grasses: usually in damp places; commonly associated with marshy heaths.

LIFE-HISTORY LHPs *Calamagrostis canescens*; *Brachypodium sylvaticum*; *Molinia caerulea*; *Phragmites australis*. Ova laid on stems. Larva feeds in a tube formed from a grass blade. Half-grown larva hibernates within its feeding station. The green pupa suspends itself within a loose structure formed from grass stems bound with silk.

Lulworth Skipper *Thymelicus acteon*

RANGE Canary Islands, NW Africa, Europe to 54°N, Turkey, Cyprus, Israel, Jordan, Lebanon, Iraq, Iran.

T. acteon acteon Rottemburg 1775 TL: Lansberg-an-der-Warthe, Germany.

DISTRIBUTION Morocco. Algeria. Tunisia. 0-1800m. Common and widespread in most of Europe to about 54°N. In Britain, restricted to the Dorset coast, S England. Recorded from Sicily, Elba, Corfu, Evia, Naxos, Syra, Tinos, Aegina, Andros, Paros, Crete, Thassos, Samos and Rhodes. Absent from Balearic Islands, Corsica, Sardinia, N Belgium, Holland, N Germany, NE Poland and Baltic countries. 0-1600m.

VARIATION In NW Africa, f. *oranus* Evans: ups darker, tending to greenish or greyish-brown. Similarly-coloured races occur in Spain, Elba, Crete and other E Mediterranean islands.

FLIGHT-PERIOD Univoltine. Mid May/early August in prolonged emergence.

HABITAT Grassy and flowery places, usually amongst scrub: often hot, dry situations. In S England, restricted to coastal chalk grassland.

LIFE-HISTORY LHPs *Brachypodium pinnatum*; *B. sylvaticum*; *Elymus repens*; *Calamagrostis epigejos*. Usually, several ova laid in a row on underside of a stem-leaf. Hibernates as a newly-hatched larva within a cocoon on grass-blade.

T. acteon christi Rebel 1894 TL: Canary Islands.

DISTRIBUTION Canary Islands: Hierro (Pic del Risco 300m); La Palma; Gomera; Tenerife; Gran Canaria. 100-1000m.

DESCRIPTION Ups gc brownish; upf yellow-orange markings well defined.

FLIGHT-PERIOD Voltinism uncertain: February/late September in two or three broods.

HABITAT Flowery, grassy places in margins of laurel forests.

Moroccan Small Skipper *Thymelicus hamza*

RANGE Morocco, Algeria, Tunisia, Libya.

T. hamza Oberthür 1876 TL: Oran, Algeria.

DISTRIBUTION Widespread but local. Morocco. Algeria. Tunisia. 500-2400m.

DESCRIPTION Resembles *T. acteon* closely: upf rarely with traces of orange pd markings; unh greyish, with orange wedge-shaped marking extending from outer margin to wing-base at v2.

FLIGHT-PERIOD Univoltine. May/late June.

HABITAT Flowery grassland; rocky gullies and slopes.

Levantine Skipper *Thymelicus hyrax*

RANGE Greece, Turkey, Iran, Syria, Lebanon, Israel.

T. hyrax Lederer 1861 TL: Antakya.

DISTRIBUTION Greece: S Parnassos massif; Askion Mts.; 600-800m: E Aegean islands of Samos, Chios, Lesbos and Rhodes. 0-250m.

DESCRIPTION Resembles *T. sylvestris*: uns hw more greenish.

FLIGHT-PERIOD Univoltine. Late April/late June.

HABITAT Hot, dry, rocky places.

BEHAVIOUR On Mt. Parnassos, both sexes are greatly attracted to the flowers of a small, bushy *Thymus* sp.

Large Chequered Skipper

Lulworth Skipper

Moroccan Small Skipper

Levantine Skipper

LARGE CHEQUERED SKIPPER

♂ ♀

LULWORTH SKIPPER

♂ upf slender sex-brand conspicuous

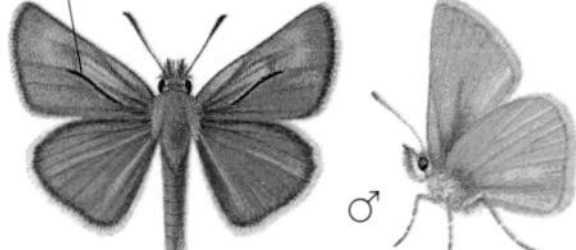
♂

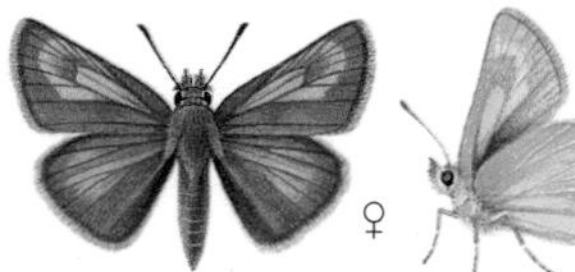
♀

♂

T. a. christi
(Canary Islands)

MOROCCAN SMALL SKIPPER

Restricted to N Africa

♂ upf sex-brand short and thick

♂

♀

LEVANTINE SKIPPER

♂ upf sex-brand short, broken at v2

♂

♀

Essex Skipper *Thymelicus lineola*

RANGE N Africa, Europe, C Asia, Tian Shan, Amur. Introduced to N America.

T. lineola Ochsenheimer 1808 TL: Germany.

DISTRIBUTION Morocco. Algeria. Throughout Europe, including S England, S Fennoscandia (including Baltic Islands), Baltic countries, European Turkey, Sicily and Corsica. Absent from Sardinia. 0-2200m.

DESCRIPTION Resembles *T. sylvestris*: generally smaller: ups narrow, black outer marginal borders more prominent; black veins usually prominent, highlighted by finely tapered, black suffusion expanding towards outer margins: male upf sex-brand short, broken at v2: uns of antennal tip black or dark brown (cf. *T. sylvestris*).

VARIATION In N Africa, f. *semicolon* Staudinger: ups black marginal borders wider, black veins prominent.

FLIGHT-PERIOD Univoltine. May/August in prolonged emergence.

HABITAT Flowery places containing tall grasses: woodland clearings; bushy places; open fields. *T. sylvestris* almost always shares same habitats.

LIFE-HISTORY LHPs *Phleum pratense*; *Holcus mollis*; *Calamagrostis epigejos*; *Dactylis glomerata*; *Agrostis capillaris*; *Brachypodium pinnatum*; *B. sylvaticum*; *Arrhenatherum elatius*; *Triticum aestivum*; *Alopecurus pratensis*; *Carex acutiformis*; *Lolium perenne*; *Phalaris arundinacea*; *Anthoxanthum odoratum*; *Elymus repens* [=*Agropyron repens*; *Triticum repens*; *Elytrigia repens*]. Ova laid between base of stem-leaf and stem. Hibernates as a fully-formed larva within ovum-case.

NOTE In S England, consolidation and extension of range in recent decades may be due, partly or largely, to new and highly integrated habitat provided by the verges of new road systems. Has spread rapidly in N America since its accidental introduction to Ontario in about 1910, and in other sites subsequently. An economic pest on *Phleum* spp., the transportation of which, as hay-bales, appears mainly responsible for the rapidity of expansion.

Small Skipper *Thymelicus sylvestris*

RANGE NW Africa, Europe, Turkey, Middle East, Iran, Caucasus, S Urals.

T. sylvestris Poda 1761 TL: Graz, Austria.

syn: *flavus* Brünnich 1763; *thaumas* Hufnagel 1766

DISTRIBUTION Widespread and very common. Morocco. Algeria. 0-2600m. From Spain, Sicily, European Turkey and Greece (including Corfu, Kithera, Limnos, Lesbos, Chios, Samos, Kalimnos, Kos and Simi) to Wales, England, Denmark (including Fyen) and Baltic states. Absent from Balearic Islands, Corsica, Sardinia and Crete. 0-1900m.

DESCRIPTION Resembles *T. lineola*: generally larger: ups black veins usually less conspicuous: upf male sex-brand extends to v3: uns of antennal tip fulvous (cf. *T. lineola*).

VARIATION Rarely, upf male sex-brand greatly reduced or absent. In S Europe, f. *syriacus* Tutt: large; ups gc brighter.

FLIGHT-PERIOD Univoltine. May/July.

HABITAT Diverse. Flowery clearings in woodland or scrub containing tall grasses.

LIFE-HISTORY LHPs *Holcus lanatus*; *H. mollis*; *Phleum pratense*; *Brachypodium sylvaticum*. Ova laid in small groups. Ovum much rounder than that of *T. lineola*. Hibernates as a newly-hatched larva within a cocoon attached to a grass-blade.

BEHAVIOUR Ovipositing females are usually very fastidious and may take 10-15 minutes inspecting LHP stems before laying.

Silver-spotted Skipper *Hesperia comma*

RANGE NW Africa, Europe, Turkey, temperate Asia to Amur. NW America.

H. comma Linnaeus 1758 TL: Sweden.

syn: *sylvestris* auct. nec Poda

DISTRIBUTION Morocco. Algeria. Widespread and common. 1500-2800m. Throughout Europe except low-lying regions of southern Iberian peninsula and much of central Scandinavia (including Baltic Islands). Largely absent from S Italy. Absent from Mediterranean islands except N Sicily. 0-2300m.

VARIATION In Lapland and at higher altitudes elsewhere, f. *catena* Staudinger: smaller; ups darker fulvous, tending to brown; uns gc darker green. In N Africa, f. *benuncus* Oberthür: ups brighter; unh pd silver/whitish spots often confluent, basal spots also fused; unh veins paler, sometimes white.

FLIGHT-PERIOD Univoltine. Late June/mid September according to locality.

HABITAT Open, flowery places with short grass containing an abundance of *Festuca ovina*. On calcareous and non-calcareous soils.

LIFE-HISTORY LHP principally *Festuca ovina*: rarely, *Lolium perenne*. Natural use of *Lotus corniculatus* and *Ornithopus perpusillus* requires confirmation: captive larvae accept *L. corniculatus* and *Coronilla varia* spontaneously. Ova laid singly, usually one per grass tuft. Hibernates as an ovum or unfed larva in N and C Europe but as a mature larva amongst roots of LHP in Mediterranean region. (In Alaska, two seasonal cycles are required for development, hibernating as an ovum in first winter and as a larva or pupa in second winter). In N and C Europe, mature larva are green, greyish-green or olive-brown: dusky-pink specimens have been recorded in S Spain, S France, NW Italy and NW Greece.

Large Skipper *Ochlodes venatus*

RANGE Europe, Turkey, temperate Asia to China and Japan.

O. venatus faunus Turati 1905 TL: Italy and S France.

syn: *sylvanus* Esper 1777 (invalid homonym).

DISTRIBUTION Widespread and common in most of Europe to 64°N. Absent from N Africa, Ireland and Mediterranean islands except Sicily and Corfu. 0-1800m: above 1000m in S Spain.

VARIATION At high altitudes and in colder, northern localities, f. *alpinus* Hoffmann: smaller; darker.

ESSEX SKIPPER

♂ upf sex-brand short, broken at v2

♂

Uns of antennal tip black

Ups dark marginal border disffuse, extending along veins

♀

Unh gc pale

SMALL SKIPPER

♂ upf sex-brand long, curved

♂

Uns of antennal tip fulvous

Ups dark marginal border well defined

♀

Ups gc brighter

♂

f. *syriacus*
(S Europe)

SILVER-SPOTTED SKIPPER

♂ upf sex-brand conspicuous

♂

♀

Unf subapex and unh silvery-white spots distinctive

♂

f. *cantena*
(Lapland)

LARGE SKIPPER

♂ upf sex-brand conspicuous

♂

♀

Essex Skipper

Small Skipper

Silver-spotted Skipper

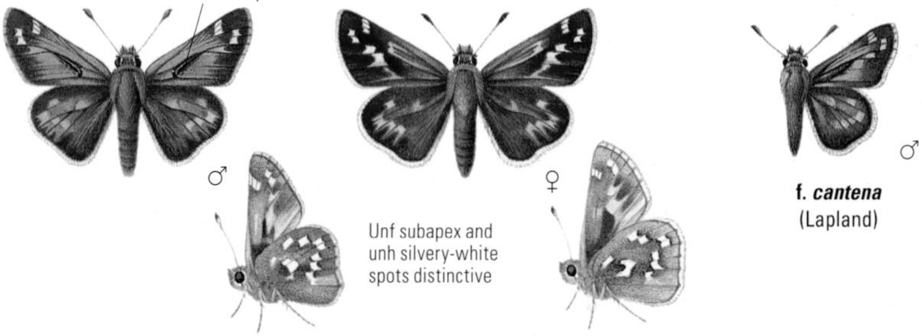

Large Skipper

FLIGHT-PERIOD Generally univoltine, June/August: (?)bivoltine in Spain, recorded in May, June, July and August.
HABITAT Sunny, grassy, woodland margins/clearings: most often with some deciduous trees, bushes and shrubs, especially *Rubus fruticosus* (bramble). Most habitats are humid and often contain an abundance of ferns, especially bracken (*Pteris aquilina*).
LIFE-HISTORY LHPs *Dactylis glomerata*; *Molinia caerulea*; *M. c. arundinacea*; *Brachypodium pinnatum*; *B. sylvaticum*; *Poa pratensis*; *Festuca arundinacea*; *Calamagrostis epigejos*; *Luzula pilosa*; *Holcus lanatus*; *Elymus repens*; *Juncus effusum*; *Agrostis capillaris*; *Phleum pratense*; (?)*Bromus erectus*. Ova laid on underside of grass-blade. Larvae feed inside a tube formed by drawing together edges of a grass-blade. Hibernates as a large larva.
BEHAVIOUR Both sexes attracted to bramble blossom and often rest or bask on the leaves of this shrub.

Mediterranean Skipper *Gegenes nostrodamus*

RANGE Mediterranean coastal region, Turkey, Middle East, Arabia, Iraq, Iran, Afghanistan, Pakistan, NW India.
G. nostrodamus Fabricius 1794 TL: 'Barbaria' (Algeria).
DISTRIBUTION Very local and sporadic in predominantly Mediterranean coastal regions. Morocco: northern coast near sea-level; Taroudannt 250m; High Atlas (Tizi-n-Test 1880m; Tizi-n-Bachkoum 1400-1600m). Algeria. Tunisia. Spain: scattered colonies from southern coast to Soria and Zaragoza. Mallorca. Corsica. Sardinia. Elba. W Italy. NW Sicily. W Croatia: Dalmatian coast. SW Serbia: Zelenika. Albania. Republic of Macedonia: Ohrid; Vardar Valley (Gevgelija). Greece: coastal districts 0-250m; NW Pindos Mts. 400-1200m; Crete 0-100m. Occurs with *G. pumilio* in some localities on Crete.
DESCRIPTION Unh cilia-like hairs on costa long and dense (cf. *G. pumilio*).
FLIGHT-PERIOD Bivoltine or trivoltine (late April/October) according to locality: in province of Soria, bivoltine (May/June and late July/August). Usually very scarce in first brood.
HABITAT Hot, dry gullies; stony/sandy flood-plains of rivers, usually amongst sparse vegetation.
LIFE-HISTORY LHP not recorded for Europe: in Sinai peninsula, ova and larvae have been recorded on *Aeluropus* and *Panicum* spp. (Poaceae).
BEHAVIOUR Flight very fast and low. Males often sit on stones or soil in full sun: extremely wary but returns quickly to original resting site when disturbed. Females perch on tall grass or flower-stems in early morning: much less in evidence at other times of day.

Pigmy Skipper *Gegenes pumilio*

RANGE Mediterranean coastal region, eastwards to Iran and Himalayas. Sporadically throughout Africa.
G. pumilio Hoffmannsegg 1804 TL: Naples.
syn: *pygmaeus* Cyrilli 1787 (invalid homonym); *aetna* Boisduval 1840; *lefebvrei* Rambur 1842.
DISTRIBUTION Generally very local in predominantly Mediterranean coastal regions. Algeria. Tunisia: Aïn Draham. S Spain. Mallorca. SE France: Var; Alpes-Maritimes. Corsica. Sardinia. Elba. W Italy. Sicily. Malta. S Croatia: Heretva Valley 0-4m. SW Serbia. Albania. Greece: mainly coastal districts (0-400m), also inland at moderate to high altitude (Pindos Mts. 500-1000m; Mt. Tymphristos 1200-1800m); Corfu (Mt. Pantokrator, 910m); Spetsai; Paros; Crete; Samos; Kos; Rhodes; Kastellórizo. Not reported from E Italy, NE Greece or European Turkey. 0-1800m. Occurs with *G. nostrodamus* in some localities on Crete.
DESCRIPTION Unh cilia-like hairs on costa short and sparse (cf. *G. nostrodamus*).
VARIATION Chromosome number in W Mediterranean region (CN=24) differs substantially from that of E Mediterranean (Turkey and Lebanon) and SW Saudi Arabia (CN=41): cytological data are very limited and do not include Italy, Balkans or Greece. Whilst two species of insect may be implicated, this observation is possibly an example of polyploidy, that is, duplication/multiplication of a chromosome set in which all superfluous sets are inactive: if so, the number of active sets – the only ones in genetic control – may be equal in different populations. (It is assumed that inexact multiplicity of CN in present example is due to experimental error: a small range of inter-population variance in chromosome number is probably tolerable (cf. *Lysandra coridon*)).
FLIGHT-PERIOD Bivoltine or trivoltine according to locality: records span mid April/late October. Generally very scarce in first brood.
HABITAT AND BEHAVIOUR As for *G. nostrodamus*.
LIFE-HISTORY LHP(s) (?)unknown in Europe. In S Africa, *Ehrhartia erecta* (Poaceae): although sometimes quoted for Europe/NW Africa, this plant genus is not known from either region. Captive larvae have been reared on *Cynodon dactylon* and *Hyparrhenia hirta* (Poaceae): both species, plus *Imperata cylindrica* [=*Saccharum cylindricum*] have been quoted as LHPs but their natural use is apparently unconfirmed.

Zeller's Skipper *Borbo borbonica*

RANGE SW Spain. Gibraltar. Throughout Africa, including coastal districts of NW Morocco, Algeria, Libya and islands of Madagascar, Mauritius and Reunion. Egypt, Israel, Lebanon, Syria.
B. borbonica zelleri Lederer 1855 TL: Syria.
DISTRIBUTION Very local in coastal districts. Morocco: Rabat; Kenitra; Larache; Tangier. Algeria: Algiers. SW Spain: Algeciras. Gibraltar. Not reported from Tunisia. 0-50m.
DESCRIPTION Upf pd spots hyaline; spot in s1b yellow; unf brown; unh yellowish-brown; palpi buff: female similar; larger; unh with 3 small, well-defined, pale pd spots. (cf. *Gegenes nostrodamus* and *G. pumilio*).
FLIGHT-PERIOD Voltinism uncertain. Records span June/November: most observations relate to August/October.
HABITAT Hot, dry, rocky, coastal gullies and sandy hills with sparse vegetation.

MEDITERRANEAN SKIPPER

PYGMY SKIPPER

ZELLER'S SKIPPER

♀

Spots clearly defined

MILLET SKIPPER

Fw ostal spots in curved row

♂ upf sex-brand pale

♂

(Samos and Rhodes)

Mediterranean Skipper

Pigmy Skipper

Zeller's Skipper

LIFE-HISTORY LHPs: N Africa *Leersia hexandra*; *Sorghum alepense* (Poaceae).
BEHAVIOUR Reputedly an occasional migrant.

Millet Skipper *Pelopidas thrax*

RANGE Greece (Aegean islands), W and SW Turkey, Israel, Lebanon, Syria, Iraq, Arabia, Africa, Kashmir, Far East.

P. thrax Hübner 1821 TL: Java.
DISTRIBUTION Greece: known only from Samos and Rhodes. 0-75m. Possibly over-looked on other Aegean islands in proximity to Turkish coast.
DESCRIPTION Male upf narrow, white sex-brand distinctive. In both sexes, fw hyaline spots distinctive (cf. *Gegenes nostrodamus* and *G. pumilio*).
FLIGHT-PERIOD Voltinism uncertain: Greek records relate to June. Reportedly bivoltine in Turkey, May/July and late September/mid October.
HABITAT Hot, dry, grassy places in low-lying coastal districts.
LIFE-HISTORY LHP unknown in Europe: in N Africa, *Panicum miliaceum*. In Lebanon, an occasional pest on cereal crops.
BEHAVIOUR Flight low and powerful. Reportedly a migrant.

Cleopatra continued from page 76

G. cleopatra eversi Rehnelt 1974 TL: Gomera.
DISTRIBUTION Gomera: Las Rosas; Hermigua; La Palmita; Las Hayas; Mt. Garajonay; Laguna Grande; Roque de Agando; Montaña Quemada; Vallehermoso. 500-1400m.
DESCRIPTION AND VARIATION Resembles *cleobule*: upf orange discal flush slightly paler, variable: female resembles *palmae*: ups lemon yellow; upf often with strong orange discal flush. Female ups non-reflective in UV-light.
FLIGHT-PERIOD Voltinism uncertain (see *maderensis*). Recorded in March/May, July/September and December.
HABITAT, BEHAVIOUR AND LIFE-HISTORY As for *G. c. cleobule*.

Spanish Fritillary continued from page 214

LIFE-HISTORY LHPs *Dipsacus fullonum*; *D. comosus*; *Cephalaria leucantha*; *Scabiosa* sp; *Knautia* sp.; (?) *Centaurea* spp. Ova laid in batches on underside of leaves. Captive larvae accept *Succisa pratensis*.

Mountain Ringlet continued from page 270

E. epiphron roosi Arnscheid and Sterba 1978 TL: Mt. Pelister.
DISTRIBUTION Republic of Macedonia (Sar Pl.; Jakupica Pl.; Pelister massif); NW Greece (Varnous Mts.: extremely local). 1500-2600m. Distributional relationship with *E. e. aetheria* in SW Balkans unclear.
DESCRIPTION AND VARIATION Male upf rust-red pd spots in s4-s5(6) contiguous and broader than those in s1b and s2, spot in s3 often vestigial, sometimes absent; pd ocelli in s4 and s5 constant; ocellus in s3 usually absent; unh pd red-ringed ocelli variable in size and number, usually vestigial, often absent; unh ocelli usually absent; pd area sometimes slightly paler. Male genitalia distinctive. On Sar Pl. above 2300m, small dark forms resembling f. *nelamus* are not uncommon.
FLIGHT-PERIOD Univoltine. Late June/mid August according to season and altitude.
HABITAT Grass-covered slopes, sometimes in very exposed situations: often associated with taller grass species and prostrate Juniper (*Juniperus communis nana*).

Large Grizzled Skipper continued from page 327

HABITAT As for nominate form.
LIFE-HISTORY LHPs *Potentilla* spp.; *Helianthemum nummularium*.
P. alveus scandinavicus Strand 1903 TL: Dovre, Norway. syn: *ballotae* Oberthür 1910.
DISTRIBUTION Local in Norway and Sweden to 63°N. Absent from Denmark and Finland. 100-1100m.
DESCRIPTION Resembles nominate form: smaller; ups white markings slightly larger, clearly defined; male genitalia distinctive. Considered specifically distinct by some authors.
FLIGHT-PERIOD Univoltine. Late June/August according to season.
HABITAT At higher altitudes, barren stony ground with damp, grassy hollows or small, sheltered streams: at lower levels, dry soils with sparse grass.
LIFE-HISTORY LHPs *Potentilla* sp.; *Agrimonia eupatoria*; (?)*Polygala vulgare*. Hibernates as an ovum.
P. alveus numidus Oberthür 1910 TL: Lambessa, Algeria.
DISTRIBUTION Morocco and Algeria: Middle Atlas; High Atlas. 1500-2800m.
FLIGHT-PERIOD Univoltine. Late May/late June.
HABITAT Grassy, flowery slopes.
LIFE-HISTORY LHP *Helianthemum croceum*.

Checklist of species

Papilionidae

Papilio machaon Swallowtail ❏
Papilio saharae Desert Swallowtail ❏
Papilio hospiton Corsican Swallowtail ❏
Papilio alexanor Southern Swallowtail ❏
Iphiclides podalirius Scarce Swallowtail ❏
Zerynthia polyxena Southern Festoon ❏
Zerynthia rumina Spanish Festoon ❏
Zerynthia cerisy Eastern Festoon ❏
Archon apollinus False Apollo ❏
Parnassius apollo Apollo ❏
Parnassius phoebus Small Apollo ❏
Parnassius mnemosyne Clouded Apollo ❏

Pieridae

Aporia crataegi Black-veined White ❏
Pieris brassicae Large White ❏
Pieris cheiranthi Canary Islands' Large White ❏
Artogeia rapae Small White ❏
Artogeia mannii Southern Small White ❏
Artogeia ergane Mountain Small White ❏
Artogeia napi Green-veined White ❏
Artogeia balcana Balkan Green-veined White ❏
Artogeia bryoniae Mountain Green-veined White ❏
Artogeia krueperi Krueper's Small White ❏
Pontia edusa Eastern Bath White ❏
Pontia daplidice Bath White ❏
Pontia chloridice Small Bath White ❏
Pontia callidice Peak White ❏
Euchloe crameri Western Dappled White ❏
Euchloe simplonia Mountain Dappled White ❏
Euchloe ausonia Eastern Dappled White ❏
Euchloe insularis Corsican Dappled White ❏
Euchloe tagis Portuguese Dappled White ❏
Euchloe falloui Scarce Green-striped White ❏
Euchloe belemia Green-striped White ❏
Elphinstonia charlonia Greenish Black-tip ❏
Elphinstonia penia Eastern Greenish Black-tip ❏

Anthocharis cardamines Orange Tip ❑
Anthocharis belia Moroccan Orange Tip ❑
Anthocharis damone Eastern Orange Tip ❑
Anthocharis gruneri Gruner's Orange Tip ❑
Zegris eupheme Sooty Orange Tip ❑
Colotis evagore Desert Orange Tip ❑
Catopsilia florella African Migrant ❑
Colias phicomone Mountain Clouded Yellow ❑
Colias nastes Pale Arctic Clouded Yellow ❑
Colias palaeno Moorland Clouded Yellow ❑
Colias chrysotheme Lesser Clouded Yellow ❑
Colias aurorina Greek Clouded Yellow ❑
Colias myrmidone Danube Clouded Yellow ❑
Colias hecla Northern Clouded Yellow ❑
Colias hyale Pale Clouded Yellow ❑
Colias crocea Clouded Yellow ❑
Colias caucasica Balkan Clouded Yellow ❑
Colias alfacariensis Berger's Clouded Yellow ❑
Colias erate Eastern Pale Clouded Yellow ❑
Gonepteryx rhamni Brimstone ❑
Gonepteryx cleopatra Cleopatra ❑
Gonepteryx farinosa Powdered Brimstone ❑
Leptidea sinapis Wood White ❑
Leptidea reali Réal's Wood White ❑
Leptidea duponcheli Eastern Wood White ❑
Leptidea morsei Fenton's Wood White ❑

Lycaenidae

Cigaritis zohra Donzel's Silver-line ❑
Cigaritis siphax Common Silver-line ❑
Cigaritis allardi Allard's Silver-line ❑
Apharitis myrmecophila Desert Leopard ❑
Thecla betulae Brown Hairstreak ❑
Quercusia quercus Purple Hairstreak ❑
Laeosopis roboris Spanish Purple Hairstreak ❑
Satyrium acaciae Sloe Hairstreak ❑
Satyrium ilicis Ilex Hairstreak ❑
Satyrium esculi False Ilex Hairstreak ❑
Satyrium spini Blue-spot Hairstreak ❑
Satyrium w-album White-letter Hairstreak ❑
Satyrium pruni Black Hairstreak ❑

Satyrium ledereri Orange-banded Hairstreak ❑
Callophrys rubi Green Hairstreak ❑
Callophrys avis Chapman's Green Hairstreak ❑
Tomares ballus Provence Hairstreak ❑
Tomares nogelii Nogel's Hairstreak ❑
Tomares mauretanicus Moroccan Hairstreak ❑
Lycaena helle Violet Copper ❑
Lycaena phlaeas Small Copper ❑
Lycaena dispar Large Copper ❑
Lycaena virgaureae Scarce Copper ❑
Lycaena ottomana Grecian Copper ❑
Lycaena tityrus Sooty Copper ❑
Lycaena alciphron Purple-shot Copper ❑
Lycaena thersamon Lesser Fiery Copper ❑
Lycaena thetis Fiery Copper ❑
Lycaena phoebus Moroccan Copper ❑
Lycaena hippothoe Purple-edged Copper ❑
Lycaena candens Balkan Copper ❑
Lampides boeticus Long-tailed Blue ❑
Cacyreus marshalli Geranium Bronze ❑
Leptotes pirithous Lang's Short-tailed Blue ❑
Cyclyrius webbianus Canary Blue ❑
Tarucus theophrastus Common Tiger Blue ❑
Tarucus rosaceus Mediterranean Blue ❑
Tarucus balkanicus Little Tiger Blue ❑
Azanus ubaldus Desert Babul Blue ❑
Azanus jesous African Babul Blue ❑
Zizeeria knysna African Grass Blue ❑
Everes argiades Short-tailed Blue ❑
Everes decoloratus Eastern Short-tailed Blue ❑
Everes alcetas Provençal Short-tailed Blue ❑
Cupido minimus Little Blue ❑
Cupido carswelli Carswell's Little Blue ❑
Cupido osiris Osiris Blue ❑
Cupido lorquinii Lorquin's Blue ❑
Celastrina argiolus Holly Blue ❑
Glaucopsyche alexis Green-underside Blue ❑
Glaucopsyche melanops Black-eyed Blue ❑
Turanana endymion Odd-spot Blue ❑
Maculinea alcon Alcon Blue ❑
Maculinea rebeli Mountain Alcon Blue ❑
Maculinea arion Large Blue ❑

Maculinea telejus Scarce Large Blue ❏
Maculinea nausithous Dusky Large Blue ❏
Iolana iolas Iolas Blue ❏
Pseudophilotes baton Baton Blue ❏
Pseudophilotes panoptes Panoptes Blue ❏
Pseudophilotes vicrama ❏
Pseudophilotes abencerragus False Baton Blue ❏
Pseudophilotes barbagiae Sardinian Blue ❏
Pseudophilotes bavius Bavius Blue ❏
Scolitantides orion Chequered Blue ❏
Chilades trochylus Grass Jewel ❏
Maurus vogelii Vogel's Blue ❏
Plebejus martini Martin's Blue ❏
Plebejus allardi Allard's Blue ❏
Plebejus pylaon Zephyr Blue ❏
Plebejus argus Silver-studded Blue ❏
Plebejus loewii Loew's Blue ❏
Plebejus idas Idas Blue ❏
Plebejus argyrognomon Reverdin's Blue ❏
Vacciniina optilete Cranberry Blue ❏
Kretania psylorita Cretan Argus ❏
Kretania eurypilus Eastern Brown Argus ❏
Eumedonia eumedon Geranium Argus ❏
Aricia agestis Brown Argus ❏
Aricia artaxerxes Mountain Argus ❏
Aricia morronensis Spanish Argus ❏
Ultraaricia anteros Blue Argus ❏
Pseudaricia nicias Silvery Argus ❏
Albulina orbitulus Alpine Blue ❏
Agriades glandon Glandon Blue ❏
Agriades pyrenaicus Gavarnie Blue ❏
Cyaniris semiargus Mazarine Blue ❏
Agrodiaetus iphigenia Chelmos Blue ❏
Agrodiaetus damon Damon Blue ❏
Agrodiaetus dolus Furry Blue ❏
Agrodiaetus ainsae Forster's Furry Blue ❏
Agrodiaetus escheri Escher's Blue ❏
Agrodiaetus amanda Amanda's Blue ❏
Agrodiaetus thersites Chapman's Blue ❏
Agrodiaetus admetus Anomalous Blue ❏
Agrodiaetus fabressei Oberthür's Anomalous Blue ❏
Agrodiaetus agenjoi Agenjo's Anomalous Blue ❏

Agrodiaetus humedasae Piedmont Anomalous Blue ❑
Agrodiaetus violetae Andalusian Anomalous Blue ❑
Agrodiaetus aroanensis Grecian Anomalous Blue ❑
Agrodiaetus ripartii Ripart's Anomalous Blue ❑
Agrodiaetus nephohiptamenos Higgins' Anomalous Blue ❑
Agrodiaetus galloi Gallo's Anomalous Blue ❑
Neolysandra coelestina Pontic Blue ❑
Plebicula dorylas Turquoise Blue ❑
Plebicula golgus Nevada Blue ❑
Plebicula nivescens Mother-of-pearl Blue ❑
Plebicula atlantica Atlas Blue ❑
Meleageria daphnis Meleager's Blue ❑
Lysandra coridon Chalk-hill Blue ❑
Lysandra philippi Macedonian Chalk-hill Blue ❑
Lysandra hispana Provence Chalk-hill Blue ❑
Lysandra albicans Spanish Chalk-hill Blue ❑
Lysandra bellargus Adonis Blue ❑
Lysandra punctifera Spotted Adonis Blue ❑
Polyommatus icarus Common Blue ❑
Polyommatus andronicus Phalakron Blue ❑
Polyommatus eroides False Eros Blue ❑
Polyommatus eros Eros Blue ❑
Polyommatus menelaos Taygetos Blue ❑

Riodinidae

Hamearis lucin Duke of Burgundy Fritillary ❑

Libytheidae

Libythea celtis Nettle-tree Butterfly ❑

Danaidae

Danaus plexippus Milkweed or Monarch ❑
Danaus chrysippus Plain Tiger ❑

Nymphalidae

Charaxes jasius Two-tailed Pasha ❑
Apatura iris Purple Emperor ❑

Apatura ilia Lesser Purple Emperor ❑
Apatura metis Freyer's Purple Emperor ❑
Thaleropis ionia ❑
Limenitis populi Poplar Admiral ❑
Limenitis reducta Southern White Admiral ❑
Limenitis camilla White Admiral ❑
Hypolimnas misippus False Plain Tiger ❑
Neptis sappho Common Glider ❑
Neptis rivularis Hungarian Glider ❑
Nymphalis antiopa Camberwell Beauty ❑
Nymphalis polychloros Large Tortoiseshell ❑
Nymphalis xanthomelas Yellow-legged Tortoiseshell ❑
Nymphalis vaualbum False Comma ❑
Inachis io Peacock Butterfly ❑
Vanessa atalanta Red Admiral ❑
Vanessa indica Indian Red Admiral ❑
Vanessa cardui Painted Lady ❑
Vanessa virginiensis American Painted Lady ❑
Aglais urticae Small Tortoiseshell ❑
Polygonum c-album Comma Butterfly ❑
Polygonum egea Southern Comma ❑
Araschnia levana Map Butterfly ❑
Argynnis pandora Cardinal Fritillary ❑
Argynnis paphia Silver-washed Fritillary ❑
Argynnis laodice Pallas's Fritillary ❑
Argynnis aglaja Dark Green Fritillary ❑
Argynnis adippe High Brown Fritillary ❑
Argynnis niobe Niobe Fritillary ❑
Argynnis elisa Corsican Fritillary ❑
Issoria lathonia Queen of Spain Fritillary ❑
Brenthis hecate Twin-spot Fritillary ❑
Brenthis daphne Marbled Fritillary ❑
Brenthis ino Lesser Marbled Fritillary ❑
Boloria pales Shepherd's Fritillary ❑
Boloria napaea Mountain Fritillary ❑
Boloria aquilonaris Cranberry Fritillary ❑
Boloria graeca Balkan Fritillary ❑
Proclossiana eunomia Bog Fritillary ❑
Clossiana euphrosyne Pearl-bordered Fritillary ❑
Clossiana titania Titania's Fritillary ❑
Clossiana selene Small Pearl-bordered Fritillary ❑
Clossiana chariclea Arctic Fritillary ❑

Clossiana freija Frejya's Fritillary ❑
Clossiana dia Weaver's Fritillary ❑
Clossiana polaris Polar Fritillary ❑
Clossiana thore Thor's Fritillary ❑
Clossiana frigga Frigga's Fritillary ❑
Clossiana improba Dusky-winged Fritillary ❑
Melitaea cinxia Glanville Fritillary ❑
Melitaea arduinna Freyer's Fritillary ❑
Melitaea phoebe Knapweed Fritillary ❑
Melitaea aetherie Aetherie Fritillary ❑
Melitaea didyma Spotted Fritillary ❑
Melitaea deserticola Desert Fritillary ❑
Melitaea trivia Lesser Spotted Fritillary ❑
Melitaea diamina False Heath Fritillary ❑
Mellicta athalia Heath Fritillary ❑
Mellicta deione Provençal Fritillary ❑
Mellicta varia Grisons Fritillary ❑
Mellicta parthenoides Meadow Fritillary ❑
Mellicta aurelia Nickerl's Fritillary ❑
Mellicta britomartis Assmann's Fritillary ❑
Mellicta asteria Little Fritillary ❑
Hypodryas maturna Scarce Fritillary ❑
Hypodryas intermedia Asian Fritillary ❑
Hypodryas cynthia Cynthia's Fritillary ❑
Hypodryas iduna Lapland Fritillary ❑
Eurodryas aurinia Marsh Fritillary ❑
Eurodryas desfontainii Spanish Fritillary ❑

Satyridae

Melanargia galathea Marbled White ❑
Melanargia lachesis Iberian Marbled White ❑
Melanargia russiae Esper's Marbled White ❑
Melanargia larissa Balkan Marbled White ❑
Melanargia occitanica Western Marbled White ❑
Melanargia arge Italian Marbled White ❑
Melanargia ines Spanish Marbled White ❑
Hipparchia fagi Woodland Grayling ❑
Hipparchia alcyone Rock Grayling ❑
Hipparchia syriaca Eastern Rock Grayling ❑
Hipparchia ellena Algerian Grayling ❑
Hipparchia neomiris Corsican Grayling ❑

Hipparchia volgensis Delattin's Grayling ❑
Hipparchia semele Grayling ❑
Hipparchia cretica Cretan Grayling ❑
Hipparchia christenseni ❑
Hipparchia aristaeus Southern Grayling ❑
Hipparchia azorina Azores Grayling ❑
Hipparchia caldeirense Oehmig's Grayling ❑
Hipparchia miguelensis Le Cerf's Grayling ❑
Hipparchia mersina ❑
Hipparchia pellucida ❑
Neohipparchia statilinus Tree Grayling ❑
Neohipparchia fatua Freyer's Grayling ❑
Neohipparchia hansii Austaut's Grayling ❑
Neohipparchia powelli Powell's Grayling ❑
Peudotergumia fidia Striped Grayling ❑
Pseudotergumia wyssii Canary Grayling ❑
Chazara briseis The Hermit ❑
Chazara prieuri Southern Hermit ❑
Pseudochazara atlantis Moroccan Grayling ❑
Pseudochazara graeca Grecian Grayling ❑
Pseudochazara hippolyte Nevada Grayling ❑
Pseudochazara geyeri Grey Asian Grayling ❑
Pseudochazara mamurra Brown's Grayling ❑
Pseudochazara orestes Dils' Grayling ❑
Pseudochazara mniszechii Dark Grayling ❑
Pseudochazara cingovskii Macedonian Grayling ❑
Pseudochazara anthelea White-banded Grayling ❑
Oeneis norna Norse Grayling ❑
Oeneis bore Arctic Grayling ❑
Oeneis glacialis Alpine Grayling ❑
Oeneis jutta Baltic Grayling ❑
Satyrus actaea Black Satyr ❑
Satyrus ferula Great Sooty Satyr ❑
Minois dryas Dryad ❑
Berberia abdelkader Giant Grayling ❑
Berberia lambessanus ❑
Kanetisa circe Great Banded Grayling ❑
Arethusana arethusa False Grayling ❑
Erebia ligea Arran Brown ❑
Erebia euryale Large Ringlet ❑
Erebia eriphyle Eriphyle Ringlet ❑
Erebia manto Yellow-spotted Ringlet ❑

Erebia claudina White Speck Ringlet ❑
Erebia flavofasciata Yellow-banded Ringlet ❑
Erebia epiphron Mountain Ringlet ❑
Erebia orientalis Bulgarian Ringlet ❑
Erebia christi Rätzer's Ringlet ❑
Erebia pharte Blind Ringlet ❑
Erebia melampus Lesser Mountain Ringlet ❑
Erebia sudetica Sudeten Ringlet ❑
Erebia aethiops Scotch Argus ❑
Erebia triaria de Prunner's Ringlet ❑
Erebia embla Lapland Ringlet ❑
Erebia disa Arctic Ringlet ❑
Erebia medusa Woodland Ringlet ❑
Erebia polaris Arctic Woodland Ringlet ❑
Erebia alberganus Almond-eyed Ringlet ❑
Erebia pluto Sooty Ringlet ❑
Erebia gorge Silky Ringlet ❑
Erebia aethiopella False Mnestra Ringlet ❑
Erebia rhodopensis Nicholl's Ringlet ❑
Erebia mnestra Mnestra's Ringlet ❑
Erebia gorgone Gavarnie Ringlet ❑
Erebia epistygne Spring Ringlet ❑
Erebia tyndarus Swiss Brassy Ringlet ❑
Erebia cassioides Common Brassy Ringlet ❑
Erebia hispania Spanish Brassy Ringlet ❑
Erebia nivalis De Lesse's Brassy Ringlet ❑
Erebia calcaria Lorkovic's Brassy Ringlet ❑
Erebia ottomana Ottoman Brassy Ringlet ❑
Erebia pronoe Water Ringlet ❑
Erebia melas Black Ringlet ❑
Erebia lefebvrei Lefèbvre's Ringlet ❑
Erebia scipio Larche Ringlet ❑
Erebia stirius Styrian Ringlet ❑
Erebia styx Stygian Ringlet ❑
Erebia montana Marbled Ringlet ❑
Erebia zapateri Zapater's Ringlet ❑
Erebia neoridas Autumn Ringlet ❑
Erebia oeme Bright-eyed Ringlet ❑
Erebia meolans Piedmont Ringlet ❑
Erebia palarica Chapman's Ringlet ❑
Erebia pandrose Dewy Ringlet ❑
Erebia sthennyo False Dewy Ringlet ❑

Proterebia afra Dalmatian Ringlet ❑
Maniola jurtina Meadow Brown ❑
Maniola megala ❑
Maniola chia ❑
Maniola nurag Sardinian Meadow Brown ❑
Maniola telmessia ❑
Maniola halicarnassus ❑
Hyponephele maroccana Moroccan Meadow Brown ❑
Hyponephele lycaon Dusky Meadow Brown ❑
Hyponephele lupina Oriental Meadow Brown ❑
Aphantopus hyperantus Ringlet ❑
Pyronia tithonus Gatekeeper ❑
Pyronia cecilia Southern Gatekeeper ❑
Pyronia bathseba Spanish Gatekeeper ❑
Pyronia janiroides False Meadow Brown ❑
Coenonympha tullia Large Heath ❑
Coenonympha rhodopensis Eastern Large Heath ❑
Coenonympha pamphilus Small Heath ❑
Coenonymphia thyrsis Cretan Small Heath ❑
Coenonympha corinna Corsican Heath ❑
Coenonympha elbana Elban Heath ❑
Coenonympha dorus Dusky Heath ❑
Coenonympha vaucheri Vaucher's Heath ❑
Coenonympha arcania Pearly Heath ❑
Coenonympha darwiniana Darwin's Heath ❑
Coenonympha gardetta Alpine Heath ❑
Coenonympha arcanioides Moroccan Pearly Heath ❑
Coenonympha leander Russian Heath ❑
Coenonympha glycerion Chestnut Heath ❑
Coenonympha hero Scarce Heath ❑
Coenonympha oedippus False Ringlet ❑
Pararge aegeria Speckled Wood ❑
Pararge xiphioides Canary Speckled Wood ❑
Pararge xiphia Madeiran Speckled Wood ❑
Lasiommata megera Wall Brown ❑
Lasiommata maera Large Wall Brown ❑
Lasiommata petropolitana Northern Wall Brown ❑
Lopinga achine Woodland Brown ❑
Ypthima asterope African Ringlet ❑
Kirinia roxelana Lattice Brown ❑
Kirinia climene Lesser Lattice Brown ❑

Hesperiidae

Pyrgus malvae Grizzled Skipper ❑
Pyrgus melotis ❑
Pyrgus alveus Large Grizzled Skipper ❑
Pyrgus armoricanus Oberthür's Grizzled Skipper ❑
Pyrgus foulquieri Foulquier's Grizzled Skipper ❑
Pyrgus warrenensis Warren's Skipper ❑
Pyrgus serratulae Olive Skipper ❑
Pyrgus carlinae Carline Skipper ❑
Pyrgus onopordi Rosy Grizzled Skipper ❑
Pyrgus cinarae Sandy Grizzled Skipper ❑
Pyrgus sidae Yellow-banded Skipper ❑
Pyrgus carthami Safflower Skipper ❑
Pyrgus andromedae Alpine Grizzled Skipper ❑
Pyrgus cacaliae Dusky Grizzled Skipper ❑
Pyrgus centaureae Northern Grizzled Skipper ❑
Spialia sertorius Red Underwing Skipper ❑
Spialia orbifer Orbed Red-underwing Skipper ❑
Spialia phlomidis Persian Skipper ❑
Spialia doris Aden Skipper ❑
Muschampia tessellum Tessellated Skipper ❑
Muschampia cribrellum Spinose Skipper ❑
Muschampia proto Sage Skipper ❑
Muschampia mohammed Barbary Skipper ❑
Muschampia leuzeae Algerian Grizzled Skipper ❑
Carcharodus alceae Mallow Skipper ❑
Carcharodus tripolinus False Mallow Skipper ❑
Carcharodus lavatherae Marbled Skipper ❑
Carcharodus boeticus Southern Marbled Skipper ❑
Carcharodus stauderi ❑
Carcharodus flocciferus Tufted Marbled Skipper ❑
Carcharodus orientalis Oriental Marbled Skipper ❑
Erynnis tages Dingy Skipper ❑
Erynnis marloyi Inky Skipper ❑
Heteropterus morpheus Large Chequered Skipper ❑
Carterocephalus palaemon Chequered Skipper ❑
Carterocephalus silvicolus
Northern Chequered Skipper ❑
Thymelicus acteon Lulworth Skipper ❑
Thymelicus hamza Moroccan Small Skipper ❑
Thymelicus lineola Essex Skipper ❑
Thymelicus sylvestris Small Skipper ❑

- *Thymelicus hyrax* Levantine Skipper ❏
- *Hesperia comma* Silver-spotted Skipper ❏
- *Ochlodes venatus* Large Skipper ❏
- *Gegenes nostrodamus* Mediterranean Skipper ❏
- *Gegenes pumilio* Pigmy Skipper ❏
- *Borbo borbonica* Zeller's Skipper ❏
- *Pelopidas thrax* Millet Skipper ❏

Glossary

Abdomen. The part of the body behind the thorax.

Aberration. An abnormal individual form of usually rare occurrence arising from an environmentally induced or genetic cause.

Aestivation. A state of torpor (diapause) in summer heat or drought.

Allopatric. Two or more forms having essentially separate areas of distribution.

Anal angle. Small apical area enclosed by inner and outer margins of the hind-wing.

Anal fold. A fold in the hind-wing inner margin.

Androconia (sing. Androconium). In male butterflies, specialized wing-scales (often called scent-scales) possessing gland cells containing special chemicals for attracting females.

Antennae (sing. Antenna). Paired, jointed sensory organs – clubbed in the case of butterflies – arising from the head of an insect.

Anterior. Towards the head in reference to axis of head thorax and abdomen. Applicable to adult, larvae or pupa. (Cf. posterior).

Apex. The point of coincidence of the costal and outer margins.

Apical area. Of fore-wing, area just inside and contiguous with apex. (Cf. subapex).

Auct. (auctorum). Indicating the use of a name for a purpose other than that intended by the original author.

Basad. Towards the wing-base.

Basal. Of the wing-base.

Bivoltine. Having two annual broods.

Caterpillar. *See* larva.

Calcareous. Referring to rocks/soils having an alkaline (basic) reaction.

Cell. In reference to wings, the generally closed area defined by the subcostal, medial and discoidal veins in the basal and discal areas of the fore-wings and hind-wings: due to the absence of one or more elements of the discoidal vein, the cell on the hind-wing is sometimes open. (See also discocellular).

Cephalic. Of the head.

Chevron. A wedge-shaped mark.

Chitin. A tough, sometimes brittle material from which the hard parts of an insect are formed, e.g. exoskeleton.

Chromosome. Within the nucleus of each living cell, small bodies carrying the genes.

Chrysalis. *See* pupa.

Cline. A progressive, usually continuous change in one or more characters over a geographical or altitudinal range. *Euchloe tagis* is an example of a geographical cline; good examples of altitudinal clines are provided by some *Erebia* spp. for which populations at highest altitudes tend to be smaller and have reduced wing-markings. The term is also applicable to equivalent change in relative proportions of individuals having two or more distinctive forms, e.g., ratio of 'brown' to 'blue' females in populations of some lycaenid butterflies. A combination of clinal types is apparent for some species, e.g. *Erebia gorge*. Although many clines correlate with climatic variables, often temperature and humidity, causal/ functional relationships are not necessarily implied.

Club. The thickened, terminal part of the antenna.

Code. See International Commission on Zoological Nomenclature.

Colony. A small, locally isolated population.

Compositae. Disused plant family name for Asteraceae.

Conspecific. Belonging to the same species.

Costa. The front (leading) edge of fore-wing or hind-wing.

Costal fold. A narrow, thin membrane folded back on the upper surface of fore-wing costa containing androconia.

Cremaster. Tiny hooks at the abdominal tip of a pupa giving support by attachment to a silk pad spun by the larva prior to pupation.

Cruciferae. Disused plant family name for Brassicaceae.

Cryptic. Colouring and/or pattern adopted for the purpose of protection from predators or concealment from prey.

Cuspidal. Two segments of curved lines meeting and terminating at a sharp point.

Cytology. The study of cells.

Dentate. Tooth-like. Often applied to small cuspidal projections on outer margin of wings.

Desiccation. In plants, excessive loss of water from plant tissues caused by high temperature and/or drought. Usually a reversible condition but relevant to the nutritional quality of plant used as a larval host-plant.

Diapause (noun or verb). Suspension of activity or development in any metamorphic stage. (See also aestivation and hibernation).

Dimorphism. The occurrence of two distinct forms within the same population: hence, sexual dimorphism, seasonal dimorphism, etc.

Discal. The central portion of wing from costa to inner margin: hence, discal band, discal markings etc.

Discocellular. Of the veins associated with the cell.

Discoidal. Of the area associated with the cell: hence discoidal spot.

Dispersion. Of adult butterfly behaviour, extension of local range. (*See also* migration).

Distad. In the direction away from the body.

Distal. The point furthest away from the centre of the body.

DNA. Abbreviation for deoxyribonucleic acid, a complex molecule from which the chromosome, and the genes it carries, is made.

Dorsal. Of the back – upper surface of the body (cf. ventral).

Dorsal Nectary Organ. In the larvae of many species of the Lycaenidae, a gland located in the dorsal region of the 7th segment producing a sweet secretion attractive to ants. Often called the 'honey-gland'.

Dorsum. The back.

Ecdysis. The process of shedding the larval skin or pupal case.

Ecology. The study of the relationships of animals and plants with each other and their environment.

Elongate. Of extended or lengthened form – stretched.

Endemic. Restricted to a well-defined region – found nowhere else: hence, endemic species, form, etc.

Exuvium. The cast skin of a larva.

Falcate. Hook-shaped.

Faculative. A beneficial, but non-essential association: e.g., that between the larval (or pupal) stages of many lycaenid butterflies and ants. (See also obligate).

Family. A basic unit of taxonomic classification, usually comprising an assemblage of genera considered to be closely related on account of certain shared characters.

Fauna. Collectively, the animals of a region.

Flora. Collectively, the plants of a region.

Form. Any taxonomic unit subordinate to subspecific classification applicable to ecological, seasonal or sexually dimorphic/ polymorphic forms.

Frons. The area between the eyes on the front the head ('face'), often bearing a hair-like tuft.

Fuscous. Smoky greyish-brown.

Genitalia. Located in the terminal abdominal segments, the male or female sexual organs, by which means the spermatophore of the male is transferred to the female during copulation.

Genotype. The total genetic characters of an organism.

Genus. A basic unit of taxonomic classification, usually comprising a number of species considered to be more closely related to each other than to other species of other genera.

Girdle. A silken thread supporting the midsection of a pupa.

Gramineae. A disused plant family name for Poaceae (the grasses).

Gynandromorph. An individual having both male and female characters. Various degrees of gynandromorphism are possible: in bilateral gynandromorphism, sexual characters/components of left and right-hand sides of an adult insect are sharply delineated by the vertical axial plane of the head, thorax and abdomen. Gynandromorphs are infertile.

Hair-tuft. A grouping of hair-like androconia.

Hibernaculum. For butterflies, a protective structure within which hibernation occurs, fashioned by a larva (or, collectively and co-operatively by larvae) for its own use or that of its pupa.

Hibernation. The dormant stage in which an animal passes the winter. (See also diapause).

Homonym. A name given (inadvertently) to two different species within the same genus. According to international code (International Commission on Zoological Nomeclature), the first published name must be adopted upon recognition of oversight.

Honey-gland. *See* Dorsal Nectary Organ.

Hyaline. Translucent, glass-like membranes: part of the wing-structure of some butterflies.

Hybrid. The progeny of two species arising from cross-fertilization: hence, hybridization. Adult hybrids are infertile: characteristically, the early-stages arising from cross-fertilization have poor viability.

I.C.Z.N. *See* International Commission on Zoological Nomenclature.

Imago. The adult or 'perfect' insect.

Infrasubspecific. Any taxonomic unit subordinate to subspecific classification.

Inner margin. Of the wings, the margin closest to the body.

Instar. A stage of larval development between skin changes.

Internal (syn: proximal). The point closest to the body.

International Commission on Zoological Nomenclature. The body responsible for the International Code of rules governing the application of the scientific names of animals.

Invalid name. A scientific name inconsistent with rules of the International Code governing the application of such names.

Irrorate. Covered with minute, coloured dots - 'dusted' or minutely speckled.

Jullien Organ. Distinctive, dark, stiff rods (or batons) present in the male genitalia of certain butterflies.

Lapsus calami. An author's error, for example, inaccuracy in the description of a type locality or the mis-spelling of a name.

Larva (pl. larvae). The second (growth) stage in the development of an insect.

Leguminosae. Disused plant family name for Fabaceae.

Lunule. A crescent-shaped mark.

Macular. Spotted.

Marginal. Of fore-wing or hind-wing, the wing area contiguous with the outer margin.

Mediobasal. Central transverse line of basal area.

Mediodiscal. Central transverse line of wing – bisecting the discal area.

Melanism. Increased development of black pigment.

Metamorphosis. Transformation of one structure into another: in butterflies, the transitions of larva to pupa, and pupa to adult.

Migrant. Of butterflies, survival strategy depending partly or wholly on dispersion and establishment of temporary breeding colonies over an extensive geographical area. (See Dispersion).

Mimic (n. or v.). A species (animal or plant) bearing a close resemblance, in part or whole, to another, used as a model: to adopt, in part or whole, the superficial characters of another species.

Mimicry. The close, superficial resemblance of one organism (animal or plant) to another of a different species, adopted for the purpose of gaining advantage through deception, e.g. to evade a predator or to conceal from prey.

Monophagous. Restricted to a single larval host-plant.

Morphology. The study of structure and form: in butterflies, in any developmental stage, includes visible external characters, such as wing-markings in the adult stage.

Nacreous. Resembling mother-of-pearl.

Nominate form. Having characters corresponding to type specimen upon which species description is based – the typical form, often referred to (more correctly according to the present Code) as the nominotypical form.

Nominotypical form. *See* nominate form.

Nom. nud. (*nomen nudum*). A proposed scientific name unaccompanied by formal description and therefore unacceptable according to the rules of the International Code.

Obligate. Of association, necessary - unavoidable. Applicable to that of the larval stage (or part of) of some lycaenid butterflies and ants.

Ocellus (pl. ocelli). An 'eye-spot': a rounded spot (often black), usually with a central white pupil or pale spot, often enclosed by a pale or coloured annulus. When the pupil is absent, the spot is said to be 'blind'.

Oligophagous. Restricted to a single genus of larval host-plants.

Osmeterium. An eversible (erectile), fleshy organ held within the first thoracic segment of the larva of certain butterflies.

Oviposit. To lay eggs.

Ovipositor. Located in the tip of the female abdomen, a specialized structure through which eggs are extruded during egg-laying.

Ovum (pl. ova). Egg.

Palearctic. Of the biogeographical region comprising Europe (including Canary Islands,

Azores and Madeira) and the extra-tropical areas of Africa and Asia.

Palp (pl. Palpi). In adult butterfly, one of pair of sensory organs located on the front of the head.

Phenotype. Pertaining to the appearance of an organism arising from the interaction of its genetic character with that of its environment.

Photoperiod. Day-length, period between dawn and dusk.

Polygenetic. A wing-character or other feature controlled by a contribution from several genes.

Polymorphism. The occurrence of two or more forms of a single species within the same population.

Polyphagous. Having a range of larval host-plants belonging to more than one plant genus.

Polyploidy. Within a cell, the multiplication of chromosome sets in which superfluous sets are inactive (non-functional).

Polyvoltine. Having two or more annual broods (number of which may be unknown or unspecified).

Population. Individuals of a species living together or in sufficiently close proximity to sustain, over time, a high probability of maintaining uniform (within limits of normal variation) genetic character.

Postdiscal. Of the wings, the area between the discal and submarginal areas.

Posterior. Towards the abdominal extremity relative to axis of head, thorax and abdomen.

Proboscis. The feeding tube of the adult butterfly.

Proximal (syn: internal). The point closest to the body.

Pupa (pl. pupae). The third developmental stage of an insect in which the final transformation to the adult insect occurs.

Race. A distinctive population of a species approximating to, but generally considered subordinate to a subspecies.

Range. The total (unless otherwise specified or implied) geographic area within which a species or subspecies occurs: distribution need not be continuous.

Reticulate. A network pattern.

Sagittate. Arrow-shaped.

Scandinavia. Geographical region of Europe comprising Denmark, Norway and Sweden.

Sex-brand. A grouping of androconia – often in conspicuous patches.

Space. Of the wings, an area of wing membrane between two veins.

Species (pl. species). A basic unit of formal taxonomic classification referring to a group of individuals of an organism capable of interbreeding and producing healthy, fertile offspring. Such groups are incapable of cross-breeding with other groups to produce healthy, fully fertile offspring.

Spermatophore. The sperm sac transferred to the female during copulation.

Sphragis. A hard structure formed on the ventral surface of the terminal abdominal segments of a fertilized (female) butterfly to prevent further copulation.

Stria (pl. striae). A narrow line or streak.

Subapex. Of the fore-wing, the area inside the apex: hence subapical area.

Subgenus. A sub-unit of taxonomic classification pertaining to a closely related group of species within a genus.

Submarginal. Of fore-wing or hind-wing, the wing area between that just inside the outer margin and the post-discal area. (Closest to the outer margin is the marginal (or sometimes antimarginal) area).

Subspecies. A population occupying a distinct geographical region, separate from other populations of the same species, and having constant and clearly different characters. Such populations have the potential to interbreed and, therefore, cannot overlap.

Symbiosis. Living together – a close and often obligatory association of two species: e.g. the associations of ants and lycaenid larvae.

Sympatric. Two or more species occurring in the same habitat or otherwise in sufficiently close proximity to sustain a high probability of inter-breeding, if biologically possible.

Synonym. Different (scientific) names given to the same taxon: only the first published name is valid.

Systematics. The study of the diversity of biological organisms and the description of their relationships.

Taxon (pl. taxa). Any defined biological unit (species, subspecies or form etc.) or group of units (genus, family, subfamily, tribe, etc). Although taxa are almost always given scientific names, a taxon may be properly defined solely according to its site of origin.

Taxonomy. The classification of animals and plants.

Thorax (a. thoracic). The middle section of an insect's body: in the adult butterfly, the clearly separate portion, bearing the wings and legs, between the head and the abdomen. The thorax itself consists of three segments, more clearly apparent in the larva – prothorax (front), mesothorax (middle) and metathorax (last).

Toponym. Name designating type locality. (Taxonomic names often derive from type locality).

Tornus. Junction of inner and outer margins, on fore-wing or hind-wing.

Trivoltine. Having three annual broods.

Tundra. Grassy, treeless, Polar regions with permanently frozen subsoil (permafrost). In lower latitudes, tundra-like zones, conforming closely to arctic climatic conditions, occur at high altitudes.

Type locality. The geographical site of capture of the type specimen.

Type specimen. The single specimen accepted as the basis of the description of a taxon.

Umbelliferae. Disused plant family name for Apiaceae.

Undulate. Wavy, scalloped.

Univoltine. Having one annual brood (generation).

Valid name. According to the rules of the International Code, an acceptable scientific name.

Variety. A poorly defined sub-unit of taxonomic classification below the rank of subspecies – in definable terms, inseparable from a form.

Vein. In an insect's wing, the semi-rigid tubes supporting the wing membrane.

Venation. The arrangement of veins in an insect's wing.

Ventral. Below the central plane of the body: hence ventral surface of the wings. (Cf. Dorsal.)

Voltinism. Number of annual broods (generations): hence, univoltine, bivoltine, trivoltine, polyvoltine.

Bibliography

The following includes source publications and botanical reference works, amongst which will be found many useful bibliographies.

Abadjiev S. 1992. *Butterflies of Bulgaria. Part 1. Papilionidae and Pieridae.* - Veren Publishers, Sofia.

Abadjiev S. 1993. *Butterflies of Bulgaria. Part 2. Nymphalidae: Libytheinae and Satyrinae.* - S. Abadjiev, Sofia.

Abadjiev S. 1995. *Butterflies of Bulgaria. Part 3. Nymphalidae: Apaturinae and Nymphalinae.* - S. Abadjiev, Sofia.

Agosti, D. and Collingwood, C. A. 1987. A provisional list of the Balkan ants (Hym., Formicidae) and a key to the worker caste. 1. Synonymic list. - Mitt. schwiz. ent. Ges., 60:51-62.

Agosti, D. and Collingwood, C. A. 1987. A provisional list of the Balkan ants (Hym., Formicidae) and a key to the worker caste. 1. Synonymic list. - Mitt. schwiz. ent. Ges., 60:51-62.

Baldock, D. W. and Bretherton, R. F. 1981. Butterflies in Corfu (Kerkyra) in late August, 1980, with a provisional list of all species known from it: (Parts 1 and 2). - *Proc. Trans. Br. ent. nat. Hist. soc.*, 14:8-10, 101-107.

Bateman, G. (Ed.) 1986. *The Oxford Encylopedia of Trees of the World.* - Peeridge Books, London.

Baynes, E. S. A. 1964. *A revised catalogue of Irish Macrolepidoptera.* - Hampton.

Benyamini, D. 1984. The butterflies of the Sinai Peninsula (Lep.: Rhopalocera). - *Nota lepid.*, 7(4):309-321.

Benyamini, D. 1990. [*A field guide to the butterflies of Israel including butterflies of Mt. Hermon and Sinai*]. - Keter Publishing House Ltd., Jerusalem. [In Hebrew].

Bernardi, G. 1961. Biogéographie et spéciation des Lépidoptères Rhopalocères des îles mediterranéennes. - *Colloques int. Cent. natn. Rech. scient.*, 94:181-215.

Bernardi, G. 1971. *C. r. somm. Séanc. Soc. Biogéogr.*, des Lépidoptères des îles égéennes. - *C. r. somm. Séanc. Soc. Biogéogr.*, 1971:21-32

Bink, F. A. 1992. Ecologische Atlas van de Dagvlinders van Noordwest-Europa. [In Dutch].

Bretherton, R. F., De Worms, C. G. M. and Johnson, G. 1963. Butterflies of Corsica. - *Entomologist's Rec. J. Var.*, 75:93-104.

Bretherton, R. F. 1966. A distribution list of the butterflies (Rhopalocera) of western and southern Europe. - *Trans. Soc. Br. Ent.*, 17:1-94.

Buszko, J. and Maslowski. 1993. *Atlas motyli Polski: Vol. 1. Motyle dzienne (Rhopalocera).* [In Polish].

Carlstrom, A. 1987. *A Survey of the Flora and Phytogeography of Rodhos, Simi, Tilos and the Marmaris Peninsula (SE Greece, SW Turkey).* - Department of Systematic Botany, University of Lund, Lund.

Chneour, A. 1954. Macrolepidoptera de Tunisie I, II, Rhopalocera, Gryocera. - *Bull. Soc. Sci. nat. Tunis.*, 7:207-239.

Chneour, A. 1963. Vingt-six ans de travail d'un lépidoptèriste en Tunisie. - *Alexanor*, 3:104-110.

Coutsis, J. G. 1969. List of Grecian Butterflies. - *Entomologist* 102:264-268.

Coutsis, J. G. 1978. List of Grecian Butterflies: additions and corrections. - *Entomologist's Rec. J. Var.*, 90:300-301.

Coutsis, J. G. 1984. Description of the Female Genitalia of *Hipparchia fagi* Scopoli, *Hipparchia semele* Linnaeus (Satyridae) and their Related Taxa. - *J. Res. Lepid.* 22(1983)(3):161-203.

Dacie, J.V., Dacie, M.K.V., Grammaticos, P. and Coutsis, J.G. 1982. Butterflies in northern Greece: July-August 1980. - *Entomologist's Rec. J. Var.* 94:18-20.

Davies, P. H. *et al* (Eds.) 1965-75. *Flora of Turkey and the eastern Aegean islands, Vols. 1-5.* - Edinburgh.

De Lesse, H. 1970. Les nombres de chromosomes à l'appui d'une systématic du groupe de *Lysandra coridon* (Lycaenidae). - *Alexanor*, 6(5):203-224.

De Lesse, H. 1970. Formules chromosomiques de quelques Rhopalocères paléarctiques (Lep.). - *Bull. Soc. ent. Fr.*, 75(7-8):214-216.

De Lesse, H. 1972. Variations géographiques des nombres chromosomiques chez les Lycaenidaede. - *C. r. somm. Séanc. Soc. Biogéogr.*, 48:32-38.

Ebert, G. (Ed.) 1993. *Die Schmetterlinge Baden-Württembergs.* Vols. 1 and 2. - Eugen Ulmer, Stuttgart.

Fernandez-Rubio, F. 1991. Guia de Mariposas Diurnas de la Peninsula Ibérica, Baleares, Canarias, Azores y Madeira.

Fiedler, K. 1991. Systematic, evolutionary, and ecological implications of myrmecophily within the Lycaenidae (Insecta: Lepidoptera: Papilionoidea). - *Bonn. zool. Monogr.*, 31:1-156.

Fiedler, K. 1991. European and North West African Lycaenidae (Lepidoptera) and their associations with ants. - *J. Res. Lepid.* 28(1989)(4):239-257.

Ford, E. B. 1957. *Butterflies.* - Collins, London.

Ford E. B. 1975. *Ecological Genetics.* - Chapman and Hall, London.

Forster, W. and Wohlfahrt, T. A. 1976/77. *Die Schmetterlinge Mitteleuropas. Vol 2. Tagfalter. (2 Auflage).* - Franckh'sche Verlagshandlung, Stuttgart.

Geiger, W. (Ed.) 1987. *Les papillons de jour et leurs biotopes.* - Ligue Suisse pour la Protection de la Nature, Bâle. [In German or French].

Gomez-Bustillo, M. R. and Fernandez-Rubio, F. 1974. *Mariposas de la Peninsula Ibérica: Ropalóceros. Vols. 1 and 2.* - Ministerio de Agricultur, Madrid.

Gonseth, Y. 1987. Atlas de Distribution des Papillons Diurnes de Suisse (Lep.; Rhopalocera). - *Doc. faun. Helv.*, 5:1-242 [In French or German].

Gozmany, L. 1968. Nappili lepkek - Diurna. - *Fauna Hungariae*, 91:1-204.

Gross, F.J. 1978. Beitrag zur Systematik von *Pseudochazara*-Arten. - *Atalanta (Würzburg)*, 9:41-103.

Hackray, J. and Sarlet, L. G. 1969-74. Catalogue des Macrolépidoptères de Belgique. - *Lambillionea* (supplement), 67(1969) *et seq*.

Hartig, F. and Amsel, H. G. 1952. Lepidoptera Sardinica. - *Fragm. ent.*, 1(1951):1-159.

Heath, J. (Ed.) 1970. *Provisional atlas of the Insects of the British Isles. 1. Lepidoptera Rhopalocera: Butterflies.* - Biological Records Centre, Huntingdon.

Heath, J. (Ed.) 1976. *The moths and butterflies of Great Britain and Ireland.* Vol. 1. - Blackwell Scientific Publications and Curwen, Oxford and London.

Heath, J. 1981. Threatened Rhopalocera (butterflies) in Europe. - *Nature Environ. Ser.*, 23:1-157.

Henriksen, H. J. and Kreutzer, Ib. 1982. *The Butterflies of Scandinavia in Nature*. - Skandinavisk Bogforlag, Odense. [In English or Danish].

Hesselbarth, G., Van Oorschot, H. and Wagener, S. 1995. *Die Tagfalter der Türkei. Vols. 1-3*. Berger-Juling Electronic Publishing, Bonn.

Higgins, L. G. 1941. An illustrated Catalogue of the Palearctic *Melitaea*. - *Trans. R. Ent. Soc. Lond.*, 91(7):175-365.

Higgins, L. G. 1950. A descriptive Catalogue of the Palaearctic *Euphydryas* (Lepidoptera: Rhopalocera). - *Trans. R. Ent. Soc. Lond.*, 101(12):435-499.

Higgins, L. G. 1955. A descriptive Catalogue of the genus *Mellicta* Billberg (Lepidoptera: Nymphalidae) and its species, with supplementary notes on the genera *Mellitaea* and *Euphydryas*. - *Trans. R. Ent. Soc. Lond.*, 106(1):1-131.

Higgins, L. G. 1975. *The Classification of European Butterflies*. - Collins, London.

Higgins, L. G. and Riley, N. D. 1984. *A Field Guide to the Butterflies of Britain and Europe*. - Collins, London.

Høegh-Guldberg, O. and Jarvis, F. V. L. 1969. Central and north European *Ariciae* (Lep.). Relationships, heredity, evolution. - *Natura jutl.*, 15:1-106.

Howarth, T. G. 1973. *South's British Butterflies*. - Warne and Co. Ltd., London.

Hruby, K. 1964. Prodomus Lepidopter Slovenska. - *Vydav. Slov. Akad. Vied*, Bratislava.

Ivinskis, P. 1993. *Checklist of Lithuanian Lepidoptera*. - Vilnius.

Izenbek, B. A. 1980. The Butterflies of the Lithuanian SSR. - *Nota lepid.*, 3(3-4):126-135.

Jong, R. de, 1972. Systematics and geographic history of the genus *Pyrgus* in the Palaearctic region. - *Tijdschr. Ent.*, 115:1-121.

Jong, R. de, 1974. Notes on the genus *Carcharodus* (Lepidoptera, Hesperiidae). - *Zool. Mededelingen*, 48(1):1-9.

Jong, R. de, 1978. Monograph of the genus *Spialia* Swinhoe. - *Tijdschr. Ent.*, 11:23-146.

Kaisila, J. 1962. Immigration und Expansion of der Lepidopteren in Finnland in den Jahren 1869-1960. - *Acta ent. fenn.*, 18:1-452.

Koch, M. 1984. *Wir bestimmen Schmetterlinge*. - Neumann, Leipzig.

Kremsky, J. 1925. Przyczynek do fauny motyli Podlasia [Macrolepidoptera of Poland. - *Polskie Pismo ent.*, 4:35-62. [In Polish].

Krzywicki, M. 1981. Anmerkungen zur Tagfalterfauna Bulgariens. - *Nota lepid.* 4(1-2):29-46.

Kudrna, O. 1985/86/90. *Butterflies of Europe*: Vols. 1, 2 and 8. AULA-Verlag, Wiesbaden.

Kudrna, O. 1977. *A Revision of the Genus Hipparchia Fabricus*. E.W. Classey Ltd., Faringdon.

Larsen, T. B. 1983. Insects of Saudi Arabia: Lepidoptera; Rhopalocera (A mongraph of the butterflies of the Arabian Peninsula). - *Fauna of Saudi Arabia*, 5:333-478.

Larsen, T. B. 1984. *Butterflies of Saudi Arabia and its neighbours*. - Stacey International, London.

Le Cerf, F. 1972. *Atlas des Lépidoptères de France. 1. Rhopaloc*ères. - Paris.

Leestmans , R. 1965/66/68. Étude biogéographique sur les Lépidoptères diurnes de la Corse. - *Alexanor* 5:17-24, 89-96, 113-120, 179-189, 194-194, 281-288, 297-304, 345-352.

Lempke, B. J. 1937/53/54/56/57. Catalogus der nederlandse Macrolepidoptera. - *Tijdschr. Ent.*, 79:238-315; 96:239-305; 97:301-345; 98(1955):283-355; 100:155-216.

Lukhtanov, V. and Lukhtanov, A. 1994. *Die Tagfalter Nordestasiens*. - Eitschberger, Marktleuthen.

Manley, W. B. L. and Allcard, H. G. 1970. *A Field Guide to the Butterflies and Burnets of Spain*. - E. W. Classey Ltd., Hampton.

Mariani, M. 1939. Fauna Lepidopterorum Siciliae. - *Memorie Soc. ent. ital.*, 17(1938):129-187.

Markgraf, F. 1931. *Pflanzen aus Albanien*. - Wien.

Niculescu, E. V. 1961. Lepidoptera. Fam. Papilionidae (Fluturi). - *Fauna Repub. pop. rom.*, 11(5):1-103. [In Romanian].

Niculescu, E. V. 1963. Lepidoptera. Fam. Pieridae (Fluturi). - *Fauna Repub. pop. rom.*, 11(6):1-202. [In Romanian].

Niculescu, E. V. 1965. Lepidoptera. Fam. Nymphalidae (Fluturi). - *Fauna Repub. pop. rom.*, 11(7):1-361. [In Romanian].

Nordstrom, F. 1955. De Fennoskandiska dagfjärilarnas utbredning. - *Acta Univ. Lund (N.F.)* 66(1):1-176.

Nordstrom, F. and Wahlgreen, E. 1935-41. *Svenska fjärilar*. - Nordisk Famijeboks Förlags, Stockholm.

Oberthur, C. 1915. Faune des Lépidoptères de la Barbarie. - *Étud. Lép. comp.*, 10:7-459.

Oberthur, C. 1922. Les Lépidoptères du Maroc. - *Étud. Lép. comp.*, 19(1):1-403; 19(2):71-90, 165-195.

Oehmig, S. 1977. Die Tagfalter Madeiras. - *Ent. Z. Frankf.a.M.*, 87:169-176, 189-199.

Oehmig, S. 1983. *Hipparchia azorina* (Strecker, 1899) (Satyridae) Biology, Ecology and Distribution on the Azores Islands. - *J. Res. Lepid.*, 20(1981)(3):136-160.

Olivier, A. 1993. *Butterflies of the Greek island of Ródos*. - Vlaamse Vereniging Voor Entomologie, Antwerp.

Pittaway, A. R. 1985. Fauna of Saudi Arabia. Lepidoptera: Rhopalocera of Western Saudi Arabia. - *Fauna of Saudi Arabia*, 7:172-197.

Popescu-Gorj, A. 1964. *Catalogue de la collection de Lépidoptères "Prof. A. Ostrogovich" du Museum d'Histoire Naturelle "Grigore Antipa" Bucarest*. - Museum d'Histoire Naturelle "Grigore Antipa", Bucarest.

Rebel, H. 1903. Studien über die Lepidopterenfauna der Balkanländer. 1. Bulgarien und Ostrumelien. - *Annln. naturh. Mus. Wien*. 18:123-347.

Rebel, H. 1904. Studien über die Lepidopterenfauna der Balkanländer. 2. Bosien und Herzegowina. - *Annln. naturh. Mus. Wien*, 19:97-377.

Rebel, H. 1913. Studien über die Lepidopterenfauna der Balkanländer. 3. Sammelergebenisse aus Montenegro, Albanien, Mazedonien und Thrazien. - *Annln. naturh. Mus. Wien*, 27:281-334.

Rebel, H. 1926. Lepidopteran von den Balearen. - *Dt. ent. Z. Iris*, 40:135-146.

Rebel, H. 1934. Lepidopteran von den Balearen und Pityusen. - *Dt. ent. Z. Iris*, 48:122-138.

Rebel, H. and Zerny, H. 1931. Die Lepidopterenfauna Albaniens. - *Denkschr. Akad. Wiss. Wien*, 103:37-161.

Romaniszyn, J. and Schille, F. 1930. Fauna motyli Polski. 1. - *Pr. monogr. Kom. fizjogr*., 6(1929):1-555. [In Polish].

Schaider P. and Jaksic, P. 1988. *Die Tagfalter von jugoslawisch Mazedonien*. - Schaider, Munchen.

Scott, J. A. 1986. *The Butterflies of North America*. - Stanford University Press, Stanford, California.

Sichel, G. 1963. Elenco dei Ropaloceri della Sicilia nord-orientale nella collezione dell'I.N.E. - *Fragm. ent*., 4:49-61.

Stoyanov, N. and Kitanov B. 1966. *Plants of the high mountains of Bulgaria*. - Sofia.

Strid, A. 1986. *Mountain Flora of Greece*. Vol 1. - Cambridge University Press (Cambridge, London, New York, New Rochelle, Melbourne, Sydney).

Stubbs, A. E. 1982. Conservation and the future for the field entomologist. - *Proc. Trans. Br. ent. nat. Hist. soc*., 15:55-66.

Tax, M. H. 1990. *Atlas van de Nederlandse dagvlinders*.

Tennent, J. 1996. *The Butterflies of Morocco, Algeria and Tunisia*. - Gem Publishing Company, Wallingford.

Thurner, J. 1964. Die Lepiddopterenfauna Jugoslawisch Mazedoniens. 1. Rhopalocera, Gryocera und Noctuidae. - *Posebno Izd. prirod. Muz. Skopje*, 1:1-158.

Thomas, J. A. and Lewington, R. 1991. *The Butterflies of Britain and Ireland*. - Dorling-Kindersley, London.

Thomson, E. 1967. *Die Grosschmetterlinge Estlands*. - Rauschenbusch Verlag, Stollhamm.

Thomson, G. 1980. *The Butterflies of Scotland*. - Croom Helm, London.

Times Books. 1994. *The Times Atlas of the World - Comprehensive Edition*. - HarperCollins, London.

Tolman, T. W. *The Butterflies of Greece*. [In prep.].

Tronicek, E. 1949. Contribution to the Knowledge of the Lepidopterological fauna of Crete. - *Acta ent. Mus. natn. Pragae*, 26:1-15.

Tutin, T. G., *et al* (eds.) 1964-80. *Flora Europaea. Vols. 1-5*. - Cambridge University Press, England.

Valletta, A. 1972. *The butterflies of the Maltese Islands*. - Valletta, Malta.

Varga, Z. 1975. Geographische Isolation und subspeziation bei den Hochgebirgs-Lepidopteren der Balkanhablinsel. - *Acta ent. jugosl*., 11:5-39.

Verity, R. Revision of the athalia group of the genus *Melitaea* Fabricius, 1807 (Lepidoptera, Nymphalidae). - *Trans. R. Ent. Soc. Lond*., 89(14):591-706.

Verity, R. 1940-1953. *Le Farfalle Diurne d'Italia*. Vols. 1-5. - Florence.

Viidalepp, J. 1966. [Baltic butterflies and their distribution (Rhopalocera and Gyrocera)]. - *Ucen. Zap. tartu. gos. Univ*., 180:3-39. [In Russian, English summary].

Viidalepp J. 1979. [Additions to the fauna of the butterflies of Tuva]. - *Ucen. Zap. tartu. gos. Univ*., 483:15-16. [In Russian, English summary].

Vikhodtsevskii, N. 1958. [New and rare butterflies in the fauna of Bulgaria]. - *Izv. zool. Inst. Sof*., 7:358-365 [In Bulgarian, French summary].

Warren, B. C. S. 1926. Monograph of the Tribe Hesperiidi (European species) with revised classification of the subfamily Hesperiinae (Palaearctic species) based on the Genital Armature of the Males. - *Trans. Ent. Soc. Lond*., 74(1):1-170.

Warren, B. C. S. 1936. Monograph of the Genus *Erebia*. - British Museum [Natural History], London.

Weidemann, H. J. 1986/88. *Naturführer - Tagfalter. Vols 1 and 2*. - Neumann-Neudamm, Melsungen. [In German].

Wiemers, M. 1995. The butterflies of the Canary Islands: A survey on their distribution, biology and ecology. - *Linn. belg*., 15(2):63-84; 15(3):87-118.

Willemse, L. 1975. Distribution records of Rhopalocera in the Greek mainland and Crete. - *Ent. Ber., Amst*., 35:141-149.

Willemse, L. 1980. Some interesting faunistical data of Rhopalocera in Greece. - *Ent. Ber., Amst*., 40:156-158.

Willemse, L. 1981. More about the distribution of Rhopalocera in Greece. - *Ent. Ber., Amst*., 41:41-47.

Willien, P. 1990. Contribution lépidoptérique française à la Cartographie des Invertébrés Européens (C.I.E.). Le genre *Erebia* (Lépidoptères: Nymphalidae: Satyrinae). - *Alexanor*, 16(5):259-290.

Zerkowitz, A. 1946. The Lepidoptera of Portugal. - *J. New York ent. Soc*., 54:51-87, 115-165, 211-261.

Index of English Names

Index of Scientific Names